DYNAMIC PERSONNEL ADMINISTRATION

— MANAGEMENT OF HUMAN RESOURCES

Om

Lead Me from the Unreal to Real

Lead Me from Darkness to Light

Lead Me from Death to Immortality

— *Brihadaranyaka Upanishad*

DYNAMIC PERSONNEL ADMINISTRATION

— MANAGEMENT OF HUMAN RESOURCES

Prof. M.N. RUDRABASAVARAJ
PRESIDENT & EXECUTIVE DIRECTOR,
MNR ASSOCIATES PTE LTD.
SINGAPORE.
FORMERLY PROFESSOR OF MANAGEMENT,
VAIKUNTH MEHTA NATIONAL INSTITUTE OF
COOPERTIVE MANAGEMENT, PUNE.
PROFESSOR & HEAD OF DEPARTMENT OF MANAGEMENT,
PSG COLLEGE OF TECHNOLOGY, COIMBATORE
AND
VISITING PROFESSOR OF HUMAN RESOURCES MANAGEMENT,
JAMNALAL BAJAJ INSTITUTE OF MANNAGEMENT,
MUMBAI.

Himalaya Publishing House
MUMBAI • NEW DELHI • NAGPUR • BENGALURU • HYDERABAD • CHENNAI • PUNE
LUCKNOW • AHMEDABAD • ERNAKULAM • BHUBANESWAR • INDORE • KOLKATA • GUWAHATI

First Edition : 1996
Second Revised Edition : 1998
Reprint : 1999
Third Revised Edition : 2001
Reprint : 2004
Reprint : 2005
Reprint : 2007
Reprint : 2008
Reprint : 2009
Reprint : 2011
Reprint : 2013

Published by : Mrs. Meena Pandey
for **HIMALAYA PUBLISHING HOUSE PVT. LTD.,**
"Ramdoot", Dr. Bhalerao Marg, Girgaon, **Mumbai - 400 004.**
Phones: 2386 01 70/2386 38 63, Fax: 022-2387 71 78
Email: himpub@vsnl.com
Website: www.himpub.com

Branch Offices:

New Delhi : "Pooja Apartments", 4-B, Murari Lal Street, Ansari Road, Darya Ganj, **New Delhi-110 002.** Phone: 23270392, 23278631 Fax: 011-23256286

Nagpur : Kundanlal Chandak Industrial Estate, Ghat Road, **Nagpur - 440 018.** Phone: 2738731, 3296733 Telefax : 0712-2721215

Bengaluru : No. 16/1 (Old 12/1), 1st Floor, Next to Hotel Highlands, Madhava Nagar, Race Course Road, **Bengaluru - 560 001.** Phone : 22281541, 22385461, Telefax: 080-22286611

Hyderabad : No. 3-4-184, Lingampally, Besides Raghavendra Swamy Matham, Kachiguda, **Hyderabad - 500 027.** Phone: 040-27560041, 27550139, Mobile:- 09848130433 Telefax: 040-27560041

Chennai : No. 85/50, Bazullah Road, T. Nagar, **Chennai - 600 017.** Phone: 044-28344020, 32463737, 42124860

Pune : No. 527, "Laksha" Apartment, First Floor, Mehunpura, Shaniwarpeth, (Near Prabhat Theatre), **Pune - 411 030.** Phone: 020-24496323/24496333/32326733

Lucknow : House No. 731, Sehkhupura Colony, Near B.D. Convent School, **Lucknow - 226 024.** Mobile : 09307501549

Ahmedabad : No. 114, "SHAIL", 1st Floor, Opp. Madhu Sudan House, C.G.Road, Navrang Pura, **Ahmedabad – 380 009.** Phone: 079-26560126, Mobiles: 09327324149,09314679413

Ernakulam : No. 39/104 A, Lakshmi Apartment, Karikkamuri Cross Rd., Ernakulam, **Cochin – 682011**, Kerala. Phone: 0484-2378012, 2378016, Mob.: 09344199799

Bhubaneswar: 5 Station Square, **Bhubaneswar (Orissa) - 751 001.** Mobile: 9861046007, E-mail:- orissa@himpub.com

Indore : Kesardeep Avenue Extension, 73, Narayan Bagh.Flat No. 302, IIIrd Floor, Near Humpty Dumpty School, Narayan Bagh, **Indore (M.P.) 452 007** Mobile: 09301386468

Kolkata : 108/4, Beliaghata, Main Road, Near ID Hospital, Opp. SBI Bank **Kolkata - 700 010.** Mobile: 09910440956, E-mail:- nkmitra@himpub.com

Guwahati : House No. 15, Behind Prajjyotish College, Near Sharma Printing Press, P.O. Bharalumukh, Guwahati - 781009 (Assam) Mobile: 07439040301; 07439040302

Printed by : Shri Krishna Offset Press Delhi-93

Dedicated with all my love and regards
to my beloved parents
Shri. M.R. Arasananjundappa
(Who is, alas, no more) and
Smt. Rudramma
(Who is thereal brain behind our family)
What I am and ever hope to be
I owe it to them.

PREFACE

The students and practitioners in the field of Personnel Administration/Human Resources Management as well as employers and industrialists will, I am sure, find this publication useful and valuable.

Contemporary business and management are complex, sophisticated and vital. In their growth, efficiency and progress lies the prosperity and well-being of the people and the nation. Perhaps today there is no other activity which is as important and dynamic as management — the oldest of arts and the newest of professions. One of the fundamental activity areas of management is the management of people — Management of Human Resources.

To say that management of people (particularly at the present juncture in our country) is not easy would obviously be an understatement. One of the chief problems is the fact that the *task* and the *process* of managing people are often imperfectly understood. There is a tendency to confuse the performance of a few welfare and employment functions with Human Resources Management. Another difficulty is that the scope and variety of the operative, advisory and service functions of Human resources Management are not properly appreciated. Yet another is the plain lack of exposure on the part of both practitioners and students to the prevailing body of systematic knowledge and literature on the subject of the management of people. There is an imperative need, now as never before, to overcome these problems and to develop a proper perspective of personnel administration with a view to sharpening the performance and efficiency of management of people.

The Present volume is designed just to meet this need. It endeavours to place before the reader the vast expansive scope, variety and dynamism of the field of Human Resources Management. The purpose of discussing Human Resources Management of both India and U.S.A. is mainly to give a total and complete picture of personnel administration and it is *not* a comparative study. The starting point for improving the methods of managing people is first of all to distinguish clearly the nature and scope of all the various elements of operative, advisory and service functions as well as the available tools and techniques of Human Resources Management. The present volume begins with a discussion of the nature and evolution and develops in the first three chapters certain concepts, theories, and principles in the field of Human Resources Management. It then sets for the policies, programmes and procedures of the various operative and advisory functions, discussing in detail the human resources tools and techniques utilised in India and U.S.A. and elsewhere.

Several personnel policies and programmes of Indian and American companies are offered to serve as examples. The last chapter points out some of the trends in the field of personnel administration and the kind of challenge facing the personnel executives.

Both philosophical concepts and practical ideas are presented. The volume sets forth commonly accepted philosophies, principles, concepts, formulas and procedures to help both the student and the practitioner. It is basically text-cum-reference book useful to the students and the companies.

The students of management and human resources management, who are future managers and who are primarily interested in gaining knowledge and learning skills not only with a view to appearing for the examinations but also to using the knowledge later in their careers, will find the detailed treatment of the subject interesting and stimulating. Those, who want to know the historical, philosophical and theoretical aspects of personnel administration, will find them in this textbook.

The personnel executives will find a great deal of assistance in this volume for the solution of their own problems. The practical ideas, several operating personnel programmes of Indian and American companies and the cold economics suggested here should make this a good reference volume. It attempts to answer such questions as what is it, why is it necessary, how is it done, where is it feasible, what is the cost the programme to suit the conditions obtaining in their companies. The volume brings together in a form convenient for reference all the systematic body of knowledge which has developed over the years on personnel administration. Any time a company wishes to introduce a job evaluation programme, an induction programme, a job analysis programme, or a training programme it can refer to this volume to get some practical ideas.

The readers — both students and managers — will find the discussion of personnel administration in India and U.S.A. in one volume particularly helpful (even profitable). This volume will be a practical help to faculty members and researchers who teach and conduct research on personnel administration.

The present volume will be of interest and value to all levels of managers and administrators in business, Government and Public Services and all areas where individuals are brought together to achieve certain goals as a team.

The present volume is the result of several years of continuous research and in writing this volume, the author has drawn rather freely upon writing and research done by outstanding scholars and those two great American institutions, National Industrial Conference Board and American Management Association, in the area of Human Resource Management, and upon the experience of numerous managers. The author has let the experts and scholars speak, wherever possible. Many Indian and American companies cooperated in giving valuable information. The author is most grateful to them.

Finally, the current volume presents the subject in 4 parts: (I) Dynamic Personnel Administration — The Concept; (II) Management of Personnel; (III) Management of Industrial Relations and (IV) Management of Human resources — Recent trends, which covers hitherto unexplored areas like (1) New Trends in Human resources Management, (2) Evaluation of Human Resources Management, (3) Computer applications in Human Resources Management, (4) Human Resources Management Education, (5) Manpower Planning, and (6) Challenge of Tomorrow.

Perhaps this is the appropriate place to remember my very dear poor little wife, Mani and to express special thanks to her, for her patience and smiling encouragement, while the author was lost in the wilderness of the world of work and authorship.

In writing a book such as this, the author is indebted to so many persons that it is impossible to give them all due credit. But to all, the author extends his sincere and grateful thanks, while bearing responsibility for any sins of omission and commission.

Singapore **M. N. RUDRABASAVARAJ**

CONTENTS

PART I
DYNAMIC HUMAN RESOURCES MANAGEMENT — CONCEPT

1. GLOBAL HUMAN GROWTH MODEL 1 - 30

What is Dynamic Personnel Administration — Changing Concepts of Management and Personnel Administration — A Historical Perspective — Definition and Scope — A Code of Ethics — Some Hurdles in the Path of Personnel Administration.

2. DYNAMIC HUMAN RESOURCES MANAGEMENT 31 - 58

3. FIELD OF HUMAN RESOURCES MANAGEMENT 59 - 103

Functions of Personnel Administration — Personnel Administration — A Staff Function — Personnel Administration and Other Areas of Management — Organisation Charts — Personnel Administrator — His Status and Qualifications.

4. PRINCIPLES OF HUMAN RESOURCES MANAGEMENT 104 - 124

Principles of Personnel Administration — Management Philosophies and Creeds — Personnel Objectives — Personnel Policies — Personnel Procedures and Programmes — Personnel Budget — Personnel Research.

PART II
MANAGEMENT OF HUMAN RESOURCES

5. HUMAN RESOURCE PLANNING 127 - 139

Perspectives in Human Resources Planning — Changes in the Attitudes of People — Manpower Planning — Executive Resources Planning.

6. SCIENTIFIC SELECTION: PLACING THE RIGHT PERSON ON THE RIGHT JOB 140 - 183

Scientific Selection — The Nature of the Job — The Nature of Personnel — The Nature and Sources of Recruitment — Selection Process.

7. HUMAN RESOURCES DEVELOPMENT 184 - 254

Training Needs and Objectives — Training Responsibility and Organisation — Training Principles — Training Types and Techniques — Management Development — Organisation Development — Training Evaluation.

8. **PROMOTIONS, TRANSFERS AND PERFORMANCE APPRAISAL** 255 - 268

Employee Promotions — Transfers — Employee Performance Appraisal

9. **EMPLOYEE MORALE** 269 - 279

What is Employee Morale — Effects of Good and Poor Morale — Measurement of Morale — Improving Employee Morale.

10. **COMMUNICATIONS AND SUGGESTION SYSTEMS** 280 - 297

The Objectives of Communications — Responsibility for Organising of Communications — Communications at Managerial Levels — Content and Channels — Rules and Principles — Barriers — Programme for Action — Suggestion Systems.

11. **WAGE AND SALARY ADMINISTRATION** 298 - 348

General Considerations — Principles — Job Evaluation — Systems of Wage Payment — Some Wage Issues in India.

12. **EMPLOYEE BENEFITS AND SERVICES** 349 - 402

Purposes — Factors Influencing Benefits and Services — Costs — Items — Added Income and Leisure — Employee Security Benefits — Old Age and Retirement Benefits — General Administration — Employee Health and Safety — Total Loss Prevention — Accident Prevention — Safety Engineering — Safety Audit — Employee Morale and Welfare — Range of Employee Services.

13. **HUMAN RELATIONS AND MOTIVATION** 403 - 432

What is Human Relations in Management — Human Relations and Motivation — How to Handle Human Relations Problems — Personnel Administration and Human Relations.

PART III
UNION AND MANAGEMENT RELATIONS

14. **UNION AND MANAGEMENT RELATIONS** 435 - 512

Unions and Their Role — American and Indian Trade Unions — Union — Management Relations — Tripartite Machinery.

15. **LABOUR LEGISLATION** 513 - 542

Laws Dealing Working Conditions — Laws Dealing with Wages — Laws Dealing with Industrial Relations — Laws Dealing with Social Security.

16. **EMPLOYEE GRIEVANCE REDRESSAL** 543 - 564

What is a Grievance — Causes of Grievances — Grievance Redressal Procedures — Evaluation.

17. **EMPLOYEE DISCIPLINE** 565 - 580

The Problem of Alienation — Principles — Areas of Indiscipline and Types of Penalties — Disciplinary Procedure — Domestic Enquiry — Role of Personnel Administrator.

PART IV

MANAGEMENT OF HUMAN RESOURCES — NEW TRENDS

18. **NEW TRENDS IN HUMAN RESOURCES MANAGEMENT** 583 - 605

The New Role — The New Concern — The New Professionalism.

19. **HUMAN RESOURCES MANAGEMENT EDUCATION** 606 - 617

A New Programme of Education — Curriculum Details — Prerequisites — Basic Corelated Core — Industrial Relations — Personnel Administration — Field Work.

20. **COMPUTER APPLICATIONS IN HUMAN RESOURCES MANAGEMENT** 618 - 642

Computer Applications in Personnel — Extent of EDP Use — Types of Applications — Some Specific Applications — Do's and Dont's — Managing Data — Personnel and Systems Men.

21. **HUMAN RESOURCES MANAGEMENT AND FAMILY PLANNING** 643 - 661

Family Planning Scheme — A Personnel Programme — Children by Choice, Not by Chance — Have You a Planning Service?

22. **EVALUATION OF HUMAN RESOURCES MANAGEMENT** 662 - 685

The Problem of Evaluation — Process of Evaluation — Cost-Benefit Analysis — Questions, Indices, Ratio — Everybody a Personnel Administrator.

23. **THE CHALLENGE OF TOMORROW** 686 - 713

Tomorrow's Manager and Management — The Job Ahead — The Challenge.

PART ONE

Dynamic Personnel Administration

CHAPTER 1

Global Human Growth Model

The Human Condition

The International Labour Organisation (ILO) in a new report on the global economy entitled "Defending Values, Promoting Change" paints a bleak picture of the contemporary human condition.[1] "30 per cent of the labour force in the world is out of work or under employed. A global job crisis is gripping both rich and poor nations. It is a crisis that in some countries could really explode and undermine the social fabric very badly" proclaimed by Mr. Ali Taqi, Chief of Staff, ILO. (*See Diagram I*)

Unemployment: ILO estimates that more than 820 million people worldwide are either unemployed or working at a job that does not pay even a subsistence wage. Releasing the report, the Director-General of ILO, Mr. Michael Hansenne points out: "Industrialised market-economy countries most of which had achieved and they thought they could sustain, virtually full employment two decades ago, now faced an unemployment rate of 8.5 per cent. But it is in the poor countries, where the crisis is most acute, that the dangers are the greatest. The situation in Africa, was troublesome, with most countries there experienced major decline in living standards. Sub-Saharan Africa is a general disaster."

Illiteracy

Illiteracy is the mother of unemployment. More than half of the world's population live in nine developing countries — Bangladesh, Brazil, China, Egypt, India, Indonesia, Mexico, Nigeria and Pakistan — which account for more than 70 per cent of the world's adult illiterates and which are also among the world's poorest, according to a United Nations Education, Scientific and Cultural Organisation (UNESCO) report in December 1993.

Poverty

The World Bank, in its World Development Report 1990 on Poverty, presents grim figures on world poverty.[2] 1115 million people or one-fifth of the world's population are poor, living on a dollar (US) a day. One-third of the population of the developing countries are poor.[3]

The Human Condition ...

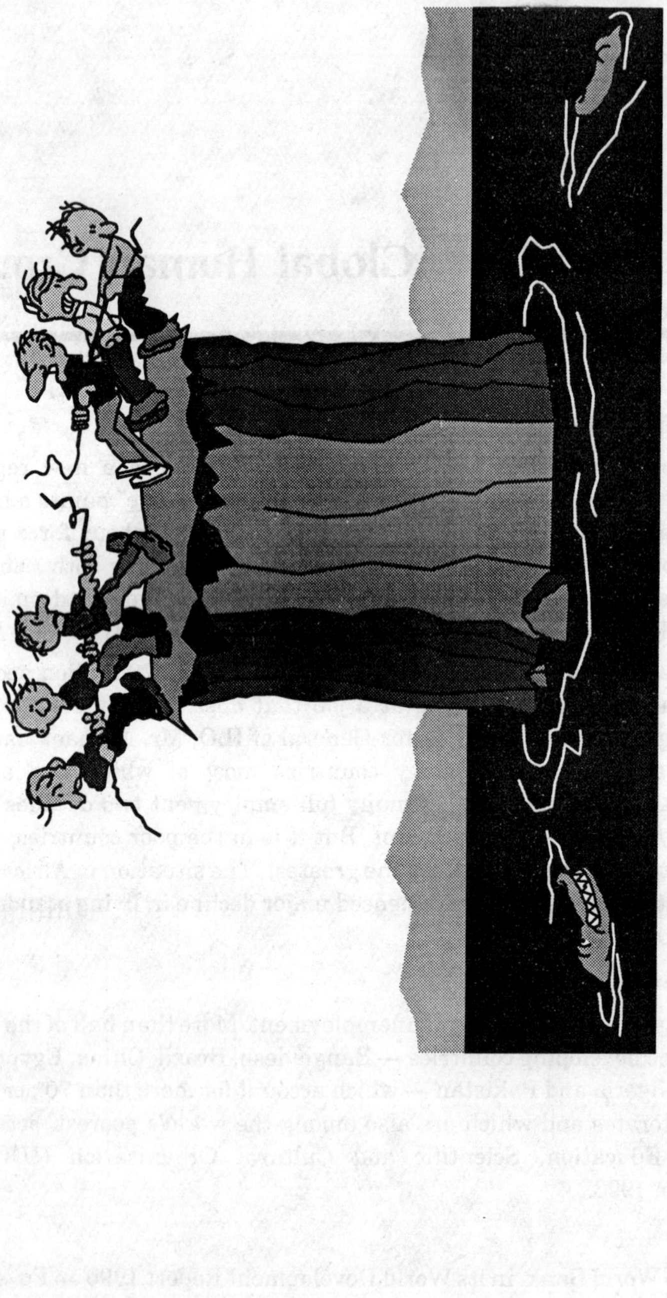

Diagram 1.1

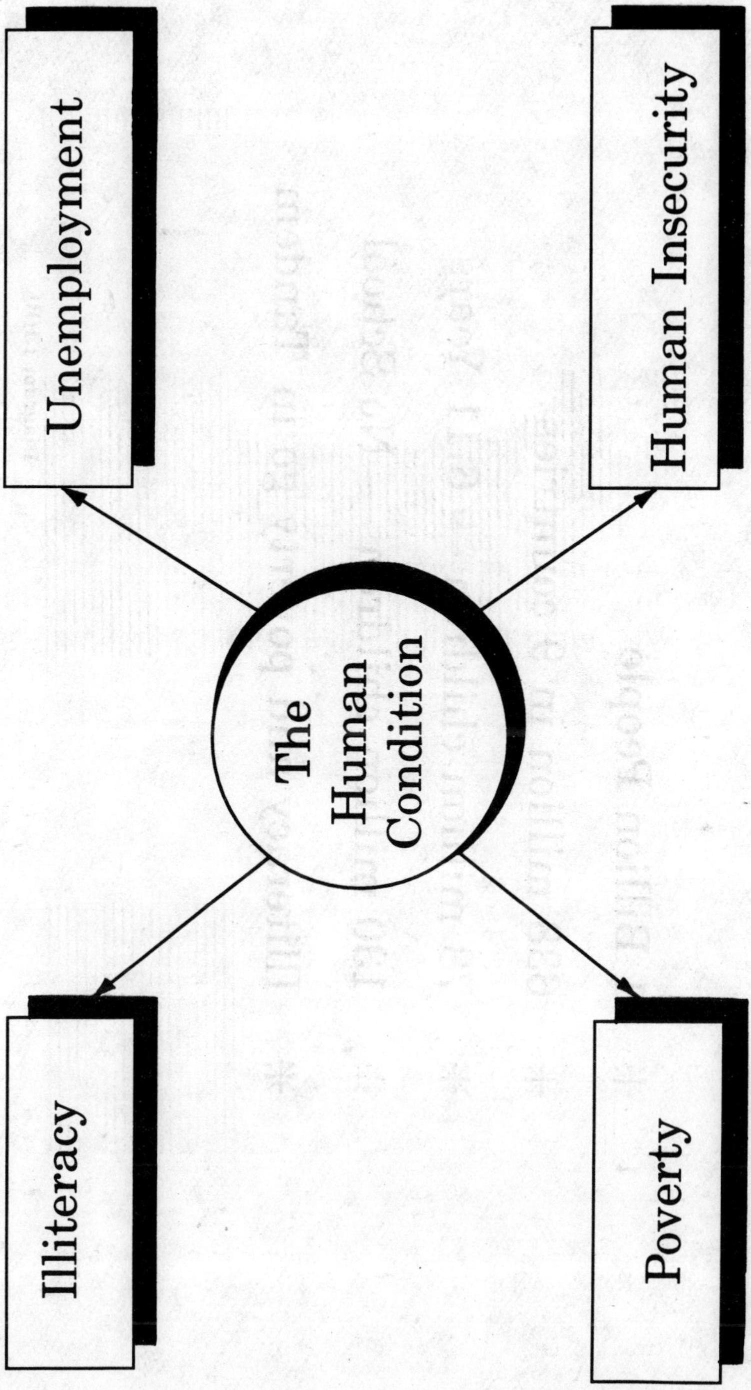
The Human Condition
Unemployment
Human Insecurity
Illiteracy
Poverty

Diagram 1.1(A)

Illiteracy

- ✻ 1 Billion People
- ✻ 638 million in 9 countries
- ✻ 78 million children — 6-11 Years
- ✻ 130 million children — No School
- ✻ Illiteracy and poverty go in Tandem

Diagram 1.1(B)

Unemployment

* 30% of world labour force
* 820 million unemployed or underemployed
* 35 million in rich countries — USA, OECD
* Poor countries — Hardest Hit
* Highest among unskilled

Diagram 1.1(C)

Poverty

* 1.2 Billion or 1/5th of the world
* 1/3 of population of developing countries
* 630 million (18%) — Extremely Poor!
* Rural Masses, Women — The Poorest
* 15% Americans Poor

Diagram 1.1(D)

Human Insecurity

- Over 100 million living outside their countries
- 37% — Refugees
- Situation worst in Sub Saharan Africa
- 17 Countries could face collapse
- Indicators — Food Scarcity, High Unemployment, HR Violations, Ethnic Violence

Diagram 1.1(E)

Human Insecurity

The 1994 Human Development Report of the UN, which ranks all the countries of the world on a Human Development Index said that 17 countries, including Mexico, Nigeria and Algeria, could face collapse. 13 countries, were in various stages of collapse and they were Afghanistan, Angola, Haiti, Iraq, Mozambique, Myanmar, Sudan, Ziare, Ruanda, Burundi, Georgia, Liberia and Pakistan. The report said Algeria was experiencing severe internal tensions and Egypt, Mexico and Nigeria had large regional disparities in income and life expectancy, which were strong indicators of disintegration. The report identified six indicators of human insecurity that could help pinpoint trouble spots and they are:[4]

1. Food scarcity;
2. High unemployment and declining wages;
3. Human rights violations;
4. Widening regional disparities;
5. Ethnic violence; and
6. An overemphasis on military spending.

Countries like Iraq, Somalia and Nicaragua, spending 3½ to 5 times more on military expenditure than on education and health care, have collapsed.

The ILO, in its 1994 World Labour Report, highlights the following world labour trends:[5]

1. World unemployment is increasing and wages falling;
2. Russia: Unemployment low but wages falling;
3. Globalisation will intensify;
4. Informal employment increasing;
5. Feminisation of the work force;
6. Line between home and workforce blurred;
7. Greater emphasis on employers' organisation;
8. Health care still low in developing countries;
9. More Asian workers covered by social health insurance;
10. Health threat from chemicals accelerated.

The report estimates that 43 million people are being added to the global labour force every year. Agriculture is still the largest employer and two-thirds of the global workforce are still employed in agriculture.[6]

Global Summit

The World leaders congregated in the World Social Summit under the aegis of UN, celebrating its 50th anniversary, in March (6-12) 1995 to tackle the human crisis brought about by poverty, unemployment and social alienation. Mr. Ali Taqi, Chief of Staff, releasing the ILO report observed: Nobody has the answer or a set of answers that could end the crisis:

Our contension is that there is a solution — albeit not a quick fix one, but a longer term, strategic and dynamic one — through the global human growth model, which aims to provide three fundamental Es —

1. Education for all;
2. Employment for all; and
3. Energising all people of the world to realise their maximum potential through global approach, global leadership and global cooperative, advantage which we shall elaborate in the following pages.

Concept of Human Growth

The central thesis of this treatise is that people are the key not only to the development of organisations but also to the development of nations and the world. So far we have placed great deal of emphasis on agricultural development, industrial development, economic development, security and defence development, and of late on environmental development, hoping somehow that this will, in the final analysis, will contribute to the common weal and human development. The World Bank in its World Development Report 1991 on the thesis, The Challenge of Development, maintained:[6] "Few policies promote development as powerfully as effective investment in human resources. An estimated 80 per cent of the world's population lives in developing countries — a proportion that is rising. Crucial issues in many of these countries include expanding primary education, alleviating poverty, and controlling population growth through better education, health care, and family planning...."

Human Growth: Unlike classical economic growth, where the concern is for the production of goods and services and economic wealth, in the new and contemporary concept of human growth, the centrepiece is the human being and his/her growth. (*See diagram II what is it?*)

The Concept

The concept of human growth is that every human being, regardless of his race, religion, age, sex, colour and nationality etc., is given the opportunity to grow to realise his maximum and unique potential. Self-actualisation is the core of the concept of human growth.

The concept of human growth goes beyond the concept of full employment, which in itself seems like a mirage, almost unattainable, in most parts of the world. In our new concept, not only do we provide a job to every able bodied and willing person but also we provide an equal and full opportunity to grow and develop his unique personality and potential. Every human being is provided full and equal opportunity to realise his maximum potential. In the growth and development of individual lies the growth and development of companies, organisations and nations. It was Adam Curle who said very aptly: "Countries are underdeveloped largely because most of the people are undeveloped, having had no opportunity of expanding their potential capacities in the service of society." Underdevelopment of nations is the function of underdevelopment of their people. Lack of opportunity is the crux of the problem of human growth. Given the opportunity, the fundamental assumption of human growth is that people strive to grow and realise whatever is their unique individual potential.

Basic Premises

1. Every human being has potential, that is unique to the individual.
2. Given the right environment and opportunity, every person is capable of realising his unique potential.

What is it?

- ✻ To enable every human being to realise ones maximum and unique potential
- ✻ Self actualisation which is the core of human growth
- ✻ Monitor human growth through a human resource inventory

Diagram 1.2

The 3 'E's

* Education: The first key to development of human potential

* Employment: The right opportunity at the right time to provide the realisation of ones potential

* Energising: Motivating every individual to realise his/her maximum potential

Diagram 1.2(A)

3. Every individual has the basic urge to fulfil himself and to realise his potential.
4. It is dynamic, not static.
5. The promotion of human growth results in the promotion of human peace, prosperity and happiness.
6. Human growth is achieved through global effort, cooperation, research and management. In modern times, you cannot realise yourself, if you do not go global. If we plan to promote the growth of all the 5.5 billion people of the world, we need global effort, cooperation, expertise and management. Long ago, Mr. Lee Kuan Yew, the dynamic leader of Singapore observed wisely. "The development of Singapore cannot be left in the hands of Singaporeans only. We need everybody in the world, who can make a contribution to the development of Singapore and we welcome them with open arms."

Definition of Human Growth

We may define human growth as the dynamic process of systematically identifying the potential and the ultimate potential of the individual through a human resources inventory, developing the potential through education, training and development, providing the right employment opportunities at the right time through the right career pathing and progression and energising the individual through the right motivation for the greatest possible realisation of one's intrinsic abilities, ideas, and dreams, contributing to the success of the organisation, nation and world and thus human progress, prosperity, happiness and peace.

Philosophy of Global Human Growth

1. Respect for humankind.
2. Respect for cultural differences of humanity.
3. Promotion of human growth.
4. Plan human development.
5. Strive for human fulfilment.
6. Achieve human prosperity.
7. Establish human peace.
8. Utilize global cooperative advantage.

Global Commitment

It is necessary for every nation to make a policy decision and national commitment to human growth, to provide the fundamental 3Es — education for all, employment for all and energising all to reach their maximum potential and convert every human being into a great asset. All the nations join together in according top priority to human growth and make a global commitment to assist each other in the development, implementation and achievement of global human growth. This is the first step towards the management of global human growth model. (*See the diagram III, Pyramid of Growth*)

Global Human Resources Inventory (GHRI)

The first phase of the model is to develop a global human resources inventory — the opening stock of global human resources which represents the human capital of the world, the wealth of the world. The first step in developing global human resources inventory (GHRI) is to develop national human resource inventories in all the nations of the world, which is a daunting task to most countries of the world and which will need expert and professional assistance to draw up national inventories. The diagram III below shows the process of formulating GHRI.

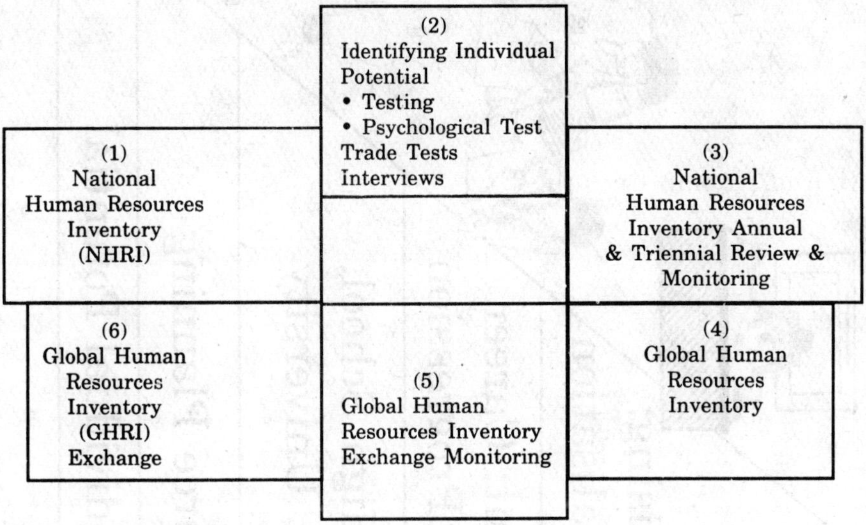

Fig. 1.1

Potential Dynamic

The reason we have the annual and triennial reviews is because human potential is dynamic, not static. They keep changing or "growing" new goals, new aspirations, new dreams, new vistas, new horizons.

Why Global

If we leave this exercise to national initiative, it might be feasible for a few nations to undertake this gigantic exercise unheard of inhuman history but the majority of the nations may not be able, in view of lack of expertise, funds or priorities or leadership. That's why the global approach and leadership is necessary. We want every child and person — 5.5 billion of the world — to benefit from the human growth process.

Global Human Resources Plan

We have to think in long terms, because developing people is a long term process. We cannot adopt an assembly line approach but we have to adopt an agricultural approach. You can produce a car on an assembly line in less than a minute as they do in USA or Japan; but it takes nine months to produce a baby, another 22 years for the baby to become a graduate, another 10 years to become a manager; another 10 to become a director and another 10 to become the chairman of the corporation!

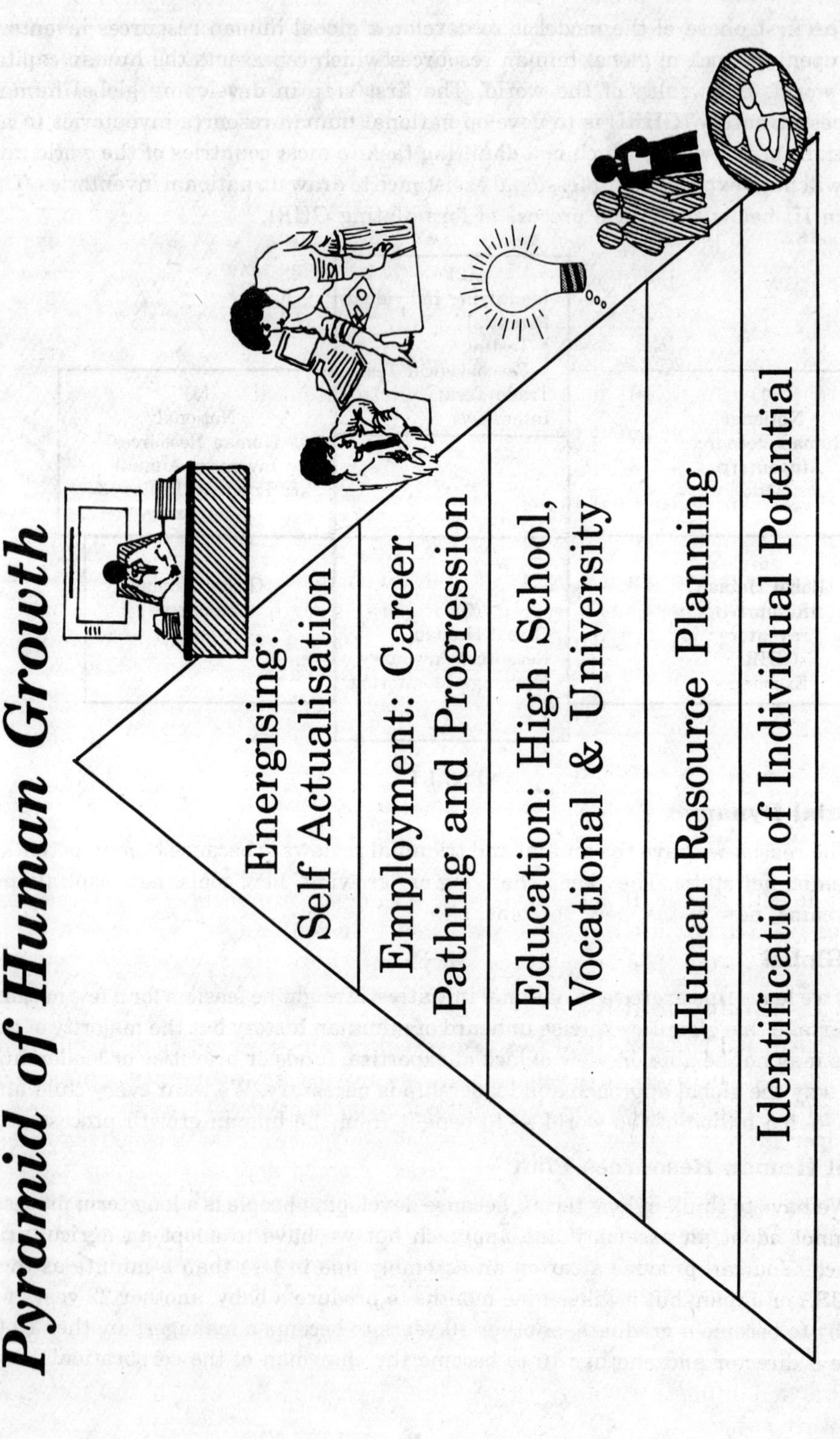
Pyramid of Human Growth
Energising: Self Actualisation
Employment: Career Pathing and Progression
Education: High School, Vocational & University
Human Resource Planning
Identification of Individual Potential

Diagram 1.3

In addition, the primary purpose of a long term plan of human and social engineering is to develop a new global person with right values, attitudes, motivation, who while maximising his potential, enriches his family, corporation, society, nation and the humanity. Every nation will have to develop long term — 100 year-plan, which may be broken down into 4 medium term plans of 25 years each, further with short term plans of 5 years each, updated annually.

GHM I: Education for All by 2010

Education is the key to not only human growth but also to human, national and global prosperity. Witness America, Switzerland and Japan, more recently Taiwan and Korea. Every nation must accord top priority to education and the national goal must be 100 per cent literacy through universal and compulsory primary and high school education. In addition, the national strategy must be to encourage the child to pursue education according to its potential and ultimate potential.

(a) Child development and home environment;

(b) Identification of potential.

35 per cent Vocational Education.

35 per cent University Education.

To achieve the above targets of 100 per cent school education, 35 per cent vocational and 35 per cent university education, every nation will have to give top priority in the national budgets to develop thousands of schools, hundreds of polytechnic and hundreds of universities in each nation and they will have to seek help of advanced countries to build schools, labs, playgrounds, productive investment, the rate of return is the highest, because their products of the educational institutions will produce wealth for nations beyond one's imagination.

A good school leaves indelible impact on students. "Mr. Le Buechler '78, President of Phamis, a technology company in Seattle told me, "The School (Harvard Business School) changed my personal expectations about what I achieve in my career, about what I do with my life. It put a monkey on my back that probably I will never shake the idea that I can achieve a whole lot more than I have so far. I attribute the awakening of that belief to my experience at the school."[7]

GHM II: Employment for All

The second phase of GHM — Employment for all — is even more daunting and challenging not only for the developing nations but also for the developed nations, all of whom are reeling under the burden of unemployment anywhere from 11 per cent to 60 per cent in some of the developed and in some of the developing nations respectively. The great potential of the people created and achieving the target of education for all will be completely dissipated and amount to nothing, if we do not create opportunity for every knowledgeable and skilled individual to put his/her knowledge and skills to great use for his/her benefit, career and growth as well as for the benefit and growth of one's organisation and nation.

That brings us to the second major policy commitment and decision to give top priority, after education, to employment for all its citizens based on their education, potential and ultimate potential, either within the country or without, in cooperation with other nations.

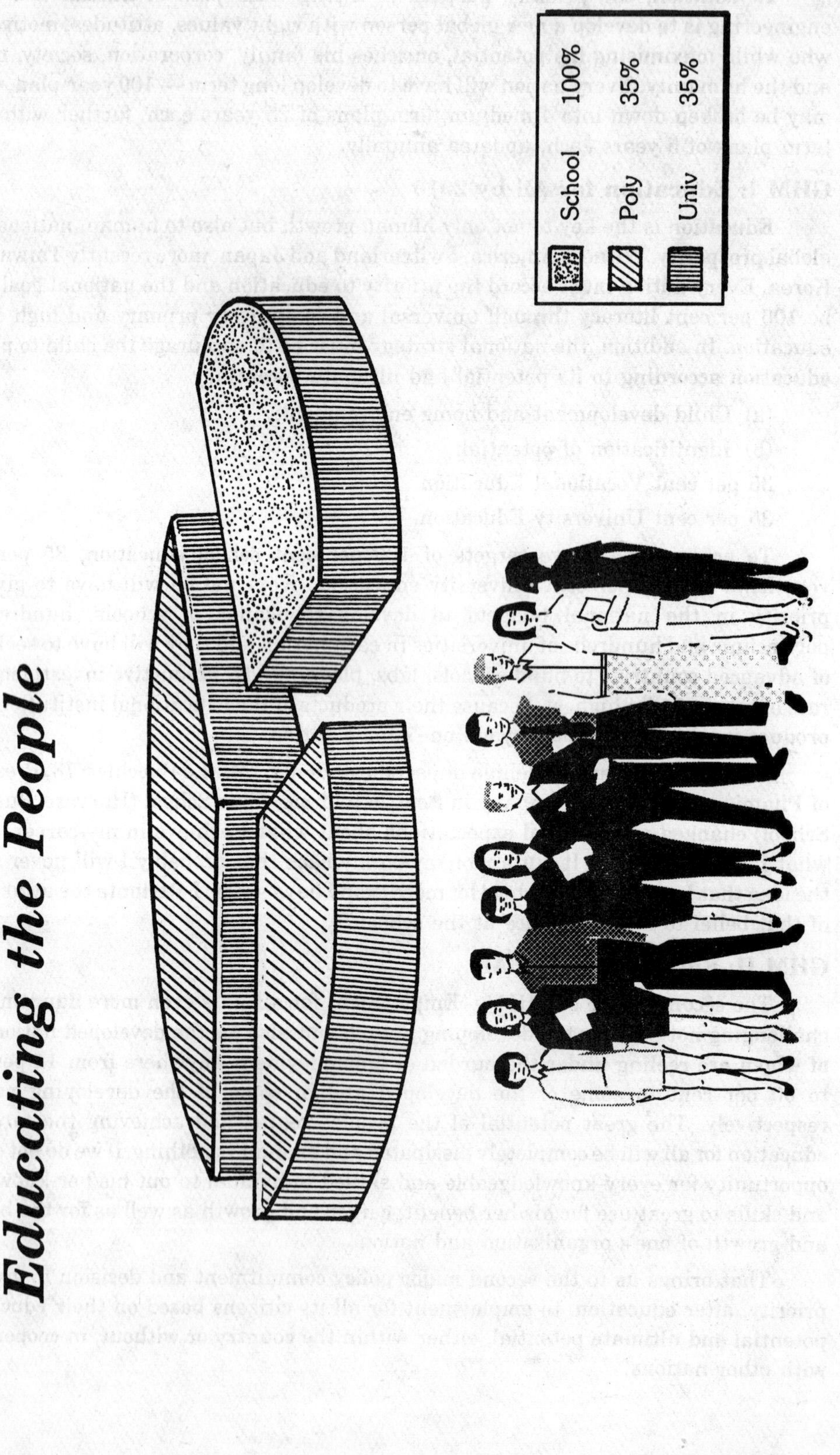
Educating the People
School 100%
Poly 35%
Univ 35%

Human Resources Development

The nations of the world must give great attention to training, development and education — human resources development — in the employment stage, the second important stage of human life, which will last most of the best part of human life — 25 to 75 years.

Konosuke Matsukshita's human resources philosophy was: "We make men, before we make products."

I must have, through our MNR Associates, international management consultancy firm, trained, developed and educated more than a million people from salesgirls to chairmen of corporations in various parts of the world and it is always amazing to see the transformation of the personality of people after systematic, training, guidance and supervision. I remember a Chairman of a large corporation in Indonesia exclaiming, "Professor, how can you ask me to smile when I am speaking?" During a coaching session for a video program. But within a year, he not only learned to smile but also to charm an international audience of top executives in a world conference. Plain Janes are converted into Singapore girls, delivering great customer service and high profits to Singapore Airlines. The potential of people always amazes me in my work around the world regardless of whether they are Indians, Americans, Japanese, Nigerians, Egyptians, Bolivians, Indonesians, Chinese, Singaporeans, British, Fijians, Australians, Seychellois, etc. etc.

Strategies of Employment for All

Employment for all is a very simple goal, but like all simple propositions, the hardest to achieve, unless there is a global coordinated and systematic effort and mechanism put in place to achieve the goal by the end of 2020. So far there is no global effort, although there are plenty of piece mean measures in USA, France, Germany, Italy, India, China, Indonesia, Thailand, Mexico, Brazil, etc.

China is trying to liberalise with market reforms to promote growth to absorb its millions in urban cities and start village enterprises to keep rural people from migrating to urban coastal cities and creating congestion and job crisis. It has worked out a strategy to develop labour-intensive enterprises in cities to absorb surplus labour, incentives like loans, tax exempting reduction to employ more people. Various training centres to train people and provide skills, project of reemployment for retrenched and unemployed for six months or more, to provide career introduction, new skills training, job seeking instruction and self-relief production.

India has opened the country with liberalised market reforms and foreign investment to create employment opportunities for the millions, particularly educated unemployed.

Some strategies for Employment for all:

1. Policy Commitment.
2. Global Co-operation.
3. Adopting Countries.
4. World Security.
5. Regional Cooperation.

Employment

* Human Resource Development
* Individual Career Development Plans
* Management Succession Systems
* Right Opportunity at the Right Time for the Right Person

Diagram 1.3(B)

Energising Potential

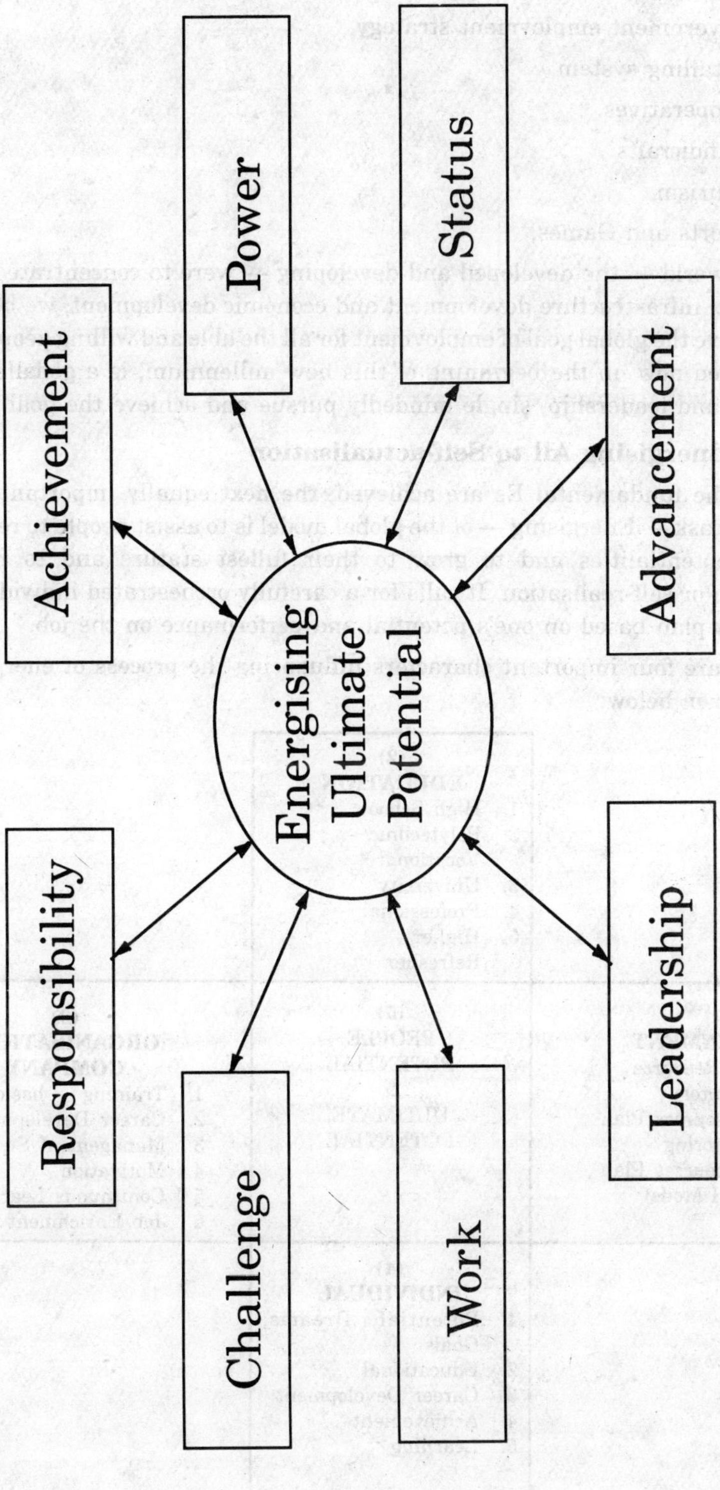

Diagram 1.3(C)

6. Keep them in school.
7. Government employment strategy.
8. Retailing system.
9. Cooperatives.
10. Handicrafts.
11. Tourism.
12. Sports and Games.

If the world — the developed and developing — were to concentrate on human development, infrastructure development and economic development, we believe that we can achieve the global goal of employment for all the able and willing people to work. What we need now, in the beginning of this new millennium, is a global solidarity, cooperation and leadership, single mindedly pursue and achieve the goal by 2020.

GHM III: Energising All to Self-actualisation

Once the fundamental Es are achieved, the next equally important but more challenging task — Energising — of the global model is to assist people to realise their maximum potentialities and to grow to their fullest stature and to reach self-actualisation or self-realisation. It calls for a carefully orchestrated individual career development plan based on one's potential and performance on the job.

There are four important characters influencing the process of energising and they are shown below:

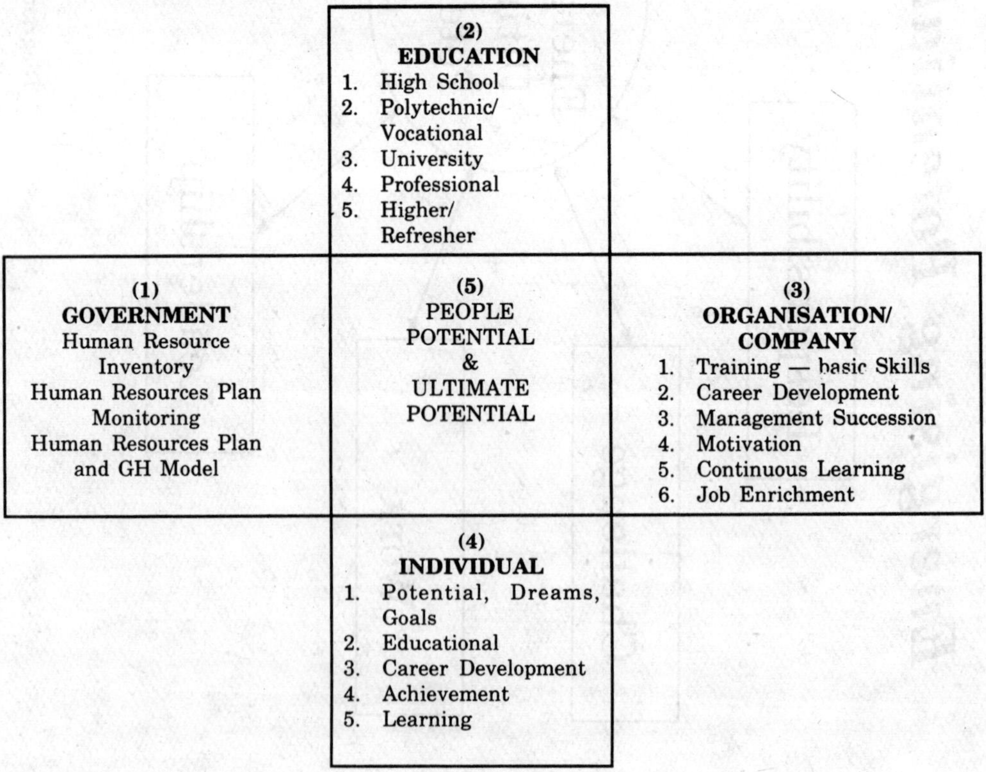

Fig. 1.2

Empowerment of People

EXXON Example: Mr. Michael Haider, former Chairman of Exxon, the largest oil company and the second largest industrial company in the world, observed the key to the success of Exxon.

"In the life of a corporation, today's success is largely product of three types of executive actions taken yesterday: selecting the right people; placing them in the right jobs; and seeing to it that they were able to grow to meet their own needs.

Shell Study

The Shell Oil is the second largest oil company and first largest non-American company in the world and one of the few companies in the world which has done considerable amount of research to evolve a methodology to spot the potential and ultimate potential of people working in Shell companies around the world. More than quarter a century ago, Shell wanted to find out who, among the hundreds of thousands of people employed in more than 80 countries are likely to become the top executives and Directors of the Main Board. They organised a global project, a top Shell executive at Shell Centre in London explained to me, to formulate a methodology, to identify the potential and ultimate potential of their people. Prof. Van Lennep of Utrecht University and Dr. Mueller, a senior executive, the Project Team, conducted a 3 year study first studying leaders in all walks of life, second, the performance appraisals of Shell executives for 10 years to identify the qualities that made them leaders and top executives, asking them to look back on their careers in order to identify the qualities that helped them to become top executives and the qualities that their superiors looked for when they promoted them. After considerable research, and discussions and rationalisation, the team came up with 5 qualities that help spot potential and ultimate potential in Shell.

Qualities

1. Helicopter quality.
2. Power of Imagination.
3. Sense of Realism.
4. Power of Analysis.
5. Power of anticipation.

Shell, introduced these qualities in the appraisal system, which contains two parts, Performance Report, which evaluates the performance of the individual in the past year and Potential Report, which looks at the potential and ultimate potential using the 5 qualities to which are added a few more qualities as shown below:

1. Helicopter Quality;
2. Power of Analysis;
3. Power of Imagination;
4. Sense of Realism;
5. Achievement Motivation;
6. Business Sense;
7. Decisiveness;

8. Capacity to Motivate;
9. Delegation; and
10. Communication.

Senior Minister, Mr. Lee Kuan Yew said recently in Parliament that after having spent 40 years selecting men for big jobs — ministers, civil servants, chairman and CEOs, and having asked many CEOs on how they selected top executives, he found that Shell, had the best system. He sent top ministers and civil servants to London to study the Shell system and implement it in Singapore.

Singapore Transformation

In an address to the undergraduates from two universities in Singapore on "what if I were a young undergraduate again?," Mr. Lee sketched the blueprint of selection and development of leaders in Singapore which is something very unique in the world. Mr. Lee, being himself top of the top 1 per cent of his class, believes in meritocracy, looked for the best and brightest in the school. They win SAF or Overseas Merit Scholarship and they study abroad in the best universities in America and the scholars are obligated to serve government for 6-8 years. They are given challenging assignments and tests. They get married to a wife, equal or better than them, because the wife has to bring up the children with the right values. Their careers are followed by the ministers. They are encouraged to participate in community, professional, social activities and evaluated. They are picked to serve as Members of Parliament and the very best are selected to serve as Ministers.

Global Human Growth Research

Global human growth has a fantastic field full of opportunities for fundamental and applied and empirical research, experimentation and experiences. Nations singly or together, or region wise or worldwide must conduct research on human growth, human resources inventory, human resources planning — long-term, mid-term and short-term, how to educate people in the rural areas, how to use multimedia information technology and interactive learning in the villages and urban area, how to spot people for polytechnic and universities and for different disciplines, how to improve methodology to spot potential and how to monitor potential, how to dovetail human resource planning with national development planning and corporate planning.

Global Human Growth Index

It is necessary to establish global standards to measure the progress of nations in achieving human growth on the basis of certain factors. The United Nations has a Human Development Index based on three factors.

1. Life expectancy, dealing with the life span of people in a country.
2. Educational level, dealing with levels of education attained by the individuals in a country.
3. Basic Purchasing Power, dealing with income and its purchasing power in the country.

The latest report studied human development in 173 countries and ranked them all in order in achievement. Canada stood first, followed by Switzerland in the second spot and Japan in the third place.

We propose a more comprehensive Global Human Growth Index based on 10 factors, with another 100 sub-factors.

The 10 Factors

The 10 factors in the Global Human Index (GHI) are as follows:

1. Life expectancy.
2. Education level.
3. Employment.
4. Energising potential.
5. Income.
6. Population growth.
7. Health & Fitness.
8. Prosperity.
9. Happiness.
10. Achievement.

Global Cooperative Advantage

Inaugurating the World Summit for social development in Copenhagen, Mr. Boutros-Ghali, Secretary General of United Nations, called for a new social contract: "A new social contract at the global level, is required to bring hope to states and nations and to men and women around the world. In making social issues a universal priority, our intention is to take responsibility for the collective future of international society and to pledge ourselves anew to the idea of global solidarity... today's global economy affects everyone. We also know that its effects are not all positive. It erodes traditional ties of solidarity among individuals. It has marginalised entire countries and regions. The gap between the rich and poor is getting wider."

It is imperative that we move away from global divide, traditional concepts of national competitive advantage, beggar thy neighbour policy, neo-imperial economic and political colonialism, zero sum game to a new mind set and a new concept of cooperation, that is highly creative, constructive and cooperative where the developed and developing nations come together in order to work together sharing knowledge, expertise, technology, science, information, research and management in order to develop every nation in the world to reach certain minimum standards of human growth, economic development and infrastructure development. Thus we operate on the principle of global cooperative advantage, collecting the wisdom of the people of the world to solve problems of poverty, illiteracy, unemployment and social disintegration and to provide for education for all, to liberate humankind from the scourge of darkness; employment for all, to break the shackles of poverty and idleness; and energise all to create a new world human order of prosperity, peace, progress and happiness.

We need, like the Marshal Plan, a very comprehensive plan and global compact between G-7 and nine countries in the Delhi meet (India, China, Brazil, Indonesia, Egypt, Pakistan, Mexico, Bangladesh) to tackle illiteracy and provide education for all. Another consortium of developed countries can work with some African countries. (See diagram V — Global coop. Advantage)

Global Human Growth Index

* Life Expectancy
* Population Growth
* Health and Fitness
* Education
* Employment
* Energising Potential
* Income
* Prosperity
* Happiness
* Achievement

Diagram 1.3(D)

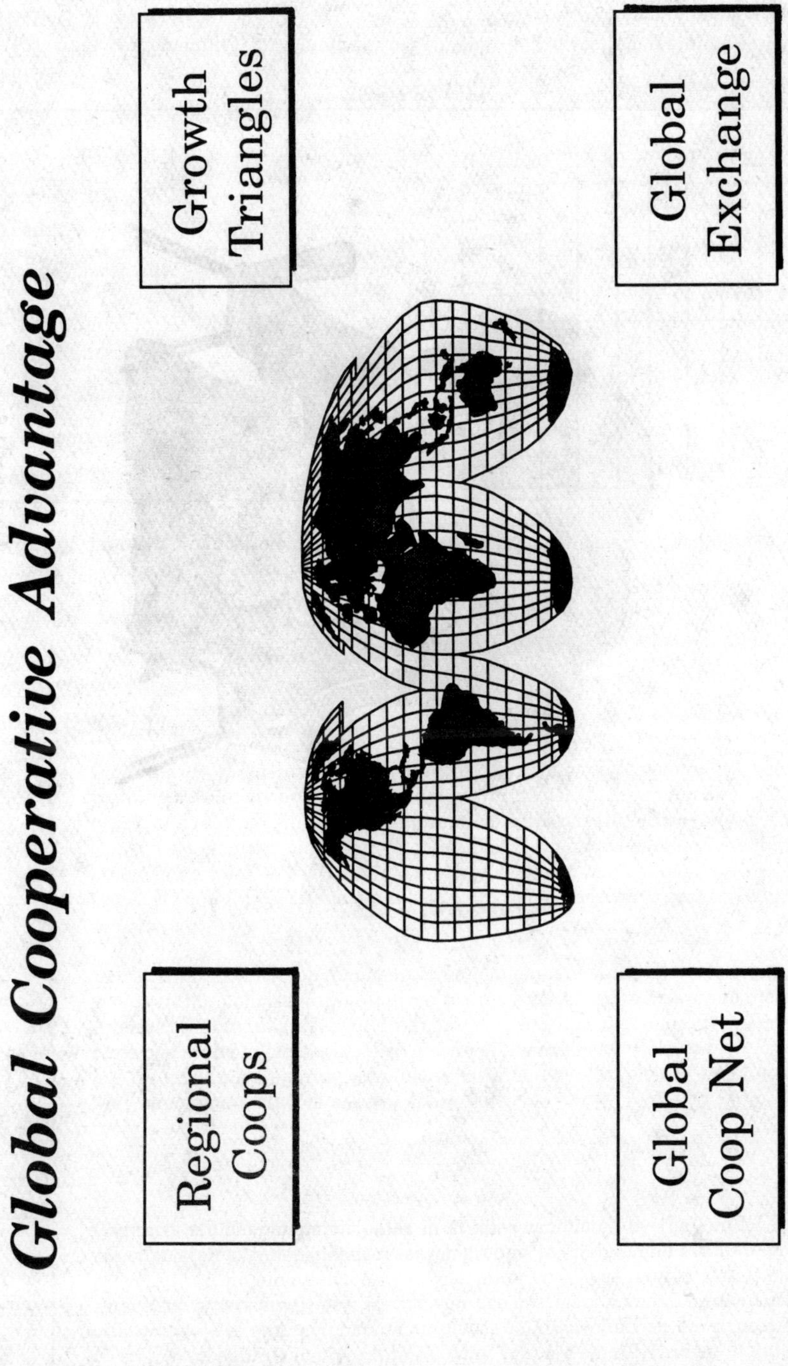
Global Cooperative Advantage
Regional Coops
Growth Triangles
Global Coop Net
Global Exchange

Diagram 1.4

Human Growth Vision ...

Diagram 1.5

Employment

Education
100% Basic Education
35% Poly Education
35% Univ. Education

Employment
100% Employment

New Global Human Order
Global Progress
Global Prosperity
Global Peace
Global Happiness

Energising
100% Self Actualisation
Equal Opportunities
100% Life Goals

Diagram 1.5(A)

Global Human Vision and Future

World population has risen from about 1 billion in 1825 to 2 million in 1925, to 4 billion in 1976 and 5.3 billion in 1990. Estimates for 2025 range between 7.6 billion and 9.4 billion. 95 per cent of the world's population growth will take place in the developing nations.

The Indian Prime Minister, Mr. P.V. Narasimha Rao, observed in his statement to the Plenary Session: "It is only now, at the end of the century, that the leaders of the world have begun to think how to live, rather than how to kill or escape killing.... Our vision for the summit should go beyond the summit itself so as to translate the vision into action. Commitments must be backed by the will to act."

Global Standard

We must aim to achieve certain standards of human growth, if we want to enhance not only the quality of life but also human prosperity, happiness, progress and peace. (*Please see diagram VI — Global Human Growth Vision*)

REFERENCES

1. International Labour Organisation, *Defending Values, Promoting Change,* 1994, ILO, Geneva.
2. World Bank, *Poverty: World Development Report 1990,* Oxford University Press, New York, pp. 1-6.
3. *Ibid.,* p. 1.
4. UN, *Human Development Report, 1994*, United Nations Organisation, New York.
5. ILO, *World Labour Report — 1994,* 1994 International Labour Organisation, Geneva.
6. World Bank, *The Challenge of Development,* World Development Report 1991, 1991 Oxford University Press, New York, pp. 153-157.
7. David Ewing, *Inside the Harvard Business School,* 1990, Random House, New York, pp. 10-11.

❑ ❑ ❑

The above article is a very brief abstract of my forthcoming 621 page book, Global Human Growth Model.

CHAPTER 2

Dynamic Human Resources Management

Personnel Administration — management of human resources — is an evolving science concerned with the management of people and people constitute the principal assets of our business and industry. Any business is as sound as its people. The mission of human resources management is to assure a steady source of sound people who can contribute to the success of business enterprise.

The chapter deals with:

1. What is dynamic Human Resources Management;
2. Changing concepts of management and Human Resources Management;
3. A historical perspective — the evolution of Human Resources Management in U.K., U.S.A. and India;
4. The definition and scope of Human Resources Management;
5. A code of ethics; and
6. Some hurdles in the path of Human Resources Management.

1. WHAT IS DYNAMIC HUMAN RESOURCES MANAGEMENT?

The central thesis is of this volume is to emphasise the dynamic nature of human resources management by highlighting its scope, range, nature, principles, functions, and philosophy. Personnel administration in India, as it is interpreted, discussed and practised, is largely static, legalistic and ritualistic. The buoyancy and dynamism of an art and a science, that seeks to influence, mould, and shape the individuals as members of a group of business organisations with a view to attaining satisfaction in work (perhaps the most important part of man's life) are conspicuous by their absence. There is a great deal of confused thinking and a plain lack of awareness of what personnel administration is and what it can contribute to an organisation. A clear and proper understanding of dynamic personnel administration is a *sine qua non* for successful management.

Mr. J.R.D. Tata observes:

"It was thirty years ago that I put forward a proposal for the creation of a full-fledged Personnel Division in Tata Steel and outlined its basic concept, structure and objectives. I am delighted that its success over the years has fully justified its establishment.

"The main role of the Personnel Division, since its inception, has been to provide functional guidance to the managers and line executives and to advise and assist them. The members of the Personnel Division have always made a sincere attempt to convince managers of the wisdom of the line of action recommended. It is a tribute as much to the managers as to the officers of the Personnel Division that a fine spirit of co-operation has been developed between them. It is only in such an atmosphere of understanding and mutual respect that the personnel officers can perform their often delicate and difficult tasks.

"For us all it is a matter of satisfaction that, apart from a brief politically-instigated strike, there has not been a single instance of a serious industrial dispute in Tata Steel at Jamshedpur since the establishment of the Personnel Division.

"The future holds many challenges for Indian industry but in none more than in the field of industrial relations. For, in this most difficult field of all in industry, we deal not with machines, materials and processes, which require only brains, knowledge, skill and experience, but with human beings, the most complex of all God's creatures, who call for something more in the form of human skills as well as sympathy and understanding."

2. CHANGING CONCEPTS OF MANAGEMENT

The science of management deals with planning, organising, direction, co-ordinating and controlling the co-operative efforts of individuals with a view to achieving certain predetermined ends. Central to the management task is getting things done through people. A study of the evolution of the management concepts as enunciated by the able President of American Management Association, Mr. Lawrence Appley[1] indicates the changing concepts of management regarding "the other fellow."

1. ***Savagery:*** The other fellow is my enemy and is to be destroyed.
2. ***Slavery:*** The other fellow is to be conquered and put at my service.
3. ***Servitude:*** The other fellow is to serve me for a consideration and ask no more.
4. ***Welfare:*** The other fellow should be helped up when down, without too much concern for what got him down.
5. ***Paternalism:*** The other fellow should be cared for, and I will decide to what extent.
6. ***Participation:*** The other fellow has something to contribute to my efforts and can help me.
7. ***Trusteeship:*** That for which I am responsible is not mine. I am developing and administering it for the benefit of others.

8. ***Statesmanship:*** The other fellow is capable of being far more than he is, and it is my responsibility to help him develop to his fullest potential.

Concepts of Human Resources Management

Assisting top management in realising the last concept of statesmanship is the central task and fundamental purpose of dynamic Human Resources Management. There are three fundamental concepts of Human Resources Management recognised in contemporary times. First is the concept of the development of people to their fullest potentialities. Personnel administration must assist individuals to grow in a business organisation to such an extent where they will have complete opportunities to realise their fullest potentialities. The second concept of dynamic Human Resources Management to facilitate the working together of groups of people toward definite predetermined ends. When individual employees are brought together it is very essential to promote the will to collaborate with a view to giving off their best as a team or a group. "The need of winning the whole hearted co-operation of people is the central, ever present problem of management."[2]

The third emerging concept is that Human Resources Management is a profit-cum-growth engineering function. In a recent study conducted by National Industrial Conference Board on personnel managers and their functions, it was found that many personnel executives expressed the opinion that their functions directly contribute to company profitability and growth. Some years ago, Mr. Lawrence A. Appley wrote: "Management is the development of people and not the direction of things; management and personnel administration are one and the same. They should never be separated. Management is personnel administration."[3] Although Mr. Appley knew that there was more to management than just the development of people he rightly pointed out the dynamic nature of personnel administration and its central importance in management.

3. HISTORICAL PERSPECTIVE

A. Evolution of Personnel Administration in U.K.

When labour was treated as a commodity and when no entrepreneur was interested in his employees, as early as in the 1800s, in U.K. Robert Owen[4] of New Lanark (1771-1858), a pioneer in Management, was paying attention to the welfare of the "vital machine" or "animate machines", i.e., the employees. He was asking his fellow manufacturers not to neglect the employees and that it would "pay" in the long run, to take care of the employees. Perhaps he was the first one to pioneer this aspect — the management of people. His ideas were far ahead of his time. He was perhaps the first one to point out and emphasise the relationship between environment and employee efficiency and he wanted entrepreneurs to pay as much attention to "vital machines: as they do to "inanimate machines." Owen had come to the conclusion that human beings behaved as they did, not because of their nature but their nurture. If, for example, that mill folk were prevailingly vicious, it is not because they were born vicious. No, said Owen, it was because they lived in a vicious environment. He renovated the mills, improved the housing, cleaned up the village streets, and opened a store where sound merchandise was sold practically at cost. He was able to accomplish much in other directions. Most important of all, he established a school. It was an extraordinary school because, though intended for the children of workers, it lacked all taint of piety. The one aim of instruction was to develop and keep happy minds in clean and healthy bodies. And, in part, Owen tried to influence that parents. He sought to make the latter take interest in their work and develop a pride in themselves. His efforts paid. "The more he spent on what his partners considered extravagance, the handsomer were the dividends he produced."[5] Robert Owen was visionary and dreamer. Perhaps most of his dreams have come true in modern and personnel practices. Prior to Robert Owen in England, Boulton and Watt Jr. (1770-1848) in their Soho Foundry (Birmingham) showed some interest in the welfare of their workers. They instituted an employees sickness benefit scheme which was run and managed by the workers as early as the 1800s. Another pioneer in the management of people was B. Seebohm Rowntree (1871-1954), who enunciated a new philosophy of industrial welfare. His philosophy was to make industry operate as efficiently as possible through scientific management with a view to offering the workers as ever-rising standard of life. As the Director-in-charge of Labour at the York Cocoa Works he conducted many experiments in promoting the welfare of the workers. With a view too providing economic security to workers after retirement, he instituted as early as 1906 a Pension Fund for the workers in the company. He wanted the industry to provide a decent living to all those engaged in it and he inculcated that no efforts should be spared in attaining this objective. In his approach to the problems of industry he had two underlying principles. First, "Whatever may be the motives which induce any given individual to engage in industry its true basic purpose must be service of the Community." And the second, "Industry is a human thing in which men and women earn the means of life, and from which men and women are entitled to expect the means to a life worth living."

Urwick and Brech make this observation regarding the managerial philosophy of Rowntree: "Business administration is a skilled job and the responsibility for it should be placed in the hands of trained and selected managers. But the workers, as a body, should be kept informed of the conditions and policies on which administration is based. Working conditions, on the other hand, affect the workers closely and hence they are mutually agreed. Every working rule in the factory is fixed by this process of mutual agreement between management and workers. Neither the Board nor an individual Director can make rules indepeendently. But yet there is discipline, the better because it is self-imposed and rests on the solid foundation of self-responsibility."[6]

The Industrial Welfare Society, the Management Research Groups, and the Oxford Lecture Conferences in U.K. Owe their origin and progress to the interest and zeal of Rowntree.

Thus in U.K. Personnel administration had its origin in the concept of welfare as propounded and practiced by some of the enlightened entrepreneurs, who were actually laying the foundations for the evolution of modern personnel administration.

B. Human Resources Management in U.S.A.

The term "personnel management" originated in U.S.A. and it may properly be called the child of scientific management. Personnel management received much impetus from F.W. Taylor's scientific management movement. As one of the essential principles of scientific management, Taylor laid great stress on scientific selection and systematic training and development of the individual worker. "Personnel administration at first became a part of scientific management, particularly in connection with employment, testing, placement, wage determination, and performance evaluation. A paternalistic philosophy of management which predominated after the First World War and during the 1920s also expressed itself through considerable emphasis on employee welfare."[7]

H.L. Gantt, a close associate of Taylor in the scientific management movement, foresaw the need for obtaining the willing co-operation of the worker. He maintained that it was not enough to tell the worker how to do a job, but it was also necessary to promote the ability and willingness to do the job not only through incentive plans but also through proper development of "habits of industry" in the worker as well as through the establishment of the faith of workers in management through a proper philosophy of management expressed in deeds. He used better psychology in his handling of the labour problem by attaching a great deal more of importance to the careful study of the workers' point of view. The human element in industry and business was of paramount importance to him. He believed that business had social responsibilities and that the doctrine of service preached in the churches as religion was good economics and eminently practical.

Along with Taylor and Gantt, F. Gilbreth and his wife Lillian Gilbreth and Mary Parker Follet were interested in the training and development aspects of management. The psychological aspects of worker behavioural patterns received considerable attention from these pioneers of scientific management. Apart from increasing efficiency, they were also interested in fighting fatigue and monotony among the workers.

Perhaps one of the most important breakthroughs for personnel management in particular and management in general was Elton Mayo's Hawthorne experiments, which created a new movement — the human relations movement — and a new school of thought — Behavioural Sciences School — which had a far reaching impact on personnel management. These studies, now world famous paved the way for using the disciplines of sociology, psychology, industrial psychology, social psychology, etc., with a view to understanding employee and organisational behaviour and influencing them through a motivational approach.

All these experiments and studies of the pioneers of scientific management assisted in the gradual evolution and development of a theory and practice of personnel management. There were also other events and influences at work aiding in the rise of personnel management. The dynamic great organisers, who built great industrial and business empires, offered revolutionary concepts such as the economy of high wages, mass production, mass distribution, and mass financing. The huge monolithic corporations employing thousands of employees were too complex to be managed without the help of managers devoted to the management of people. The labour shortages during the world wars and various labour problems on account of union organisation resulting in picketing, strikes, absenteeism and labour turnover posed a challenge to management. When the trade unions came along, employee-employer relations ceased to be simple and uncomplicated. Collective bargaining and meeting the labour's demand for "more, more, more" was not everybody's cup of tea on the side of management.

With the Great Depression in 1929, big business suffered a severe setback and the mass misery that resulted an eye opener. The State, the public and the trade unions clamoured for efficient professional management. Public policy, and the political and social climate obtaining in U.S. forced businessmen to put their house in order. Elimination of waste, maximum utilisation of resources, particularly human resources, and a national resurgence were demanded and these posed new challenges and responsibilities to the management.

All these developments in America inculcated the inevitable proposition that management of people — or personnel management — is just as important as the management of production, or the management of finance, or management of distribution, or the management of materials, etc. There were firms in U.S.A. which evinced keen interest in personnel administration and by 1923 they practised most of the fundamentals of personnel administration as enunciated in five or six standard texts.[8]

Thus it is seen in the West that the entrepreneurial interest, apart from other events, in the concept of worker welfare provided the source of inspiration for the evolution of modern dynamic personnel administration. Although a good deal of interest in the management of people was shown in the beginning by the enlightened entrepreneurs in U.K., it was in U.S.A. systematic research studies and experiments were conducted which ultimately evolved into the present art and science of personnel management. Contemporary personnel administration does not stop with welfare and as a recent research study of National Industrial Conference Board indicated it has assumed the majesty and responsibility of a profit-cum-growth engineering function in industry and business.

In recent times a tremendous responsibility is placed on the personnel function and the personnel executives, who must interpret for their corporations the implications of such things as Executive Order 11,246, The Office on Contract Compliance Revised Orders 4 and 14, The Occupational Safety and Health Act, The Age Discrimination Act, Regulations Covering Hiring Handicapped Workers, The Pension Reform Act, Health Maintenance Organisation Legislation, Environmental Acts, Social Legislation, quality of work issues, and almost daily government decisions on what personnel policies ought to be in effect. Fred K. Foulkes observes: "These expanding human resources concerns call for not only an increasingly strategic role for the personnel function, but also for creative and imaginative thinking and a new social awareness on the part of the personnel staff and line managers."[9]

C. Evolution of Personnel Management in India

While the evolution and development of personnel administration in U.K. and U.S.A. was largely voluntary, in India personnel administration had to be prodded along by governmental intervention and coercion. While in the West the pioneering work in the field of personnel management was motivated by the managerial preoccupation with the concept of welfare, in India a combination of the disquieting recruitment practices, growing labour unrest resulting in strikes and loss of production, and a consideration of numerous grievances initiated some interest in personnel management especially in the textile mills in the years prior to the Second World War.

"In the jute industry for instance, before the war, it was not uncommon for a burra sardar to import and recruit labour, supervise them, punish them, pay their wages, and dismiss them at his pleasure. Often he provided living quarters and even fed the workers during short periods of unemployment. The system was open to all the obvious abuses of corruption, and arbitrary deductions from pay. Moreover, it provided no security at all for the worker."[10]

The Royal Commission on Labour in India under the chairmanship of J.H. Whitley in its report covering all aspects of labour problems recommended the abolition of the "jobber" system of hiring and firing labour and instead, the appointment of labour officers to perform the function of recruitment and selection. "He (labour officer) should be carefully selected and directly responsible to the General Manager of the factory." "Integrity, personality, energy, the gift of understanding individuals and linguistic facility are the main qualities required, for a labour officer," The Commission commented, and added that "if he is of the right type, the workers will rapidly learn to place confidence in him and regard him as their friend. It was recommended that the labour officer should engaged all labour and that none should be dismissed without his consent except by the manager himself after hearing what the labour officer had to say; and that there should be no discharge without showing adequate cause. Finally, it was noted that labour officers can fulfil many other duties, particularly in respect of welfare."[11]

In the meanwhile a series of legal measures was being enacted with a view to regulating hours of work, work environment, payment of wages, employee benefits etc. These legal controls of business and industrial enterprise brought in their wake so many complex regulations that it became necessary for the employers to seek the assistance of specialists in the area of personnel management.

The increasing industrial disputes in the 1920s resulting in strikes industrial disharmony, and loss of production forced the government and businessmen to think seriously in terms of labour problems and promotion of personnel management. The recognition of trade unions in India with their right to organise the workers brought a new perspective to employer and employee relationship.

There were some enlightened entrepreneurs like the Tatas, Calico Mills, Empress Mills, British India Corporation, etc., who had appointed Welfare Officers as early as 1920. Though strongly paternalistic, they had shown a good deal of interest in promoting employee welfare. The social reformers and workers, who were behind the organisation of trade unions in our country and who were carrying on some welfare work, impressed upon the employers the need for a fair and equitable employee-employer relationship as well as the need for proper personnel management. But it was governmental intervention that acted as the catalyst in the evolution of personnel management. The Bombay Trade Disputes Conciliation Act of 1934 appointed Labour Welfare Officers, whose function was the redressal of employee grievances and the promotion of industrial harmony, and the Commissioner of Labour as the Chief Conciliation Officer. On the recommendation of the Bombay Government, the Mill Owners' Association also appointed a Labour Officer with a view to getting a settlement of disputes with his Government counterpart. This system worked well. In 1937 in Bengal on the suggestion of Government the Indian Jute Mill Owners' Association appointed a Labour Officer to bring about a settlement of employee grievances with the mills and by 1939 there were five more Labour Officers appointed and their duties gradually increased. Other Employers' Associations like Indian Engineering Association, Indian Tea Association, the Engineering Association of India, etc., also followed the example of IJMA in appointing Labour Officers.

In 1941 the Government of India initiated the Tripartite Labour conference with the representatives of Government, labour and employers with a view to promoting uniform labour legislation, determining a procedure to settle industrial disputes, and promoting consultations on industrial matters affecting the country. Now they have become permanent and regular features of labour policy.

The Indian Institute of Personnel Management summarises the evolution of Personnel Management in India thus: "It will be seen that it was the interaction of Government policy and the initiative of the leading employers' associations in the textile industries that brought about the rapid development of personnel management in India just before and during the war. It is noticeable also, that in textile industries personnel management developed rather from the recruitment function and the consideration of grievances than from the welfare function as in other countries. It was the problem and the discontent to which the old system of recruitment through jobbers gave rise that led the Royal Commission on Labour to advocate the appointment of labour officers. Their function as industrial relations officers to handle grievances and to prevent disputes arising was stressed from the first. The labour officer was looked on as the friend and confidant of the workers, but he was clearly to be a member of management."[12]

But the development of personnel management was slow. Finally the Factories Act of 1948 (Section 49) and Mines Act (Section 58) required all factories and mines employing more than 500 employees to appoint Welfare Officers, whose functions were stipulated by the Rules under Section 49.

4. DEFINITION AND SCOPE OF HUMAN RESOURCES MANAGEMENT

Personnel administration is variously known as 'Personnel Management', 'Labour Management', 'Industrial Relations', 'Employee Relations', 'Manpower Management' and the manager who performs this function is also known variously as 'Personnel Manager', 'Employee Relations Manager', 'Industrial Relations Manager', 'Labour Relations Manager.' In India he is called 'Labour Officer', 'Labour Welfare Officer', 'Welfare Officer', 'Personnel Officer or Manager', 'Employee Relations Officer', 'Industrial Relations Officer', etc. The term 'personnel administration' is chosen here to connote a wider meaning, which includes both personnel management and industrial relations.

Professor Thomas G. Spates, a leader in the profession, offers the following definition: "Personnel administration is a code of the ways of organising and treating individuals at work so that they will each get the greatest possible realisation of their intrinsic abilities, thus attaining maximum efficiency for themselves and their group, and thereby giving to the enterprise of which they are a part its determining competitive advantage, and its optimum results."[13]

Professor Michael Jucius defines personnel administration as:

"The field of management which has to do with planning, organising, and controlling various operative functions of procuring, developing, maintaining, and utilising a labour force, such that the

"(a) Objectives for which the company is established are attained economically and effectively.

"(b) Objectives of all levels of personnel are served to the highest possible degree.

"(c) Objectives of the community are duly considered and served."[14]

The Institute of Personnel Management in U.K. defines personnel management as follows:

"Personnel Management is that part of the management function which is primarily concerned with the human relationships within the organisation. Its objective is the maintenance of those relationships on a basis which, by consideration of the well-being of the individual, enables all those engaged in the undertaking to make their maximum personal contribution to the effective working of that undertaking."[15]

The Indian Institute of Personnel Management has adopted the above definition of the Institute of Personnel Management of U.K. and which was subsequently modified by the later in 1963 as follows:

"Personnel Management is a responsibility of all those who manage people as well as being a description of the work of those who are employed as specialists. It is that part of management which is concerned with people at work and with their relationships within an enterprise. It applies not only to industry and commerce but to all fields of employment.

"Personnel Management aims to achieve both efficiency and justice, neither of which can be pursued successfully without the other. It seeks to bring together and develop into an effective organisation the men and women who make up an enterprise, enabling each to make his own best contribution to its success both as an individual and as a member of a working group. It seeks to provide fair terms and conditions of employment and satisfying work for those employed.

In this definition three objectives are expressed:

1. To maintain good relationships within an organisation,
2. To enable each person to make his maximum personal contribution to the organisation as a member of a working group,
3. To achieve these things through respect for human personality and the well-being of the individual."

In the West, Particularly in the U.S.A., there is a greater recognition of the human element and its potential in industry and business and many businessmen and management specialists are a good deal preoccupied with shaping and influencing this element through personnel administration. In India there appear to be certain attitudinal blocks and hurdles in the path of personnel management.

Fred K. Foulkes and Henry Morgan present a total personnel concept of Human Resources Function:[16]

From our studies we have developed a way of looking at the total personnel function and breaking out aspects that are best handled at different places by different people. Thus we can identify four distinct aspects of the personnel function:

1. Formulation of personnel policy — a top management responsibility.
2. Implementation of policies by the line managers — the service function.
3. Audit and control — the establishment of standards and procedures to see that organisation policies are maintained.
4. Innovation — research and development of new practices, procedures, and programs.

We find that many personnel departments are not organised to get the whole job done. In fact, service and audit activities bog some of them down so that they can give only scant attention to policy formulation and innovation — the most important functions in the view of a number of line managers, including chief executive officers, whom we interviewed.

Most managers recognise the longer-range critical policy problems. Many of them, however, demand administrative or maintenance type of help at the expense of policy problem solving. The urgent always gets in the way of the important, and, consequently, the personnel function should be organised to get both jobs done.

Policy Formulation

Undoubtedly, a most critical issue for any organisation is the formulation of personnel policy. In an evaluation of the personnel department of a large organisation, we asked a high-level administrator how personnel policy was formulated. His answer was, "I don't know. I don't have a good picture of it." When the personnel director of the same organisation was asked the same question, his answer was, "Each policy has a different process." When pressed, he said that policies were developed on an "as needed" basis in response to some new problem or crisis.

Confusion arises because people mean different things by "personnel policy." At the extremes, policies range from simple administrative procedures such as schedules for coffee breaks to crucial institutional issues relating to growth strategy, location of plants, and attitudes toward unions.

While much input from various people and in different ways is essential, we believe that top management should formulate the critical policy decisions relating to personnel. Such decisions should not be allowed to develop in response to crises, and they should be integrated with basic corporate strategies.

In general, the formulation of personnel policy is simply too important to be left to the personnel department alone. Personnel policies need to take into account the law, ethics, and the developmental needs of people and costs. Above all, they should reflect accurately the goals and values of the organisation.

Edwin H. Land, chief executive officer of the Polaroid Corporation, describes the strategies of his company:

"We have two basic aims. One is to make products that are genuinely new and useful to the public, products of the highest quality and at reasonable cost. In this way we assure the financial success of the company and each of us has the satisfaction of helping to make a creative contribution to the society.

"The other is to give everyone working for the company a personal opportunity within the company for full exercise of his talents — to express his opinions, to share in the progress of the company as far as his capacities permit, and to earn enough money so that the need for earning more will not always the first thing on his mind. The opportunity, in short, to make his work here a fully rewarding and important part of his life."

All personnel strategies at Polaroid flow from the second basic aim. The personnel policy committee consists of top corporate officers and is chaired by a senior vice president, with members of the personnel department serving as staff to the committee. In addition, all levels of the organisation, through a "yellow draft" system, extensively review proposed policy changes before their formal adoption.

Needless to say, personnel policies have to be well administered, for the essence of policy is administration. In personnel, as in everything else, good policies poorly administered mean little.

There is no question about the role of personnel in the implementation of policy, but what should its role be in the formulation of policy? A good personnel department can provide feedback into policy from two directions. First, it knows the concerns of employees and traditionally has represented their views. Second, in response to a world of increasing complexity, it has an outward perspective on social changes and their resulting legislative and regulatory impact on policy.

Policy formulation has two aspects: the process and the content. In the personnel area, where effective implementation counts for so much, the process can be as important as the content of the policies themselves. Thus we would recommend that personnel join with others in top management as a partner in the balancing of values that is the heart of the process.

In one large company, a recent personnel policy change upset so many people that it had to be modified considerably. The company had long had a job posting system, but the change called for selecting the most senior qualified applicant as opposed to the prior policy of selecting the "best qualified." This change raised so much havoc that the company went back to the old policy for all exempt jobs. The new policy continues, amidst much disagreement, for nonexempt employees.

Regardless of the equity of the approach, the issue would have fared differently, we feel, if it had been discussed by a method similar to that used by Polaroid's personnel policy committee of line managers.

In another case, Honeywell recently formed an executive employee relations committee composed of five operating group vice presidents and five staff vice presidents. This committee serves as a senior policy board in respect to employee relations. Commenting on this, Charles Brown, Honeywell's vice president for employee relations, said: "We go to the committee with one or more proposals for changing something at every meeting, and we have had practically 100% acceptance. Once an idea is endorsed by the committee, its implementation becomes relatively easy." The executive employee relations committee at Honeywell is also responsible for evaluating the top 200 management positions in the company.

At Honeywell, proposals approved during 1976 included a significantly upgraded employee communications program, improvements in the company's merit pay plan, and increased emphasis on recruiting talented minorities and women.

Does any set of personnel policies universally fit all situations? We think not. If they did, management could simply find and adopt them. The best personnel policies are like the best organisational strategies — they are contingent upon the particular situation and they depend on the strategy of the company.

Within a company, with respect to both setting and administering personnel policy, one must ask where and when uniformity is essential and when it is unnecessary. Given the different missions and diversity of some organisations, some local autonomy and flexibility is frequently desirable. While discretion can result in inconsistency, a certain amount of inconsistency can be lived with, at least in some organisations. And the price of a detailed set of uniform rules and regulations may be very much higher than the price of discretion.

We admit, however, that inconsistent policies at times bring difficulties in equitable administration and in compliance with government regulations. Good sense suggests that sometimes people are being treated fairly when they are not being handled in a uniform manner. Yet, unfortunately, the law sometimes makes it hard these days to justify such action.

The best personnel policies for Polaroid, Xerox, or IBM arise from different contexts from those for U.S. Steel, Kennecott Copper, and the Ford Motor Company. Good personnel policies must be judged by how well they serve the particular management and employees. Do they work? Are they easy to understand and implement? Do they contribute to the attainment of corporate goals?

Good personnel policies cannot stand apart from the basic strategies for the organisation as a whole. The two aims of Polaroid, for example, each form an essential part of one inclusive corporate strategy, neither part separable from the other.

Policy Implementation

The "bread and butter" of the personnel job is service to line management. Personnel assists in the hiring, training, evaluating, rewarding, counselling, promoting, and firing of employees at all levels. Personnel administers the various benefit programs such as educational reimbursement, health and accident programs, retirement, vacation, and sick level. The department also has a role with respect to grievances.

Personnel must, however, guard against becoming a servant to, as opposed to a service to, the line organisation. As one personnel vice president put it, "if you get into that servant role, you're asked to arrange the Christmas party and the retirement parties and that's about it."

While most good managers recognise that dealing with personnel matters is an integral part of their own jobs and that they generally must retain the responsibility for final selection of job applicants and other crucial decisions, the personnel representative can provide valuable support such as the initial screening and all necessary signing-in-processes after the final decision.

Although personnel departments have had to develop specialised expertise to maintain their usefulness and justify their existence, it is often this special expertise that brings about dissatisfaction with personnel departments. For example, dealing with people is a critical part of any manager's job, and most managers believe they are competent at the practical level. They may seek help when they are overextended, but they do not want the personnel department to do things for them that they feel competent to do.

Thus the HR representative who provides service to line managers must understand their needs and provide the help asked for — help that may require little special expertise. The personnel representative at the decentralised level, working as part of the management team, must be more of a generalist. (We will discuss the role and place of the personnel specialist in a later section of this article.)

The HR department must also be accessible. We observed that wherever there is a physical decentralisation of operations, the personnel function should be similarly decentralised. Those performing the personnel function should be where the people and the problems are. There should be a strong sense of mutual "ownership" of the HR department by both management and employees at the local level. Correspondingly, personnel needs to identify with the organisation and feel a part of it.

Consider the recent experience of a large and highly decentralised company. One of its plans produces five major product lines. Within the past two years, product management teams have been established for each line consisting of two technical or operations people and one marketing person. Each team has the authority to draw on all resources available for the profitable production and sales of its set of products.

The company noted that because of the technical nature of the manufacturing and sales involved, these teams found a definite need for personnel planning within the organisation. In fact, this need became so strong that, in three of the five teams, personnel people have been physically moved to the team location and are directly participating in the work of the team. The personnel people, moreover, have the same evaluation of their work as do the line managers under the company's management by objectives program.

In smaller organisations that are physically decentralised but without the resources to employ local personnel representatives, the personnel function can be performed on a part-time basis by someone other than a member of the personnel department. We believe it better to perform the service function locally, even if it is not assigned to a specialist in personnel, than to insist that a central personnel group try to serve where its people are not seen as members of that organisation. One organisation has made the administrative assistant to a department manager the official provider of personnel service to that department.

In a bank we studied, a line officer, who is responsible for a large clerical operation, said: "I wish HR would realise that this part of the bank is a factory with three shifts. What we need are blue-collar types rather than traditional bank types. If only the personnel people would visit us sometime, they might better understand what it is we do."

While this comment says something about the staffing of the personnel department, it is also relevant to our organisational point. It would probably be better to designate someone in the department as a HR coordinator.

However, management can go too far with a decentralised approach. Decentralisation in the personnel area has both costs and benefits. Ways need to be found to lower the costs. For example, at one large company, a former senior HR administrator, who was promoted from HR to a line job, said:

> "I think our decentralised approach to personnel is one of our strengths and also one of our weaknesses. By aligning the personnel function with the line organisation, it becomes much closer to the action, really learns to understand what pressures line people are under, and becomes actively involved in working with line managers to meet their goals.
>
> "However, from a corporate standpoint, this results in a somewhat fragmented personnel function. The separate groups tend to function independently and, as a result, much effort is spent in reinventing the wheel. It is very difficult to coordinate with this type of organisation."

Therefore, as HR service is provided locally and as implementation is decentralised, there is a corresponding need to strengthen, but not necessarily enlarge, the centralised personnel function to help maintain organisational consistency and integrity. There should be strong and centralised auditing to ensure proper and consistent policy implementation by the generalists at the local level.

Audit and Control

Of the four organisational issues we are dealing with here, a most critical one today is that of audit and control. The coherence and integrity of the entire personnel service function depends on good personnel policies that, in turn, require follow-up to ensure that they are indeed being properly practiced. This follow-up requires a strong and centralised audit of actual practice.

One organisation we studied has recently implemented a job audit program. Under this program, a central personnel member checks what employees actually do on their jobs against the job descriptions to ascertain whether there are any serious discrepancies. This company adopted its approach after some women employees filed an equal-pay suit.

Management, doing what it thought proper under its affirmative action plan, had consciously given these women additional responsibilities for development purposes. The women, however, claimed they were doing more than the men were and that they were not being paid accordingly. A job audit revealed that this was indeed the case and thus the women were given back pay. Afterwards management adopted a job-audit program to avoid future legal challenges.

The various requirements of state and federal regulations (for example, the Occupational Safety and Health Act, the Equal Employment Opportunity Commission, Wage and Hour Acts, Employee Retirement Income Security Act) make increasing demands on both profit and non-profit organisations. In 1949, the U.S. Department of Labour was responsible for enforcing 16 statutes and executive orders. By 1960, the number had grown to 40. Today it is more than 130.

While the reader could argue intelligently that the regulatory list is too long to permit proper enforcement, in the meantime compliance is necessary. Responses and reports to these regulators can be made only from a central group supplied with accurate information. In addition, this centralised group must be made up of specialists — well trained in legal requirements and in accounting and reporting techniques, and well reinforced by the full power and authority of top management.

Unfortunately, too many organisations suffer from inadequate and incompetent staff in their central audit and control group. This function should be in the hands of personnel specialists. Compliance with the laws relating to OSHA, EEOC, and ERISA demands expertise. Expertise is also needed in the content of, installation of, and administration of wage and salary plans, in the increasingly complex field of employee benefits, and in surveying what is happening in the outside world. Labour relations and grievance procedures also require the knowledge of an expert. And crucial to the entire audit and control function is the need for a superior employee information system.

Separation of the service function from the auditing function can relieve a large part of the anxiety and ambiguity of the service-control conflict. This will make the personnel function more effective and better accepted as part of the management team.

There should be more innovative ways to perform the audit and control function. Line managers need to develop further their personnel knowledge and skill. Two companies use impressive approaches to accomplish these objectives: one for labour relations and one for health and safety.

- One company has added a Step 3½ to its grievance procedure (Step 4 is arbitration). At this step, managers from nearby plants hear grievances. This procedure encourages a plant manager to get involved in day-to-day labour relations in order not to be embarrassed in front of his fellow plant managers.
- Another company requires that all of its plant managers devote two weeks a year to safety and health inspections at two plants other than their own. One week is spent at each plant. The inspection team, with the help of a company safety specialist, conducts a complete safety audit. This exercise not only educates the plant managers about safety and health and their importance but also motivates them to keep their own houses in order, since the manager knows that sometime during the year a team will be inspecting his plant and making a report to top management.

Innovation Role

The final important function of the HRM department is to provide up-to-date information on current trends and new methods of solving problems. We call this the innovation role. Personnel departments can escape their errand-boy guise and gain the respect of other members of management by providing credible information on trends concerning human resources and related policy proposals. Such a role will permit top management to plan its course of action rather than operating on an emergency basis. A personnel department able to provide timely advice to management on how to shape and use its human resources will have no trouble making its voice heard in executive councils.

Naturally, the innovative role must be in tune with the times and the set of issues confronting a particular company. In periods of rising inflation and escalating wage and salary demands, the emphasis may be on compensation issues. In times of retrenchment and falling profits, creative work sharing and layoff plans may be needed.

Currently, there is a great deal of interest in improving the quality of work life to fight boredom and decreased productivity in both blue collar and white collar jobs. More and more promoting executives in their 40s are deciding to get away from high pressure, treadmill jobs and are abandoning careers they have pursued for years, thus leaving gaping holes in the ranks of the up-and-coming. Employees are demanding changes in the ways in which work is organised. There is an increasing concern and growing legislation about privacy. There are proposals to encourage employee stock ownership.

All these issues require the attention of personnel. And, since the issues change with the times, personnel must be responsible, adaptive, anticipatory, and, especially, innovative. Because of the changing nature of demands, the personnel function must be characterised as pragmatic rather than doctrinaire.

Let us look at some of the specific issues and consider how and where innovation can best take place according to our concepts of central versus dispersed operations.

Attitude Surveys: The purpose of this activity is to assess and evaluate employees' attitudes. Who needs this information? The central office of corporate headquarters? The plant or office manager? Or both?

It seems to us that attitude surveys trigger action at the local level. The local manager certainly needs to have the survey information as a measure of the local pulse. Does a central office need the same data? Is it a local situation, purely local, or is it often part of a large system trend? We believe that attitude surveys should be made locally and sent to central office for audit, since action and service belong at the local level with auditing and control at the central level.

Work hours and Work life: Can management allow flexible working hours at one location and not at another? Should local personnel managers be allowed, or encouraged, to engage in research and experimentation, or should this research be done only at a central point to maintain equity and uniformity?

Depending on the status of union contracts or the potential for union organisation, local experimentation and research can be desirable or disastrous. Basic chances in working conditions and hours of work are critical issues of policy and should be carefully controlled corporation wide. This does not mean that variations cannot be allowed or encouraged in response to local conditions, but they should be administered in the light of overall policy.

Job Design: It can be argued that job design is an integral part of a compensation system and must be developed and audited centrally. But the knowledge about the job and persons holding jobs obviously resides at the local level. Compliance with corporation-wide standards can be too rigid, so that managers have little or no incentive to try something new in job design.

Perhaps central specialists should assemble the basic tools of job design, with the information gathered and the implementation carried out at the local level. When job redesign involves new classifications and hence changes in compensation systems, some central authorisation and monitoring is necessary, but, without local initiative and participation, it is unlikely that much will ever change.

Pay and Benefits: Because of the critical factor of equity, pay and benefits must be established and controlled centrally. The requirements of various governmental regulatory bodies, on top of the continuing need to ensure conformity with corporate strategy, have forced greater uniformity and less arbitrariness in compensation.

Government regulations form part of a societal trend that is sounding the death knell for many types of merit pay plans. Too many of these plans have been administered in such a way that the recipients cannot comprehend them. As a result, most wage and salary plans have become minor variations of a straight seniority system.

This subject is too complex for detailed discussion in this article. For our purposes here, however, we should simply remark that compensation requires centralised standardisation.

Our analysis and prescriptions for the placement of different activities could be called a contingency approach to organisation. Basic to this approach is task, since we find that certain tasks are better performed in different places.

Another element of concern in the contingency approach is the environmental forces. Many of the pressures on the personnel department today arise externally, as we have discussed. It is exactly these external changes that an innovative personnel department must sense and track to anticipate the need for internal response ahead of situational crisis.

HRM as 'Change Agent'

One danger requires a strong warning. That is the self-appointment by personnel to the role of "change agent." Any HR director who appoints himself his company's change agent is presumptuous. Anybody in a business who sets out without invitation to reform his senior colleagues is headed for trouble. In addition, simply as a practical matter, the role of internal change agent is difficult, especially on a part-time basis, added to the administrative responsibilities of an entire department.

On the other hand, if the personnel director is indeed to be a part of the executive team, can he also be a satellite of the organisation? Are these two functions, personnel manager and change agent, compatible? Many organisations, struggling for stability in a stormy sea of external change, will not look kindly on the change agent in their midst.

In our experience, most of the people who try to fill this role do not see themselves as trying to institute the change, but sincerely consider that they are helping the organisation respond, adapt, and survive. But their colleagues in management see them as the proverbial messenger bringing bad news, creating change, and creating trouble. And, like the messenger, they often suffer a disastrous fate.

As a consequence, the personnel manager often works himself into the position of feeling excluded from major management decisions and then, doning the robe of missionary and reformer, the position of defender of the downtrodden with whom he identifies. This role will further alienate him from management, because he will be seen as working against things as they are, and against established policy. He will be seen as leading the charge against the ramparts of status quo. At this point, the only direction for the personnel manager to charge is out of the door.

One HR manager we knew felt it was his responsibility to educate his top management. He developed training programs to identify and deal with social change issues. Although the effort was well intended, it required that a cultural change take place within that company. The company's operative style was one of reaction to crisis, and these training programs required an anticipatory or proactive response. These programs required more than the support of top management, in fact, top management had to institute and lead them. The personnel manager as change agent, as a satellite, cannot even produce an adaptive mode, let alone produce change itself. As one company chairman put it:

> "One weakness of personnel people is that they think they are God's favourite children. Too many simply want to rock the boat rather than solve the problem. They need to take responsibility. It is easy to come up with ideas. But there is a need to think things through. Things can't be done that quickly, especially when they involve sales and production people. HR people don't seem to understand that things can't be implemented tomorrow."

With respect to change, the personnel manager plays a role similar to the one he plays with respect to HR policy. He should be the agent to look at change rather than the change agent. Personnel can be the expert staff that identifies areas of concern, researches choices, and provides certain skills in training and implementation. But personnel alone does not decide what changes are needed, nor does it deliver the solutions. Change strategy, like policy information, must be "owned by" the appropriate leaders in the organisation. There must be an institutionalised process for developing policy and for change.

In our view, it is important to recognise, however, that while it is difficult and frequently inappropriate for the personnel officer to assume a Janus role, the chief personnel officer should be sufficiently tuned to the needs of employees via his personnel network to make certain that the employees' viewpoint is given appropriate consideration on critical matters. Sometimes it is legitimate for a personnel director to play a change agent role. As one personnel vice president put it:

> "The ideal situation is when the HR guy is a consultant. But in the real world there are a number of people in responsible positions who have no interest at all in the growth and development of their people. Personnel may be the only one an employee can turn to in non-union company. Sometimes I have to be a bad guy with the manager. I have to be a change agent or a catalyst."

What makes this personnel vice president's behaviour appropriate is the fact that he has the backing of his company's president and chairman. Personally recruited for his job by the president, this man has a value system congruent with the value system of the president and chairman of this family-controlled company.

In summary, self appointment to a change agent role can be suicidal for the individual and dysfunctional for the organisation. For the change agent role to be effective, not only does the personnel officer need to be part of top management, but other members of top management need to be committed to the appropriateness of one of their members in a change agent role.

Earlier we referred to two aspects of policy formulation, process and content. In regard to change, we see the personnel manager as the custodian and protector of the process of change. In this role, he keeps channels of communication open — channels up and down and sideways, channels that flow in and out of the company.

Line management, particularly at and near the top, must be responsible for the content of change. In assuming process as a fundamental part of his job, the personnel manager gains strength and avoids the risk we have warned against.

Staffing Considerations

While the personnel function must be organised properly to be effective, competent staffing is equally important. Though we have already said a little about staffing, we wish to deal more explicitly with this subject. How large should the staff be? What is a competent personnel department member? How has he or she been trained? How can competence be recognised and rewarded?

Too often, personnel members have been called incompetent. Too often, other departments have used personnel as a dumping ground for their failures. Some personnel departments are staffed by people recruited from outside. They do not know the business, and sometimes they show no interest in learning it. Some company personnel departments are staffed by people who have been somewhat less than successful in the line organisation. Weak people who do not engender respect and who cannot hold their own at staff meetings do not add to a department's credibility. Too often, people seek personnel work because they "like working with people."

Effectiveness in much of personnel work has little to do with liking or disliking people, rather, it requires a willingness to take the time to understand the individual needs of employees in order to identify with their problems. This is true in a direct counselling session, in labour negotiations, or in dealing with another member of senior management or the chief executive officer.

While many companies have faced up to the need to get properly trained, talented, and motivated people into the personnel function, the old image is sometimes still there. Personnel people, to be effective, ought to have a working knowledge of what goes on in a plant or office.

Specialists and Generalists

We recognise the need for a wide variety of talents. We see the need for the specialist, particularly in the areas of audit and innovation. However, we also see a strong need for the generalist in the areas of service and policy.

As we have described it, the auditing function requires detailed knowledge of the legal and regulatory aspects of personnel. It requires the development and understanding of systems, and the collection, storage, and use of large quantities of information. Personnel must have the ability to understand the needs both of the line organisation and of the various branches of state and federal government.

In many respects, all elements needed cannot be found in any one person. Rather, we suggest that a team be developed. This team would include specialists trained in personnel compensation and benefits, in the uses of computers and data systems, and in law, either in the department itself or on call.

However, because a team of personnel specialists will lack the ability to understand the needs of the line client, both manager and non-manager, we suggest that people trained in other ways should supplement the auditing and control part of the department.

Line Managers and Supervisors

One source of talent will come from line managers and supervisors who have needed personnel information themselves to help them be good managers. In effect, these are the consumers of personnel services. They will bring to personnel the knowledge, language, and requirements of the line. Such managers will improve the company, and line managers will get help from someone who talks their language.

After a stay of perhaps two to five years, when the temporary member of personnel returns to the line, he or she will service as a valuable ally of, and interface with, the personnel department. Half of IBM's corporate personnel staff consists of line managers who remain in that function for no more than two or three years.

The increasing demand for personnel to be better integrated with the rest of the organisation appears in nearly every situation we have met. A woman personnel officer at a trade association talked about the changes she had noted in the caliber of people going into personnel work in an industry that increasingly draws union interest. Commenting on this, she said:

> "Top management has finally realised that the people costs are as important as other costs. Lately, I've noted more forceful people in the personnel and labour relations field. They now have more of a voice in top management. You can't just talk it; you have to do it. The person entering the field today isn't the 'has been' who used to hang around in this field."

Current and Future Superstars

Management now pays greater attention to who heads the function. Where seniority and grandfather clauses used to prevail, many organisations today ask their current and future superstars to lead the personnel department. In one company, after a long conversation about personnel's role and other topics, the vice president of personnel casually stated, "When the president is away, I run the company." Attracting and holding a person of this caliber, one who can and does take over the reins when necessary, is becoming increasingly common.

One of the immediate effects of asking a superstar from the line organisation to head the personnel function is to increase the salary of the position, for good people do not move for less money. Thus it is important not only to rotate managerial talent into and out of personnel but also to alter the reward system to show that the organisation values such service.

In addition to having credibility with top management, the line executive who becomes the personnel vice president has to, in turn, rely on the staff people because they possess the specialised knowledge that he is lacking. Staff people thus have greater influence.

It is also more natural, perhaps, to put the personnel vice president with line experience on the executive committee and on the bonus committee, positions that indicate influence to other line managers. Such status and influence have been and will continue to be obtained by the well-prepared and trained personnel specialist who becomes a personnel generalist through his training and experience.

But does this mean that there is no great future for the well-trained specialist in the personnel department? No, but the well-trained specialist must learn the language of the rest of the organisation and go beyond his own special language, jargon, and concepts. Some who have done so have become very effective personnel vice presidents.

Just as we have suggested that line managers and supervisors take a turn through personnel, so should the personnel specialist take a rotation through a line job in order to increase the ability to understand and deal with the organisation as a whole.

It may be, however, that some personnel staff jobs have become so specialised that such people cannot handle a line job. If this is so (though we suspect these cases are rarer than is so (though we suspect these cases are rarer than is commonly thought), then such people should, in addition to teaching or taking courses in psychology, law, human relations, and personnel, take courses in marketing, finance, and general management. They also need to find ways to spend more time in offices and plants so that they become more familiar with what actually happens on a day-to-day basis.

Interested Employees

Many nonunion companies have still another source of personnel talent. These companies generally have highly developed communication networks for a two-way flow of information. Employees must know what management is thinking, and managers must also know what employees are thinking.

In such companies, interested and articulate members of the non-salaried, non-exempt ranks can become important resources for personnel. In fact, the best potential new members for personnel have often been the harshest critics. Far from bringing such employees into personnel to co-opt or silence them, the company should give them an opportunity to make improvements in the very things they found to criticize.

In one company, several key division personnel managers had been at one time hourly employees. The training in personnel, coupled with their previous hourly work experience, had made them effective with both management and workers.

While such a transition may be more difficult in unionised companies, those companies ought to have people in personnel who have seen a side of the company other than that learned through the route of college, an MBA, and several years of management experience. Is just as important for personnel people to understand the language, goals, and values of top management, we should add.

Thus, we see many sources of talent for a well-rounded, effective personnel department: the college-trained specialist, the line manager taking a rotation through personnel, the line manager with a career commitment to the function after years in the line, and the hourly employee who is upwardly mobile. Above all, look for talent, not among those who "like working with people," but among those who want to be effective and who like to be part of the total organisation.

Naturally, besides selecting people for personnel, management must think about their development. To provide the focus, attention, and coordination this activity requires, IBM has a director of personnel development who reports to the personnel vice president. His sole responsibility is the development of personnel people in IBM on a worldwide basis.

Guidelines for Evaluation

We are left with one final question: How does management evaluate the effectiveness of the personnel department? This question obviously needs to be thought through in the context of the particular organisation and its specific goals. What is effective for Texas Instruments may not be for Polaroid, or vice versa. But there are some common questions and guidelines.

While people like to think that their organisation is unique, the personnel job in reality does not differ greatly, whether it takes place at Macy's, INA, Citi-bank, or IBM. Organisations do face common problems. In the area of personnel, the similarities may in fact be greater than the dissimilarities. Every organisation has to handle people and define personnel's role, particularly how it relates to top management, and to develop the appropriate policies.

From our study of personnel departments and interviews with line managers, we can define three important measures for evaluating the effectiveness of the personnel functions.

1. ***Operating measures:*** Budget for the function as a percentage of company or division sales. Size of personnel staff to size of employee group serviced.
2. ***Quantity measures:*** Number of nurse visits and of industrial accidents per month. Cost per professional employee hired. Number of days to process insurance claims.
3. ***Quality measures:*** Analysis of grievances and of the issues personnel is involved in plus the nature and the level of its involvement. Employee feedback on specific corporate issues. Effectiveness and professionalism of personnel staff (that is, group as well as individual performance).

Undoubtedly, other criteria could be added to this list. But the point, it seems to us, is that personnel, like all staff work, has to be evaluated with rigour, and not only as to its results but also as to how efficiently those results are achieved. To do so, the organisation should develop measures and criteria in accord with its objectives. Any such evaluation should include periodic checks with line managers, the clients of the personnel department.

From

"The Twelve Principles of Efficiency," by Harrington Emerson, p. 59; New York: Engineering Magazine Company, 1912.

5. A CODE OF ETHICS

The Society of Personnel Administration in the U.S.A. has adopted a 'Code of Ethics for Personnel Administration' which apart from giving a definition encompasses the scope and philosophy of personnel administration:

"Personnel administration is the art of acquiring, developing and maintaining a competent work force in such a manner as to accomplish with maximum efficiency and economy the functions and objectives of the organisation.

Those in personnel administration are pledged:

- To be ever mindful of human dignity in all relationships and personnel decisions;
- To be guided in all actions by integrity and a conscious regard for the common interest;
- To accomplish the responsibilities and authorities of office without thought or appearance of personal gain;
- To conduct the personnel function so as to recognise merit without favour to individuals or groups, and in such a manner that will secure employee confidence and management support;
- To recognise fully the relationships of the work situation, the human being and society;
- To encourage programmes which will stimulate the work force in improving efficiency;
- To assist both management and employees in the development of each employee's potential and assignment to task for which he is best suited;
- To improve employee knowledge of the purposes, policies, and programmes of the organisation and to provide effective means for employee contribution to the operations of the organisation;
- To be candid and forthright with management concerning its responsibilities to employees concerning their performance and services to the organisation;
- To seek objective solutions to employee and management problems having personnel implications;
- To treat as confidential, information received in trust."

The code of ethics, apart from setting a moral and philosophical tone and canons of conduct for personnel executives, clarifies the nature and scope of responsibilities facing personnel administration and the men in this profession.

The Indian Institute of Personnel Management has also evolved the following code of ethics for the profession of personnel management in India.

Code of Ethics

Recognizing and accepting the responsibilities of the profession of personnel management, I, as a member of the Indian Institute of Personnel Management, shall:

- "Uphold the honour and dignity of the profession and the Institute; and shall perform my professional duties with fairness, impartiality, fidelity and dedication to the cause of the profession;
- Recognise and accept the dignity and worth of an individual as a human being irrespective of race, relation, language, caste or creed, and strive for the development of his personality;

- Co-operate in maximising the effectiveness of the profession by exchanging freely information and experience with others and by contributing to the development of the profession to the best of my ability;
- Maintain at all times an open mind with regard to problems that I have to deal with in the course of my work and approach the problems of others with understanding;
- Not allow any interest other than professional to interfere with my official work;
- Strive unceasingly for self-development by acquiring ever increasing knowledge, skill and experience related to the profession;
- Endeavour to extend public knowledge on professional matters and try to eliminate misconceptions and misunderstandings about the profession;
- Express publicly an opinion on professional matters only when it is founded on adequate knowledge and honest conviction;
- Not damage, directly or indirectly, the professional reputation or practice of other members;
- Exercise due restraint in criticising the work of other members;
- Endeavour to give credit for professional work to those to whom it is due;
- Endeavour to provide opportunities for the development and advancement of professional men who work with me;
- Uphold the principle of appropriate remuneration for those engaged in professional work;
- Not associate in work with another member who does not conform to ethical standards and not hesitate to bring to the notice of the Institute unethical practice adopted by any member of the Institute;
- Be faithful to my employer or client, and present clearly to him the consequence to be expected if my professional advice is not accepted;
- Advise engagement of specialists when I am convinced that such services are in the best interest of my employer or client and shall cooperate with them in their work;
- Follow professional principles and practices tactfully and courageously keeping in mind the principles of equity in the fair distribution of work and rewards;
- Promote the concepts, methods, skills and techniques in the field that contribute to productivity, growth, profitability and employee satisfaction;
- Not disclose any information of a confidential nature that I may acquire in the course of professional work without obtaining the consent of those concerned; and
- Not accept or officer any improper gratification in any form or manner whatsoever in connection with or in the course of my professional work."

6. SOME HURDLES IN THE PATH OF HUMAN RESOURCES MANAGEMENT

Till recently in India, management, let alone the functional areas in it, did not receive much attention. While in the West as early as 1870 there was an awareness and a recognition of the management principles and concepts and a desire to test, experiment, and apply them in business, the role of management was realised only recently in India and efforts are being made to understand and utilise the managerial concepts. A fallacious notion was that just as there are born leaders, there were born managers and that you could not teach or train individuals to become managers.

It was thought exposure and experience — trial and error methods — would convert men into managers and anybody given sufficient time and opportunity, would be able to manage. Gradually it is being recognised that this might be a costly procedure and that it is possible to train and develop managers through managerial education.

There is a direct relationship between the size and complexity of business and interest in management. The larger, more complex and sophisticated the business, the greater the interest in management. As firms grow larger in size and complexity in India, scientific and professional management will come to play a more important role in moulding the destinies of business organisations. The functional areas of management such as marketing, production, sales, finance, personnel etc., with functional specialists will be brought in to manage the organisation effectively and efficiently.

Although personnel officers are introduced on the industrial scene by the Factories Act, the nature, scope, functions and philosophy of personnel administration are yet to make an impact. There are some attitudinal blocks that pose problems in the path of personnel management and prevent the appreciation of its need in India. First and foremost, perhaps, is the distinct lack of awareness that personnel administration is a functional specialisation in management with its own expertise. One top executive recently observed: "But for the law, I would not have hired a personnel officer. I do not see any need for this man in my company. There is nothing that he can do which I cannot do myself." Just as professional management has taken time to make the grade, personnel administration is yet to arrive on the industrial scene. Perhaps when industry and business grow into large organisation the need for professional managers and personnel managers will arise.

Already in larger organisations there is a distinct improvement in the status, responsibility, challenge, emoluments and prestige of the personnel executive and the function has come to play a prominent role.

Secondly, there is the master-servant relationship obtaining in employee relations, where the employer thinks that he knows what is best and stifles the employee's initiative and his behaviour. The employee should just follow his 'commands.'

Thirdly, there is the familiar paternalistic attitude where employer-employee relations are reduced to a father-son relationship. The 'children should be seen but not heard' attitude is not conducive to the promotion of proper personnel administration.

Fourthly, the legalistic attitude pervades the employer-employee relations and most of time, both the parties strictly attempt to adhere to the latter of the law and not its spirit. Instead of voluntary bilateralism both the union and management assume the eminent position: let the law take its own course. As a consequence, the legal advisers have come to occupy the front benches and personnel officers have been relegated to play the second fiddle.

Fifthly, perhaps a strong worker association in the form of trade unions would have forced employers to take more interest in the management of people. The poor organisation and finances, unstable and outside leadership, inter-union rivalry, and multiplicity of unions, political influences, and a large majority of educationally weak membership have rendered the labour movement weak and not very effective, although some unions in the country have made their impact on management.

Sixthly, the nature of the Indian labour force itself is another hurdle in the sense that there is an abundant supply of labour which is largely unskilled or semi-skilled and inexpensive. There is no compelling need on the part of the employer to use the various advanced techniques of personnel administration to select, maintain, and motivate the employees. If one employee leaves, there are many seeking his job and the baby boom in the country is constantly and continuously adding men to the total labour pool. There is another side to the problem. The non-commitment of the migrant worker, the indebtedness of the migrant worker, the various languages and customs have complicated the problem.

Finally, Professor Jucius points out these obstacles in the path of personnel management:

1. Precise methods of measuring labour's interests or contributions are lacking.
2. The human factor is difficult to interpret and its probable future actions are difficult to forecast.
3. The common human shortcomings of ignorance, selfishness, and prejudice interfere with the application of logical methods.[17]

Even in United States "the problems with the current personnel departments stem from two sources: (1) the lack of expertise in the function, and (2) disrespect for the function, deserved or not, on the part of too many top managements."[18]

There was a time when the personnel director was primarily concerned with only blue-collar workers; he had little effect on company policy. He was viewed as little more than a record keeper and director of recreation, one chief duty being to preside at retirement parties. Peter Drucker's often quoted comment about personnel management as "partly a file clerk's job, partly a house-keeping job, partly a social worker's job, and partly 'fire-fighting,' heading off union trouble or settling it," is not without substance.

Personnel people who view themselves or are viewed as "do-gooders" also pose problems. A transfer to personnel has rarely been seen as a step up the experience or promotion ladder; and surveys have shown that "a majority of major corporation personnel directors could not state the dollar volume of sales for their company, did not know the profit level and had little idea of the rate of return."[19] In fact, the comment of a chief executive who, when asked what qualifications he would like to see in his personnel director, replied: "The ability to read and understand the company's financial statement."

Unless the personnel director can affect policy, is well compensated, has room for development, and is encouraged to take on occasion an employee advocate's role, it will not be possible for chief executive officer to attract top-notch people to the field.

Fred Foulkes maintains: "It is essential that a chief executive officer helps create a personnel function that is active, creative, independent and sensitive to some of the conflicting needs of company and its employees." He quotes Richard Anton, Vice-President of human resources of General Telephones: "Far too many practitioners in the employee relations field tend to neglect basics involved of the latest fad and to the degree that this is true, they do disservice both to the profession and the business that they serve, as a result I think, you will find many companies very weak in the development or articulation of philosophy concerning their approach to their employee relations or human resources work. From my own observations many employee relations people fail or never try to identify and reconcile employee and company to objectives. One of the results is that too often employee relations programmes do not effectively support company business objectives or, sometimes, do not even reveal an awareness of their existence."

These obstacles pose serious methodological problems for personnel administrators and because of these challenges, there is a greater need and effort to understand the functions to cope with ever-changing but ever-present problems concerned with the management of people.

REFERENCES

1. Quoted by Curtis H. Gager, "Management Throughout History", in H.B. Maynard, *Top Management Handbook* (New York: McGraw-Hill Book Company, Inc. 1960), p. 69.
2. Paul Pigors and Charles Myers, *Personnel Administration* (Tokyo, Kogakusha Company Ltd., 1961, Asian Student Edition, 4th ed.), p. 11.
3. Lawrence A. Appley, "Management — the Simple Way", *Personnel,* Vol. 19. No. 4, 1943, pp. 595-603.
4. See Robert Owen, *A New View of Society* (New York: E. Bliss & E. White, 1825).
5. Curtis H. Gager, "Management Throughout History", *op.cit.,* p. 63.
6. L. Urwick and E.F.L. Brech, *The Making of Scientific Management*, Vol. 1, Thirteen Pioneers (London: Sir Isaac Pitman & Sons Ltd., 1957, 3rd ed.), p. 69.
7. Pigors and Myers, *Personnel Administration*, p. 7.
8. See Frank B. Miller, *Historical Sources of Personnel* (Ithaca, New York: Cornell University, New York State School of Industrial and Labour Relations, 1960), p. 3.
9. Fred K. Foulkes: "The Expanding Role of the Personnel Function", *Harvard Business Review*, March-April, 1975, p. 72.
10. Indian Institute of Personnel Management (IIPM), *Personnel Management in India* (Bombay: Asia Publishing House, 1962), p. 20.
11. *Ibid.,* p. 41.
12. IIPM, *Personnel Management in India*, p. 47.
13. *An Objective Scrutiny of Personnel Administration* (New York: American Management Association, Personnel Series No. 75, 1944), p. 9.

14. Michael J. Jucius, *Personnel Management* (Homewood, Illinois: Richard D. Irwin Inc., 4th Edn., 1959), p. 25.

15. IIPM, *Personnel Management in India*, p. 31.

16. Fred K. Foulkes and Henry Morgan, *Organising and Staffing the Personnel Function,* Harvard Business Review (Boston: Harvard Business School, May-June, 1977, pp. 143-154.)

17. Jucius, *Personnel Management*, p. 20.

18. Fred K. Foulkes, *Ibid.,* pp. 73-79.

19. George Odiorne, *Management by Objectives,* Newsletter, July 1974.

❑ ❑ ❑

CHAPTER 3

The Field of Human Resources Management

This Chapter deals with the field of Human Resources Management and the discussion is carried on under the following sections:

1. Functions of Human Resources Management.
2. Human Resources Management — a staff function.
3. Human Resources Management and other areas of management — organisation charts.
4. Human Resources Manager — his status and qualifications.

1. FUNCTIONS OF HUMAN RESOURCES MANAGEMENT

The Central Model Rule 7 of Section 49 of the Factories Act of 1948 stipulates the duties of the Welfare Officer as follows:

1. To establish contacts and hold consultations with a view to maintaining harmonious relations between factory management and workers;
2. To bring to the notice of the factory management the grievances of the workers, individual as well as collective, with a view to securing their expeditious redress and to act as a negotiating officer with trade unions;
3. To study and understand the point of view of labour in order to help factory management to share and formulate labour policies and to interpret the policies to the workers in language they can understand;
4. To watch industrial relations with a view to using his influence in the event of a dispute between factory management and workers and to help bring about a settlement by persuasive effort;
5. To deal with wage and employment matters by joint consultation with the factory management and workers' representative bodies;
6. To exercise a restraining influence over workers going on illegal strikes and over managements declaring illegal lockouts and to help in preventing anti-social activities;
7. To maintain a neutral attitude during legal strikes or lockouts and to help in bringing about a peaceful settlement;

8. To ensure fulfillment on the part of the factory management of obligations statutory or otherwise, concerning the applications of provisions of Factories Act, 1948, and the rules made thereunder, and to establish liaison with Factory Inspector and the Medical Services concerning medical examinations of employees, health records, supervision of hazardous jobs, sick visiting and convalescence, accident prevention and supervision of safety committees, systematic plant inspection, safety education, investigation of accidents, maternity benefits and workmen's compensation;
9. To promote relations between factory management and workers which will ensure productive efficiency as well as amelioration in the working conditions and to help workers to adjust and adapt themselves to the working environments;
10. To encourage the formation of works and joint production committees, co-operative societies and safety-first and welfare committees, and to supervise their work;
11. To ensure provision of amenities, such as canteens, shelters for rest, creches, adequate latrine facilities, drinking water, sickness and benevolent scheme payments, pension and superannuation funds, gratuity payments, granting of loans and legal advice to workers;
12. To help the factory management in regulating the grant of leave with wages and explain to the workers the provisions relating to leave with wages and other leave privileges and to guide the workers in the matter of submission of application of grant to leave for regulating authorised absence;
13. To secure welfare provisions, such as housing facilities, foodstuffs, social and recreational facilities, sanitation, advice on individual personal problems and education of children;
14. To advise the factory management on questions relating to training of new starters, apprentices, workers on transfer and promotion, inspectors and supervisors, supervision and control of notice board and information bulletins to further education of workers, to encourage their attendance at technical institutes;
15. To suggest measures which will serve to raise the standard of living of workers and in general promote their well-being.

There was a good deal of confusion in the terminology used, in the duties laid down for the Welfare Officer between the Central Rules and State Rules. In 1957 a committee of experts was appointed by the Government to make their recommendations to improve the stipulations and the committee's recommendations were as follows:

In function 2 the words "act as a liaison officer between management and labour" should replace the words "act as a negotiating officer with trade unions."

Functions 5, 6, 7 should be deleted as they are not appropriate functions of a Welfare Officer.

In function 8 "To advise on fulfilment by the concerned departments of the factory" should replace the words "to ensure fulfilment on the part of the factory management."

In function 9 "To promote relations between the concerned departments of the factory and workers which will bring about productive efficiency" should replace the words "to promote relations between factory management and workers which will bring about productive efficiency," since the Welfare Officer would be dealing with heads of departments concerned.

In function 11 "to encourage" should replace "to ensure."

In function 13 "to advise on provision of welfare facilities" should replace "to secure welfare provisions."

However, these recommendations have not eliminated altogether the initial confusion regarding the duties of Welfare Officer and in fact, it has introduced some new ones.[1] The Indian Institute of Personnel Management summarises these functions as follows:

1. Improvement of industrial relations;
2. Promotion of joint consultation;
3. Helping management to formulate a labour policy and improving communication between management and workers;
4. Advising management on the fulfilment of statutory obligations relating to safety, health and welfare at work;
5. Improving factory amenities and welfare provisions;
6. Advising management on training and further education of workers.[2]

Presenting a paper on "The Personnel Manager in India" at an IIPM Conference Dr. S.D. Punekar observed:[3]

A list prepared in the Tata Institute of Social Sciences is given below. It maybe possible that a single officer may not be able to perform all these functions.

(A) EMPLOYEE WELFARE

(I) Conditions of Work Environment

1. Working Conditions: (i) Temperature, (ii) Ventilation, (iii) Lighting, (iv) Dust, smoke, fumes and gases, (v) Noise, (vi) Humidity, (vii) Posture — simple and complex (Convenience and comfort during work, operatives' posture, sitting arrangements, etc. (viii) Hazards and safety devices.

2. Factory Sanitation and Cleanliness: (i) Provision of urinals and lavatories, (ii) Provision of spittoons, (iii) Provision for water disposal (Drainage), (iv) Provision for disposal of waste and rubbish, (v) Provision of proper bathing and washing facilities, (vi) Cleanliness, white washing and repair of buildings and workshops, (vii) Care and maintenance of open spaces, gardens, roads, etc.

3. Welfare Amenities: (i) Provision and care of drinking water, (ii) Canteen services, (iii) Lunch rooms, (iv) Rest rooms, (v) Creches, (vi) Cloak-rooms, (vii) Other amenities.

(II) Employees' Health Service

1. Factory Health Service: (i) Medical examination of employees, (ii) Factory dispensary and clinic and treatment, (iii) First-aid and ambulance rooms, (iv) Treatment of accidents, (v) Health education and research.

2. Recreation: (i) Play grounds for physical recreation (Athletics, games, gymnasium, etc.)

(III) Workers' Education

(i) Education to improve skills and earning capacity, (ii) Literacy, (iii) Library, pictorial education, lecture programmes, etc., (iv) Workers' Education Scheme and its working.

(IV) Economic Services

(i) Employees' Cooperative Societies, etc., (ii) Grain shops and Fair Price shops etc., (iii) Housing Cooperatives.

(V) Housing for Employee and Community Services

(VI) Study of the Working of Welfare Acts

(i) Factories Act, (ii) Employees' State Insurance Act, (iii) Bombay Labour Welfare Fund Act, (iv) Minimum Wages Act.

(VII) Social Work in Industrial Settings

(Application of social work techniques)

(i) Family Planning, etc., (ii) Employee Counselling.

(B) INDUSTRIAL RELATIONS

(I) Standing Order

(i) Model and Certified Standing Orders, (ii) Their variations and reasons, (iii) Application and administration of Standing Orders, (iv) Beginnings of industrial relations. How and why?

(II) Grievances

(i) Grievance investigation (causes, incidence, etc.), (ii) Model grievance procedure and company procedure, (iii) Settlement of grievances, (iv) Statistical grievance analysis.

(III) Disputes

(i) Causes of disputes (case studies), (ii) Measures for prevention of disputes, (iii) Works Committee, (iv) Settlement of disputes, (a) Conciliation, (b) Arbitration, (c) Adjudication.

(IV) Trade Union and Union Management Relations

(i) Trade Union Organisation — Open shop, Union shop, Closed shop and Check off system, (ii) Labour-Management Cooperation (mutual aims) Codes, JMCs and Joint Committees, (iii) Collective bargaining and administration of collective agreements, (iv) The role of Trade Unions in relation to matters under the "Welfare area" (v) Implementation and Evaluation Machinery at the Centre and in the States.

(V) Strike, Lock-out, Layoff, Retrenchment, Closure

(VI) Study of the Working of the Various Acts Covering Industrial Relations

(i) Industrial Employment (Standing Orders) Act, (ii) The Indian Trade Union Act, (iii) The Industrial Disputes Act, (iv) The Bombay Industrial Relations Act.

(C) PERSONNEL ADMINISTRATION

(I) Recruitment

(a) Recruitment of Personnel: (i) Knowledge of sources of employee supply, (ii) Reception of applicants and interviews, (iii) Investigation of references, (iv) Tests: (a) Physical tests, (b) Trade tests, (c) Personality tests, (v) Final selection and appointment.

(b) Job Descriptions and Job Specifications, Job Analysis, Manpower Planning.

(II) Retainment

1. Placement: (a) Job Assignment, (b) Job Enlargement, (c) Personal Development.

2. Induction: (i) Introduction to the job and work place, (ii) Introduction to the supervisor, (iii) Introduction to colleagues, (iv) Introduction to welfare amenities and other facilities, (v) Authorities and procedures, (vi) Service conditions, (viii) Sponsor system (follow-up interviews).

3. Wage and Salary Administration (Job Evaluation): (i) Wage scales — Increments and E.B., (ii) Salary and wage standardisation — Wage Boards, (iii) Incentive payments and allowances, (iv) Working hours and overtime, (v) Profit-sharing bonus, (vi) Holidays, leave, etc., (vii) Executive Compensation Plans, (viii) Fringe Benefits and perquisites.

4. Discipline and Supervision: (i) Instances of indiscipline — Misconducts, (ii) Causes of indiscipline, (iii) How to deal with indiscipline — Domestic Enquiry, (iv) Handicaps of management in maintenance of discipline and enforcement of certain rules, (v) Shopfloor supervision and its responsibilities.

5. Transfer and Promotion: (i) What is the procedure adopted? (ii) Causes for transfer and promotion, (iii) Personnel for transfer and promotion, (vi) Records of transfer and promotion.

6. Merit-Rating and Evaluation of Employees: (i) Assessment techniques, (ii) Counselling, etc.

7. Motion and Time Study and Work Study (Industrial Engineering).

8. Prevention of Losses: (i) material loss, (ii) Work Loss, (iii) Time loss.

9. Administration in relation to:

(i) Absenteeism	(a) Causes
(ii) Late-coming	(b) Incidence
(iii) Loitering	(c) Effects
(iv) Employee turnover	(d) Remedies, etc.
	(e) Statistical analysis

10. Personnel Training and Development Training programmes for:

(i) Apprentices	(a) Courses and Equipment
(ii) Workers	(b) Training Staff
(iii) Foremen and supervisors (TWI)	(c) Staff Colleges and Training Centres.
(iv) Junior Executives	
(v) Management Staff, etc.	

11. Personnel Records and Statistics (Preparation of Charts, Graphs, etc.): (i) Accident records, (ii) Employee turnover studies, (iii) Absenteeism and indebtedness, (iv) Wage levels and cost of living (C.P.I.), (v) Research into industrial relations and personnel management problems.

12. Organisational Behavioural and Behavioural Sciences. Dynamics of Organisation Theory. Line and Staff Concepts. Team Concept.

(III) Retirement

(1) Provident Fund and Pension plans; (2) Gratuity Provisions; (3) Exit interview; (4) Long Service Awards; (5) Retirement plans — Housing, Medical aid, etc.

(IV) Study of Working of Following Acts

(i) Apprentices Act, (ii) Employment Exchanges (Compulsory Notification of Vacancies) Act, (iii) Payment of Wages Act and Payment of Bonus Act, (iv) Shops and Establishments Acts, (v) Employees Provident Fund Act.

With a few glaring omissions, the statutorily fixed functions of the Welfare Officer are quite comprehensive, but the spirit and the purpose of personnel administration in India are largely vitiated by the adoption of excessively legalistic postures by the main characters on the industrial scene — management, labour, and Government. By legal measures alone, personnel administration cannot be promoted, even as law by itself cannot promote social reformation in society.

One major corporation in U.S.A. very succinctly enumerates the personnel administration functions as follows:

1. Placing the right man on the right job.
2. Starting new employees in the organisation.
3. Training men for jobs that are new to them.
4. Improving job performance of each man.
5. Gaining creative co-operation and developing smooth working relationships.
6. Interpreting the company policies and procedures.
7. Controlling labour costs.
8. Developing potential abilities of each man.
9. Creating and maintaining a high level of departmental morale.
10. Protecting health and physical condition of employees.

The simple organisation chart in Figure 3.1 highlights the major functions of personnel administration.

The most comprehensive list of the functions of personnel administrators is provided by the Indiana State Chamber of Commerce in Figure 3.2.

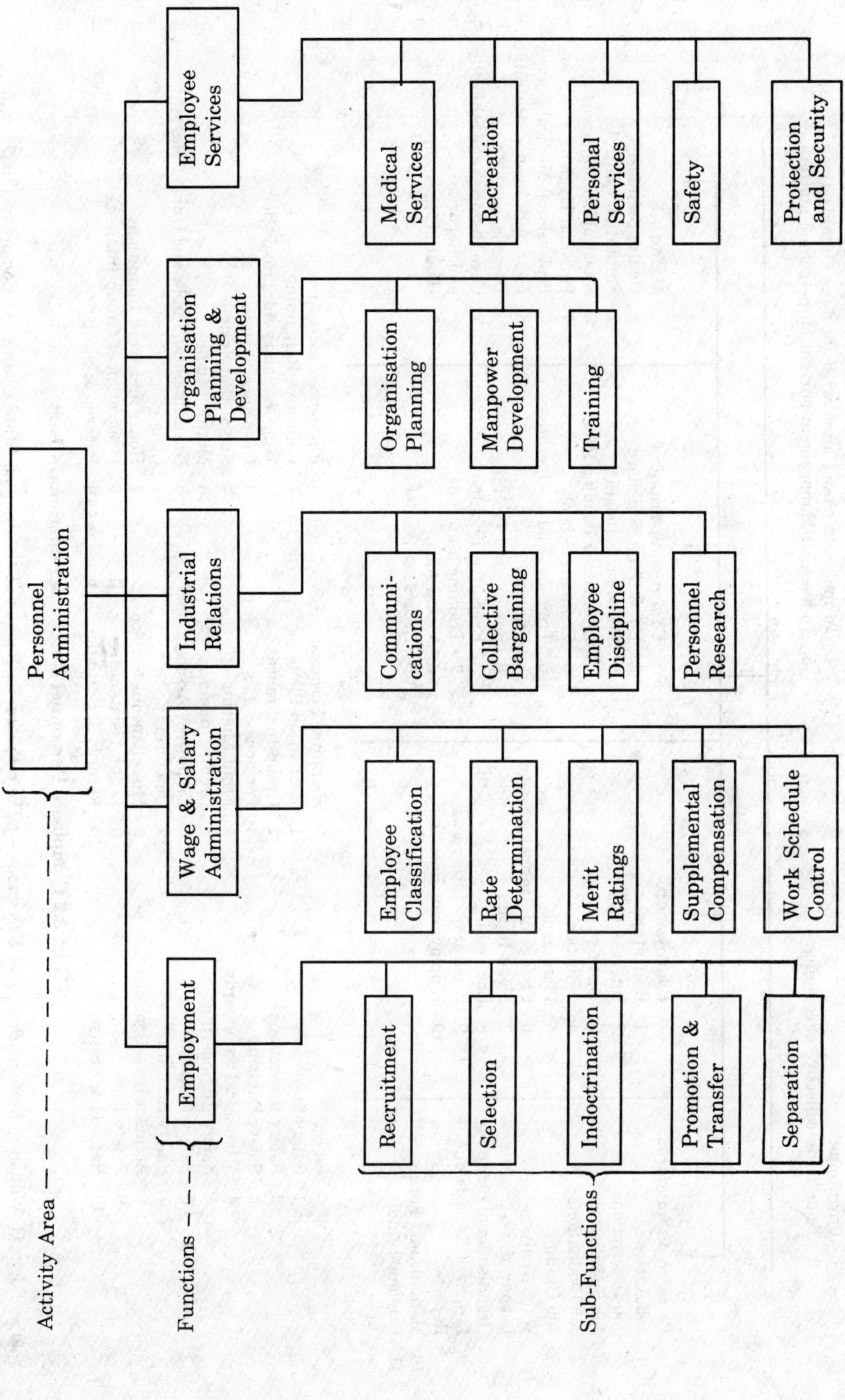

Fig. 3.1 Personnel Administration Activity Area

Personnel Relations Director

1. To plan, organise and control Personnel Relations Programme.
2. To assist in collective bargaining.
3. To assist in formulation of Personnel policies.
4. To maintain close liaison with the Line Organisations.
5. To keep all Management current on personnel matters.

Research & Standards:
1. Job Analysis
2. Job Descriptions
3. Job Specifications
4. Job Evaluations
5. Job Grading
6. Wage Analysis
7. Labour Market Surveys
8. Organisational Planning
9. Design of Records and Reports
10. Manuals and Forms
11. Personnel Audit

Employment:
1. Recruitment
2. Interviewing
3. Testing
4. Induction
5. Placement
6. Change of Status
7. Merit Rating
8. Counselling
9. Separation Interviews
10. Employment Records

Education & Training:
1. Ed. & Trng. Standard
2. Economic Education
3. Libraries & Reading Rooms
4. Company Schools
5. Training Plans. Operative Training
6. Supervisory Training, Executive Training
7. Training Materials
8. Visual Aids
9. Records & Statistics

Medical:
1. Health Standards
2. Sanitation Control
3. Physical Examinations
4. Personal Hygiene
5. Professional Medical Services
6. First Aid Rooms, Hospitals & Dispensaries
7. Case Histories and other Records and Reports
8. Health Education

Safety:
1. Safety Standards
2. Safety Inspections
3. Safety Publicity
4. Mechanical Safeguards
5. Safety Engineering
6. Safety Contents
7. Safety Education
8. Accident Investigations
9. Safety Rules
10. Records & Statistics

Employee Services:
1. Recreation Plans
2. Group Insurance
3. Pensions
4. Profit Sharing
5. Credit Unions
6. Employees Associations
7. Cafeteria
8. Miscellaneous Service
9. Legal Assistance
10. Records & Statistics

Employee Relations:
1. Collective Bargaining
2. Wage & Salary Administration
3. Grievance System
4. Suggestion System
5. Morale Studies
6. Governmental, Public and Union Relations
7. Hours and Work Conditions
8. Integration of Group Interests
9. Records & Statistics

Fig. 3.2 Composite Personnel Relations Functional Chart

Source: Edgar G. Williams, *Indiana Personnel Executives — Their Programs,* Booklet of the Indiana State Chapter of Commerce (1952), p. 5.

The following table provides more details with respect to the broad categories of functions of personnel administration.

Table 3.1

DETAILS OF INDUSTRIAL RELATIONS PRACTICE

(Adapted from the questionnaire used by the University of Minnesota Industrial Relations Centre in periodic surveys of industrial relations ratios and budgets.)

I. General Administration of the Industrial Relations Department:

1. Formulation of industrial relations policy.
2. Planning, coordinating industrial relations activities.
3. Planning recommending revisions in company organisation structure.
4. Selection, promotion, transfer of industrial relations staff members.
5. Work assignment for industrial relations staff members.
6. Supervision of industrial relations staff members.
7. Employee records.
8. Records on specific phases of industrial relations programme.
9. Reports of activities.
10. Review and evaluations of industrial relations programmes and practices.
11. Budgeting for industrial relations programmes.

II. Recruitment, Employment, Placement:

1. Forecast of personnel requirements.
2. Manning tables; personnel inventories.
3. Labour market studies: sources of employees.
4. Recruitment: recent college graduates.
5. Recruitment: non-supervisory production employees.
6. Recruitment: non-supervisory office employees.
7. Recruitment: supervisory, managerial, executive.
8. Recruitment: sales.
9. Recruitment: technical and professional.
10. Pre-employment testing programme.
11. Pre-employment interviewing.
12. Reference and experience checking.
13. Pre-employment physical examinations.
14. Placement: referring selected applicants to job openings.
15. Coordination of promotions, transfers, demotions.
16. Coordination of lay-offs and recalls.
17. Coordination of quits, discharges.
18. Exit interviews.

III. Training and Development:

1. Orientation and induction of new employees.
2. On-the job training: shop, office, sales.
3. Apprenticeship and other craft training.

4. Out-of-hours vocational courses.
5. Tuition refunds.
6. Scholarship programmes.
7. Supervisory training.
8. Management training.
9. Graduate training for professional and scientific personnel.
10. Conferences and short courses: inside company.
11. Conferences and short courses: outside company.
12. Job rotation programme.
13. Internship trainees — co-operative arrangements with schools.
14. Educational and vocational counselling.
15. Appraisals of employee potential and performance.
16. Appraisals of supervisory and managerial potential and performance.

IV. Labour Relations:

1. Collection of information preparatory to contract negotiations.
2. Preparation of company briefs.
3. Contract negotiations.
4. Contract interpretation and day-to-day administration.
5. Dealing with union representatives in administration of contract.
6. Grievance handling.
7. Preparation and presentation of cases for arbitration, mediation, NLRB Government agencies.
8. Check-off.
9. Union-management Committee: e.g., health and welfare.

V. Wage and Salary Administration:

1. Job analysis and job description.
2. Job evaluation and grading.
3. Establishment of wage rates and rate structures.
4. Rate review and adjustment.
5. Wage and salary surveys.
6. Wage incentive plans.
7. Profit sharing plans.
8. Stock purchase plans.
9. Bonus plans.

VI. Administering of Benefits and Services Programmes, including Health and Safety:

1. Life insurance.
2. Medical and hospital care insurance.
3. Unemployment compensation; supplementary unemployment benefits.
4. Severance pay.
5. Disability pay.

6. Workmen's compensation.
7. Rehabilitation of handicapped workers.
8. Sick leave.
9. Leave of absence (military and other).
10. Vacations.
11. Recreation programmes and social events.
12. Food services.
13. Employee newspapers and magazines.
14. Informational booklets: handbooks, policy manuals.
15. Annual reports to employees.
16. Bulletin boards.
17. Music.
18. Thrift and savings programmes.
19. Credit union.
20. Counselling.
21. Awards for long service.
22. Suggestion systems.
23. Periodic physical examinations.
24. First aid and dispensary service.
25. Preventive medicine and health education.
26. Occupational hygiene.
27. Safety inspections.
28. Accident investigations.
29. Accident control activities.
30. Safety training and safety promotion campaigns.
31. Safety equipment: machine guards, personal protective equipment.

VII. Research:

Plan and conduct research studies within the company on:

1. Measurement devices: tests, weighted application blanks, rating scales, etc.
2. Interviewing.
3. Supervision and leadership.
4. Supervisory and employee attitudes.
5. Job satisfaction.
6. Training needs.
7. Training techniques.
8. Training subject matter.
9. Motivation.
10. Employee-management communications.
11. Turnover and absenteeism.
12. Methods of wage payment.
13. Techniques of recruitment.
14. Employee benefit plans.

15. Records design and control.
16. Participate in studies conducted by outside research groups.
17. Maintain library of pertinent industrial relations materials.

Another major Company in U.S.A. stipulates the following duties to its Vice-President of Personnel Administration who reports in a direct line relationship to the President of the company:[4]

1. To aid in the development of general overall management policies and methods, and in the organisation and planning for supervisory control and the communication of orders, ideas, and inquiries.
2. To develop throughout the organisation an understanding of and an enthusiasm for consultative methods of management with the objectives in mind of — (a) improving leadership and supervision, and (b) obtaining participation of operating groups and opportunity for creative analysis and initiative in carrying out their assigned tasks in all levels in the development and administration of the company's personnel programme.
3. To aid the executive and supervisory organisation in developing — (a) clearly written outlines of functions, authorities, and responsibilities; and (b) simple, workable methods of measurement of their accomplishment.
4. To formulate, in collaboration with the supervisory and executive organisation, the policies of personnel administration, and to implement those policies approved by management with the best plans and practices of personnel administration.
5. To follow through, in collaboration with the appropriate supervisory and executive personnel, in making certain that the company's approved policies and practices of personnel administration are executed properly.
6. To establish and maintain contact with labour movements, to keep informed and wherever possible to participate in all collective bargaining activities, and to advise all departments of the company in the development of sound labour relations.
7. To aid in the interpretation of management's policies to employees' points of view and attitudes to management and in collaboration with the appropriate line personnel, to merchandise the company and the job to employees.
8. To aid all those who direct the work of others to become better personnel administrators.
9. To supervise the staff of the department.
10. To inform, to advise, and to caution the supervisory and executive organisation on those matters included within the context of personnel administration.

The same company lays down the following duties to the Personnel Administrator, who reports in a direct line relationship to the Vice-President:

1. To develop, and submit to the Vice-President for approval, the overall policies of personnel administration.

2. To prepare, and submit to the Vice-President for approval, written standard practice procedures and personnel bulletins for all of the personnel practices, plans, and procedures in effect.
3. To supervise the medical, store training, trainee, and other training programmes, wage and salary, benefit plans, employment and development, and labour relations divisions of the national headquarters department and the personnel director of the headquarters office.
4. To direct all activities of the department in the absence of the Vice-President.
5. To be of general assistance to the Vice-President in furnishing advisory service and in checking the efficiency and effectiveness of the regional, plant, and other local personnel offices.
6. To assist the Vice-President in his duties with respect to labour unions and collective bargaining.
7. To execute special assignments from the Vice-President.
8. To maintain at all times a list of unfinished projects and a proposed time schedule for their execution.

The same company has the following activities included within the scope of the department of personnel administration:

Personnel Practices	*Benefit Plans*	*Labour Relations*
Employee records and statistics	Recreation	Business agents
Recruiting and Interviewing	Medical	Union Officials
Selecting and placement	Hospital	Collective bargaining
Terminating	Accident	Contracts
Transfer, promotion and demotion	Sickness	Shop stewards
Leave of absence	Death	Union committee
Wage and salary administration	Old age	Conciliation
Job clarification statements	Termination	Arbitration
Earnings and incentives	Credit unions	Employer's Councils
Working hours and overtime	Analysis and Statistics	Management and Labour committees
Performance reviews		
Regulation of employment		
Selective service and veterans programmes		
	Training for:	
Job		Supervision
Production		Safety and Health
Occupation		Services
Supervision		
	Testing for:	
Selection		Employment suggestions
Placement		Channels of consultation
Studies of employees' attitudes		Principles of organisation
Employee publications		Work simplification
Standards of working conditions		Audits of Personnel Department
Standards of supervision		

Professor John F. Mee mentions the following subjects commonly found in personnel programmes:[5]

1. Employment

(a) Source of labour supply
(b) Reception of applicants and interviews
(c) Investigation of references
(d) Physical examinations
(e) Employment tests
(f) Final selection and placement
(g) Introduction to the job
(h) Provision for equipment, locker facilities etc.
(i) Continued contact
(j) Personnel records
(k) Transfers and promotions
(l) Exit interviews and terminations

2. Wages and Hours

(a) Wage scales
(b) Salary and wage standardisation
(c) Incentive plans
(d) Overtime pay
(e) Profit-sharing and Bonus plans
(f) Hours
(g) Holidays
(h) Vacations

3. Working Conditions

(a) Plant housekeeping
(b) Ventilation and lighting
(c) Sanitary facilities
(d) Reset periods
(e) Eating facilities

4. Training and Education

(a) Training on the job
(b) Company courses, conferences and lectures
(c) Co-operation with outside agencies
(d) Employee manuals
(e) Employee publications
(f) Bulletin boards
(g) Library
(h) Facts about the company
(i) Suggestion system

5. Safety

(a) Safeguarding hazardous occupations
(b) Safety education
(c) Workmen's compensation

6. Health

(a) Physical examinations
(b) Health education
(c) First Aid in company hospitals
(d) Home visiting
(e) Laboratory studies

7. Economic Security

(a) Steady employment
(b) Unemployment insurance
(c) Life insurance
(d) Accident and health insurance
(e) Retirement plan
(f) Hospitalisation plan
(g) Thrift and savings plan
(h) Housing programme

8. Contacts with Employees

(a) Opportunities for personal contacts between management and employees
(b) Open channels for grievances
(c) Consultation with employees on matters of mutual interest
(d) Collective bargaining

9. Service Activities

(a) Athletics and recreation
(b) Social activities
(c) Employees' clubs
(d) Discounts on employees' purchases
(e) Legal aid
(f) Charities

10. Research and Statistics

(a) Job analysis	(e) Analyses of the personnel
(b) Accident records	(f) Wage levels and cost of living
(c) Labour turnover studies	(g) Personnel programmes and methods
(d) Absenteeism and tardiness	(h) Labour legislation

Yet another tangible and substantial outline of the most common programmes and practices of personnel administration is provided by H.H. Carey:[6]

(i) Organisation for Personnel Administration

1. Basic responsibilities of executive, staff, line and personnel organisations with respect to employee relations.
2. Committee organisation on policy matters.
3. Staff personnel assistance to line executives.
4. Administration by personnel organisation of special services to line organisation such as employment, training etc.
5. Promotion and co-ordination of personnel policies, plans and activities — headquarters staff, committees, conferences, liaison procedures, and written instructions on personnel matters.
6. Auditing of effectiveness of personnel policies and practices.

(ii) Administration and Supervision

1. Duties, responsibilities, and authority of executive and supervisory personnel in relation to company operations.
2. Channels of communications upward and downward — both for supervisors and individuals — with respect to job information, individual problems and grievances.
3. Opportunities for participation in planning, decisions, or suggestions on job matters either as supervisors or individual workers through "multiple management" plans or "consultative supervision."
4. Supervisory skills, including job instruction, handling employee relations, job methods, conference leadership.

(iii) Employment

1. Forecast of requirements of personnel.
2. Hiring policies and standards.
3. Job descriptions, qualifications required, and rates of pay.
4. Recruitment.
5. Interviewing and testing.
6. Pre-employment medical examination.
7. Reference investigation.
8. Induction.
9. Placement and follow-up in relation to performance, ability, interests, special qualifications and handicaps and job opportunities.

10. Employee records and statistics.
11. Labour market studies.
12. Exit interviews.

(iv) Training and Employee Development

1. Induction and orientation programme, including relationship of employee's work to that of other workers, departments and branches.
2. Job-training — shop and office.
3. Supervisory training — pre-supervisory, on-the-job and conference groups.
4. Executive and supervisory development programme.
5. Out-of-hour courses.
6. Educational and vocational guidance.
7. Employee evaluation.
8. Cooperation with schools and colleges.

(v) Wage and Salary Administration

1. Job evaluation and grading.
2. Establishment of job rates and rate changes.
3. Incentive plans — time studies and standards.
4. Rate reviews and adjustments, including employee performance and merit ratings.
5. Wage and salary rates and earnings surveys — within the company and outside market.
6. Wage and salary controls — within the company and outside.
7. Pay for time not worked — vacations, holidays, disability or personal absence, jury duty, shutdowns etc.

(vi) Force Adjustment

1. Work load and requirements of personnel.
2. Promotions, demotions, and transfers.
3. Voluntary quits, layoffs, and discharges.
4. Employee inventory and rating plans.
5. Channels of progression.
6. Seniority and disciplinary matters.
7. Progress training and rotation assignments.
8. Standards and selection procedures for advancement.
9. Centralised placement and control.

(vii) Relationships between Employees and Management

1. Statement of employee relations policies.
2. Relations with employees as individuals.

3. Employee organisations.
4. Collective bargaining.
5. Grievance procedure.
6. Arbitration.
7. Employee-management committees.

(viii) Hours and Working Conditions

1. Work schedules.
2. Physical working environment and facilities.
3. Vacations and holidays.
4. Rest periods.
5. Music at work.
6. Suggestion system.

(ix) Health and Safety

1. First aid and hospital facilities.
2. Physical examination — pre-employment, occupations, and periodic health.
3. Occupational placement and control of assignments of vocationally handicapped or partially disabled.
4. Safety rules and regulations.
5. Employee consultation with company doctors.
6. Emergency and first-aid organisation.
7. Safety and health committees and training programmes.
8. Visiting Nurse service.
9. Accident investigations.
10. Research and control of hazards.
11. Safety and health handbooks.
12. Periodic inspection of plant and equipment.
13. Fire drills.
14. Publicity.
15. Safety equipment and clothing.

(x) Benefits and Employee Security Matters

1. Accident compensation.
2. Credit union facilities.
3. Sales to employees of company or other products.
4. Transportation and housing.
5. Recreational and educational facilities and programmes.
6. Payroll deduction plans.
7. Legal matters and notary public.
8. Employee counselling and assistance on personnel problems.

(xi) Communication with Employees

1. Employee publications and periodicals.
2. Informational booklets.
3. Personnel policy statements.
4. Bulletin board notices.
5. Annual reports.
6. Special meetings.

(xii) Research and Development

1. Studies on turnover, absenteeism etc.
2. Evaluation of company personnel programmes and activities.
3. Supervisory and employee morale and attitude surveys.
4. Outside company personnel practices and industry trends.
5. Labour legislation — State and Federal.
6. Employee census.
7. Controlled experimentation on working conditions, training, supervisory techniques etc.

(xiii) Relations with Local Business and Community Organisations

1. Community news — employment, financial, educational, and welfare organisations.
2. Plant visits and "open house."
3. Trade, managements, and professional associations in personnel field.
4. Outside company contacts.
5. State and Federal agencies.
6. News releases and information about personnel aspects of company operations.

A close study of the foregoing lists of functions or activities and practices of personnel administration reveal that there is a good measure of agreement among the practitioners, professionals, and academicians as to the wide range and scope of personnel functions.

The fundamental objective of these multifarious functions of personnel administration is to bring together various capable individuals in a scientific way and to create attitudes that motivate them as a group to function so effectively as to achieve the predetermined goals of the individual firm with economy, speed and efficiency.

Two Categories of Personnel Administration Functions

Despite the formidable lists of functions, there are two major categories of personnel functions and they are operative managerial functions. The operative functions of personnel management include the activities specifically concerned with procuring, developing, utilising and maintaining an efficient workforce. They are fast becoming more technical in character, requiring specialised and expert know-how.

The managerial functions of personnel management pertain to the activities concerned with planning, organising and controlling the work of those who perform the operative personnel functions. In order to be effective and efficient, it is necessary not to neglect either of these two major functions of personnel administration.

Professor John F. Mee points out that "it is essential to grasp the significance of this dual division of personnel functions if the mistake of becoming preoccupied with the demand of detailed problems to the neglect of managerial duties is to be avoided. It is easy, as many executives have learned to their regret, to become so busy with such tasks as hiring, transferring, counselling, and training that they fail to foresee shifting conditions which call for changes in operative functions, they fail to organise the work of subordinates satisfactorily, and they fail to keep good check upon the work of subordinates."[7]

Many of the various functions of personnel administration require expertise and specialist competence and now it is not enough to say that you are a personnel specialist. They ask in what field of personnel you have specialised. Specialisation is offered in interviewing, testing, job analysis, counselling, collective bargaining etc. Each of these activities of functions of personnel administration is fast reaching the status of specialisation, without which one may not be able to enter that field.

The Importance of Personnel Administration

In the management of four 'M's — money, materials, machines and men — it is needless to belabour the obvious point that, considering the nature of man, the management of men is fundamental and dynamic. Management is obtaining effective results through people and winning the willing cooperation of men in the organisation is a constant challenge to every level of management beginning from the top management to the level of supervisors. Hence personnel administration is a basic management function. It is the men, not machines, not materials, and not money, who make or mar the organisation and no organisation is sounder than the men available in it. Professors Myers and Pigors observe: "Personnel administration also permeates all types of functional management, such as production management, financial management, sales management, and research management. Unless these managers themselves expect to perform all the duties for which they are responsible, they have to secure the cooperation of other people within their part of the total organisation. In short, every member of the management group, from top down, must be a 'personnel administrator' in the vital sense that he depends on the good will and productive effort of all people in the organisation. The responsibility for personnel administration, therefore, is clearly not something that can be assigned to a minor functionary in the organisation — a glorified office boy and backslapper who will 'handle personnel problems', keep the employees happy and 'manage the men' while other more important executives manage machines, materials and money."[8]

As Walter Wriston, chairman and chief executive officer of Citicorp, has said:[9] "I believe the only game in town is the personnel game.... My theory is that if you have the right person in the right place, you don't have to do anything else. If you have the wrong person in the job, there is no management system known to man that can save you.... The selection of the people that hold the key jobs is a principal function of the chief executive officer."

In addition to selection, training and development, and manpower planning, compensation is another critical area for concern. If a company is to attract and retain good people, compensation systems ought to fit the strategy and be attractive, equitable, and motivational. Equity is extremely important, for as Strauss and Sayles point out:

"The National War Labour Board perhaps only slightly exaggerated when it said: "There is no single factor in the entire field of labour relations which does more to break down morale, create individual dissatisfaction, encourage absenteeism, increase labour turnover, and hamper production than obviously unjust inequities in the wage rates paid to the same individuals in the same labour groups within the same plant."

An effective personnel department should, with top management's support, take the initiative in researching and defining the company's personnel problems, and, as much as is possible, it should work to solve them.

Human Resource Management's New Approaches

If the personnel function is properly integrated within the organisation, the direction ought to consider developing or refining expertise in the following human resource activities: attitude surveys or other upward communication programmes; the changing workday and work life; job design; career planning and development; pay and benefits; and supplemental uses of the workplace.

Human Resource Management

The students of management are aware that the concept of line and staff was borrowed from the military organisation. The distinction between line and staff can be simply explained. While the line operates, the staff "assists" or "advises" the line in its operation. The function of the line is to get the job done and the function of the staff is to "aid the line by providing professional and technical advice, by planning and programming, and by reviewing and appraising operations."

In the line organisation, the flow of authority may be traced in an unbroken line from the top of the organisation through each set of successive executives to the lowest and final organisational unit. "The difficulties in applying the proper thought and research to a wide variety of problems in many large line organisations led to the appointment of specialists as advisors to the executives. This brought about what is recognised as the Line and Staff type of control. It is characterised by the removal from the line organisation of those planning and research functions in which specialisation is desirable, and the establishment of advisory or staff departments in which can be concentrated the work of specialists to the end of concentrating the proper amount of research, thought, and planning on the particular functions involved. In the true staff organisation, the staff departments are advisory to the line executives or to the line departments, and any specifications or orders which the staff department wish to promulgate to the line organisation must have the approval of the general coordinating officer to which the staff and line heads both report.... The use of staff permits of functional specialisation and at the same time maintains the integrity of the principle of undivided responsibility and authority within the line organisation."[10]

By its expert know-how and technical and professional advise the staff is responsible to help the line to do a better job. It is generally agreed that personnel administration is a staff or advisory function where its major objective is to assist the line to do a better job in managing people. All the afore-mentioned functions such as procuring, training, development etc. are done with a view to assisting the line to perform its duties much better. The busy line executives such as production executives, marketing executives, etc., cannot take time off to screen the applications, interview the applicants, test the candidates, or train the candidates. Nor can they effectively perform these functions, because they need a different type of expertise, which is provided by the personnel department. As Saltonstall has put it:[11]

> "The personnel executive who is dedicated to the improvement of human relationships at all levels within the organisation becomes really effective only when his basic concept of his job is to help line management to understand, adopt enthusiastically, and practise sound principles of personnel administration on the basis that to do so is good business."

Within his own section or department, personnel administrator enjoys line type of control and it is the responsibility of the top personnel manager to get the job done through his subordinates who report to him. Outside of his division, he is staff and within his division, he is line.

Responsibilities of Personnel Staff

Firstly, the personnel administrator's responsibility is to assist the top management in the formulation of personnel policies, procedures, and programmes after careful research and considering the impact of social, political, economic, and local developments.

Secondly, his responsibility is to plan and forecast the organisational manpower needs and suggest programmes that help to implement policies and achieve the organisational goals. Planning and programming assistance is provided to all levels of a firm.

Thirdly, his responsibility is to counsel and advise the line executives and supervisors on all issues involving the management of men.

Fourthly, his responsibility is to provide all levels of management various technical and professional services such as testing, counselling, contract negotiation and administration, conducting compensation surveys and morale surveys and many others.

Lastly, his responsibility is to audit and review all policies, procedures and programmes with a view to constantly improving them.

It is clear that personnel administration is a staff or an advisory function and the responsibility for getting results should rest with the line management. This point of view is forcefully expressed by Professors Pigors and Myers in their preface.[12]

"In the subsequent editions of 1951 and 1956, we retained the essential focus of our treatment of personnel administration because we believed that the responsibility for getting results with people rests with the line management. Despite this intention, some of our readers and reviewers understood us to mean that the personnel administrator — the staff man — had the primary role in handling human problems in organisations.... In this fourth edition, therefore, we have stressed even more than before the line responsibility for effective personnel administration."

They further add:[13] "The establishment of a personnel department is no guarantee that personnel difficulties will end. On the contrary, they may increase if the chief executive, lower operating management, and the personnel administrator are confused as to the proper place and functions of personnel administration in the company organisation.... The newly designated personnel administrator cannot by himself solve personnel problems. He is no miracle worker. Rather, he is an adviser to line or operating management on personnel problems and an exponent of point of view and of methods designed to help management in getting effective results with people. He cannot establish policies and make decisions about employees himself with usurping the authority and responsibilities of operating management. Yet these fairly obvious truths are frequently ignored in practice."

The Indian Institute of Personnel Management inculcates the staff role of personnel administration:[14] "...it may be said that the personnel department is a service department, and none of its staff should ever forget this. The personnel officer must himself be responsible to the executive head of unit, and all his recommendations should be made to him. When asked for advice by other executives he should give it, but he should be wary of offering advice when it is not sought...."

"The final responsibility for personnel policy must lie with top management, to whom the personnel officer acts as adviser, and its execution must run through the whole line of management if it is to be effective. But though policy decisions lie at the top, the personnel officer can do much, through his experience and intimate knowledge of the human side of business, to influence policy decisions."

We can represent the staff function of personnel administration and its relationship with other management departments in the discussion of formal organisation charts.

Mr. Robert Tenent Presents a Global Corporte Human Resources Organisation[15]

Management Values & Culture

The culture is one in which the Group seeks:

- To be the world's leading financial services organisation
- To be known for

  — Maintaining the highest standards of integrity

  — Providing the highest levels of customer service

  — Producing consistent growth in financial performance

- To have a strong management team committed to its customers, its shareholders and its staff

Diagram 3.1

Management Values & Culture

The culture is one in which the Group seeks:

- To be the world's leading financial services organisation
- To be known for
  - — Maintaining the highest standards of integrity
  - — Providing the highest levels of customer service
  - — Producing consistent growth in financial performance
- To have a strong management team committed to its customers, its shareholders and its staff
- To be a bank where teamwork is more important than individual stardom

Diagram 3.2

Group Standards Manual

- Control document
- Functional standards and principles
- World-wide application
- Reaffirms de-centralised approach to management of the Group
- Vital management tool

Diagram 3.3

Group Human Resources

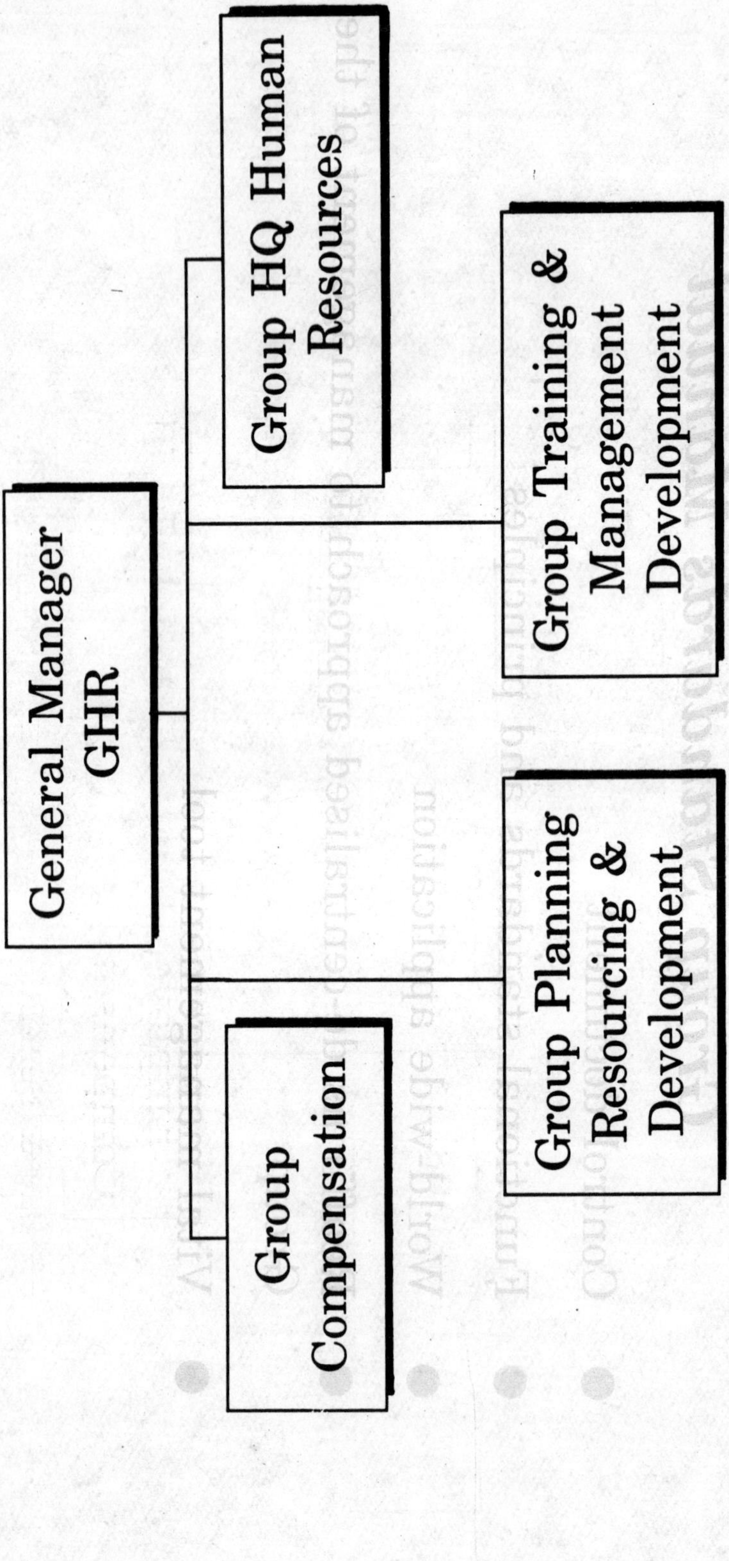

Diagram 3.4

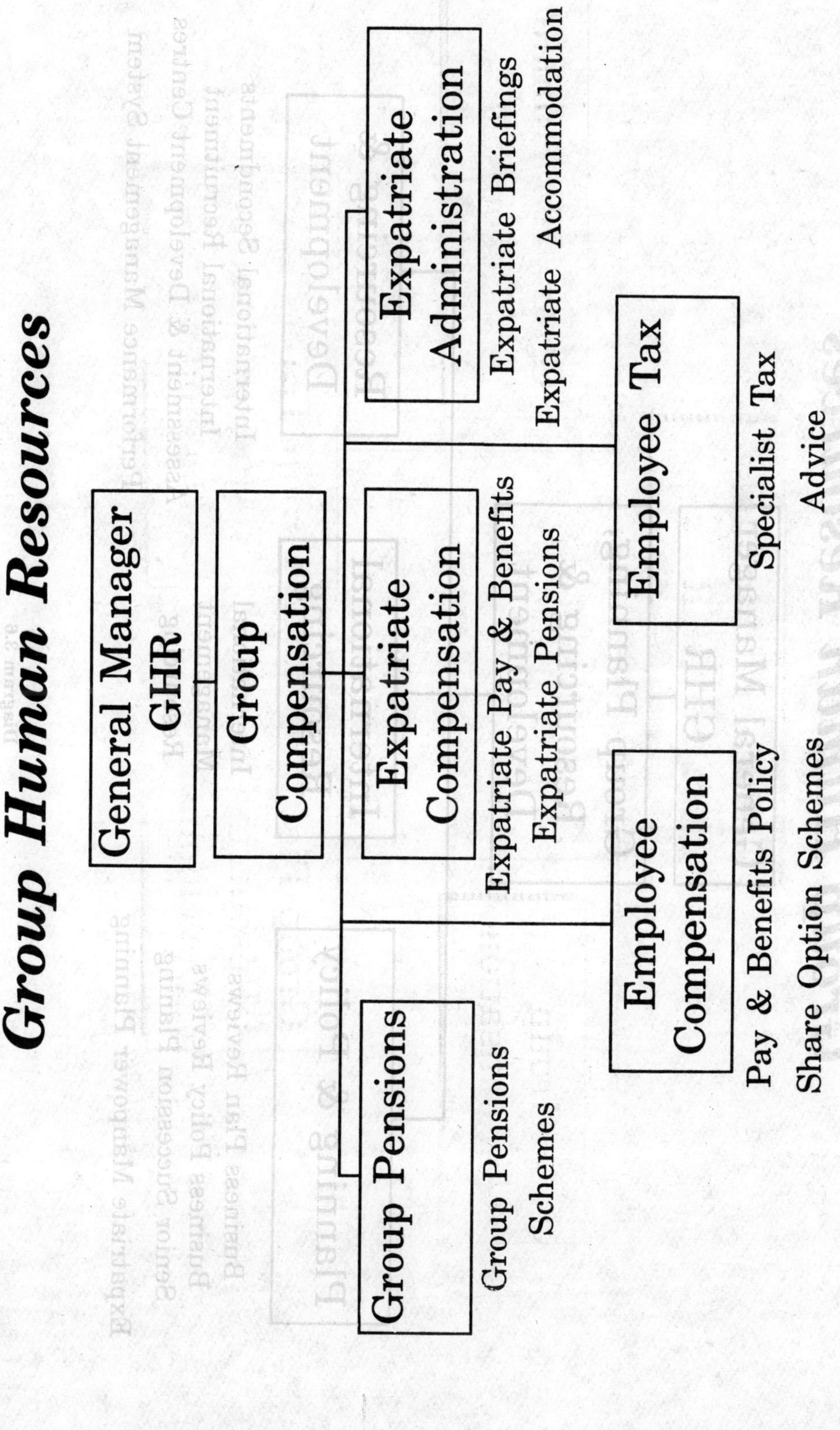
Group Human Resources
General Manager
GHR
Group
Compensation
Group Pensions
Group Pensions
Schemes
Expatriate
Compensation
Expatriate Pay & Benefits
Expatriate Pensions
Expatriate
Administration
Expatriate Briefings
Expatriate Accommodation
Employee
Compensation
Pay & Benefits Policy
Share Option Schemes
Employee Tax
Specialist Tax
Advice

Diagram 3.5

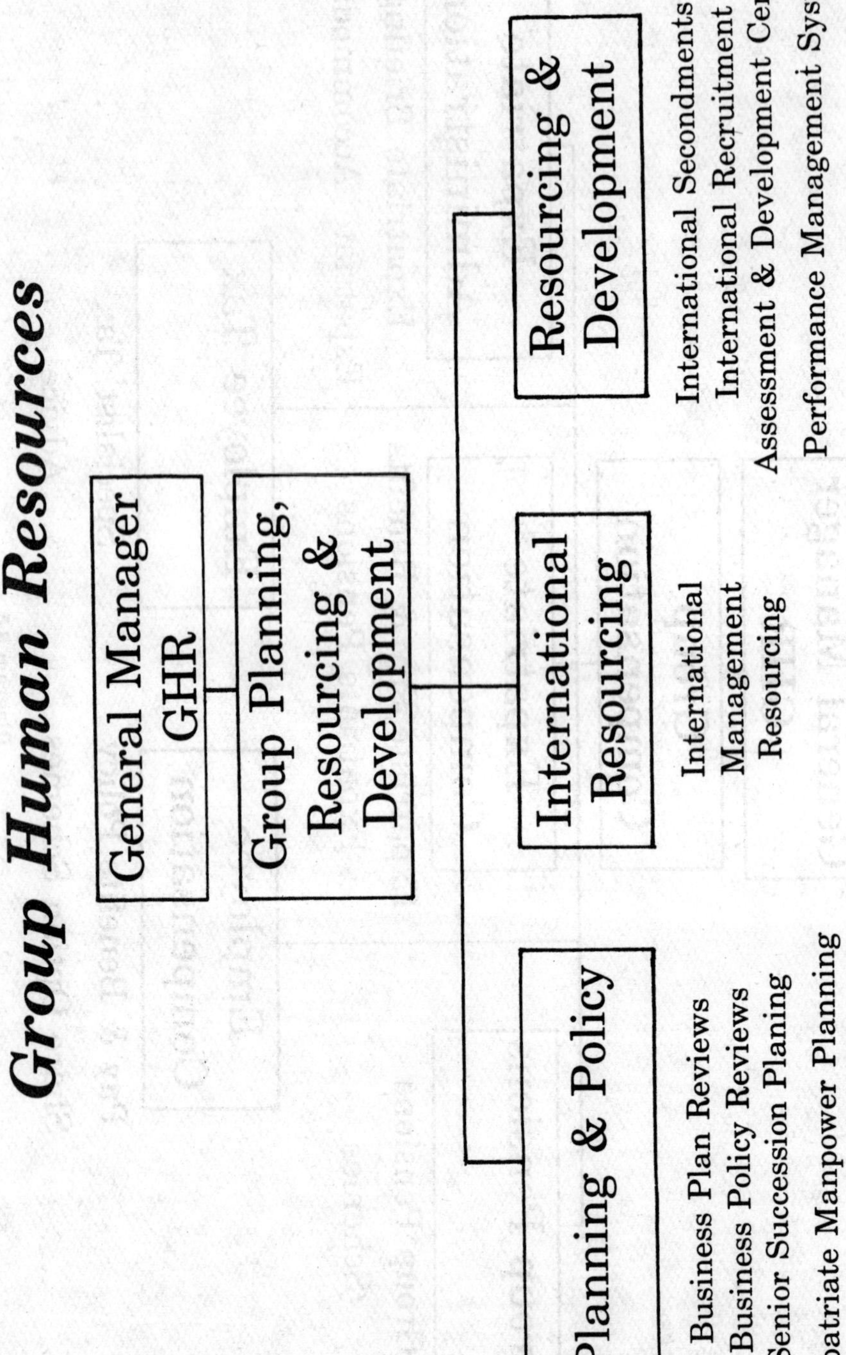
Group Human Resources
General Manager GHR
Group Planning, Resourcing & Development
Planning & Policy
International Resourcing
Resourcing & Development
Business Plan Reviews
Business Policy Reviews
Senior Succession Planing
Expatriate Manpower Planning
International Management Resourcing
International Secondments
International Recruitment
Assessment & Development Centres
Performance Management System

Diagram 3.6

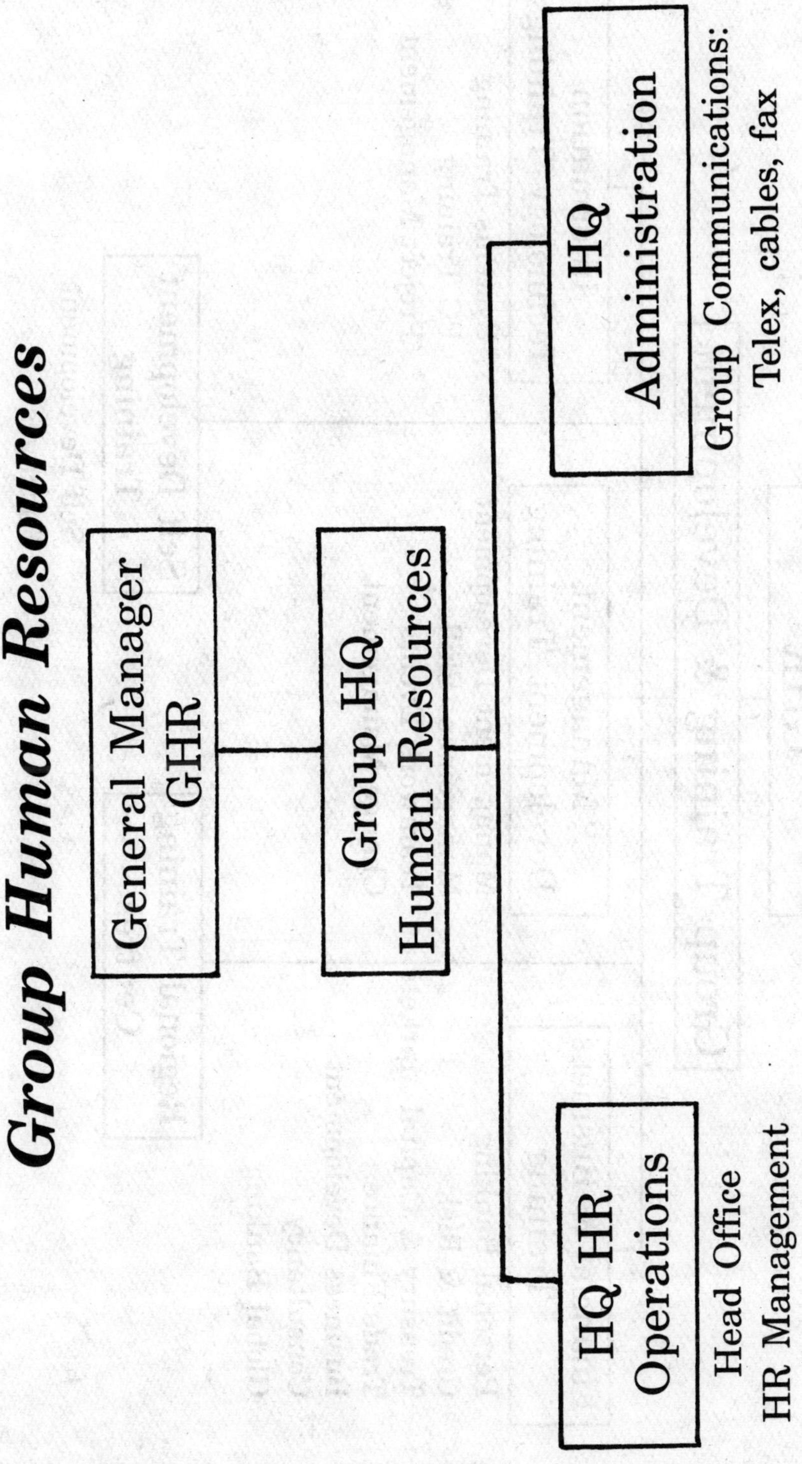
Group Human Resources
General Manager
GHR
Group HQ
Human Resources
HQ HR
Operations
Head Office
HR Management
HQ
Administration
Group Communications:
Telex, cables, fax

Diagram 3.7

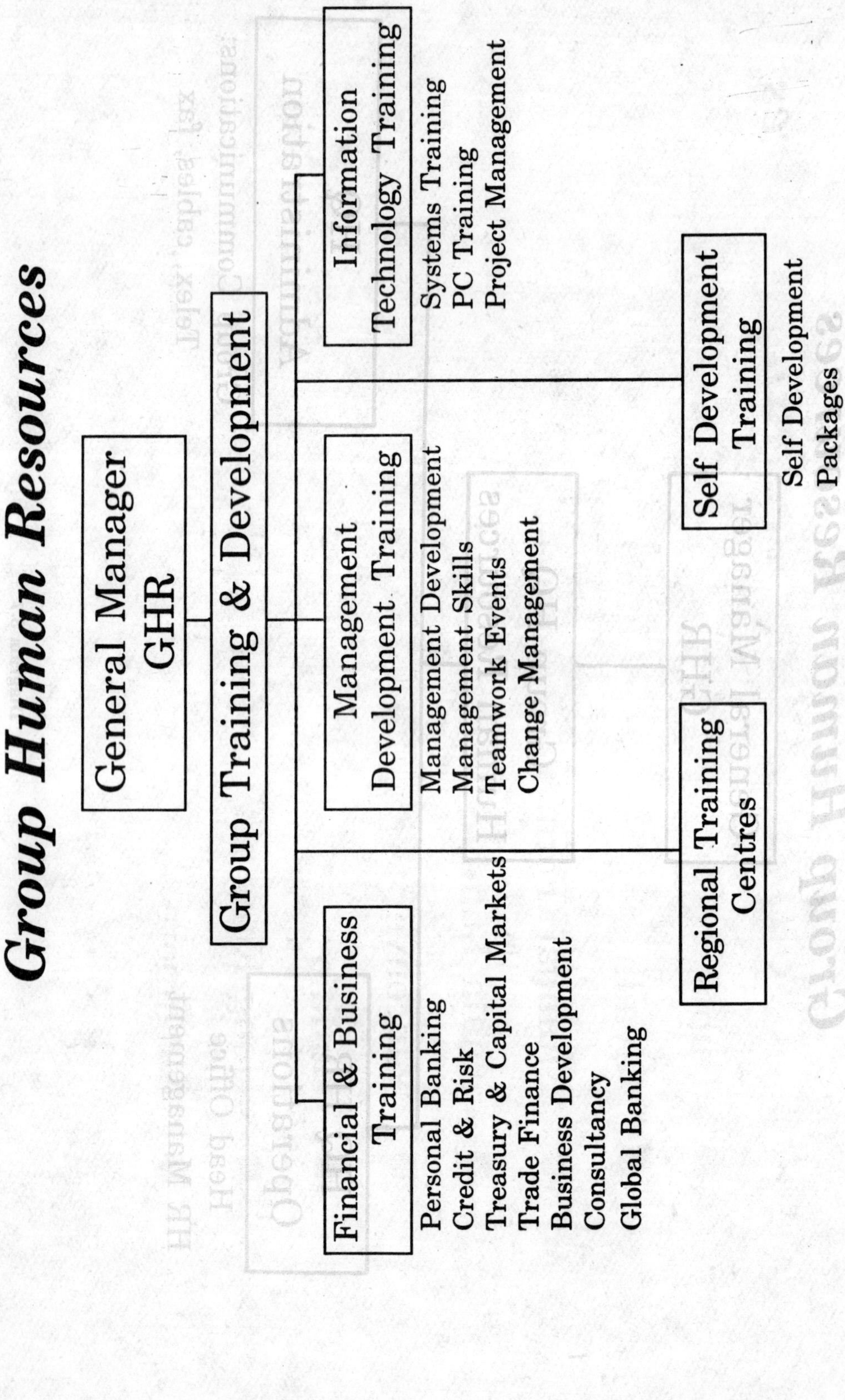
Group Human Resources
General Manager
GHR
Group Training & Development
Financial & Business
Training
Personal Banking
Credit & Risk
Treasury & Capital Markets
Trade Finance
Business Development
Consultancy
Global Banking
Management
Development Training
Management Development
Management Skills
Teamwork Events
Change Management
Information
Technology Training
Systems Training
PC Training
Project Management
Regional Training
Centres
Self Development
Training
Self Development
Packages

Diagram 3.8

Group Regional Training Centres

- Dubai
- Riyadh
- Mumbai (Formerly Bombay)
- Kuala Lumpur
- Vancouver
- Buffalo
- Hong Kong
- Singapore

Diagram 3.9

International Opportunities

- International Management Cadre
- International Secondments
- 500 Expatriate Staff

Diagram 3.10

HR Information Processes

- Strategic Plans (3 years)
- Annual Operating Plans
- HR Plans
- HR Data
- Group Executive Committee

Diagram 3.11

Human Resources Specialists

- 1,200 in Human Resources Management
- 700 in Human Resources Development

Diagram 3.12

3. HUMAN RESOURCES MANAGEMENT AND OTHER AREAS OF MANAGEMENT — ORGANISATION CHARTS

The proper relationships between a personnel administrator and management can be clearly shown on a formal organisational chart. Figures 3.3 and 3.4 illustrate current staff organisation charts of personnel and the line type of control within personnel division highlighting the grouping of various activities under varying circumstances.

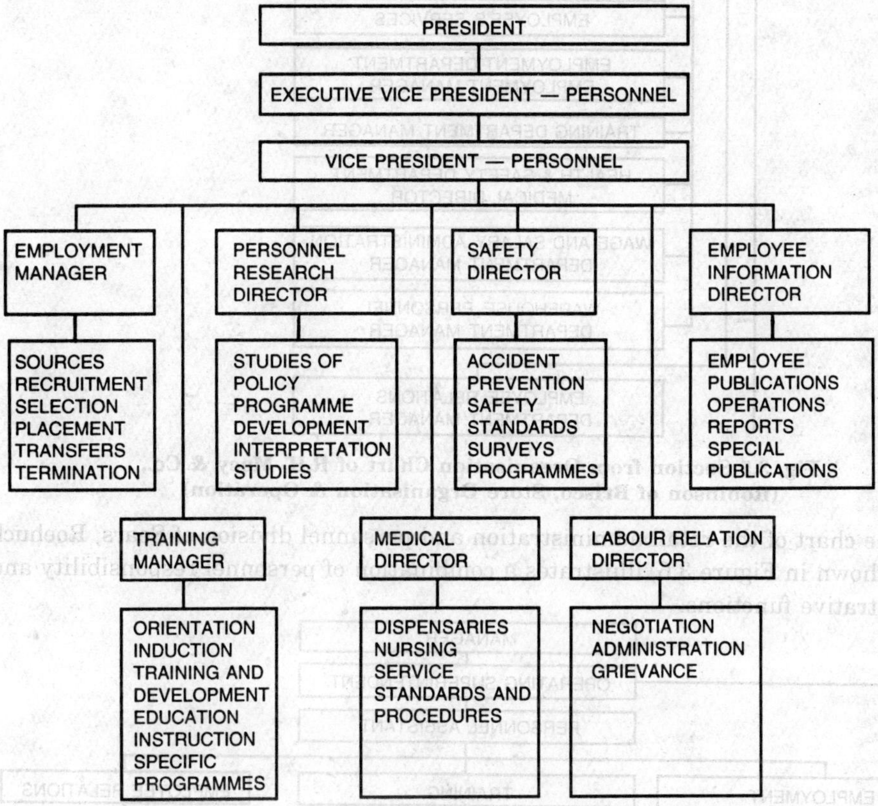

Fig. 3.3 Organisation Chart for Large Manufacturer's Staff Division

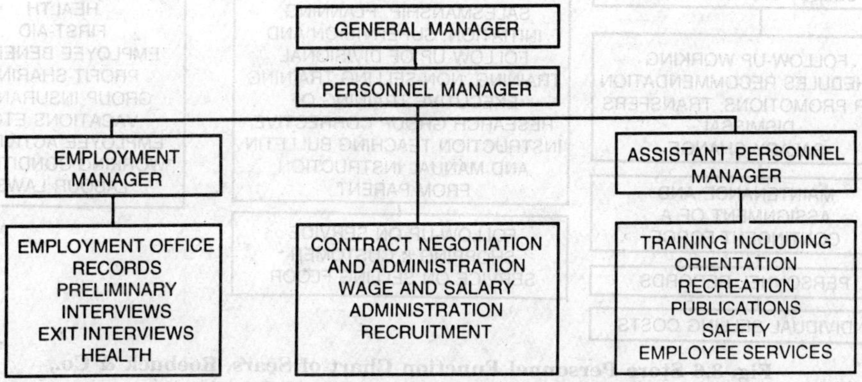

Fig. 3.4 Organisation Chart for Small Manufacturing Firm

The personnel division organisation of one of the largest department stores in the world, R.H. Macy & Co. is shown in Figure 3.5.

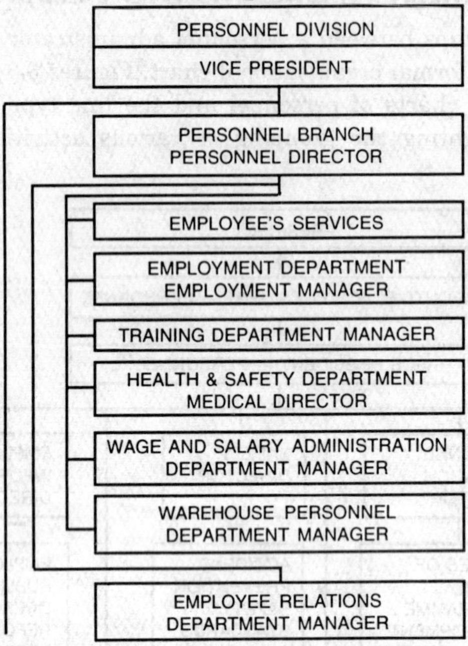

Fig. 3.5 Section from Organisation Chart of R.H. Macy & Co., (Robinson of Brisco, Store Organisation & Operation)

The chart of the retail administration and personnel division of Sears, Roebuck & Co., shown in Figure 3.6, illustrates a combination of personnel responsibility and administrative functions.

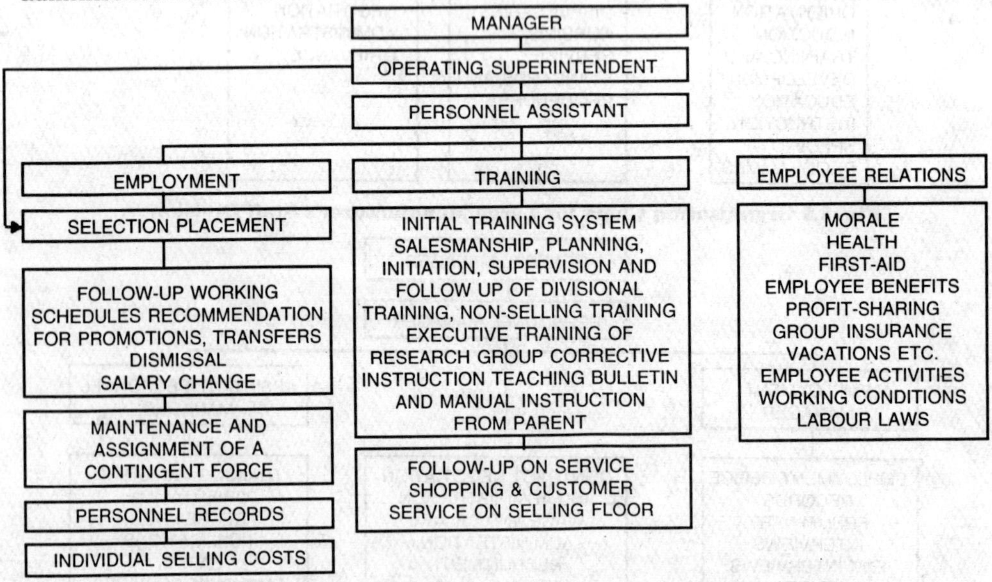

Fig. 3.6 Store Personnel Function Chart of Sears, Roebuck & Co., (Emmet and Jeuck, Catalogs and Counters)

Figures 3.7 and 3.8 illustrate centralised and decentralised personnel organisation charts.

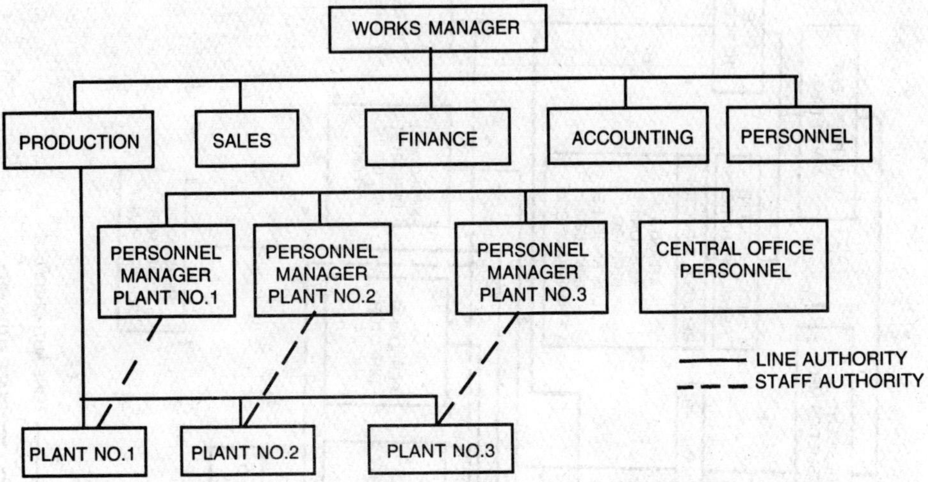

Fig. 3.7 Organisation Chart of Centralised Personnel Department

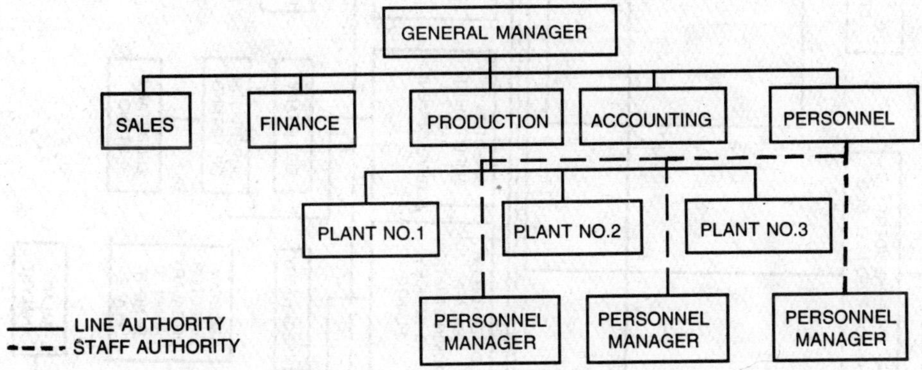

Fig. 3.8 Organisation Chart of Decentralised Personnel Department

Figure 3.9, Showing the organisation chart of department of personnel administration of a major company in U.S.A., illustrates the relationships — line and staff — existing between personnel and other management divisions.

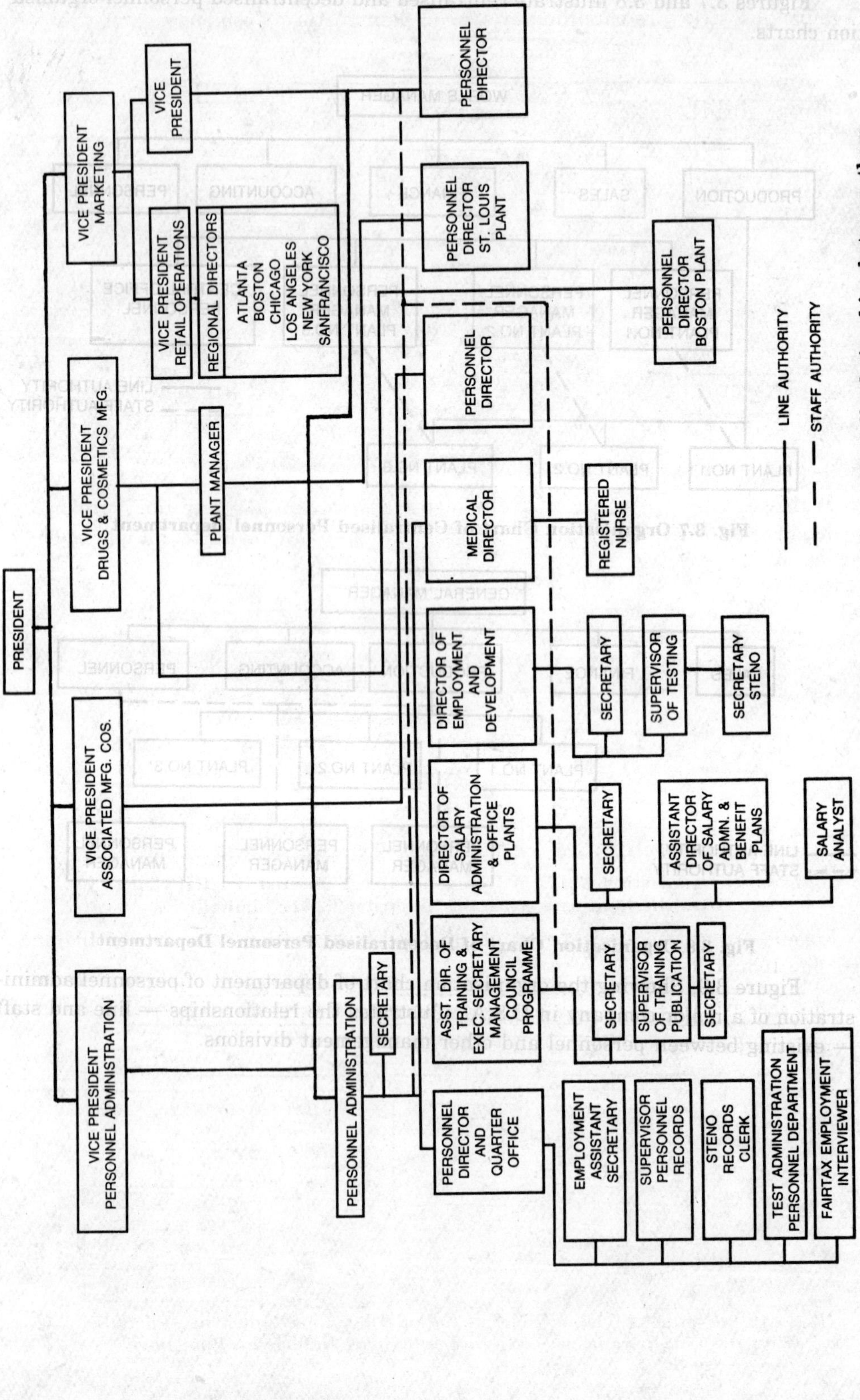

Fig. 3.9 Personnel and other management areas and the line and staff relationships between them.

Another simple diagram, shown in Figure 3.10 illustrates the line and staff form of organisation structure obtaining in a small manufacturing company.

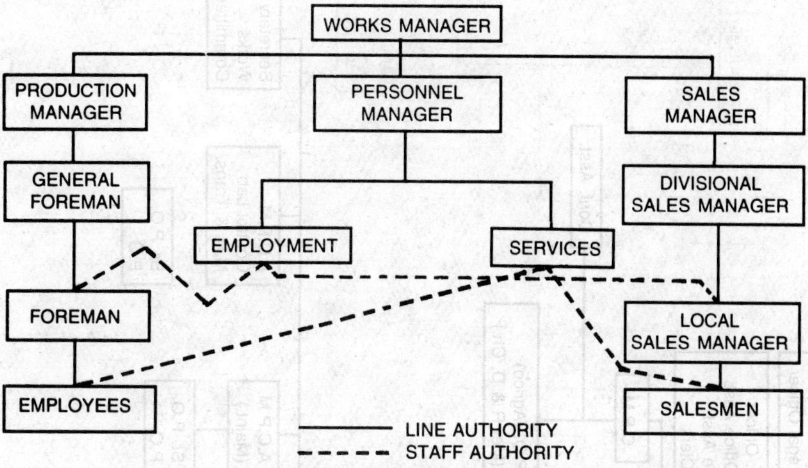

Fig. 3.10 Line and Staff Form of Organisation Chart

In the organisation structure of Hindustan Lever Limited shown in Figure 3.11 the personnel executive is on the Board of Directors — the highest executive body.

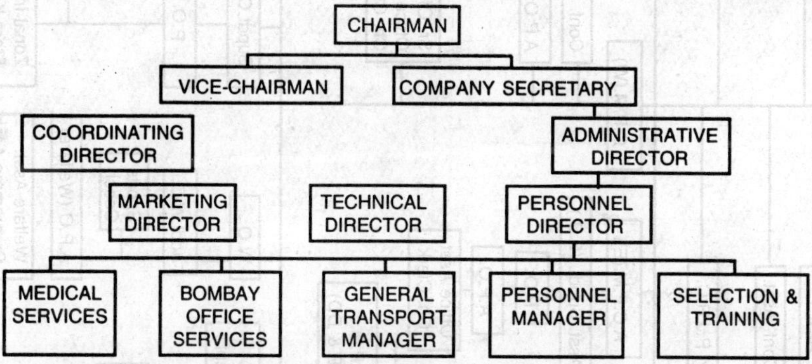

Fig. 3.11 Organisation Chart of Hindustan Lever Limited (Partial Chart)
(With the kind permission of Hindustan Lever Limited)

Fig. 3.12 represents the personnel division organisation structure of Indian Telephone Industries.

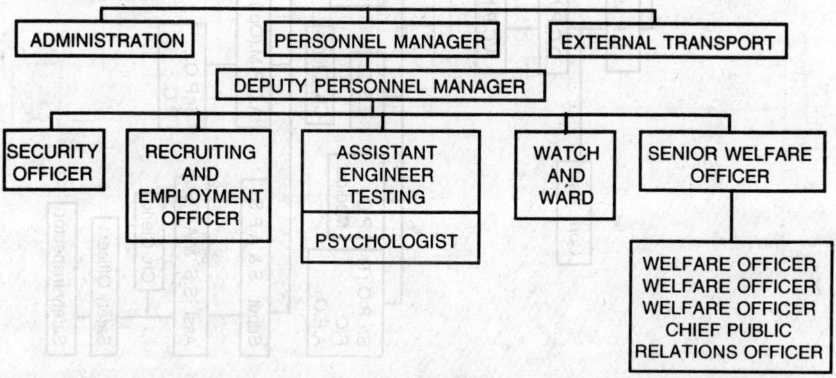

Fig. 3.12 Personnel Division Chart of Indian Telephone Industries (Partial)
(With the kind permission of Indian Telephone Industries, Bangalore)

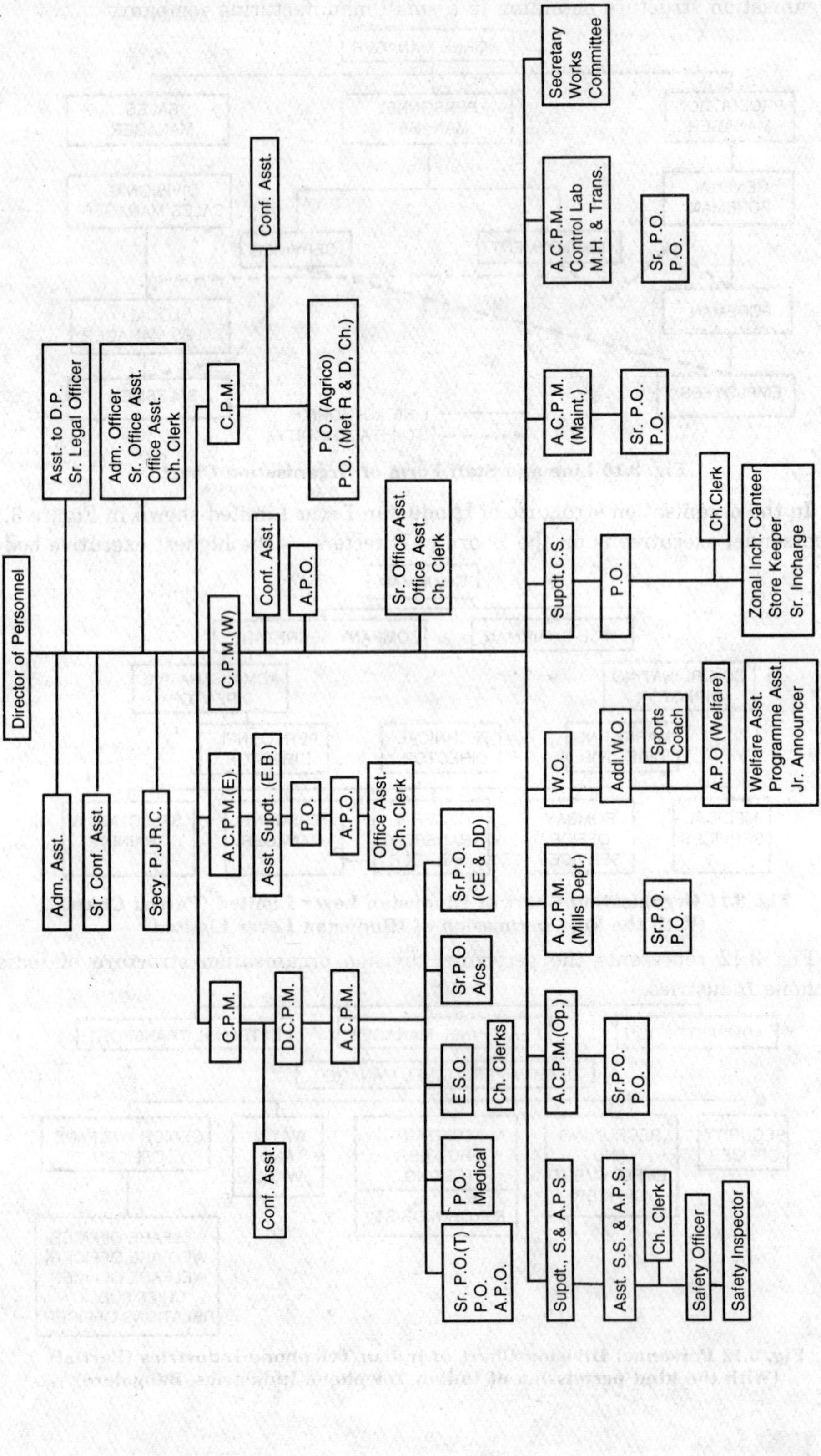

Fig. 3.13 Organisation Chart of Tisco

Professor Jucius suggests the following characteristics to be possessed by a good personnel department: [16]

1. Stability, or the ability to replace key personnel executives or employees with a minimum loss of effectiveness.
2. Flexibility, or the capacity to handle effectively short-run changes in the volume of personnel work or in the personnel problems encountered.
3. Growth, or the feature of being prepared with advance plans to handle permanent changes in personnel problems or in underlying labour conditions.
4. Balance, or the feature of having authority and resources adequate in amount to handle the functions and problems for which the personnel department is responsible.
5. Simplicity, or the feature of keeping personnel lines of relationship to other departments clear and simple.
6. Objectivity, or the feature of having definite objectives..

In most of the Indian organisations the personnel department (its function) is poorly organised and staffed. Generally, you will find one or two personnel director/ personnel managers or labour welfare officers dealing with a gamut of personnel functions in many of which they are not really experts. There is a need for sound and competent expertise in such areas as manpower planning, selection, compensation appraisals, employee services, employment benefits etc. and these seem to be lacking even in some of the leading organisations in India.

4. HUMAN RESOURCES MANAGER — HIS STATUS AND QUALIFICATIONS

(A) Status of Personnel Executive

The status of personnel executives in India seems to be not as high as that of their counterparts in the West, except in the case of a minority of companies such as the Hindustan Lever Limited, and Tata Group of Industries, where the personnel executive may sit on the Board of Directors and where their status is equal to that of other top executives. In Indian Telephone Industries, the personnel manager's status is on par with that of other top managers in the areas of Administration, Finance, Chief Engineer, Design and Development, Sales etc. But such companies are still a minute minority in India.

The Central Model Rule 6 attempts to confer a certain status on Welfare Officers:

1. "A Welfare Officer shall be given appropriate status corresponding to the status of the other executive heads of the factory."
2. "The conditions of service of a Welfare Officer shall be the same as other members of the staff of corresponding status in the factory; provided that, in the case of discharge or dismissal, the Welfare Officer should have a right of appeal to the State Government whose decision thereon shall be final and binding on the occupier." But, in spite of this stipulation, the Welfare Officer's or personnel executive's status leaves a good deal of room for improvement in India. In many instances, he finds himself at the bottom of the managerial

ladder and nobody pays any heed to him or his counsels. His compensation, which is set at as low a figure as a minimum of Rs. 200 per month as laid down by Kerala State Rules (although Central Rules lay down a minimum of Rs. 275 per month) also determines his low status. In these cases, there can be little dialogue between the top management and personnel executive. He is some sort of industrial "paraiah" unwanted and unhonoured by both management and labour. The report of 1957 committee pointed out that "where the managements were enlightened, welfare officers of suitable status and experience were employed and the system worked well. In other cases there was only nominal compliance with the rules."

The Indian Institute of Personnel Management raises the issue of status and gives an explanation.[17]

"Is the status of personnel officers in India comparable with that of their counterparts in the West? In some firms their status is so comparable, but the number of such officers is still very small. Personnel officers in India have had quite a hard battle to convince managements of their rightful role in industry, for though the number of personnel officers today is largely due to Section 49 of the Factories Act, there is no denying that in the majority of cases they were forced upon unwilling managements by legislation and so started with an initial disadvantage. There is no doubt, however, that in the last decade their position has on the whole substantially improved. Managements are now more alive to the need for personnel management and the role that personnel officers can play. There may be very many who lag behind, but since any new profession takes time to establish itself, there is no need to take a despondent view of the outlook for personnel management in India."

In the West, the advent of Scientific Management and Professional Management brought to the forefront personnel administration at a time when the growing size, complexity, and sophistication of business and industry established the need for functional specialisations. Similarly in India when industry and business grow in stature, complexity, and sophistication the need for functional managerial specialists will be felt keenly and then professional management and personnel administration will attain the majesty and stature that they have attained in the West, particularly U.S.A.

In TISCO, the status of the Personnel Director is as follows:[18]

"This arrangement was in keeping with the recommendations of the International Labour Organisation on the position and responsibility of the Personnel Division in a large undertaking which, inter alia, states that the head of the Personnel Division should be answerable to the top executive at the location of the plant. Direct control by the production line executive over this important staff function generates in the minds of the officers of the Personnel Division a bias which is not always objective.

"The head of the Personnel Division should, therefore, be in a position to give unfettered advice which, in no circumstances, should be tilted to suit the convenience of the line management. The Director of Personnel should be free to advise the management on a line of action which may not always be palatable to the line executives."

(B) Qualifications of Personnel Executive: Who can become a Personnel Executive?

Mere willingness or liking to work with people is not a sufficient qualification to become a personnel administrator. Professor Jucius maintains that success in personnel administration depends upon skill and ability in three areas: Managerial, technical, and behavioural. The personnel administrator must have the ability to plan, organise, and control. He must develop technical competency in using the personnel tools and techniques; and he must be courteous, tactful, diplomatic, and democratic. In order to be good at these three areas — managerial, technical, and behavioural — it is necessary for him to acquire some expertise, technical competence, academic training and qualifications.

In India the Central Model Rules and some States have laid down certain qualifications for an individual to become a welfare or a personnel officer and even the mode of recruitment of welfare officer and the conditions, under which he can be discharged or dismissed have also been stipulated by the Factories Act. Central Model Rule 4 lays down the qualifications necessary to become a welfare officer:

"A person shall not be eligible for appointment as a welfare officer, unless he:

(a) possesses a degree of a University recognised by the State Government in this behalf;

(b) has obtained a Degree or Diploma in Social Science from any institution recognised by the State Government in this behalf; and

(c) has adequate knowledge of the language spoken by the majority of the workers in the factory to which he is attached.

Provided that, in the case of person who is acting as a Welfare Officer at the commencement of these rules, the State Government may, subject to such conditions as it may specify, relax all or any of the aforesaid qualifications."

The States, in their Rules, specify the degrees and diplomas acceptable to them. Some States have some additional qualifications for a Welfare Officer. The State of Madras requires a degree of a University in the State or a diploma from an institute recognised by the State Government. The State of Uttar Pradesh in their Rules requires the candidate for the Welfare Officer's position to be domiciled in U.P. and in the age group between 25-35 years. The State of Bihar specifies either a degree or diploma in Social Science or practical experience of handling labour problems for at least five years. These State stipulations create certain problems, despite the intentions of the framers to the contrary. A State may not recognise the degree or diploma of another State. In one instance an applicant was rejected on the score that he did not possess the diploma of an institution of that State recognised by the State, although the applicant happened to have earned an M.B.A. specialising in Personnel Management and Industrial Relations, of a reputed American University and he had two years' experience as a personnel executive with one of the leading American meatpacking firms in U.S.A. Another problem is in the area of transfers and promotions of personnel executives in a company with plants spread all over the nation. The 1957 committee recommended that a list of institutions, whose diplomas would be recognised by all states, should be prepared "to enable welfare officers to be transferred from one State to another."

Even the procedures of recruitment of welfare officers are laid down by Central Model Rule 5:

1. The post of a welfare officer shall be advertised in all prominent newspapers of the State.
2. The selection shall be made from among the candidates applying for the post by a Committee appointed by the occupier of the factory.
3. The appointment when made shall be notified by the occupier to the State Government or such authority as the State Government may specify for the purpose, giving full details of the qualifications, etc. of the officer appointed and the conditions of his service.

West Bengal specifies in its rules that an individual recommended by the Employment Exchange or the Appointments and Information Board of the Calcutta University shall fill the position of Welfare Officer. Or the position may be filled by advertising in local newspapers.

Even the service conditions of welfare officers are specified in Central Model Rule 6, which offers a status to the welfare officer equal to that of other members of staff. But in case of discharge or dismissal the welfare officer is given the right to appeal to the State Government whose decision "shall be final and binding upon the occupier."

Bombay Rules require the employer, before dismissing or discharging a welfare officer, to place the proposed nature of action before the Commissioner of Labour, who conducts an enquiry, and advises the employer on the proposed action. West Bengal Rules prescribed that "no penalty should be imposed on him unless he is first informed in writing of the grounds on which it is proposed to take action and has been afforded an adequate opportunity of defending himself; provided that if the management terminates the service of a welfare officer otherwise than under the terms of his contract, the reasons for the termination of service shall be reported to the State Government. Bihar Rules state that "no welfare officer shall be discharged, dismissed or otherwise punished except with the previous approval of the Labour Commissioner, Bihar, obtained on proceedings drawn up against the officer." Uttar Pradesh Rules specify that management shall not impose any punishment other than censure on a welfare officer except with the previous concurrence of the Labour Commissioner, who shall give the officer an opportunity to explain the circumstances, and, if necessary, hear him in person.

All these elaborate statutory stipulations regarding the qualifications, service conditions, pay, and recruitment of welfare officers are designed, perhaps, to forestall any malpractices on the part of employers and to promote the appointment of qualified and competent officers who can deliver the goods.

Already some companies in India expect their applicants to have specialised in personnel management and industrial relations and with the increasing number of manager-development institutions we may reach a day when one cannot be an executive without a degree in management and similarly without specialising in personnel administration it may be hard to find a personnel executive position in any company. Another factor that will accelerate this process is the increasing availability of foreign trained personnel and management executives who seek positions with firms in India.

Here the employers have an obligation — that of finding and retaining competent personnel administration specialists — even as the management institutions have an obligation — that of training and developing personnel executives. We must think of tomorrow and the business of tomorrow will require competent professional personnel executives to advise and help management in the most important area of management of people.

REFERENCES

1. *Personnel Management in India*, pp. 52-57.
2. *Ibid.*, p. 53.
3. S.D. Punekar, "The Personnel Manager in India", *Industrial Relations,* IIPM, March-April, 1973, pp. 62, 64, 67.
4. A.F. Kindall, *Personnel Administration* (Homewood, Illinois: Richard D. Irwin Inc., 1961), pp. 4-7.
5. John F. Mee (ed.), *Personnel Handbook,* (New York: The Ronald Press Company, 1955), pp. 19-21.
6. H.H. Carey, "An Outline of Personnel Activities", *Personnel*, Vol. 23, No. 6, May 1947, pp. 384-387.
7. John F. Mee, *Personnel Handbook*, p. 19.
8. Myers and Pigors, *Personnel Administration,* p. 16.
9. Fred Foulkes, *Ibid.,* p. 79.
10. Thomas R. Jones, *Theories and Types of Organisation, Their History, Industrial and Economic Background and Trends,* Personnel Series No. 83 (New York: American Management Association, 1929).
11. Robert Saltonstall, "Evaluating Personnel Administration", *Harvard Business Review,* Vol. 30, No. 6, November-December, 1952, p. 93.
12. Pigors and Myers, *op. cit.,* p. v.
13. *Ibid.,* p. 21.
14. I.I.P.M., *op. cit.,* pp. 61-64.
15. Robert Tenant, Managing the Corporate H.R. Fundation Globally, Singapore, *HRD Asia,* 1996, pp. 17-28.
16. Jucius, *Personnel Management,* p. 104.
17. I.I.P.M., *op. cit.,* p. 67.
18. A.D. Singh, *Man Management in Tata Steel*, Jamshedpur, TISCO, 1973, p. 56.

❑ ❑ ❑

CHAPTER 4

Principles of Human Resources Management

This Chapter deals with:

1. Principles of Human Resources Management;
2. Management philosophies and creeds;
3. Human resources management objectives;
4. Human resources management policies;
5. Human resources management procedures and programmes;
6. Human resources management budget; and
7. Human resources management research.

1. PRINCIPLES OF PERSONNEL ADMINISTRATION

Personnel administration, just like any other profession, is incomplete without a set of basic guides or principles that guide the conduct of the personnel administrators. A mere description of functions, objectives, and programmes of personnel administration does not adequately describe the field of personnel administration. There is an absolutely essential need for certain guiding principles which assist the personnel executive in the formulation of personnel policies, procedures, and programmes, as well as in the solution of personnel problems. In view of this need, some principles of personnel administration are suggested.

1. Principle of Individual Development

Every employee must be offered full and equal opportunity to develop in order to realise his fullest potentialities.

The individual employee must be able to grow to his fullest capabilities. All the personnel policies and programmes must be geared to the individual employee development so that no employee should feel frustrated because the right type of challenges and responsibilities are not offered to him.

It must be realised that every individual has a craving to be 'somebody' in some field of occupation and unless this craving is channelised properly through effective training and development programmes, the principle of individual development will not work, resulting in harmful effects not only to the morale of the individual but also to the economic health of the organisation. It was Adam Curle who said that "countries are underdeveloped because most of their people are underdeveloped, having had no opportunity of expanding their potential capacities in the service of society."[1] In the final analysis, it is the development of the individuals that contributes to the growth and development of the company, the economy, and the nation. Every organisation, through the help of the personnel executives, must strive to train and develop the individual employee in such a way that he will derive maximum job satisfaction, having been able to utilise his talents and capacities to the maximum extent.

2. Principle of Scientific Selection Procedure

Systematic and scientific procedures must be employed in selection. A careful selection and proper usage of personnel tools and techniques are necessary to promote scientific selection. A scientific matching of men and jobs is essential. It is necessary to aid the line management in finding the right men for the right jobs after a systematic study of jobs, men and sources of recruitment. Though the decision on selection rests with the line managers, there is a good deal of room to influence this decision-making by employing proper scientific selection procedures and by assisting in proper placement. Essential to ascertain is whether the individual employee is properly placed.

3. Principle of Incentive

If we want an individual to contribute his best on his work, the principle of incentive must be utilised. The incentive may be monetary or non-monetary and it is necessary to understand the attitudes and aspirations of employee with a view to shaping and motivating them in such a way that they will contribute their maximum to realisation of organisational objectives and goals.

Unfortunately the role of incentives in the promotion of organisation health and stamina is not fully appreciated. Too often we want others to sacrifice and this sort of third person-sacrifice principle does not induce men to give off their best. Employee conduct, needs, attitudes, problems, and aspirations must be studied and analysed with a view to finding out what motives men in the shop and it may not be always money. A smile, a pat on the back, recognition of work performed, to mention a few, may often go a long way in motivating men better than money. Proper Incentives must be given at the proper time. Popular misconception is that too often employers tend to equate incentives with money, with the result they instinctively oppose giving incentives to employees.

4. Principle of Adequate Communication

Often bad communication is the root cause of many problems and misunderstandings. Secrecy breeds rumours and extreme secrecy breeds harmful rumours. As far as possible supply all relevant information to the employees. The company policies, programmes, objectives and philosophy may be made known to the employees. The channels and content of communication must be carefully prepared and developed. Effective language and proper communication styles must be adopted. All hurdles in the way of adequate communication must be removed.

The employees of organisation have great curiosity to know what the company is going to do with computers or *diwali* bonus, or rest breaks, or dearness allowance or vacancies in a department etc. If the company does not give information, the employees will concoct information that may have damaging results for the company. In order to obviate such problems, the personnel department must assist the management in supplying all the relevant information through appropriate medium at the right time to all the employees.

5. Principle of Participation

This principle is based on the consultative-participative managerial philosophy where the employer-employee relations are one of mutual trust, confidence, and give-and-take. The employees through their representatives are consulted and brought within the purview of participation in influencing decisions. The employees are offered opportunities to come up with their ideas, views, and suggestions to improve various operations of the organisation. The individual employee must feel that he is needed in the organisation and that he is making useful contribution to the company through his work, ideas and suggestions. It is a mistake to assume that only management knows what is good for the organisation and that employees have nothing to contribute. Personnel programmes must be evolved as to bring out the initiative, enthusiasm, and ideas of employees with a view to utilising them for the attainment of company goals. The employee must develop a sense of participation and belonging and he must feel that he is contributing his mite to the growth of the organisation.

6. Principle of Fair Compensation

The wage and salary structure must be fair and equitable. A fair day's work must receive fair day's wage and the personnel executive can help in arriving at what is a fair day's pay or wage for a fair day's work. Apart from pay and compensation, it is essential to provide good working conditions and environment, and good tools and equipment for the employees. Proper sanitary and health facilities must be provided.

Without establishing fair levels of wages, hours, and working conditions, it is idle to expect the employee to work well by the company. Here the personnel tools and techniques of wage and salary administration may aid management to establish a fair and just wage structure.

7. Principle of Dignity of Labour

According to this principle any labour that is productive is good and commendable. No job or task should be held as beneath one's station and neglected. Essentially it must promote the notion that any job or task must be done as best one can. If you are sweeping, you must do the best job of sweeping. It is crude and harmful to attach any stigma to any type of labour holding the man performing that job as a lowly person in society. Business-like environment must be promoted where a job is a job to be done well and reap the rewards. Any job that contributes to the material wealth and is productive is useful and good.

Efficiency in the use of labour can be promoted by the division of work and specialisation in task. There must be no structural rigidities which restrict upward mobility of an employee irrespective of his region, caste, and race. Merit, intelligence, and effort must be the sole criteria for upward mobility.

8. Principle of Team Spirit

The promotion of the will to collaborate among the employees, is essential and *esprit de corps* must be nurtured. Without team spirit business success cannot be achieved. Personnel policies and programmes must be so formulated that individuals function together as a group to attain the predetermined ends.

Individual employees, however brilliant and hard-working they may be, can dissipate their efforts if there is no feeling of group spirit. The diffused and diversified talents and efforts to individuals are brought and welded together in group effort in a true spirit of "togetherness" or "belongingness" where team work, co-operation, and collaboration may be the guiding light. It was said back in the 1950s that the Indian cricket team had brilliant individual cricket players, but as a team, they failed to win mainly because of the lack of team-spirit. Similarly in business and industry individuals with the proper team-spirit can spell success for an organisation. There is the necessity to subordinate individual interests to group interests or company interests and this is done where there is a high team-spirit.

9. Principle of Labour and Management Co-operation

Just as individual pulls in different directions sap the energy of the groups, instead of rejuvenating it, non-co-operation between labour and management will lead to industrial disharmony and unrest, which are not conducive to growth and progress of the organisation. Upon the health and profits of the organisation depend the material wellbeing of both labour and management, may, even that of a nation.

In the promotion of labour-management co-operation personnel administration has great responsibility and personnel specialist should assist management, particularly the top management, in fostering organisation conditions that remove distrust between labour and management through proper communication, creative, consultative-participative managerial philosophy, and the integration of any conflict[2] which enhance labour-management co-operation.

It is necessary not to underestimate the intelligence or the strength of labour not to ignore the reactions of labour to any particular management policy or programme. Consult and communicate with labour while building programmes and give necessary considerations to the viewpoints of labour and bring them in to participate in constructing programmes.

When labour and management realise that if they substitute friendly co-operation and mutual helpfulness for antagonism and unrest they are together able to make profits of the company so enormously greater than it was in the past that there is ample room for a large increase in wages for labour and an equally great increase in profits for employer.

This is perhaps the most difficult principle but nevertheless a fundamentally necessary principle of personnel administration.

10. Principle of Contribution to National Prosperity

Employees must be educated, through appropriate personnel programmes, to believe in the proposition that their contribution to the achievement of company goals will ultimately contribute to the economic development and prosperity of the nation as a whole. The proposition offers a higher purpose to the work of employees and they are likely to derive greater satisfaction in the knowledge that their contribution along with that of management will result in greater productivity and profits which bring in their wake prosperity to both labour and management as well as the nation.

Admittedly a need for such a personnel principle is great in developing economies like that of India where the employees, may even employers, hardly realise that they can make a significant contribution to national development and prosperity through their efforts.

These suggested principles of personnel administration are broad based guidelines that assist the personnel administrator in his conduct and behaviour. They are not inflexible or immutable laws. Inexact and imperfect as they are, they still perform a very useful function of explaining the behaviour of the personnel administrator and also in providing him a sense of direction in performing his personnel functions. Principles are concerned with the "why" of behaviour. This theoretical or conceptual framework enhances our understanding of the conduct and behaviour of personnel executives.

The principles of personnel administration are reflected in general statements or "policies" of a company. But personnel policies are largely conditioned by the management creeds and philosophies or an organisation and let us now turn to a discussion of management philosophies and then personnel policies.

2. MANAGEMENT PHILOSOPHIES AND CREEDS

Every organisation has its own management philosophy and some companies have consciously developed with great deliberation their creeds or philosophies, whereas others operate without such formal statements, but with the aid of unconsciously developed creeds or philosophies. A company or management philosophy may be defined as a general statement of beliefs, ethical values, ultimate aims and objectives, principles and policies and lastly, responsibilities and obligations that govern the behaviour, conduct, and operations of an organisation.

Delivering the KcKinsey Foundation Lectures at the Graduate School of Business, Columbia University, Thomas J. Watson Jr.,[3] Chairman, International Business Machines Corporation, very forcefully expresses the faith of his Corporation in the philosophy which expounds certain basic beliefs of I.B.M.:

> "This, the, is my thesis: I firmly believe that any organisation, in order to survive and achieve success, must have a sound set of beliefs on which it premises all its policies and actions.
>
> "Next, I believe that the most important single factor in corporate success is faithful adherence to those beliefs.
>
> "And finally, I believe that if an organisation is to meet the challenges of a changing world, it must be prepared to change everything about itself except those beliefs as it moves through corporate life."

"In other words, the basic philosophy, spirit, and drive of an organisation have far more to do with its relative achievements than do technological or economic resources, organisational structure, innovation, and timing. All these things weigh heavily in success. But they are, I think, transcended by how strongly the people in the organisation believe in its basic concepts and how faithfully they carry them out. I.B.M.'s philosophy is largely contained in three simple beliefs:

1. "I want to begin with what I think is the most important: our respect for the individual. This is a simple concept, but in I.B.M. it occupies a major portion of management time. We devote more effort to it than anything else."[4]
2. "I.B.M. means service." "It is a succinct expression of our second basic corporate belief. We want to give the best customer service of any company in the world."[5]
3. "The third I.B.M. belief is really the force that makes the other two effective. We believe that an organisation should pursue all tasks with the idea that they can be accomplished in a superior performance from its people in whatever they do."[6]

It is said that a company philosophy comprises of the guidelines that have become established as expected patterns of behaviour, either through trial and error or through leadership. Part of the foundation for a successful system of management is a philosophy that is consciously thought out, clearly spelled out, and consistently acted out in practice. I.B.M.'s philosophy was greatly influenced by the values of Mr. Thomas J. Watson, father of Mr. Watson Jr. "The important values, as he learned them, were to do every job well, to treat all people with dignity and respect, to appear neatly dressed, to be clean and forthright, to be eternally optimistic and above all, loyal."[7]

Tata Philosophy

"Personnel management in Tata Steel is older than the steel that they produce. From the very beginning of his entrepreneurial career, the Founder, Jamsetji Tata, placed man at the centre of the stage. In Tata Steel, man's precedence over machine has never been in question. Man has always been the core of Tata Steel. His management and welfare have been its prime concern. Hence, the emphasis on a sound personnel and industrial relations policy, the quest for the most modern techniques and methods in personnel management, the eagerness to accept and understand the urges and aspirations, rights and responsibilities of the workers and sound ethical and moral standards.[8]

"An intelligent anticipation and sympathetic understanding of the needs of employees, a keen foresight and breadth of vision in the formulation of policies, and sincere efforts to meet those needs have been the hallmark of Tata Steel's personnel and industrial relations policies.

"The statement of objectives of Tata Steel gives the following highlights of its obligations towards employees:

(i) Realistic and generous understanding and acceptance of their needs and rights and an enlightened awareness of the social responsibilities of industry.

(ii) Adequate wages, good working conditions, job security, an effective machinery for speedy redressal of grievances, and suitable opportunities for promotion and self-development.

(iii) Promoting feelings of trust and loyalty through a humane and purposeful awareness of their needs and aspirations.

(iv) Creating a sense of belonging and team spirit through their closer association with management at various levels.

This statement is not merely an exposition of a philosophy or attitude. In fact, it finds concrete expression in the personnel practices in Tata Steel which have been evolved through decades in accordance with the changing situations and requirement."

In a reply to an educationist, Mr. J.R.D. Tata, Chairman of Tata group of concerns, stated 'a few guiding principles,' than had 'kindled his path' and which may well be the corporate philosophy of the illustrious Tata House:

"That nothing worthwhile is ever achieved without deep thought and hard work;

"That one must think for oneself and never accept at their face value slogans catch phrases to which unfortunately, our people are too easily susceptible;

"That one must for ever strive for excellence, or even perfection, in any task however small, and never be satisfied with the second best;

"That no success or achievement in material terms is worth while unless it serves the needs or interest of the country and its people and is achieved by fair and honest means;

"That good human relations not only bring great personal rewards but are essential to the success of any enterprise."[9]

According to Steward Thompson's study on Management Creeds and Philosophies, a management creed is a general statement which:

"(1) Sets 'objectives, aims and goals'; (2) Lays down principles, policies, and ethics, governing the manner in which the objectives or aims are to be achieved; and/or (3) States responsibilities or obligations which are to be met."[10]

The statement of "Fundamental Objectives" by H.P. Hood and Sons, Inc. serves as a good example:[11]

"We recognise that industry justifies its existence to the degree that it is of service to the community.

"We also recognise that our industry is one in which competition is a dominant and beneficial influence. Competition has resulted over the years in a benefit to the community by the establishment of high standards of quality, service and efficiency.

"Therefore, our overall objective is to conduct our business so that all groups in the community will regard us as the best company in our industry and want us to prosper and grows.

"In order to accomplish this, our direct goals are:

1. To make available to consumers a combination of price, quality, variety and service through friendly and trustworthy people which will make our company the best in our industry from which to buy.

2. To provide farmers who sell to us a combination of money and worthwhile services which are greater than they can obtain by selling their products elsewhere.
3. To establish wages, working conditions, benefits, job security, opportunity, and personal recognition which combined will make our company the best in our industry in which to work.
4. To offer investors in company stocks and debentures a greater return on their money and greater security than they can obtain elsewhere in our industry.
5. To demonstrate that H.P. Hood and Sons is a good neighbour and citizen by our active support of good Government, education, health programmes and other good works which benefit the entire community in which we operate.

"To reach these objectives, we must operate more efficiently than our competitors. We must also pioneer in developing adventurous programmes and be willing to take risks, so long as the balance is in the best interest of attaining overall objectives."

Responsibility for the Formulation of Management Philosophy

Top management (often one individual at the top) must spell out clearly what they stand for and what are their basic beliefs, and must formulate general statement of beliefs or 'philosophy' of the company which governs the behaviour and conduct of all executives. The company creeds and management philosophies must be written down in unambiguous and clear language. They should be distributed to every executive, whose actions are governed by the established creed or philosophy. Apart from wide circulation, it is the responsibility of top management to see that executives live up to the creeds and philosophies of the organisation and that there is no deviation from the mainstream of business beliefs. There are two schools of thought which influence management philosophies and creeds.

Two Schools of Thought[12]

In recent years there has been a renewed search for a proper rationalisation of business operations on the horizon of the American business world. The consequence of this renewed examination of values is the possibility of an emergence of a new American business apologetic. The various facets of this development of a new apologetic are influenced by two schools of thought — one led by the Libertarians under the leadership of F.H. Knight, David McCord Wright, Henry Simmons, F.A. Hayek, Milton Friedman etc. and the other, the new business moralists led by Bengamin Selekman, Underwood, Stanley F. Teele, Ralph Cordiner etc.

The Libertarians, who represent the time-honoured traditional view, assert that business is business, meaning that a businessman is in business to make profits and that charity, sentimentality or religion have no place in business. Frank Knight[13] points out the ethical dualism in the market place:

"The spirit of life in the 'Christian' nations and the spirit of Christianity offer an interesting study in contrast between theory and practice. And all the while, there are multiplying evidences of a genuine spiritual hunger in the modern peoples. They have got away from the spiritual attitude toward life, and do not know how to get back. Science is too strong for old ideals of simplicity, humanity, and reverence.. This ethical dualism is suggested by the vernacular expression, 'business is business' meaning that business is one thing and 'charity' another. There is a strong feeling that it is 'right' to 'play' the business according to the rules to make exchanges at the ratio objectively set or made possible by the market. That is, it is assumed to be ethically legitimate and even positively virtuous, to desire to maximise one's 'income'... and to act in such a way as to do so, subject always to the sweeping reservation of mutual free consent in all relations with others." Knight further is highly critical of the current trend of posing moral values and social obligations in business and suggests that it would be wise if the principle of business-is-business is accepted.

"... the dualistic principle must be accepted whole-heartedly... if the kind of civilisation we call free is to exist. Business must be separated from 'charity' meaning all personal considerations. The principle of Business-is business-is on a par with that of Justice-is-blind, though both must be tempered with mercy. Moral obligations to persons in consequence of special relationships is the general principle of feudalism, and is anachronistic and disruptive in a commercial or enterprise economy."[14]

Here the central assumption is that the individual businessman is the best judge of his own values and interests and that he is free to pursue them in his own ways and means, and such individual pursuit of self-interest will enhance the overall efficiency of the market economy with mutual advantage through free exchange of goods and services.

Completely opposed to this libertarian apologetic is the school of the new business moralists, who reject the libertarian principle of business-is-business, for it reflects a maximum absence of moral tension. They confer a corporate conscience on the organisation and proclaim that the businessman is in business to serve the community and that he has social responsibilities and plead a 'service' apologetic. Benjamin Selekman observes:[15]

"What will no doubt be recorded by historians as the ethical awakening of American business constitutes one of the dramatic developments of past quarter century. It has always been taken for granted that the American businessman was a moral and religious man, even though his daily practices might at time have been questioned. Up until recent years, however, it did not occur to businessman to articulate the fact that what he did had moral goals. Now just the opposite is true. An explicit moral attitude is expressed again and again in literature, in meetings of business groups, in missions that go abroad, and in the reception of delegates who visit us to get a better understanding of American methods. The expression takes various forms. The social responsibility of business is a favourite theme; some leaders indeed take the unambiguous position that *'the corporation is a moral community.'* "

Management creeds and philosophies will be influenced by the viewpoints of these differing schools of thought and it is the responsibility of top management to decide where they stand and what their values are in the market place. In India also up until now the traditional libertarian theory of maximisation of profits in business ruled the day. But now there is emerging a new awareness among the businessmen and finds its expression in the theme of doctrine of social responsibilities. Ramakrishna Bajaj and other businessmen are trying to evolve a code of conduct for the businessman to adhere to in the market place. Recently two seminars were held at India International Centre in Delhi on social responsibilities of businessmen and social responsibilities of trade unions and there is a new moral awakening where the businessmen in India are willing to shoulder extra-legal self-imposed responsibilities and obligations towards the society. In a developing economy like ours, the businessmen have a great role to play in contributing to the economic growth and prosperity of the nation.

Then there are two theories of management expounded by Professor Douglas McGregor[16], which deal with two different modes in which managers manage and which will have impact on policies and programmes of an organisation.

Two Theories of Management: Theory X and Theory Y

1. Theory X states the traditional philosophy of direction and control where the central assumption is that people should be told what to do and see that they do it. Professor McGregor lists three assumptions which he states, "are implicit in most of the literature of organisation and in much current managerial policy and practice." They are:

1. The average human being has an inherent dislike of work and will avoid it if he can.
2. Because of this human characteristic of dislike of work, most people must be coerced, controlled, directed, threatened with punishment to get them to put forth adequate effort toward the achievement of organisational objectives.
3. The average human being prefers to be directed, wishes to avoid responsibility, has relatively little ambition, wants security above all.

Under the assumptions of theory X it is safe to presume that managerial policies and personnel policies are likely to put emphasis on discipline, incentive programmes, welfare measures, close supervision, pension and other benefit programmes.

2. Theory Y expands the currently growing consultative-participative philosophy of management which attempts to render the integration of individual and organisation goals. This theory is based on a completely different set of assumptions stated by Professor McGregor:

1. The expenditure of physical and mental effort in works is as natural as play or rest. The average human being does not dislike work. Depending upon uncontrollable conditions, work may be a source of satisfaction and will be voluntarily performed.
2. External control and the threat of punishment are not the only means of bringing about effort toward organisation objectives. Man will exercise self-direction and self-control in the service of objectives to which he is committed.
3. Commitment to objectives is a function of the rewards associated with their achievement.
4. The average human being learns, under proper conditions, not only to accept but to seek responsibility. Avoidance of responsibility, lack of ambition, and emphasis on security are generally consequences of experience, not inherent human characteristics.

5. The capacity to exercise a relatively high degree of imagination, ingenuity, and creativity in the solution of organisational problems is widely, not narrowly, distributed in the population.
6. Under the conditions of modern industrial life, the intellectual potentialities of the average human being are only partially utilised.

In the light of assumptions of theory Y, emphasis is likely to be placed on consultation, participation, motivation, communication, opportunities in formulating managerial and personnel policies. Professor McGregor states the contrasting managerial approaches thus: Theory X offers management an easy rationalisation for ineffective organisational performance: It is due to the nature of human resources with which we must work.

"Theory Y, on the other hand, places the programmes squarely in the lap of management. If employees are lazy, indifferent, unwilling to take responsibility, intransigent uncreative, unco-operative, Theory Y implies that the causes lie in management's methods of organisation and control." And also in management's concept of personnel administration.

As observed earlier these two theories of management with their contrasting assumptions are likely to have impact on managerial and personnel policies and programmes through which organisational objectives are achieved. Professor Charles Myers[17] rightly inculcates the fact that "the task of the personnel administrator is far different under theory Y management than under theory X."

"Specifically, under Theory Y, the personnel administrator is less concerned with personnel techniques and employee welfare programmes (even though these may still be desirable as supplements to the main purpose) than he is with helping line managers to develop managerial approaches which bring out the best efforts of free people at work. He stresses the techniques and values of consultation, of getting ideas from subordinates before reaching decisions, of assisting people to set goals and targets for themselves so that they can evaluate their own performance rather than expecting the manager to evaluate it for them, as pupils in a school. And he tries to show how this works by the way he consults with his own staff in the personnel or industrial relations department. If his company deals with a union, he attempts to build communication bridges at many levels between management and union representatives, to avoid having the only contacts confined to opposite and often antagonistic sides of the bargaining table or the grievance meeting."

Business creeds, management philosophies, beliefs, personnel principles, and theories influence and shape personnel administration and its policies and programmes in a company. Next to philosophy it is necessary to take into consideration organisational objectives and personnel objectives in order to formulate personnel policies.

Personnel Objectives: Objectives are the ends or goals toward which group activity in an organisation is aimed. They must be set at all levels of the organisation and for all the functional areas of management. It is required that everybody knows what the goals of the company and the goals of the department or division are. It may be argued that there is one and only one objective for a business unit — the pursuit of profit, but in recent years it is increasingly realised that there are various objectives, which differ from company to company. Broadly they can be grouped under economic objectives, social objectives and personal objectives. Under economic objectives we may classify the following: to make a profit; to create a customer; to produce and market cheaper goods and services; to provide employment opportunities; to pay good dividends to the shareholders; to increases sales at the rate of 20 per cent per year for the next five years; work to procure new sources of income; to seek ways for better utilisation of raw materials and by-products; to obtain additional business by filling certain needs of new industries etc.

Under social objectives the following may serve as examples: To serve the consumer, to promote ethics; to be a good corporate citizen; and encourage individual citizenship; to promote a higher standard of living; to innovate products that are useful and that bring comfort and happiness to citizens; to serve the community and the nation etc.

Personal objectives are those values that individuals and groups want for themselves.

There are short-range, medium-range, and long-range objectives and for each of the functional areas of management such as production objectives, sales objectives, design objectives, personnel objectives etc.

3. HUMAN RESOURCES MANAGEMENT OBJECTIVES

The objectives of personnel administration in any company may broadly be classified as primary objective and secondary objective. Under primary objectives fall such objectives as to manufacture and sell utilitarian and acceptable goods or services, to offer fair and satisfactory wages and salaries and satisfactory return to shareholders; and to meet the social responsibilities and obligations.

Secondary objective is to achieve the primary objectives economically, efficiently and effectively. The following is a partial list of personnel objectives of one company in the area of employment:

To provide jobs:

1. In a climate of stable employment, fair pay, good working conditions, work satisfactions;
2. With opportunities for development and advancement as members of our family of employees, having need and concern for each other as individuals;
3. For those individuals who evidence pride of company and associates, loyalty, initiative, care, effort, attendance, performance and team-work.

Personnel objectives must be in line with organisational objectives and there must be complete harmony between personnel objectives and company objectives.

Employee Needs and Interests: In the establishment of company personnel objectives, it is necessary to take into consideration the interests and needs of employees as well as employee goals with a view to formulating personnel objectives which will bring about an integration of employee interests and management interests to achieve organisational objectives. Generally the needs or wants and interests of employee centre around job security, good work environment, fair wages and benefits, opportunity for advancement and development, recognition of work, good boss, decent treatment etc.

Professor Mee has very ably illustrated the concept of integration of labour-management interests and also the relation between objectives and programmes in the following figure.

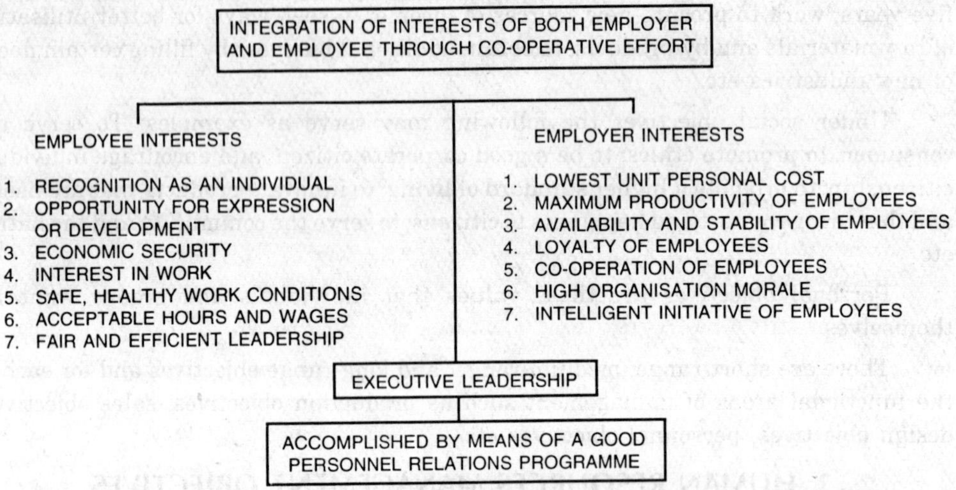

Fig. 4.1 Relation of Objectives, Personnel Programmes and Leadership

Source: John F. Mee, *Management Organisation for a Sound Personnel Relations Programme,* (Bulletin 2) (Bloomington: Bureau of Business Research, School of Business, Indiana University), p. 2.

Achievement of personnel objectives will depend upon the formulation of appropriate policies and implementation of policies through proper personnel programmes.

4. HRM POLICIES

One company defines policies as "guides which chart the course of an organisation and govern its activities toward the achievement of the purpose for which it was set up." Policies are characterised as "rules of action" or guides to thinking and action, but they are not the action. Policy refers to a continuing decision to a recurring question. For example, a policy, which states "promotion from within" has established the framework of action for the executives that whenever there is a vacancy of an executive position, you should depend upon internal sources to fill the vacancy and that nobody from outside the company must be hired to fill the vacancy.

Policies are formulated to achieve personnel and organisational objectives. Policies are not objectives. For example, the *policy of promotion from within* is formulated with the objective of individual development. Here providing the opportunity of advancement and development to individuals in the company is the objective and the policy of promotion from within attempts to carry out this objective by establishing a guide to thinking and a rule of action whenever there is a vacancy.

Policies are positive declarations and they are commands to the organisation. It helps the subordinates to make decisions without having to wait for consultation with the superior or for his concurrence.

The following serve as examples of a few personnel policies commonly found in organisations:

To promote from within, to hire only the relatives and friends of employees, and then to the others, to pay a wage slightly above the going wage in the industry in the community, to select only those who possess at least high school education, to evaluate employee performance every six months, to provide fellowships and scholarships to employees and their children, to hire only persons with engineering background. The list can be extended endlessly. But, suffice it to observe, that all the above policies are aimed at achieving certain definite personnel objectives.

Policy Coverage

There are a variety of policies covering the various areas and operations of personnel administration, for personnel functions, activities and personnel procedures and programmes are conditioned, regulated and directed by personnel policies. Professor Jucius identifies the following types of policies.[18]

1. Organisational Grouping of Policies

(a) ***General company policies*** which must be followed by all units of a company, e.g., it maybe a company policy to subsidise educational programmes of study carried on by any executive or employee in various schools.

(b) ***External policies*** which guide an organisation in relation to outside groups and agencies, e.g., it may be the policy to approve the participation of executives in part-time assistance to community, charity and welfare agencies.

(c) ***Internal policies*** which guide the internal relations between organisation units. They may be vertical or horizontal.

1. ***A vertical policy*** is intended to guide a lower level in an organisation, e.g., the sales manager may rule that all district managers are to evaluate salesmen every quarter.

2. ***A horizontal policy*** is intended to guide relationships between departments on the same level, e.g., a policy maybe set to the effect that the personnel department must consult with and get approval of departments it serves before establishing, let us say, training procedures.

(d) ***Centralised policies*** which have pertinence for companies with several locations and have reference to the degree of autonomy which local units will have in setting policies and procedures with their respective conditions.

2. Functional Grouping of Policies

(a) Policies which guide managerial functions of personnel planning, organising and controlling, e.g., it may be the policy that every manager must submit a plan of action for personnel activities in his unit by December 1 for the next operating year.

(b) Policies which guide technical functions of procuring, developing, maintaining and utilising labour, e.g., it may be the policy that any employee, who has a grievance has the unqualified right to go to his superior or the personnel division, as he may choose.

We give below a statement of the personnel policy of one of the leading Corporations of the world:

I. Fundamentals and Aims of the Personnel Policy

The Personnel Policy serves the goals of Swissair and is an integral part of the Company policy.

The economic success of any enterprise depends primarily on the quality of the employees and their initiative. The objective of the Personnel Policy is to create working conditions and a climate which will both attract and retain a willing and capable working team. This is an essential responsibility of Management.

Every business concern is part of the total social structure. Within this structure it exercises an essential social and economic function and bears part of the responsibility for the furtherance of social justice. A company cannot establish its Personnel Policy outside the social environment; there must be interaction and interdependence.

The Personnel Policy influences the public's opinion of Swissair. The prevailing working climate has a distinct bearing on the customer's confidence in our company and on the image of Swissair.

In such fundamental issues as terms of employment, wage policies, recruiting and training, Swissair adheres to and protects basic local employer practices.

A company is not only a technical and economic unit, but also a social one. Each employee is an individual personality. A Personnel Policy serving the Company's business aims not only considers technical and economic factors but also takes into account patterns of human behaviour.

It must recognise that the employee's will to perform, his achievements and his behaviour on the job are not only motivated by rational, but also by non-rational forces (feelings, attitudes, expectations). The Personnel Policy, therefore, takes psychological factors into account.

A Personnel Policy operates within the framework of often conflicting interests between employer and employees, as well as between superiors and subordinates. The reconciliation of opposite interests, and the full utilisation of those which are parallel, have a decisive bearing on the overall team achievement and the success of the enterprise. Integration of operational, technical, and organisational requirements with the employee's personal aims, expectations, preferences and desires, strengthens identification with the Company and its goals and creates an *"esprit de corps."*

The conflict created by the necessity of integration and the employee's desire for personal freedom can be largely overcome when the employee understands and accepts the reason for this integration.

Aside from putting operational, economic and social aspects into proper order, the Personnel Policy's main purpose is the motivation of employees to perform. Terms of employment, opportunities for advancement, placement according to aptitude, adequate job site and free flow of information within the organisation, must be consciously planned with a view to achieving the Company's goals.

Even under changing conditions, the basic concepts of the Personnel Policy and its rules and regulations must remain effective means of achieving the aims of the Company. Continuous technical progress and economic and social developments call for constant adoption and sensible application of a Personnel Policy.

The Personnel Policy must be implemented by all levels of management. The manager's function includes the obligation to always live up to the principles of the Personnel Policy and to secure compliance therewith.

The Personnel Policy encompasses the following areas: Contractual terms of employment, social and welfare benefits of personnel (salaries, hours of service, pension plans, meal facilities, expense accounts, personnel guidance etc.). Working conditions and facilities (organisation of work, tools and equipment, adequacy and decor of work area, accident prevention, etc.). Human factors (responsible leadership, human relations on the job, transfers, development for advancement, etc.).

The Personnel Policy is substantially affected by external factors such as: laws and government regulations; labour situation (competition on the labour market); social norms and expectations; the socio-economic aims and endeavours of employers; influence of labour organisations on working conditions.

General employment and working conditions must be especially geared towards: attraction and retention of employees; increased productivity through encouragement of individual performance and teamwork; maintenance of harmonious labour relations; awareness on the part of the Company of general economic and social situations.

These various criteria and aims should always be assessed in their totality.

II. Principles of the Personnel Policy

1. General Principles: The Personnel Policy must contribute towards the economic success of the Company.

Decisions affecting personnel are to be taken with a view to safeguarding the short and long-term interests of the Company.

The extent of the employer's freedom to establish terms of employment depends, in the long run, upon whether he — together with the employees — can find mutually satisfactory solutions within the accepted practice of private enterprise. Swissair voluntarily assumes its share of responsibility for a healthy social order by paying constant attention to general employment and working conditions, social obligations (pension and medical plans, etc.) and excellent employee relations.

Respect for the individuality and dignity of each employee is the basis of interpersonal relations in the Company.

The principle of good faith is observed with respect to both application and executions of legal, contractual and operational regulations, and in resolving conflicting interests and claims.

A good working climate prospers only where fairness, loyalty, freedom from prejudice and respect for individual privacy are the ruling criteria at all times.

The personnel policy serves to protect the interests of the employee on the job. It ensures responsible utilisation of manpower with full regard to legal, psychological and medical considerations.

2. Responsibility for Policy Formulation: Conventions, traditions and trial and error methods cause the conception of policies; but careful thinking and conscious efforts must be devoted to the formulation of right policies. While the top management is responsible for establishing company-wide personnel policies with the aid of personnel specialists, every executive should be responsible for determining personnel policies in his area of supervision with the assistance of personnel department. The following criteria may be prescribed from the formulation of good personnel policies:

1. The policy must affirm or reflect a principle.
2. The policy must aim to achieve the organisational objectives.
3. The policy must be stated clearly and in simple, but accurate language.
4. The policy must be enduring and stable for a period of time.
5. The policy must also be flexible to be applicable for any minor deviations.
6. The policy must be in line with the policies of other departments of the company.
7. The policy must be made known to all who will be affected by it.

The formulation of personnel policy must be followed by policy education and acceptance. Once all the organisational levels are educated and they have accepted the policies, it is necessary to apply the policies and interpret them. Finally a check on policies must be maintained in order to effect proper control on them. Policies are not inflexible and eternal, but they need to be constantly examined and re-examined in the light of changing environment. While policies hold good, they must be in supreme command of the situation.

In order to implement policies, we have to evolve personnel procedures and programmes.

5. HRM PROCEDURES AND PROGRAMMES

Personnel procedures detail the exact manner in which a certain activity must be accomplished with a view to implementing a certain policy. The essential distinguishing feature is while a policy is a guide to action, the procedure tells how action should take place. Procedures tend to be less general than policies and more specific in establishing the course of action and the sequence of activities necessary to implement policies. Written procedures ensure a uniformly high level of performance. It simplifies work and establishes checkposts for evaluation and appraisal of performance. One problem with procedure is that it may suppress individual initiative to some extent.

An example will help clarify the relationship of procedures and policies. A company may have a policy of granting two weeks' vacation per year to each employee. In order to implement this policy, procedures will have to be established, providing for scheduling of vacation of each employee to avoid disruption of work, methods and rates of pay, the maintenance of records to assure employees a vacation and means by which an employee may apply for his vacation.

Programmes give a step-by-step approach to guide the action necessary to reach a predetermined goal. Personnel manager has to develop a programme of action for the implementation of personnel policies and procedures and the organisational objectives. The programmes are organised within the framework of personnel policies.

Where the procedure tells how the work is to be done, the programme tells what. Personnel programmes may be combined with budgets and some companies call their total process of programming and budgeting, the "company programme." It is desirable to co-ordinate the programme with the budget, for one is the basis of the other.

6. HRM BUDGET

It is an appraisal of expected expense projected against anticipated income for a future period. Before a manager can develop a budget, he must think through the objectives he is trying to achieve and the programme he will follow. This consideration is practical and realistic, for it can be meaningful only if it is based on such data as wage rates, personnel needs, material costs, space requirements and so forth. Personnel programmes and practices should not be undertaken without preparing a personnel budget, which will throw light on the financial implications. The budget assists in planning, organising and controlling various personnel activities and it must determine the allocation of amounts to various activities over a given period of time. It also helps in arriving at decisions quickly regarding personnel activities if it is known how much a particular programme would cost, e.g., it may be a good idea to send executives to the Harvard Graduate School of Business for a short-term executive development programme. But when it is realised that it is going to cost the company Rs. 1,00,000 per executive, the idea will be quickly dropped. Alternate executive development programmes in the country itself will be utilised.

Preparation of the personnel budget assists in the classification and enumeration of all the activities or functions, the people required to perform, the time factor, equipment and facilities needed, managerial and technical staff required etc. will have to be thought of and this means forecasting, planning and organising the personnel programme more accurately and effectively.

Each of the personnel departments such as employment, medical, welfare, training, safety division, industrial relations etc. must be asked to prepare their estimates and they must be carefully checked to eliminate duplications, imbalance and gaps. All these estimates may be consolidated and a personnel budget may be prepared and at the end of the budget period of actual expenditure may be compared with the original estimates. One can draw some very useful lessons from this useful exercise.

Finally with the aid of budgets, comparisons may be made with other companies and with the industry-wide data. It will be easy to determine how much money is being expended per employee as a result of each of the personnel programmes with a view to comparing with other companies. The following Table 4.1 gives such details:

Table 4.1

PERSONNEL COSTS

Average Functional Cost per Employee per year	$
1. Administration	7.38
2. Planning policy and organisation	3.88
3. Staffing: job analysis, selection, recruitment, induction	9.06
4. Training	5.13

5.	Promotion and transfer	2.47
6.	Personnel rating	2.04
7.	Labour relations	6.08
8.	Employee services including communication	9.14
9.	Medical, health and safety	11.68
10.	Wage and salary administration	4.82
11.	Records and reports	5.66
12.	Audit and review	1.51
13.	Research	1.46
14.	Overhead and miscellaneous	6.57
	All functions	76.88

Source: A.C. Thornton, *Practical Personnel Budgeting,* Personnel Series No. 173, American Management Association, p. 55.

The following Table 4.2 shows the personnel budget of a company in our country in 1965-66.

Table 4.2
PERSONNEL BUDGET OF MANI PRIVATE LIMITED

		Rs.
1.	Personnel Officer	10,000
2.	Welfare Officer	6,500
3.	Training Officer	7,000
4.	Administrative Division (Office staff, Clerks, Attenders, Office suppliers etc.)	32,000
5.	Training Division: One Training Supervisor Two Training Assistants Two Diploma Trainers Clerks, Stationeries, Supplies etc.	32,000
6.	Management Training and Development	20,000
7.	Safety Division	5,000
8.	Medical Division (First Aid)	3,000
9.	Employee Services: (a) Picnics, tours and visits (b) Washing facilities for Uniforms (c) Soaps (d) Free fruits, milk, buttermilks etc. (e) Uniforms (f) Recreation (g) Reading room (h) Sports & games	35,000
10.	Canteen	10,000
11.	Co-operative Stores	5,000
12.	Printing Booklets, Brochures, Pamphlets etc.	6,000
13.	Technical Library	3,000
14.	Miscellaneous	5,000
	Total	Rs. 1,79,500

7. HRM RESEARCH

Good and effective personnel programmes, procedures, functions, policies and objectives, in short, personnel administration, are possible when there is good personnel research. Personnel research often influences programmes and practices. Often an employer would like to know how the suggestion system is working in another company before he will think of introducing a suggestion system in his company.

There are various research tools and techniques such as wage surveys, morale surveys, compensation surveys, job analysis, job evaluation, job description, personnel inventory, merit rating, turnover, absenteeism etc., which we shall discuss in later sections and which provide basic information with which policies, programmes, procedures and practices of personnel administration can be improved upon constantly. These tools and techniques may not be very perfect and exact, but nonetheless they assist in estimating the effects of programmes and practices and improving them.

In United States, The National Industrial Conference Board periodically has conducted surveys of personnel practices in factory and office since 1937 and on the sixth and the latest in the series I had the opportunity of assisting Mr. Harland Fox on a study which involved mailing questionnaires to 7000 corporations in U.S. These personnel surveys have been considered most useful by American corporations. The primary purpose of this study was to answer, "how is it being done", but the Board conducts many studies on personnel administration which answer "why" and "what" and "where" also. Similarly American Management Association conducts many studies which throw a great deal of light on personnel administration and which help the corporations in formulating and improving their personnel administration practices.

Unfortunately in India such research work and information is conspicuous by its absence. Furthermore there is very little of sharing of information on management practices and a lack of such exchange of views, ideas and information is a series obstacle to the growth of good management practices.

We also conducted a study on Personnel Administration Practices in the private sector, cooperative sector, and the public sector, which throws light on the state of art of personnel management in the leading companies of the three sectors in the country which would be useful to personnel administrators, students of management, employers, management institutions and research organisations. This is published under the title: *Personnel Administration Practices in India* by the Vaikunth Mehta National Institute of Cooperative Management.[19]

We are also happy to report that both the Indian Institute of Personnel Management and the National Institute of Labour Management have undertaken various studies conducted by personnel experts in the country and these are published under two separate monograph series. The Indian Institute of Personnel Management has also published a book Readings in Personnel Management in India which is a collection of articles by the leading personnel administrators in the country. The National Institute of Labour Management has published a commemorative volume of Readings in Human Resources Management in India, again a collection of articles by the leading personnel experts in the country. They have also published the papers presented in their annual conferences for the last 25 years, in a book entitled, *Personnel Management — The Indian Scene.*

In India there is a great need for good research in the areas of management and personnel administration. The purpose of research is to improve operations, programmes, policies and practices, apart from providing information and knowledge. The management institutions must give the lead in this area of research and corporations, management associations, productivity councils, Administrative Staff College and similar institutions must take upon themselves the responsibility of conducting a variety of research projects which will provide basic information regarding our management and business philosophies, policies; undoubtedly research is the 'key to effective planning of personnel activities.'

So far in the first part we have discussed the concepts, functions, and philosophies of personnel administration; let us now turn to the detailed discussion of the functions of personnel administration beginning with the Human Resources Planning.

REFERENCES

1. Adam Curle, "Some Aspects of Educational Planning in Underdeveloped Areas," *Harvard Business Review,* Vol. 32, No. 3, Summer 1962, p. 300.
2. See Mary Parker Follet, *Dynamic Administration* (Chapter 1: Constructive Conflict), ed. by Henry C. Metcalf and Lyndall Urwick. (New York: Harper & Bros. 1940).
3. Thomas J. Watson, Jr., *A Business and its Beliefs* (New York: McGraw-Hill Book Co. Inc., 1963), p. 5.
4. *Ibid.,* p. 13.
5. *Ibid.,* p. 29.
6. *Ibid.,* p. 34.
7. *Ibid.,* p. 12.
8. M.N. Rudrabasavaraj, *Personnel Administration Practices in India,* Poona, Vaikunth Mehta National Institute of Cooperative Management, 1970, p. 303.
9. J.R.D. Tata, "A Few Guiding Principles," *Tata Review,* Vol. 1, No. 3, October 1965, p.2.
10. Steward Thompson, Management Creeds and Philosophies: *Top Management Guides in Our Changing Economy* (New York: American Management Association, Research Study No. 32, 1958), p. 10.
11. *Ibid.,* p. 117.
12. For greater discussion on these Schools of Thought, see my, "Towards a New Business Apologetic: An American Adventure," *Eastern Economist,* Special Budget Number, March 11, 1966, p. 530; also my "The Evolution of Business Thought", *Industrial India*, issues of April, May, June, 1966.
13. Frank H. Knight, *Freedom and Reform* (New York: Harper & Brothers, 1941), p. 57.
14. Frank H. Knight, "Theory of Economic Policy and History of Doctrine," *Ethics,* Vol. 63, 1952-53, p. 24.
15. Benjamin Selekman, *A Moral Philosophy for Management* (New York: McGraw-Hill Book Co. Inc., 1960).
17. Charles Myers: "New Directions in the Management of Human Resources", *Indian Management*, September-October 1962. Most of the material in this section is borrowed from this paper and from Douglas McGregor's, *The Human Side of Enterprise.*
18. Jucius, *Personnel Management,* pp. 73-74.
19. M.N. Rudrabasavaraj, *Personnel Administration Practices in India,* Poona, Vaikunth Mehta National Institute of Cooperative Management, 1970.

❑ ❑ ❑

PART TWO

Management of Human Resources

CHAPTER 5

Human Resources Planning

In the discussion on Management of Human Resources we must begin at the beginning — manpower planning or planning for resources. We shall discuss:

1. Perspectives in human resources planning;
2. Changes in the attitudes of people;
3. Manpower planning;
4. Executive resources planning.

1. PERSPECTIVE IN HUMAN RESOURCES PLANNING

Management of human resources in contemporary times is highly complex, sophisticated and difficult. The momentous changes taking place in education, science, technology, management, business and society have rendered many age old concepts and stereotypes obsolete. The human resources planner has to have some understanding of the new perspectives both with regard to the challenge of change and the changing attitudes of people. I should like to place before you what Prof. Daniel Bell calls the five dimensions of contemporary and post industrial society.[1]

1. First of all for the first time in human history we are moving towards a service society, not just a good producing society. Today more than half the labour of an advanced country no longer is engaged in production of goods by the production of services in the sense of trade, finance, real estate, transport, insurance, education, health, research, government, etc.

2. A second dimension is that a service society requires an increasingly technical character, particularly the white collar employees. And one finds that the professional and technical class is the largest single occupational class of the advanced industrialised society. We in India are also moving towards that. You have here an extraordinary shift in the kinds of work that people do and where they work with enormous consequences in all other ways. A service industry to a great extent is based more on a person-to-person relation rather than a man-to-machine relation.

3. The third and most important and revolutionary factor of our times is that increasingly innovation takes place through the codification of

theoretical knowledge. This has enormous consequences of the changed relationship of science to technology. Every society is dependent upon knowledge, but not always upon the codification of theoretical knowledge as a way of advancing other dimensions of society.

If one looks at the major industries — steel, auto, telephone, electricity — almost all of them are 19th century industries (exceptions include steel beginning in the 18th and aviation in the 20th). Almost all of them were made by talented tinkerers, who worked quite independently of the laws of science. Darby with the first coking process, Bessemer with the steel hearth process, Siemens with the dynamo, Edison with the electric light, Bell with the telephone, Wright Brothers with aviation, the various people who created the automobile industry, whether it be a Renault, a Ford, or various others — all of these were people who worked quite independently of basic laws, thermodynamics, metals etc.

The first modern industry, to a crucial extent, is chemistry. Because one has to have a knowledge of the property of the macromolecules one is manipulating in order to know where one goes. You have to have some foreknowledge in order to see what you are going to get and one sees this not only in the relation of science to technology, but in all areas of life, increasingly in economics, management and political science. For example, one finds the extraordinary situation of a British Labour Government or an American Republican Government, deliberately engineering a recession in order to redeploy manpower resources based upon some notion of economic theory.

However, it is this codification of theory, the primacy of theory over empiricism, which to a great extent is the real revolutionary change which is taking place in our lives. And to a considerable extent, it is responsible for the new centrality of the university, of the research organisation and of those corporations which are oriented to research, to the national laboratories, to the university based laboratories, etc.

The interaction of business corporations with these sectors rather than simply within the corporations themselves becomes a new relationship with which the contemporary manager is concerned. This is why intellectual institutions have become so crucial to the future. It also means to a great extent that the most scarce resource of society is no longer money capital, but human capital. The idea of human capital is very different. Planning for it regards a different time cycle. You have to think over a 20 year basis of locating talent when talent is young, husbanding it, developing it, making sure in a sense that it is given a rich curriculum, going ahead in terms of accurate choices, etc. This is one of the most crucial problems of management.

4. The fourth dimension is the fact that increasingly we will see the growth alongside the machine technology of an intellectual technology. The growth of new techniques such as linear programming, model construction, simulation, game theory, systems analysis, systems engineering, much of it hitched to a computer, gives a different and decisive and increasingly technical character to managerial decision-making. Techniques can never define the goals of the society or business, but how they are used and the extent of their effect provide greater power for the managers and the technocrats.

5. The fifth dimension is the notion of technological forecasting. One of the things which belied, to a considerable extent, the predictions about the demise of advanced industrial society, is the fact that technology has provided an open frontier to this business and society. Almost all the economists of the 19th century, Mill with his notion of a stationary state and Marx with the notion of crises — predicted that there were finite limits to this system based in large part on population and resources.

Technology did provide an open frontier and it is an indeterminate frontier. If there is possibility of sustained technological forecasting, one can therefore chart out the necessary areas of capital and business growth, expansion of society as a whole. The lack of understanding of these dynamic environmental forces and response to them will increasingly render the managers obsolete.

2. CHANGES IN THE ATTITUDES OF PEOPLE

The attitudes of people in general and workers, supervisors and managers in particular industry are changing. No longer the stereotypes of uneducated and unambitious workers, hard working devoted supervisors, and managers totally loyal to their companies all the 24 hours hold good. There has been an evolutionary process of changing attitudes of workers, supervisors and managers over a period of time influenced by a variety of factors.[2]

1. Political: The State is playing a major role in not only promoting economic growth but also controlling business enterprises in order to improve the standards of living of people as well as the quality of life. In the U.N. designated Second Development Decades, the State has initiated and nurtured an era of rising aspirations of people. In industry the concept of industrial democracy which promotes participation at all levels is increasingly pursued through such programmes as workers' participation in industry, greater managerial autonomy and managers' participation in management.

2. Economic: There is a greater concern for promotion of economic development, particularly in the developing economics with a view to raising the standards of living of people, particularly the workers in the organised sector. Overriding concern seems to be not in the area of gross national product as much as in promoting the concept of net economic welfare of people. Economic growth must result not only in abundance of goods and services but they must also contribute to greater happiness and welfare of people.

3. Sociological: The quality of working life and quality of life are the major sociological concerns. The trend towards an egalitarian society is pushed further by combating discrimination of any sort — sex, race, religion, age, old school, etc. There is also an erosion of authority in all walks of human life. In fact, blind authority is frowned upon.

4. Educational: The explosion of knowledge in the 20th century has contributed to knowledge industry with knowledge workers and professionals as supervisors and managers dealing with more automated, sophisticated and complex systems in industries. They operate more on the basis of a codified theory, principles and systems rather than trial and error, seat of the plants and guess work methods. There is a great sense of self-confidence among these people because of their knowledge, expertise and competence. Their life goals and career goals are self-fulfilment and self-actualisation.

Managers who deal with employees in industry and need to be aware of the various factors which have influenced the changing attitudes of the workers, supervisors and managers so that they may evolve better and more systematic policies, procedures, and tools to manage these people in a fruitful fashion.

Changing Attitudes

(a) Workers: The stereotype of an Indian worker used to be that he was uneducated, lazy, unaccustomed to urban industrial environment and unwilling to participate in the industrial process actively and productively. This may no longer be so. Various studies reveal that the modern factory worker is educated, quite attuned to the urban industrial life process, quite willing to work hard not only with his hands but also with his mind and capable of making suggestions to improve technical, production process. In other words, we are dealing with knowledge workers. They are no longer awed by the authority of managers and supervisors. They have ideas about the work process, work design and quality of working environment and life. Furthermore, they want a sense of participation at least in areas which affect their working life closely. This sense of participation is encouraged by such State schemes as workers' participation in industry, Joint Management Councils, workers directors on the Board etc. In addition to job security they demand greater job satisfaction, better working environment through job enrichment and work redesign programmes. The knowledge worker also wants to be treated as unique individual human being with his own aspirations, needs and problems and he is greatly concerned about optimising his own talent and reaching his own maximum potentialities. In short the modern factory worker has become more demanding, selective, assertive and difficult.

(b) Supervisors and Managers: Increasingly we find professionals entering into the ranks of supervisors and managers.

1. Their loyalty is no longer to their companies but, first, to themselves and secondly to their profession. They want to fulfil themselves in the sense they want to realise their maximum potentialities and capabilities through an organisation.

2. They also want to make a contribution to their discipline, thus help advance knowledge and experimentation in the discipline with a view to not only helping the companies but also the nation and the world.

3. There was a time when a manager joined a company and remained with the company for the rest of his life. He was largely a one company man. There is gradual change in this aspect also. Today the manager will stay with the company as long as he has opportunity to fulfil himself and failing that, he may move to another organisation where he sees better opportunities of self-fulfilment. Sometimes, the manager may become redundant as a result of technological change and he may be no longer needed by the company.

4. There was a time when a person went to school once and prepared for the rest of his professional career. That is also changing today because of the knowledge explosion. It is necessary for the managers and supervisors to go back to school and get a retread in education as often as necessary.

5. The life styles and life goals of managers and professionals are also changing. They want to do their own thing. They are more selective, demanding and difficult.

There was a time when in a large organisation if the organisation wanted its manager to go on transfer to another unit in another place or another country, it was expected of the manager to be ready to do so. He also was willing. But today there are many aspects and questions regarding education of the children, health of the wife or dependent parents, safety and security in the region, career prospects, etc., which are taken into consideration by the manager before he makes a decision.

6. Another interesting facet of the changing attitude of the managers is that more young people want to be their own bosses and want to be entrepreneurs. They do not want to be workoholics and neglect their other responsibilities towards family, children, parents and society, profession, nation and humanity at large. They want to be a well-rounded personalities who are interested in discharging their social responsibilities not only towards the society, profession and the country but also towards their family.

These have grave consequences on human resources planning and management. The most interesting prospect of this phenomenon is that we cannot take people for granted and the function of planning for human resources is rendered challenging, complex and even exciting, albeit harassing, to all organisations and managers. Let us now proceed to an examination of the mechanics of human resources planning.

3. MANPOWER PLANNING

What is Manpower Planning?

Manpower Planning may be defined as a strategy for the acquisition, utilisation, improvement and preservation of an enterprise's human resources.

Objectives of Manpower Planning

The objectives of manpower planning are mainly:

1. To ensure optimum use of human resources currently employed;
2. To assess or forecast future skills requirements if the organisation's overall objectives are to be achieved; and
3. To provide control measures to ensure that necessary resources are available as and when required.

A number of more specific reasons for attaching importance to manpower planning and forecasting exercises are:

1. To determine recruitment level;
2. To anticipate redundancies and avoid unnecessary dismissals;
3. To determine optimum training levels;
4. To provide a basis for management development programmes;
5. To cost the manpower in new projects;
6. To assist productivity bargaining; and
7. To assess future accommodation requirements.

What are the Types of Levels of Skill for which Forecast should be prepared?

One of the main purposes of manpower planning is to enable the company to identify "trouble spots." Since the effort of preparing forecasts can be considerable, it is clearly desirable to concentrate as far as possible on critical skills in occupation groups, i.e., those where shortages are most likely to upset the company's programme where recruitment is more difficult, where the period of training is longest, or where skill costs have been rising steeply. Considering these, we suggest that unit manpower planning should involve from first level supervisors to Junior Assistant level and the Central Personnel Department from Senior Assistant upwards.

Are Forecasts to be Prepared for the Whole Unit or by Department?

We suggest to prepare plans by departments like Spinning, Weaving, B.D.P., Engineering, Manager's Office.

What is to be the Length of Forecasting Period?

In many companies, five years are felt to be as far ahead as it is possible to make a reasonable estimate of economic, social and technological developments; but this may be too ambitious for some organisations and too short for those who are accustomed to long-term planning of large-scale capital plant like our chemical units. Five years will, however, give most units the "lead time" they will require to take remedial action where manpower is concerned. The best practice is to draw up forecasts for the first two years in detail, then each of the subsequent years and have a procedure for annual, or even half-yearly revisions. A useful technique is to roll on the forecast by a year at each annual revision, thereby keeping the length of the forecasting period unchanged whilst making any amendment necessary in the light of changing circumstances.

Human Resources Inventory

How to Compute Manpower Forecasting? To compute manpower planning for a particular period, we should know (i) demand of different skills in that forecast period and (ii) how to supply those skills.

Demand: Broadly speaking, four main approaches to medium and long-term manpower forecasting can be distinguished at the level of the unit.

1. The first of these relies on the informal opinion of managers within the company.
2. The second is based on the idea of projecting past trends in employment by statistical techniques like extrapolation, regression and co-relation etc.
3. In the third, the results of work study/job description etc. exercises form the basis for forecasts; and
4. Lastly and in many circumstances the most difficult to apply, predictions are based on measure of productivity. Although in practice these approaches are treated as alternatives, we should use all these to supplement each other whenever we have sufficient data to do so.

For our units, to begin with, we can:

1. Estimate the manpower implications of one or more alternative assumptions about rate of company growth etc. (expansion rate C.P.D. has assumed is 4% per year);
2. Monitor, at regular intervals (half yearly done by C.P.D.), the effects of change in order to be in a position to revise forecasts without delay where this becomes necessary.

In tabular form it will be as follows:

	1972	1973	1974	1975	1976	Total (1972-76)
1. Number required at the beginning of year (present + vacant positions)						
2. Additional requirement due to expansion at the rate of ... % per year						
3. Total requirement at the end of the year. (Item No. 1 plus Item No. 2)						

Supply: We should make an analysis here for forecasting for replacements of losses through wastage. Broadly speaking, the wastage elements are:

(a) Normal Retirement: Normal retirement is a natural wastage which depends on the company policy. Our company policy is 60 years for normal retirement. This can be estimated for the forecast period through the personnel records and through an analysis of the age distribution of employees. If the company encourages employees to stay on after reaching retirement age, some estimate will be necessary of the numbers doing so, or it may be preferred to regard this as an extra margin of error in case other types of wastage prove higher than anticipated.

(b) Actual Wastage: Natural wastage can be defined as losses of staff due to death, illness or disability. This can be computed through the past experience and the age structure and general health of the employees.

(c) Discharges: Some units may wish to take into account the loss of personnel as a result of discharge or dismissals. Again, previous experience should provide the guidelines.

(d) "Voluntary" Wastage: The units will have to consider another constituent of the wastage rate, that is loss of personnel through "voluntary wastage" or resignations. It is clear that wastage for reasons such as conditions of work, morale, job satisfaction, opportunities in the unit and elsewhere will vary widely from unit to unit and between industries. Here, again, the past experience and future trends in the industry will provide the guideline.

(e) Transfer and Promotions: An allowance which must be allowed when arriving at an overall estimate of wastage, will be the extent to which particular occupational and hierarchy group is lost to other occupations of promotion. Given careful analysis like succession systems analysis, transfer analysis, etc. it will be very easy to predict the proportion of employees in particular categories who are likely to be promoted or transferred between departments in the future.

(f) Expansion, Diversification, Modernisation:

In tabular form, it will be as follows:

	1972	*1973*	*1974*	*1975*	*1976*	*Total (1972-76)*
1. Number available at beginning of the year						
2. Losses through wastage:						
(a) Actual retirement at the age of 60 years						
(b) Early retirement (% per year)						
(c) Discharges (% per year)						
(d) Voluntary resignations (% per year)						
(e) Transfers and Promotions (% per year)						
3. Total available at the end of the year (Item No. 1 minus Item No. 2)						

Reconciling Supply and Demand Forecasts

The stages already discussed in Demand and Supply columns are intended to provide the management the extent and nature of shortages or surpluses of manpower given certain business objectives. The following table provides a simplified picture of the way in which size of the manpower gap can be calculated and a recruitment and control schedule for the succeeding five years derived. This table gives a hypothetical case and is not related to any of our units.

COMPANY X

SPINNING DEPARTMENT (DEPT. ASSTS.)

		1972	*1973*	*1974*	*1975*	*1976*	*Total (1972-76)*
	1. Number available at beginning of the year (1st January)	100	108	112	116	120	—
SUPPLY	2. Losses through wastage:						
	(a) Actual retirement at 60 years	2	3	7	1	3	16
	(b) Early retirement (1%)	1	1	1	1	1	5
	(c) Discharges (1%)	1	1	1	1	1	5
	(d) Voluntary resigntions (5%)	5	5	5	5	5	25
	(e) Promotions & Transfers	7	4	4	2	3	20
	3. Total (Item No.1 minus Item No. 2)	84	94	94	106	107	—
DEMAND	4. Vacant Position	4	—	—	—	—	4
	5. Expansion (4% per annum)	4	4	4	4	4	20
	6. Total Required (Item No. 1 + Item No. 4 + Item No. 5)	108	112	116	120	124	—
	Additional number required during the year (Item No.6 – Item No. 3)	24	18	22	14	17	95

Explanation:

Item No. 2(a) : In 1972, Mr. Y (5.6.1912), Blow-room Section and Mr. Z (5.11.1912), Carding Section are due to retire.
(Likewise in other years)

Item No. 2(b) : One vacancy due to early retirement each year.

Item No. 2(c) : One vacancy due to allowance for discharges each year.

Item No. 2(d) : The vacancies arising out of voluntary resignations (turnover) are estimated to be 5 each year.

Item No. 2(e) : In 1972, 7 vacancies are due to promotions and transfers.
In 1973, 4 vacancies are due to promotions and transfers.
(Likewise in other years)

Item No. 3 : Total number available after losses due to wastage is estimated by deducting Item No.2 from Item No.1.

Item No. 4 : 4 positions are vacant
(To specify particular positions vacant)

Item No. 5 : Vacancies due to expansion are estimated to be 4 each year.

Requirement and Supply Profile

Year	*Total Requirements*	*Supply Plan*	
		Internal	*External*
1972	24	19	5
1973	16	13	3
1974	22	18	4
1975	14	11	3
1976	17	14	3
Total:	93	75	18

Recommended Recruitment Schedule

Please write recommendations of yours for 5 years.

4. EXECUTIVE RESOURCES PLANNING (ERP)

Executive resources planning is perhaps the crucial element in an effective and successful executive development system and without this critical input, everything else done in E.D. effort proves fruitless.

Dovetailing Executive Resources Planning with Business Plans

It is essential that efforts to develop executives are put into effect with thorough consideration of the probable growth and changes in various functions of the companies. There are two major problems that crop up if E.D. is not dovetailed with the total plans of the future of the company. First, the effort that is dictated by whim or fad may well be useless. Secondly, and more seriously, the problems can arise when business plans do not guide E.G. and executive personnel implications are taken up only as an after thought. For example, many companies have committed themselves to EDP facilities and equipment or rural banking with scant attention to the knowledge and skills which are required to operate such facilities. When it is determined that branches in urban, semi-urban and rural areas should attempt to be total banking centres for their communities, it is apparent that major efforts to reeducate present managers and to find additional people with different knowledge, skills and habits would be required.

There are four major elements in the process of executive resources planning that would claim the attention of the companies:

1. Executive resources inventory.
2. Executive resources forecasting.
3. Career development plans.
4. Management succession systems.

Executive resources planning is concerned with the implementation of the basic human resources objective of having the right people in the right places at the right time. Viewed in this light, the activities necessary to implement executive resources planning become as much an integral part of the human resources function as any other activity in the human resources development.

The need for a practical approach to executive resources planning is based on the obvious requirements of the organisational situation. As many companies are aware, the situation calls for advance planning and preparation with respect to executive manpower in much the same way it does with respect to buying and selling.

(a) Executive Resources Inventory

As a starting point, for executive resources planning in a going company, information about future requirements would be just worthless unless accompanied by adequate information about present executive resources. In addition to knowing how many executives there are in the companies, in various categories and levels, we must find out in detail many other relevant aspects. In planning future utilisation of manpower, particularly at the managerial level, it is not enough to know that the present executive calibre is made up of so many executives in this and that kind of position. It is essential to have certain information about each executive individuality. What kind of training and experience has he had? How old is he? Is his health an asset or liability to his qualifications? What kind of ability has he demonstrated? Is he reliable, dependable? Is he capable of assuming greater responsibilities?

The importance of having information which will answer these and other similar questions is quite obvious. Effective planning to utilise present executive resources on future requirements simply cannot take place without it.

Each company should design an Executive Resources Inventory file containing basic information regarding the individual, his education, training and development, experience for executive resources requirements. This must be constantly updated so that the information is adequate and in readily usable form. Three simple tests are suggested for determining whether executive resources inventory is adequate and put up in readily usable form:

1. Is it portable?
2. Is it in constant readiness to be taken into a meeting on short notice?
3. Will it quickly provide the pertinent information needed to make personnel decisions objectively with respect to filling vacancies, recruitment needs, development programmes, etc.?

Development of Executive Resources Inventory: The approach consists of: (1) Establishing and maintaining an inventory of present executive resources. (2) Setting up and maintaining a separate record of employees considered immediately qualified for promotion.

(b) Executive Resources Forecasting

Once we know "what we do have" the next step is "what we do need" taking into consideration our future growth plans. Forecasting executive resources requirements is the means of gaining the necessary time to meet future requirements in the most effective manner possible. The dependence of advance planning and preparation on forecasting information raises two issues: What kind of information is needed? How can it be developed?

The Kinds of Information Needed: Forecasting executive resources requirements is essentially nothing more than trying to determine in advance what kind of executive employment requisitions to expect in the future. How many can be expected from the various parts of the organisation? In what lines of work? When? If the problem is visualised in this manner, the specific type of information which should go into the forecast for each part of the organisation can be readily determined.

How it can be Developed: Forecasting, if it is to be satisfactorily, must be approached in an objective manner. The problem of developing forecast information is primarily one of seeking out and systematically utilising information which will most reliably indicate future needs.

Future executive resource needs can be expected to reflect:
1. Loss of present executive resources
2. Expansion or contraction in business
3. Growing or declining needs for certain types of executives.

In the first instance, the resulting need will be for replacements. In the latter two, the resulting need will be for more or fewer executives, depending on the nature of the development or the direction of the trend. What kind of information is available in each of these which can be used in forecasting what future executive resources requirements will be?

For the purpose of forecasting replacement needs:
1. An analysis of future separations under the retirement programme will provide one source of definite and reliable information.
2. Early retirements, disability or otherwise, can frequently be determined in advance with reasonable accuracy. These can be reflected in the forecast.
3. An analysis of past experience will provide a basis for projecting future loss through other types of separations such as resignations, involuntary quits, dismissals, etc.

To summarise:

1. Determine the number of replacements;
2. Adjust figure up and down in light of —
   (a) Expansion or contraction requirements;
   (b) Growing or declining requirements for certain types of executives;
   (c) Any long-term trends which should be reflected.

Project executive requirements sufficiently ahead to allow the necessary time to get ready to meet them. In actual practice this may mean anywhere from two to five or more years, depending on the nature of the requirements.

The Use of Forecast and Inventory Information

Forecast and inventory information is one of top management's most useful human resources management tools. It is especially useful in such fundamental areas as:

(a) Planning and making personnel moves — promotion, transfers, demotions, lay-offs etc.

(b) Determining recruitment needs.

(c) Determining training and development needs.

(d) Insuring management the services of the best qualified executives and potential executives, available.

(e) Insuring consideration to all qualified candidates on an equitable basis.

(f) Planning changes in organisational structure.

Besides these obvious applications and uses, there are other very substantial benefits to be derived from its development and use. For example, it will stimulate more effective personnel communications. It will serve to get attention focused in the right direction, by getting executives thinking in terms of performance, abilities, capacities, potential etc. It will cause executives up and down the line to get better acquainted with their immediate subordinates and other employees. These benefits should not only make for a more constructive approach to dealing with the problems directly involved in meeting future executive requirements, but they should also have definite carry over value in dealing with executive resources, problems in general.

(c) Executive Resources Individual Development Plan (ERIDP)

The next basic phase in executive resource planning is to get down to the specifics from general executive resource planning to individual career development plan, which would be essential for effective E.D. effort. Determine career paths or development plans for every individual executive, because an individual executive when he joins a company expects a certain career within the company and it follows that the company should develop a career plan for the next immediate period of a year or two, then extend it to long-term of 4 or 5 or even 10 years as some organisations do. ERIDP is designed to provide a record of current job assignments and performance, a projection of near and long-term potential and the developmental needs of the individual. It will be reviewed and revised periodically and shall be available for review by the management. The steps involved are suggested:

1. What is the current position, responsibilities, along with the month and year assigned to the current position?
2. What is overall current performance appraisal?
3. What is his promotability? Be specific. List positions to which you feel the individual is promotable either now or within two-three years.
4. What is his possible ultimate potential?
5. Why do you say so and on what basis?
6. What are his development needs?
7. What is your development plan?
8. The ERIDP must be prepared and reviewed by the principle line and staff executive and dated.

(d) Management Succession Systems (MSS)

MSS is next important phase in the executive resource planning relevant and significant in the EDS. MSS should be worked out in the case of every executive position on an executive resource replacement table or a Management Succession Chart.

1. Determine the current executive position and incumbent.
2. Determine the age and date of appointment on the current appointment.
3. Establish the date due for replacement.
4. Determine the next appointment to which the incumbent could be promoted (unless he is retiring or quitting the company).
5. Is the incumbent ready for promotion? If no, what further training or development or experience is required?
6. Identify the possible successors or replacements? Immediate and long-term.
7. Determine the successor's or replacement's current position responsibilities and capacities.
8. Determine what further training or development or education or experience is required to fit successor for promotion.
9. Determine the date when the successor would be ready for promotion or succession and match this date with the date due for replacement of the incumbent.

We shall now proceed to a discussion on scientific selection and how to go about placing the right man on the right job.

REFERENCES

1. See Daniel J. Bell, *Structural Changes in American Society: A Preview of the Next 30 Years,* Commission on the Year 2000 of the American Academy of Arts and Sciences.
2. See M.N. Rudrabasavaraj, "Managerial Obsolescence," paper presented at the 23rd All-India Conference of NILM, 1973.

❑❑❑

CHAPTER 6

Scientific Selection: Placing the Right Man on the Right Job

With this chapter, we commence a study of the operative functions of human resources management, which are procuring, developing, maintaining and utilising labour, supervisory and managerial force and this chapter is devoted to a discussion of procurement, using the principle of scientific selection procedure.[1] In the subsequent chapters the other operative functions are discussed.

SCIENTIFIC SELECTION

The promotion of productive efficiency through an effective utilisation of men and machines is one of the primary objectives of personnel administration and the attainment of this objective largely is contingent upon the function of finding and placing the right man on the right job at the right time in the right place. This poses problems even in the industrially advanced countries of the West, where the employment opportunities in industry and business are vast and this is more so in a country like ours where too many people are chasing too few jobs. In a lighter vein, a wage observed that proper placement is an exception and misplacement is common in our country. In order to avoid the pitfalls of wrong selection and placement, it is necessary to adopt the principle of scientific selection procedure. The use of science and systematic procedures in selection is essential if we want to find the right man for the right job. A wrong man on a wrong job will mar the development and progress of the organisation, even as the right man on the right job will contribute to organisational growth. The function of scientific selection is one of the most important functions of personnel administration and this encompasses the following sub-functions:

1. Determining the nature of the job to be filled.
2. Determining the nature of the personnel required.
3. Determining the nature and sources of recruitment.
4. Selection process:
   (a) Preliminary interview;
   (b) Application forms;

(c) Reference letter;
(d) Group discussion;
(e) Interviews;
(f) Handling an Interview;
(g) Tests;
(h) Physical examination;
(i) Selection and placement;
(j) Induction;
(k) Follow-up.

Policy Framework

Before an examination of the scientific selection procedure, it must be made clear that the personnel administrator must operate within the framework of employment or selection policies. It may be a company's policy to hire only South Indians or North Indians or the close relatives of the employees. Many a company may have a policy of promotion from within and recruitment from within and the objective of this policy is to promote good morale in the organisation. It may be a company policy to hire only high school graduates. Another company may have a policy of hiring only engineering graduates. And the list may be extended endlessly. But it maybe sufficient to emphasise that these employment or selection policies will guide the selection process and procedures, which must operate within the policy framework.

Central Employment Office

Another important factor is that all hiring activities may be conducted through a central employment office, a division of personnel administration, which can give the line and top management in a plant the required expertise in hiring. It can keep records and take follow-up measures and use various personnel tools in hiring. It can maintain an organisational balance through an analysis of manpower requirements of the various departments. It can establish a skills inventory along with personnel inventory and plan and forecast manpower requirements. Promotional possibilities and transfer lines may be suggested. Unnecessary waste of other executives' time may be eradicated if all employment enquiries and applications are directed to be routed to the central employment office.

Where a company has branches all over the country and the plants are geographically dispersed it would be good to decentralise hiring procedure and give complete autonomy to plant employment offices to hire. But at the company headquarters may be located the central personnel administration, which would advise the plant's personnel divisions and provide research and other allied services to them.

The Responsibilities of Employment Office

The main responsibilities of the employment offices and selection are enumerated by Northcutt:[2]

1. To consider the form and content of the employment policy of the company and advise how best the employees needed maybe obtained; to keep in touch with information concerning the general factors affecting the supply and any new trends therein.

2. To this end, to maintain liaison with the Ministry of Labour and with sources of supply, including those other than local.
3. To become conversant with statutory and collectively agreed terms and conditions of employment affecting the company, advise on any that are a functional responsibility and ensure that all are observed.
4. To engage new workers in accordance with a defined functional responsibility which may mean, for example, that the final word in selection may rest with a foreman in the case of a skilled man or formally with the appropriate line executive in every case.
5. In all such instances, to engage new workers, and introduce them into the company's service, assist in placing them where required to the advantage of both the worker and the company, and follow up their progress to ensure that they are becoming both efficient and happy in their work.
6. To transfer workers to meet varying needs of different sections of the establishment or assist in a more satisfactory placement of individuals, carrying out, in particular, the company's policy of promotion.
7. To receive notice from persons who wish to leave and to give notice to such as must be dismissed from the company's service or are no longer necessary to its labour requirements.
8. To interview all employees who leave either voluntarily or on due notice and, in particular, those who leave on pension; in addition, to take necessary action on the death of a worker.
9. To keep records and statistics required (1) by statute and regulation; (2) for the due fulfilment of personnel activities and responsibilities; (3) for adequate knowledge of each person, including any grading or rating system.
10. In the light of this knowledge, to carry out a company policy of appointments and promotions.
11. To answer inquiries from official sources and from fellow executives, in so doing observing the privacy of records.
12. To afford the fullest opportunities for employees to express their grievances or difficulties.
13. To represent the company on any Governmental or industrial committee concerned with this function.

Having considered the employment or selection policies and responsibilities, as well as the advantages of centralised hiring, let us now turn to the specific methodology and detailed activities of the already mentioned various sub-functions of the important operative function of personnel procurement. It is appropriate to sound some warning notes here. There are two employment extremes. One is where the recruitment and selection procedures are initiated after the notification of an existing vacancy. It is necessary to anticipate and forecast the actual and potential personnel requirements and to initiate procedures to procure personnel in time. The second extreme is where, as is happening in some industries, enormous number of people are hired now a year or two ahead of time, when the employees will be utilised. For a year or two the employee waits around doing practically nothing, when the plant is erected and the machinery installed. These two extremes ought to be eliminated.

1. DETERMINING THE NATURE OF THE JOB TO BE FILLED

This is the first stage in the process of placing the right man on the right job at the right time in the right place, through the adoption of a scientific selection procedure. It is essential for the personnel executive to find out the specific nature of the job to be filled before initiating the process of selection.

The personnel administrator has various tools with which it is possible for him to understand the nature of the job for which the process of procurement is to be initiated. To fill a job effectively, it is necessary to select a candidate, whose actual and potential qualifications match the present and future requirements of the job. So, the first stage of procurement deals with the description of the job to be filled and many problems are created when this aspect is taken for granted or completely ignored.

Job Terms Defined

A 'job' is defined as an assignment of work calling for a set of duties, and conditions that are different from those of other work assignments. A job may include many positions, but a 'position' is a task performance by and related to a particular employee. Whereas the job is impersonal, the position is personal. The term 'station' is somewhat similar to 'position', but there are more positions or stations than jobs in a company. The term 'occupation' refers to a group of jobs with common or related characteristics and another term, "job family" is used to indicate the same notion of grouping of similar jobs. Within a job, two or more 'grades' may be identified, where the work assignments may be graded according to skill, difficulty or quality of workmanship. Among clerks, there may be Grade I Clerk, Grade II Clerk, Grade III Clerk, and Grade IV Clerk with varying skills and carrying varying compensation arrangements.

Job Analysis: The personnel tool with which the duties, responsibilities, operations, conditions and organisational aspects of a particular job are studied, specified and clearly enumerated is job analysis. Job analysis is a procedure by which the facts with respect to each job are systematically discovered and noted. From such analyses, general statements are obtained known as 'job description.' A job description describes the work performed, the duties and responsibilities involved, the skill or training required, conditions under which the job is done, relationships with other jobs and personal requirements of the job. Fig. 6.1 serves as an example for job description.

The 'job specification', a product of job analysis and a reined form of job description, may contain the duties of the job and the type of employee required, in terms of skill, education, experience, special aptitudes etc. The 'job classification' refers to a system of relating jobs with similar or family characteristics into a logical order of groupings. The 'job evaluation' refers to the process whereby the relative values of employees on particular jobs are measured. Job evaluation will be discussed in a later chapter.

Job analysis, also known as job study, is often considered basic in the management of people, because the results of job analysis are so widely used and so distinctly important. This provides complete job information which is useful in the following areas of personnel administration:

JOB DESCRIPTION

(i) Identification Data

Job Title:	Code Number:
Alternate Title:	Department:
Date of Analysis:	Division:

(ii) Job Summary

Under the direct supervision of the General Office Manager, performs such secretarial and clerical duties as typing, takes dictation, interviews, handles confidential data, handles mail, answers telephone and performs other similar and related duties while relieving the General Office Manager.

(iii) Work Performed (job content)

Routine or Daily Duties:

1. Performs general office work in relieving company officers of minor executive and clerical duties (3 hrs.)
2. Takes dictation, transcribes from notes and uses Ediphone (1 hr.)
3. Interviews persons seeking General Office Manager, determines importance of their calls, makes decisions on those warranting time of the General Office Manager (1 hr.)
4. Makes appointments and reminds General Office Manager of them and of other meetings (1½ hr.)
5. Types routine correspondence on own initiative; prepares confidential correspondence as directed (1 hr.)
6. Answers telephone as relief for Telephone Operator.
7. Sorts and distributes personal mail in the general office.

Periodic Duties:

1. Reminds General Office Manager of weekly staff meetings, organisational reports, records and statistics that are prepared on a scheduled basis.
2. Accompanies General Office Manager to weekly staff meetings, takes and transcribes notes for his files.

Occasional Duties:

1. Files confidential materials.
2. Performs other similar and related duties as may be prescribed by the General Office Manager.

(iv) Minimum Job Requirements (job specifications)

Education:	Sex:	Age:

Experience:

Abilities:

Responsibilities:

Knowledge:

Job Analyst E.G.W.

Fig. 6.1

Source: Edgar G. Williams, "Planning for Job Evaluation," *Business Information Bulletin No.19,* Indiana University Bureau of Business Research, February, 1954, p. 10.

1. Recruitment, selection and placement.
2. Transfers, promotions and demotions.
3. Training and development programmes.
4. Wage and salary administrations.

5. Settlement of grievances.
6. Work measurement and method study.
7. Improvement of working conditions.
8. Setting production standards.
9. Increasing productivity.
10. Organisational planning.

Through the job analysis we would like to know what a worker is doing and expected to do on a particular job; how the job is performed; skills required to do the job; the organisational relationships of the job. In short job analysis provides the following relevant information:

1. Job titles, including alternate or trade nicknames.
2. Number of employees on the job and their organisational relationships.
3. Names of immediate supervisors.
4. Materials, tools and equipment used or worked with.
5. Work or instructions received from and to whom delivered.
6. Salary or wage levels.
7. Hours and conditions of work.
8. Complete list of duties — daily, weekly, monthly, seasonal or casual — and time spent on each.
9. Educational requirements.
10. Experience requirements.
11. Skills, aptitudes and faculties required.
12. Promotional and transfer routes from and to the job.
13. Other information, comments and observations.

Responsibility for Job Analysis

The responsibility for sponsoring a job analysis programme lies with the top management, who usually authorise the personnel division to execute the programme. The personnel division can train some of its staff to conduct job analysis or they can hire a job analyst from outside to do the job for the division. Very often, particularly in India, the usefulness of a job analysis programme is not realised by the top management and it falls upon the shoulders of personnel people to 'sell' this programme and its utility value.

In some good companies with good personnel divisions, there may be a small team of specialists headed by a job analyst, who organises, directs, co-ordinates and controls the work of the specialist team. The job analyst may hire specialists or train personnel to become specialists. They may be given proper training in their work about the company organisation structure, policies and programmes and to get along with line executives, without whose co-operation job analysis becomes very difficult. Where there are trade unions, their co-operation should be sought and they must be consulted and educated as to the purpose and uses of job analysis programme.

Methodology of Job Analysis

Job information is obtained through three sources: (1) employees on the jobs; (2) supervisors; and (3) managers. Generally, the methods of obtaining information and necessary facts with regard to the job are: (1) Questionnaires; (2) Personal interviews; and (3) Observation.

1. Questionnaire Method is one of the common methods, where a job questionnaire is submitted to each employee and an illustration of a job questionnaire is given in Fig. 6.2. The job analysts can help the employees in filling the questionnaire and the completed questionnaire may be submitted to the immediate supervisors for their comments and get complete information regarding jobs under their supervision. Questionnaire method is less time consuming and easy. Supervisors and foremen may be given special training and asked to analyse jobs under their supervision.

JOB QUESTIONNAIRE

Title of Position ....

Department .... Section ....

Division .... Date ....

Please read all of the questions before making any entries; then answer each one as briefly as possible, consistent with complete information. Return this description within one week to the Job Analyst, Personnel Department.

Description of Duties

1. What is the general purpose of your work?
2. What duties do you personally perform in the usual course of work? (Tell from where you receive your work, what you do with it and where you send it. In answering this question discuss your daily routine.)
3. What duties do you perform only at stated periods, such as weekly, monthly etc.?
4. What occasional duties do you perform at irregular intervals?
5. How many employees do you supervise? (List job names and number of people in each job.)
6. To whom are you directly responsible?
7. What, if any, instructions do you receive as to how the work is to be done and from whom are they received?

Performance of Duties

A. Mental Requirements

8. What is the lowest grade of grammar school, high school, or college education that should be required of a person starting in position?
9. If any special courses are needed in order to perform your duties satisfactorily, name them.

B. Skill

10. What past experience is necessary for a new employee to have in order to learn to perform the duties of your position? Name the kind of experience, where and how it could be obtained and the time required to secure it.
11. Having the above education and experience, what would a new employee have yet to learn and how long would it take the employee to obtain sufficient practice in doing the new work to reach the point at which he would be barely satisfactory?
12. In what lower positions could an employee receive training for your position?
13. For what higher positions in the company does your present work train you?

14. What, in your opinion, is the most difficult part of your work and why is it difficult?

C. Physical Effort

15. Roughly, what proportions of your time are spent in: Standing ...%, Sitting ...%, Moving about ...%, other ...%?
16. What machines or other equipment do you personally operate; regularly or only occasionally?
17. Roughly, what proportion of your time is spent in operating each machine you use? State also what degree of speed is required on each machine.
18. What, if any, are the physical requirements for the proper performance of your duties? (strength, height, dexterity etc.)
19. Please list any other requirements not covered above and any personal qualifications and characteristics which you believe a candidate for your position should have.

Responsibility

20. What is your responsibility for money, securities, or other valuables?
21. What is the nature and extent of your responsibility for the employees under your supervision?
22. Give the nature and extent of any responsibility you may have other than for men and money.
23. What personal dealings with customers do you have in performing the duties of your position? State the nature of your business with the customers.
24. Roughly, what proportion of your time is spent in dealing with customers?

Working Conditions

25. What are your usual working hours?
26. What are the disagreeable features of your work?

Use this space and additional sheets of paper, if necessary, for any special features of your work not covered above, and for answers to questions for which more space is needed.

Your name ....

Years in this position ....

Fig. 6.2

Source: Dale Yoder, Personnel Management and Industrial Relations, pp. 284-285.

2. Personal Interviews: The job analyst can obtain information through personal interviews with the employees. Although this is more time consuming, the interview may bring out all the relevant information. A trained job analyst knows what to ask and how to get the relevant information. He will interview not only the employees but also the supervisors and managers connected with the jobs under analysis.

3. Observation: The questionnaire and interview methods may be supplemented with independent observation. By observing the worker at work over a period of time a job analyst can accurately analyse the job and its various components.

A job analyst is careful in using these methods and he is also familiar with analyses of similar jobs. He carefully should avoid describing the employee and his traits and personality and stick to only information concerning the job. The jobs on the surface may appear similar but he should note the distinguishing feature of a job or aim to discover the crucial task in a job. Now all the relevant information concerning a job is ready.

Written Job Description

After a thorough job study, tentative job descriptions should be written, which may be submitted to various interested supervisors and executives for review, change and final approval. Then, acceptable job descriptions are written out in simple and clear language, avoiding semantics, confusion, ambiguity in sentences. Overestimation or underestimation of job requirements must be avoided. A 'catchall' clause must be used where management will reserve the right to add or delete certain aspects in a job. The job analysis procedures look complicated, but it is a very useful personnel tool in determining the nature of the job to be filled. Now that completes the first stage of personnel procurement, i.e., understanding the nature of the job to be filled; let us now turn to the second stage.

2. NATURE OF THE PERSONNEL REQUIRED

After the nature of the job is determined, the characteristics of the manpower required to full the job assume prominence and also the number of employees that must be procured.

Man Specifications

The personal characteristics or 'man' specifications have to be determined and they encompass the following:

(a) Physical Specifications: Various types and degrees of physical faculties are required for different jobs. For some jobs, such as assembling a TV set, accurate and good vision is required. For a typing job, good finger dexterity and memory are required. For boosting jobs, one has to be strong, thickset and heavy. To be a cop (policeman) in New York City, you have to be over 6 feet in height and around 165 pounds in weight. So the necessary physical abilities and skills necessary to do the job must be specified. Under physical specifications the following may be mentioned: height, weight, physical abilities like walking, vision, pulling, pushing, finger dexterity, hand steadiness, stamina etc.

(b) Mental Specifications: Here the mental processes required to do the job to be filled are specified. This has reference to the following: intelligence, memory, judgement, ability to plan, ability to estimate, to read, to write, to think and concentrate, scientific faculties, arithmetical abilities etc. Particular types and degree of mental requirements for different jobs may also be specified.

(c) Emotional and Social Specifications: There is a growing awareness on the part of the employers that emotional and social characteristics are important although specifying these requirements is not easy. Recent research emphasises the impact of a man's ability to get along with people, his relations with the group etc. With the help of research and psychologists, sociologists, and psychoanalysts, some emotional and social specifications are listed. Some of them are: ability to remain calm, social adaptability, personal hygiene, dress, poise, features etc.

(d) Behavioural Specifications: This is specified in higher levels of management. Certain management personnel are expected to behave in a certain way. These are not formally listed out, nevertheless these play an important role in selection. The corporate image requires the executive to conduct himself in society in a certain fashion.

The status of the individual and prestige of the company help direct the behaviour of executives. With the determination of man specifications and the estimation of manpower requirements, the second stage is completed. Now I proceed to the third stage.

3. THE NATURE AND SOURCE OF RECRUITMENT

After obtaining information regarding job requirements and manpower requirements and before instituting the selection procedures, it will be necessary to find out the nature of recruitment. The nature of recruitment is dependent upon the nature and stage of economic sophistication of the industrial society. In industrially advanced countries like America, the channels of recruitment tend to be formalised and institutionalised, e.g., Union, Private Employment Agencies, Public Employment Agencies etc. But in less advanced countries like our own, there is a tendency to be less formal and non-institutional in character, e.g., friends, relatives etc. In America, studies have indicated definite recruiting patterns that vary with the size of the firm, the type of workers being sought, and with the structure of industry. In India also, despite the lack of research studies, one may identify certain definite recruiting trends. Certain industries look for certain types of workers coming from a particular background and from certain regional areas.

It is also recognised that there is a direct correlation between recruiting practices and changing conditions of labour market. According to Professor F.J. Malm, the firm's reactions in its adjustment of recruiting methods of changing labour conditions are influenced by two factors:

1. Firm's Position in the Labour Market: The firm's own size, location and reputation will tend to have a persistent effect on its ability to attract labour. Hindustan Lever, TISCO, TELCO, DCM, Union Carbide, Lakshmi Mills attract an abundant supply of labour, whereas others may not find much response even when they are looking for manpower.

2. The Degree of Tightness of the Labour Market: This is part of the environment within which every firm operates, but its actual effect on any given firm will depend in part on the factors mentioned under: (a) when the market is most 'loose' or when labour supply is abundant, there may be a surplus of applicants at the employer's door; (b) when the market is most 'tight' or when labour supply is scarce, the employer is likely to resort much more extensively to formal or institutional channels of recruitment and also to imaginative or even unorthodox methods. In West Germany the shortage of labour has forced many an employer to offer various incentives to attract labourers from neighbouring Italy. One company gives a motor cycle to the Italian employee free, so that he may come into Germany to work in the plant in the morning and go home to Italy after work.

In U.S.A. the shortage of manpower is critical in many areas and *Time Magazine* reports some unorthodox recruitment procedures:[3] "On posters plastered all over the Lockheed Missiles and Space Co. grounds in Sunnyvale, California, an Indian sends up smoke signals above the caption: 'Spread the Word'; the word is that Lockheed has an immediate need of 2000 workers. Douglas Aircraft Co. has been hiring engineers with a $ 100,000 savings plan that is above and beyond normal retirement benefits.

In Cincinnati, General Electric is offering present workers bonuses of upto $ 200 for every new employee they successfully recruit. Monsanto has started running help wanted advertisements on TV in Dayton. Ford's Lincoln-Mercury assembly plant in St. Louis is using spot radio commercials, has set up portable employment offices at several shopping centres. According to San Francisco's Ampex, the necessity of looking farther a field for technicians has increased its recruitment costs from $ 3000 to nearly $ 5000 a man.... Detroit automakers have imported unemployed mountaineers from Appalachia to sweep floors at $ 3 an hour.... Inland Steel has 600 openings for unskilled workers, has had to hire 150 college students just to fill vacancies in its week-end cleaning gangs."

In India, the abundance of human resources poses peculiar problems when we are going through a socio-economic revolution by subjecting recruiting process to informal modes.

The IIPM observes:[4] "The most striking feature in the Indian labour market is the apparent abundance of labour. Yet, despite tremendous unemployment, the right type of labour is not too easy to find. Since new workers are still mainly drawn from the rural population, they take time to adjust themselves to the new life. Sometimes they cannot adjust themselves to the new life and eventually they return to their native villages. Others may return for long spells and some wish to return at least once a year to their homes. Labour turnover and absenteeism therefore constitute a continuing problem in industry. This underlines the need for properly planned recruitment policy in order to minimise the disruption of work by constantly changing personnel. Illiteracy among the working population also raises problems in recruitment and selection."

The Sources of Recruitment

The sources of manpower supply are many and varied and the company must know what and where these are in order to fill their personnel needs. Some organisations have established recruitment policies. It may be a company's policy to hire only the relatives of the employees and one Indian textile mill has a hierarchy of preferences. First they prefer wives or husbands, then sons or daughters, then cousins and then other close relatives. This mill has a hierarchy of intimating its employees of the vacancy or potential vacancy and of inviting employees to recommend a person, who must be his relative. For this purpose the firm uses an Employee Recommendation Form. Many companies have a policy of hiring only friends and relatives. In one U.S. pharmaceutical firm, summer jobs are available only to the children of the employees and if there are not enough children, only then other students are offered job opportunities. These recruitment policies guide the procedure of hiring and where to look for to fill the vacancies.

There are a variety of sources of recruitment for manual, clerical, sales, professional, technical, and managerial personnel and in U.S.A. the following sources of recruitment are widely used:

1. Direct Hiring: This has reference to those who come to the door of the company looking for employment. This is a very common source of recruitment. Those firms, which have a good reputation regarding wages, working conditions, and other facilities, attract a good number of people, from whom the company may think of selecting some men.

2. *Friends and Relatives:* As already pointed out, friends and relatives of employees are another good source of supply and some companies prefer to utilise this source extensively. Often the employee may tell his friend or relative that his company is hiring people and so the word spread. This is also a popularly used source of recruitment and this is sort of a recommended labour. Some companies encourage and invite employees to recommend their friends or relatives and the companies feel that this promotes employee loyalty. The employees feel happy at the opportunity of having had a hand in the employment aspect of the company and they are also careful in recommending somebody to the company. There is some sort of preselection available to the company. Companies dependent on this source declare that there is a high degree of morale and loyalty and good group relationships and friendliness among the employees. The work atmosphere appears congenial and even enjoyable.

3. *Advertisements in Newspapers:* This is one of most commonly employed source. The corporation needing manpower to fill certain job, advertises the available job, likely pay, duties and responsibilities of the job — job specification — and also man specifications in a newspaper, magazine or journal and invites applications. But advertisements must be carefully written giving all relevant data, and they must attract only the right type of people with right qualifications. If the advertisement is vague and general, it may attract hundreds or even thousands of applications, rendering the process of screening time-consuming and costly. The advertisement must clearly state the educational qualifications, experience, and skills necessary to do the job to be filled, with a view to discouraging the unsuitable candidates from applying.

4. *Unions:* This is another source of recruitment and in some industries such as the building trades, unions have provided the employer the necessary number of workers. In some industries in U.S.A. the unions have completely taken over the function of hiring semi-skilled and unskilled labour force. There are "hiring halls" of the unions. The union may also advise a worker where he can find a job. If its member losses his job in one company for some reason, the union may find him a job in another company.

5. *Public Employment Agencies:* The United States Employment Services or 'USES' as it is popularly known, started in 1918, has a network of several state employment services, which act as public employment agencies. In the early years they were not found very useful, but they were, after the passage of the Social Security Act, which provided unemployment compensation to the unemployed for a short time till they found another job. In order to obtain this compensation, the unemployed has to register with USES, providing a roster of all who were unemployed and desired to work. The Second World War gave a strong stimulus to USES, when there was a great demand for all types of manpower.

USES with 1800 offices located all over U.S.A. serves both the worker and employer by acting as a clearing house for jobs and job information. Counselling, testing, labour market surveys etc., are some of the services provided by USES. The unemployed register themselves with employment services and USES helps them find jobs with some companies.

6. *Private Employment Agencies* are another important source, which many companies cultivate for hiring purposes. The firms can find suitable men through these private employment agencies. In New York city alone there may be hundreds of such agencies. Usually they specialise in supplying certain types of personnel and some specialise in clerical and secretarial personnel and others in executives, accountants, engineers, economists, salesmen, dieticians, beauticians, top executives etc. They usually charge a fee for their services and they may collect the fee either from the applicant or the employer or from both. They also provide employment counselling and guidance service, resume service and other services to the people seeking employment.

7. Employers' or Trade Associations: Meetings, conferences, seminars, and other social functions organised by these associations are another source through which the firms try to recruit the needed people. A few come to these conferences looking for a change in positions and some others attend to recruit the right man.

8. Professional Associations and Journals are yet another source for finding some professional and technical people. Advertising in the professional journals will bring in good response. Again the seminars, symposia, meetings, conferences, and other functions sponsored by the professional associations provide opportunities to recruit professional personnel. Through the journals, the employers can identify some, who contribute articles and papers and who may be tapped.

9. Schools and Colleges: Recruitment from educational institutions is a popular practice of thousands of firms in U.S.A. For clerical, labour and apprentice help, high schools are extensively used. Many colleges have their own placement offices, through which students find their jobs. The placement office is in touch with various firms and displays employment opportunities on its bulletin board for the benefit of students who may apply for some jobs. Their applications are processed and sent to the companies by the placement office. The companies usually send their recruiters to college or university campus to interview candidates and those who are successful, are invited to the company for further interviews. Schools and colleges are a very widely used recruitment source of the companies. Even in India, many of the leading universities and institutes of management & technology provide a variety of placement services to both to their own students and industries.

10. From other Firms: Recruiting personnel from other firms is a popular practice. There are corporations which have made a name for themselves in training and developing people, particularly executives. In the auto industry, they would like to recruit an executive from General Motors. Similarly Dupont, General Electric, Standard Oil, N.J. have an established reputation for good executives and other firms would like to recruit from these corporations.

11. Management Consultants: Specialised executive selection services are offered to the companies by many consultants. Executive search is really big and fascinating business in U.S.A. Many firms rely on consultants for executive recruitment. In our country there are many consultancy firms which offer their services to the companies.

12. Radio and Television: Through radio and TV many companies recruit their employees and particularly when the labour market is very tight, these sources of recruitment are used much.

13. Internal Resources: So far we discussed external sources of recruitment. But to many organisations, internal source is the main source of recruitment. Through transfer, promotions and demotions the firms try to fill their personnel needs. Recruitment from within policy is a common policy with many organisations. This policy has many merits. Firstly, it improves the morale of the men. Secondly, it promotes loyalty among men to the organisation. Thirdly, the employer has tried and familiar employees to evaluate.

But the problem with this policy is that it leads to the danger of "inbreeding." People, when they work for an organisation, develop attitudes and notions that are moulded by the organisation and the danger here is the lack of new initiative, ideas and views. Growth and development of any organisation needs certain amount of exposure to the new ideas and initiative that may come from people who come from outside the organisation. They view the company methods and practices from a new perspective and may contribute views that help in the progress of the firm.

Another danger is that internal source may dry up. It may not be possible to find a certain type of skilled labour within the organisation. Another problem is that promotion based on seniority principle is inherent in this policy of recruitment from within. Seniority alone should not be the criterion for promotions. This aspect, we shall discuss in a later chapter.

14. Other Sources: In some areas, churches, fraternal organisations and lodges serve as effective employment agencies. There are some institutions, where deaf, dumb and blind workers are available for employment if you need them.

In India, the popular sources of recruitment are listed by IIPM:

1. Within the organisation.
2. Budli or temporary workers.
3. Employment Agencies.
4. Casual callers.
5. Friends and relatives.
6. Advertisements.
7. Labour Contractors.

To this list may be added radio, management consultants, schools and colleges and other firms.

Many Indian firms, particularly textile mills, employ budli or temporary workers and whenever they need permanent help they turn to these budli employees and make them permanent. There is an advantage here, because the employer knows the worker and his efficiency at work.

Just like USES, we in India have National Employment Service, which has employment exchanges all over the country. These employment exchange register the names of candidates, seeking employment and try to place them with some employers. In our country compulsory notification of all vacancies to the employment exchange is required by law. Our employment exchanges are not as high powered as those of the USES, but they serve some useful purpose as an employment agency. For professional and technical personnel the University Employment Bureaux or Placement Offices and the Council of Scientific and Industrial Research set up by Government may also be tapped.

The practice of recruiting through labour contractors, who may themselves be employees, is peculiar to our country. Although this breeds many malpractices as pointed out by even the Royal Commission on Labour and though the Industrial Courts frown upon them, it is still prevalent in some areas, but there is growing feeling that it needs to be abolished altogether.

In Japan many firms depend upon University professors, particularly Kayo University and University of Tokyo, to recruit professional, technical and managerial personnel.

Recruitment procedures may be improved, if the personnel executive carefully studies the correlation between sources of labour supply, methods of recruitment and subsequent job performance. The idea is to know from where and through what methods, good and efficient workers can be hired.

After the completion of these three stages — determining (1) the nature of the job to be filled, (2) the nature of personnel required and (3) the nature and sources of recruitment-selection procedures are set in motion to ensure proper selection and placement. Before initiating selection procedure, a hiring requisition is necessary.

Requisitioning Employees

In case of a vacancy or expected vacancy, the executive or supervisor or foreman in need of help should request the personnel department (or Employment Section) on a 'hiring requisition' form to help him hire the needed personnel. This requisition should give all necessary information about the job, the experience, qualities, skills, and qualifications to be looked for in the applicant. In short a job and man specification must be given. In requisitioning, the line executives must also take into consideration the time factor in recruitment and selection and request for help sufficiently ahead of time. Sufficient time period must be given to the personnel department to employ its scientific selection procedures with a view to hiring the proper personnel. Hasty selections may prove costly to the company in the long run.

It is the duty of the personnel department in its staff advisory capacity to meet the needs of line management by recruiting and screening. There should be close and effective co-operation and collaboration between executives and supervisors on the one hand and personnel division on the other. There is need for good team spirit and team work between line and staff personnel.

After the personnel division knows precisely what kind of man is needed for a particular type of job, it may start its scientific selection procedures.

4. SELECTION PROCESS

The selection procedures must take into consideration the public policy and operate within the framework of the provision of the State or Central statutory controls. Public policy may prohibit any kind of discrimination against any person on grounds such as colour, race, sex, creed, or caste. Public policy may prohibit employment of children or even women in certain industries or limit the hours when women may work in a plant. Former employees with good standing, who were laid off for some reasons, may be considered for employment and in some union-management contracts, management will be required to hire the former employees first and then consider others for employment. Often employers prefer employees who are known to them and who have a good service record to their credit.

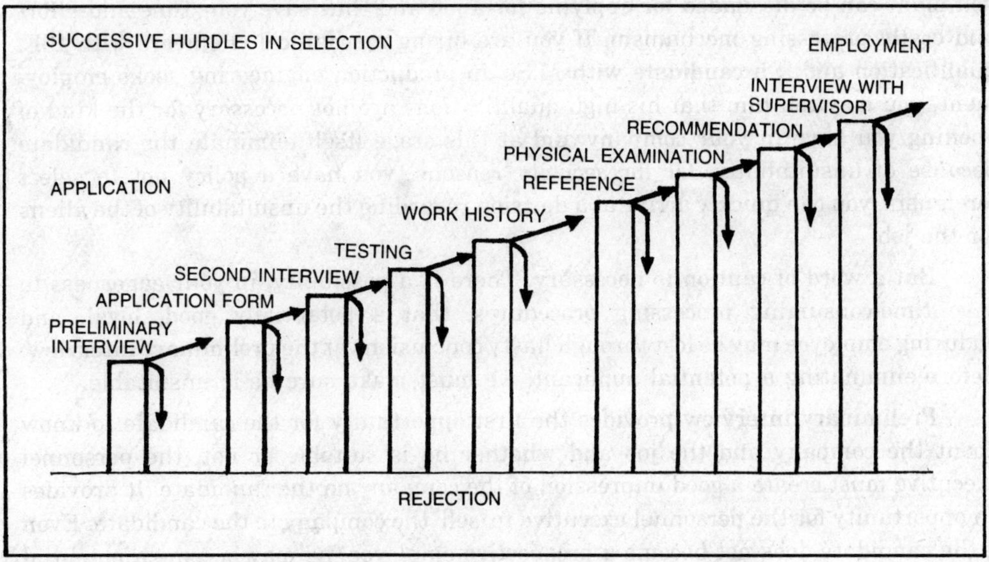

Fig. 6.3 Successive Hurdles in Selection Process

Source: Dale Yoder, *Personnel Management and Industrial Relations,* p. 324.

Within the framework of public policy and company policy, proper selection standards must be prescribed with a view to placing the right person on the right job. The selection process involves a series of obstacles which have to be overcome by the candidates and the winning candidate wins the job. The series of hurdles is well illustrated in the Figure 6.3.

Generally a good selection process will include the following steps, which act as a sequence of obstacles to be surmounted by the candidates seeking employment.

1. Preliminary interview;
2. Application forms;
3. Reference letters;
4. Group discussions;
5. Interviews;
6. Handling interview;
7. Tests;
8. Physical examination;
9. Selection and placement;
10. Induction;
11. Follow-up.

(a) Preliminary Interview

Preliminary interview, which maybe conducted by a junior executive in personnel department, is the first hurdle which a potential candidate has to overcome and it is possible to screen and eliminate unsuitable candidates. For example, if you have a policy of hiring only male employees, any female candidate looking for employment in you plant can be dissuaded for applying for a job and thus save your time and effort and costly processing mechanism. If you are hiring mechanical engineers with B.E. qualification and if a candidate with M.Sc. in production engineering seeks employment, you may tell him that his high qualifications are not necessary for the kind of opening you have in your company and at this stage itself eliminate the candidate because of unsuitability. Or for security reasons, you have a policy not to select foreigners, you can quickly arrive at a decision regarding the unsuitability of the aliens for the job.

But a word of caution is necessary. There is a possibility, in your eagerness to save time-consuming processing procedures, that a potentially good, loyal, and enduring employee may be lost through hasty conclusions at the preliminary interview. Before eliminating a potential applicant, we must make sure he is unsuitable.

Preliminary interview provides the first opportunity for the candidate to know about the company and the job and whether he is suitable or not, the personnel executive must create a good impression of the company on the candidate. It provides an opportunity for the personnel executive to 'sell' the company to the candidate. Even if the candidate does not become a prospective employee, he may become a potential consumer of your product. Besides it never hurts to build the corporate image and the opportunity should not be lightly passed up. Informality, courtesy, kindness, listening patiently and giving relevant information will impress the candidate very much. Rudeness and discourtesy will make you lose not only a potential employee, but a potential consumer also. If a candidate is found suitable, an application blank may be given to him to fill in and return.

(b) Application Forms

Application forms are widely used everywhere and constitute one of the fundamental media through which information is gathered about the applicant. Quite a few companies in India do not have any application blank, but will ask the applicant to apply on white paper giving details about age, marital status, educational qualifications, work experience, references. But most companies design different application forms for different types of employees — managers, supervisors, employees etc. and while some application forms are simple, general and easily answerable, some others may require elaborate, complex and detailed information from the applicant. Figure 6.4 serves as an illustration of a simple application blank and figure 6.5 will serve for a detailed one.

QUESTIONNAIRE TO BE COMPLETED BY APPLICANTS FOR EMPLOYMENT IN THE COMPANY

1. Name. 2. Father's Name

....

3. Age 4. Married/Single

....

5. Home Address & Nearest Police Station ....

....

....

6. Present Local Address ....

....

7. Educational Qualifications ....

....

8. Previous Experience:

Employed in	Capacity in which worked	Duration	Reason for leaving
(a)	....	....	....
(b)	....	....	....
(c)	....	....	....
(d)	....	....	....

9. Give names of 2 respectable persons for reference purposes:

1. .... 2. ....

10. Medical Officer's Remarks:

Place: ....

Date: ....

....

Signature of Applicant

P.S.: If you have any relative already working in this Company, please give his name, Tally No. and designation.

Introduced by:

....

Fig. 6.4 Simple Application Blank

APPLICATION FOR EMPLOYMENT

(This form is to be completed in the candidate's own handwriting)

photograph of the applicant

Personal data

Position desired ....

Name (in block letters, surname first) ....

Permanent address ....
street & number city

....
state telephone number

Present address ....
street & number city

....
state telephone number

Date of birth .... Place of birth ....

Are you a citizen of India? .... Male ☐ Female ☐ weight .... height ....

Community .... single/engaged/married/widowed/divorced/separated (cross whichever is not applicable)

Number of dependents ....children .... adults ....
ages

Father's name and occupation ....

Condition of health: excellent ☐ good ☐ fair ☐

Have you any physical disabilities? If so, of what nature? ....

....

Time lost due to illness during the past three years ....
days months

Explain causes: ....

....

Who referred you to KALPA?

....

Have you any relatives in KALPA?

....

Names of present employees you know in KALPA?

....

Have you ever been employed by KALPA? when?

....

Which division and department?

....

Have you been arrested for any offence?

....

If 'yes', what were the outcomes?

....

Education

Names of schools, colleges, and universities attended in chronological order	from	to	Examinations passed with subjects	Position attained in examination
....	....	....	....	....
....	....	....	....	....
....	....	....	....	....
....	....	....	....	....
....	....	....	....	....

Thesis or special studies Professor

....

Publications and patents

....

What languages can you speak fluently? 1. 2.

....

mother tongue

3. 4.

....

What languages can you write well? 1. 2.

....

3. 4.

....

Prizes, honours or awards

....

Extra-curricular activities:

School

....

College/University

....

Business and professional experience: List present or last employer first, then next previous in order

1. Company or equivalent Employment from to

....

Address

....

street and number city state

Type of business or equivalent

....

Name and title of Supervisor

....

Title and description of your work

....

Reason for leaving

....

Starting monthly salary .... Current or last monthly salary ....

basic allowances basic allowances

2. Company or equivalent Employment from to

....

Address

....

street and number city state

Type of business or equivalent

....

Name and title of Supervisor

....

Title and description of your work

....

Reason for leaving

....

Starting monthly salary .... Current or last monthly salary ....

basic allowances basic allowances

3. Company or equivalent Employment from to

....

Address

....

street & number city state

Type of business or equivalent

....

Name & title of Supervisor

....

Title and description of your work

....

Reason for leaving

....

Starting monthly salary .... Current or last monthly salary ....

basic allowances basic allowances

4. Company or equivalent Employment from to

....

Address

....

street and number city state

Type of business or equivalent

....

Name and title of Supervisor

....

Title and description of your work

....

Reason for leaving

....

Starting monthly salary — Current or last monthly salary

....

basic — allowances — basic — allowances

May we contact your present and/or previous employer as a reference?

....

....

References: School and personal (Not relatives or previous employers)

Name	Address	Business	Years known
1.			
2.			
3.			
4.			

Interests:

Hobbies	Sports	Civic, business and professional organisations	Offices held

General Information: Please discuss here any information not already covered that will help in giving us a comprehensive picture of yourself as a person and as a potential employee:

....

....

What Indian territories are you familiar with?

....

What type of commodities have you been selling and to what class of customers? Give as much data as possible:

....

....

Have you ever embarked upon an independent enterprise of a professional and/or commercial nature? If so, give details:

....

What are your outstanding qualities which will aid you in being successful?

....

In what areas do you think you may require development?

....

Outline briefly your career goals and objectives

....

What considerations led you to apply to us for a job?

....

....

What minimum consolidated monthly salary would you consider?

....

If offered a position, when can you start?

....

Do you or your family object to going to any part of the country?

....

Are you prepared to undergo training at our laboratory at a nominal remuneration for any length of time required?

....

Are you a member of a Provident Fund covered by the Employees' Provident Funds Act, 1952?

....

Note: Employment is subject to physical examination and investigation of data and references given on this form.

....

I understand that any false answers or statements made by me on this application will be sufficient grounds for immediate termination.

....

Date Signature

Please do not write below this line

Date employed Department Division

....

Additional or replacement Job level Starting salary Rs.

Requisition number Approved by

....

....

Remarks:

....

Interviewed by

....

....

Interviewer's comments

....

....

Fig. 6.5 Detailed Application Blank

Reference to nationality, race, caste, religion, and even place of birth has been regarded as evidence of discriminatory attitudes and the fair employment practice regulations have required the employers to delete any such references. In some instances, requiring photographs may be objectionable.

Generally the information sought to be gathered through the applications refers to the following:

1. Name of applicant, his address, telephone number.
2. Personal information such as sex, marital status, number of children, other dependents, if any, parent's names, and their occupation and birthplaces.
3. Education.
4. Physical characteristics, such as height, weight, health, vision, other defects.
5. Experience, usually with the past three or four employers.
6. Hobbies and interests.
7. Membership of Associations.
8. Financial status.
9. Statement of purpose.
10. References — personal and business.
11. Wages and salary required.
12. Comment and remarks.

The crucial factors, generally, are education, employment record, place of residence, sex, etc.

Weighted Application Forms: Application forms may be designed to serve as highly effective preliminary screening device. By careful study, such items as age, education, dependents, earnings, and years on previous jobs may be found to be closely correlated with success in the job for which the candidates are applying. On the basis of past experience, a scoring system may be provided for all such items and a cutting score may be established for the total. Such a weighted application form may quicken the process of recruitment and selections.[5]

Professor Yoder observes: "In a somewhat similar procedure, six biographical items have been identified as 'knock-out-factors' in a preliminary screening programme for salesmen. They include instability of residence, failure in business within two years, divorce or separation within two years, excessive personal indebtedness, too high a standard of living, and unexplained gaps in the employment record."[6]

Apart from providing information on the applicant, the application forms provide the starting off point for interviews, the basis for reference checking, and also testing. Seldom should applications be the sole criterion for selecting and seldom they are.

It is just one more hurdle. Often it is possible to screen quite a few candidates on the basis of applications. In a country like India, where too many persons are chasing too few jobs, many will respond to an advertisement, even when they know that they do not possess the qualifications needed to get the job. They hope against hope that the right candidates possessing the needed qualifications may not apply or may not be aware of the opening and in which case the employer may have to settle for candidates with lesser qualifications. Often this is true to experience requirement. Although it may be difficult to find a candidate with seven years' experience, the employer will go ahead and demand seven years' experience in the advertisement. Then when there is no applicant with seven years' experience he maybe forced to settle for a chap with four or five years' experience. The usual problem is that the emloyer may stipulate impossible requirements, particularly in India, where skilled, technical, professional and managerial personnel are in short supply. In the final analysis, he will settle for what is available. There is a need to be realistic in fixing qualification requirements.

It is common in our country to receive hundreds or even thousands of applications in response to an advertisement and many will be found unsuitable by a cursory glance at their applications. Those, who are found to be suitable, may be recruited and invited to face another hurdle — interviews. Before the interviews, the references given by the applicant may be checked in order to get some more information from the referees.

(c) Reference Letters

Generally the applicant will be asked to give two or three referees — preferably former employers, or professional acquaintances or friends or professors or famous persons, and the applicant will give the names of those who may speak well of him. It is possible to get impartial assessment or evaluation of the applicant from some of the referees. Some other referees, in order to avoid any unpleasantness will speak in generalities, which will be of no use to the employer in evaluating the applicant. Hence many companies do not place much reliance on the referees' letters. In fact Pigors and Myers maintain: "Letters of recommendation are not discussed here since they seem not to be a sound device for getting reliable information. The writers are sometimes more concerned with avoiding disagreeableness than in stating their considered opinion or describing their experience with the candidate."[7] I maintain that contacting the referees has some usefulness, although too much reliance may not be placed and there are some referees, who will give a dispassionate evaluation of the applicant's strengths and weaknesses, which will be useful to the personnel executive and the line executive.

Regarding contacting the previous employers, in some applications, the applicant will be asked whether it is all right to contact his former employers and if the applicant does not want this, his former employers may not be reached. There may be a need to investigate the employment history of the applicant and to check the veracity, accuracy and candour of the applicant.

(d) Group Discussions

Next in the sequence of obstacles for the applicant is the group discussion. The group discussion is a method where groups of the job applicants are brought around a conference table and they are given either a case study or a subject for discussion. Any subject, barring religious or political, but mostly topical or relevant subjects are given for group discussion. For instance, if we are hiring management trainees the subject may be the practices of management in Indian industry or the image of an Indian manager or management education in India. Suppose we are hiring a transportation manager the subject may be rural transportation and communication.

If we are hiring an economist the subject may be methods to contain inflation or the virtues of the balanced budget. The other variation is to give a short case study highlighting a problem.

It is for the group to analyse, discuss, find solutions and articulate their views, in a completely leaderless situation and they are being observed by a selection panel who judge the group discussion on the basis of such activities as:

1. Initiating the discussion
2. Explaining the problem
3. Providing information
4. Clarifying issues
5. Influencing others
6. Summarising
7. Speaking effectively
8. Mediating arguments among the participants

It gives the opportunity for the selection panel to observe and judge how well the participants can think, analyse problems, substantiate arguments, find solutions, cogently reason and take decisions. Another variation of this method is to ask the participants to rate the others in the group and interestingly it is found that the group will always rate quite objectively who are the No. 1, 2, 3, and nobody will over-rate himself. Still another variation of the method is to ask the participants in the group to write up the summary of the group discussion which gives an opportunity for the selection panel to observe writing abilities of the participants.

Next in the sequence of obstacles for the applicant is the interview.

(e) Interviews

Interviewing is the most universally used tool in any selection procedure and interviews are designed to serve in the important areas of employment, training, human relations, and labour relations. In many companies interview may be the only tool used. Interview maybe for a period of five minutes or for sixty minutes. Interviews may be informal and oral or they may be highly planned and carefully conducted.

Invitation for the Interview: When a company invites an applicant for an interview at the head office or the plant, some companies meet his travel expenses and some do not. Some meet the applicant's staying expenses also. Executives may be paid first class or air fare, whereas blue collar employees may be given second class far. According to the type and status, employee's expenses will be met. Then there are many companies that do not defray any expense incurred by the applicant appearing for the interview. Here the ability of the company to defray full or any part of the expenses of the applicant is crucial and its policy is important.

The letter inviting the application to appear for the interview must be sent at least three to four weeks ahead of the time of interview, so that the applicant may plan his trip. The interview letter must also state the place of interview and time of interview.

Place of Interview: The place of interview in the employment office must be neat, and good-looking and it must create a good impression on the applicants. Many companies provide a lounge for the applicants to sit and relax, while they wait for the interview. Magazines, newspapers and company materials like the house organs, employee handbooks, company reports etc. Maybe also displayed for the applicants to browse through. Some companies serve coffee or tea to the candidates.

Time of Interview: Generally all the candidates are asked to appear for the interview at the same time. For example, let us say a company invites 10 candidates for the interview and all of them are asked to report for the interview at 9 a.m. at the company office. Even if the interviewer or the interviewing committee or the selection board were to take 10 minutes for each candidate the last of the 10 candidates will have to wait for more than 90 minutes. If the interview takes longer time, the candidates will have to wait for a longer period.

Some companies meet this situation by staggering the interview time in such a way that no candidate will have to wait for more than five minutes. This will call for careful planning of interview time, but this will assist the candidates and also the interviewers.

Some Interview Rules: Interviews must be planned with care and the interviewers may observe some of the following rules:

1. Be courteous to the candidate and let him feel "at home."
2. Listen attentively and patiently.
3. Do not ask leading or tricky questions.
4. Never argue or interrupt or change the subject abruptly.
5. Ask questions in a simple language under stable to the applicant.
6. Be tactful in asking direct and personal questions.
7. Keep the candidate talking encourage him to talk.
8. Try to get the relevant information.
9. Respect the interests of the candidate.
10. Answer the candidate's questions.
11. Do not 'oversell' the job opportunities in the company.
12. Lead the interview to its conclusion.

Training for Interviewers: To observe all these rules, the interviewer must plan the interview and the questions he is going to ask, with particular care. Many companies train their interviewers in conducting interviews. The interviewers may be asked to beware of their first impressions, hasty inferences, bias, prejudice, likes and dislikes. Despite all the interview techniques, the personal observations and impressions of the interviewer are important in appraising the candidate and this element of subjectivity cannot be eliminated altogether. By pointing out the warning signals, this subjective element can be minimised.

The Bell Telephone Company at Philadelphia, U.S.A. trains its interviewers with ten lessons:[8]

1. Establish tentative job qualifications.
2. Review application for employment.
3. Preparation for conducting practice interviews.
4. Conducting practice interviews.
5. Recording the findings.
6. Interpretation of the findings.
7. Introduction of job specifications.
8. Evaluation of findings.
9. Closing the interview.
10. Practising the complete interview.

Some companies employ those trained in psychology and psychiatry in the personnel department to interview candidates. Others hire and train people to become expert interviewers.

Purpose of Interviews: The primary purpose of the interview is to complete and get the correct picture gained through application forms. It measures the ability of the candidate to speak and present his views, his sociability, poise, appearance, that almost undefinable personality, etc. Through the company policies, programmes and opportunities may be given to the candidate.

There may be just one main interview. In the case of supervisory or managerial personnel more than one interview may be conducted. Interviews are the most widely used personnel tools to selection and some companies may have no other hurdles than this and on the basis of the interview, a candidate may be selected or rejected.

Types of Interviews: There are various types of interviews employed by the companies. In India most of the interviews may be oral and informal. Then there are some whose interviews are well-planned and well-conducted. The following are the different types of interviews and they are briefly discussed:

1. Informal interview.
2. Formal interview.
3. Planned interview.
4. Patterned interview.
5. Non-directive interview.
6. Depth interview.
7. Stress interview.
8. Group interview.
9. Panel interview.

1. Informal Interview: An informal interview is an oral interview and may take place anywhere. This type of interview is perhaps followed very widely in India. The employer or the manager or the personnel man may ask a few almost inconsequential questions like name, place of birth, names of relatives etc., either in their respective offices or anywhere outside the plant or company. It is not planned and nobody prepares for it. This interview is used widely when the labour market is tight and when you need workers very badly. In India, a friend or a relative of the employer or manager may take a candidate to the house of the employer or manager, where this type of interview may be conducted. In some instances, the candidate may not open his mouth at all, for his friend or relative may be doing the talking with the employer. The employer or the manager may hire the candidate. This happens not only in our country, but, perhaps, in other countries also.

2. Formal Interview: Formal interviews may be held in the employment office by the employment officer in a more formal atmosphere, with the help of well-structured questions. The time and place of the interview will be stipulated by the employment office. The formal interview will attempt to elicit the relevant information from the candidate and the interviewer may have a prepared list of questions that he is proposing to ask the candidate.

3. Planned Interview: It is a formal interview, which is carefully planned. Here the interviewer may have a plan of action worked out in his own mind and he knows how much time he is going to devote to each candidate, what type of information he is seeking and what he proposes to give, how to open the interview and how to close the interview and how to conduct the interview. He may use the plan with some amount of flexibility. He may deviate from his plan, but he can come back to his original plan and continue the interview.

In a planned interview there need not be any waste of time, embarrassing moments of silence, and failure to obtain some relevant information.

4. Patterned Interview: A patterned interview is also a planned interview, but it is more carefully pre-planned to a high degree of accuracy, precision, and exactitude. With the help of job and man specifications, a list of questions and areas will be carefully prepared, and it will act as the interviewer's guide. With the help of this formal list covering all aspects the interviewer can go down the list of questions, asking one after another and this list is also a memory aid to the interviewer. But the interviewers' guide may be supplemented to gather any other significant information and this is dependent upon the skill of the interviewer.

5. Non-directive Interview: Non-directive interview or unstructured interview is designed to let the interviewee speak his mind freely. The interviewer has no formal or direct questions, but is all attention to the candidate. He encourages the candidate to talk by a little prodding whenever the candidate is silent. In recent times this type of interview may start off thus: " Mr. Raj, please tell us about yourself after you graduated from high school" and keep the interview going by prodding questions or suggestions.

The idea is to give the candidate complete freedom to "sell" himself, without the encumbrances of the interviewer's questions. But the interviewer must be of a higher calibre and must guide and relate the information to the objective of the interview. Interpreting the information given by the applicant and relating it to the job requirements calls for great skill on the part of the interviewer.

6. Depth Interview: Depth interview is designed to intensively examine the candidate's background and thinking and to go into considerable detail on particular subjects of an important nature and of special interest to the candidate. For example, if the candidate says that he is interested in tennis, a series of questions may be asked to test the depth of understanding and interest of the candidate: who was the Wimbledon men's champion in 1995 and women's champion in 1995? Who was responsible for India's defeat in the recent Davis Cup match? Where was the match played ? What are the different types of grips used by tennis players? What are various types of surface on which tennis is played? What is the bounce of the tennis ball like on these different surfaces? How long have you played tennis? Do you like singles, doubles, or mixed doubles play? Similarly great many questions may be asked about tennis to test the candidate's understanding.

The theory is that this gives the interviewer the necessary insight to evaluate and assess the individual candidate and if the candidate is found good in his area of special interest, the chances are that if he likes the given job, he may take serious interest in the job and deliver the goods for the company.

These probing questions must be asked with tact and through exhaustive analysis; it is possible to get a good picture of the candidate.

*7. **Stress Interview:*** This type of interview is designed to test the candidate and his conduct and behaviour by putting him under conditions of stress and strain. The interviewer may start with, "Mr. Raj, we do not think your qualifications and experience are adequate for this position," and watch the reaction of the candidate. A good candidate will not yield, on the contrary he may substantiate why he is qualified to handle the job.

This type of interview is borrowed from the military organisation and this is very useful to test behaviour of individuals when they are faced with disagreeable and trying situations.

*8. **Group Interview:*** The group interview is designed to save busy executive's time and to see how the candidates react to and against each other. All the candidates may be brought together in the employment office and they may be interviewed.

In another type of group interview, the candidates may be given a topic for discussion and observe who will lead the discussion, how many will participate in the discussion, how each will make his presentation, and how they will react to each other's views and presentation.

*9. **Panel Interview:*** A panel or interviewing board or selection committee may interview the candidate, usually in the case of supervisory and managerial positions. This type of interview pools the collective judgments and wisdom of the panel in the assessment of the candidate and also in questioning the faculties of the candidate.

In the case of executive positions, the candidate may be asked to meet the panel of interviewers individually for a fairly lengthy interview.

In U.S.A. the wives of executives are also interviewed by some companies in order to find out how she would like her husband working for the company in a particular place. If the wife does not like her husband travelling a great deal, the company would like to know that if the job involves extensive travelling. If the wife does not like living in the place where the plant is located, then there will be problems in the home of the candidate and the company would like to know that. The idea is that if the wife is unhappy at home, her husband will also feel unhappy not only at home but also at the office and on the job. That means his efficiency on the job will not be 100% and will be low.

Interview Rating: A method widely accepted in vocational guidance and personnel selection is "The Seven-Point Plan" which provides a framework for listing and examining the important aspects of personality to be sought under the following headings:[9]

Physical Make-up	: Health; physique; age; appearance; bearing; speech.
Attainments	: Education; occupational training and experience.
Intelligence	: Basic and "effective."
Special Aptitudes	: Fluency, written and oral; numeracy; organisational ability; administrative skill.
Interests	: Intellectual; practical; physically active; social; artistic.
Disposition	: Self-reliance; nature; motivation; acceptability.
Circumstances	: Domestic; social background and experience; future prospects.

To this may be added position requirements and family background, which would give important relevant information on the upbringing and moulding of his personality, family conditioning, values in life, parental influences. This would act as an interview guide and the candidates may be rated on a five-point rating scale by the selection committee.

It must be admitted that most people do not know the art and skill of interviewing. It must be learnt and practised. Many companies offer courses on selection processes to top executives which are of benefit.

Limitations of Interviewing: As earlier pointed out there are certain limitations of interviewing. The subjective element cannot altogether be eliminated. The prejudices, likes, dislikes, first impressions, bias of the interviewer because of his human nature, introduce the subjective element and this may distort the evaluation or assessment of the candidate. The interviewer may unconsciously dislike men with long noses, Brahmins, Negroes, aliens, Jews or Muslims, or Hindus. He may, in our country, dislike quite unconsciously Bengalis, or Punjabis, or Madrasis etc. This unconscious dislike will show up on the surface in his reception and appraisal of the candidate.

Professor Dale Yoder points out these limitations of interviewing:[10]

"One of the most common types of interviewing errors has been widely *described as halo or the halo effect*. It is the tendency to allow one prominent characteristic of the candidate to dominate appraisal of the entire personality, to colour the interviewer's judgement on other traits. If the individual being interviewed has a pleasant voice and speaks well, that quality makes all his other qualifications look better. Any one of many individual characteristics may create the halo — dress, physical appearance, small mannerisms."

"Closely related is what has been called *stereotyping*. The interviewer's experience may have created a close association between some particular trait and a distinctive type of personality. Whenever the interviewer discovers that the trait is present, he tends to ascribe to the interviewee all the other characteristics of the type. The interviewer may, for example, associate red hair with fiery temperament. He may relate a single physical characteristic with racial types. He may stereotype all applicants from Oklahoma as Okies, all those from Minnesota as Scandinavians, all those from Stanford as "eggheads", or all graduates of your *alma mater* as playboys."

Another problem is that some managers believe they are good at character analysis even now and they are guided by their own abilities at character analysis. But this seems to be giving place to systematic selection procedures.

Interpreting Information: The information gathered through different types of interviews has to be interpreted and a scoring system may be used. Then interviewers may be asked to rate the interviewees and these may be interpreted with a view to finding the most suitable candidate. A five point rating scale may be used, such as (1) outstanding, (2) good, (3) above average, (4) below average, (5) unsatisfactory, and total the points in making the final evaluation.

As earlier pointed out, interviews may be the only tool of selection, but most companies supplement the interviews with tests, physical examinations etc.

(f) Handling an Interview

David Lim suggests how candidates should prepare for interviews:

Going for an interview can be scary. Your resume may have already sold your qualifications, skills and experience to your potential employer, but the interview is where you have to impress with your personality as well.

So before you go for your next one — be it for a job, scholarship or university admission — arm yourself with these tips doled out by Mr. David TK Lim, vice president at AT Kearny, an executive search firm, at a Career '98 seminar:

Relax ... or at least look it: "But don't be so comfortable that the moment you go in, you put your legs on a chair," said Mr. Lim. "You need to keep a professional distance."

Prepare in advance: "You need to show (your interviewer) that you are interested, that you know at least a little bit about the company."

Answer and ask questions attentively and to the point: "Answer more than ask," advised Mr. Lim. But if you do not know the answer, just say so, "(Interviewers) would prefer honesty rather than have you go round and round and, in military terms, throw smoke. At the end, they will think you have no depth."

Never argue or be "too cocky" or show you are losing interest: Mr. Lim cautioned: "If you have been given an introduction by somebody, don't go in there thinking that you already have the job."

Dress suitably and professionally: It shows that you respect your interviewer enough to look smart.

Be on time: "If you do show up late, please apologise. But don't spend 10 minutes explaining why you are late." A related point — "after you get the job, show up for work on time. You might laugh at this, but it happens and it creates a negative impression of you."

What HR Managers Look For

Mr. Lim also shared nuggets of information on what human resource managers look out for when screening candidates:

Qualifications: Sound and relevant academic qualifications help you get a foot in the door at the very least.

Mr. Lim said that if possible, get a professional degree (like engineering, law and architecture for example) instead of a generic degree (like business administration, science and arts).

His reason — professionals can do jobs that generic degree holders can, but the opposite is not true.

Years of experience: Nothing quite beats hands-on relevant experience.

Reputation of previous company or university: Mr. Lim said this is becoming increasingly important. He urged: "When you're looking around at which university to choose, find out first about how recognised the university is."

Career-wise, having worked for a reputable company means you have probably received good training.

Personality: Desirable traits include self-confidence, decisiveness, adaptability, willingness to learn and the ability to think analytically. According to Mr. Lim, some companies use psychological tests to pick out candidates with these traits.

Communication skills: It is now no longer enough to know much. The ability to communicate effectively is becoming increasingly important.

"Verbal communication is very important," emphasised Mr. Lim, "especially in English; because come year 2000, we're going to see more multinationals here ... and English is their main business language."

He warned: "You may be the best Research and Development engineer for example, but if you cannot present (your thoughts, ideas and plans) in English, you will never climb up the hierarchy."

(g) Tests

Tests are used to gather some more accurate information about the candidate and thus, they supplement the other selection techniques, and they cannot supplant them. Since the First World War, when psychological tests were used by U.S. Army to select army personnel, much interest has been shown in U.S.A. in the usage of tests as a selection technique. Tests are not infallible and they depend upon correct construction and interpretation. There are many hazards when tests are used as the sole criterion for selection. But tests are found useful as one of selection techniques. The use of psychological tests is widely prevalent in the West and for their usage it is necessary to get the benefit of specialists. Tests are used in the areas of employment, guidance, promotion, training, placement and transfers.

The use of tests in industry today is not so widespread as the volume of literature on the subject would lead one to believe. Their use has steadily expanded, however, and testing has definitely earned a place in a scientific selection procedure. One survey of personnel practices in business has revealed that 81 per cent of 473 firms having 250 employees or more indicated that they were using one or more tests in hiring. Most smaller firms do not make use of standardised tests, but rely more heavily upon interviews, and background checks. Many have tended to abandon testing in the light of validation requirements made evident by the Supreme Court decision in the *Griggs vs. Duke Power Company* case.[11]

But in India their usage is limited to some of the large established Indian companies and some foreign subsidiaries. Many others do not use any of the tests for the purpose of selection. Some common tests used in the West are as follows:

1. Aptitude tests.
2. Intelligence tests.
3. Mechanical tests.
4. Trade tests.
5. Character tests.
6. Achievement tests.
7. Combination tests.
8. Personality tests.
9. Interest tests.
10. Various tailor-made tests.

The candidate must be assured that the tests are to help the company to assess the candidate and the information will be strictly confidential.

(h) Physical Examination

In U.S.A. it is common to give a prospective employee a thorough medical check-up, known as the pre-employment physical examination. If the employee's health is found satisfactory, a job offer is made. This is yet another selection hurdle that has to be surmounted by the candidate. Again there is a need to assure the candidate that his health information will be kept strictly confidential and this will help both the candidate and the company.

Generally the medical examination is both general and thorough, conducted by a qualified doctor and the findings will be interpreted and transmitted by the doctor to the employment office.

In India, physical examinations are not very common for the purpose of selection. But some companies do use these physical examinations and they are used after the employee is hired and only a few give pre-employment physical examination.

(i) Selection and Placement

In the selection process, particularly in India, we should not forget to mention the role played by the letters of recommendation and influence. Many a candidate is selected mainly on the basis of a recommendation letter from the right individual. Though unfortunate, the letters of recommendation are often a very good passport to a job. And influence plays also a significant role. Without the influence of some godfather, many candidates may not find a job, let alone a decent job. These render the selection process unsystematic and inefficient and in the long run this will reflect on the efficiency, productivity, and profits of the organisation.

In U.S.A. and even with some firms in India the in-basket technique is used in the selection of executives. We are familiar with correspondence separated as incoming and out-going in a basket on the executive desk. Mr. John K. Hemphill, Director of Executive Study, Educational Testing Service writes:[12] "An in-basket test is a collection of documents which presumably have accumulated in the in-basket of a manager and are awaiting his attention. The particular documents in the in-basket constitute the test items. The examinee responds to these test items by taking action as though he were actually on the job, and whatever results he produces in taking the test are his "answers" to the test items...." "Our research studies in this area have been oriented toward the solution of problems involved in performance measurement on in-basket tests. We have devised systems by which we can score or evaluate the output of a subject. The first system developed yielded measures of his performance in a wide variety of areas, including:

1. The manner in which he analyses the problem.
2. The types of decisions that he makes.
3. The kinds of actions he takes.
4. The way he communicates with others.
5. His method of organising or approaching the work.
6. The amount of initiative he shows in solving problems.
7. The way in which he delegates work.
8. The way in which he interacts with his staff.
9. The amount of consideration displayed towards others."

The in-basket approach is also a useful selection technique and is being used in some companies in India.

Interpreting the findings made through interviews, application blanks, references, tests, personal observation, and physical examinations is the next process of selection, although at each of these selection hurdles, the selection process is taking place. On the basis of the findings, decisions to select or not to select have to be made. The responsibility for such decisions should rest with the line executives, save in the case of recruitment for the personnel division.

The employee may be, after selection put on a period of probation, after which his employment will be regularised. The new employee needs to be properly placed and here proper matching of the employee with the job is essential. In a case of continuous hiring, and when there is no job opening, but the candidate is a good one, an interim placement may be made, until a suitable job is ready. The newly selected employee may be intimated through a letter of appointment, the terms of appointment and service conditions and when and where he should report to work.

It is necessary to maintain records of rejections also and in case, a rejected candidate applies again for the same job, the records will show that he had been found unsuitable for some specific reason and thus all the elaborate procedures of selection can be avoided. Records of selected candidates should be maintained and into them all additional data regarding service, merit rating, grievances, disciplinary cases, health history etc. are reported.

(j) Induction

The selection procedure does not end once the selection is made, for the new employee has to be inducted in to the organisation. The purpose of induction is to educate the employee and provide orientation on the following subjects:

1. Company history, products, processes, and major operations;
2. Company policies, objectives, and regulations;
3. Relation of foremen and personnel department;
4. Rules and regulations regarding wages, hours of work and overtime, safety and accidents, holidays and vacations, methods of reporting tardiness and absences, discipline and grievances, uniforms and clothing, parking, badges and parcels;
5. Economic and recreational services available, insurance plans, pensions, athletic, social, and cultural activities;
6. Opportunities, promotion and transfer, suggestion systems, and job stabilisation.

To 'sell' the company to the new employee so that he may feel proud of his association with the company is the primary purpose of induction.

In some companies in U.S.A. induction is done through the 'buddy system' where a senior or older employee inducts the new employee. More conventional is the practice of inducting the new employee through one of the personnel staff. A wide variety of printed material, employee handbooks, pamphlets, picture stories, comics and cartoons, movies and slides are used to educate the new employee about the company. A programme of induction helps the new employee to understand and develop a sense of identification with the company.

(k) Follow-up

The objective of a follow-up is to see whether the right man has been placed in the right job or there has been a mistake. This also provides an opportunity for the supervisor or the manager to assess the contribution of the employee. If the new employee is not functioning well, it is necessary to find out his problems. Through interviewing, guidance, and counselling, the problems of the new employee have to be brought in to the open and ways and means have to be suggested to eradicate the issues.

If the individual is functioning well in his present capacity and is 'happy' with his job where he has been able to realise his full potentialities, the personnel executive will have had the pleasure of assisting in the placement of the right man on the right job.

The contemporary recruitment, selection, and placement procedures are systematic, professional, and technical in character and they are designed not only to place the right man on the right job but also to see that there is an enduring employee and employer relationship. The personnel administrator's responsibility is to provide a loyal, effective, and enduring work-force to the company and to promote a sense of membership and belongingness in the organisation among the work-force. The long term association and loyalty of employees to TISCO may be cited as an example. Mr. Bhabha observes:[13] Many of today's workers, foremen, supervisors, and superintendents are the children of former employees of the Company who earned their livelihood, built their homes, and settled down in the steel city and who have a sense of 'belonging' to Jamshedpur. There must be very few plants in India where there is, for instance, such a sense of personal loyalty to the head of the organisation, Mr. J.R.D. Tata. This is something you cannot help feeling whenever you go around the Steel Works with the chairman. The newer companies have yet to achieve the same degree of fellowship and sense of partnership and this is where the Personnel Officers have a prominent role to play. Today you cannot, as in the past, wait for many decades for the sense of 'belonging' to be gradually developed. You have got to telescope this process into a short period of years, or even months. And in doing so, you have to achieve one of your primary purposes, which is to relieve the line management men of the burden of looking to the needs, problems and grievances of the workers and imbuing them with a sense of loyalty to the organisation and the will to improve their productivity."

We should like to contrast the scientific procedure with some historic selection practices noted by Professor Lundy.[14] "Some of the darkest days in the history of personnel administration occurred when phrenologists, physiognomists, palmists, graphologists, and astrologists were selling their services throughout the business world. Each of these groups specialised in impressive, but unproven, methods of personality evaluation. For example, phrenologists studied the bumps on one's head and judged character accordingly. Franz Gall, the Austrian who proposed the theory of phrenology, contended that each of many traits is associated with a particular portion of the brain, and the contour of the skull indicates the prominence of portions of the pseudoscientific techniques of brain and their corresponding traits."

"Physiognomy is quite similar to phrenology, except that the physiognomist judges character by such features as the shape and size of one's chin, nose, and ears, and the colour of one's eyes and hair. Of all the unsound techniques, physiognomy seems to be the most enduring. How often have you heard red-heads described as short-tempered or people with eyes close together described as cruel or mean? Many interesting studies have been performed to disprove physiognomy as a valid technique for determining character traits."

"Palmists and graphologists have not been very active in the field of employee selection, but they still can be found at fairs and amusement parks. Palmists claim to be able to judge character and predict one's future by scrutinising the lines of one's hand, while graphologists provide the same type of information by analysing handwriting. Again, the predictability of these techniques has been shown to be no better than chance, though there is a feeling that graphology, if developed more thoroughly, might become a useful approach."

"The most dubious of these pseudoscientific techniques is that of astrology. Not only do the astrologists claim to be able to foresee the future, but they also claim that the position of the stars on one's date of birth determines one's character and therefore can be used in appraising individuals."

"Although the heading for this section implies that techniques just discussed are of historic interest only, this represents, unfortunately, just wishful thinking. One still can find medicine men in the field of personnel management. Perhaps with more widespread and improved education in the field, pseudoscientific approaches to problems of personnel management eventually will become extinct."

"One should not conclude from this discussion, however, that such things as appearance and handwriting are not suitable criteria, but rather their utility is doubtful in the prediction of personality traits. To be sure, in the selection of a chorus girl or a secretary, one might be interested in appearance and handwriting respectively. This is different from hiring or rejecting a machine operator because he has blue eyes, a crewcut, round, chin, short upper lip, long nose, or moustache."

Fortunately in modern days, there are more reliable tools available to the men in the field of personnel administration and the selection procedures are more systematic and scientific. It is possible that we may hire once in a while an unsuitable or wrong candidate even after adopting all the scientific selection procedures but the fact is that we leave ourselves wide open to chance and errors if we do not adopt a scientific selection procedure."

The Problem of Discrimination

The problem of discrimination in selection has assumed great importance in modern scientific selection procedure. We find various types of discriminations based on sex, age, race, caste, region, practised in organisations. We find that in certain companies women are not provided employment. In some others minority groups like the Muslims, Christians etc. may be discriminated against. In some cases age becomes a candidate for discrimination, and older employees are scrupulously avoided. It is also interesting to note that there are companies where Hindus are discriminated against. In the United States, U.K. and other countries black people are discriminated against, and various other minority groups like Chinese, Japanese, West Indians, Puerto Ricans face discrimination. Now the state is interfering in order to prevent such discriminations. It is considered an unfair labour practice. Now in fact, the whole selection procedure and instruments have come under sharp attack. Now companies are required to justify the instruments in the sense that they are being used for the purpose of scientific selection, objectivity and fairness and not use the instruments with a view to eliminating some groups of people because of their race, caste, religion, region, sex and age. We are sure that even in our country the state will intervene to see that the entire selection instruments and procedures are used fairly, objectively and justly and any discrimination on any ground will be considered not only unfair but illegal also in the very near future.

Asia Magazine Features Some of the Discrimination Problems in Selection

Many employers still espouse archaic hire-and-fire policies which discriminate on the bases of sex, age, disability and even marital status. Will recently enacted laws be enough to alter this mindset?[15]

Shoji Furuya, a 30-year-old nursery school teacher, and Nobuo Taguchi, an interpreter, are both well-qualified professionals who would sail through any job interview — if they wore a skirt. As it is, they have to convince potential employers that their masculinity is not a handicap — or a threat.

"People think because I like working with kids, I must be a child molester," says Furuya. "I answer to 'male only' advertisements and try hard at interviews to convince school principals that it is handy to have a man around. I usually end up moving lots of furniture."

Interpreter Taguchi faces similar discrimination, as his profession attracts mainly women. Japanese men, anxious to get on the executive fast track, shun the temporary nature of interpreting as a vocation.

"I studied hard for years to gain a valuable work skill because I was determined not to enter the salary man grind," he says. "My female classmates at the language school work for a while, travel abroad, then work again when they run out of money. I want this same lifestyle — but because I am male, society does not give me this flexibility. Employment agencies always tell me clients prefer a soft female voice for interpreting. This is discrimination — if I speak in a falsetto voice, will I get hired?"

If Furuya and Taguchi were living the US, they would most likely have had their day in court, and a victorious one too. But this is Asia, and few disgruntled employees are willing to confront their employers — in or out of court. Furthermore, only a handful of Asian countries have a specific legislation against discriminatory employment practices. An even in those which do — such as Hong Kong, Japan and the Philippines — deeply ingrained Asian attitudes and social mores regarding gender roles, age, sexual orientation and disability perpetuate discriminatory practices at work.

But the cases of Furuya and Taguchi — where men complain of employer prejudice — are the exception. By and large, employment practices in Asia are skewed against women. As Thai Senator Srisavang Phuavongphatya points out, Asian society is still slowly accepting the concept of the successful career woman, as traditional views emphasise a woman's role as primarily that of wife and mother.

Gender discrimination can be outright and blatant. Certain companies in Thailand and Japan have different retirement ages for men and women employees — with men usually enjoying a longer working lifespan.

Notes Rangsee Phanthumchinda, Director of Measures for the Thai National Women's Commission: "It is common to see ads asking for good-looking women as receptionists or secretaries, while ads seeking engineers specify men only. The main reason given by employers for this unequal treatment is 'flexibility or efficiency' at work — but uppermost in their minds is the risk of female employees getting pregnant and taking 60 days of paid maternity leave. Yet being pregnant is not a woman's fault, is it?"

To compound the overt sexual discrimination in the workplace, Thailand's universities have an unequal quota system for entrance to various courses. According to the Ministry of University Affairs, there are 18 fields of study in public universities which have an entrance quota favouring male students. These courses — such as archaeology, biotechnology, veterinary science, agronomics, forestry and physical education — lead to highly paid jobs. Only four fields have an entrance quota skewed towards women — all are in lower-paid service sectors such as nursing, hotel services and secretarial duties.

In 1996, a group of female lecturers in the Veterinary Science Department of Chulalongkorn University wrote a letter to the National Women's Commission asking for an investigation into the biased quota system. The letter noted that their department in 1995 had a quota system which accepted 114 men and only 30 women. Commenting on the case, Supalak Boranin of the NWC states: "The lecturers felt it was unreasonable to give opportunities to boys with poorer scores than girls who could do better."

But despite a cabinet order to rescind any discriminatory practices in tertiary institutions, the Ministry of University Affairs' stand is that a quota system is necessary — because "the nature of each discipline makes it better suited to one sex or the other." The ministry also argues that the quota system was initiated based on market demand — for example, only female nurses are in need in the market, while the military wants only male doctors.

Singapore and Malaysia, like Thailand, do not have specific legislation regarding sex discrimination. A flip through the classified ads in The Straits Times, Singapore's leading daily, reveals ads headlined "male technicians", "female receptionists", or even "marketing assistants below the age of 25." Farah Namazie, a practising lawyer dealing in employment matters, confirms that Singapore does not have equal opportunities legislation, and sexual discrimination *per se* is not illegal. However, employees who feel discriminated against can seek redress under the Employment Act, which states: "There shall be no discrimination against citizens of Singapore on the grounds of religion, race, descent or place of birth with respect to an appointment to any office or employment under public authority or the establishing or carrying on of any trade, business, profession, vocation or employment."

The Ministry of Labour has a Commissioner for Labour who acts as mediator when complaints of discrimination are filed. But as a lawyer specialising in employment law admits: "At this point, I find little prospect for reinstatement for those who claim to have been dismissed because of discrimination. The most you can do is negotiate for an agreeable settlement."

Indeed, job discrimination is a taboo topic that is often swept under the carpet as the Lion City aspires to a system of meritocracy. Laletha Nithyanandan, managing director of employment agency Business Trends, says the reality is a different picture. "Five years ago, women were generally paid 20 per cent less than men," she says. "Women were not favoured because their family and children were deemed disruptive for business. But now, many employers are beginning to realise it costs more to hire men because they have to go to army reservist training every year."

Industrial engineer Sng Gim Hong recalls her uphill battle to overcome sex discrimination and become Director of Manufacturing at Aztech Systems.

"When I first started work at a Japanese electronic appliance manufacturing company," says Sng, "my boss sent my male colleague for training in Japan, although I was just as qualified. I went to ask him about it and he just said, 'because you are a lady.' I was very angry, but it made me work harder just to make up for this disadvantage. In the male-dominated field of information technology, I have to prove I know the business before the men will open up and share information. But once they know I know my stuff, the guys are fine."

Malaysian professionals say there is no overt hiring based on sex, although a glass ceiling does exist for the working women. Jessica See, editor of *Women at Work*, a magazine targeted at women executives, notes: "It is an employee's market and employers are just keen to hire — and keep — someone with the right qualifications. I don't see them worrying about whether to pay women less than men."

Taiwan, although lauded as one of Asia's industrial tigers, is an equally conservative society when it comes to fairness in the workplace. A survey conducted in 1993 revealed that women in the private sector earn about 30 per cent less than their male counterparts; while in the public sector they make about 24 per cent less. Recruitment ads seeking "women aged between 24 and 30 with a pleasant personality" are common place, as the perception is that women give a certain "decorative value" in the office.

Berdie Lo, product manager for a French cosmetics company, recalls the chauvinistic attitudes of her former colleagues in a multi-national company. "There were lots of jokes and sexual insinuations like 'if you make your sales target, you'll get a kiss from Miss So-and-so' (usually the prettiest girl in the office)" she notes. The worst part, laments Lo, was that the women did not object, but merely smiled and even played along.

Chih-poung Liou, employment attorney at the Taiwanese firm Formosn Brothers, has dealt with gender discrimination issues for more than a decade, and has been at the forefront of drafting an Equal Employment Act for Taiwan. The final draft of this act — published in 1989 — is now under review at the Legislative Yuan. The new laws will include restrictions on the placing of gender-specific employment advertisements in the media. Male and female employees will have to be treated equally as regards promotion, training, salary and benefits, while the law also allows for the creation of an equal employment commission to handle disputes. Until this law comes into effect, any discriminatory disputes between employer and employee are covered by the Employment Services Act.

According to Liou, so far only one suit concerning sex discrimination has hit the headlines — two years ago, Yangming Co-operative Bank forced a female employee to quit after she got married. The bank was found guilty and received the maximum fine from the Council of Labour Affairs.

While legislation may allow the victims of discrimination to seek justice in the courts, it does not erase social prejudices. Japan is a case in point. Despite being the first Asian country to introduce equal employment legislation in 1985, only 1.2 per cent of Japanese women today hold executive positions. The majority of working women are relegated to clerical and support roles — and even as such, they face blatant discrimination in the office.

There is a saying that "an office flower wilts within three years" — so during her third year, hints in the form of jokes about how she should spend more money on her looks to catch a husband start coming a woman's way. It continues with comments about how tea tastes better when served by her younger colleagues.

"It's ridiculous being called 'Auntie' at 25," says Yoshiko Takahashi. "Sure, men work long hours, but we who type up their reports and photocopy their research information are alongside them the entire time. They got recognition and more money but we are replaced within a few years. It's exploitation."

In September 1996, Hong Kong introduced three pieces of legislation to deal with employment discrimination — the Sex Discrimination Ordinance, Disability Discrimination Ordinance and the Family Status Discrimination Ordinance. Recruitment ads asking for "pretty young unmarried female secretaries" are no longer permitted. But although the tools are in place to combat discriminatory practices during the recruitment process, there is no guarantee that selection will be based solely on merit. Says Ian Strutton, general manager of recruitment company Gemini Personnel: "The law still needs to filter down and change people's attitudes. A man has the right to apply for a receptionist's position. But will he get the job? I doubt it."

The Equal Opportunities Commission was created to enforce the new legislation. However, critics have labelled the commission as a tiger with no teeth, as it does not have the power to act against employers suspected of discriminatory practices. Rather, it offers to "conciliate between the parties."

Last October, a survey by the Democratic Party revealed that up to 20 per cent of job applicants faced discrimination. The survey revealed that nine companies out of 50 that had placed ads in newspapers had immediately rejected certain job seekers over the phone. "People are being turned down during phone interviews because they are not of the right sex. We have a law to make sure people are given jobs according to their abilities, but the fact is few employers follow the law," notes party spokesman Tse Wai-ming.

But in the Philippines — the only Southeast Asian country to have had a woman head of state (Cory Aquino, 1986-1992) — many women professionals say sex discrimination is not a burning issue. "Sure, there is the Boys' Club," says Dolores Amor, a lawyer. "It exists in professions traditionally dominated by men, such as banking and finance. And there is a tendency to think that certain roles are more suited to men and women — for instance, clients may prefer to deal with a woman lawyer in domestic cases because she is perceived, rightly or wrongly, as having more heart. And trade unions may prefer a man to handle negotiations.

"But by and large, Filipino men recognise competence, capability and intelligence. There is no taboo about a man asking a woman colleague for professional advice. And more importantly, there is no feminist aggression among the working women."

While sex discrimination is more obvious and emotive a topic, other forms of discrimination — age, sexual orientation and stability — are equally damning but attract less media attention. Hong Kong, Singapore and the Philippines have specific legislation against hiring and firing based on age, but only Hong Kong has an ordinance to address the issue of discrimination against the handicapped. As yet, no country in Asia has drawn up legislation to combat discrimination based on sexual orientation — not surprisingly, considering that homosexuality is a topic not mentioned in polite circles.

Singapore has taken more concrete steps to encourage employers to hire senior citizens. Instead of the usual 20 per cent Central Provident Fund contribution, employers need only pay 7.5 per cent for employees over the age of 60.

Phua Kok Tee, acting CEO of the Singapore Action Group for the Elderly (SAGE), explains: "Up to a point, it is logical, because a retiree has got less energy — physically and mentally — than a younger person, so he's not expected to perform at the same rate. Still, one shouldn't assume that old people should be paid less because they spend less."

As part of the Hong Kong government's campaign to promote its stand against age discrimination, a series of ads encouraging employers to hire "old hands" has been aired on local television. But again, changing a social mindset is a uphill task. Gemini Personnel's Strutton notes: "We've come across many situations where, for example, a 35-year-old manager will not consider employing a 45-year-old staff member. Age discrimination legislation is one thing, but it is employers' attitudes that count, not those of lawmakers."

Indeed, in countries such as Taiwan and Japan, age discrimination can be blatant. Recruitment ads in Japan, which has a tradition of life-long employment, specify an age limit of 25. In Taipei, Ligawaty Alamsgah of Price Waterhouse say many clients refuse to interview job applicants older than 48 years.

Gilbert Wang, managing director of Taipei's golden Wheel Group, a trading and manufacturing company, is a case in point. Wang admits he is hesitant to hire older workers, noting that while age often equals experience, it also means that the person could be resistant to change and personal improvement.

While it is usually the elderly who get discriminated against, sometimes the situation is reversed. Says Maria Samad, a senior advertising agency executive in Kuala Lumpur: "When a young person is bright and capable, his age can be a handicap because he is seen as an upstart, or as inexperienced and not ready for responsibility, while an older person may be regarded as very experienced — even though he may have reached the limit of his competence."

There are also employers who try to get away with paying disabled workers less. Nithyanandan of Singapore's Business Trends recalls: "There was this typist who could type faster than most typists. She had two fingers on one hand, while her other hand was normal. The employer who saw this automatically offered to pay her less than the norm. Luckily, we came in to stop them. But many employers actually feel they are doing these minority groups a favour by hiring them."

Mrs. Lua-Lieng, an employment executive at Biz Link, a specialised employment agency under the Singapore Council of Social Service, agrees that employers take advantage of employers with a disability, however small.

"At this point, employment of disabled workers is based purely on employers' goodwill," she says. "When we get a complaint of discrimination in the workplace, we offer the disabled worker two choices — either accept the situation and come to a settlement with the employer, or leave the company and wait for another job placement."

Wheelchair-bound Razak Bin Ismail has been unemployed for six months now. "My last job at a local hospital was very good. Unfortunately, I was asked to resign because the boss wasn't happy with the medical problems I developed from sitting for too long. Every time I turn up in response to an ad, they take one look at me and say there are no vacancies. Or they give excuses, such as the office isn't accessible to wheelchairs. It's very discouraging to face such obstacles."

Discrimination on the job — whatever the basis — has no role in a progressive society. But sadly, because it is the norm, the people who suffer can do very little to address the issue.

Nithyanandan sums it up succinctly: "at the end of the day, it's going to take more than legislation to fight job discrimination. There needs to be more responsibility from the community and society in terms of raising awareness against such discrimination.

"The problem stems from our ingrained values and prejudices, so we have to change the way we think and give everyone a fair chance to show what they can do. Some of these people can be real gems in the work force. I think we owe it to the community to accept them instead of shutting them out."

Scientific selection is one of the most important principles of scientific management and there is enough knowledge and experience to prove that these selection techniques are useful in the recruitment, selection and placement process.

REFERENCES

1. See my, "The Right Man on the Right Job", *The Textile Magazine,* Annual Number, October 7, 1966, p.56.
2. C.H. Northcott, *Personnel Management* (London: Sir Isaac Pitman & Sons Ltd., Third Ed., 1955, p. 218.
3. U.S. Business, *Time Magazine*, Asia Edition, March 25, 1966, p. 49.
4. I.I.P.M., *Personnel Management in India*, p. 199.
5. For greater details on weighted application blanks see J. Welch, C. Harold Stone, and Donald G. Paterson, "How to Develop a Weighted Application Blank", *Research and Technical Report II*, University of Minnesota Industrial Relations Centre, 1952; Marvin D. Dunnette and James Maetzold, "Use of Weighted Application Blank in Hiring Seasonal Employees," *Journal of Applied Psychology,* Vol. 39, No. 5, May 1955, pp. 308-10.
6. Dale Yoder, *Personnel Management,* p. 329.
7. Pigors and Myers, *Personnel Administration*, p. 267 (footnote No. 11).
8. N.A. Moyer, "Non-directive Employment Interviewing," *Personnel*, Vol. XXIV, No. 5, p.395.

8(A) David Lim, Handling an Interviewing, *The Straits Times.*

9. Quoted by Central Training Council in *Training and Development of Managers: Further Proposals* (London: Her Majesty's Stationery Office, 1969), p.27.
10. Yoder, *op. cit.*, p. 334.
11. Edwin B. Flippo, *Principles of Personnel Administration* (4th edn.), Tokyo, McGraw Hill-Kogakusha, 1976, p. 154.
12. John K. Hemphill, "Plans and Progress in Personnel Research", *The Personnel Job in the 1960s,* A M A Management Report No.63, Personnel Division, American Management Association, New York, 1961, pp. 85-86.
13. See "The Fifth Tata Personnel and Labour Relations Conference," *Tata Review*, Vol. 1, No.4, December 1965-January 1966, pp. 5-6.
14. James L. Lundy, *Effective Industrial Management* (New Delhi: Eurasia Publishing House (Pvt.) Ltd., 1964), pp. 487-88.
15. *Asia Magazine,* February 20-22, 1998, pp. 9-13.

❑ ❑ ❑

CHAPTER 7

Human Resources Development

WORLD BANK SKILLS FOR DEVELOPMENT*

Increasing the skills and capabilities of workers is a key to economic success in an increasingly integrated and competitive global economy. Investing in people can boost the living standards of households by expanding opportunities, raising productivity, attracting capital investment, and increasing earning power. Better health, nutrition, and education also have value in their own right, enabling people to lead more fulfilling lives. The importance of investing in human capital, especially education, for economic growth and household welfare is recognised worldwide; this realisation has contributed to unprecedented global increases in schooling in recent decades. Yet these investments alone do not always lead to more rapid growth; in the wrong environment investments in people may only yield misspent or idle resources.[1]

This chapter examines why human capital is important, why many countries have not been able to reap its benefits, and what role governments can play in supporting household investments in human capital.

What is Human Capital?

The livelihoods of farmers, industrial labourers, and service workers depend increasingly on their acquiring such basic skills as literacy and numeracy, as well as more specialised skills and the ability to manage complex tasks and organise the work of others. The human resources investments required to learn these skills — investments in health and nutrition, and in education and training — begin at an early age and extend over a lifetime. Such investments in health and nutrition, and in education and training — begin at an early age and extend over a lifetime. Such investments create the human capital necessary for raising the productivity of labour and the economic well-being of workers and their families.

Lowering protein-energy malnutrition, and increasing consumption of micronutrients such as iron and iodine, can increase labour productivity by improving mental and physical capacity. Analyses of farm households in southern India and on

* See World Bank, *The Challenge of Development*, World Development Report, 1991, New York, Oxford Univesity Press, 1991.

the island of Mindanao in the Philippines found that increased weight-for-height (a measure of long-term nutritional status) and height (a proxy for childhood nutrition) are both closely associated with greater adult output per worker. The quantitative impact on future productivity of better nutrition early in life appears in these cases to be at least as large as that often reported for primary schooling.

Education is essential for raising individual productivity. General education gives children skills that they can later transfer from job to job and the basic intellectual tools necessary for further learning. It augments the ability to perform standard tasks, to process and use information, and to adapt to new technologies and production practices. Evidence on the adoption of high-yielding varieties of food grains in China and India illustrates the point. After accounting for farm size and other production factors, studies found that better educated farmers in China's Human Province were more likely to adopt the more productive hybrids. In India, areas where relatively few farmers had primary schooling at the onset of the green revolution experienced less growth than areas with the same technological opportunities but better educated farmers.

Training for work exhibits a similar relationship with productivity. Enterprise-based training in Taiwan, China, has been associated with a significant rise in output per worker, with the largest gains realised in firms that invested simultaneously in training and technology. As in the case of the green revolution, human capital bears an especially high return when the opportunity to take advantage of new ideas is present.

Investments in people are often highly complementary. Adequate nutrition and health increase the ability of children to learn. Analysis of four Guatemala villages indicates that protein-enriched food supplements delivered in childhood significantly improved scores on educational achievement tests administered some ten years later. Improving a country's general education increases the probability that workers will receive training after their formal education. In Peru male workers were 25 per cent more likely to receive training from their employers if they had some rather than no secondary schooling; if they had completed secondary school, they were 52 per cent more likely to receive training.

Increasing the human capital of workers boosts their earning power, because market-oriented economies reward the skilled worker who is able to deliver more output, or an output that is more highly valued in the marketplace. Rewards for education and skills, relative to those for unskilled labour, are now rising in some former centrally planned economies, where administrative rules rather than the market long determined wages. In Slovenia workers with education and prior work experience have seen their wages increase, as newly released market forces have begun to expand the wage structure in line with differences in the value of worker productivity.

Human Capital: Necessary but not Sufficient

More education usually means more productive individuals. So it is not surprising that, since 1960, world enrollments at all levels of education combined have increased. Today more than five of every ten secondary graduates live in low- and middle-income countries; years ago only three in ten did. In 1960 roughly one of all adults in developing countries were literate; now more than half were. This trend spans all regions, although the variance in outcomes remains large. Worldwide, men are increasingly better educated, although the distance of schooling between men and women remains unequal in most regions.

It explains why has economic growth remained elusive in many developing countries of the world, despite rising levels of schooling and increasing forms of human capital. There are two reasons. First, investment in human capital can be poorly used. Greater investment in human capital can neither compensate or overcome factors inimical to economic growth. Second, human capital investments can be of the wrong type or of poor Capital Expenditures on human resources often fail to provide quantity, quality, or type of human capital that it should have if the funds had been better spent. There are various examples — food supplements having little effect on recipients' nutritional status; of increased school attendance yielding little change on standardised test scores; high school graduates of public training institutes finding no improvement in their new skills.

Underutilisation of the education and skills of workers is due to the problem of lack of labour demand due to inadequacies in development strategies. This is evident in many countries including Southeast Asia. The work forces of Vietnam and the Philippines have historically had higher rates in adult literacy and educational attainment than other countries in the region. Yet both of these economies have developed relatively slowly, largely because countries adopted development strategies — central planning in Vietnam, import substitution in the Philippines that proved incapable of taking full advantage of investment of human capital. Some of the successful countries in Southeast Asia, in contrast, initially had low levels of human capital but pursued strategies expanded education and the demand for labour technical skills.

Philippines and Vietnam did realise a return on human resources investments. Many educated utilised their skills abroad, and their remittances became economy's largest source of foreign exchange. In Vietnam today, past investments in human capital are contributing to improved economic performance that the country has adopted a more market oriented approach to development. But what the Philippines and Viet Nam demonstrate is that the expansion of human capital delivers its full potential only when there is a high increase in market-driven demand for human skills and technology.

Government's human resources policy also is part of the reason why investments in people do not always pay dividends. There are many examples; here we focus on education. Excessive spending on education bureaucracies and school infrastructure, rather than on teaching staff and supplies, depresses the quantity and quality of schooling. So do poorly trained teachers and failure to set high standards for students. Finally, human capital tends to be relatively unproductive where the skills acquired in school do not match market opportunities, or where higher education is promoted at the expense of primary and secondary schooling.

In all of these cases, improvements in education policy are needed to ensure that expenditures on schooling yield productive investments in human capital.

Supporting Investment in People

Households willingly invest in their members' good health and education, because the benefits, which include the economic benefit of higher lifetime earnings, usually far exceed the costs. Yet often households under invest in human capital. When they do, governments have an essential role in supporting these investments in people.

Households are often poorly informed about the returns to human capital, especially in the areas of health and nutrition. Government-sponsored health and nutrition education can encourage them to undertake these high-return investments. Governments also intervene when families are willing to invest in human resources but cannot, because lenders are unwilling to extend credit against expected future earnings. Finally, the value to society of human capital investment can exceed its value to individual families; a more educated society is better able to adopt new technologies, and shared schooling experiences contribute to nation building. To capture these social benefits, governments can change the incentives households face, by targeting subsidies at the poor or, as in the case of primary education, providing the service for free.

Special efforts are often needed to offset the tendency for girls to receive less education than boys. Beyond the benefits it offers women in the labour market, education is linked to lower fertility, lower maternal mortality, and better health, nutrition, and education of children. These may not be fully realized without strong public intervention. The goals of combating discrimination, reducing poverty, and promoting equity therefore justify government action to promote the accumulation of human capital, especially among the poor.

Training as an Investment

Productive learning does not end with school. Most individuals continue to build their skills throughout their working lives, through training on the job and in formal training centers. Training is an investment from the perspective of both workers and employers. Workers often willingly incur fees for training courses, or accept lower wages than they would receive if not engaged in on-the-job training, in return for expected higher wages in the future. Firms have an incentive to invest in their employees' training because they frequently need workers with certain skills. Neither side is completely sure that it will be able to appropriate fully the returns to its investment: workers may quit and transfer the gains to another employer, or may lose their jobs and find the skills they have acquired are not transferable. Employers and employees have found ways to work around this problem so that both sides can still gain: employers provide job security to reduce turnover; workers may agree to training contracts whereby they repay the employer if they leave before the employer's investment has been recouped; and workers and their employers can share the productivity gains associated with training.

Because training is often a good investment, most training takes place with little government involvement. The amount of training firms undertake varies, sometimes greatly between countries and sectors, and even across firms within the same sector, depending on their size and type of ownership. In 1991, 24 per cent of Mexican workers reported receiving some form of training to improve their skills on the job; the corresponding figure in Japan was 37 per cent. Firms in high-technology industries in Indonesia are more likely to train their workers than those in low-technology sectors. Export-oriented enterprises in the chemical sector in Taiwan, China, are three times more likely to invest in training than those producing for the domestic sector, and six-times more likely than the average Taiwanese textile firm. Export orientation, the pace of technological change, the education of the work force, and economic cycles and growth prospects all appear to determine a firm's willingness to train its workers.

If training is in the interest of both workers and employers, and in market economies takes place in response to underlying economic circumstances, should governments get involved? Governments should intervene in the market for training if there are particular market failures or imperfections, or to pursue goals other than economic efficiency. As with general education, individuals may underinvest in training because of lack of information or credit market failures, or because spillover effects drive a wedge between private and social returns. However, at least in the case of within-firm training, many of these problems form investing in skills.

When the level of skills in the labour marker is low, firms may invest too little in training despite prospective returns that would justify the investment, for fear that their workers, once trained, will find other employment. How great a problem this is remains unknown. Where returns to training have been high, as in the Republic of Korea, firms still invested in training despite employee turnover that, throughout the 1970s and well into the 1980s, often amounted to 5 or 6 per cent of the manufacturing work force leaving their employers every month.

Lack of training may also result from labour market regulations — including high minimum wages and rules governing job ladders within firms — that prevent firms from paying lower wages to trainees or restrict the placement of trained workers. In Mexico, federal labour legislation placing strict seniority-based rules on promotion reduces the incentive to train workers. The ideal solution would be to remove these policy constraints; failing that, alternatives.

By how much does Education Raise Wages?

In every country, workers with more education tend to earn more than workers with less education. Detailed statistical analyses of the studies confirm a positive association between wages and schooling for both men and women. The association was found both in economies that were growing (Indonesia and Thailand) and in those with falling in per capita (Cote d'Ivoire, Peru, and Slovenia).

The wage premium associated with education varies from country to country and appears related to the relative scarcity of educated — higher rewards where educated workers are in high demand (Thailand) or low supply (Cote d'Ivoire), lower rewards where educated workers are relatively abundant (Slovenia and the United States). The wage premium also depends on the level of education — among the low- and middle-income countries in the figure, the wage ratio between secondary and primary school graduates exceeds that between secondary and primary school graduates exceeds that between primary graduates and those with no schooling in all but one case. Wage premiums to education are sometimes higher for women than for men (in Indonesia, Peru, and Thailand, for example). This does not mean that women earn more than men, but only that the economic return to their schooling can be higher.

Information about what skills are in demand in the presence of scale economies in training are other government involvement. These constraints sought particularly relevant within the informal sector, but on-the-job training is common there, especially in the form of traditional apprenticeship schemes. A recent survey of workers in Ghanaian small-scale manufacturing found that 44 per cent of workers had been trained as apprentices in their fields, and that 52 per cent of firms were training apprentices at the time of the survey. Studies in other countries confirm that skill deficiencies are rarely cited as a major problem confronting small-scale entrepreneurs.

Training in the informal sector may be sufficient for perpetuating current activities, but lack of knowledge about marketing, new technologies, and general business skills may constrain the expansion of informal sector firms. Training services targeted at small enterprises and aimed at remedying these deficiencies have shown some promise. One example is Mexicos' Multiple Support Service Program (known by its Spanish acronym CIMO), which provides technical assistance and training services to micro and small enterprises. Numerous case studies document cost-effective improvements in productivity and increases in employment and profitability among CIMO participants. The scope for replicating and expanding such programs, however, is limited. For many public interventions aimed at microenterprises, costs are high because of program administrative expenses and the high failure rate of small enterprises.

In many countries, governments use training to address such problems as low skill levels among the employed work force, high youth unemployment, displacement of workers during economy-wide transitions, and the structural unemployment and poverty associated with disadvantaged workers. But whether public expenditures on training are warranted depends on the underlying cause of the problem, and on the opportunity cost of public resources.

Low work force skill levels appear to be less the result of failures in the market for training than of a generally low level of labour demand. The same may hold true for youth unemployment. But the rationale for government involvement in training displaced workers is more compelling. Displacement due to major economic transitions or aggregate shocks may call for government support of retraining, because of absent markets, excessive risk, and the need to ensure social stability and public support for the broader reform program; unfortunately, the direct economic benefits often are limited.

Enterprise-led training is usually the most-effective means of developing worker skills. By comparison, government delivery in most countries, in state-sponsored training centers and especially in vocational education, has proved expensive and often has provided trainees with few marketable skills. Ways must be found to reorient public training institutions to respond to consumer and market demands. The best way is often to shift public financing from providers of training to the demand side of the market, enabling targeted workers to purchase training within a competitive environment of alternative suppliers.

This shift has happened in some Latin American countries. Training institutions had been guaranteed financing from payroll levies to perform reemployment training, even though frequently they were unable to place their graduates. But with the right incentives many of these same institutions have evolved and now sell valued services directly to private enterprises and individuals. Chile's use of training vouchers for workers and tax credits for employers is one example of successful reform in this area. Vouchers are distributed to targeted groups — young, unemployed workers, usually women. At the same time, rights to offer training courses are auctioned by a government agency to a competitive market of training organisations, both public and private; their cost recovery is conditional on a minimum rate of trainees finding jobs after completing training. In this way the burden of designing successful training programs is shifted to where it belongs — the training institutions themselves.

Private training provides are also emerging in the transitional economies of Eastern Europe and Asia, for example in foreign language, education, and computer skills. Prior to the transition all training institutions were public, and few were oriented to the new skills required by a modern market economy. Government can support private sector initiatives by removing prohibitions on the private supply of training: price controls on tuition fees, excessive regulation of curricula, and competition with subsidized public institutions all limit the private sector's response.

Households and firms need an environment that encourages good decision-making with respect to investing in skills. What should governments do? Where private returns to human capital are high but the investments are not being undertaken, government must first try to understand why before designing and implementing interventions, especially pricing strategies. In primary education, free public provision usually makes sense, to reap the gains to society as a whole and reach the poor. But for most other human resources programs, free provision more often is not justified. Especially in the area of training, governments should focus more on financing and less on production. Government intervention, whatever its form, should avoid benefiting the privileged few. The highest priority should be placed on investing in children, because their health, nutrition, and basic education are the foundation of a nation's future.

One of the central and legitimate purposes of modern management and business is the development of people by providing the right environment where the individual may grow to his fullest stature and realise his fullest potentialities. Development of people is a specialised function and is one of the fundamental operative functions of personnel administration, though the responsibility for the training and development of people rests with the line management. In the development and growth of people lies the organisational growth and progress.

In our century the great issue facing not only the industrially developed nations but also the fast developing nations is the problem of change and combating this problem of change and adapting to change the primary concern of thinking individuals. Change, that is induced by business and industry through science and technology, demands rapid individual and social adjustment and it renders obsolete, products and processes, skills and attitudes and with them men and jobs. Meeting this challenge of change is a necessary responsibility of management.

The above two challenges facing management and business are met by manpower training and development programmes offered in a company by the personnel administration staff. In a Voice of America broadcast the Training Director of Lockheed Aircraft Company in California, U.S.A. observed that in 1965 out of their

22,000 work-force, as many as 16,000 underwent some sort of training programme within the company or without all through the year.[1] Formerly Lockheed used to have a training programme once in three years; but now they feel that the aerospace technology is advancing so fast that without continuous training and development programmes, many of the employees will be rendered obsolete. The company counsellor may recommend some course to some people and many others may take courses on their own within the company or without. The company offers a tuition aid or tuition reimbursement programme whereby all or a part of the course expense will be met by the company.

In developing countries like ours, there is a great demand for trained personnel at all levels and this is created by the tremendous growth in number, size, and complexity of industrial organisations in recent years. There is a need for industrial and business organisations to conduct their own programmes and an increasing number of firms is recognising the training needs of their personnel and are sponsoring a variety of programmes to meet these needs. Lawrence Appley has maintained that the basic objective of the personnel executive is to assist the entire organisation from top to bottom in bringing about an improvement in knowledge, skill, habits, and attitudes that will ultimately express itself productively in work and constructively in human relations.[2]

The essential purpose of training is to develop that knowledge and those skills and attitudes, which contribute to the welfare of the company and employees. Further, all training programmes aim at making the employees more effective and productive on their present jobs and increasing their potential on higher level jobs.

The importance and the problem of training in U.S.A. is expressed by some personnel experts:[3]

"Training is a widely accepted problem-solving device. Indeed, our national superiority in manpower productivity can be attributed in no small measure to the success of our educational and industrial training programs. This success has been accompanied by a tendency in many quarters to regard training as a panacea. It is almost traditional in America to believe that if something is good, more of the thing is even better. Hence, we take more vitamin pills to solve personal health problems and more training to solve our manpower problems. Over and/or underemphasis on training stem largely from inadequate recognition and determination of training needs and objectives. They stem also from lack of the professional nature and professional techniques of modern industrial training."

Manpower training and development is discussed under the following sections:

1. H.R.D. Training Needs and Objectives.
2. H.R.D. Training Responsibility and Organisation
3. H.R.D. Training Principles.
4. H.R.D. Training — Types and Techniques.
5. H.R.D. Management Development.
6. Organisation Development.
7. Training Evaluation.

1. H.R.D. TRAINING NEEDS AND OBJECTIVES

Training is no panacea to all manpower problems and so it is necessary to establish where it would be useful and where it would meet a problematic situation. When a new high school graduate is hired, there is a need to give him some sort of on-the-job training so that he may be effective and productive. When a college graduate is hired to sell, there is a need to give him some sort of sales training. When a new machine is brought into the organisation, the people, who are going to work on this machine may need some training. There are many industrial and business problems or situations when training and development programmes will be of great use. In modern business, there are various changes — job changes, organisation changes, method changes, changes in personnel, changes in the volume of business etc., that are constantly taking place and that necessitate modification of understanding, attitudes, and skills on the part of the personnel. They create needs that may be met by training and only needs that can be met by training are training needs.

Professor John F. Mee indicates how training needs can be located in the figure 7.1 and indicates the training programmes required to meet some typical problems.

The following formula is suggested to indicate the specific training needs:

Training Needs = Job Requirement – Employee's Present Job Skills

This indicates that there is a need for careful job analysis and job specification and a careful analysis of the individual employees. A survey of overall training needs of an organisation may be conducted periodically with the active support to top management. There may be a few doubting Thomases, who may just pay lip-service to training, who may think it is just another personnel gimmick and it is of no practical value to the organisation at all. They must be converted by pointing out the specific results of training. And that training is a practical necessity which results in the reduction of waste and spoilage, improvement of methods, reduction of absenteeism and labour turnover, reduction of learning time, reduction of supervisory burden, reduction of machine maintenance costs, reduction of grievances, improvement of quality, encouragement of upgrading, reduction in accident rate, improvement of communications, improvement of morale, and improvement of efficiency and productivity. Some methods of determining training needs are through job analysis, tests, morale and attitude surveys, personnel audits, activity analysis etc.

Table 7.1
HRD Needs Identification

Training Needs Reported by	*Nature of Typical Problems*	*Corrective Form of Training*
	PERSONNEL PROBLEMS Supervisors	Supervisor training
Employees and Personnel Department	Supervisors pass the buck; lack of authority	Presupervisory training
	No clear-cut job definition (Responsibilities poor — overlap)	Management training Aid-operator training Role-playing, leadership conference
Compared Production Report	Failure to meet production standards	Improved consultation and communication
Grievance Analysis	Poor leadership — favouritism — unfair decisions	

	EMPLOYEES	
Written personnel Form	Job carelessness — absence of job pride	Orientation training Personnel department memos Public address system
	Poor co-operation — cliques — gossip — rumours	General education — attitude training
Supervision Observation	Excessive number of complaints and grievances	Supervisor training — general education
Supervision Reports and Comments	Ignorance of policy — Uncertainty and misunderstanding of policy	Orientation training and conference
Company Grievance	Experience Limitations of new and old employees	Operator training — general education
	Number of job transfer requests. False and unproven claims of job attitudes	Improved placement orientation training Job training — general education
	Over-all job dissatisfaction	General education — attitude training
	Skill limitations of local area Labour market	Job training — technical conference — I.C.S.
	High labour turnover	
Production Forms	Employee insecurity and job uncertainty	General education — supervisory training
	Employee questions — individual sessions	General education attitude training — role playing
	Inability to interpret business data	
	Personality conflicts	
	PRODUCTION PROBLEMS	
Department Heads Supervisors	Delivery delays — poor rating	Supervisory Training Conference
Production Records Operator Charts	Scheduling errors — wrong parts	Demonstration training Safety tours
Monthly Department Reports	Poorly inspected parts	Orientation training
	Poor housekeeping — congested aisles	Technical engineering training
	No classification of job duties	
Production Charts	Skill limitations — limited technical "know-how"	Operator training Production conference
Rework Sheets	Work defective — work not upto standard	Quality conference
	Failure to meet production schedules	
Salvage Costs	High rate of work spoilage	
	Scarcity of skilled job applicants	
Budget	High unit costs — new equipment — re-engineered jobs	Business training
	SAFETY PROBLEMS	
Medical Records	Shop housekeeping poor	Safety conferences
Accident Reports Safety Committee	No appreciation of job hazards	Employee orientation
Sickness Reports Meetings Fire Loss	Safety equipment ignored, not used	Safety tours
	QUALITY PROBLEMS	
Sales Records Customers	Too much rework — work not up to inspection standards	Conferences

Fig. 7.1 Training Needs Locator.

Source: John F. Mee *Personnel Handbook*, pp. 960-61.

Identification of Training Needs in a Leading Corporation

With a view to organising management development on systematic lines the corporation appointed a task force comprising the senior line management executives and personnel executives to conduct a training needs survey and to formulate a management plan based on the survey.

The Objectives of the Study

The objectives were as follows:

1. To conduct training needs survey of selective sample in respect of Dy. Managers, Officers, Senior Assistants and Junior Assistants and Departmental Assistants in different functions;
2. To identify their needs of training and development keeping in view their present assignments as well as the potential;
3. To suggest the broad outline of formal in-group and out-group training and development programmes to meet their needs.

Methodology

The task force conducted the survey using a questionnaire based on training by objectives model and interviewed the chief executives, the managers and the heads of the department. The chief executives pointed out the broad organisational objectives/needs, group objectives/needs, problem solving objectives/needs, regular training objectives/needs and the innovative and training objectives/needs. The manager of the unit indicated the unit level training needs and the needs of the individuals reporting to him. The heads of the departments specified the department level needs and the needs of all individuals from deputies to departmental assistants under them. Suggestions were solicited from them regarding training and development plan in general and post training and follow-up in particular. As a result of this survey the task force identified: (1) The organisational objectives, (2) Problems solving objectives, (3) Regular training objectives, (4) Innovative training objectives, (5) Unit level objectives, and (6) Individual training and development objectives.

In the light of these needs the task force formulated a five-year management development plan which was approved by their central management and was put into operation.

An Overview of the Methodologies: There are a variety of methods in order to identify and determine the needs of training and development of individuals. We shall briefly cover each one of them.[4]

Methods of Determining Needs

1. ***Analysis of an Activity (Process, Job, Operation):*** To list as steps in a logical sequence the activities involved in producing a product or service, or part thereof, and determine what new knowledge or skill is called for or present knowledge or skill is to be modified.
2. ***Analysis of Problems:*** To analyse problems and determine what additional skills, knowledge or insight is required to handle it.
3. ***Analysis of Behaviour:*** To analyse typical behaviour by individuals or groups and determine the corrective action involving training.

4. ***Analysis of an Organisation:*** To analyse organisational weaknesses to produce clues to training needs, both individual and group.
5. ***Appraisal of Performance:*** To analyse performance and determine if someone should get something, be it additional knowledge, skill or understanding.
6. ***Brainstorming:*** To bring together a homogeneous group and to ask individuals in the group to call out any ideas they have for answering a "how to" question and identify items which call for additional knowledge, skill, or attitude.
7. ***Buzzing:*** To ask an audience of supervisors, managers, professional personnel, or others (as long as it is homogeneous) can be given a question such as, "what are desirable next steps in our training," or "what additional areas of knowledge (or skill or understanding) do we need to handle our work better."
8. ***Card Sort:*** To write statements or potential training needs on cards; hand them over to the person whose ideas are sought to arrange these cards in what he feels is their order of importance for him.
9. ***Checklist:*** To break down a job, process, program, activity, or area of responsibility into a list of detailed parts or steps arranged in logical sequence and check off by each individual the items about which he feels he would like to have more skill or knowledge.
10. ***Committee:*** To constitute an advisory committee composed of persons responsible for, or with a direct interest in, an activity to identify training needs.
11. ***Comparison:*** To compare what an individual is doing (or contemplates doing) with what others are doing or have done to learn about new ways to handle old problems, keep up to date on new techniques and procedures, fight his own obsolescence.
12. ***Conference:*** To identify training needs and make decisions on ways these needs will be met in a conference of persons concerned with an operating problem.
13. ***Consultants:*** To employ outside consultants to determine training needs and develop ways to meet them.
14. ***Counselling:*** To discuss between a training practitioner and a person seeking guidance regarding ways he can improve his on-the-job performance or prepare for advancement.
15. ***In-basket:*** To measure or test a manager's ability to handle some of the day-to-day challenges which come to him in writing in his "inbox" from various sources.
16. ***Incident Pattern:*** To note in terms of success or failure, the responses to special situations and to study the pattern of deviation.
17. ***Information Talks:*** To meet and talk informally with people for finding clues to training needs.

18. ***Interviews:*** To arrange a formal meeting with the person or group concerned employing the interview technique.
19. ***Observation:*** To observe such things as may have value as indicators of training needs, especially needs which are just under-the-surface or emerging.
20. ***Problem Clinic:*** To arrange meetings of a homogeneous group to discuss a common problem and develop a solution.
21. ***Research:*** To identify implications for training and development as a result of research.
22. ***Role Playing:*** To get clues to his training needs in a skill, an area of knowledge, or in understanding or attitude by observing how each role player acts in a role playing situation.
23. ***Self-analysis:*** To self-evaluate and know what is needed in theory of additional knowledge, skill, or insight.
24. ***Simulation:*** To analyse performance in simulation exercise to reveal individual and/or group training needs.
25. ***Skills Inventory:*** To establish and annually update an inventory of the skills of their employees and to identify gaps or blind spots in reserve or stand-by skills.
26. ***Slip Writing:*** To write on a slip the type of training needed and analyse the information on these slips.
27. ***Studies:*** To undertake studies which can turn up training needs which will have to be met if the plans are adopted.
28. ***Surveys:*** To undertake surveys that can be used to take inventory of operations, employee attitudes, implications of advanced planning etc.
29. ***Tests:*** To perform tests to measure skill, knowledge or attitude and to identify gaps.
30. ***Task Force:*** To constitute a task force which, in analysing the problem may unearth training needs which must be met before their recommended solution to the problem can be implemented.
31. ***Questionnaire:*** To develop a questionnaire to elicit information which can be used to determine training needs, delimit the scope of the training, identify course content etc.
32. ***Workshop:*** To identify in a workshop the need for further understanding or insight about organisation goals or operations.

Sources of Training Need Information

Clues to training needs can come from a number of written sources. Even such sources as complaints, requests, suggestions, while usually oral at first, should be reduced to writing if they are to be used as a basis for determining training needs. The discipline of writing makes the information more precise and useful and of course official. Some of the methods described earlier produce written sources — studies and surveys for instance. However, for our purpose here, we consider written materials already in existence. Some sources for the same are:

1. Articles
2. Books
3. Case Studies
4. Complaints
5. Crises
6. Experience of others
7. Factual Data
8. Grievances
9. Plans
10. Policies
11. Records
12. Reports
13. Requests
14. Statements
15. Suggestions
16. Symptoms
17. Other Sources.

Case Study of: Training Needs Survey — GM Group — 1987-1988

Rudrabasavaraj presents a case study of GM training Needs Survey and Human Resource Plan for 1987-88.

As per the advice of Bapak Hari Darmawan, a training Needs Survey was conducted by Prof. M.N. Rudrabasavaraj in the Matahari group from December 29th to February 20th for a period of 93 consulting hours.

Objectives of the Survey

1. To identify the training and Development needs of the employees in:
   (i) The Store
   (ii) Super Bazars
   (iii) Head Office
2. To develop a Human Resource Training & Development Plan for 1987-1988.
3. To assist in the implementation of HRD Plan in 1987-1988.

Nature and Scope

The Consultant conducted personal interviews with the following Division Heads, Department Heads, Managers of Stores and Managers of Super Bazars with the help of a questionnaire to identify the Training and Development needs of their suggestions to meet the objectives of Training and Development.

Stores

1.	Bp. Ronny H. Hidayat	Store Operation Manager Head Office
2.	Bp. Freddy Zakaria	Store Manager MDS Ps. Baru
3.	Bp. Jozef Budi Prakasa	Regional Manager Jak-sel & Bogor
4.	Bp. Djoko Sutrisno	Regional Manager Jak-pus & Jak-tim
5.	Bp. Fandawan Ramali	Regional Manager Bonding
6.	Bp. Glenn Yahya	Store Manager MDS Surabaya
7.	Bp. Mulyana Adi Saputra	Store Manager MDS Hayam Wuruk Plaza
8.	Bp. V. Hutomo Santoso	Store Manager MDS Ratu Plaza
9.	Bp. Wahyudi Hidayat	Store Manager MDS Melawai
10.	Bp. Eddy Effendi Irawan	Store Manager Ps. Busana JP
11.	Bp. Budi Mulyono Saliman	Store Manager Sinar Matahari Bogor
12.	Ibu Endah Sulistyawati	Store Manager MMF Bandung
13.	Ibu Evie Sulvia	Store Manager MMF Senen

Super Bazaars

1.	Bp. Setyadi Surya	Regional Manager Super Bazaar
2.	Bp. Bambang Winarto	Store Manager Super Bazaar 120-122
3.	Mr. Koh Boon Kim	Consultant

Head Office

1.	Bp. Lukman Djatisutikno	Gen. Ass. to the Pres. Dir.
2.	Bp. M. Th. Soemargono	Manager SDM
3.	Bp. Hengky Citra	Finance & Accounting Manager
4.	Bp. Sumedi Surjadi	Internal Audit Manager
5.	Bp. Harry Kurniawan	Accounting Manager
6.	Bp. Hermanto	Warehouse Koordination
7.	Bp. Petrus Gunawan	General Affair Manager
8.	Bp. John Mampuk	Promotion Manager
9.	Ibu Tina Iskandar K.	Tr. & Dev./SDM

Recommendation for Action

A. First, we must continue the following basic programs for all new employees at all levels before they are placed on the job:

1. Basic Salesmanship program for Pramuniaga
2. Basic Counter Chief Development program for Counter Chief
3. Basic Cashier Development program for Cashiers
4. Basic Junior Supervisory program for new Supervisors
5. Basic Management program for Senior Supervisors (with potential)
6. Basic Store Managers program for new Store managers
7. Management Development program for Senior Managers
8. Faculty Development program for Prospective Faculty.

B. Secondly, we need to provide continuing professional training, development and education for all personnel with a view:

1. Upgrading skills, knowledge and attitudes
2. Updating with new knowledge, habits and attitudes
3. Refreshers and continuously improving professional development.

The following training and development plan is recommended for action in 1987-1988.

In addition to Matahari Group HRD effort, we recommend that we depute our Senior Staff to external programs on a selective basis in the country and outside the country.

STORES

Chart 3
TRAINING & DEVELOPMENT PLAN 1987-1988
BASED ON TRAINING NEEDS SURVEY JAN-FEB 1987

No.	Groups (1)	Needs (2)	Program (3)	Faculty (4)	Days and Dates (5)	
1.	Pramuniaga	— Upgrading & updating selling skills	Selling techniques-1	M.N.R., SDM & Store Managers	2 days	20 × 80 = 1600
		— Refreshers	Understanding the Customer	M.N.R., SDM & Store managers	2 days	
		— Lack of knowledge of merchandise	Merchandising knowledge	Merchandising Division (visit to suppliers fabric)	1 day	
			Improving Customer service-1	M.N.R., SDM & Store Managers	2 days	
2.	Cashiers	— Upgrading & updating Customer service skills	Customer service-1	M.N.R., SDM	2 days	3 × 80 = 240
		— Refreshers in Accounting	Understanding the Customer	M.N.R., SDM	2 days	
		— Improving skills	Basic Accounting	Accounting Division & SDM	2 days	
			Credit cards	Store Managers, Regional Managers	1 day	
			Selling techniques	M.N.R., SDM & Store Managers	2 days	
3.	Counter Chief/Jr. Supervisors	— Upgrading & updating Supervisory skills	Leadership	M.N.R., SDM & Stores Managers	2 days	5 × 80 = 400
		— Knowledge of Merchandising	Merchandising knowledge	Merchandising Division (visit to Suppliers Fabric)	2 days	
		— Improving Customer services	Customers services	M.N.R., SDM & Store Managers	2 days	
			Understanding the customer	M.N.R., SDM & Store Managers	2 days	
			Selling techniques-1	M.N.R., Store Managers, Regional Managers	2 days	

(1)	(2)	(3)	(4)		(5)
4. Supervisors	— Upgrading & updating supervisory skills - 1	Role & responsibilities Checklist & activities	M.N.R., SDM, Regional Managers, S.O. Manager	3 days	3 × 40 = 120
	— Upgrading Merchandise of knowledge	Merchandising knowledge	Merchandising Division (visit to Suppliers Fabric)	2 days	
	— Customer service skills-1	Customer Service-1 Understanding the customer	M.N.R., SDM, Regional Managers, S.O. Manager	2 days	
	— Skills of Motivation	Motivation	M.N.R., SDM, Regional Managers, S.O. Manager	2 days	
5. Store Managers,	— Upgrading & updating Managerial skills - 1	Changing role & responsibilities of store manager	M.N.R., SDM & Regional Managers	2 days	
		Understanding the Customer & Customer service	M.N.R., SDM, S.O. Manager, President Director	3 days	
	— Knowledge of Merchandising	Strategy of merchandising	M.N.R., SDM & S.O. Manager	3 days	
	— Leadership skills	Leadership	Merchandising Division	2 days	
	— Refresher	Management theory & Practice	M.N.R., SDM & PD	2 days	
			M.N.R.	3 days	
	— Motivating skills	Motivation	M.N.R.	2 days	
	— Marketing skills	Marketing Management	M.N.R. & GF	3 days	
6. Regional Managers Division Managers	— Upgrading & updating	Management theory & Practice	M.N.R. & Guest Faculty (GF)	3 days	
	— Refresher	Understanding the customer	M.N.R.	3 days	
	— Merchandising skills				
	— Enrichment skills	Strategies of Merchandising	Merchandising Division & GF	3 days	
		Management Development-2	M.N.R. & GF	3 days	
		Role & responsibilities systems & manuals			
	— Improving coordination skills	Meeting on coordination	M.N.R. & S.O. Manager	1 day	

(1)	(2)	(3)	(4)	(5)
7. Security Staff	— Upgrading & updating security skills	Fire prevention & Evacuation procedure	M.N.R. & GA	2 days
	— Customer service skills-1	Understanding Customer & Customer service	M.N.R., Store managers, Regional Managers	2 days
8. Kebersihan	Basic skills	Kebersihan, keindahan & ketertiban	M.N.R., GAS, Store Managers	2 days
	Customer service skills - 1	Understanding the Customer & customer service		2 days
9. Staff in MDS Surabaya	Knowledge business philosophy	Matahari Philosophy	M.N.R. & Pres. Dir.	1 day
10. Staff in Bandung	Knowledge & business Philosophy	Matahari Philosophy	M.N.R. & Pres. Dir.	1 day
11. Pramuniaga & Cashier in Bogor	Stock taking skills	Stock check (physical & continuous)	M.N.R., Gudang, & Store Managers	2 days
12. Staff	English speaking skills	Bahasa Inggris - Business Communication	M.N.R. & AEI	3 hours/2days a week

HEAD OFFICE

Chart 4

TRAINING & DEVELOPMENT PLAN 1987-1988

No.	*Division/Dept. Groups* (1)	*Needs* (2)	*Program* (3)	*Faculty* (4)	*Days & Dates* (5)
1.	Merchandising Division	— Upgrading & updating technical skills	Merchandising knowledge	Merchandising Division	2 days
		— Refresher	Strategies of Merchandising	Merchandising Division Consultant	3 days
		— Customer service skills	Understanding the Customer & his needs	M.N.R. & Consultant (MD)	3 days
		— Marketing skills	Marketing Management	M.N.R. & GF	3 days
	Head of Dept., Head of MD A1-A7	— External programs on Marketing Management & Retail Merchandising			
		— Coordination skills	Meeting between Merchandising Division & Store Manager, Regional Managers, S.O. Manager	M.N.R. & Consultant	1 day
		— Negotiating skills	Skills of Negotiation	MD Consultant	
2.	Internal Audit Division	— Upgrading & updating	Management Audit	SDM & GF	3 days
		— Refresher	Operations/efficiency Audit	SDM & GF (External program)	
		— Refresher	Understanding the customer & his needs	M.N.R. & Regional Managers & S.O. Manager	2 days
			Retail Management	M.N.R. Reg. Manager, SDM & Pres. Dir.	2 days
3.	Finance Division	— Upgrading & updating	Finance Management	SDM & GF	3 days
		— Budgeting & Planning skills	Operation Budget & Performance Review	M.N.R. & GF	3 days

(1)	(2)	(3)	(4)	(5)
Supervisors	— Supervisory skills	Capital budgets	M.N.R. & GF	3 days
Accounting Staff	— Accounting skills & knowledge	Basic Management	External programs	3 days
		Basic Accounting	M.N.R., Finance, SDM	5 days
	— Computer skills	Advance Accounting	Finace & Acct. Division	
Senior staff	— Upgrading English	Computerised Accounting	External programs	3 days
	Business communication skills	Business Communication in English	M.N.R. & GF	3 hours
			M.N.R. & AEI	2 days/week
4. Gudang Dept.	— Upgrading & updating for Staff (below Kepala Seksi)	Stores & Inventory Control	SDM & Gudang & GF	4 days
	— Refresher for Head of Gudang & Kepala Seksi	Inventory Management		3 days
		Management & Distribution Center	M.N.R., MD Consultant, GF	
	Deputation to External Programs			
	— Supervisory skills for Kepala Seksi	Basic Management	Ext. M.N.R., SDM, MD	3 days
	— Staff Expedisi	Administration of Expedisi	Ext. SDM, MD, Gudang	2 days
5. Promotion Dept.	— Upgrading skills in promotion	Sales Promotion	M.N.R., Promotion, MD, GF	3 days
			External Programs	
	— Technical skills in graphic design printing display		"	
6. Gen. Affair Dept.	— Technical skills for: 1. Electricians	Electrical preventive Maintenance	SDM, GA & GF	2 days
	2. Drivers 3. Security	Technical care & maintenance (Discussed in Stores)	"	2 days

(1)	(2)	(3)	(4)	(5)
	External skills programs			
7. Sumber Days Manusia	— Upgrading & updating	Modern Human Resource Management	M.N.R. & GF	3 days
	— Technical skills	Job evaluation & Compensation system	M.N.R. & GF	2 days
		Man-power planning	M.N.R. & GF	2 days
		Organisation design & structure	M.N.R. & GF	3 days
		Curriculum development	M.N.R. & GF	3 days
	External Programs			
8. Business Planning & Development	— Upgrading & updating	Modern project-Management	External programs	
		Computer design layout		
		Estate Management		
9. Decoration Dept.	— Upgrading & updating	Modern decoration & Store ambience Management	External programs	
	— Technical skills	Designing & Fixtures		
10. Public Relations & Customer Service Dept.	— Upgrading & updating	Retail Management	External programs	3 days
		Understanding Customer & his needs & customer service	M.N.R. & GF	
11. All H.O. Sr. Staff	— Upgrading skills in planning	Corporate planning	M.N.R. & GF	3 days
12. "		SWOT Analysis	M.N.R. & GF	3 days
13. "	— Upgrading Managerial skills	How to improve managerial performance	M.N.R. & GF	3 days
14. "	"	Raj's Human Growth dynamics	M.N.R.	3 days
15. "	"	Time Management	M.N.R.	2 days

Chart 5
SUPER BAZAARS
TRAINING & DEVELOPMENT PLAN 1987-1988

No.	Groups (1)	Needs (2)	Program (3)	Faculty (4)	Days & Dates (5)
1.	Managers - SB	— New Orientation and skills managerial and technical	MG Super Bazaar management	M.N.R., Mr. Koh, RMS, PD	3 days
		— Improving customer services	Understanding the Customer * improving customer advice	M.N.R., Mr. Koh, RMS	3 days
		— Skills in merchandising	Strategies of merchandising	MD, Mr. Koh, RMS	2 days
		— Skills Management	Management theory & practice	M.N.R., Mr. Koh	
			Marketing management	M.N.R., Mr. Koh, RMS	3 days
2.	Supervisors	— New orientation & skills	MG Super bazaar management	M.N.R., Mr. Koh, RMS, PD	3 days
		— Supervisory skills	Basic management	M.N.R., Mr. Koh, RMS	3 days
		— Improving customer service	Merchandising Customer	M.N.R., Mr. Koh, RMS	
			Improving customer service		
		— Merchandising skills	Strategies of merchandising	MD, Mr. Koh, RMS	3 days
		— Leadership skills	Leadership		
3.	Pramuniaga	— Selling skills	Basic salesmanship in super bazaars	M.N.R., Mr. Koh, RMS	3 days
		— Customer service	Understanding the customer & improving customer service-1	M.N.R., Mr. Koh, RMS	3 days
			Stock check		
		— Stock managing skills	Product knowledge	M.N.R., Mr. Koh, RMS, SMS	3 days
		— Knowledge of merchandising	(visit to supplier company)	Mr. Koh, RMS, SMS	3 days
4.	Cashiers	— Customer service	Understanding the customer & customer service	MD, Mr. Koh, RMS, SMS	3 days
		— Technical skills	Basic Accounting	M.N.R., Mr. Koh, RMS	3 days
		— Selling skills	Basic salesmanship	Fin. & Acct. Division	3 days
				Mr. Koh, RMS, SMS	
				M.N.R., Mr. Koh, RMS	3 days

Training Objectives

Training policy should be established by top management, who may ask the personnel administrator to advise the line management on framing policies. The personnel executive should evolve policies that reflect the primary and secondary objectives of the management. Determining the basic objectives of the organisation, determining which of these objectives can be met through training and reducing these objectives to specific programmes are important functions of personnel division. Generally training objectives and policy formulation must be able to provide answer to the following questions:

1. What do you want and hope to accomplish through training?
2. Whose responsibility is training?
3. Is training to be formal or informal?
4. What are your priorities in training?
5. What types of training do you need?
6. When and where shall training be given?
7. Shall training be continuous or continual?
8. How much do you wish to pay employees in training?
9. What outside agencies will be associated with training?
10. How is training related to your labour policy?

Training policy, objectives and goals must be thought through carefully and stated before instituting a training programme.

2. H.R.D. TRAINING RESPONSIBILITY AND ORGANISATION

Responsibility for training and development rests with the top management. That does not mean that the individual employees have no responsibility at all; on the contrary acquisition of any skill or knowledge is largely dependent on the receptivity of the individual and his willingness and eagerness to learn and this is a matter of self-development. Further, all the other levels of management are equally responsible for the success of a training programme, for their co-operation and interest is essential. Through training and development programmes management provides an opportunity to the employees to improve their skills, attitudes and knowledge.

Because of the expertise and specialist know-how required to organise training and development programme the personnel administrators are asked to evolve the training programmes and conduct them with the help of the line management. The line organisation must be 'sold' on training and Andrew Daly makes the following suggestions to attain this purpose:[5]

We have all many methods of improving the attitude of the line organisation towards training. Among the means I recognise are:

1. Invite them to visit or participate in training programs.
2. Select them as conference leaders or instructors.
3. Contact them for assistance in program planning, based on their experience.
4. Organise a training committee from the line organisation to recommend, plan and evaluate programs.

5. Distribute copies of programs and the results of training activities.
6. Route papers, professional journals or books containing items of interest to them.
7. Invite them to attend conferences or meetings of professional organisations.
8. Invite them to visit other business organisations with successful training programs.
9. Prepare proposed programs to serve the need of their operations.
10. Visit with them and discuss training methods and activities.
11. Publicise training activities through the house organ.
12. Initiate training in areas where management is receptive to training. Start all programs with a pilot group.
13. Show better quality and quantity of products at lowered costs.

Now in U.S.A. Robert R. Blake and Jane S. Mouton point out in recent Grid Team Training programmes that an unusual feature is the use of trained line managers from the company, rather than behavioural scientists as in T-group approach, for laboratory trainers. As they point out "when the organisation members take responsibility for such teaching, they also feel increased responsibility for seeing to it that the learning is used in work."[6]

Training Organisation Principles

There are certain general principles to be considered while organising a training programme. The National Industrial Conference Board lists the following training organisation principles:[7]

1. The purpose of training is to help meet company objectives by providing opportunities for employees at all organisational levels to acquire the requisite knowledge, skills and attitudes.
2. The first step in training is to determine needs and objectives.
3. The objectives and scope of a training plan should be defined before its development is begun in order to provide a basis for common agreement and co-operative action.
4. The techniques and processes of a training program should be related directly to the needs and objectives.
5. Training is properly the responsibility of anyone in management who has a need or objective to be reached.
6. The function of training personnel is to assist line management in the determination of training needs, and in the development, administration, conduct and follow-up of training plans.
7. To be effective, training must use the tested principles of learning. (These principles are discussed in psychological texts under such headings as: individual differences, best learning rates, learning by doing, mind set, morale and motivation, the whole person, and group dynamics.)
8. Training should be conducted in the actual job environment to the maximum extent practical.

Steps to follow in Setting up the Training Programme

Richard Crow of the United States Rubber Company provides the following outline of steps in the organisation for training:[8]

1. Classify the phases of the job involved.
2. Outline the background knowledge.
3. Develop skill breakdown or procedure outlines.
4. Prepare written programme.
5. Determine training method and location.
6. Review plan with key supervision and top management.
7. Train instructors.
8. Outline the basis of trainee selection.
9. Develop evaluation and follow-up plan.

The scope of the training programme will depend upon the size and resources of the organisation. For many of the companies in India, although there is a great need for training employees at various levels of the organisation, the financial resources come in the way of organising a programme, whereas some companies have many well-organised training programmes for their employees.

Mistakes to be Avoided

A word of caution is appropriate in the organisation of training programmes. They must guard against (1) overtraining, (2) use of poor instructors, (3) too much training on skills not needed on the job, (4) imitation of other company training programmes, (5) misuse of testing techniques, (6) inadequate tools and equipment for required training, and (7) overreliance on slides, or films or lectures, and not enough on practice.

One company has an interesting method to find out what is wrong with its training programme. Trainees are asked to write down their 'gripes' and these are classified and analysed in order to rectify the training mistakes and problems.

3. H.R.D. TRAINING PRINCIPLES

Unwarranted and enormous waste can result by the usage of improper training methods and techniques. There are certain basic principles of industrial training built upon the principles of learning. In Zen Buddhism the master tells his disciple: "First empty your cup. Then I will pour tea." First of all you must be ready to learn and that readiness to learn is greatly dependent upon your emptying of all your half-knowledge, prejudices, bias, likes, and dislikes about the subject you are going to learn. If you assume the attitude, "Oh! well, what is there in this operation (or job) to learn" your ability to learn is strictly limited. Next, you must have an open mind, not a closed mind. You must be receptive to new ideas, suggestions, views — in short, new learning. Any individual, who believes that he knows everything worth knowing and what he does not know is not worth knowing, is a man of extremely limited vision and horizon and is a poor pupil (or trainee). William J. Michels lists the important aspects of learning as follows:[9]

1. Learning requires purposeful activity.
2. Learning is a process of the whole individual.

3. Learning is problem solving. Challenging problems stimulate learning.
4. Learning is based on past experiences.
5. Learning results from stimulation through the senses.
6. The more vivid and intense the impressions, the greater the chance of remembering.
7. Interest is essential to effective learning. Learning requires motivation.
8. Friendly competition stimulates learning.
9. Recognition and credit provide strong incentives for learning.
10. People learn more when they are held to account and made to feel responsible for learning.
11. Knowing 'why' makes learning more effective.
12. Knowledge of the standards require makes learning more effective.
13. Things should be taught the way they are to be used.
14. Teaching should be logical or orderly.
15. The most effective learning results when initial learning is followed immediately by application.
16. Early successes increase chances for effective learning.
17. Repetition, accompanied by constant effort toward improvement, makes for effective development of skill.
18. Feelings of both teacher and student affect learning.
19. Students learn many things in addition to skills and information (attitudes, interests, appreciations, etc.)
20. Continuous evaluation is essential to effective learning.

Principles of Teaching Basic Work Skills

Morris Viteles provides the following principles of acquiring work skills:[10]

1. The work must be taught and must practise only correct methods of work. This is the basic principle.
2. First establish the best way of doing a job — use job analysis and/or time and motion study techniques.
3. Follow the principles of best movements in work.
4. Job training under actual working conditions is superior to classroom and formal training.
5. *Emphasise* accuracy first — speed second.
6. Training is more efficient when distributed over short periods of time.
7. Remember the practice aims — efficiency increases with repetition of the task. However, you should expect learning plateaus when no apparent progress is made, follows by additional spurts of improvement. Therefore, you should carry out distributed practice over longer period than is commonly believed (otherwise workers settle down at production speeds lower than their real abilities).

8. *When* a plateau is reached, use incentives and other devices to get *more* improvement.
9. *Age and learning:* You can train older workers as well as younger ones. Learning ability does not deteriorate rapidly with age — instead, older workers have learned more bad habits and therefore need retraining.

Principles of Teaching Basic Physical Movements

Viteles also gives the following principles:[11]

1. Successive movements should be so related that one movement passes easily into that which follows, each ending in a position favourable for the beginning of the next movement.
2. The order of movements should be so arranged that little direct attention is needed for passage from one to another. In other words, they should be so arranged that the mind can attend to the final aim or end of the operation instead of being distracted by the work of initiating successively the several movements which are involved in a task.
3. The sequence of movements is to be so framed that an easy rhythm can be established in the automatic performance of the various elements of operation.
4. From the principles which have been stated follows the corollary that a continuous movement is preferable to angular movements involving sudden changes in the direction of movement.
5. The number of movements should be reduced as far as possible within the scope of limitations suggested above. In general, reducing the number of movements will facilitate a rhythmic method of working and automatisation as a means of reducing the volitional direction of work.
6. Simultaneous use of both hands should be encouraged.
7. When a forcible stroke is required, the direction of movement and placement of material should be so arranged that, as far as practicable, the stroke is delivered when it has reached its greatest momentum.

Training Principles for Supervisors

The Federal Security Agency in U.S.A. lists some ways to help speed employee learning by the supervisors:[12]

Five Ways to Speed Learning

1. In getting across information, emphasise its use and application on the job.
2. Stir the learner to activity; get him to participate.
3. Give the employee time to digest what he learns.
4. Help the employee see what is especially important.
5. Help the employee understand the meaning of what he is learning.

Application of these sound principles of training will make the training programme very effective resulting in various advantages to the employee and the employer and in the final analysis, to the nation and national economic growth.

Now let us turn to the types and techniques of training.

4. H.R.D. TYPES AND TECHNIQUES OF TRAINING AND DEVELOPMENT

Training means to educate somewhat narrowly, mainly by instruction, drill, and discipline, whereas development inculcates an unfolding process and carries an implication of growth and maturisation. Lately it is increasingly being realised that men or employees are the human assets in an organisation and expenditure on training and development programmes is an investment in human capital. So a variety of methods, types, and techniques of training are being utilised in order to cash in on the human capital, whose potential is much greater than any other thing. Broadly, the following types of training and development programmes can be identified: (1) Initial or preliminary training; (2) Non-supervisory training; (3) Retraining; (4) Special purpose courses; (5) Supervisory training; (6) Management development.

1. INITIAL OR PRELIMINARY TRAINING

Initial or preliminary or learner training is designed to meet the needs of new employees of an organisation, who have had no industrial experience. The new employees may not have seen the insides of a factory and they are 'green' hands. Either through a company training institute or public vocational schools, the learner may be given training for a period of several weeks in two broad categories of employee training: (1) general education and (2) job training. The learner, as one company does, may be given training in elementary arithmetic, shop science, economics, mathematics, reading blueprints, operation of machines, reading and using gauges, fire fighting, safety and good housekeeping.

The foreman may be asked to teach the learner what is the job, what he has to do on the job, how he has to do it, when and where he has to do it and why.

The first few weeks are critical for both the learner and the company and the training the learner receives, hence, is all the more important.

2. NON-SUPERVISORY TRAINING

During the Second World War, with a view to meeting the job training needs of companies, the War Manpower Commission under the sponsorship of the Council of National Defence in U.S.A. developed 'standardised' training programmes, that could be used in almost any company, known as Training Within Industry or popularly TWI. TWI programmes have been enormously successful and these were introduced in our country with the assistance of I.L.O. experts. Apart from the actual job training; TWI also instructs the instructor as to how he should instruct.

Under the TWI method, here is how a job training programme is planned and developed:[13]

THE PROGRAMME DEVELOPMENT CARD

The four steps were established as:

(a) Spot a Production Problem

* Get supervisors and workers to tell about their current problems. Uncover problems by reviewing records — performance, costs, turnover, rejects, accidents.

(b) Develop a Specific Plan

* Who will be trained?
* What content? Who can help determine?
* How can it be done best?
* Who should do the training?
* When should it be done — how long will it take?
* Where should it be done?
* Watch for relations of this plan to other current training plans and programs.

(c) Get Plan into Action

* Stress to management evidence of need — use facts and figures.
* Present the expected results.
* Discuss plan — content and methods.
* Submit time-table for plan.
* Train those who do the training.
* Secure understanding and acceptance by those affected.
* Fix responsibility for continuing use.
* Be sure management participates.

(d) Check Results

* How can results be checked? Against what evidence?
* What results will be looked for?
* Is management being informed — how?
* Is the plan being followed?
* How is it being kept in use?
* Are any changes necessary?
* Is the plan helping production?

Job training may be broken down into various types of training and the figure 7.2 gives some types of training in the automobile industry in U.S.A.

The most common types of non-supervisory training programmes are discussed below:

*1. **On-the-Job Training:*** This type of training is usually adopted where jobs are too varied to permit the establishment of group instruction. It is also used where machinery to be provided for trainees is too costly. The general set up is to assign a new employee to an older and experienced employee so that the new employee learns the skills of the job gradually by observation as well as occasional handling of the job. Sometimes a supervisor may be there to train him while he is doing the job. Sometimes training on the job is supplemented by instruction in a classroom.

It has been found that this type of training is carried in a haphazard manner for a variety of reasons such as lack of ability of the experienced employee to impart skills to the trainee, lack of breakdown of the job for the purpose of instruction, and lack of motivation on the part of the trainer to impart skills.

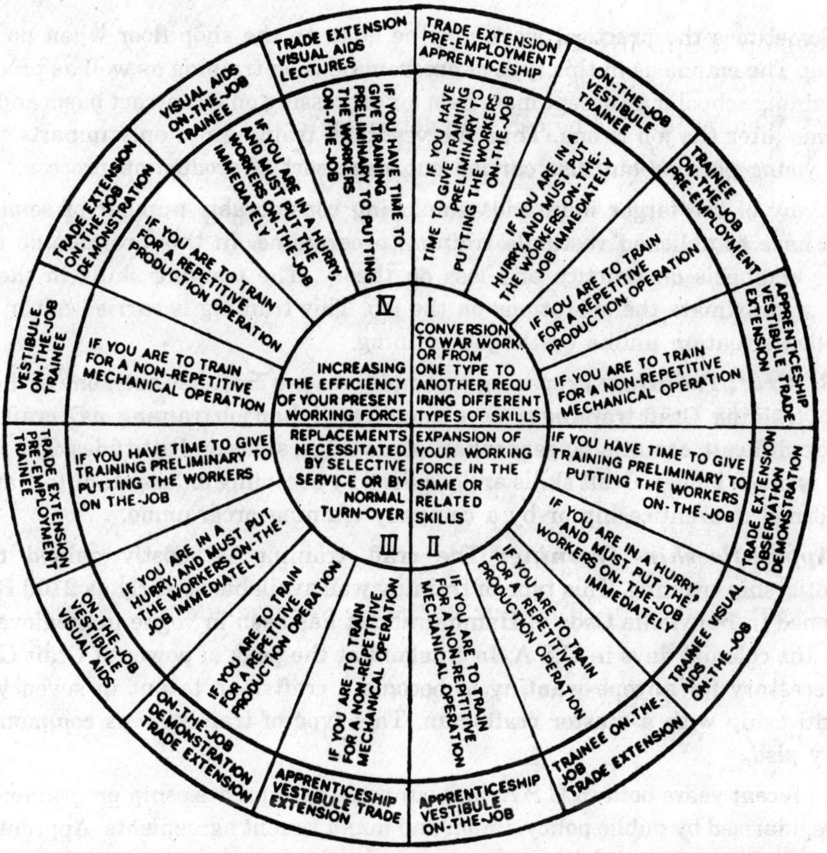

Fig. 7.2 Graphic Presentation of the Approach to non-Supervisor Training Programmes in the Automotive Industry

In the centre circle are listed the problems generally faced; in the second circle, the different situations involved; and in the outer circle, the methods recommended to meet the specific problem.

Source: Training and Upgrading (Report of Automatic Council for War Production Detroit), p. 6.

However, on-the-job training is being commonly used in a large number of organisations, mainly because it requires no special school and trainee's contribution adds to the total output of the department. Careful selections of a trainer and assigning a new employee to the proper trainer are very important. There is a need to train the trainer also. This type of training is a reasonable alternative for a company where there are almost as many jobs as there are employees. On-the-Job training is applicable to all levels of job-operatives, supervisors and executive trainees.

2. ***Vestibule Training:*** It refers to job skill training which is shorter than the apprenticeship programme and is given in a regularly established school. It is designed to equip the learner to only onc phase of training, to operate one machine or to perform a single operation. The training is carried out in a miniature situation of the real plant so that the trainee can practise those skills which he will later use on the job. Thus his training is closely geared to job duties. The theoretical instruction is given in the class room while the practical work may be conducted on the production line. Sometimes the practical work may be done on the shop floor when no shift is working. The emphasis in this type of programme is on training as well as production. The training school may accept materials for processing on a contract basis and return the same after the job is one. Thus the vestibule training not only imparts training to the young persons but also carried out some sort of production process.

Many of the larger industries employing considerable number of semi-skilled people have established vestibule training programme. In this programme there is greater emphasis on practice and less on theory. The training skills in the school closely approximate the operations on the job. This training is carried out in a well-controlled situation unlike on-the-job training.

3. Craft Training: Preparing an employee for a craft has been one of the oldest types of training. Craft training is more complicated than job training, as a craft is more complex, difficult, comprising generalised knowledge, skills and attitudes. The training period is much longer. Craft skills are acquired by becoming an assistant to craftsman, by a formal apprenticeship or by a company training programme.

Apprenticeship Training: The craft training is mostly gained through apprenticeship training. This type of training was available as early as 2100 B.C. and mentioned in Babylonia Code of Hammurabi. It has been in vogue in medieval times and in the colonial days in U.S.A. In England at the peak of power of Craft Guilds it was necessary for anyone wanting to become a craftsman to put in seven years of apprenticeship with a master craftsman. This type of training was common in our country also.

In recent years both in U.S.A. and our country apprenticeship programmes have been regularised by public policy, union and management agreements. Apprenticeship involves training for total job where acquiring the knowledge and skills of a trade requires fairly long period — anywhere from two to seven years. The fields in which apprenticeship training is offered are numerous such as Boiler Attender, Draughtsman, Machinist, Printer, Tool Maker, Pattern Maker, Mechanic, Carpenters, Shipfitters, Jewellers, Die Sinkers, Plumbers, Engravers, Coremakers, Electricians, Millwrights.

Training is mainly concerned with development of skill and knowledge and basis of extensive theoretical and practical study. Where skilled persons are not readily available it becomes necessary to establish apprenticeship programmes. These programmes may be delegated in part or in whole by the company to a vocational school. Larger companies that employ enough craftsmen can run these programmes economically at any rate until their requirements are fulfilled.

A modified form of this type, namely, co-operative programme, can be tried out wherein shop practice is only on the job under the direction of a skilled craftsman, while classroom instruction is given in a local school or institute. Apprenticeship programme extends over a long period and is too costly for smaller companies particularly when trainees leave the company soon after the training is completed. But it is the only alternative where ready skilled help is not available. Sometimes it involves on the part of the trainee signing an agreement to serve the company. This programme is carried on in an informal set-up without having a separate training department. It has been generally charged that not enough attention and facilities are provided for apprenticeship training programme because of the long time it takes to prepare the trainees for work. Sometimes these trainees are used by companies to augment their permanent work force.

The Federal Bureau of Apprenticeship lists the following advantages of apprenticeship training:[14]

1. Maintenance of skilled work force.
2. Immediate return from training.
3. Quality workmanship.........
4. Satisfied customers.........
5. Higher production.........
6. Lower hiring costs because of reduced turnover.........
7. Lower production costs.........
8. Increased loyalty of employees.........
9. Opportunity for youth..........
10. National security.

Apprenticeship Scheme in India: Considerable fillip has been given to the apprenticeship training in India by the Apprenticeship (Amendment) Act 1973 and also the recent public policy:[15]

Freshers as well as trainees of the ITIs are eligible for apprenticeship and latter rightly enjoy some exemption in the term of apprenticeship. This period for most trades is of 3 years but for a few it varies between 6 months and 4 years. In England, the normal period is of 5 years, while in the United States it varies between 3½ years to 4 years. In all countries, apprentices are paid a stipend which generally carries an annual increment. In India, too, the stipend increases from, say, Rs. 130 p.m. in the first year to Rs. 200 p.m. in the fourth. Graduate engineers receive a minimum of Rs. 280 p.m. Though a trainee is not a worker, he does produce some goods and services. The stipend may therefore be interpreted as remuneration for work done. The cost of the scheme in India is borne entirely by an establishment, if it employs 500 or more workers, and is shared with the Government if it employs less. The financial burden on the establishment and the Government would be made a little lighter if levies are imposed on establishments which default. But this suggestion has not been acceptable to the Government despite the failure of the employers to co-operate.

Penalties Prescribed: As in other countries, so in India, the Act requires that a contract shall be signed between the employer and the apprentice or his guardian (if he is a minor). This contract binds the trainee to observe certain rules and regulations and the employer to train the apprentice in a trade. An employer can be fined or imprisoned for 6 months if he fails in his obligations and a trainee has to repay Rs. 35 p.m. upto a maximum of Rs. 500 if he abandons his training half-way. The provisions regarding refund may deter some candidates, especially those coming from the weaker sections, participating from in the apprenticeship scheme.

A distinguishing feature of the Indian Act is the final trade test, which it is necessary for every trainee to pass. In England, no final examination is held, while in the United States an examination is held for the licence to practise the trade; but the system lacks standardisation. The Indian Act provides for prizes and medals for the best apprentice and the best establishment.

This review of the working of the Act is seriously handicapped by the non-availability of some of the latest statistics. Table 7.1 shows that, between 1962 and 1975, the number of specified industries has quadrupled and that of designated trades has increased sevenfold. Considering the substantial increase in specified industries and trades, the number of apprentices passing out must have increased substantially, but the relevant data are not available. The number of establishments covered has registered a threefold increase between 1964 and 1974, while the number of apprentices undergoing training has shot up from 3,383 in 1963 to 1,17,836 in 1975 and to 1,45,464 by the end of October 1976.

Table 7.2 represents a snapshot of the position in 1974. It shows, among other things, that the vast potential of the programme is yet to be tapped. Out of 55,113 establishments, 38,180 (69.03 per cent) had no arrangements for training facilities. Only 8.34 per cent of the surveyed establishments (47,508) were taking on apprentices, presumably according to the prescribed ratio for trades; while 7.60 per cent did not observe the prescribed ratio.

Table 7.1

PROGRESS IN APPRENTICESHIP (1962-75)

Year	*No. of industries specified*	*Trades designated*	*No. of establishments in which apprentices were engaged*	*No. of undergoing training*	*No. of apprentices passed out*
1962	53	14	—	—	—
1963	75	12		3,383	—
1964	—	—	1,414	14,130	74
1965	—	—	1,333	22,544	698
1966	14	14	2,061	29,854	2,405
1967	53	—	2,365	34,816	4,937
1968	—	10	3,249	35,200	6,163
1969	—	—	3,514	38,265	7,691
1970	—	4	4,385	42,112	10,954
1971	—	2	4,154	45,582	11,731
1972	6	5	5,103	52,454	13,999
1973	—	—	6,809	60,347	14,002
1974	—	—	7,573	56,263	N.A.
1975	15	42	N.A.	1,17,886	N.A.

Figures relate to the month of September in each year except 1967 and 1975. From them they refer to the position in August and December respectively.

N.A.: means "Not Available."

Table 7.2

STATE OF THE PROGRAMME IN 1974

	Establishments					*Apprentices*			
Region	*Covered*	*Surveyed*	*Engaging apprentices*	*Engaging below ratio*	*Not engaging*	*No. training facilities at present*	*Facilities located so far*	*Apprentices undergoing training*	*% of col. 8 to 9*
A. Western	18,192	16,802	541	480	1,054	14,367	49,749	12,540	63.4
Northern	13,747	12,570	1,846	1,631	2,001	7,092	20,821	11,659	55.8
Eastern	9,044	5,032	478	427	547	3,580	16,690	11,646	69.7
Southern	13,640	12,444	1,024	469	1,065	2,886	15,879	10,012	63.0
Total (A)	54,623	46,848	3,889	3,367	4,667	34,925	73,139	45,857	62.0
B. Western	119	111	16	58	27	10	7,052	4,972	70.5
Northern	209	192	15	68	25	84	6,467	3,936	60.8
Eastern	242	242	27	72	25	118	9,169	5,292	57.7
Southern	120	115	15	45	11	43	8,496	6,206	73.0
Total (B)	690	660	74	243	58	255	31.185	20,406	65.4
(A + B)	55,313	47,508	3,963	3,610	4,755	38,180	1,04,323	66,063	63.5

A = State/Private Sector B = Central Sector.

The best indicator of performance is the ratio, expressed as percentage, of the number of apprentices undergoing training to the seats located. The national average of 63.5 per cent for the utilisation of these seats speaks of a fairly high performance; and the improvement in this indicator since the declaration of emergency is very impressive. As on 31st December 1975, 1,23,295 seats were located, of which 1,17,886 were utilised, raising the percentage of utilisation to 95.6. In March 1975, the utilisation ratio was only 63 per cent; but, under the impetus provided by the emergency, it improved to 96.52 per cent by the middle of May 1976 when, of the 1,34,980 located seats, as many as 1,30,283 were utilised. By the end of October 1976, the utilisation ratio had further improved; for, out of the 1,45,464 located seats, as many as, 1,41,601 were utilised — a little over 97 per cent utilisation. While the position regarding craftsmen is extremely satisfactory, that relating to engineering graduates and technicians calls for a great deal of improvement. Out of 7,334 seats located for degree-holders, only 3,017 were utilised, while out of 7,960 seats located for technicians, only 3,202 seats were utilised.

The performance of the Southern region, with a utilisation ratio of 73 per cent in the Central sphere, is quite high compared to its performance in the State/private sector at 63 per cent. In the latter sector, the Eastern region reports the best and the Northern region the worst performance. In the Central sector, the Eastern region shows the worst utilisation.

Out of the 1,30,283 utilised seats in May 1976, as many as 28,914 belong to the scheduled groups, the physically handicapped and the minorities.

4. Internship Training: Internship training is a work and study programme where the trainee attends a school for theory sessions and works in the plant for practical experience in order to learn the skills and knowledge required to do a particular job. The training periods may range three to nine months and the trainee alternates from school to the plant and vice versa, until the course is completed. This kind of programme is offered through the cooperation between industries and schools — trade schools, high schools, and vocational schools.

A distinct advantage of this programme is that there is balance between theory and practice, which enables the trainee to pick up the skills, knowledge, and attitudes. But the problem is that it is a slow process and when the business is in a bad state, these trainees may be laid off first.

5. External Training: In our country in recent years there is some sort of a boom in external training programmes, which are offered by various agencies such as Industrial Training Centres, National Productivity Council, Small Scale Industries Service Institutes, Training Institutes and Schools, Correspondence Courses, Night Schools etc. Vocational training is offered to the trainees here.

In U.S.A. there is a number of agencies and groups such as vocational, correspondence, trade, and evening schools, offering training facilities. To meet the needs of high school drop-outs various job training centres have been opened all over U.S.A. In many communities, the local chapters of Personnel Association, local Chambers of Commerce, Human Relations Councils and other civic bodies cooperate in providing training facilities to people in their communities.

6. *Retraining:* One of the grave problems facing an industrial worker is job obsolescence, where his job may become obsolete because of changes brought by technology. Automation has introduced new problems. Workers with years of loyal and long service find their jobs becoming completely useless to the company. That is why many workers fight the introduction of automation. In India this problem is a very familiar one. The dock workers, L I C employees, banking employees, to name a few, are in the grip of fear of losing their jobs. This is at once a challenge and a responsibility to the management. In U.S.A. management has been able to meet this problem through retraining programmes. Many union-management contracts are signed providing for such retraining programmes. Generally the employee, whose job has gone obsolete, is retrained on the payroll and is retrained to do another job, so that the advancing technology can be harnessed to the benefit of the company without any adverse effects on the employees.

In Europe for years retraining programmes are supported by public financial assistance.[16] In U.S.A. a beginning was made in the Federal Area Redevelopment Act of 1961 whereby the law provided 4.5 million dollars of federal funds to assist State and local retraining programmes in areas of substantial and persistent unemployment. Such grants are further bolstered by an additional 10 million dollars per year available to provide subsistence payments to trainees. Yet there are some problems. An older worker, who has worked for 30 or 35 years or more on a job and when he loses his job, can he learn a new job? Then what job is he going to learn? What retraining programme is suitable to him? Who is going to decide it? Perhaps the struggle for survival will suggest a course and the employee and management have to work out a programme of rehabilitation through retraining.

4. SPECIAL PURPOSE COURSES

Various special purpose courses are offered by companies to meet special and unusual needs of certain employees. In U.S.A. special courses are designed to help alien employees prepare for American Citizenship, to teach economics, home economics, civics, basic English, reading, telephone etiquette, personnel hygiene, time study, standard setting, reading dietetics, public relations, public speaking etc. In India similarly Hindustani and English are taught to jawans. Hindi may be taught to non-Hindi speaking employees. Family planning instruction is common among some companies. Some companies offer courses in housekeeping, flower arrangement, casting votes, Indian Constitution, Five Year Plans, productivity, education of children, safety etc.

The Banker's Trust in New York offer a charm course to their Tellers, who are young and attractive ladies in their late teens or early twenties. They are taught telephone etiquette, personal hygiene, good grooming. They are taught how to dress, how to talk to customers, how to walk, how to keep a pleasing personality, how to keep 'wolves' at a distance and how to be courteous always. They are given every Friday, a free hair dressing and a new hair-do which in some beauty parlours in New York costs anywhere from 5 to 50 dollars.

Training Facilities

Various facilities and equipments are provided by companies for training purposes and the following may be mentioned:

1. Training institutes and schools (company sponsored).
2. Films, Slides, Projectors, Movies, Stills.
3. Charts, Graphs, Flash Cards, Flannel boards, pictograms.
4. Pamphlets, Brochures, Handbooks, Manuals.
5. Libraries and Reading Rooms.
6. Teaching machines, closed circuit TV.
7. Exhibits, Posters and displays.
8. Notice Boards, Bulletin Boards, Enlarged Drawings.
9. Cartoons, Comic Books, Books.

Trainers and Instructors

Any training programme's success, regardless of how well it is organised, planned and developed, depends upon competent trainers and instructors. The selection and training of instructor also is important, particularly when foremen or supervisors are asked to teach. We shall discuss under supervisory training programmes techniques that enable the supervisors to teach and train in the next section.

Professor John F. Mee gives the following generalised formula:[17]

1. The training department should assume primary responsibility for doing the following types of teaching; instruction of trainers in method of teaching; formal orientation; training of supervisors in human relations aspects of their jobs; development of executives; co-operative education with schools and colleges; general education of employees.
2. Line supervisors and employees should carry the bulk of the teaching load in the following areas; on-the-job instruction of employees; instruction in the technical or professional aspects of the business; daily development of supervisors and executives through counselling; departmental communications and staff meetings as part of an overall training programme.

The job of specialised Training Director or Administrator is given in Figure 7.3, and the job of training specialists, who are non-administrative staff members in the training division, is given in Figure 7.4 by the American Management Association.

THE TRAINING ADMINISTRATOR JOB

Supervisor of:

TRAINING:

(Principal responsibility for planning, organising, and directing training activities in a company).

JOB PROFILE

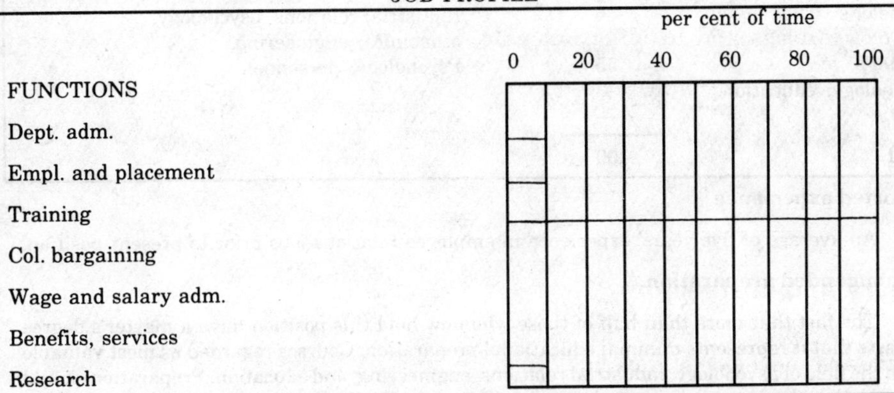

Reported Titles

Director of training; education and training director; manager, personnel training and development; training coordinator; personnel supervisor.

Job Dues

Principal Duties

Training Time 45%

Coordinates the training activities of the company, supervising one or more training specialists and maintaining programmes which may include the following types of training: on-the-job, apprentice, supervisory, sales and management. Consults with other managers to determine training needs. Prepares manuals and other materials — for use in training sessions. Arranges training schedules. Conducts training sessions. Counsels employees concerning training opportunities.

Administration and Planning Time 24%

In consultation with top management and members of the employee relations staff, sets training policies and organises training activities to carry out these policies. Advises other managers, including those on the employee relations staff, concerning revisions of the organisational structure of the company. Responsible for maintaining records and preparing periodic reports and summarises of training activities. May supervise a staff of several specialists.

Allied Duties

All others Time 31%

Conducts studies, or participates in studies conducted by the employee relations research staff or independent research groups, to analyse and evaluate present and proposed training methods. May advise other employee relations staff members in establishing personnel specifications for use in selection and placement. May advise other managers and members of employee relations staff on development and use of employee appraisal programmes. May prepare and distribute handbooks and manuals. May consult with staff members who counsel employees on vocational or personal problems.

QUALIFICATIONS FOR EMPLOYMENT

Reported education

Highest Degree Received	Per cent	Most frequently reported areas of specialisation.
No degree	9	
Bachelor's	36	Industrial relations, psychology, economics, engineering.
Master's	55	Psychology, personnel.
Psychology, education.		
Ph.D.	—	
Total	100	

Reported experience

An average of five years' experience in employee relations jobs prior to present position.

Recommended preparation

The fact that more than half of those who now hold this position have a master's degree suggests that it represents minimal educational preparation. Courses regarded as most valuable fall in the field of psychology, industrial relations, engineering, and education. Preparation should also include experience in other industrial relations staff jobs.

Fig. 7.3 The Training Administrator Job

Source: "Jobs in Employee Relations," Research Study No.38, New York: American Management Association, 1959, pp.26-27.

THE TRAINING SPECIALIST JOB

Specialist in:

TRAINING

(Member of a training staff, usually in medium-size and large companies).

JOB PROFILE

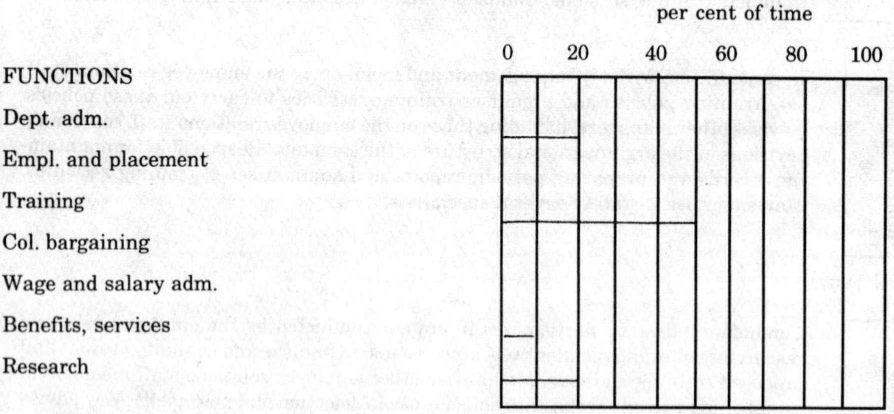

Reported Titles

Assistant director of training; assistant to the training director; assistant training consultant, training director; management development and training director.

JOB DUTIES

Principal Duties

Time	Training 84%

Devotes major portion of time to training activities which may include on-the-job, apprentice, sales, supervisory or management training. Consults with other managers to determine training needs. Prepares manuals and other materials for use in training sessions. Counsels employee concerning opportunities.

Allied Duties

Time	All Others 16%

Participates in planning and organising training activities. Keeps records and prepares periodic reports and summarises of training. May maintain a library of pertinent training materials. May advise other managers, including members of the employee relations staff, on problems of recruiting and on the development and use of employee appraisal procedures.

Qualifications for Employment

Reported Education

Highest Degree received	Per	Most frequently reported areas of specialisation
No. degree	8	
Bachelor's	69	Business Administration, Economics, Sociology, Psychology, Education
Master's	23	Psychology, Education.
Ph. D.	—	Engineering.
Total	100	

Reported Experience

An average of five years' experience in employee relations jobs prior to present position. However, this is frequently an entrance job; 30 per cent of the incumbents report on experience in employee relations.

Recommended Preparation

Educational preparation for these positions should include at least the bachelor's degree. There is distinct preference for graduate work and the master's. Appropriate major and minor fields include psychology, education, business administration, economics, engineering, and sociology. For many positions, a minimum of one or two years of experience in other employee relations staff jobs is required.

Fig. 7.4 The Training Specialist Job
(From "Jobs in Employee Relations," *op. cit.,* pp. 37-38)

A good trainer or instructor must:

1. Know the job or subject he is attempting to teach.
2. Have the aptitude and abilities to teach.
3. Want to teach.
4. Have a pleasing personality and a capacity for leadership.
5. Have a knowledge of teaching principles and methods.

Planning Training Sessions

Don Copell suggests a procedure for trainers in planning their sessions:[18]

1. Every lesson should be planned.
2. Know how many and what kind of students you are teaching.
3. Lay out the subject matter.
4. Select the best method of instruction.
5. Decide what the students need in the way of preparation.
6. Make plans to capture and maintain student interest.
7. Plan summary of points to be emphasised.
8. Plan for using of training aids, if any.
9. Have a rehearsal of the lesson.
10. Plan for examination questions.

The trainees also must be carefully selected and except for the most routine job training, training must be optional. The employees must be made to understand that the right to receive training is a privilege and an opportunity. The careful selection process of trainees may be made through employee counselling in selection or exit interviews, recommendation of supervisors and managers, employee attitude and morale surveys, suggestion systems and study of in-plant problems.

5. SUPERVISORY TRAINING

The terms 'supervisor', 'leadman', 'straw boss', 'departmental head' are often used interchangeably and they are all alike in that they supervise employees. But the supervisor is often associated with office staff and foreman with hourly-rated production employees. The supervisor is the main communication link between managers and employees and he is the one who has to get things done through his men. It is often charged that he is the 'step-child' of management and an 'orphan', because many times he is not considered as one of management and he is not one of labour also. But the supervisor has a very important role to play and many firms with a policy of promotion from within, must largely limit the selection of future junior and middle managers to choices among foremen and supervisors. Supervisory experience is the first step up in the management ladder.

Management is interested in supervisory training and development programmes for a variety of reasons. First, as a company expands it needs more supervisors; hence there is a need to augment the source of supply. Secondly, supervisory development programmes are often the basis of executive development programmes. Thirdly, each department needs a good supervisor as its head. Fourthly, good supervision is responsible for good team spirit and team work. Fifthly, top management realises that there is a need to keep the supervisors in good shape all the time.

A. Top Management Support

In setting up and conducting a supervisory training programme the support of top management is essential. The programme must be of longer duration and someone of top executive stature must be assigned for this function.

B. Supervisor-trainee Selection

This training programme must be provided after a careful selection of supervisors is made on the basis of their training needs. Supervisory training needs are usually determined in one of the five principal ways: (1) by employees, (2) by supervisors, (3) by top management, (4) by the training department, and (5) by outside consultants.

C. Supervisory Training Policy

The supervisor must become an expert (1) in his handling of machines and materials and (2) in his leadership and management of people.

Generally supervisory training policies propose:

1. To help present supervisors improve their performance.
2. To help them to prepare for greater responsibilities in higher levels of management in the future.
3. To build up the security and status of supervisors.
4. The above policy is supplemented by salary objectives that seek to insure stability in supervisory salaries at levels above the earnings of blue collar workers, usually 20% to 30% more.
5. To assure technical competence with a view to helping him know and understand all about the process and operations in which his crew participates.

Training policy proposes to help supervisors develop (1) technical competence, (2) ability to delegate, (3) skill in communications, (4) use of consultation in supervision, and (5) personal interest in members of their crews.

D. Supervisory Training and Development Programmes

Supervisors and foremen have great variations in duties, responsibilities, authority, status, pay and privileges. In short, supervisory jobs differ greatly and hence training needs show greater variation. Various supervisory training programmes are offered and here are discussed the common types. The following Figure 7.5 is a graphic presentation of the various programmes for supervisors in the Automotive Industry in U.S.A.

1. Technical Training: Technical training for supervisors, has a heavy concentration on products and processes.

(a) They describe firm's operations, its policy and practice in purchasing, requisition, inventories, cost control, overtime, shop rules and other standard operating procedures.

(b) They provide instruction in planning, scheduling, and record keeping. Some companies offer special training in mathematics, science, book-keeping, time study, job evaluation, legal regulations, and other technical fields.

(c) Training in personnel procedures is given, inculcating the following aspects:

1. Personnel policies, programmes, and procedures. Supervisors learn how employees are selected, transferred, promoted, trained, paid, why job evaluation, about morale surveys and services and benefits provided by the company to the employees.

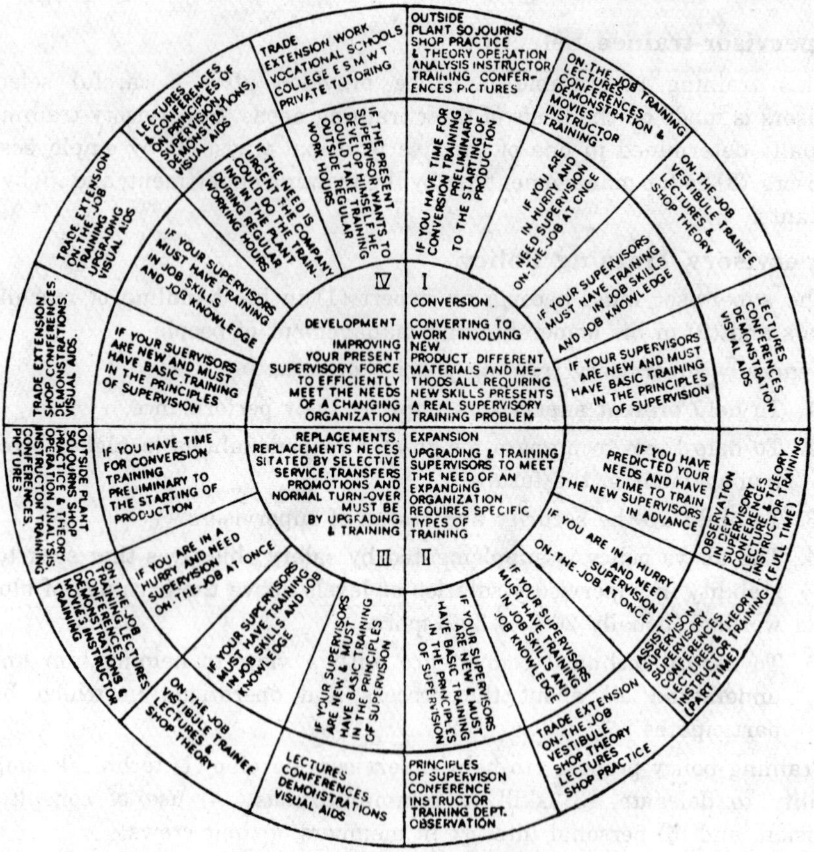

Fig. 7.5. Graphic Presentation of the Approach of Supervisory Training Programs in the Automotive Industry

Source: Training and Upgrading (Report of Automotive Council, War Production, Detroit), p.6.

2. Dealing with common problems such as absenteeism, tardiness, indiscipline, and insubordination.
3. Appraising employees and rating them and maintaining personnel records.
4. Procedures of contract administration and grievance handling.
5. Guiding and helping superior managers and suggesting changes of improvement.

2. Leadership Training: This type of training is common for supervisors and the aim is to develop leadership qualities in supervisors so that they may become effective leaders. Most programmes emphasise the importance of communications, especially listening; they stress participation as a factor in incentivation and identification, and try to develop empathy and sensitivity; they consider methods of overcoming resistance to change, the influence of informal organisation and the advantages of non-authoritarian leadership.

It is emphasised that Hitler-like approach to supervision cannot increase the efficiency and productivity of the group. A supervisor, who says "you do this operation this way and I want it ready by sundown," is ultimately going to realise that authoritarian supervision does not bring good results. But the supervisors, who say "How shall we do it? We have a deadline to meet. Let us try to do it fast," is likely to get better and better results these days. Leadership programmes attempt to train the supervisors:

1. To become effective communicators, to adopt a constructive attitude and to become effective listeners listening to the employees.
2. To aim at consultative supervision, cultivate suggestions, ideas, advice from employees, advise them of assignments and problems; ask their advice, receive, consider, and discuss their suggestions; delegate authority to make decisions, recognise ultimate responsibility; and adopt a "how-shall-we-do-this" approach.
3. To adopt "employee-centred" supervision. Likert, Seashore, and others report that both employee productivity and morale are likely to be high in case of employee-centred supervision and they note that employee interest and performance correlate positively with high employee membership in a work-group with high group-pride, cohesion, and solidarity.[19]
4. To become proficient in human relations, training in human relations is provided. We shall discuss human relations in a separate chapter later.

3. Training within Industry: The already mentioned T.W.I. has made a signal contribution to supervisory training first by pointing out specific skills and knowledge required by the supervisor to do his job effectively and second, by providing four different supervisory training programmes. T. W. I. maintained that the supervisor has the following needs:

Every supervisor has five needs:

1. Knowledge of the Work: Materials, tools, processes, operations, products, and how they are made and used.

2. Knowledge of Responsibilities: Policies, agreements, rules, regulations, schedules, interdepartmental relationships.

These two knowledge needs must be met currently and locally by each plant or company.

Such knowledge must be provided if each supervisor is to know his job and is to have a clear understanding of his authority and responsibilities as a part of management.

3. Skill in Instructing: Increasing production by helping supervisors to develop a well-trained work-force which will get into production quicker; have less scrap, rework and rejects, fewer accidents, less tool and equipment damage.

4. Skill in Improving Methods: Utilising materials, machines, and manpower more effectively by having supervisors study each operation in order to eliminate, combine, rearrange, and simplify details of the jobs.

5. Skill in Leading: Increasing production by helping supervisors to improve their understanding of individuals, their ability to size up situations, and their ways of working with people.

These three skills must be acquired individually. Practice and experience in using them enable both new and experienced supervisors to recognise and solve daily problems promptly.

In order to acquire these skills and knowledge, the T W I recommended four different training programmes, which have been highly successful and which can be used by almost any company. The training programmes are:

1. *Job Instruction Training* or J.I.T. which is designed to teach the supervisor how to instruct and train the employees.
2. *Job Methods Training or J.M.T.* which is designed to help the supervisor improve methods in his department, using principles of work simplification.
3. *Job Relations Training or J.R.T.* which is designed to help the supervisor determine the most effective arrangement for handling human relations problems among his employees in his department.
4. *Programme Development Training*, which we have discussed in the earlier discussion dealing with job training of employees.

The TWI report explains these various programmes in detail and they are as follows:[20]

(1) Job Instruction Training or J.I.T.

HAVE A TIME TABLE —

How much skill you expect him to have, by what date.

BREAK DOWN THE JOB —

List important steps.

Pick out the key points. (Safety is always a key point).

HAVE EVERYTHING READY —

The right equipment, materials, and supplies.

HAVE THE WORKPLACE PROPERLY ARRANGED —

Just as the worker will be expected to keep it and the 4 steps of "how to Instruct."

Step 1 PREPARE THE WORKER

Put him at ease.
State the job and find out what he really knows about it.
Get him interested in learning the job.
Place in correct position.

Step 2 PRESENT THE OPERATION

Tell, show, and illustrate one Important Step at a time.
Stress each Key Point.
Instruct clearly, completely, and patiently, but no more than he can master.

Step 3 TRY OUT PERFORMANCE

Have him do the job — correct errors.
Have him explain each Key Point to you as he does the job again.
Make sure he understands.
Continue until You know HE knows.

Step 4 FOLLOW UP

Put him on his own — Designate to whom he goes for help.

Check frequently. Encourage questions.

Taper off extra coaching and close follow-up.

If the worker hasn't learned, he Instructor hasn't taught.

(2) Job Methods Training or J.M.T

The following steps are used in J.M.T.: [21]

THE JOB METHODS CARD

Step (i) BREAK DOWN the job.

1. List all details of the job exactly as done by the present method.
2. Be sure details include all:
   - — Material handling.
   - — Machine work.
   - — Hand work.

Step (ii) QUESTION every detail.

1. Use these types of questions:
   WHY is it necessary?
   WHAT is its purpose?
   WHERE should it be done?
   WHEN should it be done?
   WHO is best qualified to do it?
   HOW is the "best way" to do it?
2. Also question the:
   Materials, Machines, Equipment, Tools, Product Design, Layout, Workplace, Safety House-keeping.

Step (iii) DEVELOP the new method.

1. ELIMINATE unnecessary details.
2. Combine details when practical.
3. REARRANGE for better sequence.
4. SIMPLIFY all necessary details.
   - — Make the work easier and safer.
   - — Pre-position materials, tools, and equipment at the best places in the proper work area.
   - — Use gravity-feed hoppers and drop delivery chutes.
   - — Let both hands do useful work.
   - — Use jigs and fixtures instead of hands, for holding work.
5. Work out ideas with others.
6. Write up your proposed new methods.

Step (iv) APPLY the new method.

1. Sell your proposal to the boss.
2. Sell the new method to the operators.
3. Get final approval of all concerned on Safety, Quality, Quantity, Cost.
4. Put the new method to work. Use it until a better way is developed.
5. Give credit where credit is due.

(3) Job Relations Training or J.R.T.[22]

The Job Relations steps are:

DETERMINE OBJECTIVE

1. Get The Facts
   Review the record.
   Find out what rules and plant customs apply.
   Talk with individuals concerned.
   Get opinions and feelings.
   Be sure you have the whole story.

2. Weigh and Decide.
   Fit the facts together.
   Consider their bearing on each other.
   What possible actions and policies.
   Consider objective and effect on individual, group, and production.
   Don't jump to conclusions.

3. Take Action
   Are you going to handle this yourself?
   Do you need help in handling?
   Should you refer this to your supervisor?
   Watch the timing of your action.
   Don't pass the buck.

4. **Check Results**
   How soon will you follow up?
   How often will you need to check?
   Watch for changes in output, attitudes, and relationships.
   Did your action help production?

Facilities in India: In India with the help of the experts of International Labour Organisation, the TWI training programmes are available for the companies to train their supervisors. The TWI Centre in Mumbai offers facilities to the companies in the country to conduct and use the TWI training programmes which have been very successful. The Central Training Institute for Instructors also offers various supervisory training programmes. The other agencies that offer programmes in this area are Small Scale Industries Service Institute, National Productivity Council, Management Training Institutes and Colleges, National Institute for Training Industrial Engineers, Administrative Staff College etc.

Apart from these, there are facilities made available by companies for supervisory training in company schools and institutes and one of the notables in our country is the Staff Training Institute of Tata Iron & Steel Company Limited, which offers courses in Foremanship and Supervision.

Institute of Industrial Supervisors: In 1962 a professional association of foremen and supervisors in India known as the Institute of Industrial Supervisors was founded under the initiative of successful supervisors of part-time course in foremanship and supervision offered by TISCO at Staff Training Institute. The institute started with a membership of only 26 and it has grown considerably, to about 300 members, under the able guidance and dynamic of its president, Mr. K.H. Kutar, General Manager of TISCO. The institute has the following aims and objectives:[23]

(a) To foster the spirit of fellowship among the supervisors and provide opportunities for their professional development.

(b) To provide means for increasing co-operation with the management for efficiency and economy of production and safety of employees and equipment.

(c) To organise and develop the activities of the Institute for furtherance of effective supervision through social, educational and training programmes.

(d) To facilitate holding of group discussion, case studies, seminars etc.

(e) To sponsor observation and study tours to other industrial units.

(f) To undertake such activities conducive to the attainment of the objects of the Institute.

The institute has local chapters spread all over the country and it aims to bring the supervisor in our country up-to-date regarding skills, attitudes and knowledge required for effective supervision.

E. Supervisory Training — Techniques and Methods

The techniques and methods available for companies to train supervisors and foremen are many and they are discussed in this section.

1. Reading Material: Extensive reading materials are provided to the supervisors to educate themselves. Many companies, as part of supervisory training, circulate or mail weekly or fortnightly or monthly supervisory letters emphasising techniques of supervision. Some training departments prepare abstracts, digests, or summaries of articles and papers on supervision and give them to the supervisors. Some provide reading lists and journals. Some companies have established in-plant libraries and reading rooms and the trainee is given regular reading assignments, assignment to prepare a paper, or report, or a review of book, with a view to making the supervisor use the library and learn in the process. Some libraries have promotional activities also with open houses, announcement of new purchases, book reviews, compilation of books of current importance, book exhibits. Usually the libraries buy standard basic texts covering management, personnel administration, production, training, economics, mathematics etc. Some companies put out magazines and house journals which are given to the trainees. Some companies give a gift subscription of some magazines to their trainees. Summaries of research reports are also prepared by the training department and mailed to the supervisors.

2. Job Rotation: Carefully planned job rotation programmes are used to give wide-in-plant experience and to get to know all the operations, processes, products of the company. The supervisor may be moved from section to section and from department to department in the capacity of assistant supervisor. He has the opportunity to observe, to learn, to handle and to lead. The rotation period varies from one week to one year depending on the trainee and the programme.

3. Staff Meetings: Regular weekly or fortnightly or monthly staff meetings for training purposes are common and it is training of an indirect nature. Here discussions, participation, action and interaction help the trainees to learn and it gives an insight to their behaviour, ideas and views. The training manager may take up part of the programme to show a firm, to review a book, to conduct discussion, or to discuss an article.

Some of these are brainstorming sessions, where you are asked to come up with all kinds of ideas regarding various things, from naming a new product to handling a smoking problem of an employee. Thinking and learning are stimulated by these meetings and sessions.

4. *Interplant and Industrial Visits:* Many companies arrange for supervisors to visit other plants and offices of their companies or those of other companies. The visit is carefully preplanned. The supervisors are prepared for the visit in the sense they are advised what to observe, what questions to raise and what to learn from the visits. These visits do a great deal to stimulate and motivate supervisors. They may discuss problems with other supervisors and managers and what kind of problems are common and how they are being tackled.

5. *Individual Assignment with the Department:* The supervisor needs various skills and a certain supervisor is found lacking in one of the specific skills. He may be good at everything but weak in the concept of factors entering into cost. Then he maybe assigned to the cost department and given training in the fundamentals of cost control and data.

6. *Participation in the Work of Other Departments:* Some supervisors develop excessive loyalty to their department and do not attempt to realise the inter-departmental relationships and their impact on organisational health. In large organisations the supervisor's knowledge of the operations and problems of other departments may be very limited and often from this stems his criticism of this or that department for a variety of reasons.

So some companies ask their supervisors to work with the personnel department in the area of recruitment and selection or contract negotiation or organisational planning. Or he maybe asked to work with the quality control or purchase or stores departments in order to enable him to learn the operations of other departments and the problems they face. And he will have a better picture of the organisation as a whole and the critical role played by each of the departments.

7. *Problem-solving Sessions:* For training purposes, purely problem-solving meetings are held with specific problems facing the company. Some people, who believe that experience is the best teacher, think that this is the best type of learning. But some others argue there is very little learning in these sessions.

This technique is useful when the problems posed are used for training and developing skills and attitudes, rather than arriving at a solution and the chairman of these sessions must recognise the primary purpose and that is to train and develop supervisors.

8. *Lectures and Teaching:* These are perhaps the oldest and most common techniques to train supervisors. Well prepared and thought-provoking lectures delivered by competent teachers will be very useful in training. Lectures may be by professional teachers and line people trained in teaching.

9. Role-playing: In the role-playing technique of supervisory training the supervisors assume different roles — that of a production manager, personnel director, president, secretary, worker — and play out a typical problem situation. Hence through the role-playing, thinking and doing are brought together and many times a supervisor would say that the personnel executive must be doing this or that and when he is in that position in a class-room session faced with a problem, he gains altogether a different insight into the problems facing other executives and supervisors.

Professor John F. Mee writes that several companies which have used this technique, have noted certain advantages:[24]

1. It tends to give the men playing roles an insight into their own behaviour; they are looking at what they are doing in terms of their relationships with others and begin to realise their strengths and weaknesses in this area.
2. Since many roles are played in this type of training by each of the members of the group, the individuals are forced to look at a problem from many points of view. It broadens their perspective and gives them an insight into the feelings and thinking of other people.
3. Supervisors learn the skill of handling themselves in relation to others by actually doing rather than telling about what they would do.
4. Role playing has the advantage of giving many members of the group an opportunity to discuss the procedure and technique used in the role played. This not only broadens the group members but also gives the "role players" an opportunity to see how their actions are evaluated by other men holding similar positions.

10. Case Studies: In this method, the supervisors are given typical situations in various areas such as personnel, sales, labour relations, administration and finance and they are asked to discuss the case. These cases are based on actual business situations and present various problems which require management action. This technique develops individual's ability to spot problems to be solved, to discover and analyse relevant facts in order to reach a decision, to find alternative courses of action and to decide on a course of action. He may be asked to substantiate why he decided to choose a particular course of action or a solution.

Each presents his case analysis and is exposed to view points of the others. This discussion opens out new areas a particular supervisor may have left out. Study of cases forces him to consider many facts and opinions in an effort to reach a solution.

This method was developed and largely used at Harvard Business School. It is designed to stimulate analytical thinking and provide opportunities for learning. Bias, prejudices, likes and dislikes all come into the open and they are exposed to the group and once these are brought out into the open, many times the individual gets rid of them because he sees the mistakes himself.

11. Conferences: The conference method is a pretty common method of training and development. It provides an opportunity for the exchange of views and experiences and thus learning is promoted. One of the great advantages of the conference method is the development of analytical abilities and the inquiring spirit. Fundamental ideas, concepts and principles can be put across easily. It also helps in changing the attitudes of the conferences.

12. Programmed Instruction: The American Management Association has developed PRIME, Programmed Instruction for Management Education, for supervisors and it has shown impressive results. PRIME has two essential phases: one a step-by-step series of bits of knowledge, each building upon what has gone before and the second, a mechanism for presenting this series and checking on the trainee's knowledge. The machine can ask questions in proper sequence and indicate promptly whether answers are correct.

13. Selection of Trainers: The success of supervisor-training and development programme depends upon the people who offer the programme. There is need for engaging training specialists and professional instructors. More and more line executives must be trained by the training division to impart instruction. There must be some sort of an optimum manager-instructor mix.

Then a careful selection of the trainees is also necessary. Often not much thought is given to this aspect and mostly it is the boss who says that somebody needs to be trained. On what basis, he will not know himself.

5. H.R.D. — MANAGEMENT DEVELOPMENT[25]

A. The Need and Importance of Management Development

Mr. John Marsh, Director of the British Institute of Management, believes that "increase in productivity depends *inter alia* upon the vitality of the management's initiative, sustained enthusiasm, competence and technical know-how."[26]

To Dr. Herbert B. Schmidt, formerly of German Management Institute, it was apparent that there was one area which showed significant difference between U.S.A. and Europe and that area was management, its philosophy and proper realisation of its functions. He suggested that management and not capital or technology had been the greatest bottleneck in modern economic growth.[27]

Dr. Stefan H. Robock, Director of International Business Studies at Indiana University and a past Director of Committee of Economic Development, Wrote:[28]

"If any single factor is the key for unlocking the forces for economic growth in the underdeveloped areas of the world, that factor is management."

In U.S.S.R. after Mr. A.N. Kosygin became the Premier, there has been a great deal of attention and interest focused on industrial and business management. In his report to the plenary meeting of the Central Committee of the Communist Party of the Soviet Union in 1965, Mr. Kosygin stated:[29] The Presidium of "the C.P.S.U. Central Committee and the Council of Ministers of the U.S.S.R. are of the opinion that in tackling the problems of the further development of industry and the raining of people's living standards, the greatest attention should be focused on improving the methods and forms of industrial management. The forms of management, planning, and incentives which are now operating in industry are no longer in conformity with modern techno-economic conditions and the present level of productive forces."

In our country, the Third Five Year Plan Report observed:[30] "Lack of quality of managerial personnel is another factor prejudicing the success of an enterprise." There is a great dearth of professional managers and there are differing estimates as to our managerial requirements.

The Management Personnel Committee set up under the chairmanship of Sir A. Ramaswamy Mudaliar by the Ministry of Education assessed the requirements of executive personnel during the Third Five Year Plan period as 6,970 for Technical Management and 13,070 for General and Commercial Management. The corresponding requirements for the Fourth Plan are 13,243 and 26,496.

The Institute of Applied Manpower Research at Delhi estimated that there were about 55,000 managerial personnel in the beginning of the Third Plan.[31] The Institute estimates that the managerial manpower requirements in the Third, Fourth and Fifth Five Year Plans are likely to be of the order of 52,800, 79,500 and 1,08,000 respectively. Other management experts believe, perhaps with good reason, that both these estimates are on the low side. Suffice it to say that there is a great need for executive talent and to train individuals to become executives.

In U.S.A. also there is a dearth of managerial manpower as pointed out by Mr. Leo Cherne in his address to the U.S. Chamber of Commerce. "In fact, there will be fewer people in 1975 available to manage and grasp the opportunities — almost a million less in 1975 than there will be this year.... Management is not only the most urgent calling, but it is perhaps the most critically short resource facing us in the years immediately ahead."[32]

The outlook for the years ahead suggests that the development of business managers will continue to require substantial effort. Several conditions point to this:

1. ***The competition for talent capable of development:*** This competition is more acute at the moment among technical people graduating from college. But the long-run prospect is that all who draw on the pool of available talent will continue to find it difficult to get the numbers they need of the kinds of people they would like to have. This is likely to be especially true of people capable of becoming managers.

2. ***The continued growth and development of business:*** This outlook will vary with the company, but most businesses see a good deal of undeveloped opportunity ahead, although at the moment for some, the outlook is bleak.

3. ***Increasing complexity of business:*** Growth and the problem of size, new forms of product competition, new technology, competition for capital, will combine to present new problems for all managers.

4. ***Probable continued unsettled political, economic, and social conditions — both domestic and foreign — that add to the demands on managers:*** It does not seem that the pressures on managers brought about by inflation, aftermath of war, population growth, social change are likely to diminish — and there may be new ones.

5. ***The need to press for continually improving performance despite these complicating factors:*** The effort of a business to improve its product, lower its cost and extend its use will continue to be a major aim of managers.

6. ***The need to compress the time taken for a manager to become fully competent:*** Growth, complexity, competition for talent, new demands, plus the cost of inexperience in the management staff will make this increasingly important.

B. Aims of Management Development

The following are some of the major aims:

1. To assure managers in required numbers and with the required skills to meet the present and anticipated future needs of the business.
2. To encourage managers to grow as persons and in their capacity to handle greater responsibility.
3. To improve the performance of managers at all levels in the jobs they now hold.
4. To sustain good performance of managers throughout their careers.

Executive development programmes embrace long time horizons and the stress is on manager manpower planning. Though recent in origin, management training programmes have become popular with many corporations in the West and the accent is on the manager-in-the-making. Considering the shortage of available managerial talent, this phenomenon is hardly surprising. The nature of these programme has introduced a new dimension in the Organisation of business enterprises, that is the concept of an 'everlasting firm' and a prompt availability of managerial 'heirs' ensures the longevity of the enterprise, which in turn not only enhances the importance of executive development programmes but also perpetuates the calling of the managers. The process of executive development acts as the very elixir of the business enterprise. Peter Drucker writes, "In fine, manager development must embrace all managers in the enterprise. It must aim at challenging all to growth and self-development. It must focus on performance rather than on promise, and on tomorrow's requirements rather than on those of today. Manager development must be dynamic and qualitative rather than static replacement based on mechanical rotation. Developing tomorrow's managers means in effect developing today's managers all of them to be bigger men and better managers."

The Problem of Managerial Training

The full purport of the management training programmes is to encourage the development of men in whom others can have confidence. But no organisation should take the obligation or responsibility to develop men into managers, without the keen interest and complete co-operation of the individuals involved. To take such a responsibility would be 'unwarranted paternalism' as well as 'foolish pretension.' Every manager in a business has the opportunity to encourage individual self-development or to stifle it, to direct it or to misdirect it. He should be specifically assigned the responsibility for helping all men working with him to focus, direct, and apply their self-development efforts productively. And every company can provide systematic development challenges to its managers.

"Managerial training is an effort to provide knowledge and experience, an integral part of the material needed for the development of judgment. Indeed, the knowledge and experience acquired in educational institutions and practical pursuits are the whetstones upon which natural intelligence is sharpened."

By and large a managerial programme is justified by its contribution to the development of skilled managers. But a few students of management contend that executive training programme might deaden the initiative and creative thinking in the case of young college graduates who may possess high potentialities to become exceptional managers. It is better to pick the right man than one who needs training.

Managerial training cannot be standardized, in the sense manager development ought to be tailored to the needs of the person. There is no standard formula that can be applied to all the candidates for executive development. Furthermore there are levels of executive training, i.e., supervisor training, junior executive training, senior executive training, and all such levels should be exposed to the programmes, as long as we subscribe to the theory that there is room for growth and development on the part of a manager regardless of his rank in the organisation. Often the fallacious reasoning is advanced that senior executives need no further development programmes and that all such training should be concentrated on foremen and junior executives. It is essential to think through the objectives of training before starting a training programme.

Strategy of Executive Development (ED)

Talking about the strategy of E.D., it is essential to bear in mind that 90% of the development occurs as a result of on-the-job experience — the way he manages, the way he is allowed to manage, the way his superior manages and the impact of his style on the subordinate, and the general environment created by the management system in vogue. Formal training and development programmes affect only 10% of his development. Hence the best of formal development programmes cannot help the individual much if he is unable to use new learning, knowledge, skills and techniques.

We suggest a combined unified strategy of ED as depicted in the chart.

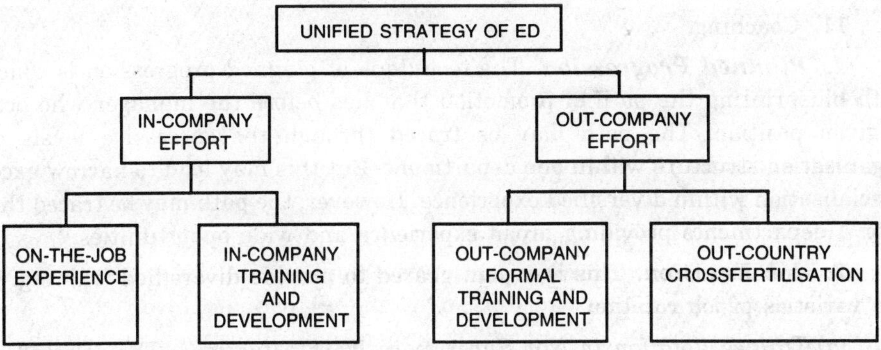

In our scheme the in-company on-the-job experience plays critical role in the strategy of ED. It is fair to concede that the executive or manager "manages" and uses the process of management.

Types of Training

One of the oldest forms of training was the exposure of the potential manager to the vagaries of business enterprise and it was hoped that experience would mould him into a manager. But this form of training can be very costly in the present complex nature of the industrial organisation. While practical business experience is necessary the executives believe that a formal training, which is carefully designed and planned, would go a long way in alleviating the problem of the paucity of managerial talent.

Creation of opportunities for diversified experience would be the most effective means of: (1) orienting the candidate to the inter-relationships of departments and the view points held by their personnel; (2) understanding the people in other departments; (3) forestalling the growth of unseemly departmental loyalties; and (4) broadening the vision and thinking in terms of company as a whole. The primary objective of training programmes is to develop a pool of manpower capable of succeeding the managers at higher levels. "The smart businessman has of course, always known that it has never done a company harm to be known as 'the mother of President.' On the contrary, the power of a company to attract good men is directly proportionate to its reputation as a developer of successful men for itself as well as for other companies."

The various types of formalised programmes may be listed as follows:

1. Planned Progression;
2. Job Rotation;
3. Creation of 'assistant-to' positions;
4. Role-playing;
5. Temporary Promotions;
6. Understudy;
7. Committees and Junior Boards;
8. Conference Programmes;
9. University Management Programmes;
10. Management Workshop Programmes;
11. Coaching.

1. Planned Progression: The technique of planned progression is concerned with blueprinting the path of promotion that lies before the manager who occupies a given position. The path may be traced through the successive levels of the organisation structure within one department. But this may lead to narrow excessive specialisation within diversified experience. However, the path may be traced through 3 or 4 departments providing broad experience and wide opportunities.

2. Job Rotation: This is a plan geared to provide diversified training. There are varieties of job rotation.

(a) Trainee Rotation in Non-Supervisory Work Situations: The selected candidates for training are assigned to predetermined jobs within a list of departments for a given period of time. The purpose is to acquaint trainees with the range of activities undertaken by the firm. But the problem is that employees may resent the trainees and their preferred position and also the fact that trainees may take away the jobs from the permanent help. The trainee also may be discouraged during this type of training.

(b) Trainee Rotation in Observation Assignments: This concept envisages the creation of opportunities for trainees to observe a group of department managers on a rotating basis. The purpose is to acquaint the trainee with various managerial problems and their solutions. This gives an opportunity for the trainee to 'sell' himself and to learn the type of work he would like to do. But observing and doing are two

different things and it does not provide any practical experience. Many executives also feel that candidates do not know what to observe and how.

(c) Rotation among Managerial Training Positions: This involves the designation of certain managerial positions on the same level in the organisation structure as training stations to be successively occupied by trainees. The purpose is to give actual supervisory experience in a variety of positions in several departments. But when suitable placement is not forthcoming after training, disillusion grows greater on the part of the trainee.

(d) Middle-level Rotation in "Assistant" Position: This involves shuffling trainees as assistant managers in several departments. The purpose is to broaden their experience at a high level in each department. This creates a pool of trainees for later appointment to department managerships.

(e) Unspecified Rotation among Managerial Positions: This is an unplanned and unspecified rotation of managers from one department to another. The purpose is to give managers responsible experience in a variety of positions.

3. *Creation of "Assistant-to" Positions:* This training device permits the candidate to broaden his viewpoint by exposure to many areas of managerial practice. Here the superior can act effectively as the teacher and he can judge the assistant's decision making and his leadership ability in selected cases. The training period can be tailored to assistant's needs. But if the superior fails as a teacher or is authoritarian the training will be poor and ineffective.

4. *Role-Playing:* This consists of creating situations in the classroom where the candidates in pairs assume roles of executive and subordinate and discuss the issues and at the end conclusions as to the most effective means of handling a situation can be arrived at. The problem here is creating the environment of work situation.

5. *Understudy:* The executive is expected to train the understudy to fill his place when he may be away for sometime because of vacation, business trips, illness or other reasons. This is to develop flexibility and stability in the organisation as well as to provide opportunity to the candidate to show his mettle. The understudy system should be a part of an organised promotion system.

6. *Temporary Promotions:* They may be found as an ideal way to train executives in medium-sized and small firms. The candidate may be moved upto the next rung of managerial hierarchy and tested for his performance and made accountable during that period of temporary tenure. In some corporations to arrange for such temporary promotion may be impossible.

7. *Committees and Junior Boards:* These are composed of middle level managers, selected on the basis of merit rating, who meet regularly and act as idea 'men' and their proposals will be considered by the responsible general executive and may be referred to the Board of Directors if found suitable. The advantage is that the perspective of the members is broadened and a sense of responsibility for the firm is instilled in them.

8. *Conference Programmes:* These imply group exposure to ideas developed by a leader or speaker. It is direct and economical. Thus a class of trainees may be instructed effectively in company policies, history, objectives, customer attitudes etc.

9. University Management Programmes: Some Universities organise courses, institutes, conferences and formal programmes to train managers for a specific period. These establish valuable group contacts, which act as an aid to the efficiency of individual managers. But much depends on the quality of these programmes.

10. Management Workshop Programmes: Through workshops or seminars instruction is provided in a wide variety of subjects and classes are restricted to a small number so that there might be a free exchange of varied experiences. The leader of each workshop is usually an operating business executive, who possesses both experience and teaching ability.

In view of the variety of training programmes, the right training programme to achieve the predetermined objectives must be instituted after careful deliberation and planning.

11. Coaching: This is an old technique discovered anew and the distinctive feature is face-to-face counselling. Its success depends on the ability of the superior to counsel the subordinate and on the receptivity of the candidate. Counselling is an effective way to get a new subordinate oriented in his job. It involves continuous analysis of the subordinate's performance by the superior. This enables the candidate to understand clearly how the superior operates regarding inter-departmental relationships and personalities. Counselling cannot be standardized and should be personal in nature. When mutual confidence is developed, the exchange of ideas and views between the superior and subordinate can be extremely valuable. It may be necessary to teach superior the ability to coach well, for on this rests the success or the failure of the entire coaching programme. If the superior lacks the capacity to counsel, then the coaching programme will be ineffective.

These executive development programmes provide for much needed managerial manpower.

Recent Trends in Executive Development

The Science of Management does not have all the answers regarding the training and developing of executives. But there is a constant effort through research and analysis to improve the existing training programmes and to develop new ones to meet the problem of executive development. It is appropriate here to make a brief mention of the recent trends in training programmes and new techniques adopted to train and develop managers.

Self-renewal

Mr. John Gardner advocates a theory of self-renewal for the development of individuals and the organisation.[33] If the individual has a commitment to self-renewal, the organisation can remove some of the obstacles and even provide opportunities, but the emphasis remains on the self. In a society capable of self-renewal, men not only welcome the future and the changes it may bring, but believe that they will have a hand in shaping that future. Professor Charles Myers observes:[34] "In other words, if the educational system prepares the individual for an accelerating rate of change, and the business organisation gives him opportunities to gain versatility and responsibility in a variety of jobs and assignment situations, that individual will not be dragged screaming into the future. He will welcome it."

Laboratory Training

The National Training Laboratories (NTL) in U.S.A. pioneered "laboratory training" associated with "T-Groups" or "sensitivity training" for executives, middle managers and people from non-business organisations and many executives have been exposed to this type of programme. Schein and Bennis state:[35] "this important new educational strategy.... is capable of releasing some important forces which can enhance man's ability to control more effectively and creatively his human environment."

Although the unstructured T-Groups, in which the real "learning experience" takes place, are the core of the programme, they are supplemented by "information or theory sessions," in which staff members lecture or demonstrate the relevance of research findings in the behavioural sciences, and "focused exercises," including role playing, interview groups, seminars and other sessions.

Schein and Bennis point out that increased awareness of his own feelings and the feelings of others is a vital necessity for the adoption of the individual to the organisation. The manager who is insensitive to the impact of his behaviour on others is the cause of resentment, withheld effort and often lack of initiative in his associates and subordinates and the consequence is reduced organisational effectiveness.

The "stranger" T-Groups where participants come from different organisations offer psychological safety — the individual does not have to go back and face the same people who have helped him learn about his own behaviour. This safety does not exist in laboratory training conducted for executives within a particular company.

Schein and Bennis report that companies such as ESSO Standard, Pacific Finance, Aluminium Company of Canada, Hotel Corporation of America, U.S. Rubber, General Electric, I.B.M., Eli Lily and many others have made laboratory training an essential part of their management development and organisation improvement efforts.

Grid Team Training

Associated with the managerial Grid concept, "grid team training" is developed by Robert R. Blake and Jane S. Mouton.[36] There are five principal managerial styles with interesting and descriptive labels:

"Impoverished Management (1, 1) — Effective production is unobtainable because people are lazy, apathetic and indifferent. Sound and mature relationships are difficult to achieve because human nature being what it is, conflict is inevitable."

"Country Club Management (1, 9) — Production is incidental to lack of conflict and good fellowship."

"Middle of the Road Management (5, 5) — Push for production but don't go all out. Give some, not all. Be fair, but firm."

"Task management (9, 1) — Men are a commodity just like machines. A manager's responsibility is to plan, direct and control the work of those subordinate to him."

"Team management (9, 9) — Production is from the integration of task and human requirements into a unified system of interplay toward organisational goals."

Table

Comparative Value of Different Methods

Primary Purpose	*Method*
1. Explaining facts and procedures. Expounding general principles.	Lectures, guided discussion.
2. Developing analytical skills & ability to ask oneself questions.	Case Method (Incident Process).
3. Developing awareness of oneself and one's impact on others.	Sensitivity Training (T-Groups) Role-Playing.
4. Carry-over from class to the job.	Problem-solving Conferences (to a lesser extent: Role Play).
5. Inducing change in behaviour.	Role Play, T-Groups, Problem-solving Conferences.
6. Opportunity for emotional catharsis.	T-Groups, Case Method, Problem-solving Conference.
7. Insuring good training with unskilled trainers.	Lectures, Incident Process.

Source: Strauss & Sayles: *Personnel, The Human Problems of Management* (New York, Prentice Hall, 1960), p. 566.

These represent different mixes of "concern for people" and "concern for production." Blake and Mouton describe how their training approach can be applied in six phases to vertical and horizontal levels of management within a company. An unusual feature is the use of trained line managers from the company, rather than behavioural scientists as in T-Group approach, for laboratory trainers. As they point out, "when organisation members take responsibility for such teaching, they also feel increased responsibility for seeing to it that the learning is used in the work."[37]

6. H.R.D. — ORGANISATION DEVELOPMENT

What is Organisation Development?

Organisation development may be defined as an effort (1) planned, (2) organisation-wide, and (3) managed from the top, to (4) increase organisation effectiveness and health through (5) planned interventions in the organisation's "processes," using behaviour-science knowledge.

An OD programme involves a systematic diagnosis of the organisation, the development of a strategic plan for improvement, and the mobilisation of resources to carry out the effort.

To understand the goals of organisation development, it is necessary to have some picture of what an "ideal" effective, healthy organisation would look like. An effective organisation is one in which: (a) The total organisation, the significant subparts, and individuals manage their work against goals and plans for achievement of these goals; (b) The problem, or task or project, determines how the human resources are organised; (c) Decisions are made by and near the sources of information regardless of their location on the organisation chart; (d) The reward system is such that managers and supervisors are rewarded (and punished) comparably; (e) Communication laterally and vertically is relatively undistorted; (f) There is a minimum amount of inappropriate win/lose activities; (g) There is high clash of ideas about tasks and projects but little of interpersonal difficulties; (h) The organisation is an "open system"; (i) There is a shared value of trying to help each person (or unit) to maintain his (or its) integrity and uniqueness in an interdependent environment; (j) The organisation and its members operate in an "action research" way.

Organisation development achieves its goals through planned interventions using behavioural science knowledge. A strategy is developed of moving into the existing organisation and helping it, in effect, examine its present ways of work, norms, and values, and look at alternative ways of working, or relating, or rewarding.

OD efforts usually have some of the following operational goals: (1) To develop a self-renewing, viable system that can organise in a variety of ways depending on tasks; (2) To optimise the effectiveness of both the stable (the basic organisation chart) and the temporary systems; (3) To move toward high collaboration and low competition between interdependent units; (4) To create such conditions where conflict is brought out and managed; (5) To reach the point where decisions are made on the basis of information source rather than organisational role.

Most successful organisation development efforts have the following characteristics: (1) There is a planned programme involving the whole system; (2) The top of the organisation is aware of and committed to the programme and to the management of it; (3) It is related to the organisation's mission; (4) It is long-term effort; (5) Activities are action oriented; (6) It focuses on changing attitudes and/or behaviour; (7) It usually relies on some form of experience-based learning activities; (8) OD efforts work primarily with groups.

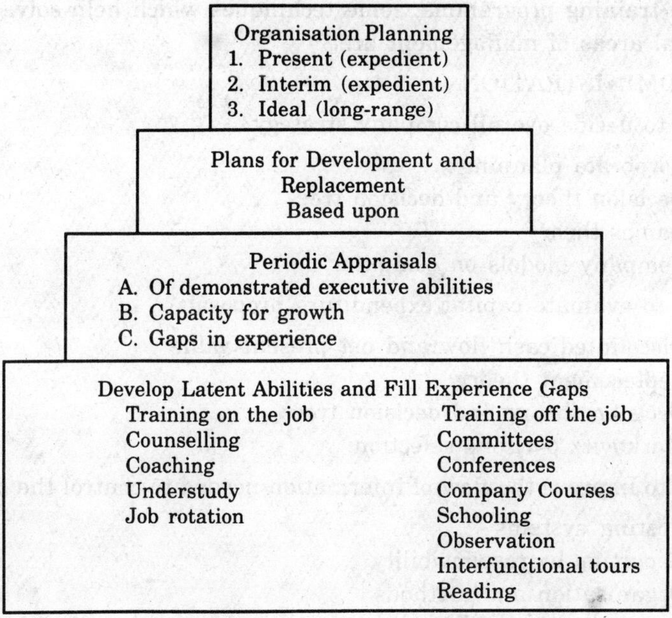

Fig. 7.6 Steps in the programme for systematic development of executives in Standard Oil Company, (New Jersey)

Source: George B. Coreless, *The Development of Executive Talent,* Chapter XXXI, "Case 1: The Standard Oil Company (New Jersey) Programme for Executive Development." (New York: American Management Association, 1952), p. 312.

Some In-Company Programmes in India

Many companies in U.S.A., U.K. and India offer training facilities and programmes within their companies. The larger ones have their own schools, institutes and centres for the purpose of training, development and research. Corporations like General Motors, Standard Oil, N.J., Sears Roebuck, I B M, General Electric, Bell Telephone, A. T. T., Chase Manhattan, Ford, DuPont and others are known for their executive development programmes. The Figure 7.6 gives the steps involved in Standard Oil Company (New Jersey).

In India in recent years there is increasing awareness of and interest in management development programmes. On January 6, 1966 the Tata House which has always been in the forefront in this area, founded The Tata Management Training Centre at Pune and inaugurating the centre, Mr. J. R. D. Tata, the dynamic leader of the Tata Group of Industries, declared: "Trained managers are vital to the economic development of the country.... We have always been, from the early days of Jamsetji Tata, interested in anything new. In fact, we have built up a reputation for pioneering, so that it was natural that we should eagerly look towards and adopt some of these new ideas. And we realised that this business of executive development was one of the most crucial, essential and, at the same time, one of the most difficult elements in providing continuity and efficient management."[38]

This new centre, established at a capital cost of Rs. 22 lakhs for the first stage, is wholly residential in character. It accommodates about 36 participants at a time. As part of the training programme, some techniques which help solve problems in some functional areas of management are:[39]

GENERAL ADMINISTRATION

How to decide overall company strategy?

- Corporate planning
- Decision theory and decision trees
- Games theory
- Company models on computer.

How to evaluate capital expenditure proposals?

- Discounted cash flow and net present value
- Replacement theory
- Decision theory and decision trees
- Markovitz portfolio selection.

How to improve the flow of information needed to control the organisation?

- Costing systems
- Reporting by responsibility
- Organisation and methods
- Systems and analysis
- Computers for data processing
- Management by exception
- Computers for information retrieval
- Random observation studies
- Information theory
- Cybernetics.

How to launch a new project?

Critical path including PERT
PERT/COST
Branching networks
Resource allocation
Using a computer with these techniques.

MARKETING AND SALES

How to forecast demand?

Exponential smoothing
Market research
Moving averages
Regression analysis
Box/Jenkins
Time series
Leontieff input-output tables
Use of computer with these techniques.

How to generate new product ideas?

Market research
Brainstorming
Value analysis.

How to launch a new product?

Critical path method including PERT
PERT/COST
Branching networks
Using a computer with these techniques.

How to determine the profitability of a product or product line?

Marginal costing
Contribution analysis
Profit-volume ratio
Break-even charts
Linear programing.

How to improve product design?

Market research
Value analysis
Ergonomics.

PRODUCTION

How to remove factory bottlenecks?

Production control by computer
Critical path methods including PERT
Branching networks
Resource allocation
Using a computer with these techniques

Simulation including Monte Carlo method
Queuing theory.

How to improve product quality and reliability?

Statistical quality control
Process control by computer, including
Evolutionary operation, and
Adaptive control.

How to cope with complex mixes? — such problems as: several factories, delivery to many customers, or several products from many raw materials available from many different sources, or several products profitability made by several processes, etc. Mathematical programming by computer, including

Linear programming
Quadratic programming
Separable programming
Integer programming
Dynamic programming.

How to cut labour costs?

Method study
Incentive schemes
Ergonomics
Productivity bargaining.

How to improve labour relations?

Job relations programme.

PERSONNEL

How to improve training methods?

Teaching machines
Business games.

How to bring order and equity into wages and salary schemes?

Job description
Job evaluation
Merit rating
Salary progressing curves
Time-span discretion.

How to recruit the right number of the right type of people?

Manpower planning
Intelligence, personality and aptitude tests.

PURCHASING

How to check quality and reliability of raw materials?

Statistical quality control including quality protection
Statistical sampling methods including sequential analysis.

How to cut down the cost of purchasing and holding stocks?

Statistical stock control
Methods of forecasting demand (see under marketing)
Economic batch re-ordering quantities
Simulation by computer.

RESEARCH

How to reduce the time taken to complete research?

Method study
Critical path methods including PERT
PERT/COST
Branching networks
Research allocation
Using a computer with these techniques
Statistical design of experiments
Scientific calculations by computer
Simulation by computers.

Other companies like D C M, Hindustan Lever, Larsen & Toubro, I T I, H M T, etc. offer training programmes from the work level all the way up to the top executive.

Basic Philosophy of Executive Development in a Leading Group

1. Executive Development, to be effective, touches all the bases of the executive cadre and the potential executive cadre from top to bottom. Executive Development will be ineffective if the needs of all levels are not ministered to. All levels of management in Group need to be exposed to contemporaneous management concepts, techniques and tools through appropriate executive development effort aimed at different levels.
2. A corollary to the above principle is that organisational development results through a balanced and integrated executive development effort which encompasses the needs of training and development of different levels. Strengthening different and all functional management areas contributes to greater organisational effectiveness and development.
3. A systems approach to executive development effort is a *sine qua non*, where executive resources planning, career development plans, executive succession systems, evaluation of the impact of the executive development effort and organisational development constitute interrelated and interlocked phases of a total executive development system. What happens before and after is as (perhaps more) important as what happens in a programme. Mere executive development programmes are of not much consequence. Executive development effort must constitute an integral component of general personnel and management processes of an organisation.
4. The strategy of executive development effort is to (a) strengthen the manager and the potential in his basic functional area, (b) develop him, gradually over a period of time, to higher and higher capabilities through a vertical planned progression and to raise to the highest position in the organisation to which he is uniquely capable of rising, (c) provide opportunities of broadening his

horizons through cross-functional experiences, inter-disciplinary approaches, cross-fertilisation of ideas and views, and exposure to socio-economic, politico-cultural and religious forces as well as to the internationalisation of dominant values of our society.

5. Two specific goals for every manager and the potential in the Group are necessary as an integral part of executive development effort: (a) First is that every manager accomplishes results. (b) Second, he develops his subordinate to succeed him (even at a very short notice). These goals offer tremendous fillip to executive development effort.
6. The executive development effort must strive, as far as possible and feasible, to integrate the organisational needs and interests with individual needs and interests. Catering to only one type of needs and interests will not result in executive development and organisational effectiveness.
7. Executive development effort embraces both in-company, out-company and out-country programmes as well as a variety of on-the-job development experiences. The latter two topologies must receive greater attention and usage, since they are likely to be more effective and useful.
8. Equal opportunities are available to every individual in the Group to rise to the highest position.
9. The high talent personnel receive greater attention in executive development effort and management progression.
10. Initiative, enterprise, creativity, innovativeness, hard work and dedication are to be developed and nurtured in our managers and potential. These are the qualities that lead to success not only in the present but also in the distant future.

Apart from in-company programmes, there are many institutions which offer management development programmes.[40] They are universities and colleges, professional associations and institutes, research institutions, management institutes and schools, and management consultancy firms. In U.S.A. the well-known graduate Schools of Business Administration are at Harvard, Columbia, U.C.L.A., New York University, Stanford, Wisconsin, Yale, Cornell, Minnesota, Indiana, University of Michigan, M.I.T. etc. The work of American Management Association is well known. Among the research institutions, the National Industrial Conference Board is easily the most outstandings and the courses, seminars, conferences and programmes conducted by N.I.C.B. and A.M.A. are perhaps the most useful to the executives.

In India professional bodies like Indian Institute of Personnel Management, Institute of Chartered Accountants, National Association of Purchasing Executives, Institute of Industrial Engineers and others offer programmes in their areas. There are about 20 management institutions offering management development programmes. Perhaps the Andhra University was the first one to offer M.B.A (Master of Business Administration) programme in India. The other prominent ones are School of Industrial Administration and Business Management at University of Delhi, Jamnalal Bajaj Institute of Management Studies at Mumbai, Institute of Social Welfare and Business Management at Calcutta, University of Kerala, Chennai,

Osmania, Thiagarajar School of Management at Madurai, P. S. G. College of Technology at Coimbatore, St. Xaviers Institute of Labour Relations at Jamshedpur and recently Indian Institute of Management at Calcutta and Ahmedabad in collaboration with M.I.T. and Harvard respectively. Birla Institute of Technology and Engineering offers M.B.A. and Ph.D. programmes.

Then we have All India Management Association and various Management Associations in large cities which offer training programmes.

The other agencies are Administrative Staff College, National Productivity Council and local Productivity Councils, NITIE, Small Scale Industries Service Institutes and many private management consultancy firms.

Some companies are sending their executives abroad to such countries as U.S.A., U.K., West Germany, Japan, France, Switzerland, Sweden, Italy and others. With the increasing trend of collaborations with foreign companies, often Indian executives are sent to the foreign collaborating company for training. The foreign subsidiaries headquartered here in our country also send their executives for training to the parent company. Sometimes the parent company may sent its specialists to train executives in its subsidiary in our country.

Despite these in-company and external training facilities available to companies, there are many companies in various parts of our country relatively unexposed to any supervisory or executive development programmes. Then there are some who merely pay lip-service to such programmes and some who think it fashionable to be "with it." Increasing complexity, size and sophistication of business and industry will force employers to think seriously in terms of operating efficiency and management and developing supervisors and managers.

7. H.R.D. — EVALUATION OF TRAINING[41]

A. Evaluation of Employee Training

In many instances, there is no follow-up and evaluation of training programmes. Walter R. Mahlen of the Psychological Corporation in U.S.A. reported:[42]

1. most companies don't know what industrial training has accomplished;
2. training needs are determined primarily on the basis of what the boss wants;
3. most companies have no idea what training methods work best;
4. 1 in 10 companies use systematic research to determine training needs;
5. 1 in 40 companies evaluate efficiency of training methods; and
6. testimony or subjective opinion is the basic system of evaluation.

This situation is possible only when there is little care and deliberation devoted to training needs of employees and analysis of training programmes that could meet these needs.

The following criteria are suggested for the purpose of evaluation of training programmes:

1. Increased output.
2. Reduced time to turn out a unit of production.

3. Reduced training time.
4. Reduction in scrap, breakage and supplies used.
5. Improvement in quality of output.
6. Improvement in morale.
7. Reduction in absenteeism, grievances, turnover, and accidents.
8. Reduction in overhead.

As earlier pointed out, training is provided to meet a need or to solve a problem. If safety training is offered to prevent accidents, the follow-up must evaluate whether there have been fewer accidents. The following techniques may be used to evaluate the effectiveness of training programmes.

1. Tests.
2. Checklists.
3. Attitude surveys.
4. Learning curves.
5. Cost accounting.
6. Employee appraisals.

B. Evaluation of Supervisory and Executive Development and Training

Once attending a management development programme conducted by a professional management association in our country, I asked the Secretary in charge of the programme, "What are your follow-up and evaluation measures, after this programme is over?" He replied disarmingly, but definitely with authority, "Oh! no follow-up and evaluation, Professor. You see, in programmes like these, particularly for executives, it is not at all possible to evaluate. And we are very busy with other similar programmes all over the country. But then evaluation of management development programmes is always impossible."

The Chairman of Hindustan Lever, Mr. P.L. Tandon has some caustic words for some programmes: "There is thus a large and growing body of institutions to serve our needs, and their contribution to industry is indeed valuable; but one point has perhaps to be watched. Is the training they give realistic and concrete and built around the day-to-day needs of the executive or does it tend to make diffused theoretical sweeps over wide fields? Does it fill the men with mostly knowledge or does it also develop ability to analyse, choose from a set of alternatives and to decide? There are instances of courses organised where the participants hear as many as a dozen speakers on a dozen subjects in one day. This is not executive development. It is like much of our education, filling the head with a lot of knowledge while the need is to sharpen the ability to choose, to apply, to decide."[43]

Often the training needs and objectives are not determined; there is no follow-up and evaluation; and there is the mistaken notion that 'management development programme' is the answer. It is a fallacious notion to believe that the objectives of management development programmes are so complex that the evaluation of results is practically impossible.

These programmes were instituted to meet a serious need or to solve a problem and *it should be possible to define that need and measure the extent to which these programmes are meeting it.* We suggest a programme of follow-up and evaluation.

The evaluative process will largely depend on the objectives which we set out to organise training and development programmes. Broadly speaking the objectives of training and development are: (1) Knowledge Change; (2) Attitude Change: (3) Skills Change; (4) Behaviour Change; (5) Performance Change.

As a result of changes in the first four, changes in performance occur.

One type of evaluative process would be at three levels:

First Approach

1. Endorsement level refers to what the executive trainees think about the course through a questionnaire.

2. *Learning level* examines the measured changes that occur in training in on-the-job test situation.

3. Results level examines the desired outcomes of economic or quasi-economic terms. In regard to our ultimate evaluation criterion, the results level hits the bull's eye.

Second Approach

We suggest another four-step evaluative process along with the tools to be used in the process.

Step I — Reaction: How well did the participants like the Programme? (Tools: Questionnaire — observation — interview).

Step II — Learning: What principles, facts and techniques were learnt? (Tools: tests — examinations — quiz — projects)

Step III — Behaviour: What changes in job behaviour resulted from the programme? (Tools: (1) Systematic appraisal of on-the-job performance before and after the programme. (2) Appraisal of performance by (a) self-appraisal; (b) by his superior/s; (c) by his subordinates; (d) by his peers; (3) Post-training appraisal 3 months, 6 months, 1 year; (4) Statistical analysis to compare before and after performance and related changes to programme; (5) A control group not receiving training should be used.

Step IV — Results: What were the tangible results of the programme in terms of reduced cost; improved quality, improved productivity etc.? (Tools: tests — checklists — attitude surveys — learning curves — cost accounting — employee appraisals — depth interviews — mailing questionnaires — follow up).

1. Ask the participant to submit a report on training, and what he learnt from it.
2. Set up and maintain detailed personnel records of the participant, showing from month to month and year to year what has happened.
3. Conduct a follow-up interview with participant after 3 months, to find out how he is using his learning, whether there has been an improvement in his operations, and whether he has any problems.

4. Incorporate a programme of periodic polling of participants, superiors, peers, and subordinates whose opinions may help you judge the effects and values of your departmental activities.
5. Insist on periodic audit of the whole training programme at least once a year.
6. Have informal conferences and discussions for the participant with the superiors, who shall appraise the participant.
7. Ask him to make a weekly report indicating progress in various aspects of his work such as reduction of indirect labour and costs, waste, materials or supplies, increase in productivity, improvement of operations, reduction of work stoppage, improvement of personnel relations etc.
8. Use examinations, tests, ratings.
9. Conduct periodic interviews and counselling session.

Follow-up and evaluation of training programmes are essential considering the fact that so much money is spent on the programmes. There are many companies who have evolved successful evaluation systems so that they can determine what is the return for their investment in training programmes. Groht and Mallick describe a convincing demonstration of this tool at Westinghouse Electric Company.[44] After finding that 36 per cent of their labour dollar goes to material handling, they set up a material handling course. The total cost of the programme was $ 6,000. Savings from this programmes were $ 53,000, a 900 per cent return on the training cost.

REFERENCES

1. An Interview with Lockheed Aircraft Company, Voice of America Broadcast, 7-15, A.M. 19-12-1966.
2. Quoted from James L. Lundy, *op. cit.,* p. 502.
3. Dale Yoder and others, *Handbook of Personnel*, pp.12.2-12.3.
4. Condensed from the American Society for Training and Development, *Training and Development Handbook*, New York: McGraw Hill Book Company, 1967.
5. Andrew Daly, "Building Training Attitudes," *Supervision*, Vol. 14, No. 9, September 1952, p. 18.
6. Robert R. Blake and Jane S. Mouton, *The Managerial Grid: Key Orientations for Achieving Production through People* (Houston, Texas: Gulf Publishing Company, 1964) p. 175.
7. Evolved by the Council on Training of the Conference Board, *The Conference Board Management Record,* National Industrial Conference Board, New York, Vol. 12, No. 12, December, 1950, p. 447.
8. Richard R. Crow, "An Organised Approach to Training," *Personnel*, Vol. 23. No. 6, May 1947, p. 447.
9. William J. Micheels, "Use of Audio-visual Materials," The Third Annual Industrial Relations Center Labour Conference, Industrial Relations Center, University of Minnesota, Minneapolis, Minnesota, February, 1951, p. 6.
10. See Morris S. Viteles, *The Science of Work,* New York: W.W. Norton and Company, Inc. 1934, pp. 227-270.
11. *Ibid.*, p. 247.
12. Federal Security Agency, "Staff Development: The Supervisor's Job," *Training Manual No. 6,* Washington D.C. 1948, p. 16.

13. *Training within Industry Report,* 1940-1945, Washington, Bureau of Training Within Industry Service, War Manpower Commission, September 1945, p. 45.

14. See "Apprentice Pays Dividends," Bureau of Apprenticeship, U.S. Department of Labour, 150, pp. 3-6.

15. L.K. Deshpande, "Evaluation of Apprenticeship Programme," in S.D. Punekar (ed.), *Economic Revolution in India,* Bombay, Himalaya Publishing House, 1977, pp. 459-464.

16. See Phyllis P. Groom, "Retraining Unemployed," Monthly Labour Review, Vol. 84, No.8, August 1961, pp. 823-28; also No. 9, September, 1961, pp. 939-43.

17. John F. Mee, *Personnel Handbook,* p. 958.

18. See Don Copell, "A Scientific Approach to Training and Public Speaking," *Modern Management,* Vol. 5, No. 5, October 1945, pp. 24-25.

19. See Stanley E. Seashore, in Rensis Likert and Samuel P. Hayes, Eds., *Some Applications of Behavioural Research* (Paris: United Nations Educational, Scientific and Cultural Organisations, 1957), pp. 62-63; also Rensis Likert, New Patterns of Management (New York: McGraw-Hill Book Company. Inc., 1961), Ch. 2.

20. TWI Report, p. 274.

21. *Ibid.,* pp. 37-38.

22. *Ibid.,* pp. 40-41.

23. From the Constitution, Institute of Industrial Supervisors, Staff Training Institute, Jamshedpur.

24. John F. Mee, *Op. cit.,* pp. 1006-7.

25. For greater details see M.N. Rudrabasavaraj, *Executive Development — A Model and A Point of View*, Calcutta, Indian Institute of Personnel Management, 1972; M.N. Rudrabasavaraj, *Executive Development in India.*

26. Quoted by Kuldip Singh Aneja, "Exacting Requirements of Successful Executives," *Machine Tool Engineer,* Vol. VII, No. 3, July-September 1966, p. 16.

27. See Dr. Herbert B. Schmidt, "Developing Business Leadership," *Business Horizons*, December, 1956.

28. Quoted by John F. Mee, *Management Thought in a Dynamic Economy* (New York: New York University Press, Third Printing, 1964), p. 27.

29. A. N. Kosygin, *Report on Improving Management of Industry, Perfecting Planning and Strengthening Economic Incentives of Industrial Production, Soviet Review,* Vol. II, No. 51, pp. 10-11.

30. *The Third Five Year Plan Report,* Planing Commission, p. 268.

31. Institute of Applied Manpower Research, *Job Outlook For Managerial Personnel in India,* February 1965, pp. 1-17.

32. Quoted by *Personnel,* American Management Association, July-August 1965, p. 50.

33. See John Gardner, *Self-Renewal: Individual and Innovative Society* (New York: Harper & Row Publishers, 1963).

34. Charles Myers, "Behavioural Sciences for Personnel Managers," *Harvard Business Review,* July-August 1966, p. 155. Most of the material in this section comes from this scholarly review.

35. See Edgar E. Schein and Warren G. Bennis, *Personal and Organisational Change Through Group Methods: The Laboratory Approach* (New York: John Wiley & Sons, Inc. 1965), p. 9; and also Alfred Marrow, *Behind the Executive Mask* (New York: American Management Association, Inc. 1964).

36. For greater details see Robert R. Blake and Jane S. Mouton, *The Managerial Grid: Key orientations for Achieving Production Through People* (Houston, Gulf Publishing Company 1964).

37. *Ibid.,* p. 175.

38. The Tata Management Training Centre, *Tata Review,* Vol. 1 No. 4., December 1965-January 1966, p. 3.

39. R.P. Billimoria, "A Guide to Planning Managerial and Training Requirements," *TISCO Technical Journal of the Tata Iron & Steel Company,* Vol. 13, No. 4., October 1966, pp. 170-171.

40. See for greater details, Prakash Tandon, "Executive Development and Economic Growth," *Business Herald*, May 1966, pp. 7-10; G.F. Asthana, "Institutional Programmes for Developing Managers," *Business Herald*, July 1966, pp. 5-9; A. Das Gupta, "Nature & Scope of Executive Development Programmes," *Productivity,* Vol. VII, No. 2, Monsoon 1966, pp. 173-185.

41. See for an excellent discussion on this subject, "Evaluating a Management Development Program," *Conference Board Management Record*, Vol. 16, No. 17, July 1954, pp. 264-265; also Kenneth R. Andrews, "Is Management Training Effective", *Harvard Business Review,* Vol. 35, No. 1, January, February 1957, pp. 85-94.

42. From "A Quiz on Training Methods," *Business Week,* No. 1198, August 16, 1952, pp. 160 ff.

43. Prakash Tandon, "Executive Development and Economic Growth," *Business Herald,* May 1966, p. 10.

44. W.J. Groth and R.W. Mallick, "Materials Handling Training," *Factory Management and Maintenance,* Vol. 110, No. 11, November 1952, pp. 84-87.

❑ ❑ ❑

CHAPTER 8

Promotions, Transfers and Performance Appraisal

After procuring and training the employee, maintaining and utilising him in the organisation effectively to the satisfaction of the company and the employee is the concern of management and personnel administration here has a distinct responsibility to assist and advise the top and line management in this area of maximum utilisation of the employee force to the maximum advantage. You do not retain and utilise the skills of an employee effectively keeping the sweeper, a machinist, or an oiler in the same job for which he was hired originally. Good service of an employee has to be rewarded. So also long and loyal service. The employee has an urge to improve and move up in the organisation. Then vacancies have to be filled from within by moving an employee from one job to another. Both the employer and the employee is doing on his job and how he can improve his performance. These requirements are met by (1) promotions, (2) transfers, and (3) performance appraisal.

1. EMPLOYEE PROMOTIONS

A promotion may be defined as an upward movement or advancement of an employee in the organisation to another job, which commands better pay or wages, better status or prestige, and higher challenges, and responsibilities and opportunities. Better working environment, hours of work, facilities and location may accompany the change.

Purpose of Promotion

The following objectives of promotion may be cited:

1. It is a recognition of a job well done by an employee.
2. It is a device to retain and reward an employee for his years of service to the company.
3. It is to increase the employee and organisational effectiveness.
4. It is to promote job satisfaction on the part of the employee.
5. It is to build loyalty, morale, and belongingness on the part of the employee.

6. It is to impress upon others that opportunities are available to them also in the organisation if they perform well on their jobs.

Watkins, Dodd, McNaughton, and Parasow summarise the human relations purposes of promotion:[1]

1. Furnishes an effective incentive to initiative, enterprise and ambition.
2. Is useful in conserving proved skill, training, and ability.
3. May be a means to reduce discontent and unrest.
4. May be helpful in attracting suitable and competent workers.
5. Promotional plans suggest logical training for advancement.

Promotion is often a loaded issue and promotions must be based on a clear-cut policy and the personnel administrator must not only help the management formulate the company policy of promotion but also educate all the employees as to the company promotion policy through effective communication. The Indian Institute of Personnel Management suggests a promotions policy:[2]

(a) Encouragement of promotion within the organisation instead of looking outside to fill vacancies in higher places;

(b) An understanding that ability as well as seniority will be taken into account in making promotions;

(c) Drawing up an organisation chart to make clear to all the ladder of promotion. Where there is a job analysis and a planned wages policy, such chart is quite easy to prepare;

(d) Making it clear to all concerned who may initiate and handle cases of promotion. Though departmental heads may initiate promotion, the final approval must lie with the top management, after the personnel department has been asked to check from its knowledge whether any repercussion is likely to result from the proposed promotion;

(e) All promotions should be for a trial period, in case the promoted person is not found capable of handling the job. Normally during this trial period he draws the pay of the higher post, but it should be clearly understood that if "he does not make the grade" he will be reverted to his former post and former pay scale.

Systematic Promotion Procedures

1. Establish a plan of job relationships, after job analysis.
2. Trace promotion routes.
3. Define lines of advancement.
4. Keep detailed personnel and service records, to provide a summary of the facts upon which promotions are to be based.
5. Make a definite allocation of responsibility for selecting individuals for promotion at various job levels.
6. Have overall co-ordination by some central agency.
7. Announce the openings for promotion and invite the interested employees to apply within a specific period.

8. Prepare the employee for promotion through the provision of some type of training.

Should promotion be based on merit or ability or seniority?

This is the bone of contention between management and labour. Trade unions generally insist that years of service or seniority should be the main criterion for making promotions. From the point of view of management, this policy would not be a wise and efficient one. It is correct to assert that an employee, who has stayed with a company for number of years, needs some amount of consideration, but many a management would not like to promote an employee all because he has been with them for a number of years.

Management would like to base their promotions on merit or ability or competence, although no management would like to ignore the seniority of an employee altogether whenever there is an opening to be filled and there is one senior employee and there is another with less seniority but more competence. In this situation the unions insist that the senior employee must be promoted to fill the opening, while management would prefer the more competent, but junior employee to fill the opening.

A compromise between labour and management is suggested, where each meets the other halfway, as many union-management contracts provide for. Both seniority and merit could be considered as the basic criteria for promotions. Whenever there are two employees of equal seniority, ability or merit should clinch the issue and promotion should go to that employee who is more competent between the two. Where there are two employees of almost equal competence, seniority should be the decider as to who will get the promotion. Pigors and Myers observe:[3]

"...management should stress ability above seniority in promotion.... Seniority should be considered, but only when the qualifications of two candidates for a better job are, for practical purposes, substantially equal." They also point out that management cannot expect this type of promotion policy to be accepted unless it is objectively and fairly operated. This is not possible without a good objective, acceptable performance appraisal programme.

Seniority Problem

Management is also faced with the problem of establishing who is senior. Is seniority to be based on occupation, department, plant or company? Even within this unit computing seniority is not easy. A good plan has to be established with the help of personnel division using occupational, departmental, or plant or company seniority as criterion. Another related issue is when an employee's seniority is lost if he is moved from one job to another. This is a troublesome issue and a careful analysis and programme is necessary.

Merit Versus Seniority

The utilisation of seniority in making various employment decisions has a number of advantages, the most outstanding being that it is an objective means of distinguishing among personnel. There is no doubt that the person who has ten years and two months of continuous recognised service is superior in service to the one with nine years of such service. The measurement is exact. It is also contended that the measurement is simple; and it does have the advantage of simplicity, provided that the seniority system is explicitly set up and defined. A reading of the preceding section would suggest that the measurement of seniority is not so simple as many people believe.

In the realm of human relations, seniority has the value of being accepted by employees. As we stated earlier, the use of length of service in awarding rights and privileges is very old and widespread. Thus, when employment decisions are made strictly on the basis of an objective measurement of length of service, it is probable that the majority in a group will accept the decisions. Thus, the use of seniority promotes more peace than does the use of merit, the latter being more easily affected by bias and favouritism. Another value in the use of seniority is security; an employee is able to predict when and how certain changes will be made. The use of this objective measure protects one from the whims and biases of management by removing the decision-making power from management and giving it to a system.

A final value of the use of seniority, which is more acceptable to members of management, is that it effects a reduction in labour turnover. An asset as valuable as seniority is not easily given up. Employees will remain with an organisation even when they are aware of better opportunities elsewhere, one reason being the loss of seniority that will result from quitting.

There are several reasons against the use of seniority, particularly when it becomes the sole base for decision-making. In the first place, seniority often ignores merit or ability. The job must be done if the organisation is to accomplish its objective. Length of service will not do it, and there is no guarantee that the experience indicated by seniority will produce ability. In one study in a steel firm, it was discovered that there was little relation between ability to do the job and length of service of journeyman machinists. Ten tests of ability were correlated with length of service and only four tests showed a positive relationship, the highest correlation being a plus 30. Thus, though experience is a great teacher, there is no guarantee that a person will consent to be taught or that one will be able to learn. In addition, if the seniority system is rigidly followed, where is the incentive to learn and improve? The only incentive one has is to "stick around" and accumulate service. The use of length of service, therefore, places a considerable burden on the use of seniority will not prevent good employment decisions from there on. This may be good logic, but it is practically impossible to demonstrate in practice; as indicated earlier, our selection techniques are not that good.

The use of seniority overvalues experience. It does not guarantee the selection of competent personnel. It provides no incentive toward preparation for advancement. It drives the ambitious and able person, with little service, out of the firm. A rigid seniority system makes it extremely difficult to attract and recruit capable new personnel unless they are placed in the exempt category.

From the viewpoint of productivity, the stronger argument is on the side of merit and performance. However, if the organisation makes little or no attempt to measure merit or performance systematically, it has a very poor case to put against the more objective values of seniority. It should be recognised that much of the clamour for recognition of seniority is founded on a fundamental distruct of management.[4]

Promotion from within

Many companies follow the policy of promotion from within and the following advantages are usually noted:

1. Systematises promotions
2. Builds employee morale
3. Builds employee loyalty
4. Permits a more rational allocation of manpower, benefiting both the employer and employee.
5. Enables the company to retain the employees.

Furthermore the company is not dealing with an unknown entity, when it is promoting one of its own men. The organisational morale will be adversely affected whenever an 'outsider' is brought to fill a better job.

But there are certain demerits:

1. It leads to "inbreeding', which is undesirable.
2. The source may dry up and you may not have the right type of candidate to fill a job.
3. The lack of fresh views and ideas is a serious lacuna. Often companies have a 'diplomatic exit' where they may stipulate that "as far as possible" the policy of promotion from within will be followed and when there is no competent candidate available within the company, they may go 'outside' to fill the job.

Upgrading: Upgrading is used to connote a 'minor promotion' or a promotion from within a grade. A second grade machinist is upgraded to a first grade machinist. This type of promotion is also described as a horizontal promotion. Sometimes upgrading may imply an increase of pay on the same job. This is also an important variety of promotion.

Demotion and Downgrading: Demotion and downgrading are the reverse counterparts of promotion and upgrading. An employee may be moved from his job to a job which carries less compensation, status, and responsibilities. Demotion is a punishment procedure evolved for a variety of reasons — a disciplinary action, incompetence, preliminary to a lay-off.

Demotions have serious repercussions, hence have to be handled carefully. Yodern Heneman, Turnbull and Stone suggest a minimum set of provisions when disciplinary demotion is done:[5]

1. A clear and reasonable list of rules, violations of which would subject the violator to demotion as a penalty.
2. The careful communication to employees of this information.
3. Competent investigation of any purported violation.
4. If violations are found, the consistent and equitable application of the penalty, preferably by the immediate supervisor.
5. Provision for review. In the unionised case this will be automatic via the grievance procedure; in the non-unionised situation the employer will need to make other provisions for review.

Downgrading may imply a loss of some pay on the same job. Or the job may fall into a lower grade carrying less status, pay, and responsibility. Or the employee may receive the same pay but he is on a lower grade job. Demotions and downgrading serve a necessary function. Just as the company rewards efficient employees, the inefficient ones must face the threat of demotion and downgrading even when it is very infrequently used.

2. TRANSFERS

A transfer is a lateral movement of employees from one position or department or plant to another, generally without involving any significant change in compensation, duties, responsibilities and status.

Purpose of Transfers

The following are the purposes of transfer:

1. To increase the effectiveness of thé organisation;
2. To increase versatility and competence of key positions;
3. To deal with fluctuations in work requirements;
4. To correct erroneous placement;
5. To relieve monotony;
6. To correct incompatibilities in employee relations;
7. To move an employee in the interests of health or age of employee;
8. To provide creative opportunity;
9. To train employees for later advancement or promotion.

Types of Transfer

There are various types of transfers and the following are the main types:

*1. **Production Transfers:*** This type of transfer is effected to meet the company requirements and at times to forestall lay-offs. When production is declining in one department, and production is strong in another department, where additional help is needed, some employees from the former may be transferred to the latter. A special order or rush order in one department may need more employees temporarily who are moved.

When production in a plant is down and instead of laying off its employees, some employees may be transferred to another plant. Sometimes there may be some downgrading where a skilled worker may be asked to do an unskilled job.

Such production transfers are an essential part of employment stabilisation programmes.

*2. **Replacement Transfers:*** Replacement transfers are similar to production transfers and to forestall lay-offs, but here they are to protect the senior and long service employees. Because of business conditions, production may have to be drastically reduced resulting in lay-offs. But the long service employees or senior employees are transferred to replace an employee with less service or 'bumps' an employee with shorter service.

3. Versatility Transfers: This type of transfer is designed to benefit both the company and the employee. Here the employee may be moved from one job to another to provide a broad background of varied job experiences. This type of transfer is resorted to in order to prevent the employee from developing proprietary interest in the job, materials and equipment used on the job and workloads.

4. Personnel or Remedial Transfers: This type of transfer is effected to correct erroneous placement, where the employee is ineffective or unhappy and uninterested. For reasons of health or age of the employee such transfers are resorted to. If the employee is unable to get along with his colleagues, he may be transferred. Generally remedial transfers are used to promote employee interest in the job and job satisfaction.

5. Shift Transfers: Shift transfers are pretty common, where there is agreeable employee transfers are used here. Man on the day shift may like to work on the 'graveyard' shift and Kamakshi on the night shift may like to work on the first shift and they may agree to change shifts. They notify the personnel division, which notifies the interested supervisors and with their approval transfers may be affected.

Transfer Policy and Programme

Most of the companies use all these types of transfers sometimes or the other. In order to be impartial and objective, transfer policy and procedures must be established and all the employees must be aware of these policies and procedures.

A good transfer policy and programme must answer these questions:

1. What types of transfers are to be used? When?
2. What is the area over which transfers will be effected?
3. What is the basis used for effecting transfers?
4. Who is responsible for initiating and approving transfers?
5. Whether a transfer should be permanent or a temporary one?
6. What is the rate of pay the transferred employee should receive on his new job?
7. Whether training is necessary to effect a transfer?

The industrial practices greatly vary and there is no need to be dogmatic in suggesting the policy framework and programmes. But management must think through these questions and with the help of personnel experts come up with answers that are suitable to its organisation.

For any efficient promotion and transfers policy and programme, what is needed is a device to evaluate the performance of the employee. Let us turn to the performance appraisal, which is the personnel tool used to evaluate the performance of the individual.

3. EMPLOYEE PERFORMANCE APPRAISAL

In any organisation there is some sort of evaluation of the employees and subordinates. Subordinates evaluate the superior and employees also evaluate the management. This is something natural and is one of the oldest and most universal practices. This evaluation is often subjective, unsystematic and even irrational. But in this section the discussion centres on systematic employee performance appraisal which is variously known as employee evaluation, employee efficiency rating, performance rating, merit rating, employee development programme, development report, personnel development or progress record or report, personnel performance record, employee progress report, employee service rating, personnel rating, employee ability rating; and they all mean the same thing.

An employee performance appraisal is a systematic, orderly and objective method of evaluating the present and potential usefulness of the employees to the organisation. Systematic performance appraisal is adopted by many organisations in the West and a few in our country as a means of helping supervisors to evaluate the work of each employee.

Purpose of Appraisals

Joseph Tiffin lists the following objectives of appraisal:[6]

1. Prevent grievances.
2. Improve job performance.
3. Increase analytical abilities of supervisors.
4. Assist management in promotion, demotion, and transfer problems.
5. Reveal areas where training is needed.

A National Industrial Conference Board study of several industrial employee attitudes pointed out how the employee felt and it was typified in the words of an employee: "I don't know how I am doing — no one ever tells me where I stand."[7] But every employee wants to know how he is doing on the job and he wants, even craves for, assurance from his superior. Norman Maier[8] includes the need for emotional security as one of the five primary needs all employees seek to satisfy on the job. He lists the elements of emotional security as *the need to belong, the need to know where one stands, and the need for approval.* A performance appraisal programme will meet this vital need of the employee and at the same time the company will come to know about employee performance.

Personnel Rating Principles and Policies

C.E. Jurgensen stipulates the following ten basic essentials of a rating programme:[9]

1. Policies with regard to rate ranges, promotion, lay off, incentives and other policies which are related to merit ratings of employees in a background sense must be available before we can expect to have an adequate rating programme. Provision for implementing these policies is, of course, included in this point.
2. A clear-cut definition of the purposes of the rating plan.
3. A programme for training the raters in how to rate and a continuing programme for improving that ability.
4. Adequately constructed rating scales.
5. Qualified overall supervision of the plan's development and administration. This includes what we might call a watchdog responsibility over the validity and reliability of ratings.

6. Willing participation on the part of all persons who are making ratings.
7. Private interviews with the employees who have been rated.
8. A programme to improve the rater's interviewing abilities. That again must be a continuing programme.
9. Full understanding of the plan by all persons concerned.
10. The acceptance of the plan by the union.

Joseph Tiffin gives some additional principles:[10]

1. Train the raters.
2. Have ratings made in conference or under supervision.
3. Be extremely cautious in comparing the ratings of men in different departments or on different jobs.
4. Interpret the ratings in terms of actual job demands.
5. Avoid the use of numerical values in interviews with ratees.
6. Don't rate factors for which quantitative data are available.
7. Avoid pooling poor ratings with good ones.
8. In using ratings, don't use them alone; be sure to make sure of all possible supplementary information to be obtained from other sources.

Major Types of Appraisal Plans

There are various types of appraisal plans and the following are the major type:[11]

1. Point system with weight for each factor.
2. Non-point system with a chart or form describing the factors to be appraised.
3. The rank-order or forced-distortion method, in which each supervisor ranks his employees on overall performance or divides them into groups such as the top 10 per cent, the next 20 per cent, etc.
4. The field-review method in which the performance of each employee is reviewed in detail by the supervisor with the help of the personnel department.
5. The critical incident method.

In the 1950s companies used elaborate appraisal or rating forms, but in 60s there was a move away from this and a different appraisal plan became popular. Mr. Richard A. Enion discusses the mechanics of performance appraisal, which meets the company's personnel needs and the appraisal procedure should fit into the company's normal way of doing things.[12]

Most appraisal procedures generally include the following four steps, in order:

1. An appraisal of the subordinate's job performance is written by his superior.
2. The superior submits the written appraisal to a committee which reviews and approves it.
3. The superior discusses the appraisal with the subordinate in a private interview.
4. The superior and the subordinate together create a personal development programme for the subordinate.

Mr. Enion in the light of the experience with several large industries mentions that there is a definite trend towards the narrative or "open-end" type of appraisal form. A typical form requires the appraiser to write answers under heading:

What are the employee's strengths?

What are the employee's weaknesses or areas that need development?

What is the employee's overall job performance?

He adds:[13]

"Thus, the appraisal is custom-made to the individual being appraised by comparing his actual job performance with the performance expected of him by his superior. Conspicuous by its absence in this type of form is a list of traits or characteristics that might be checked off in varying degrees, ranging from poor to superior. Many times, degrees of such items as "leadership", "enthusiasm", and, "loyalty" have led to bickering between the author of the appraisal and the man being appraised and have thus diverted all concerned from the true purpose of the appraisal. They also soon lead to a discussion of personality. The Foundation for Research on Human Behaviour at Ann Arbor, Michigan, in a recent report entitled 'Performance Appraisal and Review', makes this statement: 'Personality ratings are notoriously unreliable, for the same will be rated differently by different people. Appraisal of performance is more reliable, and consistent. People can be more objective about their jobs, for they generally know how to improve results while they seldom know how to change their personalities'."

Review and Check

The written appraisal must be checked and reviewed by several people. Preferably in a committee, so that it may be based on more objective consideration and deliberation and it may have the complete support of management. Often there are complaints that the superior was prejudiced or there was snap judgment.

Appraisal Interview: The next important step is the appraisal interview where the employee finds out where he stands and what they think of his performance. This also gives the appraiser an opportunity to fully explain the details of the appraisal so that the employee is fully aware of his strengths and weaknesses. This interview provides the appraiser an opportunity to find out what the employee thinks of the facilities and job conditions provided by management and what improvement management could make in them.

Personal Development Programme: Mr. Enion points out that "a successful appraisal interview will provide time for a joint determination by the appraised employee and his superior of just what steps the employee should take to capitalise the joint aspect of this determination, for the final analysis only the employee himself can bring about the desired changes in his job behaviour and attitude."

A Seven-point Training Programme:[14] Mr. Enion suggests a seven-point training programme to 'sell' the appraisal programme to the top and line management and to prepare a company to launch a new appraisal programme or revise an existing one. The training programme accomplishes the following ends:

1. Points out the value of an appraisal programme to management.
2. Points out the value of an appraisal programme to employees.

Model of Performance Management Processes

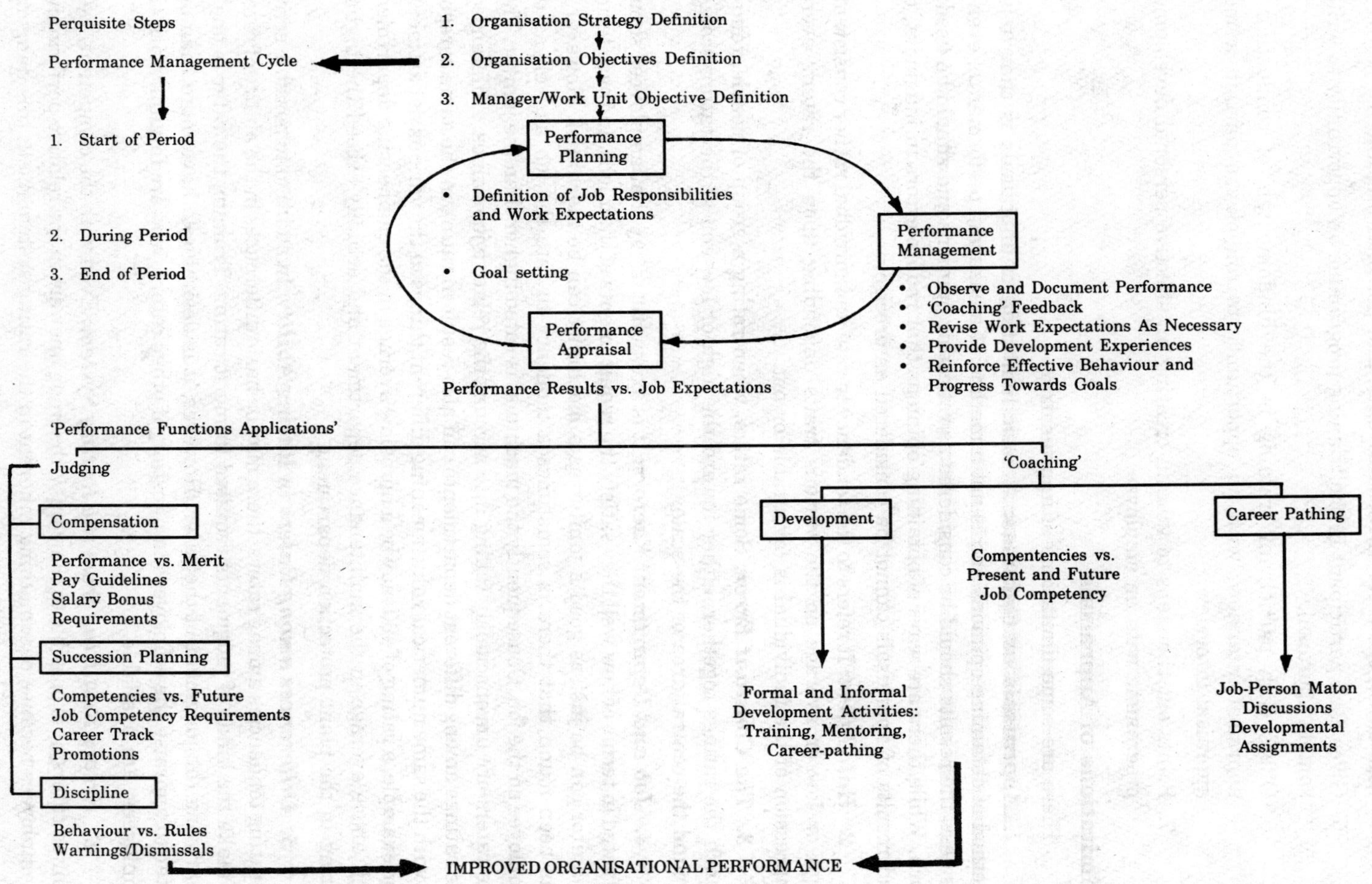

Source: Schneir, C.E., Implementing Performance Management and Recognition and Rewards (PMRR) at the Strategic Level: A Line Management-Driven Effort, Human Resource Planning, Vol. 12(3), 1989, pp. 205-220.

3. Instructs in the techniques of writing appraisals.
4. Points out the pitfalls to be avoided in writing appraisals, for example, the halo effect, the error of recent events, and personal prejudices.
5. Gives each participant in the training programme an opportunity to write a sample appraisal.
6. Offers each participant training in the fundamentals of conducting an appraisal interview, with an opportunity to role-play a part in a mock appraisal interview.
7. Points out the steps to take in creating an effective personal development programme with an employee.

Limitations of Appraisals

There are some limitations of appraisals:

1. Appraisals as Opinions: A basic limitation of appraisals is that it is a method of obtaining opinions and is not a method of measuring performance; even at its best, the results should be considered as reflecting opinions and should be used as such. While there are ways of obtaining opinions that reduce errors in judgment, the end results of appraisals cannot be considered as precise.

2. Halo Effect: It refers to the tendency to rate an individual rather consistently high or low or average on the various traits depending upon the rater's overall impression of the individual is favourable or not.

3. The Constant Error: Some raters, when rating a group of people, tend to bunch the ratings together, either toward the high or low end of the rating scale or around the central area of the scale.

4. Job and Department Factors: It is axiomatic to say that employees should be rated in terms of how well they satisfy the requirements of their jobs. In these terms, a janitor can be just as good a janitor as a machinist can be machinist. However, it has been found that there is sometimes a tendency to rate the job as well as the employee on the job. Consequently the machinist is rated higher than the janitor. Thus the raters are unconsciously taking into account the relative job values. Difference in the ratings among different departments can also result in rating in the same category or with the same numerical value meaning different things in the various departments. For example, a rating of 400 may be a bit below average in the engineering department, well above average in the maintenance department and actually exceed the highest rating in the plant protection department.

5. Differences among Raters in Rating Ability: In addition to possible errors in rating tendencies among raters, there may be basic differences in the ability of raters to make the kinds of judgments required in merit rating. Training the rater is one of improving the judgment of the rater. However, it is desirable to have more than one rater to appraise the employees in question, if other raters, who are familiar with the employees, are available.

6. Errors Resulting from the Rating System: Even with the competent, well-trained raters, it is possible to come up with wrong answers in the relative performance of employees because of something inherent in the rating system itself; this danger of course suggests the use of extreme care and research in the development of the system itself.

Ethics of appraisals

Another basically important factor is the ethics of performance appraisals and there will arise many problems and organisational morale issues if this aspect is ignored. The very purpose of appraisals will be at stake also. Marion S. Kellog suggests a manager's check list to keep your appraisals ethical:[15]

1. Don't appraise without knowing why the appraisal is required.
2. Appraise on the basis of *representative* information.
3. Appraise on the basis of *sufficient* information.
4. Appraise on the basis of *relevant* information.
5. Be honest in your assessment of all the facts you obtain.
6. Don't write one thing and say another.
7. In offering an appraisal, make it plain that this is only your personal opinion of the facts as you see them.
8. Pass appraisal information along only to those who have good reason to know it.
9. Don't imply the existence of an appraisal that hasn't been made.
10. Don't accept another's appraisal without knowing the basis on which it was made.

She maintains that these "ethical standards are most certain to be met if appraisals are accompanied by such qualifiers as (1) the facts on which the appraisal is based; (2) time period covered; (3) the purpose for which the appraisal is made; (4) the situational factors that shed light on the facts presented; (5) the nature of the appraiser's working relationship with the employee; (6) an explanation of how and where the facts were obtained."[16]

In conclusion, we may add that personnel experts must assist and advise the top and line management, who should participate in the appraisal programme and it should be the line management's responsibility to evaluate employee performance. An appraisal plan keeps the supervisors on their toes and forces them to carefully study the performance of their employees, to analyse their strengths and weaknesses and finally to help the employees to overcome their weaknesses and capitalise on their strengths.

REFERENCES

1. See Gorden S. Watkins *et al.*, *The Management of Personnel Relations* (New York: McGraw-Hill Book Company, Inc., 1950, 2nd ed.), pp. 447-449.
2. IIPM, *Personnel Management in India,* pp. 212-213.
3. Charles Myers and Paul Pigors, *Personnel Administration* (New York: McGraw-Hill Book Company, Inc., 1951, 2nd ed.), p. 206.
4. Edwin B. Flippo, *Principles of Personnel Management,* p. 254.
5. Yoder *et al.*, *Handbook of Personnel Management*, p. 9.19.

6. Joseph Tiffin, *Industrial Psychology*, Englewood Cliffs, N.J.: Prentice-Hall, Inc., 1947, 2nd ed., pp. 328-333.

7. Quoted by Richard A. Enion, "The Custom Appraisal of Job Performance," *The Personnel Function: A Progress Report,* A M A Management Report Number 24, Personnel Division, American Management Association, p. 87.

8. See Norman R. F. Maier, *Psychology in Industry* (Boston: Houghton Mifflin, 1955).

9. Clifford E. Jurgensen in "What Makes Merit Rating Tick?," *Management Record,* Vol. 12, No.1, January 1950, p. 5.

10. Tiffin, *op. cit.*, pp. 358-460.

11. For details on various types of appraisals, see (1) John F. Mee, Personnel Handbook; (2) Yoder *et al., Handbook on Personnel Management and Industrial Relations*; (3) M. Joseph Dooher and Vivienne Marquis (eds.), *Rating Employee and Supervisory Performance* (New York: American Management Association, 1950); (4) *Employee Rating,* National Industrial Conference Board, Inc., Studies in Personnel Policy, No. 39, 1942; (5) Jucius, *Personnel Management.*

12. Richard A. Enion, *Op. cit.,* p. 87. Most of the material in this section is borrowed from this paper.

13. *Ibid.*, p.88.

14. *Ibid.,* p.89.

15. Marion S. Kellog, "The Ethics of Employee Appraisal," *Personnel*, July-August 1965, p. 37.

16. *Ibid.,* p. 39.

❑ ❑ ❑

CHAPTER 9

Employee Morale

Modern managers and personnel administrators are greatly interested in forthcoming and influencing the morale of the employees in such a way that it will contribute to the maximum effectiveness, growth, and progress of the organisation. Contemporary personnel administration, particularly since the Second World War, is interested in designing programmes that help provide optimal employee morale.

In this chapter we shall discuss:

1. What is employee morale?
2. Effects of good morale and poor morale;
3. Measurement of morale; and
4. Improving morale.

1. WHAT IS EMPLOYEE MORALE?

Though the term 'morale' is frequently used, many would be at a loss to define what is morale. Simply put, morale is an attitude of mind or a state of mind of the employee which has impact on the individual and company goals and purposes. Feelings, emotions, and motives combine to provide certain attitude and behaviour on the part of the individual, which in turn represents the employee morale.

Morale is a relative concept. When an employee has few frustrations, he has 'high' morale and when he has many frustrations or deep frustrations, he has 'low' morale. Professor Mee observes:[1] "Good employee morale is the mental attitude of the individual, or of the group, which enables the employee to realise that the maximum satisfaction of his drives coincides with the fulfilment of the objectives of the company. In other words, the employee identifies his objectives with those of the company, not merely subordinates his own desires to those of the company."

Professor Jucius sums up the definition of morale thus:[2]

"Definitions of morale are many. A review of them all would show that they define it in terms of what it is, what it does, where it resides, whom it affects, and what it affects." Thus to use the foregoing classification, morale is composed as follows:

1. What it is — an attitude of mind, an esprit de corps, a state of well (or unwell) being, and an emotional force.
2. What it does — affects output, quality, costs, co-operation, discipline, enthusiasm, initiative, and other aspects of success.
3. Where it resides — in the minds, attitudes, and emotions of individuals themselves, and in their group reactions.
4. Whom it affects — immediately, employee and executives in their interactions; ultimately, the customer and the community.
5. What it affects — willingness to work and to co-operate in the best interests of the enterprise and in turn of the individuals themselves.

A favourable attitude towards the job, the group, the boss, and the company indicates good or high morale and an unfavourable attitude towards the job, the group, the boss, and the company reflects a low or poor morale.

Then there is individual morale and group morale and constant interplay between them, which in turn affects the company and individual interests. Milton L. Blum contends that industrial morale is a group phenomenon involving group solidarity, group goal, observable progress toward the goal, and individual participation in reaching the goal.[3] Morale, motivation, and attitudes are interrelated and personnel administrators seek to increase motivation by taking steps to improve attitudes and morale and they strive to provide optimal employee morale. There is no doubt that modern management understands what impact good or bad morale of the employee will have on the organisational objectives and it is not enough to say that a certain employee's performance is bad or he has low morale. Increasingly top management wants to know through the aid of manpower managers, why the employee behaves the way he does and how to reshape and influence his attitudes, his behaviour, and his morale. They also want to know, how the employee feels and why he feels that way. More and more executive realise that there is need for considerable 'empathy' — the ability to put themselves in the shoes of the other person — in order to find out his feelings, attitudes and emotions.

Whenever the management adopts the I-don't-care attitude or the employee-is-stupid attitude, sooner or later it is bound to land the company in trouble. Many companies may feel that they simply do not have the time to 'care' about what the other person feels and why he does so, but in the long run, the time spent on caring for the employee is well worth it. Admittedly, the employee morale is a very complex phenomenon influenced by so many factors on or off the shop floor. Such factors as the job, supervisor, company and its working conditions, its policies, the group, and interpersonal relations, certain co-worker, pay, other benefits, employee's family life, his social life, his community life, his friends, top management policies and attitudes, and his union have impact on employee morale. If the employee has a nagging wife or he is harassed by his debtors, or he thinks he has a hostile foreman or he thinks his co-worker fools around too much, he may hit a 'low spot' or his morale may be low.

While considering employee morale, both the business character and non-business character of the individual, i.e., the whole person, have to be reckoned with and as a personnel executive pointed out: "We cannot isolate the non-business character of the individual from the work-place and the individual carries with him to the shop-floor his emotions, feelings, and attitudes induced at home or in society. We have to contend with the whole persons." It is necessary to understand the employee and his feelings and emotions wish a desire to influence them positively for the good of the employee and the company. They can take the necessary steps to realise improved job performance, job satisfaction, and stability of employment.

2. EFFECTS OF GOOD MORALE AND POOR MORALE

Good or high morale among the employees is likely to bring the following good results:

1. Job satisfaction.
2. Higher productivity.
3. Better goods and services.
4. Cheaper goods and services.
5. Lower costs.
6. Higher profits.
7. Better wages.
8. Employment stability.
9. Employee identification with company.
10. Employee initiative, regularity and punctuality.

People with high morale generally tend to increase productivity, to show more initiative and drive, to take an added responsibilities, to come up with various ideas and suggestions to improve the operations, eliminate waste, cut costs and save raw materials, to show great loyalty to the boss and the company. But it may be hasty to conclude that high employee morale alone will contribute to all the beneficial results cited, but given proper management, tools, equipment, and environment, high morale can help cause many good results for the organisation, management, and the employees. For, in spite of high morale, without the required raw materials or proper management and leadership, high productivity or high profits cannot be realised. Conversely given every other factor, management cannot operate efficiently if the employee morale is low.

The popular notion is to believe that high morale is synonymous with productivity. But available evidence, report Brayfield and Crockett, does not support the general proposition that high morale and high productivity go hand in hand.[4] But this should not hasten one to the conclusion that employee morale has nothing to do with increasing productivity. Other things being equal, employee morale can cause productivity of the organisation to increase.

Poor Morale and its Effects

Poor employee morale manifests itself in many ways and may contribute to the following:

1. Apathy and non-involvement.
2. Fatigue and monotony.

3. Labour stoppages.
5. Absenteeism.
6. Disciplinary problems.
7. Restriction of output.
8. Increased grievances.
9. Labour unrest.

Employees with low morale tend to show the least interest in their jobs and in what they are doing. Work is drudgery and misery to them. They are generally dissatisfied. They show their dissatisfactions in various ways, by being irregular to work, by taking leave often, by pleading sickness, by not putting forth their best, by criticising foremen and by a distinct lack of interest.

In many a case low employee morale may be caused by many misconceptions and unwarranted fears, which reflect in employee attitudes which seem to say:

1. They (management and shareholders) make all the money for themselves.
2. They believe that they have all the answers.
3. They benefit when we work hard.
4. They may fire us if we increase output.
5. They want to introduce changes all the time at our expense.
6. They are fallible and neglectful.
7. They don't care.
8. They hire and fire as they please.
9. They don't share.
10. They think we are stupid and dumb.

Such employee misconceptions and the like lend to deliberate 'soldiering' or withholding of energy and they create attitudinal blocks, which cause injury to the organisational effectiveness and development. This results in poor morale and an unwillingness to do the best he can on the job, because he believes that his interests will not be served when he contributes to the company interests.

Having taken into consideration the effects of good employee morale and bad employee morale, it is no wonder that management is interested in finding out what the employee morale and attitudes are and how to provide for optimal or high employee morale.

3. MEASUREMENT OF MORALE

The most common practice of personnel administration to determine current employee morale is to conduct morale or attitude surveys among the employees. Generally morale is indicated by various attitudes and behaviour of the employees, such as actions, expressions, oral comments, criticisms, suggestions, and answers to questions. But the problem lies in the correct interpretation of these indicators to determine what kind of morale is prevalent at a given point of time. A certain employee may not be working upto the standard, and it is easy to conclude that he has poor morale. But it is quite possible that the same person may excel in his work under a different supervisor or with another crew. Hence there is a need to be careful in interpreting personal behaviour and associating it with morale.

But the external behaviour of employees on the shop floor is very revealing. Whether they are cheerful or morose, satisfied or dissatisfied, enthusiastic or indifferent, co-operative or complaining, dull or alive, regular or irregular, punctual or unpunctual, indicate the state of employee morale.

Management wants to measure employee attitudes and morale pertaining to matters about which management can do something. Hence they are interested in the direction, intensity, and interrelations of attitudes and increasingly managers are resorting to morale and attitude surveys using various techniques in gathering data on employee morale.

(a) Objectives of Morale-attitude Surveys

Mr. S. A. Raube of N I C B reported five major reasons for conducting morale-attitude surveys.[5]

1. To find out what employees think;
2. To improve morale and check on effectiveness of personnel programme;
3. To determine training needs;
4. To find out what education and information are needed by employees; and
5. To find out what employees like.

These attitude surveys are used not only in the case of employees, but also in the case of supervisors, managers, professional employees, older employees, minority groups and some of these may be special purpose surveys. The attitude surveys have been made to determine employee reactions to such diverse subjects as employment tests, wage rates, music in industry, and employee-rating programmes.

(b) Methodology

Morale and attitude surveys are important because they provide an orderly channel of finding out how employees feel. Various techniques are used in these surveys. The N I C B survey of 111 companies in U.S.A. measuring employee attitudes showed that in these companies:[6]

1. 75 per cent used written techniques, 19 per cent used interviews, and 6 per cent used both;
2. 75 per cent included rank and file and supervisor;
3. 40 per cent included executives;
4. 92 per cent of firms using interviews used sampling;
5. Average cost of questionnaire method (excluding time of responding employees) was \$ 2.50 to \$3 for a wide variety of subjects and 50 cents to \$ 1 for a few questions;
6. Average interview cost was \$ 5 to \$ 6;
7. Average time for reply (excluding explanation and conditioning) was 30 to 44 minutes.

In the most recent N I C B study, out of a total of 473 respondents, 98 companies (21%) had conducted employee morale surveys. Of the 98 companies, 72 used written questionnaires and 12 used individual interviews. The rest (14) used a combination of questionnaire and interview techniques.

Frequency of Surveys

Among the 98 companies that have conducted employee attitude surveys, the approximate number of surveys made to date and the number of companies reporting each number is as follows:

Frequency of Surveys	*Companies*
1 survey	45
2 surveys	26
3 surveys	13
4 surveys	1
5 surveys	3
7 surveys	1
8 surveys	3
12 surveys	4
Semi annually	1
"Continuing programme"	1

To conduct the survey, out of 98 companies, 63 used a specialist from the outside the company, whereas 35 companies used their own staff.

Some companies use the method of observation. Many of the employee's actions, replies to questions, behaviour speak for themselves and indicate how they feel. It takes close, systematic, and conscious observation to detect employee's favourable and unfavourable attitudes. But there is a real hazard in that the supervisor may not accurately observe and he may be carried away by an insignificant external action. Observation must be supplemented with other methods of morale measurement.

Another method of measuring attitudes is by studying and analysing service records, output, quality, absenteeism, tardiness, grievance records of individuals and department. But these records must be always kept up-to-date and accurate.

Yoder, Heneman, Turnbull and Stone provide the following outline of major steps to be considered in planning an employee survey:[8]

1. Decide what information is needed and why (should be general or specific?)
2. Sell top management.
3. Sell employee and advise the union that the survey is coming up. (If they resist strongly, it is probably best not to do the survey since the employee answers may be biased).
4. Select scaling technique, write up questions, and build questionnaire.
5. Decide upon face-sheet information, e.g., department, age, and sex — these will give so-called "breakdowns."

6. Pretest the questionnaire in a small "pilot" study (this is essential).
7. Make a preliminary posting of anticipated findings to work sheet table and then to summary reports.
8. Decide on who the respondents will be — in general random sampling will provide satisfactory results in large firms and/or large departments.
9. Develop administration and scoring techniques and train questionnaire administrators preferably through "role-playing" techniques.
10. Make plans on how to deal with refusals and those absent from work.
11. Select and secure an appropriate room or rooms for administration.
12. Make arrangements with department heads for employees to be absent from work while the poll is being conducted.
13. Make plans to interview those who can't read or write.
14. Conduct the poll.
15. Score results — use of mechanical means, such as I B M, is highly recommended.
16. If "open-end" or "write-in" items are called for tabulate and analyse these.
17. Prepare work sheets.
18. Do any needed statistical tests.
19. Analyse and interpret results, preferably through a diagnostic clinic or conference, if qualified technicians are available.
20. Decide on what data can be eliminated as relatively unessential.
21. Prepare report — for management, employees, and possibly the union, if desired.
22. Make plans to interpret report to top management.
23. Recommend needed improvements in industrial relations policies, and practices as a result of opinion survey findings.
24. Begin development of company norms to be used in future surveys.
25. Prepare plans for follow-up surveys.
26. Write up report of details of the survey including methods and costs.

These attitude and morale surveys should be conducted and the results interpreted by professionally trained and experienced specialists. Some companies in U.S.A. not only publish the findings of the survey but give each employee a copy also. The survey findings are discussed among supervisors and staff and line executives, where they may evolve an action programme to improve company practices and programmes and rectify errors and mistakes. As a result of the survey, an economic education programme, or a supervisory training programme, or a safety training programme may be called for. Furthermore attitude surveys must be conducted periodically and it is not enough to conduct one survey, for attitudes are changing from time to time which may affect the company performance.

Directions

Below and on the following pages you will find a number of statements about your job.

1. Read each statement.
2. Choose the word below the statement which best tells how you feel about that statement, and put an "x" in the box above that word. Do not write in answers for questions where you can just put an "x" in the box.
3. Do this for all the statements.
4. Please answer every question.
5. If you need help in filling out the questionnaire, please raise your hand.
6. There are no "right" or "wrong" answers. Just tell how you feel about each statement.

Your answers are secret. No one in the company will see them.

Section 1

—— (1) The lighting for my job is

☐ Excellent ☐ Good ☐ Fair ☐ Poor ☐ Very poor

—— (2) The ventilation where I work is

☐ Excellent ☐ Good ☐ Fair ☐ Poor ☐ Very poor

—— (3) The job that the top executives are doing in this company is

☐ Excellent ☐ Good ☐ Fair ☐ Poor ☐ Very poor

—— (4) All in all, as a place to work, this company is

☐ Excellent ☐ Good ☐ Fair ☐ Poor ☐ Very poor

—— (5) Considering the present cost of living, my pay is

☐ Excellent ☐ Good ☐ Fair ☐ Poor ☐ Very poor

—— (6) Considering everything, my working hours are

☐ Excellent ☐ Good ☐ Fair ☐ Poor ☐ Very poor

—— (7) The spirit of co-operation among employees in my department is

☐ Excellent ☐ Good ☐ Fair ☐ Poor ☐ Very poor

—— (8) The reputation of this company in the community (how people feel and talk about this company) is

☐ Excellent ☐ Good ☐ Fair ☐ Poor ☐ Very poor

—— (9) Considering everything, my present job is

☐ Excellent ☐ Good ☐ Fair ☐ Poor ☐ Very poor

Fig. 9.1 Excerpt from the Triple Audit Attitude Scale, University of Minnesota Industrial Relations Center

4. IMPROVING EMPLOYEE MORALE

After determining the current state of employee morale, it is necessary to institute an action programme which would result in the eradication of the conditions that bring about low morale among employees and in the promotion and maintenance of higher morale, for which the responsibility rest with the top management. The personnel staff may be asked to shoulder the responsibility of conducting morale surveys, testing the morale implications of various company plans, policies and practices, interpreting results and suggesting programmes of remedial action. The line management must assume the responsibility for administering the morale-building programmes and maintenance of high morale in the organisation.

Promotion and maintenance of high morale is possible when the employee enjoys job satisfaction; when he identifies the attainment of his interest with the interests of the company; and when he is proud of his association with the company.

Professor Mee suggests in the Figure 9.2 what is necessary to maintain high morale.[9]

DESIRES OF WORKERS AND MANAGEMENT

Worker desires	*Management desires*
1. Fair and efficient leadership	1. Cooperation of employees
2. Opportunity for expression and development	2. Intelligent initiative
3. Recognition as an individual	3. Availability and stability of workers
4. Acceptable hours and wages	4. Maximum productivity of employees
5. Safe, healthy working conditions	5. Lowest cost per unit
6. Interest in work	6. High organisation morale
7. Economic security	7. Loyalty of workers

Fig. 9.2 Some of the Desires of Workers and Management which are Basic in Maintaining High Morale

Any morale improvement programme of management must embrace the following rules:

1. Respect the individual.
2. Be fair and just.
3. Encourage initiative.
4. Design effective communication.
5. Give fair compensation.
6. Provide good work environment.
7. Provide job security.
8. Be alert.
9. Leave door open.
10. Be courteous.

11. Point individual prosperity in company prosperity and company prosperity in national prosperity.
12. Adopt a how-shall-we-do-it attitude.

Any discussion of morale improvement is incomplete without reference to human relations, but because of its importance and need in our country a chapter is devoted to its discussion in the end. Influencing employee attitudes and maintaining high morale in the organisation demands continuous vigilance and care on the part of management. Every action, policy, programme, plan, practice must be carefully reviewed with an eye on what reaction it will bring forth from the employees. A production manager once pointed out that he never said to his employees "Do it this way" but he always said "how shall we do this" and that he always got good results from his crew. Much depends on management behaviour towards employees. Improvement of morale among employees is possible when management removes conditions that may give birth to unfavourable employee attitudes and remove misconceptions and fears of employees. Many companies use interviewing, guidance and counselling to overcome many morale problems.

Pointing out that proper employee attitudes can attributes to increasing productivity, Mr. R.S. Livingstone writes of developing a new state of mind:[10]

> We have to convince people that only through higher productivity and lower costs can they fulfil their ambitions for a higher standard of living. We must make clear to them that in the larger sense our role as managers is to help them achieve higher productivity and that with this will come the progress that we are all seeking. By using the analogy of the division of income we can prove that, by producing more, we will have more to divide, wages can be raised, the stockholder can be paid more, there will be money for reinvestment in the business and the consumer interests will be protected.
>
> This understanding will lead to the state of mind which is essential to obtaining the free release of energy.

He stresses the responsibility of personnel man.[11]

> The constructive forming of employee opinion should be made the primary duty of the personnel man, working with his chief executive .... The top personnel executive should make his principal task the problem of developing and applying appeals to the mind, mental concepts that will induce the people who comprise the nation's businesses to give more fully and freely of their human energy.

How the employees feel, what they think, why they think so, what their attitudes, opinions and morale are and how their opinions, attitudes, morale can be moulded to advantage both the employee and management should be the concern of all levels of management — both line and staff. Personnel staff must assist management in measuring employee morale and in evolving action programmes that aid management in the promotion and maintenance of high employee morale, that will bring in beneficial results to the organisation.

REFERENCES

1. John F. Mee, *Personnel Handbook,* p. 926.

2. Michael Jucius, *Personnel Management,* p. 338.

3. See Milton L. Blum, *Industrial Psychology and Its Social Foundations* (New York: Harper & Bros., 1949), pp. 132-135.

4. See Arthur H. Brayfield and Walter H. Crockett, "Employee Attitudes and Employee Performance," *Psychological Bulletin,* Vol. 52, No. 5, September, 1955, pp. 396-414.

5. See S. A. Raube, "Experience with Employee Attitude Surveys," NICB Studies in Personnel Policy, No. 115, April 1951, pp. 9-11.

6. *Ibid.,* pp. 17-21.

7. National Industrial Conference Board, *Personnel Practice in Factory and Office: Manufacturing,* Studies in Personnel Policy, No. 194, 1964, pp. 55-56.

8. Yoder, *et al.*, *Handbook of Personnel Management,* pp. 14. 21-14. 22.

9. Mee, *Personnel Handbook,* p. 926.

10. R.S. Livingstone, "Employee Attitudes and Productivity," *The Personnel Job in the 1960s*, pp. 19-20.

11. *Ibid.,* p. 20.

❑ ❑ ❑

CHAPTER 10

Communications and Suggestion Systems

What the nerves are to a human organism, the communications are to an industrial organisation.[1] The keynote of a good communication system is to help establish understanding, that is complete and effective in producing productive efficiency and industrial harmony. One of fundamental problems of personnel management is "the problem of obtaining the willing co-operation of the people employed in divergent activities within an enterprise towards the common goal." A discussion of communications can be undertaken under the following heads:

1. The objectives of communications.
2. Responsibility for the organisation of communication.
3. Communications at the managerial levels.
4. Communications — content and channels.
5. Rules of communications and principles.
6. Barriers to good communication.
7. A suggested programme for action.

1. THE OBJECTIVES OF COMMUNICATIONS

Since management involves tasks done through people, it is essential to communicate what the management wishes to accomplish by the various tasks that the organisation has undertaken. The Indian Institute of Personnel Management enumerates the following objectives:

1. Satisfying basic human needs like recognition, self-importance and sense of belonging.
2. Discouraging misinformation.
3. Preparing for a change.
4. Encouraging ideas from subordinates.
5. Releasing emotional strain.

The main spirit here is to share information and to keep all levels within the organisation well-informed of the company philosophy, policies, and objectives and responsibilities and duties. There are formal and informal communication structures and every level and segment of the organisation must concern itself with communication. There must be a two-way flow of communication. Upward must come ideas, comments, reactions, attitudes, and reports through all levels from the very lowest. Now downward must flow clarifications, interpretations, orders, instructions and policies. Each direction of flow should stimulate and be stimulated by the other. As a matter of fact, several exchanges up and down, may be needed to complete the education on some subjects. For this reason the phrase "sharing information" is perhaps a clearer term of best practice.

2. RESPONSIBILITY FOR THE ORGANISATION OF COMMUNICATIONS

Although "everyone" is responsible for good communications, specific delegation of authority for leadership of an education and communication programme is desirable and here the personnel division is a natural choice: "He should provide leadership of ideas, but always submit programme proposals to the appropriate line executives for suggestion and approval. The latter with line authority would then spearhead the execution of approved plans using the help supplied by the personnel division. Moreover, the personnel division can seek out help on communication matters from management consultants, educational institutions, professional institutions, professional societies, and business and trade associations. Such an organisational set up would serve to insure proper design of programmes, minimum conflict between organisation units, a strengthening of the work and support of line executives and advantageous use of all sources of communication measures and opportunities."

3. COMMUNICATIONS AT THE MANAGERIAL LEVELS

Top management must support the communication programme with all its authority to ensure confidence and stability within the industrial organisation. Communication programmes cut across the various levels of management, (a) top management, (b) middle management and (c) supervisory levels.

(a) Top Management Groups

One of the most significant movements in recent years has been that concerned with top-level executive development. This is a most encouraging trend because good communications must be based upon intelligent leadership. Since the top executives represent the power centre of the organisation and the policy-making and decision-making body, they must have a clear picture of the enterprise in order to communicate with workers and they must be in a position to answer such questions as the following:

1. What are the social responsibilities of management?
2. To what extent is business liable for the various risks which endanger employees?
3. What is an optimum balance between reasonable profits and fair wages?
4. Can workers be loyal to both the company and union?
5. What are the realistic policies toward political activities on the part of the company?

6. How do the roles of management and workers interact?
7. To what extent and how should employees participate in managerial decisions of importance to them?

While no one executive may be able to provide all the answers, there is the encouraging trend to seek counsel when necessary.

(b) Middle Management Groups

Occupy a strategic position affecting labour-management relations. They must be adequately prepared to receive and transmit accurately and to control constructively, the plans, policies and ideas of the top-levels. Middle management groups need (1) To learn precisely the educational plans to top-management. (2) To co-ordinate the educational responsibilities horizontally of various line and staff units. (3) To transmit specific educational plans to lower supervisory levels and ultimately to employees.

However, though the main flows of communication may be up and down, cross-wise to co-ordination is increasingly important as the company grows.

(c) Supervisory Levels

Supervisors comprise the critical level of management affecting employee communications. The supervisor is in immediate contact with the work force and it is through him that most information will be channelled downward and upward. They can interpret correctly or grossly misinterpret information to labour force causing efficiency or bottlenecks as the case may be. The strategic position of supervisors makes it imminent that they should be properly educated and provided with all the necessary information.

Graicuna's Theory: This great French mathematician propounded a theory which stated that as the subordinate executives are increased arithmetically, the resulting relationships among them tend to increase geometrically. The Table 10.1 illustrates the increasing relationships.

Table 10.1

TOTAL POSSIBLE NUMBER OF RELATIONSHIPS WITH INCREASING NUMBER OF SUBORDINATES

No. of Subordinates	*No. of Possible Relationships*
3	18
4	44
5	100
6	226
7	490
8	1080
9	2376
10	5210

More the number of levels and relationships, more complicated will be the problem of communication, particularly oral communication is likely to present a great many issues.

Why Does Communication Matter?[2]

The following extracts from the booklet, *The Manager's Responsibility for Communication,* published by the Industrial Society, London, in 1971, may be read with interest:

"Why does communication matter? Because failures in communication are costly. Examples:

1. Out of 35 stoppages in a large organisation 18 were due to failures of communication. The cost of these stoppages cannot be measured in the hours lost alone; the stoppages upset the whole rhythm of production and lessened cooperation between employees and their managers.
2. An executive with good potential leaves the staff because he is unaware of his prospects within the company. Finding and training a successor is costly and will have repercussions in his section and also lowers morale among his colleagues. Failures in communication are not limited to shop floor level.

Secondly, the benefits of change can only be achieved where there is an adequate communication mechanism for explaining face to face, directly to employees, what is required, and why? Examples:

A large company negotiated centrally a productive deal with the unions, to achieve greater flexibility in the use of manpower. The only sections of the company that succeeded in getting the flexibility in practice, were those with a direct and systematic method of communication through managers and supervisors to their own employees.

Thirdly, adequate communication can result in greater productivity through more effective work and greater cooperation. Example:

In a production job where a new manager was appointed, but all other variables were the same, a saving of five per cent was achieved amounting to £ 80,000 per annum, because the new manager laid down an effective system of communication. The main difference, as far as the employees were concerned, was that under the new man they knew what the problem was, what they were trying to achieve, how he wanted the problem tackled and what part they had to play in order to get improvements. They knew too the extent to which they succeeded in reaching the individual targets set.

The need for a properly organised system of communication applies as much in offices, research laboratories and drawing offices as it does on the shop floor. If effective communication is to be achieved it cannot be left to casual methods.

People will only give of their best to their work if they understand:

(a) what they have to do; why they have to do it; to what extent they are achieving the targets set;

(b) what their conditions of employment are and the reasons for them.

In small organisations much of this information is readily available. In larger organisations, however, many of these matters are, of necessity, settled at many levels above the employee concerned. Unless communication is systematically organised, people immediately affected by a change in conditions of employment will not understand the reasons behind it: this will cause unnecessary antagonism, misunderstanding and lack of cooperation. All will result in loss of efficiency."

4. COMMUNICATION — CONTENT AND CHANNELS

Content: The keypoint of communication is to mould employee attitudes, opinions, information — in short, employee behaviour. In a country with innumerable languages and dialects, the problem of communication are important, the language to be chosen to express also is equally important. It may be useful to use regional languages and vernacular expressions to carry the message.

In U.S.A. the following topics are included in communication programmes:

(a) Company history, objectives and services.

(b) Company organisations, finances and operation.

(c) Personnel objectives, policies and practices.

(d) Economics and the American system.

(e) Political and community relations.

(a) Company History, Objectives and Services

It is generally felt that an employee will take pride in his company when he knows its history, objectives and services. The induction programme is a common way of communicating the message of the company's background. Films to highlight the story of the founding of the company and its trials and tribulations and also the story of the founder will serve the purpose also. Booklets are often used to cover these subjects. In order to induce the workers to read, well-designed, excellently illustrated and carefully worded topics are helpful. Plant publications are also used to provide materials about the background of the company. Product display boards are used to help employee visualize their contributions to the final product. Plant tours are also a convenient channel. Museums are also used and the Ford Museum in Detroit is one of the most famous in the world. Some companies display competitive products so that employees understand the task facing the company in maintaining its position in the industry.

(b) Company Organisation, Finances and Operation

These have received a great deal of attention in many companies. This is to acquaint the employee as to how he fits into the organisational structure of the company. It is characteristics of organisations that persons are structured into different systems of relationships. A work structure exists: Certain persons are expected to perform certain tasks together with other persons. An authority structure exists: Some people have responsibility for directing the activities of others. The status structure determines which persons have what rights and privileges. The prestige structure permits certain persons to expect deferential behaviour from others. The friendship structure is based on feelings of interpersonal trust. It is necessary to understand the various formal and informal relationships within an organisation.

Group meetings have been widely used to explain current problems of the company to the employees. Some companies require their executives to explain the cost and profit position of the company. Supervisors are briefed about these matters so that they may be articulate when dealing with employees. Television is used to highlight company operations and films may be utilized showing the decision-making process involving the chairman and the board of directors. The comic-book format is used in presenting its annual report to the employees. In one company the public address system is used once a week during a few minutes rest period to tell employees about new orders or cancellations, about training courses and about their interesting news items.

(c) Personnel Objectives, Policies and Practices

Information regarding wages, pensions, hours of work, overtime, job-security, employment condition, personnel services etc., is provided through every conceivable conveyor by almost every company. The personnel interviews and the supervisors are the best conveyors. Booklets are widely used to describe pension benefits and grievance procedures etc., are covered in employee handbooks. Group meetings have also been used in this area of communications. Panel discussions are also held. Personnel policies may be geared to bring about mutual understanding between unions and management. Many companies also use conference and meetings with supervisors to gain their views and to clarify their understanding of labour-management problems.

(d) Economics and the American System

One of the most interesting phases of education has been along the lines of increasing economic understanding of not only the firms but also the American system of free enterprise. This movement has gained strength particularly in the last several years because of the belief that an employee who does not comprehend how the economic system works cannot feel confident about the fairness of his wages, the reasonableness of profits or the significance of the capitalistic system. Hence industry as well as various public and private institutions have interested themselves in disseminating economic knowledge. One company has developed a series of four films which attempt to show the following:

1. How we got what we have
2. What we have
3. How to lose what we have
4. How to keep what we have

A discussion is held after each film. The Dupont have developed a conference method programme concerning American economic system, its accomplishments, the place of competition, the place of the individual freedom in the system and the place of the company in the American system.

(e) Political and Community Relations

Some industries educate employees and the community in community projects on such matters as the following:

1. Every citizen benefits from industry's growth.
2. You are entitled to facts.

3. Collective bargaining is the one practical means to assure fair wages, reasonable hours, satisfactory working conditions.
4. All employees, as well as management, benefit by improving productive efficiency.
5. Citizens should be protected in their right to work.
6. Management and wage earners have mutual interests, need close personal relations.
7. Management is obligated to give a square deal to every employee in the shop.

COMMUNICATIONS AND SUGGESTION SYSTEMS

1. Downward Communications	
Oral	*Written*
1. Personal Instructions	1. Instruction and orders
2. Lectures, conferences, committee meetings	2. Letters and memos
3. Interviews, counselling	3. House organs
4. Telephone, public address systems, movies, slides	4. Bulletin boards
	5. Posters
5. Whistles, bells etc.	6. Handouts and information racks
6. Social affairs, including union activities	7. Handbooks and manuals
7. Grapevine, Gossip, Rumour	8. Annual reports
	9. Union publications
2. Upward Communications	
1. Face to face reports and conversations	1. Reports
2. Interviews	2. Personal letters
3. Telephones	3. Grievances
4. Meetings and conferences	4. Suggestion systems
5. Social affairs	5. Attitude and information surveys
6. Grapevine	6. Union publications
7. Union representatives and channels	
3. Horizontal or Crosswise Communications	
1. Lectures, conferences, committee meetings	1. Letters, memos, reports, carbon dittos, and mimeographs
2. Telephone, intercom systems, movies, slides.	2. House organs
3. Social affairs, including union activities	3. Bulletin boards and posters
4. Grapevine, rumour	4. Handbooks and manuals
	5. Annual report
	6. Union publications

Fig. 10.2 Communications — Downward, Upward, and Cross-wise

Rumours, Gossip, and Grapevine

Whenever there is inadequacy in formal structure, informal communication process develops. Informal structure develops when workers find it difficult to transmit or receive messages or they feel they should receive messages.

Rumour and gossip are prominent in the messages carried by informal system. Gossip indicates the attitude of organisational members towards different topics at a particular time and smoothens the function of the organisation.

Grapevine is also one of the forms of informal communication. Grapevine discourages frankness since confidential information may be spread. It is a channel through which disturbing rumours are passed and accurate information distorted and coloured. This often brings dissatisfaction to members who require accurate information. It can be reduced or made harmless by giving relevant information promptly and directly through appropriate official channels.

According to Robert Hershey[3] rumour is the information heard from an unofficial source. The factors that appear to govern the rumour generation are: (1) lack of effective communication and (2) the position of employees in the company hierarchy. The first factor depends on the formula that communication misses what it wants to tell its employees and what the employees want to know. The second factor, on which rumours are sparked, are wages, hours of work, working conditions, supervisory relationships, job security, benefits and layoffs. These are the factors on which the emotion-laden rumours keep spreading.

Channels of Communication

Major Groups of Communication Channels in U.S.A.

(a) Individualized, personal contacts.

(b) Group personal contacts.

(c) Written media.

(d) Demonstrations and displays.

(e) Radio, Television, films and recordings.

The Indian Institute of Personnel Management lists the following channels of communication:

1. Employee Handbook.
2. Notice Boards.
3. Standing Orders.
4. Posters.
5. House Magazines.
6. Wall Newspapers.
7. Brochures & Bulletins.
8. Broadcast Messages.
9. Museums and Exhibitions.
10. Works Library & Reading Room.
11. Training Courses.
12. Suggestion Schemes.

Although the management may have chosen the contents and channels of communications, the problem of application is still there and it entails certain ground rules in order to be effective.

5. RULES OF COMMUNICATIONS

Certain rules and principles have to be formulated in order to overcome certain obstacles and among these are the following:

(a) The Factor of Change — Resistance to Change

People resist changes and the labour force more so, owing to the problems of automation and job security. To gain acceptance of the particular change requires effective communication with all about the relevant information. Communications can be helpful in checking psychological frictions: Explain the significance of the change — why changes are needed and why they are desirable should be communicated. It is also possible to invite suggestions to meet the changes necessary and thus involve employees in decision-making.

(b) Educational Process

It involves shaping the thinking process of the employees. It is often 'indoctrination.' Every executive must possess the skill to coach and teach employees and must project 'human interest' into his lessons. This involves understanding of the enterprise on the part of the executive and also the best techniques of coaching. To get employees to apply themselves, various educational devices must be used. Much could be learned in this regard from the comic books and movies of Walt Disney for he has the peculiar facility to educate extremely well in a most interesting and 'painless' manner.

(c) The Individual

The problem of reaching an individual is nowhere felt as acutely as in communication. We assume that he is receptive and when is not receptive or open to consideration of our messages, we have a real problem on hand. Moreover employees have personal problems that demand their attention and management will have to compete with these demands for his attention. Besides the ability of the employee to absorb the message has to be taken into consideration. A complicated balance sheet may be above his lead but a simple rupees and paise system of profit and loss statement will be within his grasp.

(d) Language

Language barriers can be considerable in a country like ours. It may be necessary to use the local or regional language or dialect to get across the ideas and information. The problem of semantics is there and certain words carry certain symbols or images to certain people. 'Profit' may means something to the worker and something else to stockholder. We have to avoid problems of provincialism and regionalism which are the bane of our society. It is necessary to choose the words carefully and the language carefully to transmit, ideas and information.

(e) Classes

Another difficulty in communications that must be overcome is the obstacle created by the class attitude and cast attitude taken by various groups. Thus, workers as a class may be opposed to management and in our country cast provide obstacles. The class consciousness is there even among executives — the staff may have friction with line. There may be overlappings of political, racial, religious, colour and job groupings and to address communications in terms of one grouping alone here will certainly antagonize the others. Hence management must design communications with all these class groupings in mind and the communications must be designed to minimise some of these class distinctions.

The design of communications to minimize class distinctions must begin, therefore, with a revision of acts which tend to raise class barriers. Management, for example, must live so that employees will not consider executives as natural enemies.

Similarly, staff people would not act as if they alone are repositories of all that is good; line people should have confidence in their abilities and not reflect characteristics manifestations of an inferiority complex in relations to staff people; upper management should put more managerial responsibilities upon lower supervisors; and the lower levels should take a broader company view and seek to earn the confidence of upper executives.

Principle of Communication

Koontz and O'Donnell have suggested the following sound principles of communication:[4]

1. ***Principle of clarity:*** Communicate in commonly understood language.
2. ***Principle of attention:*** Give full attention to receiving communications from all sources.
3. ***Principle of integrity:*** Make communications support organisational objectives.
4. ***Principle of strategic use of informal organisation:*** Use informal organisation constructively as a means of communication.

6. BARRIERS TO GOOD COMMUNICATION

There are many barriers to good communication and they may be summarised as follows:[5]

1. Badly expressed language.
2. Faulty translations and poor retention.
3. Loss by transmission.
4. Inattention.
5. Unclarified assumptions.
6. Insufficient adjustment period.
7. Distrust of communicator.
8. Premature evaluation.
9. Fear.
10. Failure to communicate.

These common barriers have to be removed if you plan to promote effective communication, which can bring in good results for the organisation. It is the responsibility of the personnel staff to devise communication channels and design and word communication content properly and effectively. Efficient usage of content and channels of communication in order to get result is the responsibility of line management.

7. A SUGGESTED PROGRAMME FOR ACTION

Mr. A.S. Hatch, Director of Communications, Whirlpool Corporation, U.S.A., has suggested a programme for action:[6]

1. Make it your mission to secure recognition of the fact that communication does not take place automatically — that its successful handling may be as complex a problem as the development of a new product, and worth as much to the company.

2. Analyse the channels through which communications can flow, and work actively at the job of securing recognition of their existence, the uses to which they can be put, and the conscious and studied effort necessary to determine which channels are most appropriate for transmitting specific kinds of information in various situations and at different times.
3. Recognise that channels rapidly become clogged through disuse and, conversely, become more effective to the degree that they are properly employed.
4. Build understanding of the degree to which the climate for reception is an integral part of the process of transmitting ideas.
5. Check the adequacy and accuracy of the information which is getting through to people in the organisation.
6. Be alert for opportunities to check out the effectiveness of every possible aspect of our total communications pattern through objective research.
7. Finally, in all of the above-mentioned considerations recognise that transmission of the essential information of the business with maximum efficiency ought to be the first concern of communications study, counsel, and training.

8. SUGGESTION SYSTEM

Employee suggestion systems are designed to encourage active co-operation of the employees in the activities of business and industry through seeking ideas for cost-reduction or cost-prevention or increasing productivity or efficiency from the rank and file. The suggestion systems facilitate upward flow of communication — a type of communication that is very much needed in industry. The suggestion systems were first instituted in 1880s in U.S.A. and they grew rapidly during the Second World War. Presently they are quite popular with many firms. Though employee suggestion schemes may not be as common in India as they are in U.S.A., there are many firms in India which have operated suggestion schemes quite profitably to themselves as well as to their employees. This section attempts to discuss the benefits of the suggestion system, some standards for the scheme, processing and operating suggestions, some suggestion schemes in operation in India and lastly some of the limitations.

1. Benefits of the Suggestion System

The proponents of the scheme claim that the employee suggestion system:

(a) Improves employer-employee relationships;

(b) Is an employee benefit scheme;

(c) Tends to increase the morale of the labour force;

(d) Acts as a good means of communication;

(e) Commits the labour force to take more active interest in their work and the company;

(f) Affords the essential incentive and device for employees to co-operate in contributing their ideas;

(g) Provides management with an organised way of handling their ideas; and

(h) Constitutes an important tool of management "to feel the pulse" of the rank file.

2. Standards for the Scheme

Some suggestion plans are well planned and more successfully operated. It is not unusual to find in U.S.A. the percentage of accepted suggestion between 25 and 35 per cent and about one out of every three employees submitting suggestions. Suggestions systems that have achieved this high degree of success usually have met the following standards:

1. The scheme has the wholehearted support of the top management and definite responsibility for the operation is assigned to a management official, usually in the personnel department, who has to find ways and means to stimulate employee ideas.
2. The rules and the processing operation of suggestions are clearly explained to the employees. Some even go to the extent of informing the employees as to the kinds of problems facing the company and so to the kinds of suggestions wanted.
3. All suggestions are promptly acknowledged and evaluated. If a particular suggestion is rejected, an explanation is given for the rejection.
4. Awards for acceptable suggestions are monetary and on the liberal side, usually 15 to 30 per cent of the first year's net savings.
5. The award winners are given full publicity through house journals, newspapers, company reports, meeting etc.

3. Operating and Processing Suggestions

(a) Introducing Suggestion System: In introducing and operating an employee suggestion scheme it is necessary for management to formulate safely the following premises:

(i) The employees are intelligent enough to think constructively about their jobs;
(ii) There is always room for improvement in the company operations;
(iii) Management can gain from the ideas of employees; and
(iv) The brighter employees want to contribute more than just a day's work.

(b) Receiving Suggestions: The suggestions are received either through a suggestion box or through the supervisor. The former is more common in our country. When an employee has a suggestion to improve some operation he puts his suggestion in the suggestion box for consideration. Another practice is when he has a suggestion, he makes the suggestion to his supervisor who takes up this suggestion with management. At General Electric in U.S.A., when an employee has a suggestion there in no need for him to look for paper and pencil. He can pick up the phone and this is recorded on a tape through a recording device which will be considered by management. In order to make a suggestion if the employee needs any expert help, such help is also provided. Making blueprints, designing and planning etc., are some areas where the employee may need technical help which is provided.

(c) Does It Improve Operation: The most important thing management look for in a suggestion is whether it will improve any of the operations in the firm. If the employee's suggestion is tested and found to be of direct value to the firm, this value is the pay-off to the industry for operating the suggestion system and the suggestion award is the pay-off to the employee for his contribution. Besides these values, it is quite possible that the employee has got stronger feeling of personal achievement, which is an excellent by-product. Through the scheme management comes to know of the fairly bright, intelligent and alert employees and the departments where they are working.

A suggestion system that is operated as a management device for getting improved operations is actually an incentive plan for employees. No member of management can think of all the attainable efficiencies in any operation; but all the employees in an operation know most of the practical improvements that should be made by enlisting the voluntary co-operation of employees in getting the job done as efficiently as possible. A company which is considering the adoption or revision of a suggestion system might wisely decide what return, in the form of provable results, it expects for the money it will cost to administer the system.

(d) Processing Suggestions: The suggestions are processed either by management alone or by a suggestion committee comprising both management and employee representatives.

Management Alone: In U.S.A. it is not unusual to find a "Suggestions-system Administrator" — a management official — who handles the details of the system and management committee then takes action on suggestions received. There may be more suggestion systems operated by management alone than by a joint-committee. It is often suggested that a suggestion system operated exclusively by management might be more efficient, in the sense that investigations are made by trained plant engineers or methods men and decisions can be swiftly reached.

On the other hand, in some cases, employees or their representatives may raise doubts as to the fairness of management decisions regarding an employee's suggestion. Charges of favouritism, buck-passing and delays are not uncommon.

Joint Committees: There are suggestion systems where suggestions are processed by a joint committee of management and union representatives. The rank-and-file employees are likely to have greater confidence in the fairness of the suggestion operation if their representatives are on the suggestion committee.

A joint committee offers management a valuable opportunity to share certain types of information with the employees and to develop understanding of the mutual problems confronting labour and management. If management stops short of encouraging participation of employees in the process of deciding upon suggestions, the suggestion system is likely to retain an air of paternalism — a means of passing out a few extra rupees to the boys in the shop.

It is also necessary to encourage the supervisors or foremen to help the workers in various ways in coming up with useful suggestions.

Let us now turn to some suggestion schemes already in operation in some of the companies in India.

4. Some Suggestion Systems in India

At TISCO and TELCO: Tata steel proudly claims that it pioneered the Suggestion Box Scheme in India to encourage initiative from the shop floor. In an advertisement TISCO claimed: "At Jamshedpur, during the last twenty years, employees have put forward over 12,000 suggestions, of which nearly 1,000 have been accepted. These suggestions have helped to increase productivity and make operations safer, and have led to the utilisation of local knowhow and materials for self-reliance."

How Suggestions are Invited: TELCO exhorts its employees to come up with suggestions this way:

"Did you know that almost Rs. 25,000/- was paid out last year for suggestions? And they were certainly valuable suggestions."

"Why don't you come out with suggestions — suggestions for saving manhours, saving materials, improving procedures?"

"Through the Suggestions Box scheme each and every one of us can have a hand in running the company and not just a few top officers."[7]

What is the Suggestion and the Award? In 1964-65 of the many awards made, there were five big awards for suggestions. Mr. M.A. Latif, General Foreman (Operation), Coke Ovens, was given a reward of Rs. 5,000/- for an outstanding suggestion. "Mr. Latif solved an intricate problem by his ingenuity. Three of our coke ovens could not be operated owing to bulging chamber walls. Repeated attempts at straightening the bulged portion of the walls proved futile, and even a special gadget, made by Simon Carves and fabricated in our shops, failed to produce results. It was felt by all concerned, including foreign technicians, that there was no alternative but to rebuild the ovens, keeping them idle till the bricks, ordered for, arrived and the job completed."

"At this stage, Mr. Latif came forward with his suggestion for removing the bulge. He proposed partial charging the ovens and pushing them. By repeating the process and increasing the charge every time, the bulged-out portion, he pointed out, could be pressed to the side by the pressure of the coke at the time of pushing. This partial charging and controlling of the flue temperature produced the desired results, and finally, the ovens could be fully charged and put into normal operation. It prevented production loss to the extent of 40 tonnes of coke per day."[8]

Besides the award, Mr. Latif was given due publicity and he appeared on the front cover of TISCO house journal.

The other four awards were (1) Rs. 3,000/- reward for Mr. R.C. Bagat for his suggestion to modify the Jaw Operating mechanism of the New Floor Charger Crane at Plate Mill which enabled the Crane to be put into operation; (2) Rs. 1,000/- for Mr. A.R. Chakravarthy for building up an instrument known as Defibrillator, which is capable of defibrillating the heart and making it beat in the normal manner; (3) Rs. 1,000/- for Mr. Balwant Singh for his suggestion for cleaning C.O. gas lines in the Plant by flushing them with service water, instead of the conventional methods which involved considerable time and labour; (4) Mr. Balwant Singh was also given a reward of Rs. 400/- for modifying the design of Top Coolers of furnaces at Steel Melting Shop No. 2 using steel flats for fabricating the coolers, replacing special hydraulic pipes which used to be imported.[9] At TELCO, apart from individual suggestion awards, they have a Suggestion Box Cup which can be won by the division that gives more acceptable suggestions through the employers of the division. This promotes healthy competition among the divisions to make a better use of the suggestion box scheme.

HOW SUGGESTIONS ARE PROCESSED AT TISCO

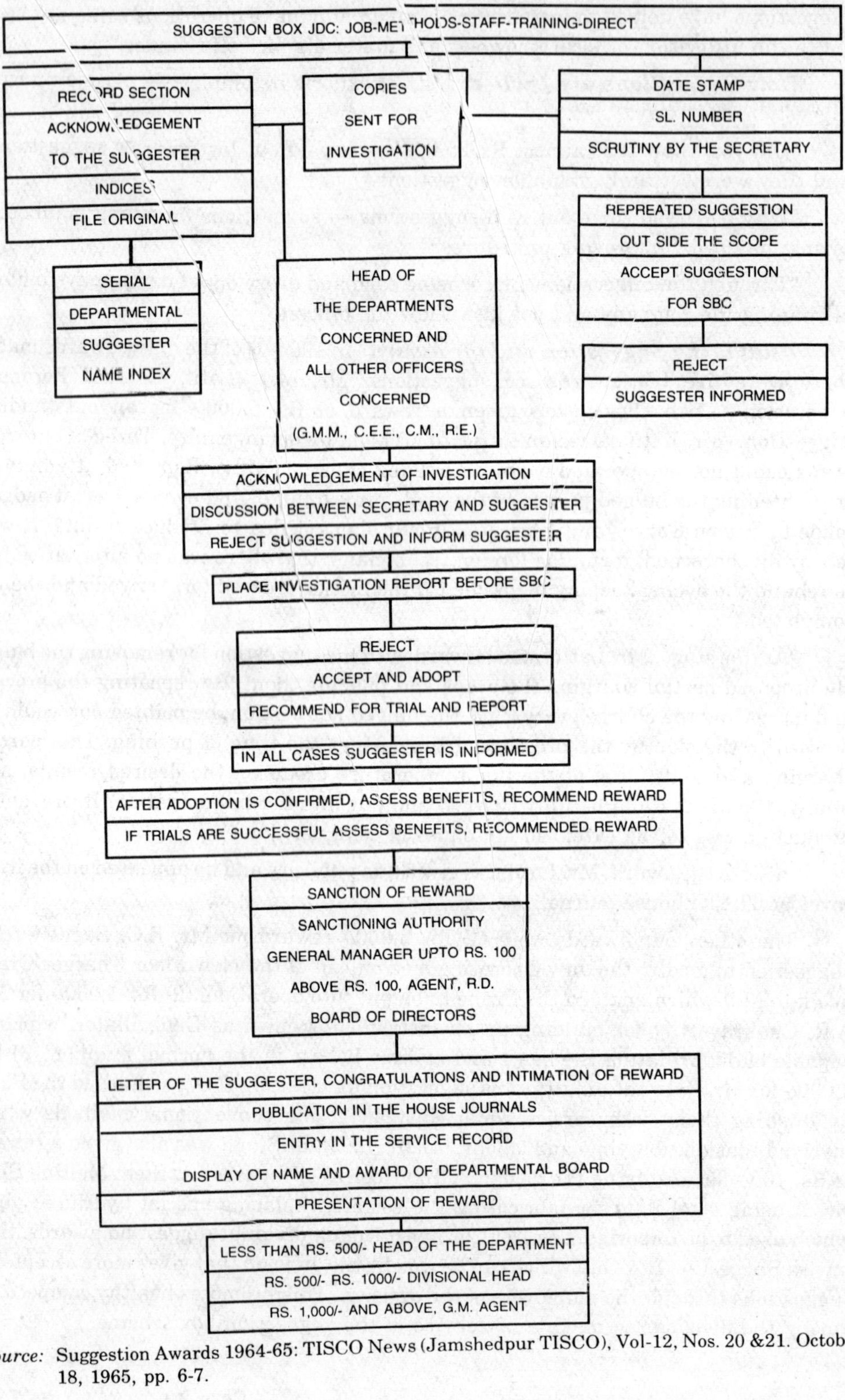

Source: Suggestion Awards 1964-65: TISCO News (Jamshedpur TISCO), Vol-12, Nos. 20 &21. October 18, 1965, pp. 6-7.

The "Current" reported that TISCO gave an award of Rs. 9,000/- to Mr. V.A. Murari, an Assistant Electrical Engineer, for his suggestion relating to one of the rolling mills, that would save several lakhs every year for the company.[10]

At Hindustan Lever: In a special ceremony at Head Office Mr. P. Tandon, Chairman of Hindustan Lever presented a cheque for Rs. 3,750/- to Mr. R.N. Bharadwaj, Area Sales Control Representative, Foods, Mumbai — the highest award at Hindustan Lever — "for the best suggestion so far received under Suggestion Box Scheme."[11]

The scheme has been in operation at Hindustan Lever for many years and in 1960 under a revised scheme the prize money awarded was increased from Rs.50/- to a maximum of Rs. 5,000/-. There are categories of suggestions and in the first are those that result in financial benefit to the company and suggestions may pertain to improving "any aspect of business, such as working conditions, methods of work, advertising or trade relations." For this category of suggestions, a reward, equivalent to 30 per cent of what the company estimates will be the first year's savings from the implementation of the suggestion or Rs. 5,000/- whichever is less, is offered.

Under the second category there are suggestions, which basically offer a good idea; but which cannot be evaluated in monetary terms. For such a suggestion the employee is awarded as much as Rs. 500/-. In the third category are included suggestions that may not bring any financial gain. Nevertheless they are considered good enough to merit a prize, whose value may go upto Rs. 50/-. Matters relating to trade marks or prices of products are specifically stated to be out of the purview of the scheme. At Hindustan Lever the suggestions are processed by a joint committee of three senior management members and two employees union representatives. But it was stated that there was not very good response from the employees to the scheme in spite of attractive awards offered since 1960 and "the number and quality of suggestions left much to be desired."[12] There were only 80 suggestions in the last five years and only 10 had won awards at Hindustan Lever.

At Larsen and Toubro: The suggestion scheme was introduced in Larsen and Toubro at Powai years ago and it has been quite popular with its employees, "During 1965-66, 800 suggestions were received as against 240 in the previous year. In 1964-66, 8 employees from every 100 participated in the scheme while last year 25 per cent of our employees sent in suggestions. Thus employee participation increased by 312 per cent."[13]

Two special annual departmental awards — one for production shops and the other for office departments — are instituted with a view to further increasing employee participation. These awards are based on: "(a) number of prize-winning suggestions received from a shop department during the year; (b) total value of these suggestions to the company; (c) number of persons participating in the suggestion scheme during the year in relation to the total strength of the shop/department. The awards will be declared after the end of the year in April and every employee in the winning shop/department will share the award."[14]

L & T operates the suggestion scheme in its Head Office and Regional Office in Ballard Estate. Suggestions to improve the company efficiency such as methods of work simplification, improvement in systems and procedures, reduction in paper work and stationery, elimination of unnecessary delays etc., are welcomed from the staff.

At Hindustan Machine Tools: During the period between January 1, 1966 and March 31, 1966, at HMT there were 13 suggestion award winners and the highest award went to Mr. H.R. Ramaswamy of Grinding Assembly for suggesting that the T-slot pieces on the tables of G-17 Grinding Machines can be eliminated by making them integral with table casting. These pieces were hitherto being manufactured in shorter lengths, selected according to the size of the machine and then fixed on to the table in the assembly section. Mr. Ramaswamy's suggestion resulted in savings of Rs. 5,195 to the company.

Mr. K. Gangadharan and Mr. M. Shivaram of Milling Assembly won an award of Rs. 490/- for suggesting a simplified design of fork used on M-2 Milling Machine.[15]

All the above companies give due publicity to the suggestion system, suggestion awards and suggestion award winners in their house journals and also through advertisements in newspapers.

5. "Shram Vir" National Awards Scheme

In addition to the company suggestion systems, the Ministry of Labour and Employment, Government of India, has instituted the "Shram Vir" National Awards Scheme for employees who give useful suggestions leading to higher productivity, economy or greater efficiency in industries.

27 awards have been made to the employees of various companies so far and TISCO has won no newer than five "Shram Vir" awards worth Rs. 500 to Rs. 2,000. These awards are made annually. This scheme is a further incentive to the employees to think and contribute ideas leading to higher productivity at less cost.

6. Limitation of Suggestion System

In spite of the success of suggestion systems there are certain limitations that preclude full-fledged employee participation in production problems.

First of all, there are suggestion schemes which do not carry the necessary monetary incentives for the employees to think constructively about their job. By fixing the suggestion awards as low as Rs. 50 to Rs. 5, as is the case with some companies, management is not encouraging the employees to come up with ideas to improve operations. To many workers management appears to be unwilling to share fairly the savings made, by suggestions. Secondly, in some schemes there is no definite policy with regard to the payment for suggestions and with regard to the processing suggestions. Arbitrary selections and awards tend to create frustration among the employees in the long run and ultimately they will resent the whole scheme.

Thirdly, where the employee suggestion results in the elimination of some jobs, it creates morale problems in the organisation and frictions among interpersonal relationships and weakens team spirit.

Lastly, the success of the suggestion scheme is prejudiced by the lack of enthusiasm on the part of management for the scheme. "What we can't think of nobody else can" attitude on the part of members of management is not helpful in creating the kind of atmosphere that encourages upward flow of ideas from the rank and file.

7. Conclusion

While suggestion systems have become a common industrial practice with some of the leading concerns in India, it is yet to gain momentum among many industrial units. A well-organised and well-operated suggestion system can afford a very good opportunity for management and labour to collaborate with a view to cutting costs, increasing efficiency and promoting higher productivity.

REFERENCES

1. See my "Communication in Industry", *The Financial Express,* March 22 & 23, 1966 and also my "Suggestion System in Industry", *Indian Management,* March-April 1967.
2. Employers Federation of India, *Industrial Bulletin,* Bombay, May 1, 1972, pp. 35-36.
3. Robert Hershey, "The Grapevine... here to stay but not beyond control", *Personnel,* January-February 1966, pp. 62-64.
4. Abstracted from Harold Koontz and Cyril O'Donnel, *Principles of Management* (New York: McGraw-Hill Book Company, 3rd edition 1964).
5. *Ibid.*
6. A.S. Hatch, "The Line Approach to Industrial Communication", *The Personnel Function; A Progress Report,* AMA Management Report No. 24, Personnel Division, American Management Association, Inc. 1958. pp.79-81.
7. *TELCO News* (Jamshedpur: TELCO) Vol. XIV, No.3, 1965, p.24.
8. *TISCO News* (Jamshedpur: TISCO) Vol. 12, No.26, December 27, 1965, p.3.
9. *TISCO News* (Jamshedpur: TISCO) Vol. 12, Nos. 20 & 21, October 18, 1965, pp. 6-7.
10. *The Current,* December 27, 1966, p.21.
11. *Hamara,* Bombay: Hindustan Lever Ltd., Vol. XX, No. 2, p.4.
12. *Ibid.*
13. Larsen & Toubro Ltd., *News Letter,* Vol. 7, No.2, July 1966, p. 5.
14. *Ibid.*
15. "Suggestion Award Winners", *Machine Tool Engineer,* Bangalore Hindustan Machine Tool, Vol. VII, No.1, January-March 1966, p. 43.

❑ ❑ ❑

CHAPTER 11

Wage and Salary Administration

Wage and Salary Administration is one of the vital areas of personnel administration, for sound wage and salary policies and programmes are essential to procure, maintain, develop, promote and transfer employees and to get effective results from them. Wages are perhaps the most important single element in the conditions of employment. Organisational morale cannot be maintained at high level without a fair, equitable and sound remuneration programme. Modern wage and salary administration is very complex and sophisticated requiring expertise and specialist know-how and in this chapter we shall discuss how personnel administration, through its tools and techniques, assists and advises top management in developing sound wage and salary administration policies and programmes under the following sections:

1. General considerations in wage and salary administration.
2. Principles of wage and salary administration.
3. Job evaluation and wage determination.
4. Systems of wage payment.
5. Some wage issues in India.

1. GENERAL CONSIDERATIONS IN WAGE AND SALARY ADMINISTRATION

A retrospective view of wage and salary administration indicates the successive stages of development and change. Some four steps are discernible and they may be broadly identified and classified. First of all, in the primitive era, when man's needs and wants were relatively few, the worker was paid in kind, mainly in the form of foodgrains and the employer determined what wage he was going to pay to the worker. The second stage brought forth the traditional labour market supply where the autonomous forces of demand and supply of labour in the marketplace determined what wage the employer was going to pay to the worker. The conditions of labour market (whether they were "tight" or "loose") as well as the competitive forces in the market determined the level of wages. There was only individual bargaining, where the individual employee was at a disadvantage.

In the third stage, we come across the institutional labour market supply, where labour organised itself in the form of trade unions with a view to protecting the economic interests of the workers. The bipartite system of wage fixation developed where union and management negotiated to determine the wage scales. In the fourth stage, we perceive a tripartite system of wage determination coming into vogue. The State is also interested in wage determination and establishes certain policy framework within which labour and management must negotiate and fix wages work and salaries. In India under the influence of a tripartite machinery — Indian Labour Conference and Standing Labour committee — Wage Boards are set up for different industries to establish certain policy guidelines to determine wages in industries. Wage Boards have been set up in industries such as Cotton industries, Sugar, Cement, Jute, Iron & Steel, Tea plantations, Rubber plantations, Coffee plantations, Coal mining etc.

Wages mean different things to different people. To management, wages and salaries constitute a cost and a wage is a price they are prepared to pay for hiring the services of an employee. To the worker, a wage is an income and it is a return he gets for offering his services to the company. By offering to sell his services the employee expects a remuneration or compensation in the form of wage or salary. To the State, the wages and salaries mean the level or standard of living of its citizens.

Wage and Salary Terminology

Wages may be defined as the aggregate earnings of an employee for a given period of time such as a day or a week or a month and equal to the product of an hourly rate times the number of hours, or the product of a piece rate times the number of pieces, plus any premiums or bonuses earned. These earnings maybe expressed in terms of money, in which case they are called *nominal wages,* or in terms of goods and services purchasable with money, in which case they are called real wages.

Salary is a compensation to an employee for personal services rendered on a weekly, monthly, or annual basis. Salary is usually associated with office employees, supervisors, managers and professional and technical staff.

Wage Rate is the wage received by an employee for a unit of time, excluding special payments for overtime, night work and incentive earnings.

Standard Wage Rate is one established by job evaluation as the basic rate of wages to be received by employees for satisfactory performance on a given job.

Wage Scale is an assembly of all properly evaluated standard wage rates set forth in sequence according to the evaluation of the job and size of the rate.

Wage Schedule is an assembly of rates applying to a given classification of work.

Income refers to total of all compensation, including wages and special pay, interest, profits, rent and dividends.

Real Wages are wages divided by a cost-of-living or consumer price index; what wages will buy.

Fringe Benefits refer to compensation, given to employees over and above wages, that often is not directly related to output, performance, or time worked.

Premium Rates refer to special rates for certain periods, such as overtime, sundays and holidays.

Take-Home-Pay refers to earnings minus deductions for taxes, social security or E.S.I.S. or Provident Fund, union dues, contributions, etc.

A good wage and salary structure, which is essential to sound wage and salary administration, consists of prices paid for various jobs and their interrelationships. The starting point of a wage and salary programme is the wage structure, which is job structure that has been priced in monetary terms, usually in terms of wage rates.

Process of Wage and Salary Administration

Professor David Belcher gives the basic processes of wage and salary administration.[1] First, job analysis is used to provide job descriptions, which are used in many personnel functions and which we have discussed in an earlier chapter. When jobs are related, they constitute a job structure. There are two principal methods of framing objective job structures — job evaluation and time study. These may be used separately or in combination, as in the case of incentive wage systems. Pricing job structures to form wage and salary structures involves numerous and complex considerations.

Factors Affecting Wage and Salary Structures and Administration

The following factors must be taken into consideration in determining wage and salary structures:

1. Government Legislation and Public Policy: Compensation legislation such as Minimum Wages Act, Payment of Wages Act etc. in India and The Fair Standards Act, The Walsh-Healy Act and The Bacon-Davis Act in U.S.A. have to be taken into consideration in wage and salary administration and programmes, which must conform to the legal requirements.

The labour policy of the State also must be reckoned with as also the social and public policies of the State.

2. Going Wages and Salaries: The wages and salaries paid for comparable jobs by other firms in the industry and in the community have an impact on your wage policies. Without paying at least the going wage or salary, your ability to attract and retain personnel will be strictly limited.

3. Labour Supply and Demand: The supply and demand factors have to be noted and analysed and there must be flexibility in the wage and salary policies. When the labour market is 'tight' and when it is 'loose', has to be determined with a view to formulating your wage structure.

4. Union Demands: The trade unions play a significant role in wage and salary administration. It is necessary to carry the union with you and to have its co-operation and acceptance. Union demands and strategies must be taken into consideration. Otherwise, the implementation of the programme will be jeopardised.

5. Productivity: Increasingly there is a trend towards gearing wage increases to productivity increases. Productivity is the key factor in the operations of a company. High wages and low costs are possible only when productivity increases appreciably.

6. Ability to Pay: Another factor, that is taken into consideration, is the ability of the company to pay. Generally the unions demand that companies, which are able to pay high or better wages, must do so and the management's contention is that this should not be the criterion for giving better or high wages.

*7. **Labour Costs:*** As pointed out earlier wages and salaries paid to the employees constitute a cost and no wage programme can ignore the total labour costs and the return that the company is getting. An increasing wage bill has serious repercussions on company operations, prices and profits.

All these above factors, which influence the wage and salary structure and administration, must be taken into consideration.

Wage and Salary Differentials

A company employs various types of personnel — workers, supervisors, professional, technical, managerial and clerical personnel. Among workers, there are unskilled, semi-skilled, skilled workers and craftsmen. Then these personnel may belong to different occupations and functional areas carrying different grades of skills, knowledge, duties, responsibilities, assignments and workloads. They have to be remunerated differently according to these various considerations.

Hence, differential in pay for various jobs constitute the core of wage and salary administration and structure. Differentials reflect not only job content and difficulty, but numerous other factors also such as occupational, geographical, sex, shift, age, handicapped workers, older workers, methods of payment, unionisation, size of the company and the industry. For example, skilled employees are paid more than the unskilled. Supervisors are paid more than skilled workers. Managers are paid more than supervisors. Men may be paid more than the women. Highly industrialised areas may pay more than not so industrialised areas. Even among nations, we may note that highly industrialised and advanced nations pay better wages and salaries than the developing nations.

Thus wage and salary differentials reflect a variety of factors and serve many useful purposes, including: (1) to induce employees to change jobs, (2) to get employees to learn and acquire new skills, (3) to channel employees from declining industries to new industries, and (4) to get employees to accept more responsible positions. No firm can afford to ignore the impact of the various wage and salary differentials, and an alert personnel administrator can often capitalise upon distortions in outside structures to improve the competition position of his own firm. He should be constantly aware of changes in differentials in order to keep his own wage and salary programmes current. Furthermore they are of significant importance in connection with collective bargaining over wage issues.[2]

Typical Assumptions

Professor David Belcher points out that the practice of wage and salary administration appears to be based upon assumptions such as these:[3]

1. Pay is an incentive to job performance.
2. Pay in the form of money has more incentive value than pay in the form of benefits.
3. Employee satisfaction with pay is evidence of its incentive value.
4. Consistent treatment of employees in the matter of pay is a prerequisite to obtaining incentive value from pay.
5. Incentive value is lost when employees are over-paid.

6. Employees react negatively to pay inequities.
7. Pay inequities are similarly defined by all types and levels of employees.
8. Employees regard internal pay inequities as more serious than external inequities.
9. Employees react only to gross external inequities.
10. Employees comparisons of pay are made first in terms of job, and second in terms of performance on jobs.
11. Employees comparisons of pay are uninfluenced by levels of aspiration and pay history.
12. Managers make pay comparisons that are essential similar to those of rank-and-file employees.
14. Professional employees make external rather than internal comparisons.
15. Employees accept the concept of a hierarchy of jobs and pay.
16. Employees' determinants of the job hierarchy are similar to managements' determinants.
17. Employees agree with management on what they are paid for and weigh the factors (performance, seniority, job knowledge and skill, labour market, and so on).

But he admonishes that "Little is known about the accuracy of these and other assumptions on which wage and salary administration is based. What is more serious, wage and salary administrators appear neither to question these assumptions nor show any inclination to test them, despite the excellent position they are in to gather data and even to experiment."[4]

2. PRINCIPLES OF WAGE AND SALARY ADMINISTRATION

A wage and salary administration programme must follow certain basic principles, otherwise they are not sound. Often there is more emphasis placed on the techniques and processes than on the objectives and principles of wage and salary administration.

Objectives of Wage and Salary Administration

A sound wage and salary administration programme aims:

1. To attract and retain the service of employees.
2. To pay employees according to the content and difficulty of the job.
3. To reward employees according to effort and merit.
4. To improve employee morale and productivity.
5. To satisfy the employees as to how and why they are paid.
6. To facilitate payroll administration, budgeting and wage and salary control.
7. To simplify collective bargaining.
8. To promote employee organisational flexibility, including promotions and transfers.

Mr. Lawrence Appley states:[5] "A fair day's pay for every job well done, from the least skilled to the most complex, is a fundamental goal and responsibility of good management and a foundation stone of industrial peace. It is a desirable objective not only from the standpoint of business ethics but of enlightened self-interest, for the level of productivity and morale in any company is directly responsive to the degree and accuracy with which its jobs have been priced."

Principles of Wage and Salary Administration

Mr. Herbert S. Fuhrman enumerates the basic principles that any wage plan must follow:[6]

1. Job evaluation (or rating) plan and compensation plan must be separate and distinct and so understood by all.
2. Both the job evaluation and compensation plans should be sufficiently flexible to accommodate peculiarities of local labour conditions.
3. Evaluation (or rating) must be scientifically sound and easily comprehensible.
4. Individual responsible for the administration of the wage administration plan should, wherever possible, report directly to the same administrative level as director of personnel.
5. Extreme caution should be exercised in selection of wage and job analysts and others who are to be concerned with the execution of the programme.
6. The plan offers satisfaction to the just or reasonable interests of the employer or, in the case of a corporate enterprise, the stockholders.
7. Wage administration plan must at all times be consistent with management policies or programmes.
8. The job rating and compensation plans should be understood by and acceptable to the employees affected, in order that they may appreciate the objectivity and impartiality of the procedure.
9. There should be employee representation in the administration of the plan, in the conduct of locality wage surveys, and in the original rating of new positions.
10. The wage administration plan itself must be acceptable to, and in the interest of, that portion of the public which is affected, directly or indirectly, by the enterprise.
11. The wage administration plan must be flexible and responsive to changing circumstances growing out of locality conditions.
12. The wage administration plan must be consistent with nature and objectives of the organisation.
13. The plan, therefore, must be geared to the type of conditions which prevail in the particular organisation, with due regard for the consequences of size, frequency of job changes and reorganisations, etc.
14. The wage administration plan must simplify and expedite, rather than impede, the other administrative processes.
15. The wage administrator must occupy a responsible niche in the organisation, and his responsibility must be to coordinate with, and in reciprocal relationship to, that of the other phases of administration.

These basic considerations or principles must guide the development, implementation and modification of wage and salary administration system.

Wage and Salary Programmes

A sound programme must achieve the organisation's objectives at minimum costs and it is a vital programme. Many large organisations appoint a wage and salary committee or several such committees to develop and guide a good programme. Mr. William S. Wilcox of Socony Mobil Oil Company has described the nature of the duties and responsibilities and operations of wage and salary committees and their technical advisers in large organisations as follows:[7]

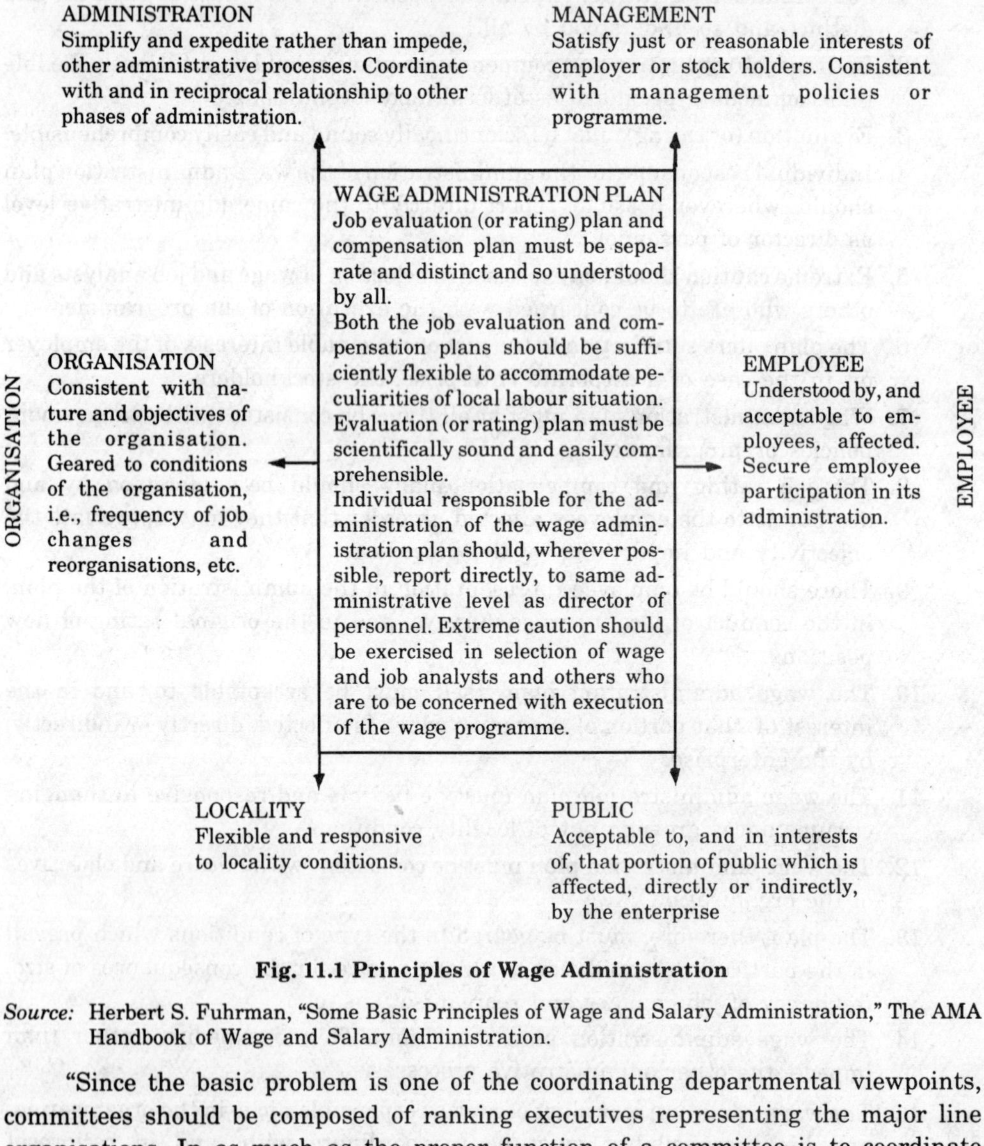

Fig. 11.1 Principles of Wage Administration

Source: Herbert S. Fuhrman, "Some Basic Principles of Wage and Salary Administration," The AMA Handbook of Wage and Salary Administration.

"Since the basic problem is one of the coordinating departmental viewpoints, committees should be composed of ranking executives representing the major line organisations. In as much as the proper function of a committee is to coordinate viewpoints and pass collective judgment upon specific proposals, rather than to carry on research work, the responsibility of thee committees include:

1. Approval, and/or recommendation to management, of job evaluation methods and findings.
2. Review, and recommendation to management, of basic salary scales.
3. Consideration, and recommendation to management, of salary policies.
4. Endorsement of classification of new jobs and reclassification of others.
5. Review of salary rates by departments to insure conformity.
6. Review of budget estimates for salary increases by departments for the forthcoming year."

Division or Plant Committees

The committees should be formed at two organisation levels. The first level is that which takes in a plant, or a specific geographical area. This should be headed by one executive who reports to a home office and who is removed not more than three supervisory levels from the rank and file. The membership of this committee should include the ranking representative for each major function. Broadly speaking, the committee should be considered responsible to management for the recommendation of sound policies and practices on job evaluation and salary administration, and for the effective application of approved methods within the division, plant, or department. Its duties are as follows:

— To make recommendations on salary administration policies.
— To make recommendations job evaluation group limits.
— To make recommendations on additions and changes in job analysis groupings and titles.
— To review annual survey of job analysis and evaluation data.
— To review salary administration procedures and practices.
— To review periodic salary and wage surveys.
— To make recommendations on annual salary budget estimate.
— To review and make recommendations on material for policy manual.
— To review and endorse organisation charts.

The Home Office Committee

The Home Office Committee should be responsible to the Board of Directors for recommending sound policies on job evaluation and salary administration and practical methods of application, and for reviewing the administration. Its duties are:

— To review proposals and make recommendations to the board on salary administration policies.
— To review and endorse statements of policy adoption and cancellation.
— To review proposals and make recommendations to the board on job evaluation group limits.
— To review proposals and endorse additions and changes in job analysis titles and groupings.

— To review proposals and make recommendations to the board on negotiated wage rates.

Role of Technical Advisers

To provide technical guidance, the industrial relations department should assign staff assistants for salary administration to serve these committees. The staff assistants at home office and in the field would be charged with the responsibility for getting the facts, formulating plans, developing methods, making recommendations and coordinating the efforts of the departments and divisions concerned with job evaluation and salary administration. They must accomplish this purpose without authority and without conflict with the line responsibilities; yet they should be held accountable for determining that approved policies are followed and that acceptable methods are applied. The relationship between the different levels should be guided by the following principles:

1. The functions and aims of salary administration are to be determined by the board and should be equally applicable to all divisions, departments and plants.
2. Uniform understanding and appreciation of the general programme and policies are essential to overall coordination.
3. Each field staff assistant should be chosen from candidates within the division, plant or department he is to represent, and his selection should be acceptable to the home office.
4. The field staff assistants should be inducted and trained through the headquarters staff office to develop a common understanding of the functions and policies of the salary administration programme.
5. The headquarters staff assistant should maintain current and close liaison through visits to the field, by headquarters conference with the field staff assistants and by direct correspondence. The object of these contacts should be to ensure that approved policies are uniformly administered through the organisation.

The home office staff assistant would be responsible for the initiation of policies, the formulation of plans, development of methods, and the coordination and application of approved practices throughout the company. His duties should be as follows:

— To coordinate methods of job evaluation throughout the company.

— To prepare statements of policy adoption, change, and cancellation on salary administration matters for review by the headquarters committee and management approval.

— To review and/or develop material for policy manuals.

— To develop methods for job evaluation and salary surveys.

— To initiate review of changes in policies affecting job evaluation and salary administration.

— To maintain headquarters files on salary studies and research data.

— To prepare all material for headquarters committee's consideration.

— To maintain liaison with field staff assistants.

— To consult with industrial relations staff and with management on trends and conditions affecting the salary administration programme.

Procedures for follow-up

Continuing control can be maintained by:

1. Reviewing all employees' performance not less than once a year.
2. Making warranted salary adjustments according to an approved schedule and in accordance with accepted salary policies.
3. Reviewing application of the schedules periodically.
4. Analysing the distribution of actual rates and their relationship to approved limits.
5. Reviewing conformance to budget estimates.
6. Making audits of job descriptions and evaluation.
7. Maintaining a consistent and continuing procedure for:
   (a) Reviewing job duties and writing job descriptions.
   (b) Reviewing job classifications and evaluating jobs.
   (c) Reviewing employees' performance and merit rating.

Some companies have separate wage programmes, and salary programmes, and some operate a combined wage and salary programme. There are several advantages claimed for separate programmes and several for combined programmes. Raymond E. Kirkpatrik has summarised the advantages of a combine wage and salary programme.[8] He argues that the aims of wage administration and salary administration are identical. Both seek to attract and retain good people; a company wants both groups to have confidence in the firm; both programmes should encourage employees to do their best work; a company's economic position cannot be ignored in dealing with either group. He argues that because of these sound industrial relations concepts there is no reason to have separate programmes and good reason to have a combined programme. He states that this will place all employees on an equal basis and be conducive to optimal employee morale.

In order to promote optimal employee morale and satisfaction with company wage and salary administration, the programme must take care to be objective, scientific and impartial. To attain this end, increasingly more and more companies are using the job evaluation techniques to establish acceptable internal wage and salary relationships. The technique of job evaluation aims at providing a more systematic and objective basis for the comparison of job contents as an in the establishment of a more rational wage structure. There is no need to emphasise that wage and salary administration is a management function and the determination, implementation and administration of wage and salary structure is primarily a management responsibility and in order to discharge this responsibility, there is a need for management to evolve a rational and objective wage and salary structure.

3. JOB EVALUATION

A. What is a Job Evaluation?

The International Labour Organisation (I.L.O.) has defined job evaluation thus:[9] "Job evaluation may be defined simply as an attempt to determine and compare the demands which the normal performance of particular jobs makes on normal workers without taking into account of the individual abilities or performance of the workers concerned."

The British Institute of Management offers this definition:[10]

"Job evaluation is the process of analysis and assessment of jobs to ascertain reliably their relative worth using the assessment as a basis for a balanced wage structure."

In the words of The Netherlands Committee of Experts for Job Evaluation:[11]

"Job evaluation is a method which helps to establish a justified rank order of jobs as a whole, being foundation for the setting of wages. Job evaluation, therefore, is the only one of the starting points for establishing the relative differentiation of base wage rates."

The Bureau of Labour Statistics of U.S.A. describes job evaluation:[12]

"Job evaluation is the evaluation or rating of jobs to determine their position in a job hierarchy. The evaluation may be achieved through the assignment of points or the use of some other systematic rating method for essential job requirements, such as skill, experience and responsibility. Job evaluation is widely used in the establishment of wage rate structures and in the elimination of wage inequities. It is always applied to jobs rather than the qualities of individuals on the jobs."

In another description, I.L.O. observes:[13]

"The aim of the majority of systems of job evaluation is to establish, on an agreed logical basis, the relative values of different jobs in a given plant or industry. Job evaluation does not, of course, take the place of established procedures for bargaining between the representatives of the employers and workers; but the use of a system of job evaluation may facilitate the development and maintenance of an equitable relationship among the rates for different jobs. The principle upon which all job evaluation schemes are based is that of describing and assessing the value of all jobs in the firms in terms of a number of factors, the relative importance of which varies from job to job."

Job evaluation is a technique of evaluating jobs and it is similar in principles and methods to employee or personnel rating, save that the latter evaluates employees. It is important that this basic distinction be kept in mind.

Objectives of Job Evaluation

The following objective of job evaluation are enumerated:[14]

1. To secure and maintain complete, accurate and impersonal descriptions of each distinct job or occupation in the entire plant.

2. To provide a standard procedure for determining the relative worth or value of each job within the plant.
3. To determine a rate of pay for each job which is fair and equitable with relation to other jobs in the plant, community and industry.
4. To ensure that like wages are paid to all qualified employees on like work.
5. To promote fair and accurate consideration of all employees for advancement and transfer.
6. To provide a factual basis for the consideration of wage rates for similar jobs both within the community and within the industry.
7. To provide information for the work organisation, employee's selection and training and numerous other important purposes.

Principles of Job Evaluation

A.L. Kress, a leader in the development of job evaluation, has set forth the following principles of job evaluation:[15]

1. Rate the job and not the man. The requirements of the job are usually definite and fixed. The man may have plus qualifications or may not quite measure up to the job requirements. A job rating plan should not be confused with any plan to grade employees. The man on the job may be paid more or less than the job itself is worth, in relation to other jobs. Each element should be rated therefore on the basis of what the job itself requires.
2. The elements selected for rating purposes should be easily explainable in terms that will avoid any overlapping which might lead to rating the same qualifications under several headings. The elements should be as few in number as will cover the necessary requisites for every job.
3. Success with job rating is absolutely dependent on a uniformity of understanding with regard to the definitions or the elements and on consistency in the selection of the degrees of those elements.
4. Any job rating plan must be sold to foremen and employees. Success in selling it will depend on a clear-cut explanation and illustration of the plan.
5. Foremen should participate in the rating of jobs in their own departments.
6. The greatest degree of co-operation from employees, in job rating, will be achieved where they themselves have an opportunity to discuss the ratings.
7. In talking to foremen and employees, avoid discussion of money values. Talk point values and degrees of each element. Discussion of money values will lead to juggling.
8. Too many occupational wages (or rate ranges for given labour grades) should not be established. It would be unwise to adopt an occupational wage for each total of point values.

The Fundamentals of Job Evaluation[16]

1. The job must be broken down into its component parts — in other words prepare a job analysis.

2. The job must be adequately described — or prepare a job description.
3. After job analysis and job description, compare one job with another.
4. Having made job comparisons, it is imperative to have some form of numerical measure.
5. The jobs having been placed on some form of progressive scale, it is necessary to relate them to money terms in order to ascertain its relative worth.

Methods of Job Evaluation

There are four main types of job evaluation schemes:

(1) The ranking method; (2) the grade or classification method; (3) the point rating method; and (4) the factor comparison method. The first two are usually referred to as "non-analytical: and sometimes as "non-quantitative" or "summary" methods and the latter two as "analytical" or "quantitative" methods.

Non-Analytical Methods

The Ranking Methods: It merely entails placing the jobs — in order of demands they make on those who perform them on the basis of their titles only or of simple description of each job as a whole. The various steps involved are:

1. *Selecting the job* — preferably administrative and clerical jobs are separated from manual or factory jobs. In this connection it must be remembered that certain jobs in inspection and foremen category may be more clerical or administrative than manual despite the manual work done as part of the job.

2. *Choosing rankers* — Generally the departmental heads who are familiar with all jobs in their department are employed to judge the rankings.

3. *Job analysis* — This should start with the statement of job. Give the duties and include a specification of the worker in terms of training and education. The greater the details given the smaller the likelihood of later conflict in ranking.

4. *Ranking jobs by departments* — A general method is to write a summary of each job analysis on separate cards and get the departmental managers, supervisors and foremen etc., to put the cards in order of difficulty. Where the jobs are clear-cut and reasonably spaced in difficulty the order given by each person should be similar. Differences are then resolved by discussion between the assessors. Where the jobs are less widely spaced the system of "paired comparison" may be employed. Here each job is paired with every other job in turn and the more difficult job of the pair is indicated by the assessor as shown in the Table 11.1. They are then ranked according to the number of times they are judged more difficult as in Table 11.2.

5. *Integrating departmental ranking* — The rankings of first department are set out vertically in their order. The jobs of second department taken in its ranking order are compared with those of the first department and are inserted in between. This process is known as "job-slotting."

Advantages and Limitations: Relatively simple, easily understood and explained to others, it involves less paper work, is inexpensive and speedier. Paired comparison becomes lengthy if the number of jobs in a department are too large. All it does is to put jobs in order without any indication of how much difference exists between them. The judges must be thoroughly familiar with all jobs which can be difficult in large organisations, the rank positions likely to be unduly biased by prevailing wage rates because of incomplete information and lack of standards.

Classification or Grading Method: This predetermined grading is widely used for salaried jobs, including those in Government and service occupations. This method differs from ranking method in that labour grades are established before actual characteristics are examined. The number of grades is decided upon and the functions corresponding to these grades defined. Only then the descriptions are prepared for each job and matched with those of the different grades established already.

Table 11.1

In each pair underline the job you believe is more difficult. Be sure to make choice of each pair.

Information clerk	MAIL ORDER CLERK
Mail order clerk	ADJUSTER
COLLECTION CLERK	Transfer clerk
REFUND CLERK	Information clerk
COLLECTION CLERK	Mail order clerk
ADJUSTER	Collection clerk
Information clerk	COLLECTION CLERK
Transfer clerk	ADJUSTER
Information clerk	TRANSFER CLERK
REFUND CLERK	Transfer clerk
Mail order clerk	REFUND CLERK
Refund clerk	COLLECTION CLERK
Transfer clerk	MAIL ORDER CLERK
ADJUSTER	Refund clerk
ADJUSTER	Information clerk

Table 11.2

Positions	*No. of times judged more difficult*	*Rank*
Information clerk	0	6
Mail order clerk	2	4
Refund clerk	3	3
Transfer clerk	1	5
Adjustment clerk	5	1
Collection clerk	4	2

Adopted from Job Evaluation, A.Mc.C. Norris.
Proceedings of the Institute of the Mechanical Engineers, London, 1964-65, Part I (Vol. 179) Number II.

The grade descriptions are formed in such a manner as to cover describable differences in degrees of skill, responsibility and other job characteristics. The lowest grade may cover jobs which merely require the worker to follow the instructions under close supervision. Each succeeding grade will reflect a higher level of skill and responsibility with less and less supervision. The jobs, as in ranking method, are considered as a whole.

Advantages and Limitations: Relatively inexpensive, simple and easily applied. In organisations with relatively small range of jobs, the results achieved may be fairly satisfactory. When the range increases, it becomes more and more difficult to compress so many jobs into a limited number of grade descriptions.

Sometimes this method is preferred because of its comparative vagueness and hence greater flexibility. When the nature of job changes owing to new production methods its classification will normally have to be negotiated anew and analytical methods with their predetermined definitions of factor and degrees, leave less freedom to the parties in such negotiations. As a result trade unions have sometimes expressed a preference for a classification method on this ground.

Analytical Methods

Point Rating Method: In short, degrees or scales of various factors are established. Each factor of a job is compared to the scale and a point value is allotted. The sum of points for the various factors places the job quantitatively as well as qualitatively. The various steps involved are:

1. *Selection of factors:* Factors should be pertinent to the type of positions included. If no supervisory posts are included, there is no point in having 'supervision of others.' However 'supervision received' may be appropriate. It is suggested that 10 to 15 factors are chosen covering all jobs. Factors should be unique, in the sense that they should not overlap in meaning. They should be defined clearly. Also they must be quantifiable and be able to be described in varying degrees. Factors which are given the same rating for all jobs need not be included as they do not contribute to differentiate among jobs. If all jobs are performed under the same physical conditions, this factor may be omitted. Also if a job is highly repetitive the factor monotony should be included.

2. *Defining the factors:* Explicit definitions must be prepared for each one so that people using the plan will have the same concept of what aspects of job are covered by the factor. Positive statements in simple language lessen ambiguities.

3. *Defining degrees in each factor:* Each factor is subdivided into degrees, six being a reasonable range. Each degree needs to be defined clearly and concisely, preferably in some quantifiable manner, e.g., 'Responsibility to equipment' could be defined in terms of money, being the maximum amount of possible loss due to lack of precaution.

Table 11.3 shows an example.

4. *Determining relative values of job factors:* As all factors will not have equal importance to the needs of an industry they must be weighted. This is not easy because the whole universe of jobs must be looked at and not a particular job. This is best done by a committee of supervisors and executives. The committee should ask themselves such questions as 'should jobs be paid more for physical effort or working conditions'? or 'should education receive more consideration than hazards, and if so, how much

more'? The individual weightings are agreed upon among the members. The weightings are then expressed as a per cent of this weighted per cent as it becomes the number of points for the first degree of each factor. The typical weightings are shown in Table 11.4 and the point for various degrees are merely the points of the 1 degree multiplied by the grade number.

Table 11.3

RESPONSIBILITY FOR MATERIAL AND PRODUCT

1st degree:	Value of material which may be wasted, damaged or lost is small $ 10
2nd degree:	Probable loss in damage is low $ 100
3rd degree:	Probability of occurrence is low upto $ 250
4th degree:	Probable loss is high $ 500
5th degree:	Loss very high — several thousand dollars.

Adapted from: *The A M A Hand Book of Wage and Salary Administration,* Editors: M. Joseph Doover and Vivienne Marquis. A M A, 1515 Broadway, New York 18. Third print Feb. 1952.

Table 11.4

WEIGHTING OF FACTORS, DEGREES AND POINTS

Factors	*Weighting*	*Percent Weighting*	*Degrees and Points*					
			1	2	3	4	5	6
Education & Mental Devt.	40	15	15	30	45	60	75	90
Experience & training	75	30	30	60	90	120	150	180
Judgment & initiative	40	15	15	30	45	60	75	90
Physical effort	18	7	7	14	21	28	35	42
Mental application	18	7	7	14	21	28	35	42
Monotony of work	12	5	5	10	15	20	25	30
Responsibility for equipment	10	4	4	8	12	16	20	24
Responsibility for material	15	6	6	12	18	24	30	36
Working condition	15	6	6	12	18	24	30	36
Unavoidable hazards	12	5	5	10	15	20	25	30

Adopted from A. Mc. C. Norris, *op. cit.,* pp. 399-400.

5. *Constructing job evaluation manual:* Certain selected key jobs are ranked in degrees under each factor headings, thus showing up anomalies which can then be corrected. Finally a job evaluation manual is prepared with *these key jobs listed as examples future evaluation of other jobs.*

6. Job descriptions and job specifications are prepared. They are expressed in terms of the factors already established.

7. Rating of jobs are done with the help of the manual and the final point values ascertain the position of the job and its worth.

Advantages and Limitations: This method is most common and widely used. In a way this method is more systematic compared to non-analytical methods. Also agreement between raters is high which aids in bargaining. This method is said to suffer from lack of flexibility, is complicated and requires more time to construct. It is also charged to contain too many refinements, point values being assigned arbitrarily. Perhaps the chief criticism is that the unit of measurement is not defined. Also a large number of jobs has to be covered by a limited number of factors which is said to restrict the scope of evaluation.

Factor-comparison Method

As originally developed this method involves ranking of jobs in respect of certain factors and usually involves the assigning of money wages to the jobs depending upon the ranking. However it may be applied in a different way, as will be shown below. The process consists of:

1. *Selection of factors:* They may be skill, mental and educational requirements, physical requirements and responsibility, working conditions.

2. Having fixed the factors, job analyses are prepared expressing job requirements in terms of these factors.

3. *Selection of key jobs:* The ranking of jobs and subsequent fixing of wages are carried for a number of 'key jobs' which serve as points of reference for later evaluation. The key jobs should be a good sample representing the entire range. It is suggested that 15 to 20 jobs should be picked. They should be clearly describable and capable of analysis in terms of factors.

4. Evaluation may be done by 'paired comparison' in each of the factors as in ranking. A typical evaluation has been shown in Table 11.5. If the method of immediate fixing of wages is to used, the jobs are ranked as follows. The wage rate of each key job is broken down and distributed among or apportioned to the factors in the proportion in which these are considered to contribute to the total 'price' paid for each key job in the form of its wage rate. For example, if tool making is chosen as a key job and its wage rate is 20 money units, it may be decided to allot 9 of these to skill, 5 to mental requirement, 2 to physical requirement, 3 to responsibility and 1 to working conditions and so on. When the rates of all key jobs have been divided this way, they have been implicitly ranked with respect to each other.

The two rankings of key jobs are undertaken independently of each other. Any differences present have to be adjusted by re-examining. If it is not possible to reconcile for a particular job, this is eliminated from the list of key jobs. Table 11.6 shows ranking by allocating money values.

5. The results are used to rank other jobs in plant and fix their wage rates.

Advantages and Limitations: E. J. Bengel, the leading advocate of factor comparison, claims the following advantages for this method. It facilitates merit rating, selection, training, improving working conditions etc. The fact that the method leads directly to the determination of wages had been regarded as an undesirable feature by those who consider that only task of job evaluation is the comparison of job contents which is logically different from the fixing of wages. Another disadvantage is that many people do not accept the prevailing rates of key jobs to form a basis of whole wage structure.

Factor-Comparison

Table 11.5						Table 11.6										
Ranking by factors						Allocation of money value & ranking										
Jobs						Wage rate in money units	Skill		Mental requirements		Physical requirements		Responsibility		Working condition	
	Skill	Mental requirement	Physical requirement	Responsibility	Working condition		Money value	Rank	Money value	Rank	Money value	Rank	Money value	Rank	Money value	Rank
Tool maker	1	2	2	1	4	20	9.0	1	5.0	1	2.0	3	3.0	1	1.0	5
Machinist	2	2	3	2	3	18	8.0	3	4.0	2	1.0	5	2.0	2	3.0	3
Electrician	3	3	4	3	5	16	6.0	3	3.0	3	3.0	2	2.5	3	2.5	4
Assembler	4	4	5	5	2	14	4.0	4	2.0	4	1.5	4	1.0	4	5.5	1
Janitor	5	5	1	4	1	12	2.0	5	1.0	5	4.0	1	0.5	5	4.5	2

Adopted from: "Job Evaluation" I.L.O. *op. cit.,* pp. 28-29.

Installing Job Evaluation

Lytle outlines the steps to be taken in installing a plan of job evaluation:[17]

1. Choose the most suitable method and the main techniques.
2. Choose the major job characteristics, then the minor ones and apportion limiting values.
3. Start selling the proposition to all concerned; seek suggestions.
4. Build definitions, measuring scales, or comparison techniques, and assign relative values.
5. Design forms or questionnaires and collect preliminary descriptions.
6. Edit preliminary descriptions and establish grades or classes.
7. Identify and evaluate key jobs, first on major characteristics, then on minor characteristics (keeping within limits of No.2).
8. Evaluate remaining jobs on all characteristics (keeping proper relativity to key jobs) and harmonise jobs titles.
9. Now if not sooner, be sure union representatives concur in weightings.
10. Make intercompany survey on key jobs only, but try to find at least one per class.
11. Translate abstract values in to money values tentatively.
12. Plot the end jobs and the most sure key jobs on a scatter diagram, bargain on wage levels.
13. Discover line of reference, i.e., the trend line, and decide range limits.
14. Read just all values relative to line, standardise and put into working form; finally, fix all operating procedures.

Advantages and Limitations of Job Evaluation

The I.L.O. summarises the advantages and limitations of job evaluation:[18]

Advantages of Job Evaluation

1. Job evaluation is a logical and, to some extent, objective method of ranking jobs relatively to each other. It may thus help in removing inequities in existing wage structures and in maintaining sound and consistent wage differences in a plant or industry.
2. In the case of new jobs, the method often facilitates fitting them into existing wage structure.
3. The method helps in removing grievances over relative wages and thus may improve labour-management relations.
4. The method replaces the many accidental factors occurring in less systematic procedures, of wage bargaining by more impersonal and objective standards, thus establishing clear basis for negotiation.
5. The method may lead to greater uniformity in wage rates, thus simplifying wage administration.
6. The information collected in the processes of job description and analysis may also be used for the improvement of selection, training, transfer and promotion procedures on the basis of comparative job requirements.
7. Such information also often reveals that workers are engaged on jobs requiring less skill and other qualities than they possess, thereby pointing to the possibility of making more efficient use of the plant's labour force.

Limitations of Job Evaluation

1. Although there are many ways of applying job evaluation in a flexible manner, rapid changes in technology and in the supply of and demand for particular skills raise problems of adjustment that may need further study.
2. However logical and consistent a system may be, account has to be taken of various limits to the possibility of changing apparently illogical elements in an existing wage structure. Certain external rates may have to be paid for "hiring jobs" whether they are compatible with the job evaluation system or not; traditional wage relationships, however inconsistent they may be, cannot always be altered.
3. When job evaluation results in substantial change in the existing wage structure, the possibility of implementing these changes in a relatively short period may be restricted by the financial limits within which the firm has to operate.
4. When there is a large proportion of incentive workers, and especially when incentives have to be changed frequently, it may be very difficult to maintain a reasonable and acceptable structure of relative earnings.
5. Job evaluation does not provide a complete answer to the wage problem. It has nothing to say about the absolute wage level and little about the absolute size of the wage differentials appropriated to the evaluated job structure.

6. In particular, the process of job rating is to some extent arbitrary because few of the factors and degrees can be measured with great accuracy.
7. Job evaluation takes a long time to install, requires specialised technical personnel and may be quite costly. One Canadian estimate put the cost of installing a scheme at $ 45 per job evaluated and maintenance charges at about 25 cents per employee per month.
8. The drawing up of job descriptions tends to formalise job contents, which may lead to abuses by workers who acquire a vested interest in maintaining the requirements for certain jobs.
9. Trade unions often regard the method with suspicion and in some cases with hostility.

Conditions Necessary for Operation of Job Evaluation

In one of the most comprehensive surveys undertaken by the Industrial Relations Section of the Department of Economics and Social Institutions of Princeton University, covering some 73 companies employing 278 to 140,000 workers, the following conditions are indicated to be necessary for the successful operation of a job evaluation scheme:[19]

1. It must be carefully established by ensuring (a) that management's aims are clear to all concerned and that not only manual workers but also all levels of supervision and management fully understand its implications, and (b) that all relevant internal and external factors have been taken into account in arriving at the final form of the scheme.
2. It must have full approval and continued backing of top management.
3. The trade union's acceptance of the scheme must be obtained.
4. Adequate administrative controls must be set up to ensure (a) centralised co-ordination of the scheme, (b) the evaluation of new and changed jobs, (c) the proper control of individual rate ranges and (d) the conduct of wage surveys to provide the necessary information about intra-plant wages.
5. The importance of factors other than job content in wage rate determination, for example, employment market conditions, sex, wage differentials, geographic wage differentials and the relative bargaining power of management and the trade union concerned, must be recognised.

Trade Unions and Job Evaluation

I.L.O. reports that various unions all over the world have expressed favourable views regarding job evaluation and some others have given their unfavourable view also.[20]

Favourable Views: Unions such as United Steel Workers of America, Commercial Telegraphers Union, International Ladies' Garment Workers' Union etc. in U.S.A., High Authority of the European Coal and Steel Community, The Italian Confederation of Trade Unions, Italian Workers' Union, General Confederation of Labour, French Confederation of Christian Trade Unions, Netherland's Federation of Trade Unions, etc. have expressed favourable views regarding job evaluation schemes.

They may be summarised as follows:

1. Job evaluation is objective.
2. It replaces arbitrary determination of wages and salaries.
3. It reduces current and potential wage grievances.
4. It gives an opportunity to unions to participate in the fixation of firm's wages on the basis of complete equality.
5. It enables unions to obtain suitable wage adjustments more quickly and effectively.
6. It limits the power of unilateral management decision in wage matters.
7. It is an important instrument in improving union-management relations.
8. It can bring about a more rational and equitable wage structure.
9. It ensures the elimination of all discrimination.
10. It relieves the workers' representatives of daily discussions, explanations and debates about certain wage questions.

Unfavourable Views: There are some unions which have expressed unfavourable views with regard to job evaluation. The Indian National Trade Union Congress, I.L.O. reports, considers the job evaluation scheme used in India to be very defective.[21] "... because of the absence of consultation with the workers in the evaluation of a scheme... the failure to inform them of the details of the scheme the absence of union co-operation in the conduct of job evaluation, the failure on the part of the evaluator to carry out essential foundational procedures such as job analysis and job description, the failure to evaluate working conditions and hazards and the assumption of differentials instead of their ascertainment as a result of job evaluation."

The International Association of Machinists in U.S.A. are highly critical of job evaluation technique itself for various reasons expressed in their manual, "What is wrong with Job Evaluation?"[22]

I. Basically, job evaluation tends to limit collective bargaining. This reflects in the following ways:

1. It tends to freeze the wage structure and thereby creates an obstacle to the correction of inequities. It restricts the right of negotiating on a rate of pay for each job year after year. It usually limits negotiations to bargaining for a fixed amount or fixed percentage for all jobs, or establishing rates of pay through some "predetermined formula" that usually does not result in equitable treatment for all.
2. It fails to consider all forces which determine wages, such as supply and demand, other contract or area rates, etc.
3. It tends to create a barrier between the employees and his understanding of his own job rate, because his rate is set in a manner not understood by him.
4. It tends to disregard the ability of the individual.
5. It places a ceiling upon wages which is contrary to a traditional objective of organised labour.

6. It disregards compensation for loyalty, i.e., years of service, etc.
7. It tends to dilute traditional skills, creating many new occupations and many new classifications and thereby reducing wages.
8. It affects the seniority of employees by the creation of additional classifications.
9. It makes the promotion of employees into higher-paying jobs considerably more difficult because of the limiting characteristic of job descriptions.
10. It provides the company with a tool to downgrade employees during times of cutbacks.

II. Job evaluation presents a threat to the stability of our organisation because of the following:

1. It necessitates the constant attention of additional trained representatives, thereby increasing the cost of representation to the local, district and Grand Lodge.
2. It provides management with a tool to play one group of employees against another.
3. It creates dissension within a local lodge (where members are from more than one firm) where all firms do not have job evaluation. It tends to hamper the efforts of the lodge in establishing uniform area rates.
4. It tends to place the responsibility upon the union for inequities that are not properly corrected since the union accepted the job evaluation plan and must, therefore, share in its shortcomings.
5. It compels the continuing and almost impossible task of educating job study committees and shop stewards in the many ramifications of the job evaluation plan in effect.
6. It encourages management of different plans to work together and provides them with a basic method to achieve jointly desired results in the determination of wages; it strengthens management's opposition to the wage demands of the union.

III. The effects of job evaluation upon the general welfare of our society is discernible as it affects the supply of skilled workers. It tends to discourage bonafide apprenticeships and, therefore, reduces the reservoir of overall skilled workers so that in the event of a future crisis a serious shortage of skilled manpower would result.

A Survey of Job Evaluation Programmes

Mr. John A. Patton, Executive Vice President, George Fry and Associates, reports the significant findings of his survey (with more than 500 respondents) about job evaluation programmes throughout U.S.A. conducted in March 1960.[23]

1. In examining the responses of those companies that rated their job evaluation programmes from "rather successful" to "highly successful", we discovered that 93 per cent of the organised companies and 86 per cent of the unorganised companies so rated themselves. The small difference in these percentages would seem to indicate that success of job evaluation programmes has little or no relation to the question of whether the company's employees are organised or not.

2. Among the organised companies, 18 per cent indicated that their unions participated in their job evaluation programmes. Of these, 53 per cent rated their programs "highly successful", as compared with only 40 per cent which so rated themselves among those organised companies whose unions did not participate in their job evaluation programmes. These figures suggest that, in an organised company, job evaluation is more likely to succeed when the union participates in the programme.

3. Of the companies using a standard job evaluation plan, 93 per cent rated themselves "rather successful" to "highly successful." Of those using a modified plan, 92 per cent rated themselves likewise. Of these percentages, 43 per cent and 46 per cent, respectively, fell within the "highly successful" category. The small difference in these figures suggests that the type of plan used is not an important determinant of the success of a job evaluation programme.

4. In correlating the length of training of job evaluation personnel with the success of the programme, we discovered that only 38 per cent of those companies employing job evaluation personnel with less than six months' rated themselves "highly successful", while 49 per cent of those companies whose job evaluation personnel had more than six months' training rated themselves in the category. It is evidently important that job evaluation personnel be adequately trained.

5. The responding companies expressed a definite preference for candidates for the position of job evaluation analyst who have a university degree or its equivalent and some previous experience in industrial engineering or personnel administration. Seventy-three per cent expect candidates to have at least two years of college training, the remaining 27 per cent accept candidates with high school diplomas. Thirty-eight per cent, however, said that they prefer to choose their job evaluation analysts from within the company. Among these, the backgrounds of analysts were described as falling into the following major areas of experience: Shop, 46 per cent; office, 17 per cent; engineering, 35 per cent; and others, 2 per cent.

6. Of the four types of job evaluation plans in general use, the responding companies indicated the following preferences: point rating, 85 per cent; factor comparison, 10.5 per cent; ranking, 3.5 per cent; and classification 1 per cent.

7. When we compiled answers on a geographic basis, we came up with these highly revealing correlations:

	East Percentage	*Midwest Percentage*	*West Percentage*
Union protested initiation of job evaluation programme	26	10	1
Job evaluation has been a significant issue in contract negotiations	50	36	21
Management made concessions to get union arrangement	34	22	—
Union has attempted to eliminate job evaluation by negotiation	15	12	6
Union has a special job evaluation committee	49	31	27

These figures raise some interesting questions. Why have unions in the East protested against job evaluation so much more than unions in the West and Midwest? Do multi-plant companies fully understand the implications of these significant geographic differences? Have companies in the West and Midwest done a better job of educating their unions and achieving union participation in their job evaluation programmes than companies in the East? Are unions in the East more aware of the importance of job evaluation as a tool of management?

8. In response to the question whether the company would now initiate a job evaluation programme if one did not already exist, the following percentages answered affirmatively:

Companies with	*Responding 'Yes' Percentage*
More than 5,000 employees	100
1,001 to 5,000	99
500 to 1,000	94
Fewer than 500	92.3

9. Fifty-five per cent of the responding companies answered the question, "How many union or employee grievances have you had about job evaluation?" The average number of grievances over the past three year was 31, but this average figure includes one large company which alone had 2,700 grievances! Subtracting this extraordinary figure, we found that the average dropped to 15, or only five grievances per year.

10. Over the past three years the responding averaged 18 regrades: 15 upward, 3 downward. Eighty-three per cent of the upward regrades were the result of changed duties, while 17 per cent were the result of re-evaluations of the same duties. The downgradings were made on the same bases: 90 per cent and 10 per cent respectively. Twenty-six per cent of the companies reduced the pay rates of employees in downgraded jobs.

11. Only 26.5 per cent of the responding companies reported cases of arbitration which involved job evaluation. The companies won 73 per cent of these cases.

12. Fifty-two per cent of the companies relied upon the questions of their affected employees to guide them in explaining their job evaluation programmes. Twenty-four per cent asked their analysts to explain their programmes. Only the remaining 24 per cent actually devised a formal instruction programme for their employees. This finding is, I feel, one of the most significant of the whole survey. It certainly has a direct bearing on the surprising figures on managers', supervisors', and employees' understanding of the job evaluation programme that emerged from the survey:

Understanding by	*Good to Average Percentage*	*Little or None Percentage*
Top management	86.3	13.7
Middle management	95	5
First-line supervisors	86.5	13.5
Employees	45.3	54.7

Note that employees, the group most directly and importantly affected by job evaluation, were considered to have the least understanding of it.

Some of the companies reported that, of the four groups identified above, employees:

(a) Are most suspicious of the job evaluation programme.

(b) Are most inclined to regard it as a necessary evil.

(c) Are least convinced that job evaluation is the best tool the company could use.

(d) Are second only to organised labour in feeling that it is a plan manipulated by management to arrive at predetermined "result."

(e) Feel the most indifference toward and the least enthusiasm about the programme.

These comments reflect the opinion of only 3.2 per cent of the employees of the responding companies, so they do not detract greatly from the validity of my earlier observation that job evaluation is generally accepted today as an important tool of management. They do, however, emphasise the need for achieving understanding and acceptance of job evaluation among employees in order to enhance its effectiveness and value.

Mr. John A. Patton summarises the findings of his survey:[24]

1. Job evaluation is regarded as an effective and valuable management tool in most companies which have job evaluation programmes today.
2. Job evaluation programmes are just as effective in organised companies as they are in unorganised companies. In organised companies, however, the chances of the programmes' success are increased if union participation is achieved.
3. The success of the job evaluation depends more on the way the programme is explained and "sold" to supervisors, employees, and the union (if one exists), and on the way it is subsequently administered, than on the type of job evaluation plan used.
4. The need for formalised job evaluation programmes become greater as the size of the company increases.
5. Too many top company executives know too little about job evaluation; its effectiveness, its potential uses, and its limitations.

Mr. Patton suggests the keys to the success of any job evaluation programme:[25]

1. Well trained job evaluation personnel.
2. A supervisory force that understands and believes in job evaluation;
3. Employees, organised or not, who recognise the need for and benefits of a job evaluation programme; and
4. A top management which is aware that job evaluation is neither a cure-all nor a one-shot operation, but a valuable, effective management tool that requires its continuing attention and support.

Pricing Jobs: After determining the job content and difficulty and establishing job relationships, which give job structures, job can be priced. Job structures, which priced, give wage and salary structures, which indicate money relationships between and among jobs. Figure 11.2 serves as an illustration of typical job evaluation chart of salary grades and ranges.

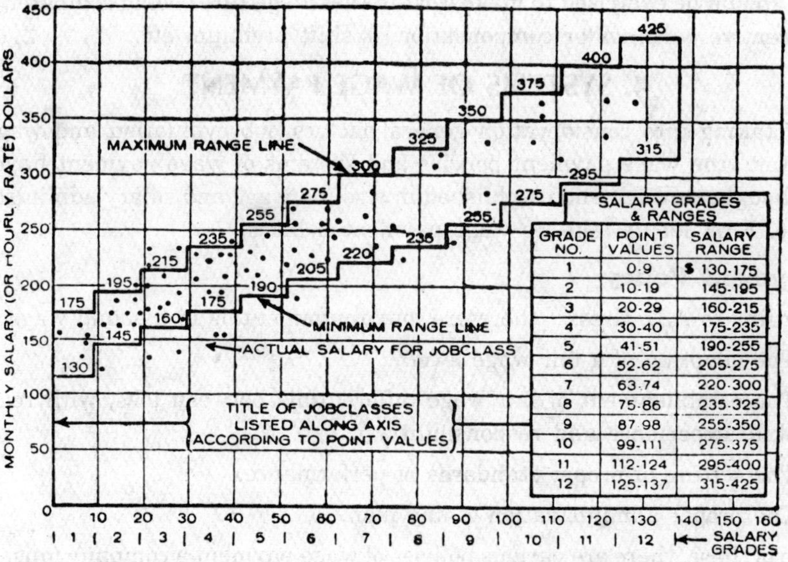

Fig. 11.2 Typical Job Evaluation Chart of Salary Grades and Ranges (for illustration only) (Business Research Corporation)

Wage Surveys: Wage surveys play an important role in wage and salary administration. It enables the company to know what kind of wages and salaries for various jobs are ruling in the market within a community and industry. Some companies wish to be 'wage leaders', i.e., where the companies pay a slightly higher wages and salaries than the going rates with a view to attracting and holding good and efficient people and have an edge over the other competitors. But most firms at least try to relate their wage policies and structures to the patterns established in the community and industry. It is indeed surprising to hear companies complain that they do not get good people and retain good employees any more and often such companies have fallen behind in the wage area without realising it.

A wage survey enables your company programme to keep in top tune and systematic wage surveys may be conducted by research institutions, leading firms, professional associations, employer associations. Usually systematic surveys include the following steps:[26]

1. Select the area, industry to be included in the survey.
2. List key jobs and positions common to most firms in the survey.
3. Get detailed descriptions of the job, so that valid comparisons may be made.
4. Prepare schedule of information to be obtained, i.e., hourly rate, weekly earnings etc.

5. Collect accurate wage and salary data on jobs that are essentially similar by questionnaires and follow it up with interviews in each firm.
6. Compile the wages and salary data for each job.
7. Present results and recommendations.

Care should be exercised to make certain that wage rates being compared do not include incentive earnings or compensation or shift premium etc.

4. SYSTEMS OF WAGE PAYMENT

After taking into consideration general factors, job evaluation and wage rate determination, the wage payment policies and systems of wage payment have to be carefully thought through and established in a sound wage and salary administration programme. First let us take up wage payment policies.

Wage Payment Policy

According to A.L. Kress[27] there are four fundamentals in a sound wage policy:

1. The adoption of a fair wage level.
2. The establishment of fair wage differentials between jobs, with regard to skill, experience and responsibility.
3. The setting of proper standards of performance.
4. The proper administration of any plan.

Aside of these, there are various policies of wage payment a company must evolve and they relate to:

1. What should be a normal work day?
2. What should be a normal work week, both regarding hours and days?
3. What should be overtime policy?
4. What should be pay for overtime work?
5. What should be the pay for sixth day or servant day or Sunday work?
6. What should be the premium for second shift or third shift? Whether there should be a premium?
7. What should be the reporting pay?
8. What pay should be guaranteed to employee called in for emergencies?
9. What should be the pay period?
10. What should be the pay day?
11. How should the employees be paid? In cash or cheque or kind?
12. Where should they be paid?
13. What should be the method of handling letters to the company from creditors of employees?
14. What should be deducted from employee's pay?
15. What should be company-paid rest period for employees?
16. Should company advances be given?

On all these matters, it is better to establish policies and they must be written down and all the companies including supervisor and management must be made aware of the company policies.

A.L. Kress summarises the salient points which should be covered in a wage payment policy:[28]

1. The general wage level should be at least equal to the prevailing wage level for similar work in the community.
2. The wage for each job or operation in the plant should be determined relatively with other jobs, with due regard for skill, responsibility, experience, physical demands, hazards.
3. Industrial or group effort should be rewarded through the use of an incentive method of wage payment, where such a plan can be applied.
4. Fair standards of performance should be set which can be reasonably and consistently attained.
5. A reasonable normal work-week should be adopted, with a suitable overtime premium.
6. Employees should be compensated for waiting time due to reasons beyond their control.
7. Full information should be given to any employee regarding the wage payment policy or plan. Management should discuss with employees, whenever requested, the setting of standards, the fixing of occupational wages, the computation of earnings, or the standards themselves.
8. Complaints arising from the operation of any payment plan should be investigated and adjusted promptly.
9. Hourly, weekly and annual earnings should be systematically analysed and studied as a basis for constructive action by management.
   (a) To raise performance standards through better training and supervision.
   (b) To stabilise employment.

Systems of Wage Payment

There are essentially two major systems of wage plans, first system, the oldest related to time and the other system related to output, quality and quantity of output. The former system is usually referred to as 'day work' or 'time wage' system and the latter is composed of incentive plans or payment by results. Under these major systems, there are several wage plans, of which the following are important and are discussed.

Day Work or Time Wage System

One of the oldest systems of wage payment, the worker is paid a definite amount of money for a specific period of work, which may be a day, week, or a month, irrespective of the amount of work he does in that period. This system is simple and can be understood by the employees. It assures a guaranteed wage to the employee. Trade unions and employees also prefer this system because it helps to create and maintain the solidarity of the work group. There is harmony among the employees. Where units of output are not distinguishable or measurable, this system is most suitable.

But this system does not offer any incentive to the worker. Since the employee is paid for his time, not output, there are chances that the employee may waste his time doing nothing and hence, he may have to be closely supervised.

Payment by Results[29]

There are many different systems of wage payment under which the worker's earnings are related directly to some measurement of work done either by himself or by his group. Such systems are generally classified in four main groups according to whether the worker's earnings vary: (1) in the same proportion as output, (2) proportionally less than output, (3) proportionally more than output, or (4) in proportions which differ at different levels of output.

1. Systems with Worker's Earnings Varying in the Same Proportion as Output

(a) The straight piece-work system, which may be applied either to individuals or to groups of workers, and the worker is paid at a specific rate per unit of output measured in terms of, for example, pounds of yarn, tons of coal, number of pieces of garments. Direct labour costs per unit thus remain constant as output increases above standard, but total unit costs decrease because fixed and semi-variable overhead unit costs decrease.

The worker's time rate is guaranteed and with a guaranteed time rate the earnings curve for rates of output below standard is horizontal upto standard output, at which it becomes a straight line having a slope of unity. This means that a one per cent increase in output results in a one per cent increase in earnings.

(b) The standard hour system: This system, which is also known sometimes as the Standard Time, Time Piece-work, or 100 Per cent Gain Sharing System is strikingly similar to the straight piece work, except here a standard time is allowed to complete a particular job and the worker is paid for the standard time at his time rate if he completes the job in standard time or less. Thus if a man completes in eight hours a job for which the standard time is ten hours, his earnings for this job will amount to ten times his time rate. If, on the other hand, he takes more than the standard time to complete the job, he will, if he is guaranteed his time rate, be paid at this rate for the time he actually spent on the job. But if he is not guaranteed his time rate, he will be paid only for the standard time.

The chief characteristics of the above systems is that any gains or losses resulting from changes in his output accrue to the worker (leaving to the employer any gains or losses in overhead costs per unit of output). In contrast, when the worker is paid by the hour or day all gains or losses resulting from changes in his output accrue to the employer. But the successful operation of this type of system of payment by results requires however that the measurement of standard and individual outputs must be extremely accurate. Inaccuracy in these matters gives rise to inequities and may lead to the ultimate failure of a scheme due to worker classification.

2. System with Worker's Earnings Varying Proportionally Less than Output

These systems are often referred to as sharing plans, because the worker's earnings vary proportionally less than output and the worker shares with his employer the gains or losses resulting from changes in output.

Halsley System: Under this system, a standard time is allowed for a job. For work done in correct time or more, the actual rate is paid. Thus the minimum wage is guaranteed even if the output falls below standard. If the job is completed in less than standard time, the worker receives as a bonus a payment at his time rate for a specified percentage of the time saved. This percentage may vary anywhere from 30 per cent to 70 per cent, but usually it is fixed at 50 per cent (the other 50 per cent, going to the share of employer). Thus if a worker does the work in 6 hours against 10 hours standard, he gets paid for 6 hours plus 50 per cent of 4 hours, i.e., 2 hours as bonus. The other 50 per cent (2 hours) is shared by the employer.

Rowan System: Under this system also a standard time is allowed for a job, and a bonus is similarly paid for any time saved. This percentage is equal to the proportion which the time saved forms of standard time. Thus if a worker does work in 6 hours against 10 hours standard, the wages payable is 6 hours' wages plus 40 per cent of the wages as bonus.

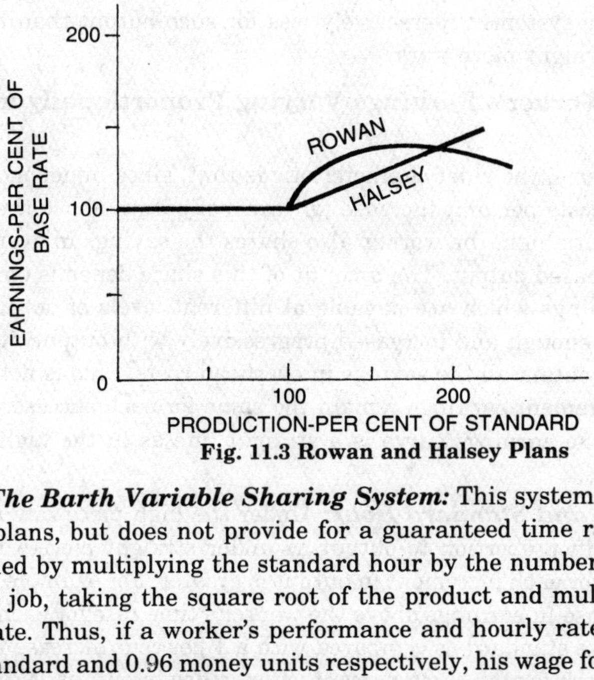

Fig. 11.3 Rowan and Halsey Plans

1. The Barth Variable Sharing System: This system is similar to Rowan and Halsley plans, but does not provide for a guaranteed time rate. The worker's pay is ascertained by multiplying the standard hour by the number of hours actually taken to do the job, taking the square root of the product and multiplying by the worker's hourly rate. Thus, if a worker's performance and hourly rate are 7 hours against 10 hours standard and 0.96 money units respectively, his wage for completing the job will be $(\sqrt{10 \times 7}) \times 0.96$, or 8.06 money units. For levels of output above standard the worker's earnings under the Barth system are always lower than under straight piece-work for standard task, but are, for low task, higher than under straight piece-work at certain levels of output above standard.

The Bedaux System: The standard time set is divided into a number of points at the rate of one minute per point. The bonus is calculated at 75 per cent of the points earned in excess of 60 per hour. Thus, if the standard time is 10 hours and if the worker completes the job in 7 hours and if his hourly rate of 0.96 money units, the standard number of points for completing the job is 600 points. The worker thus earns 600 points in seven hours. His bonus, therefore, will be 75 per cent of 180x0.96/60 which is equal to 2.16 money units. Since his time wage for seven hours' work is 6.72 money units, his total wage will be 8.88 money units. If a worker does not reach standard, he is paid at his time rate.

The Bedaux system is really more than an incentive system, since it enables the management to record the output of any worker or department in units which show at once if the production is upto the standard that management desires. In recent years, the percentage allowed to workers has, in some cases, been raised from 75% to almost 100%. If 100 per cent is allowed, the worker's earnings become the same as under the straight piece-work, but in all other cases his earnings are, under the Bedaux system, always less than under straight piece-work.

These systems are often applied in cases where it is not possible to set standards or to measure the worker's output accurately. Under some of these schemes it is possible for a worker to earn more for certain levels of output than he would, under piece-work when production difficulties are encountered. But, of course, if no such difficulties are encountered, and the worker is able to increase his output significantly, he receives under these systems progressively less for such output than he would if he were working on straight piece-work.

3. Systems with Worker's Earnings Varying Proportionally more than Output

Under these systems, the chief characteristic is that, since under most of these systems direct labour costs per unit increase for levels of output above the standard, which is usually set quite high, the worker also shares the savings in overhead costs which result from increased output. The amount of this share depends on the size of the increments in earnings which are payable at different levels of output. If these increments were large enough and increased progressively with output, it is obvious that the workers could obtain all the savings in overhead costs. This is not, of course, the case where the increment earnings remain the same for each successive increase in output, i.e., where the earnings curve is a straight line as in the high piece-rate system described below.

High Piece-rate and Standard Hour: Under the high piece-rate system the worker's earnings are in proportion to output as under straight piece-work but the increment in earnings for each increment in output is greater. For example, there may be a $1^1/_3$ per cent increase in earnings above the worker's time rate for each 1 per cent increase in output above standard as compared with a 1 per cent increase in earnings under straight piece-work for the same percentage increase in output. A $1^1/_3$ per cent increment will yield earnings $33^1/_3$ per cent above the time rate when normal or standard production is reached, save for the fact that it provides in all cases for a guaranteed time rate. The standard hour system described above, with the increment in earnings larger than the increments in output, is in effect the same as the high piece-rate system.

4. Systems with Worker's Earnings Varying in Proportions which Differ at Different Levels of Output

Under these systems earnings vary from minimum to maximum at different levels of output. Earnings for part of the rate may vary proportionally less than output and for another part proportionally in the same proportion as output. It is, therefore, not possible to classify any of these systems with any of the three other types described above although many of these systems closely resemble some of the systems of these other types. The main features of the most important systems of this type are the following:

The Taylor Differential Piece-rate System: This system, developed by F.W. Taylor in 1880 has a low piece-rate for output below standard and a higher piece-rate for output above standard with a large bonus of 50 per cent of the time rate when standard output is reached. This system therefore penalises the slow worker; but rewards handsomely workers with a high output.

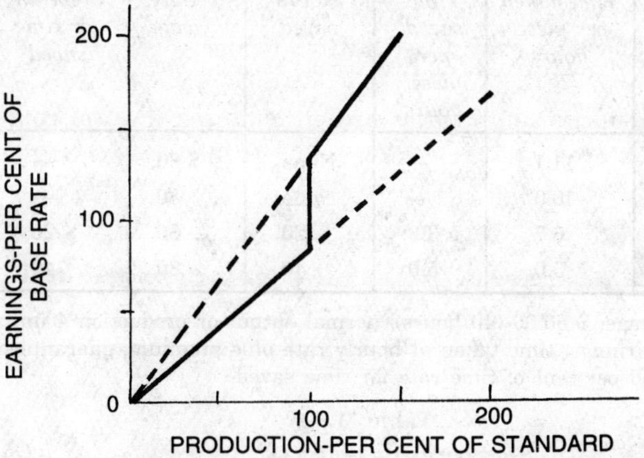

Fig. 11.4 Taylor's Differential Piece-rate Plan

The Merrick Differential Piece-rate System: This system is a modification of the Taylor system, with three instead of two rates. The one large step is broken into two so as to encourage new and average workers. Straight piece-rates are paid upto 83 per cent of the standard output, at which a bonus of 10 per cent of the time rate is payable, with a further 10 per cent bonus on reaching standard output. For output above standard, high piece-rates are paid.

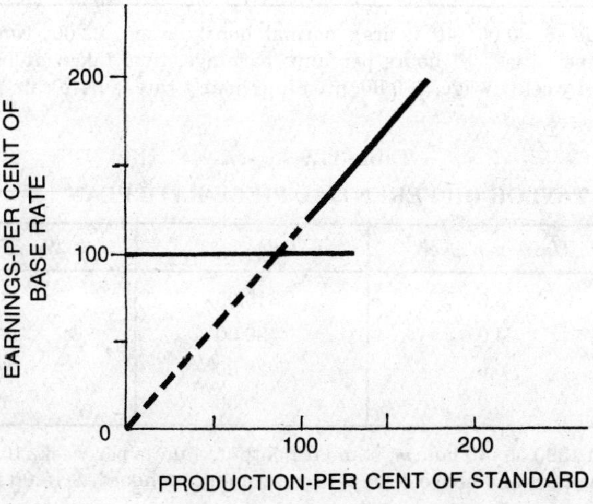

Fig. 11.5 Gantt Task and Bonus Plan

The Gantt Task and Bonus System: Under this system, the worker is guaranteed his time rate for output below standard. On reaching standard output of the task, which is set at a high level, the worker is paid a bonus of 20 per cent of his time wage. For output above task, high piece-rates are paid. The Taylor, Merrick and Gantt systems are, it will be noted, based on a similar principle — that of rewarding workers for reaching task which is set at a high level.

Table 11.7

THE HALSLEY PLAN

Employee	*Units per week*	*Time taken per piece, hours*	*Time saved per piece, hours*	*Hours saved*	*Base wage*	*Premium for time saved*	*Weekly earnings*
A	3.6	11.1	—	None	$ 80	—	$ 80
B (Standard)	4.0	10.0	—	None	80	—	80
C	6.0	6.7	3.3	20	80	$ 20	100
D	8.0	5.0	5.0	40	80	40	120

Data: Normal weekly wage, $ 80.00 (40 hours); normal output or production 4 units per week, 10 hours per unit; earnings, time taken at hourly rate plus premium, guaranteed weekly wage, $ 80; premium, 50 per cent of time rate for time saved.

Table 11.8

THE ROWAN PLAN

Employee	*Units per week*	*Time taken per piece, hours*	*Time saved per piece, hours*	*Percent normal time taken per piece*	*Percent normal time saved per piece*	*Hourly rate*	*Weekly earnings*
A	3.6	11.1	—	111.0	—	$2.00	$80.00
B	4.0	10.0	—	100.0	—	2.00	80.00
C	6.0	6.7	3.3	66.7	33.3	2.66	106.40
D	8.0	5.0	5.0	50.0	50.0	3.00	120.00

Data: Normal weekly wage, $ 80.00 (40 hours); normal hourly wage, $2.00; Normal output or production, 4 units per week, 10 hours per unit; earnings, time taken at hourly rate plus premium; guaranteed weekly wage, $80.00; premium hourly rate is base rate plus percentage of time saved.

Table 11.9

THE TAYLOR DIFFERENTIAL PIECE-RATE PLAN

Employee	*Units per week*	*Price rate*	*Weekly earnings*
A	3.6	$15.00	$54.00
B (Standard)	4.0	20.00	80.00
C	6.0	20.00	120.00
D	8.0	20.00	160.00

Data: Normal weekly wage, $80.00 (40 hours); standard output, 4 units per week, 10 hours per unit. Two piece rates; standard and above $ 20 per piece; under standard, $ 15.00 per piece.

Table 11.10

THE GANTT TASK AND BONUS SYSTEM

Employee	*Units per week*	*Standard hours allowed*	*Wage for time allowed*	*Premium*	*Weekly earnings*	*Labour cost per piece*
A	3.6	36	$80.00	—	$80.00	$22.22
B	4.0	40	80.00	$16.00	96.00	24.00
C	6.0	60	120.00	24.00	144.00	24.00
D	8.0	80	160.00	32.00	192.00	24.00

Data: Guaranteed weekly wage $ 80.00; standard output or production, 4 units per week, 10 hours per unit; standard time rate, $2.00 per hour; earnings and above, time allowed at standard time rate plus premium: below standard, guaranteed weekly wage; premium, 20 per cent of payment for time allowed.

The Emerson Empiric or Efficiency Plan

A standard time is established for each job. The efficiency of the worker is determined by dividing the time taken into the standard time. Upto 67 per cent efficiency the worker is paid at this time rate and from this point upto 100 per cent a bonus of 1 per cent is paid for every additional 1 per cent output. At 100 per cent efficiency, a bonus of 20 per cent is paid. Thereafter an additional bonus of 1 per cent is paid for additional 1 per cent efficiency.

It would appear, at first sight, that from 100 per cent the system becomes one of straight piece-work. Actually this is not the case. Thus, if output increased from 100 to 101 per cent a bonus of 21 per cent of the hourly rate would be payable under the Emerson System. With the straight piece-work, the bonus would be 21.2 per cent of the hourly rate.

Various other systems, such as the Wennerlund, Knoeppel, Bigelow, Bigelow-Knoeppel, Atkinson and Allingham systems, are simply modifications of the Emerson system. All have steps in the earnings curves to encourage workers to reach the high task which is set in all these systems. For example, in the Knoeppel system, for 98, 99 and 100 per cent efficiency, the bonuses are equal to 18, 19 and 25 per cent of the basic rate respectively. There is thus, at 99 per cent efficiency, a jump of 6 per cent in bonus for a 1 per cent increase in efficiency.

Other non-individual systems: Where individual systems of payment by results are not possible, because several workers are required to perform a single operation, there are various group systems, and department or plant systems. Separate methods for indirect workers such as janitors, maintenance workers etc. are used based on group or department bonus earnings. A combination of time rates and price-rates may be utilised.

Other Important Incentive Schemes

There are numerous other incentive schemes through which the managements stimulate the employees to increase their productivity and a brief mention is made of such schemes.

Profit-sharing plans: These plans, which started in France in the middle of 19th century, are established by the companies to share some gains in productivity within a company. J.J. Jehring reports that in U.S.A. anywhere from 8,000 to 16,000 companies have profit-sharing plans, with 100 firms implementing new plans monthly.[30] According to Pigors and Myers, "... growth of profit-sharing within the past 20 years is attributable in large measure to Government excess profit taxes and wage and salary controls during World War II to deferred payment plans which now enjoy certain tax advantages, and to the general growth of pension plans in private business."[31]

The profits may be shared in cash or in deferred payment or in a combination of both. The recent NICB study[32] reports that, out of 110 companies with profit-sharing plan, 17% (19) have a *current distribution* plan, i.e., all profit shares for a given year are paid to participants during the year or soon after the close of the year. Another 62% (68) of the companies have a *deferred* profit-sharing plan, i.e., all profit shares for a given year are put into a trust for deferred distribution, usually at the termination of employment. The remaining 21% (23) have a *Combination* plan.

Aims of profit-sharing plan: Aims are generally (1) to share some gains in productivity of the firm; (2) to promote more and more employee cooperation; (3) to promote increased effort and output; and (4) to promote loyalty to organisational objectives. A survey of 298 companies reported the following company motives:[33] (1) to instil a sense of partnership; (2) to offer a group incentive; and (3) to provide employee security.

Employee suggestion schemes: This is another scheme, which we have already discussed in greater detail in the previous chapter 8.

The Scanlon Plan

The Scanlon plan, evolved by Joseph N. Scanlon, who was a union president, suggests a scheme of Union Management Co-operation, where joint committees, with labour-management representatives, are formed to stimulate employee interest in production problems, to share gains with all employees and to promote joint-consultation. This plan is in operation in nearly 30 companies in U.S.A. This plan has two main aspects:

1. Adopting measures for increased productivity; and 2. Sharing the gains accrued from that increased productivity. Ernest Dale has described four degrees of cooperation between labour and management in the Scanlon Plan.[34]

(i) Informal cooperation; parties cooperate to gather information;

(ii) Advisory cooperation; each party consults the other;

(iii) Constructive cooperation; each party makes suggestion for improvement; and

(iv) Joint determination; union and management make decisions jointly.

The Scanlon Plan seems to be working well in U.S.A., but in our country Indian Institute of Personnel Management suggested that there was a need for some study regarding its appropriateness here.[35]

Pigors and Myers outline the steps necessary for a successful cooperation plan:[36]

1. Find a ratio of labour cost to total production value, which can be used as the basis for computing the savings over normal labour costs under the plan. Or set up a profit-sharing formula.

2. Provide for sharing the savings (the productivity bonus) each month with all the employees in the firm according to their base rate and earnings.
3. Include in the memorandum of agreement a provision for changing the ratio or formula for sharing gains as business circumstances demand.
4. Hold back some portion of each month's productivity bonus to build a reserve for paying out in the months when none is earned due to a sales slump etc.
5. Establish departmental production committees of management and union representatives.
6. Discuss all problems facing the business at these joint committees.
7. Distribute minutes of the meetings to everyone in the plant.
8. Arrange for transfers to equally good jobs if action under the plan results in displacement of workers.

Bonus System

Various bonus systems are offered, most common of which are cash bonuses, stock bonuses, merchandise bonuses and special leave with pay.

Some Requirements for Incentive Plans

The Regional Conference of the Indian Institute of Personnel Management held at Rourkela has outlined the following important requisites of incentive schemes in India.[37]

1. Under the existing conditions in India, it is necessary to provide monetary incentives to the workers for putting in an extra effort to increase production and productivity.
2. Whereas monetary incentive must form the main ingredient of any effective scheme, it would be advisable to ensure a minimum standard of amenities and other welfare measures in order to build up a contended work force, which could be depended upon to be responsive to such schemes.
3. Great care should be exercised for fixing up norms. These norms should be fixed on scientific basis after detailed time studies and should be based on sound data.
4. Before instituting or revising any incentive scheme it would be advisable to consult the employee's representatives or recognised unions, where they are functioning.
5. To begin with, there should be some elbow-room left for adjustment on starting point for these schemes. This maybe suitably changed as the scheme gets established and productivity improves.
6. While introducing incentive schemes, care should be exercised by management that in an effort to increase production and earnings, no damage is caused to the machine and the health and safety to the worker is endangered. The effcct on cost and quality should also be closely watched so that these are not adversely affected.
7. In view of the rapidly changing technology, it is necessary to review and evaluate the incentive schemes continuously in the light of the changing conditions.

8. Though production forms the primary basis of incentive payment, it is advisable to use another related criterion, viz., productivity, for making such payments. The extent to which production or productivity could be used as a criterion for incentive payment would depend on the circumstances of each unit. The measurability of productivity, fixation of a firm standard force on a scientific basis and similar other factors would have to be considered for the purpose.
9. As regards the coverage of incentive payment, the consensus was to evolve suitable incentive schemes for all categories of workers, direct or indirect, instead of excluding certain categories or paying them at a rate lower than the direct or production workers, while using the same basis for calculating the incentives. For example, it was felt that a suitable scheme could be drawn up for office workers or other such workers and for them the criterion for payment would be the office production index and not the factory production index. Care should, however, be taken to ensure that the incentive earnings of the different groups are kept within certain reasonable range and the differentials which arise do not make their earnings disproportionate.
10. No incentive scheme can be a substitute for good management and harmonious industrial relations. These two along with other environmental factors would ultimately determine the success or failure of any incentive scheme.

The conference felt that the Scanlon Plan, under which monetary incentive is combined with the non-monetary incentive by providing a formally established machinery of employees' participation in management, needs further study before any definite conclusion could be arrived at regarding its appropriateness under Indian conditions.

The human aspects of the incentive schemes must not be ignored. The employee's fears and aspirations must be taken into consideration. The schemes must be simple, easy to understand, easy to calculate employee's earnings, related to effort and difficulty, and be acceptable to employee and unions.

Executive Compensation

In modern business the executives hold the most pivotal place in an organisation and the modern corporations are constantly trying to come up with a compensation plan to attract, hold, and motivate the executives. The compensation plans are a legion and every company attempts to innovate a compensation plan that is better than the other. Most executive compensation plans emphasise current and deferred salary provision and usually a combination of them is offered. Mr. Nicholas L.A. Martucci, Industrial Relations Director of Kennecott Refining Corporation, U.S.A., writes:[38] "No single form of compensation is, in any case, best suited to the needs of all interested parties. Pay plans and practices are usually assembled from many elements to create in the management team the attitudes, motivations, and behaviour patterns that are compatible with a company's role in the national economy. Salary, of course, is basic; combined with other forms to achieve specific objectives, it is the keystone."

He further adds: "Executive compensation plans are designed to meet the needs of the majority. Over a period of time, the amount and form of compensation influence the make-up of the management team, because only those executives who are satisfied will remain as employees. Direct monetary rewards do not have the same appeal to all high level personnel; some prefer liberal insurance, pensions, and similar benefits. Others look for what they term opportunity. Perquisites of office tailored to individual needs, in some cases, are given more weight. A chance to build an estate in the face of high personal income taxes is favoured by some. And the professional or research-minded executive looks for adequate facilities and ideal working conditions that are in keeping with company requirements regarding research and development."

The first step in the establishment of executive compensation is to provide an adequate executive job-evaluation and rating plan. Payment for results philosophy must be adopted. What an executive has done and what is he likely to do in the future must be critically appraised.

Professor Dale Yoder observes:[39]

> "Policy to be implemented in management and executive compensation is not distinctly different from that inherent in other wage and salary administration, but somewhat greater emphasis is placed on incentivation through financial rewards. Put another way, managers appear to give less acceptance to broad, complex work theory in their compensation policy for themselves. They rely principally on dangling the carrot of greater financial rewards to stimulate superior performance. Present or deferred monetary rewards to be the principal answer to the question as to what makes the manager perform."

Arch Patton has listed the following requirements for a successful executive compensation plan.[40]

1. The top management must believe in the value of incentive compensation and make the necessary effort to see that it is productive.
2. The bonus should be substantial. When it averages below 30% of salary in a good year, evidence indicates it is probably too low.
3. Payment should be made on the basis of individual contribution, not on base salary received or group accomplishment.
4. The bonus "kitty" should be set up at a specific percentage of profits, after allowance for invested capital. In other words, executives should be organised so that individual responsibility is clear cut, permitting the most factual evaluation of contribution possible.
5. Allocation of bonus to division should be based largely on profits of each division.
6. The bonus should be available to everyone above a specified level. Payment is not necessary unless contribution warrants, but opportunity is.
7. The bonus should be a continuing force, approved by stock-holders and not subject to the whim of an individual or a group.
8. Time appears to be an essential ingredient in a successful incentive bonus plan... it takes (time) to bring an organisation to the creative, highly competitive frame of mind required by the successful incentive bonus.

One executive recruiter was quoted as pointing out that a man does not need more than $ 50,000 to live on. Beyond that point he is interested in building his estate. "So the ingenuity of experts in balancing the proper ingredients in package has become the prime weapon in luring executives from one corporation to another", the recruiter said. Another recruiter recalled a financial genius who explained, "I am making more salary than a man can stand. I need a salary of about $ 150,000 — for prestige purposes — a deferred compensation plan, payments to my wife, and insurance spread among five or six companies." The stunned recruiter added it up and discovered that all told it came to a neat $ 300,000 a year. Mostly a balanced package of current and deferred compensation as well as tax-exempt services such as a company car and driver, housing, club memberships and other fringes are used to attract and hold competent executives, who are always in scarce supply.

In recent years the various deferred compensation plans including stock options and bonus plan have lost much of their value and significance because of the changing tax structure as well as the recent decline in the stock market.

The recent trend in compensation is towards flexible compensation systems and fringe benefits using what is popularly known as the cafeteria approach where the idea is to match compensation plans and systems to individual needs which vary according to age, family, region, and the changing needs. The following table highlights the summary of new practices in compensation systems.[14]

SUMMARY OF NEW PRACTICES

	Major Advantages	*Major Disadvantages*	*Favourable Situational Factors*
Cafeteria fringe benefits	Increased pay satisfaction	Cost of administration	Well-educated, heterogenous workforce
Lump-Sum salary increases	Increased pay satisfaction: greater visibility of pay increases	Cost of administration	Fair pay rates
Skill-based evaluation	More flexible and skilled workforce; increased satisfaction	Cost of training; higher salaries	Employees who want to develop themselves; jobs that are interdependent.
Open salary information	Increased pay satisfaction, trust, and motivation; better salary administration	Pressure to pay all the same; complaints about pay rates	Open climate; fair pay rates; pay based on performance.
Participative pay decisions	Better pay decisions; increased satisfaction, motivation, and trust	Time consuming	Democratic management climate; workforce that wants to participate and that is concerned about organisational goals.

Executive Compensation Policy: One of the leading business groups in India has laid down the following policy regarding executive compensation.

"The formulation of executive compensation policy and systems is an important responsibility of management. Generally, executive compensation has three considerations: (1) the basic, (2) the fringe benefits, and (3) retirement benefits.

The consideration in evolving the compensation policy and system is:

(i) To keep it administratively simple;

(ii) To keep it favourable with other companies;

(iii) To maintain internal parity within certain levels;

(iv) To keep certain positions in certain grades on some rational basis;

(v) To consider the impact of grade revision on other grades;

(vi) Generally, to provide a compensation structure which will attract, retain and motivate.

In our society pay has come to be a status symbol. Similarly, power is a status symbol and that is why some people prefer to higher pay.

It must also be remembered that whereas compensation for bargainable employees is settled through the medium of collective bargaining or awards, that for executives is settled by the management. Therefore, greater responsibility is cast on the management in this respect.

It is generally a policy of a Group to compare its Company's systems and schemes with other leading companies in the industry and in the country. A compensation survey once in every two years is carried out to obtain up-to-date data on the current compensation systems in industry and to review its own compensation scheme in light of the changes taking place in the external business environment. Compensation for new occupations like some EDP occupations pose difficult problems.

As regards the base salary which should be determined by job documentation and evaluation, it is the policy of the Group to have grades and also overlapping grades. There are six grades in the Group. Generally, the size of the grade will depend upon the dearness allowance; where there is no dearness allowance, the size of the grade will be higher. Also, where there are no fringe benefits, the size of the grade will be higher. Theoretically, the grade differential may be anywhere from 30% to 50%. The executive positions are to be divided and placed in different grades. In case of additional duties, the positions may be placed in higher grades. Sometimes a person due to retire may be placed in a higher grade in order to reward him for his services and also to provide a sense of satisfaction to him that he has retired in a higher position and grade. Increments are to be synchronised on 1st January regardless of when he joins. The Group has uniform grades for all managerial personnel in all centres.

Increments are granted for several reasons, e.g., when a person has completed a year of service and thus, gained experience. Outstanding performance, loyalty, higher family responsibilities, longer service, inflation, are considered in granting increments.

What should be the normal rate of increment?

Normally it may be 10 per cent at the start and decline as one goes higher. Average increment in the Group grades maybe around 6½%. Generally, 30 per cent people get extra merit increments. There was an attempt in the last year to link merit increments to performance only. However, this attempt did not quite meet with success. Other methods of rewarding practised by Indian Companies are club membership, foreign tour, use of car, etc.

The reasons behind retiral benefits are to hold the employee, to help his family and to relieve him legitimately from taxation, and, more important, to provide economic security.

Retirement benefits comprise provident fund, gratuity and pension. Retirement benefits become important as an executive grows older in the organisation whereas the younger executive would be more interested not in retirement benefits but in current compensation and the take-home-pay.

There is a trend to provide a choice of compensation schemes for an executive and the executive is free to choose in what form he would like his compensation to be. However, in our country this is not the general practice."

5. SOME WAGE ISSUE IN INDIA

In our country, the Constitution in its Directive Principles of State Policy assures that the State shall endeavour to secure a living wage and equal pay for equal work. But the principle of equal remuneration for work of equal value and the provision of an adequate living wage, which are I.L.O.'s objectives, are yet to be realised.

The wage policies and determination in India are influenced and guided by various forces such as tripartite machinery of Government, management and union representatives, Government's legislation and recommendations, union's demands, demand and supply of labour, management policies, wage boards, committees, tribunals and courts. The wages are bread and butter issues to the employees, for the physiological needs of Indian workers are largely yet to be met. The abundant supply of manpower, the dearth of skilled workforce, the weaknesses of unions, large unemployment, near-sighted policies of many managements have all combined to produce circumstances where mere subsistence wages are available in many company in many areas. The wage situation is pretty chaotic and confusing, but generally four wage concepts have been suggested for adoption.

Wage Concepts

1. The Minimum Wage: Represents not only the subsistence wage but also some provision for some measure of education, medical and other amenities. A need-based minimum wage formula based on the following guideline for calculating minimum wage was suggested: (1) a working class family of 3 consumption units; (2) minimum food requirements on the basis of a net in-take of 2700 calories as recommended by the nutrition expert, Dr. Akroyd, for a worker doing moderate work; (3) clothing requirements at a per capita consumption of 18 yards per annum; (4) in housing rent corresponding to the minimum area provided by Government's Industrial Housing Scheme and (5) fuel, lighting and other expenses such as children's education and medical requirements should constitute 20 per cent of the minimum wage.

2. The Fair Wage is the wage based on the ability to pay principle and is equal to that received by workers performing similar work. It should not be less than minimum wage but should be a step towards a living wage and the actual wages to be based on labour productivity, going wages, level of national income and its distribution, and place of industry in the economy.

3. The Living Wage is a wage sufficient to ensure to the workmen food, shelter, clothing, fuel, frugal comforts and some provision for evil days. All these above three wage concepts were recommended by the Fair Wages Committee, appointed as a result of Government's Industrial Truce Resolution in 1948.

4. The Saving Wage: In 1955 Indian Labour Conference, Shri Bishwanath Dubey of United Trade Union Congress suggested the concept of a saving wage, where, he said, the worker should be paid such a wage as would enable him to save something for a rainy day.

The Supreme Court has held that no industry has a right to exist if it cannot pay the bare minimum wage to its worker, but above this level, when it comes to the fixation of a fair wage, capacity to pay must be one of the guiding factors, and this was also recognised by the Fair Wages Committee. Tribunals usually take as their criterion the particular industry in a specified region, so that, as far as possible, the same rates of wages should be prescribed for all units of that industry in the region.[42]

Wage Policy

The wage policy of the Second Five Year Plan had the following objectives: (1) raising real wages, (2) linking wages to productivity and (3) laying down principles to bring wages in conformity with the expectations of the working class in the future pattern of society (socialist pattern of society). But the planners wrote.[43] "A major difficulty experienced in the fuller implementation of the principle of fair wage is the "drag" exercised by marginal units in determining the wage structure."

At the 15th session of the Indian Labour Conference held in 1957, the following principles regarding wages were accepted: (1) A need based minimum wage, (2) Earnings beyond the minimum wage to be related to productivity, and (3) The system of payment by results above should not lead to increased workload, undue speed-up and fatigue.

Wage Boards

In order to evolve a wage structure based on the principles of fair wages set forth in the report of the Committee of Fair Wages, Wage Boards are set up in more than 13 industries (mentioned earlier) to bring the workmen within the scope of the proposed wage fixation. V.V. Giri observes:[44] "Statutorily constituted wage boards are set up in India for selected industries of national importance, where as in other countries, only in industries where 'sweated' labour conditions exist, wage boards are set up. Industries with organised labour fix wages by direct bargaining in such countries and are found to achieve maximum wages. It has been the experience in India that wage boards provide the starting point for disputes rather than solve problems." In our country, the largest number of industrial disputes are caused by wage issues. All the three parties — management, labour and Government — in the tripartite machinery blame each other for the non-implementation of many of the recommendations. The adjudication machinery is slow and time consuming and there is not much reliance on collective bargaining. But the IIPM[45] maintains that "reference of many cases of wage claims to adjudication has had the fortunate result of bringing about quite a large degree of standardisation of wages within industries. Before 1947 there had been tremendous variations in wage rates not only between industry and industry but company and company within the same industry. The Royal Commission on labour, referring to the Jute industry, made the comment that perhaps in no other industry in the world, situated in such a circumscribed area, was the wage position more inchoate. The major awards in this industry have now introduced standard rates, and the same thing has happened in a number of other industries. Even so there are still wide variations in wage patterns in industry. The census of manufacturers for the year 1954 showed variation in average earnings per manhour from 35 pieces in the rice milling to 112 in soap and 141 in iron and steel."

Dearness Allowance

Dearness allowance forms an important part of the employee compensation structure, although it has introduced various anomalies. During the last war, the dearness allowance was introduced as a device to meet the needs of the employees in the light of price increases, which reduced the purchasing power of regular money wages. Now with steady increase in the cost of living, it has become a very important permanent feature of remuneration, for there are situations where the companies pay only Rs. 35 as basic wage and Rs. 130 or more as D.A. for obvious reasons. Generally the industrial tribunals have granted 70 to 75 per cent neutralisation of the rise in cost-of-living through dearness allowance but all the national unions demand a 100 per cent neutralisation and also merger of D.A. into basic wages which has not been found acceptable. The national unions also demand a 25 per cent increase in wages.

The Indian Institute of Personnel Management makes the following observations on the study of Dearness Allowance in the country.

The National Commission on Labour has recommended a 95 per cent neutralisation to those drawing the minimum wages in nonscheduled employment.

There are considerable variations in the method of calculating dearness allowance in different States and industries. Thus, in the Bombay textile industry, dearness allowance is based on a points system; in the West Bengal engineering industry, a flat rate on a slab system which fluctuates on an annual review of the cost of living, was awarded in 1958.

Now, in most industries dearness allowance fluctuates either quarterly, or six-monthly with the rise or fall in the average cost of living index during the preceding quarter or six months, as the case may be, the rate being fixed per point of such rise or fall.

The National Commission on Labour felt that the capacity to pay is not a relevant consideration for payment of Dearness Allowance at the minimum level. It suggested a 5-point slab wage of the consumer price index (Base 1960) on the basis of the current All India Series or the current (1960 Central Series) would be appropriate for adjustment in Dearness Allowance.

The Commission also considered the compensation requirements of people drawing wage higher than the minimum and felt that the amount of dearness allowance to be paid to such employees should be the same as given to employees at the minimum.

The proportion of dearness allowance to total remuneration had become quite unrealistic in certain industries, representing more than 100 per cent of basic pay. To bring about a more rational state of affairs the Gadgil Committee, set up in 1952, recommended the merging of 50 per cent of the dearness allowance in basic pay, but this recommendation was not carried out. The question of the proportion of dearness allowance in total earnings was a vital one when contributions to provident funds were calculated on basic pay only, but since under the Employees Provident Fund Act contributions are now based on total pay, the question has become less important. Government has now accepted the recommendation of the Second Pay Commission that the former dearness allowance of Central Government employees should be merged with basic pay, and that a new dearness allowance should be introduced for lower paid staff at the rate of Rs. 10 for those earnings less than Rs. 150 and Rs. 20 for those earning between Rs. 150 to Rs. 300. Although in some undertakings as also in some industries a portion of the dearness allowance has been merged with the basic pay under individual agreements or wage boards' recommendations, the general pattern continues to be that the dearness allowance is disproportionately high compared to basic wages. The National Commission on Labour has suggested merger at the 1960 level and suitably changing it when a new family living survey is undertaken. The aim of such merger is to rationalise the existing wage structure and make basic wages more realistic that at present, "this merger should not be construed to imply *ipso facto* any basic change in general wages or conferment of additional benefits." (Report of the National Commission on Labour, para 16.4). It is however, difficult to visualise merger of dearness allowance into basic from time to time particularly when the dearness allowance proposed is to be the same for different levels of wages, not affecting the wage differentials as between scales within an organisation. The differentials in actual money terms in earlier years might remain the same but in terms of percentage differentials, this will be reduced so much as to leave no incentive for an unskilled person to move to semiskilled or skilled jobs. Also in respect of piece rates, the effect of change on these rates, of merger of dearness allowance need to be studied carefully, since the person with a production higher than a norm would automatically earn more than what he was previously earning and those below the norm would earn less than their previous earnings on the same production.[46]

In order to make the wage structure more realistic and rational, the Gadgil Committee, set up in 1952, recommended the merger of 50 per cent of D.A. into the basic wage, but this was not accepted. As a consequence, a peculiar situation in the wage structure continues where D.A. is often 3 or 4 times the basic pay. There are computation problems regarding consumer price indices, which have been found to be defective and which have not been updated. With the prices increasing day by day the problem of D.A. will become very grave.

Bonus

The Indian National Trade Union Congress, replying to the Bonus Commission questionnaire, declared.[47] "The term 'Bonus' might mean, according to the dictionary, "a boon or a gift over and above what is nominally due as remuneration to the employees. But bonus has not been a boon either to management or trade union executives; far from it, it has been and still continues to be, an annual headache to both of them." The annual or profit bonus was given during and immediately after the First World War in the textile industry in Bombay, Ahmedabad and Sholapur and TISCO. Such annual bonus on a country-wide basis came into vogue only after World War II. There are various types of bonuses such as good attendance bonus, good conduct bonus, efficiency bonus, production bonus, pooja bonus, profit-sharing bonus. In the beginning, the bonus was a 'gift' offered by the employer annually, when he made good profits hold bonus as a 'deferred wage.' The Bombay Labour Appellate Tribunal in 1950 held that the bonus could no longer be regarded as an ex-gratia payment, as, a claim to bonus by employees, if resisted, would result in an industrial dispute and where industry could not pay living wages, "bonus must be looked upon as the temporary satisfaction, wholly or in part, of the needs of the employee." Later the Labour Appellate Tribunal Formula resulted in determining 'surplus available for distribution as bonus' after making certain prior charges, which are (1) Statutory normal depreciation, (2) Income-tax, (3) A fair return at a lower rate on the reserves employed as working capital, (4) A fair return on the paid-up capital, and (5) Provision for rehabilitation and modernisation of machinery and buildings over and above the depreciation already provided for. According to INTUC, "how much of the available surplus should be distributed as bonus became yet another point of controversy, not thought of in the original formula. Thus where formerly there was a single dispute, i.e., the bonus dispute, now there emerged several disputes relating to each of these prior charges."[48]

Nearly 20 to 25 per cent of industrial disputes are caused by bonus issues. The employer's contention is that, while the employees share in profits, when bonus is liked to surplus benefits, losses are not shared and the employers get a raw deal.

The Bonus Commission retained the core of the LAT formula, but gave a higher return to both paid-up capital (7%) and reserves (4%) while removing altogether the claim for rehabilitation. The Government amended the formula by providing 8.5% return on paid-up capital and 6% on reserves. Labour protested against this change and the Government introduced a further provision to safeguard higher bonuses received in the past by the introduction of Sec.34 (2). This section provided for the payment of bonus on the basis of bonus paid in the base year (the year prior to the application of the Bonus Act), the proportion of bonus paid to gross profits being ensured. The employers were required to pay 4% minimum bonus to the workers.

The Supreme Court struck down Sec. 34 (2) as violating Article 19 of the Constitution of India. The Government is considering further amendments to the Act to safeguard the existing rights of labour in the light of the Supreme Court judgement.

After persistent demand from the trade unions for a minimum bonus of 8.33% Government of India appointed the Bonus Review Committee which acceeded to this formula in spite of the dissenting note from the employers' representatives of the private sector. However, Payment of Bonus (Amendment) Act 1976 changed the entire formula of bonus by linking bonus to either profits or to productivity wherever such productivity agreement obtained.

The payment of Bonus Act 1965 was superseded by the Payment of Bonus (Amendment) Ordinance 1975, which was later replaced by an Amendment Act. The Amendment Act came into force on 25th Sept. 1975, the day on which the Bonus

Ordinance came into force. The salient feature of the Amendment Act is that minimum bonus of 4% is payable only if there is an allocable surplus. However, an exception was made for the financial year 1974 for paying minimum bonus of 4% irrespective of allocable surplus. In case of availability of higher allocable surplus proportionately higher bonus will be payable but subject to the maximum of 20%. If minimum bonus of 4% is less than Rs. 100/- then the minimum bonus payable is Rs.100/- for an adult employee and Rs.60/- for employee below the age of 15 years.

There is a provision for payment of bonus to employees upto 20% under an agreement reached before or after the Amendment Act if such bonus is linked with production or productivity, in lieu of bonus based on profits payable under the Act.

A unique and trail-blazing agreement on bonus linked to production and productivity and capacity utilisation was entered into by TISCO and the Tata Workers Union as follows:

TISCO AGREEMENT

Short Recital of the Case

WHEREAS after signing the Memorandum of Agreement dated July 30, 1975 by the Joint Negotiating Committee for Steel Industry discussions have been held from time to time on possibilities of evolving a common plant-based Annual Performance Scheme for the Steel Industry as a whole;

WHEREAS subsequent to the above agreement, the Payment of Bonus Act, 1965 has also been amended;

WHEREAS the Steel Plants during the period April-September 1975 have shown record performance;

WHEREAS the National Joint Consultative Committee for Steel Industry has agreed, in principle, to the introduction of a Bonus Scheme based on production and productivity in terms of Section 31-A of the Payment of Bonus Act, 1965 as amended by Act No. 23 of 1976;

WHEREAS a Scheme based on capacity utilisation and labour productivity was evolved and proposed by the Employers' Group;

WHEREAS certain issue of the Scheme have been raised by the workers representatives in the NJCC;

WHEREAS in the meanwhile it has been agreed further to discuss the Scheme at the plant level;

WHEREAS the parties have sought the assistance of the Conciliation Officer with a view to arriving at a satisfactory settlement;

In view of the above, a Scheme based on capacity utilisation and labour productivity has been worked out on the lines of the principles discussed at the National Joint Consultative Committee and after prolonged discussions and mutual consultations, the Scheme in terms of Section 31-A of the Payment of Bonus Act 1965 as amended by the Act No. 23 of 1976 is mutually agreed to as hereunder:

1. Scope and Coverage

1.1. The Scheme cover all employees eligible under the Payment of Bonus Act 1965 of the Company and having total emoluments (Pay plus Dearness Allowance) upto and including Rs. 1600/- per month.

2. The Scheme

2.1. The Scheme shall be a two factor performance scheme:

(a) Based on capacity utilisation;

Saleable steel production will be taken into account for this purpose.

(b) Based on productivity expressed as saleable steel produced per man year — annual saleable steel production will be divided by the average manpower. Manpower will include executives as well as non-executives (regular, temporary, casual etc.) but will exclude employees not covered by this scheme.

2.2. The details of the Scheme are as follows:

(a) Based on capacity utilisation:

The cut-off point below which no payment will be made shall be 80% of rated capacity utilisation.

Given below are the details of payments at different levels of capacity utilisation and range of pay.

	Range Rs. (Basic Plus D.A.)		
	Upto 500 *Rs.*	*501-749* *Rs.*	*750 & above* *Rs.*
Payment at the cut-off point	102.00	129.00	169.00
For every per cent rise in capacity utilisation between 81% and 95% point.	5.00	7.00	9.00
For every per cent rise in capacity utilisation between 96% to 99% point.	10.00	13.00	16.00
Payment for 100% capacity utilisation	16.00	22.00	26.00
Payment for 100% capacity utilisation	233.00	308.00	294.00

Note: In determining capacity utilisation, decimals below 0.5 will be ignored and decimals of 0.5 and above will be rounded off to the next higher digit.

(b) Based on Labour Productivity:

The cut-off productivity index below which no payment will be made shall be 25 metric tonnes of saleable steel per man-year.

Given below are the details of payments to all eligible employees at different levels of productivity achieved.

Payment at cut-off point of 25	Rs. 60.00
For every point rise in productivity index from 26 points to 50 points	Rs. 3.00
For every point rise in productivity index above 50 points	Rs. 5.00

Note: In determining labour productivity decimals below 0.5 will be ignored and decimals of, 0.5 and above will be rounded off to the next higher digit.

3. Implementation of the Scheme

3.1 The Scheme shall operate for the years 1976-77, 1977-78 and 1978-79 unless modified/substituted by a Scheme evolved and agreed to by the NJCC. The workers representatives demanded that the same formula, which is being recommended for adoption for those years, should be made applicable to 1975-76 also which the representatives of the Management were not agreeable to consider. However, this Agreement shall not prejudice the claims, if any, for the year 1975-76 arising out of the calculation of allocable surplus under/amendment to the Bonus Act, 1965, if any.

3.2 If the amount paid by the Company in accordance with this agreement is determined by any competent authority or otherwise found to be less than the amount payable according to any law, then and in that event any payment made by the Company in accordance with this agreement will be deemed to have been appropriated for and made by way of bonus under any Act or any other law to the extent of the amount paid under this agreement.

4. Payment

4.1 The payment for the year 1976-77 shall be made on the basis of performance for the period April-September 1976, prorated the annual performance. The final adjustment will be made at the end of 1976-77. The same practice will be followed for the years 1977-78 and 1978-79.

In acceptance of the terms of the Settlement both the parties have given their signature to this Memorandum of Settlement this Fifth day of March 1977.

Conclusion

In India there is too much disparity and lack of uniformity in wage rates not only among centres and different industries, but also among companies in the same industry. The dearness allowance, peculiar to our country, varies widely in rates, scales and methods of computation. The adjudications and industrial tribunals do not follow a uniform policy. The National Wage policy is changing constantly and some critics go to the extent of saying that there is no wage policy at all.[46] There is also a demand for a high-power wage commission to go in to the wage structure obtaining in the country and make suitable recommendations. At the country and industries levels, we believe that factors such as large unskilled labour force, unemployment, abundant supply of labour, lack of employee mobility, ignorance of workers, poor employee motivation; multiplicity of weak and poor unions, lack of big industrial unions, political unionism, outside and political union leadership, huge unorganised sector, on the part of trade unions; on the side of management, large number of owner-entrepreneurs, greed and exploitation of employers, poor and inefficient management, under-capitalised industries, short-range policies, and legal restriction; on the part of the government, lack of proper policies, hazy thinking, excessive dependence on legal measures, and ever changing policies; and above all, on the market side, the free play of autonomous economic forces of demand and supply have rendered the wage and salary picture disperate, chaotic and confusing. There is a need for good and efficient industrial business leadership to formulate and 'sell' a wage and salary programme that will meet not only the needs of organisational objectives and the needs of workmen, but also the needs of the nation in raising the standards of living of our citizenry.

In all this, the personnel administrator has a key role to play in impressing upon top management the constant need for effective wage and salary administration, which requires close attention to broad economic changes in community wage levels, uneven changes for certain occupational groups and changes in the needs of the company. It is necessary to emphasise that wage and salary administration requires attention to the internal alignment of wages — though not to the exclusion of maintaining necessary external relationships. It requires day-by-day administration so that management can bring the same care and thought to this aspect of business as it does to production, finance and sales. The personnel administrator's responsibility is to help develop wage and salary administration that induces the workmen to contribute to the organisational goals and the management to contribute to the needs and wellbeing of the workmen. In the interests of one lies the interests of the other. Some 50 years ago F.W. Taylor said in Shop Management: "What the workmen want from their employers beyond anything else is high wages, and what employers want from their workmen most of all is a low labour cost of manufacture. These two conditions are not diametrically opposed to one another as would appear at first glance. On the contrary, they can be made to go together in all classes of work, without exception, and... the existence or absence of these two elements forms the best index to either good or bad management."

REFERENCES

1. See David W. Belcher, *Wage and Salary Administration* (Englewood Cliffs, N.J. Prentice-Hall. Inc. 1955).
2. For a detailed discussion of differentials see: (1) Adolph O. Berger, "Wage and Salary Structure and Differentials", *Research and Technical Report,* No. 13. (Minneapolis: Industrial Relations Center, University of Minnesota, 1953); (2) Richard A. Lester, "A Range Theory of Wage Differentials," *Industrial and Labour Relations Review*, Vol. 5, No. 4, July 1952, pp. 483-500; (3) Elizabeth M. Coselli, "Wage Differentials, by Skill; 1920-48", *Conference Board Management Record,* Vol. 11, No. 8, August 1949, pp. 348-350; (4) "Pay Differentials for Supervisors" *Management Review*, Vol. 36, No. 11, November 1947.
3. David W. Belcher, "Ominous Trends in Wage and Salary Administration", *Personnel,* September-October, 1964, pp. 45-46.
4. *Ibid.*, p. 46.
5. Lawrence A. Appley, Foreword to *The AMA Hand-book of Wage and Salary Administration,* (New York: American Management Association, Third printing, 1952), p. 5.
6. Herbert S. Fuhrman, "Some Basic Principles of Wage and Salary Administration", *The AMA Handbook of Wage and Salary Administration,* (New York: American Management Association, Third Print, 1952), pp. 15-19.
7. William S. Wilcox, "Keeping Wage and Salary Plans up-to-date", *Personnel*, Vol. 23, No. 4, January 1947, p. 284.
8. Raymond E. Kirkpatrick, "Relationships between Wage Policies and Programmes and Salary Policies and Programmes" in "Compensation Principles and Practices", *Research and Technical Report* 13, Industrial Relations Center, University of Minnesota, 1952, pp. 35-40.
9. I.L.O., *Job Evaluation,* Studies and Reports, New Series, No. 56, Geneva, 1960. p.8. For greater details, this is a very good reference source. I have borrowed a good deal of material for this section from this excellent report.
10. British Institute of Management, *Job Evaluation,* A Practical Guide, Personnel Management Series 4 (London, 1951), p. 77.
11. Netherlands Committee of Experts for Job Evaluation, *Standardised Method of Job Evaluation* (The Hague, January, 1951, mimeographed), p. 1.
12. United States Department of Labour, Bureau of Labour Statistics, *Glossary of Currently Used Wage Terms,* Bulletin 983. (Washington: U.S. Government Printing Office, 1950), pp. 11-12.
13. I.L.O., *Payment by Results,* Studies and Reports, New Series, No.27 (Geneva, 1951), p. 42.
14. J.K. Louden and T.C. Newton, *Job Analysis* (New York: Funk and Wagnalls Company, 1948) p. 23.
15. Quoted by L.P. Alford, *Principles of Industrial Management* (New York: The Ronald Press Company, 1951) p. 655.
16. For information and details about some job evaluation programmes in operation in India, see Appendix VII on Job Evaluation in IIPM's *Personnel Management in India,* pp. 308-311.

17. Quoted by L.P. Alford, *Principles of Industrial Management,* pp. 655-656.

18. Abstracted from I.L.O., *Job Evaluation,* pp. 99-113.

19. See Helen Baker and J.M. True, *The Operation of Job Evaluation Schemes* (Princeton, N.J.: Princeton University, 1957). But the summary is taken from I.L.O., *Job Evaluation,* p.87. See Chapter IV, for greater details, on various surveys conducted all over the world regarding Job Evaluation Programmes.

20. For a detailed account of the various employer and trade union responses to job evaluation, see I.L.O's *Job Evaluation,* Chapter V, "Advantages and Limitations of Job Evaluation," from which I have borrowed most of the material for this section.

21. *Ibid.,* p. 104.

22. International Association of Machinists, *What's Wrong With Job Evaluation* (Washington:1954), pp. 3-5.

23. John A. Patton, "Job Evaluation in Practice; Some Survey Findings", *Industrial Relations Forum,* AMA Management Report Number 54 (New York. A M A Personnel Division, 1961), pp. 74-77.

24. *Ibid.,* p. 77.

25. *Ibid.*

26. Pigors and Myers, *op.cit.,* p. 368; see also Ernest Dale, "How to Conduct a Wage Survey", *AMA Handbook of Wage and Salary,* pp. 89-105.

27. A L. Kress, "Sound Wage Payment Policies" in *The AMA Handbook of Wage and Salary Administration,* p. 27. See this chapter for more details.

28. *Ibid.,* pp. 37-38.

29. See for greater details, "Payment by Results", *Productivity* (Journal of National Productivity Council), Vol. 2, No. 5 June-July 1965. Most of the material of this section is borrowed from this article.

30. J.J. Jehring, *Profit Sharing, The Capitalistic Challenge* (Evanston, III: Profit Sharing Research Foundation, 1956), p. 2.

31. Pigors and Myers, *Personnel Administration,* p. 409.

32. NICB, *Personnel Practices in Factory and Office: Manufacturing, Studies in Personnel Policy,* No. 194, p. 110.

33. Pigors and Myers, *Personnel Administration* (New York: McGraw-Hill Book Co., Inc., Fifth ed., 1965), p. 525.

34. Ernest Dale, "Increasing Productivity through Labour-Management Co-operation", *Industrial and Labour Relations Review,* Vol. 3, No. 1, October, 1949, pp. 33-34.

35. Also see N. Mukherjee, "Scanlon Plan" and Nitish R. De, "How Successful is the Scanlon Plan" both articles in *Industrial Relations,* Vol. XVII, No. 5, September-October 1966.

36. Pigors and Myers, *Personnel Administration,* pp. 417-18.

37. Report of the Indian Institute of Personnel Management Regional Confederance at Rourkela, *The Economic Times,* dated 7-9-1966.

38. Nicholas L.A. Martucci, "The Organisation, the Man," *The Personnel Job in the 1960s,* p. 69.

39. Dale Yoder, *Personnel Management,* p. 486.

40. Arch Patton, "Incentive Compensation for Executives," *Harvard Business Review,* Vol. 29, No. 5, September, 1951, p. 38. For additional and detailed material Executive Compensation, see (1) G.T. Washington and V.H. Rothschild, *Compensating the Corporate Executive* (New York; The Ronald Press, 1951); (2) J.K. Lasser and V.H. Rothschild, "Deferred Compensation for Executives", *Harvard Business Review,* Vol. 33, No.1, January-February 1955 pp. 89-102; (3) P.W. Dickson, "Executive Compensation" N I C B Studies in Labour Statistics, No.12, 1954; (4) Executive Compensation: Company Policies and Practices, American Management Association, Financial Management series No.97, 1951; (5) "Trends in Executive Compensation Plans-A. Dartnell Survey, *American Business,* Vol. 25, No. 2, February 1955; (6) "Executive Compensation — How Much to Whom?" *Acme Reporter* (official Publication of Association of

Consulting Management Engineers, Inc.), 1959 series, No.3, August 1959; (7) Harland Fox and Mitchel Meyer, "Top Management Compensation Trends in Manufacturing", *Management Record,* Vol. 21, No.10, October 1959, pp. 318-21; (8) N.B. Winstanly, "Practical Guides for Executive Compensation", *Advanced Management,* Vol. 24, No. 1. January 1959, pp.9-13; Harland Fox, "Deferred Compensation for the Executive", *Business Management Record*, July 1963.

41. Edward E. Lawler III, "New Approaches to Pay: Innovations that Work", *Personnel*, Sept.-Oct., 1976, p. 20.

42. IIPM, *op. cit.,* p. 116.

43. See Wage Policy during the Second Five Year Plan, *Second Five Year Plan Report.* The Government explained that studies had to be undertaken to determine the marginal units, but that was the last that was heard of the studies on marginal units.

44. See chapter on National Wage Policy in V.V. Giri, *Labour Problems in Indian Industry,* (Bombay: Asia Publishing House, 2nd edition 1959).

45. I I P M, *op. cit.,* p.116.

46. *Replies to the Bonus Questionnaire,* Indian National Trade Union Congress, New Delhi, 1962, p.4.

47. *Ibid.,* p. 6.

48. See the excellent work of Dr. Shreekant Palekar, *Problems of Wage Policy For Economic Development* (Bombay: Asia Publishing House, 1962).

❑ ❑ ❑

CHAPTER 12

Employee Benefits and Services

Extra wage and salary compensation systems in the form of employee benefits and services have become commonplace in modern industrial and business oganisations. These are also referred to as wage supplements and more popularly in U.S.A., as fringe benefits and they are adjuncts and complementary to the basic systems of wage payment. Every year more and more benefits and services are being added. Generally the main purposes of these fringe benefits may be summarised as follows:

1. To promote better employer-employee relations.
2. To promote employee loyalty to the company.
3. To promote employee welfare.
4. To meet legal requirements.
5. To promote high morale among the employees.
6. To provide economic security to the employees.
7. To provide a congenial work environment.
8. To promote employee health and safety.
9. To promote employment stabilisation.
10. To promote team spirit and employee identification with the company.

Employee benefits and services programmes are the products of — (1) Governmental legislation and public policy, (2) Management initiative, (3) Employee and union demands and (4) Community relations.

1. Government Legislation and Public Policy: Many wage supplements such as old age pensions or provident fund and gratuity, maternity benefits, workmen's compensation, sickness insurance etc. are required to be provided by the statutory provisions of the State and companies merely follow the legal requirements in establishing such benefits. Public policy, through various legal measures, has sought to provide economic security through such benefits as unemployment insurance, public pensions, provident fund, workmen's compensation, maternity benefits etc. The State has also sought to reduce hours of work to provide better working conditions etc. In India, public policy requires the companies to institute most of the employee benefits and services.

*2. **Management Initiative:*** In order to promote employee morale, to encourage wide participation and to help employees identify their interests with company interests, managers have initiated and sponsored many employees benefits and services in the areas of employee health, recreation, safety, welfare, counselling, legal aid etc.

*3. **Employee-Union Demands:*** There are various fringe benefits such as rest pause, paid holidays, over time shift differentials, paid time for various activities like Jury duty, Christmas shopping, credit unions, cooperative stores, housing and the like which have come into being as a result of employee-union demands.

*4. **Community Relations:*** There are other types of employee benefits and services that are offered by companies because local traditions demand them. If in a community certain paid holidays or puja gifts or free morning meals or night meals are traditionally common practices with the companies, it will be necessary for you also to fall in line and offer these benefits and services in order to obtain and retail workforce.

TISCO Philosophy

The philosophy of TISCO is to promote the well-being of the employees not only within the company but also without. TISCO has embraced the tremendous responsibility of developing the employees not only in the portals of the company but also outside it. The philosophy is inherited from the vision and values of its founder, Jamshedji Tata. Back in 1902, five years before the discovery of Sakchi and the starting of the TISCO, Jamshedji wrote to his son about the establishment of the town of his dream: "Be sure to lay wide streets planted with shady trees. Be sure that there is plenty of space for lawns and gardens. Reserve large areas for football, hockey and parks. Earmark areas for temples, mosques and churches." All this was revolutionary indeed for those times. This vision has always guided the builders of Jamshedpur and set the pace for a tremendous employee welfare programme. The Resident Director of TISCO explained very succinctly: "Many employers will say to their employees that they are all one happy family. If the employees is a member of the family, then why is he not taken care of outside the premises of the company, just as a member of the family is looked after whether he is in the four walls of the home or outside? If he is a member of the TISCO family we must take care of him when he is inside the company as well as outside it. The main thing is to treat the employee as a whole person and to take care of him inside and outside the company. That is why we have a whole programme of community development, medical treatment, family planning, education etc. A happy and contented employee will do his best for company as the company wants to do its best for him." How did the company go about establishing the welfare programmes? "The layout of the services and facilities of the industrial complex of Jamshedpur was planned with meticulous care and eminent planners and leaders in the field of community development were engaged not only to provide a clean, pleasant and uncrowded environment, but also to ensure an orderly growth and development for the future. No expense was spared in looking after the welfare of the workers by providing a full range of services and facilities, because as Mr. R.D. Tata told the shareholders in 1923, 'We are not putting up a row of workmen's huts.' Schemes of welfare services were draw up in consultation with such eminent sociologists as Sidney and Beatrice Webb, Prof. Urwick, and A.V. Thakkar, popularly known as Thakkar Bapa. Many of the amenities that are taken for granted in a welfare state today were introduced in Jamshedpur far ahead of legislation enacted in post-independence years." The result is that Jamshedpur stands out in the country as a shining example of what great business leadership and vision could achieve. Jawaharlal Nehru, paying a visit to Jamshedpur observed: "Jamshedji had the vision of industrial India, based on a foundation of steel. He formed himself into a one-man-planning commission and embarked upon his own Five Year Plan, and indeed even longer-range plans."

What is Fringe?

Although everybody is familiar with fringe benefits, it is very difficult to define it and pinpoint it, as explained by Robert H. Hoge, Director of Wage and Salary Administration of Owens-Illinois, U.S.A.,:[1] "The word "fringe" itself is a semantic blur; it was almost unheard of in industry before World War II. The term was first used in the course of wage and salary stabilisation to describe labour costs and employee benefits which were on the periphery of, but actually outside, direct wage payments. At this late date, however, it has become so firmly fixed in the industrial vocabulary that there is little choice but to accept it.

"In describing fringes, everyone would agree that they are something which costs money. At this point, however, agreement ends. May we go so far as to say that all costs on behalf of the employee, over and beyond the basic wage or salary payment, constitute fringes? If so, incentive earnings and similarly earned supplement payments of any sort would be included, as well as paper drinking cups. Nor does a fringe necessarily take the form of a remuneration. For example, the expenditures of the company group insurance represents a fringe benefit; although the employee never sees the monies thus expended, he may reap the benefit of them later. In short, what is spent on behalf of the employee and how it is spent are not criteria which can be used to determine what constitutes a fringe; a deeper analysis is necessary." After many studies, some definition of the fringe began to take shape and Mr. Hoge has offered this definition:[2]

"A fringe is a labour cost which is in addition to the regular wage or salary for time worked. A fringe may accrue from company policy, a bilateral agreement, or legal requirements. It may take the form of monetary payments, services, privileges, benefits, or awards. It represents pay for hours not worked or extra pay for hours worked. It is a labour cost for which no tangible return may be apparent to the employer, but which in turn provides the employee with extra pay, added security, or more desirable working conditions."

But there are some writers and personnel administrators, who would include under fringe benefits only certain wage supplements such as overtime pay or premium pay, call-in pay, wash-up time, shift premiums, paid holidays and paid vacations, but there are others who would include all employee benefits and services under the fringe category.

Cost of Employee Benefits and Services

Because of increasing number of employee benefits and services, the costs are going up tremendously as indicated by various studies and companies. Austin M. Fisher and John F. Chapman write:[3] "Fringe payments alone have soared to a point where their cost exceeds the whole of that very controversial minimum wage which the New Deal put through back in 1938." Leory M. Hanford of The Carrier Corporation, reports Robert H. Hoge,[4] "came up with starting statistics at a meeting of the Midwest Compensation Association in Cincinnati in the spring of 1958. He pointed out that, while the national income rose 240 per cent and compensation rose 300 per cent during the past 25 years, the cost of fringes rose 2,400 per cent."

Hoge observes:[5] "The cost of fringes, like the meaning of fringes, is a nebulous matter. There seems to be no common denominator by which the costs are measured; therefore, company-by-company comparisons are something less than invalid. We do know, however, that the cost of fringes in our company has risen 108 per cent in the seven-year period from 1950 to 1957." Furthermore he adds:[6] "It is interesting to note that in 1957 the cost of fringes was almost exactly double the amount of dividends paid to the owners of the company."

The U.S. Chamber of Commerce report for 1955 showed that, dollarwise, the average payment amounted to 39.2 cents per payroll hour, or $ 819 per year.[7] Fringe payments varied widely for the 1,000 reporting companies, ranging from less than 5 per cent to over 50 per cent of payroll. A breakdown of fringe payments by type is given in Table 12.1.

Table 12.1

AVERAGE FRINGE PAYMENTS AND COSTS

1955 fringe payments average 20.3 per cent of payroll for all companies.

These payments included:

Legally required payments (employer's share only)	3.6%
Pension and other agreed-upon payments (employer's share only)	6.3
Paid rest periods, lunch periods, etc.	2.2
Payments for time not worked	6.3
Profit-sharing payments, bonuses, etc.	1.9
Total	20.3%

The manufacturing companies paid 18.5 per cent, somewhat less than the all-company average, while the non-manufacturing companies paid 22.9 per cent, as shown below:

The hotel industry is better represented in this than in previous surveys (88 reports in 1955, 9 in 1953). Low fringe payments by hotels reduced the average payments for all industries and all non-manufacturing. Inclusion of only hotel reports would make the all industries averages about 20.9 per cent, 41.4 cents and $ 863 per year, and the all non-manufacturing averages about 25.5 per cent, 48.2 cents and $ 979 per year.

Type of Payment	*Total All Companies*	*Total All Manu-facturing*	*Total All Non-manu-facturing*
Total fringe payments as per cent of payroll	20.3	18.5	22.9
1. Legally required payments (employer's share only)	3.6	3.8	3.2
(a) Old-Age and Survivors Insurance	1.8	1.8	1.8
(b) Unemployment compensation:			
(1) 0.3 per cent Tax to Federal Government	0.2	0.2	0.2
(2) State tax (net)	0.8	0.8	0.6
(c) Workmen's compensation (including estimated cost for self-insured)	0.7	0.9	0.6
(d) Railroad Retirement Tax, Railroad Unemployment Insurance, State Sickness Benefits Insurance etc.	0.1	0.1	0.1
2. Pension and other agreed upon payments (employer's share only)	6.3	5.0	8.2
(a) Pension-plan premiums and pension payments not covered by insurance-type plan	3.8	2.8	5.3
(b) Life insurance premiums, death benefits, sickness, accident and medical-care insurance premiums, hospitalization insurance etc.	2.0	2.0	2.0
(c) Contributions to privately financed unemployment benefit funds	+	+	+
(d) Separation or termination pay allowance	+	+	0.1
(e) Discounts on goods and services purchased from company by employees	0.2	+	0.3
(f) Miscellaneous payments (free meals, compensation payments in excess of legal requirements, payments to needy employees, tuition refunds, savings and stock purchase plans, etc.)	0.3	0.2	0.6
3. Paid rest periods, lunch periods, washup time, travel time, clothes change time, get ready time etc.	2.2	2.3	2.0
4. Payments for time not worked	6.3	5.8	6.9
(a) Paid vacation and bonuses in lieu of vacation	3.5	3.5	3.4
(b) Payments for holidays not worked	2.0	2.0	2.1
(c) Paid sick leave	0.6	0.2	1.1
(d) Payments for State or National Guard duty, jury, witness and voting pay allowances, payments for time lost due to death in family or other personal reasons etc.	0.2	0.1	0.3

Type of Payment	*Total all companies*	*Total All Manu-facturing*	*Total All Non-manu-facturing*
5. Other items	1.9	1.6	2.5
(a) Profit-sharing payments	0.7	0.7	0.8
(b) Christmas or other special bonuses, service awards, suggestion awards, etc.	1.0	0.7	1.4
(c) Special wage payments ordered by courts, payments to union stewards etc.	0.2	0.2	0.3
Total fringe payments as cents per pay-roll hour	39.2	37.7	41.4
Total fringe payments as dollars per year per employee	819	801	847
Number of companies	1,000	601	399

Source: Fringe Benefits — 1955, Washington, U.S. Chamber of Commerce, 1956, p. 10.

In 1961 NICB[8] reported that the dollar costs of these more or less indirect incentives were quite impressive, ranging from $ 300 to almost $ 2,000 per employee, not including the costs of similar benefits for executives, which might be many times these amounts. Employee contributions to these costs, represented a small fraction of the total, probably less than 5 per cent of earnings. Costs in the United States of America were higher in cents per hour but lower as a proportion of earnings than in most other nations. In 1960, reported NICB, average costs in U.S.A. were about 47 cents per hour and about 22 to 23 per cent of the total payroll. In the United Kingdom, they amounted to about 17 per cent of the payroll; in Canada, 24 per cent; in the Netherlands, 30 per cent; in Japan, 40 per cent; in West Germany, 45 per cent; in Italy 75 per cent.

Personnel Administration and Employee Benefits and Services

Generally it is the personnel division, which administers the employee benefits and services programme, but it works closely with the accounting division, which handles payroll and record work, and the law department, which provides expert help on legal issues connected with pension plans, workmen's compensations, medical plan, etc., and also with the finance division. In India most of these benefits and services are included under welfare category and the Welfare Officers are asked to develop and administer these programmes.

In large plants, where more such benefits and services are offered there is also a greater degree of specialisation and generally practices in the methods of administration of employee benefits and services vary widely depending upon the service offered, the size of the company, and the accidents of growth. Often the line managers tend to dismiss many of these benefits and services as 'gimmicks' from the 'welfare boys' in order to keep themselves busy and have some work to do. They would argue that most of these services yield no tangible return to the organisation. The personnel administrators have a definite point of view, which is well summarised by Pigors and Myers:[9] "Management should offer employee benefits and services, not because they have to, not only within legal limits, and not as a camouflaged form of bribery, but because such benefits and services are in line with the whole personnel programme...." Every worker is a whole person, not only while he is on the job but wherever he is, throughout the 24 hours of each day. When any person has a serious problem to which he cannot satisfactorily adjust, his preoccupation is likely to affect both his productivity and morale. Management depends for success on the efficiency and stability of workers, as well as on their support of the principle of mutual responsibility, both while they are at work and in their attitude towards the company at all times. It is, therefore, to management's advantage to provide plant conditions that are satisfying both on and off the job and to give each employee whatever help can properly be offered in meeting his personal problems."

The very fact that more and more companies are planning on introducing more and different types of such benefits and services is sort of an admission that they are considered necessary and useful. Sometimes fringe benefits can make up what is lacking in a basic wage and salary compensation system up to a point. This incentive value of the fringe can be illustrated by an example given by Robert Hoge:[10] "In our company we have an employees' organisation known as the OnIzed Club. Its purpose is social and recreational, and it sponsors dances, picnics, sports contests, and other such events. In some communities, especially the smaller ones, the OnIzed Club is the prime source of social relations for many employees. How much the club really means to some employees was forcibly illustrated to me recently when I overheard a minor clerk complaining about his salary and his "tightwad" boss. Finally, he concluded if it wasn't for the OnIzed Club I would go somewhere else and get a job right now." Perhaps, this may be an extreme example, but nevertheless there are people who would be motivated by benefits and services to give off their best to the company goals.

What are the Items included in Employee Benefits and Services?

A concise but comprehensive list of items included in fringe items by category are provided by Robert H. Hoge:[11]

PAY FOR TIME NOT WORKED

1. Pay during illness
2. Vacation pay (off the job)
3. Pay for holidays (not worked)
4. Paid rest and relief time
5. Paid lunch periods
6. Jury pay allowance
7. Voting pay allowance
8. Bargaining time
9. Grievance time
10. Military service pay
11. Death in family
12. Wash-up time
13. Travel time
14. Supplemental pay
15. Quarantine call-in pay
16. Personal time off

EXTRA PAY FOR TIME WORKED

1. Premium pay (daily, weekly, days as such, etc.)
2. Vacation pay (no time off)
3. Shift premium
4. Old age and survivors insurance
5. Workmen's compensation and temporary disability insurance
6. Unemployment compensation
7. Pension or retirement plans
8. Profit-sharing
9. Christmas, year-end or special bonuses
10. Group insurance (life, hospitalization, health and accident, surgical and medical, and total and permanent disability)
11. Death benefit (in addition to group insurance)
12. Food cost subsidy
13. Housing subsidy
14. Shoes and clothing (not essential to job performance)
15. Terminal pay
16. Service awards
17. Employee recreation (athletics, hobbies, parties, etc.)
18. Personnel services (education subsidies, employee loans, physical examinations, employee purchases, medicine and medical supplies, credit union and services, legal services etc.)
19. Administrative costs (direct wages and salaries, working space and utilities, telephone, travel expenses, supplies, proportionate share of general overhead, etc.)

A more detailed list of employee benefits and services under various categories is as follows:[12]

1. Extra payment for time worked:

Holiday premium	Week-end premium
Overtime premium	Cost-of-living bonus.
Shift premium	

2. Payments for time not worked:

Call-back pay	Portal-to-portal pay
Call-in pay	Religious holidays
Paid lunch periods	Reporting pay
Paid sick leave	Reserve military pay
Clean-up time	Rest period
Clothes-changing time	Room and board allowance
Dental-care time	Severance pay
Down time	Supper money
Family allowance	Time spent on contract negotiation
Holidays paid for but not worked	Time spend on grievances
Jury duty pay	Vacation time
Layoff pay	Voting time

Medical time
Military induction bonuses
Military service allowance
National Guard duty
Paid death-in-family leave
Witness time
Machine set-up time
Enforced absences
Travel allowances or expenses.

3. *Payments for employee security:*

Contributions toward:
Accident insurance
Disability insurance
Group hospitalization insurance
Individual hospitalization insurance
Life insurance
Medical insurance
Individual surgical insurance
Group surgical insurance
Supplements to unemployment compensation
Credit unions
Employees' loan associations
Health and welfare fund
Home financing
Mutual benefit associations
Contributions to workmen's compensation
Supplements to workmen's compensation
Contribution to:
Employees' thrift plans
Employees' stock purchase plans
State disability insurance
Old age and survivors' insurance
Unemployment compensation
Payment of optical expenses
Pensions
Savings bond administration
Death benefits
Railroad retirement tax
Railroad unemployment insurance
Sickness benefits insurance.

4. *Non-reproduction awards and bonuses:*

Anniversary awards
Christmas bonuses
Quality bonuses
Safety awards
Service bonuses
Suggestion awards
Waste elimination bonuses
Year-end bonuses.

5. *Payment for employee services:*

Annual report to employees
Beauty parlour
Cafeterias
Canteen service
Charm courses
Company athletic teams
Company housing
Company orchestra
Company stores
Cooking Schools
Dietetic advice
Educational assistance
Employee counselling
Employee discounts on purchases
Income tax services
Information racks
Legal aid
Lunch period entertainment
Medical exams (voluntary)
Music at work
Nursery
Paid club memberships
Paid magazine subscriptions
Parking space operation
Purchasing service
Reading room facilities
Recreational facilities
Rest room facilities

Employee parties	Safety clothes at company expense
Employee pleasure trips	Safety programmes
Employee publications	Scholarships
Financial advice	Showers and locker rooms
Flowers for ill and deceased employees and families	Transportation
	Vacation facilities
Free laundry	Visiting nurse
Functions for retired employees	Vitamins and salt tablets
Free meals	Wedding gifts
Hospital facilities	Work clothes at company expense
Health education	Moving expenses
	Libraries.

This broad range of benefits and services, though quite exhaustive at first glance, may still have left out some benefits and services in practice in U.S.A. but they do indicate the kind of programmes and its scope. Except for some, there are many similar employee benefits and services used in India. For purposes of discussion here, the employee benefits and services are broadly categorised as follows:

1. Added Income and leisure.
2. Employee security.
3. Old age and retirement.
4. Employee health and safety and accident prevention.
5. Employee morale and welfare.

1. ADDED INCOME AND LEISURE

Some of the benefits that bring added income to employees are negotiated between union and management and usually shift premiums, paid holidays, paid vacations, rest pauses, reduced hours of work, overtime, pay, leave of absence for a variety of reasons fall in this category. Both in U.S.A. and India, public policy has also intervened in fixing normal hours of work per day and per week and over and above that management are required to give an overtime pay. Employers and managements have also shown initiative in providing the most satisfactory and effective combination of leisure and working hours as well as suitable premiums.

Hours of Work and Pay Practices

In the United States federal policy has stipulated 40 hours per week and 8 hours per day as normal in interstate industry and in India public policy has fixed 48 hours per week and 9 hours per day as normal. Over and beyond the normal hours in U.S.A. the employee must be compensated at time and one-half and in India at double time in scheduled employments, mines, and plantations. In U.S.A. many firms offer attractive additional premium pay to their employees when they work on week-ends, holidays, Sundays, sixth and seventh days. In the recent NICB survey[13] the pay practices are reported as follows: Out of 426 respondents, some 46 companies (11%) paid straight time for *work on the sixth day;* 255 (60%) paid time and a half; 3 (less than 1%) double time; and 1 company equal time off. Some 158 companies (37%) do no schedule sixth day work.

Out of 426 respondents, 38 companies (9%) paid straight time for *work on the seventh day;* 109 (26%) paid time and a half; some 171 (40%), double time; and one company, triple time. Some 185 companies (43%) do not schedule work on the seventh day. Out of 426 respondents, 68 companies (16%) paid straight time for Sunday work; 104 (24%) paid time and a half; 255 (60%), double time; and only one company, equal time off. Some 111 companies (26%) do not schedule Sunday work. For *work on Saturday,* out of 426 respondents, some 130 companies (31%) paid straight time; 281 (66%) paid time and a half; one company, double time and another two, equal time off. Some 69 companies schedule no work on Saturday.

Typically under these practices an employee whose base pay is $ 3 per hour, on Saturday or beyond 8 hours a day will receive time and a half or $ 4.50 per hour. If he works on Sunday he will make $ 6 an hour or double time. If he works on a national holiday, he may make $ 9 an hour or triple time. Through these provisions leisure can be converted into additional income by the employee.

Unions also negotiate for shorter hours per day and per week and in 1962 the International Brotherhood of Electrical Workers (IBEW) wanted a 20 hour-week and finally settled for a 35 hour-week. NICB[14] reports that among the 55 companies with a normal work week of under 40 hours per week for only white collar employees (typists, stenographers, clerks non-supervisory), 28 companies pay straight time rates for work over schedule upto 40 hours; 19 companies pay time and a half; 2 give equal time off; and 6 companies do not pay for extra hours upto 40 hours.

In U.S.A. there is a good deal of moonlighting — employee holding more than one full time job — and in 1966, 5.2 per cent of the total employees, according to Executive Digest,[14A] were moonlighters. One out of every 14 employees is a moonlighting male, one out of every 50 a woman. About 70 per cent of moonlighters hold down a full-time job and a part time one; 6 per cent hold down two full-time jobs. This information was provided by the Bureau of Labour Statistics. In our country there is some moonlighting going on. But this may not be on any considerable scale although figures are not available. Generally managements ignore this sort of thing, although it might impair the efficiency of the worker in his full time job sometimes. But they view with disfavour if the worker went to work for a competitor or engaged in activity that is inimical to the interests of the primary firm.

Shift Premium: Companies operating a second and third shift pay a shift premium, varying from less than 5% of the base rate to 19% or from 5 cents to over 20 cents per hour for second shift. The third shift premium varies from less than 5 cents to over 20 cents per hour and from 5% to over 20% of the base rate. Some companies pay 8 hour pay for 6½ hour shift (this practice is the common among many Coimbatore textile mills in the case of the night shift), usually in the case of night shift. The third shift or the night generally receives the highest premium. Most of the companies pay 7 to 10 cents premium per hour for the second shift and 12 to 17 cents premium per hour for third shift.[15] These shift differentials provided additional income to the employee.

Of course, some companies do not pay any shift premium and usually they just rotate their workers, so that everybody gets to work on all the shifts. It is necessary to evolve a policy, when there is shift premium, as to who will get work on the first, second and third shifts. Some may not like to work on the night shift and some may prefer it because it gives more shift premium. The practice varies. Some decide this issue on the basis of seniority.

Paid Holidays: The pressure for holidays has been increasing and this is particular so in the case of 'paid' holidays. Under the Factories Act, 1948, every worker is to be given a weekly holiday and under the Minimum Wages Act it is recommended that the weekly day of rest should be allowed with wages in all schedule employments other than agriculture. When the worker is deprived of the weekly holiday, a compensatory holiday must be given.

In India there are eight commonly observed paid holidays and there are many regional and state variations. In Madras, Republic Day, Independence Day, Gandhi Jayanthi, Deepavali, Ayudha Puja, May Day, Tamil New Year's Day, 18th of Adi, Pongal holidays are paid holidays. The National and Festival Holidays Act enacted in Madras State stipulates eight paid holidays, but Republic Day, Independence Day and Gandhi Jayanthi are compulsory paid holidays. Regarding the rest of 5 paid holidays the union and management may mutually agree and notify to the Factory Inspector. Apart from these, there are other religious paid holidays and some holidays peculiar to certain States.

In the U.S.A.[16] nearly 97 to 99% (out of total of 361 respondents) offer 6 paid holidays: Christmas Day, Thanksgiving Day, New Year's Day, Independence Day, Labour Day, Memorial Day. Other paid holidays, which are not so common, yet prevalent, are Washington's birthday, Veterans' Day, Columbus Day, Lincoln's Birthday, Christmas Eve, New Year's Eve, Thanksgiving Friday, Easter Monday (the last four are usually given to stretch the holiday period and provide a big weekend), Good Friday, Yam Kippur, Rosha Hoshana, and employee's birthday.

Holiday Pay: Overtime premium pay for work on paid holidays is at double time or at triple time. Most of the other details regarding eligibility, quantum and calculation of pay etc. are usually negotiated between union and management.

Paid Vacation: In manufacturing, mining and plantations, every employee, who has worked for at least 240 days during a calendar year, is entitled, during the subsequent year, to leave with wages at the rate of one day for every 20 days worked if an adult or one day for every 15 days with wages, which may be treated as paid vacation and normally an employee can accumulate his leave upto 30 days. In shops and commercial establishments the leave practices vary from State to State, and the annual paid leave ranges from 10 to 16 days. The majority of the state laws, in addition, provide for the grant of casual leave ranging from 10 to 14 days with pay in a year. This type of leave cannot be accumulated and must be taken within the course of the year.

The practice in many leading organisations is to provide a month's leave for a year of actual service (1 day leave for 11 days work) which can be accumulated anywhere from 90 days to 120 days. Some organisations also provide for encashment of a part of this earned or privilege leave. Another very common practice among the leading organisations is to provide leave-holiday travel facility every year, whereby the employee can go to his home town or any other part of the country and he is reimbursed to the tune of actual return fare by air or train or he is entitled to a certain lump-sum payment related to his salary.

In the United States of America, paid vacations, which were originally meant for only the salaried employees, are a common feature for workers also and are usually negotiated between union and management. Paid vacations are usually designed to give rest and to permit the employee to escape from the fatigue, monotony, and work strain and to come afresh for the work year ahead. Summarising a study of vacation goals, Mary Owen notes: "The empirical knowledge which has led to the establishment of paid vacations, with the motivation of improving employee health, is established as scientifically valid."[17]

Types of Vacations: Basically in the U.S.A. there are three types of vacations: (a) length of vacation is the same for all eligible employees, (b) length of vacations is graduated according to length of service, and (c) length of vacation is the same, but the amount of vacation pay varies with length of service. Ninety per cent of the collective agreements, filed with Federal Department of Labour, provide for graduated vacations, based on length of service and the most common pattern allows paid vacations of 1 week for 1 year's service, 2 weeks for 5 years, 3 weeks for 15 years, and 4 weeks for 25 years.[18] Another issue with paid vacations is whether it should be a staggered vacation or shut down and the practice of companies varies — while some shut down their operations for a week or two enabling all the employees to go on a vacation at the same time, others stagger the employee vacation in such a way that operations can go on without being hindered and many companies in U.S.A. hire vacation replacements, who are usually school and college students who would like to pay their way through college with their own funds.

Leonard Smith has provided a check-list of questions that should be carefully considered while planning a vacation programme.[19]

1. What shall be the length of vacation to be granted to employees?
   (a) Fixed number of hours, days, or weeks per year?
   (b) Pro-rata amount for less than yearly periods?
   (c) Percentage of time worked?
2. What eligibility requirements shall be established for employees to receive vacations and vacation pay?
   (a) Length of continuous service as of a specific date?
   (b) Lateness or absentee record better than established standards?
   (c) Specific number of hours of work during given period?
3. How shall the amount of vacation pay be determined?
   (a) Specific number of hours at straight-line base pay?
   (b) Average hourly rate for a given period?
   (c) Percentage of previous earnings for a given period?
   (d) Flat sum payment?
   (e) Shall provision be made for the maximum amount of pay or of hours of pay?
4. Shall provision be made for the payment to employees of their vacation pay in lieu of vacations?
   (a) Permitted?
   (b) Prohibited?
   (c) At the option of the company?
   (d) Required in emergencies?
   (e) Cash bonus granted by the company?

5. What shall be the effect on the payment of vacation pay of:
   (a) Discharges?
      1. Inefficiency?
      2. Dishonesty or similar reasons?
   (b) Lay-offs?
      1. Slack periods?
      2. Cut-backs or curtailment of war contracts?
   (c) Leaves of absence?
      1. Personal illness?
      2. Family reasons?
      3. Union business?
   (d) Military leaves?
      1. When leaving company to enter service?
      2. When returning to company's employ from the service?
   (e) Resignations?
   (f) Shall employees receive:
      1. Full vacation pay due?
      2. Pro-rata vacation pay?
      3. No vacation pay?
   (g) Terminations before vacation period?
   (h) Terminations during vacation period?
   (i) Re-employment of terminated employees?
      1. Seniority rules governing service credit?
      2. Before vacation period?
      3. During vacation period?
6. Shall vacation pay be considered as part of dismissal or severance pay?
7. What period of time shall be established during which vacations shall be taken?
   (a) Entire year?
   (b) Summer months?
8. Shall the company shut down its operations for the vacation period?
9. Shall employees be required to stagger their vacation periods?
10. Shall all vacation periods selected by employees be subject to approval by the company?
11. Shall employees be permitted to split their vacations?
    (a) Request of company?
    (b) Approval of company?
12. What provision shall be made for holidays falling during employees' vacation periods?
    (a) When holiday is worked by company?
    (b) When holiday is not worked by company? Employees paid for holidays?
    (c) Extra day added to vacation period and vacation pay?
    (d) Disregarded?
    (e) Shall this provision be changed if the vacation period is assigned by the company rather than selected by the employee?

13. Shall employees be permitted to accumulate vacation credits?
    (a) Maximum amount permitted to be accumulated?
    (b) Time limit during which vacation credit is valid?

Wash-Up Time: Quite a few companies allow 5 to 10 minutes to the employees to wash-up and to change clothes. It is a general tendency among many workers — even good ones — to relax during the last 15 minutes of the shift when uppermost in their minds is the thought to go home. As one manager said, "We don't give any wash-up time, but they take it any way."

Where employees have to make a report, like in the case of a bus conductor, at the end of day, this period is also considered working time by some companies. Often these items are bargained. Some companies in U.S.A. give wash-up time of 2 to 15 minutes before lunch time and quitting time.

Call-in, Call-out and Call-back Pay: A 'Call-in' is when an employee reports to work and finds that there is no work owing to some reason and 'call-out' or 'call-back' is a situation when an employee is asked to report to work outside of regular hours and finds he has no work for some reason or the other. In both the cases, he is guaranteed what is known as 'reporting pay' or 'reporting allowance' or 'reporting time' and the reporting pay maybe to the tune of 4 hours' pay to employees. It is not uncommon to pay him for all the full eight hours' work and usually the white-collar employees are guaranteed full eight hours pay, though they may have no work at all.

Usually, in order to avoid such payments, careful planning and scheduling of work is required. When there is a machine break-down, which prevents the worker from working, he is guaranteed a downtime pay, usually a minimum of 2 to 4 hours' pay. When a worker is asked to remain in the plant, even though he may not have any work, he is paid *standby pay* of so many guaranteed hours' pay.

Rest Periods: Rest periods have become pretty common with many companies in U.S.A., where pre-lunch coffee break, a lunch break, and a post-lunch coffee break are common. Coffee breaks may be for a period of 10 to 15 minutes and lunch break for 30 minutes. A number of State laws require lunch breaks to be given to the employees during the course of the work day. The practice of employees having lunch on company time is also widespread. But coffee breaks and rest pauses — paid or not — are of recent origin and employers claim various benefits from rest pauses: (1) Reduces monotony and fatigue, (2) Increases productivity, (3) Improves communications, (4) Improves attention to work, (5) Improves employee morale.

But there are organisational problems in scheduling and controlling rest periods and coffee breaks. It is not enough to give a coffee break. There must be space for employees to get together and there must be good coffee. Often bad coffee may put off a man than no coffee. Usually companies conduct experiments with these breaks and try to come up with a satisfactory system and apply it. Sometimes the employees may tend to overshoot the break period and this problem will have to be met.

In our country, law in factories, mines, plantations, shops and commercial establishments requires that no worker should be made to work continuously for more than 5 hours unless a rest pause of half an hour is given. Some employers in addition, give short rest-pauses and half an hour to one hour lunch break, which is generally unpaid. Coffee breaks are more informal than formal, where a mobile coffee service is provided to the worker who can get his coffee at his workspot and he drinks it there. He will probably spend 5 minutes in the process and managements do not mind this. Some larger companies have formal 5 to 10 minutes coffee breaks which are on company time and some are unpaid coffee breaks, where the worker is expected to take coffee at his own time and where he has to put in 8 full hours of work.

Organising and scheduling rest-pauses, locating the cafeteria, time factor in reaching cafeteria or canteen are all important issues.

Leave of Absence: The policy on leaves of absence must be clearly spelled out and implemented. Generally in U.S.A., time-off-with-pay plans are granted to an employee:[20] (1) When there is death in his family, (2) When there is illness in his family, (3) When he has to act as the trial witness, (4) When he has religious feasts, (5) When he has to vote on Election Day, (6) When he has to do some Christmas shopping, (7) When he has to go to Summer Military Encampment, (8) When he has to serve on the jury, (9) When he has medical appointments, (10) When he is getting married. In our country we have casual leave, privilege leave, sick leave and maternity leave which are similar to time-off-with-pay plans. Generally the request for leave of absence must be made ahead of time — anywhere from 24 hours to a month. Shorter leaves may be granted by the supervisor, but longer leaves must be taken up at a higher level. Employees may be paid or not while on leave, depending on such factors as length of leave, length of service, eligibility, etc. While on leave, what is his status regarding seniority and is he covered by insurance are matters on which policy must be clear. For the recall of the employee, who has gone on indefinite leave or leave on false reasons, rules must be framed to deal with such situations.

2. EMPLOYEE SECURITY

Employee security, well-being and stability are of primary importance in any programme of manpower management. The policy on employee security, is to provide for assurance of a reasonable income, job security, and removal of employee financial worries. While some of the employee security programmes are provided by union-management negotiations, and some by management initiative, some are required by the statutory provisions. It is the objective of employee security policy to not only protect the employee's interests but also the interests of his family.

Guaranteed Wage or Employment

There is a trend toward promoting individual and family security and employment stabilisation by certain programmes such as guaranteed wage or employment clause (which guarantees the employee of wages or employment for a definite time period) and putting all employees on a salary basis. This programme offers the worker a sense of job and financial security, which will enable him to be more effective on the job than when he is uncertain about his employment and income. In India the "Payment of Wages Act" stipulates that wage period shall not exceed one month and that wages should be paid within seven days of expiry of the wage period in establishments employing less than 1,000 persons and within ten days in others.

Severance Pay

One of the two fundamental programmes designed to alleviate the financial problems arising out of unemployment is the private system of severance pay or dismissal compensation. The other basic programme is public unemployment insurance system.

Unemployment may be caused by a variety of causes such as technological progress, business slump, bad management, product or process obsolescence, change in consumer demand. A man who has lost his job, is immediately worried over the financial problem of maintaining himself and his family while he looks for another job and the severance pay or severance wages or dismissal compensation affords certain amount of financial solace during the problematic transitional period. In the words of Everett D. Hawkins,[21] "Dismissal compensation may be defined as the payment of a specific sum, in addition to back wages or salary made by an employer to an employee for permanently terminating the employment relationship primarily for reasons beyond the control of the employee." But only in a relatively few cases are payments made to workers dismissed for cause such as incompetence, incapacity or fault. Severance pay is paid for breaking employment relation rather than for the period of unemployment. Some companies have a formal plan, while others have an informal plan. In the NICB study[22] out of a total 427 respondents, some 189 companies (44%) had severance pay programmes and the maximum severance pay for both white collar and blue collar workers ranged from one week's pay to one year's pay. While some plans make a uniform payment to all employees, most of them graduate payments according to length of service. While earlier plans covered only the office employees, the present trend seems to be towards a wider coverage including blue collar workers. There are usually eligibility requirements; usually one to five years' employment is necessary to be eligible and the quantum of severance pay is computed on the basis of earnings of the employee, length of service, age, and need (the former two being most commonly employed). A fairly common pattern allows one week's pay for each year of service in excess of five years. There appears to be a trend toward giving severance even in the case of temporary lay-offs.

Lay-Off and Retrenchment Compensation

In India The Industrial Disputes Act, 1947 requires employers in non-seasonal establishments employing 50 or more workers to give a month's notice or wages in lieu thereof and also pay compensation to all those workers who are retrenched after at least one year's continuous service. The compensation is paid at the rate of 15 days' average pay for every completed year of service. The maximum number of days for which a worker is to be paid compensation is limited to 45 in a year. But if he is laid off for more than 45 days in a year, then compensation for the subsequent period will be paid only in respect of those days when he is laid off continuously for a period of one week or more unless there is an agreement to the contrary between him and his employer. No compensation is payable if the worker refuses to accept alternative employment offered to him or fails to report for work at the appointed time; or if the lay-off is due to a strike or slow down tactics of workers employed in other parts of the organisation. According to the recent amendment there is no 45 days limit.

Unemployment Insurance

Unemployment insurance is another device to meet the financial problems of an unemployed employee. Around 1935 in U.S.A. unemployment insurance was introduced by the Social Security Act by creating a federal tax on employer payrolls and by permitting States to recover 90 per cent of that tax if they created acceptable state programmes. The unemployment insurance system is a combined Federal-State programme, where the Federal law sets down a framework within which the States are free to operate and the object of this system is to provide benefits to those who had lost their jobs and who were looking for employment and who had established eligibility for benefits by earlier working experience. The coverage of the type of workers is left to the States to determine. In 1961 total coverage was about 46.5 millions and the unemployment insurance protects four-fifths of all wage and salary earners. Benefits under this system generally cover the basic worker-living requirements barely, but not enough to discourage job hunting. Probably an unemployed worker may receive nearly 50 per cent of the usual wages and most States have a fixed maximum payment, which, under rising cost-of-living, may become as much as the going rate. Several States have flexible maximum rates and have also increased the benefits by adding a variable allowance for the number of dependents. The duration of the benefit payments vary from State to State, averaging about 24 weeks. In order to be eligible for benefits, he must have actually earned a minimum from $ 150 to $ 300 in a base quarter in his previous employment and benefits may be claimed only if he is available for suitable or comparable work. Unemployment insurance, despite some limitations, has proved to be an invaluable aid not only to the unemployed but also to the entire American economy by providing purchasing power. Richard Lester points out that more than 5.8 million workers were helped in 1957, 8.2 million in 1958 and 6.1 million in 1959 and the programme gave benefits to the tune of $ 1.8 billion in 1957, $ 4 billion in 1958 and $ 2.6 billion in 1959.[23]

Supplemental Unemployment Benefits

As a result of negotiations between United Automobile workers and Ford Motor Company in 1955 supplemental benefits came into vogue and are now prevalent in steel, aluminium, rubber industries etc. and total coverage probably includes at least 2 million workers. The supplemental benefits provide an added benefit to the unemployed who are drawing unemployment insurance benefits and some plans bring workers' total income to about 65% of normal straight time earnings and these benefits may be provided for anywhere from 39 to 62 weeks. Funds for these supplemental benefits come from employer contributions — usually 5 cents per manhour. Eligibility to receive these benefits is based on eligibility for unemployment insurance.

In the N I C B study,[24] out of 427 respondents, some 37 companies (9%) have supplemental unemployment benefit plans. The supplemental unemployment benefits along with unemployment insurance payments have rendered the unemployed secure for a while when they are making the transition from one job to another.

Retraining

Whenever jobs are rendered obsolete due to the introduction of a new machine or new technology or as is popularly called automation, there arises the problem of technological unemployment threatening employee job security. This problem is very intelligently met by collective agreements which require managements to provide for retraining facilities or technological adjustments pay (TAP). Usually the men displaced by automation are retrained for other different jobs, while they continue on the payroll and they do not face lay-off problems. Under Tap agreements, companies give sufficient advance notice to the employees and a certain amount of pay depending on length of service, if other jobs are not found for them. Some companies create automation funds, mainly from employer contributions, and they guarantee workers against lay-off, assure them of a minimum of 35 hours per week, protected employees against any speed-up and provide for early retirement benefits.

Social Security Legislation in India

Social Security legislation in India, which is discussed in Chapter 12, provide for employee security against the hazards of sickness, injury and unemployment. The main schemes of social security are: (1) the Workmen's Compensation Act of 1923, which provides for payment of compensation in case of death, permanent disablement or temporary disablement; (2) Maternity benefits passed by various state laws, which provide the employees with leave and other benefits; (3) Employee's State Insurance Act, 1948, which provides five types of benefits for sickness, maternity, disablement, dependents and medical benefit; (4) The Employees' Provident Fund Act, of 1952, which aims to offer a measure of economic security to the employees. All the provisions of these above Acts are discussed in a separate chapter (13), because they form a very important component of the complex labour and industrial legislation in the country. The employee services and benefits provided under these Acts are also discussed in the thirteenth chapter.

3. OLD AGE AND RETIREMENT

The economic freedom and financial security during old age and retirement are of major concern to the employees, who not only wish to provide for themselves, but also for their families. Both the employers and the State have taken keen interest in meeting these employee needs and many enlightened employers introduced employee services in this vital area even before the State came up with social security measures. Collective agreements include old age and retirement benefits. State programmes provide old age pensions and some old age assistance and private programmes provide supplementary pensions and retirement assistance programmes in U.S.A.

OASDI (Old Age and Survivor's and Disability Insurance)

A major scheme under the Social Security Act, 1935 and amendments in 1958 designed to provide financial aid to the aged worker and his dependents is Old Age and Survivors Insurance programme, under which four kinds of benefit payments — retirement, survivors, disability and veteran — are made. Retirement benefits are provided to the wage-earner and his family upon retirement at legal age. Survivor's benefits are payable to the insured's family, no matter what the age is at death. Disability benefits are payable to the workman if the insured becomes totally disabled between the ages of 50-65. Veteran benefits primarily refer to special allowances granted to veterans of the time they were in the services.

This programme is financed by way of taxes shared equally by workers and employers, or paid entirely by the self-employed. Available tax rate is collected on earnings up to $ 4,800 a year and in 1959 the tax rate was 2½ per cent for employers and employees and for the self-employed, $3^3/_4$ per cent. The tax rate is schedule, according to present legislation, to increase to 4½ per cent for employers and employees and $6^3/_4$ per cent for self-employed persons in 1969. The taxes are designed to pay the entire cost of benefit payments and of the cost of administering the programme. The employer collects the taxes and pays over the sum to the U.S. Internal Revenue Service where this payment is credited to the account of each employee, to whom has been assigned a social security number. The exact amount of benefits can be calculated largely on the basis of average earnings, period of contributions and particular type of claim.[25]

Private Pensions

In U.S.A. the provision of pensions by employers was instituted as early as 1900 and antidate the retirement benefits provided by the Social Security Act, 1935. Private pension programmes have increased rapidly, sometimes spurred on by unions and they are regarded as supplementary to OASDI. The main aim of pensions is to give a reasonable amount of financial security to the retired employee. The following advantages of pension plans may also be enumerated:

1. Pensions attract and retain employees.
2. They attract a better class of people who stay with the firm, thus reducing turnover and recruitment costs.
3. They permit retirement of the superannuated employee.
4. They improve employee morale.
5. They promote employee goodwill and loyalty.

Prentice-Hall spells out the general requirements of a good pension plan:[26]

1. Plan is for exclusive benefit of employees.
2. Sole purpose of plan is to offer employees (or their beneficiaries) an income after retirement.
3. Plan is permanent.
4. Plan is in writing.
5. Plan is communicated to employees.

Pensions may be contributory or non-contributory and they may be administered by the employer or an insurance company. According to Professor Dale Yoder,[27] "coverage of private pensions extended, in 1960, to some 22 million employees. It was, at that time, growing at a rate of about one million per year. While heaviest coverage is among white collar workers, growing proportions of blue collar workers are covered. More than 40,000 plans were operating in 1960. Many of these plans are pensions with profit sharing. Less than one-fourth of the coverage is provided by insured plans, but they are gaining wider acceptance, especially in small firms. Coverage of private plans now extends to about one-fourth of the labour force. "Most private plans are financed by employer contribution; in about one-sixth of all plans, employees also contribute. Benefits are administered by insurance firms or by trustees of non-insured plans. For bargained plans, the most common benefit, after 30 years of service, is about $ 175 per month, including OASDI benefits. In general, benefits represent a higher percentage of wages and salaries for low-paid workers. Thus for those earning $ 3,000 annually, total monthly benefits, including OASDI, amount to about 64 per cent of earnings. At the $ 6,000 salary level, benefits amount to only about 40 per cent. In most plans, workers become eligible to participate after one year of employment. Full benefits become available after 15 years in the most common pattern."

In a recent NICB study,[28] out of 427 respondents, 332 companies (78%) reported to operate a pension plan (not including 'pension' based on company profits) and in a majority of the cases (65%) the entire cost was financed by the companies and in 23% of the cases employees and the companies shared the cost. Only in a lone case, the employees paid the entire cost of the pension plan.

Administration of Pension Plan: Jay V. Strong provides the following useful summary of the fundamentals involved in the administration of a pension plan:[29]

General Administration

"Usually an administrative committee, often called the pension committee, supervises the general administration of a retirement plan and interprets its terms when unusual situations arise....

The question is frequently raised as to what department the administrator should be in and to whom he should report. Actually the proper administration of a retirement plan cuts across departmental lines since legal, financial and industrial relations aspects are involved.... Usually the administrator works out of the office of, and is responsible to, either the general counsel, the treasurer, or the industrial relations director.

In some large and medium-size firms, separate insurance, social security, or employee benefit departments have been organised to administer not only the retirement plan but also the other employee-benefit plans. These departments appeared to be functioning well.... In large companies with multiple locations, these centralized insurance departments help to maintain a uniform employee-benefit policy in branch offices....

An employee's immediate supervisor is the person to whom he should first turn for information concerning his company's retirement plan or any other benefit. A retirement plan is one phase of personnel administration, a function of management which is exercised by every department head who is assisted by people in the achievement of his department's objectives. For this reason each department head should be a deputy of the company in administering its programme in so far as that programme affects his employees.

The staff and technical work regarding retirement plans may be delegated to the personnel department. (Two reasons appear for this recommendation.) First, the personnel department already contains most of the records and facilities needed. Second, its major interest pertains to employee relations and its interest should insure that retirement and pension questions from supervisors and employees will receive careful and sympathetic treatment. *The personnel department call well serve as a central co-ordinating agency, a source of information and advice, the custodian of personnel records, and the point of contact with the insurance company or pension trustees.* Also it can assist in preparing instructions and information for supervisors regarding retirement policies and pensions....

Administrative Manual: The responsibilities attached to the proper administration of a retirement plan involve: (1) technical aspects, that are legal, financial and tax matters; and (2) personnel aspects. A manual prepared by an insurance company or an independent consultant can greatly assist the administrator of employee-benefit plans with regard to the technical aspects and will give him some help with regard to personnel aspects. Such a manual should give detailed instructions concerning the compilation of all necessary information or data, the place to which it should be sent and the time of transmittal. The manual should answer all questions concerning the operation of the plan.

Personnel Aspects: The personnel aspects involved in the administration of a retirement plan refer to the contacts with employees regarding their rights and privileges under it. Employees may need to be contacted regarding eligibility, enrolment, contributions, vested interests, death benefits, settlement options, lay-offs, leaves of absence, disability, termination of employment, changes in compensation, transfers, date of retirement and changes in beneficiaries...."

The Federai Welfare and Pension Plans Disclosure Act, 1958, amended in 1962, requires the administrators to be bonded and the submission of annual reports for plans. The Federal Department of Labour is authorised to require such reporting and even to subpoena records. Severe penalties are imported for mismanagement of pension plans.

Retirement Assistance: Many companies offer various retirement programmes designed to assist the employee in making the transition from active working life to a retired life. Normal retirement age is around 65, but may be extended. Many companies in U.S.A. provide preretirement education for employees, which prepares them for retirement, attempts to develop some healthy hobbies and interest, and encourages them take part in community, educational, social, cultural and church activities. Some companies purchase and develop a locality in good places with salubrious climate for their retired employees and some of them are so attractive enough to make employees want to retire and go on a well earned rest. Some companies offer club, recreation, reading room, library, travel facilities to the retired employees, all of which are designed to promote employee well-being after retirement.

4. EMPLOYEE HEALTH AND SAFETY

In any industrial or business organisation, employee health and safety are of major concern and public policy, managements and unions are all interested in promoting the health and safety of workers. A few musts regarding industrial health and safety are:

1. Employee health and safety must have top management approval, sanction and support.
2. They must have competent staff direction.
3. They must have strong support and involvement of line executives.
4. They must be given equal consideration with other factors of production.
5. They must be made known to all through proper communication.

A good employee health and safety programme increases employee efficiency, employee productivity, employee morale, employee interest and employee loyalty and decreases employee tardiness, apathy, absenteeism and indifference and all these, in addition to promoting employee health and safety. The Factories Act 1948 in India has stipulated certain conditions, covering in detail such matters as safety, first aid, sanitation, cleanliness, lighting, washing facilities, drinking water, canteens and rest rooms. But the I.I.P.M. notes:[30] "There can be no doubt of the employer's liability in these matters. Unfortunately, compliance with the provisions of the Act still leaves much to be desired and Factory Inspectorates are understaffed and unable to cope with their ever-expanding territory. Therefore, the first care of the personnel officer must be to see that the Act is implemented in the spirit as well as the letter of the law. The approach should be not merely to comply with the law, but to follow to their logical conclusion the pointers to good working conditions indicated by the law."

Health

Employee health service may range from the provision of simple facilities for first aid, at one extreme, to the provision of complete medical care for employees and their dependents at the other. Its proper scope depends upon the size, character, location, financial facilities of each establishment. In India one of the very incipient employee service programmes was in the area of industrial medical service in the form of provision of maternity wards and competent medical staff. While some large units in our country provide a wide range of medical and health services to the employees, some units discontinued the provision of this service after the establishment of Employee's State Insurance Scheme (ESIS) whose sole purpose is to provide medical service to the employees. Generally it is complained that the facilities provided under ESIS, in the form of hospitals, medical staff — doctors and nurses, hospital, beds, medicine etc. — are found to be inadequate. It is also said that ESIS has imposed some additional burdens on the personnel officer, who is expected to make necessary return to the ESI Corporation and also handle issues, complaints and grievances of workers that arise out of the administration of State Health Insurance.

The Employee State Insurance Scheme provides medical benefits in the form of medical attendance, treatment, drugs and injections to insured persons and to members of their families where the facility has been extended to the families.

Facilities of full medical care including hospitalisation are now available to nearly 24.11 lakh families and would be extended further to over 10 lakh families during 1977 with the commissioning of more hospitals already under construction. There are presently 59 hospitals with over 11,000 beds operating under this Scheme and another 20 hospitals are under construction with an expected capacity of 7,000 beds. There are also 865 dispensaries and 4,588 insured medical practitioners to look after the workers.

Medical benefits are administered by the respective State Governments, except in Delhi where the E.S.I. Corporation is administering it directly. 7/8 of the expenditure on medical benefits is borne by the Corporation and 1/8th by the State Government.

The Factories Act requires initial and periodical medical examination of young persons between the ages of 15 and 17 employed in factories and it is the duty of the personnel office to see that the company meets these statutory requirements.

Scope and Range of Health Service: An extensive health service programme of a company may be as follows:[31]

1. To estimate physical and mental capacity for intelligent placement.
2. To provide a human maintenance service.

   Services available:

   (a) Prompt emergency care.
   (b) On-the-job treatment for minor non-occupational conditions.
   (c) Early detection of chronic diseases.
   (d) Better diagnosis of occupational diseases.
   (e) Health counselling.
   (f) Plan tours and active preventive programme.
   (g) Medical supervision in rehabilitation.
   (h) Medical re-check before promotion or transfer of personnel.

3. To advise and work with management on company policies relate to health such as:

   (a) Optimum hours of work per week.
   (b) Plant feeding programme.
   (c) Accident and sickness prevention.
   (d) Sanitation and public health within the plant.
   (e) Health education programme.
   (f) Selection of employee insurance and welfare plans.
   (g) Retirement plan.
   (h) Preparation of employees for retirement.
   (i) Employment of the handicapped.
   (j) Special problem employees such as alcoholics and accident-prone individuals.
   (k) In-plant and community recreation projects.
   (l) Training and use of first aid attendants.

4. To conduct medical research for the benefit of industry.
5. To coordinate the individual plant health service unit with those in neighbouring plants and the community civil defence organisation for the care of casualties in a severe disaster.

Mr. Park[32] further points out that a good health service programme effects cost reduction through reduction in compensation costs, absenteeism, labour turnover, lost time, accident frequency, occupational diseases and also by protecting company-operated sick-benefit plans from unjust claims. Another authority estimated that for every dollar spent on health service, \$ 3.50 to \$ 5 will be saved.[33]

General Features of Health Service Programme: The following general features may be mentioned:

1. A well organised plan for the medical service.
2. A competent and definitely designated staff of qualified physicians, surgeons, nurses, attendants, with one physician in charge of service (smaller units may be unable to afford such elaborate facilities, but they may use external facilities).
3. Adequate emergency, dispensary or hospital facilities.
4. Adequate medical records including physical examination records and case histories.

Before introducing a health service programme, it is necessary to carefully consider the cost factors, services offered in similar establishments, the needs of the company, standards of medical service and justification of the expenses.

Group Health Benefits: In U.S.A. most of the companies use the group insurance technique in meeting employee health needs. There are certain general features of a group insurance programme listed by Prentice Hall:[34]

1. Some central agency, such as the employer, collects the premiums and manages the details.
2. The employer receives a general policy, and each employee receives a certificate evidencing the insurance.
3. Except for comparatively new "permanent" life policies, the policy is for one year.
4. Except in those States where compulsory disability insurance laws are found, an individual must usually be employed for a given period before he is eligible for the insurance. The amount of time involved varies.
5. Premiums may be paid jointly (employer-employee) under a contributory plan, or singly (employer) under a non-contributory plan. In some cases the employee may pay the entire premium.
6. Rates are based partly on the experience of the particular risk, except in cases where carriers other than regular insurance companies underwrite hospital, medical and surgical expense.
7. Certain minimum requirements must be met. A minimum number of lives must be covered, depending upon state laws and the type of the insurance. In non-contributory programmes, the plan is not effective until 75 per cent of eligible employees have subscribed. In non-contributory plans all employees must enrol unless they sign a waiver.
8. The policy is issued on a basis precluding selection of employees to be covered.

Basic Types of Group Insurance

Basically, there are three types of group insurance:

1. Health Insurance has three types: (a) Hospitalisation Insurance, which either provides cash indemnity to meet hospitalisation plans, which provide for hospital services instead of cash allowances; (b) Medical Care Plans, which provide benefits, not for hospitalisation, but for the services of physicians and surgeons; and (c) Major Medical Plans, where the insured pays for 'minor' costs upto $ 500 and above that costs are met by a 'catastrophe' policy.

2. *Group Accident and Sickness Insurance* involves the payment of compensation for wages to employees who are temporarily disabled and unable to work.

3. *Life Insurance* involves the protection of dependents consequent upon the death of the breadwinner.

In 1954 a NICB survey of 884 reported that [34A] (1) The vast majority of plans provide the employee with hospitalisation benefits (98%), surgical care (94%), life insurance (90%), and accident and sickness insurance (85%) and (2) about half the plans are paid for via joint contributions, about 40 per cent by employer contributions only and about 10 per cent via employee contributions only.

The recent NICB survey of about 427 companies in 1963 reported the group insurance types and the extent of prevalence as given in Table 12.2.[35]

For most of these plans either the company pays the entire premium or both company and employees share the premium and only in a very few plans employees pay the entire premium.

Table 12.2

GROUP INSURANCE PREVALENCE

Practice	*Total companies*	
	No.	*%*
Total Respondents	427	100
Companies with group life insurance for employees	425	99
Companies with group dental Insurance	8	2
Companies with group life insurance for dependents of employees	8	11
Companies with group accidental and dismemberment insurance	317	74
Companies with paid sick leave	332	78
Companies with accident and sickness insurance	344	80
Companies with paid sick leave and group accident and sickness insurance	161	38
Companies with non-insured benefits used only to supplement workmen's compensation	58	14
Companies with comprehensive major medical insurance	114	27
Companies with supplemental major medical plan	206	48
Companies with Blue Cross plan for employees	220	52
Companies with a commercial group health insurance base plan	258	60

Nursing: Full-time or part-time or visiting nurse system is increasingly becoming important both in India and U.S.A. Smaller firms, which cannot afford to pay for the services of a doctor, often engage a nurse on a full-time or part-time basis. The industrial nurse can provide some very useful health services to the employees:[36]

An experienced industrial nurse at your plant for as little as two hours a day, three days a week can:

— Put into operation a plan for safe emergency care.

— Watch injuries for possible complications.

— Keep accurate records of injuries and illness pertinent to work.

— Give treatments prescribed by the doctor.

— Provide practical, commonsense counselling on physical and mental health problems.

— Help prevent accidents by observing and reporting physical and mental signs that indicate hazards in work processes or practices.

— Make standard tests needed by the physician for:

— Physical examinations.

— Improving placement of workers.

— Detecting preventable disabilities.

— Controlling communicable diseases.

— Maintaining health at a high level.

First Aid Training: The Factories Act 1948 requires the availability of first aid facilities and it is the responsibility of the personnel officer to see that these requirements are met. It may involve regular inspection, replenishing supplies and provision of first aid training for some employees.

Working Conditions — Science of Ergonomics and Anthropometry

There is a whole new science of ergonomics dealing with the study of working environment and anthropometry dealing with fitting machines to men instead of the other way round which used to be the practice after the industrial revolution. A study of working environment and considerable research and experimentation in working conditions and working environment has clearly established the close correlationship between working environment, productivity and efficiency on the one hand and fatigue on the other.

The importance of working conditions in promoting employee health and welfare need not be overemphasised. The physical working environment has a significant bearing on the psychological well-being of employees. The Factories Act, 1948 dwells at great length on the provision of good working conditions, emphasising good housekeeping, cleanliness, sanitation, lighting, ventilation, colour, humidification, heat. In this section we shall take into consideration the factors that have an important bearing on work environment and employee health such as plant layout, illumination, colour, noise, atmospheric conditions, sanitary facilities and plant housekeeping.

(a) Plant Layout: Apart from functional utility, maximum utilisation of space and engineering efficiency, plant layout must be considered in terms of employee comfort and productivity. Now this has become a sophisticated field and it is better to consult layout experts. There are many instances where a redesigning to layout increased productivity considerably. Generally physical facilities must enhance personal comfort and safety facilities should minimise risks of accidents. Work spaces should be of proper height and layout.

(b) Lighting and Illumination: Good lighting and illumination is essential and acts as a tonic. Generally the following common features of illumination may be noted:

1. Provide for general brightness.
2. Avoid glare.

3. Vary the intensity of light with the type of work.
4. Avoid heavy shadow and strong contrasts.
5. Provide uniform and diffused lighting.
6. Fluorescent tubes, though expensive, may be preferred.
7. Consult illumination engineers.
8. Install a proper maintenance programme.

There is no doubt that proper illumination brings in a good bit of cheer to the employees just as dim light may depress an employee and make him miserable, apart from increasing hazards of the light of the employees.

(c) Colour: There is evidence to show that colour increases productivity, economy and safety and reduces accidents, fatigue, strain and absenteeism.[37] Colour is perhaps the least expensive of all devices that can be used to improve the physical appearance of an office and plant. The Wire and Rope Division of The Jones and Laughlin Steel noted a reduction of absenteeism from 5 to less than 2 per cent and a reduction of labour turnover from 4.5 to 0.45 per cent after a colour engineering project had been introduced. The value of colour is most impressive in safety engineering. The Portsmouth Rod & Wire Division of The Detroit Steel had an accident frequency record of 9.2 in the first quarter of 1951. After a colour conditioning plan had been adopted, the figure for the same period of 1952 was 2.3, a drop of 73 per cent.[38]

Generally, it is better to avoid strong colours, and to use pleasing colours, to use subdued and quiet colours, to use reflective colours such as cream or white, and to have an overall colour scheme and plan. Colour dynamics is increasingly becoming important in factories and offices. Before any general painting programme is undertaken, there must be an over-all colour plan that takes into account the size, shape, orientation, special architectural features, type and amount of lighting, number of employees and class of work in each area.

(d) Noise: There is no doubt that constant exposure to noise in industrial situation will produce certain deleterious effects on the employees, their efficiency and productivity; though most of the reactions are psychological they do have a significant impact on employee behaviour and functioning. One is familiar with the employees complaining, "All this noise in here is driving me nuts." There are many industrial experiences where noise control and abatement has yielded many beneficial results. For example, Williams C. Hunter reports[39] that The Leukart Machine Company Inc., cut its noise 35 per cent and boosted productivity 7 per cent through the use of acoustical baffles and also noted these results: (1) increased output — a wage saving of about $ 140 per day for a shop of 150 employees, (2) fewer absentees — a reduction 12 per cent, (3) less personal time, (4) reduced scrap — from 1.2 to 0.8 per cent, or a reduction of 33 per cent, and (5) fewer misunderstandings in order giving and taking. Some suggested techniques for reducing employee exposure to noise are[40] (1) reducing number of employees exposed to noise, (2) reducing exposure time, (3) reducing time of engine operation at full speed, (4) providing silencers for intakes and exhausts, (5) providing acoustical barricades or blast furnaces.

(e) Atmospheric Conditions:

1. *Temperature and Humidity:* Proper temperature and humidity control, air circulation, air conditioning are all of prime importance and these must be tailored to the needs of industrial in such a way as to yield optimum personal comfort.

2. *Ventilation:* Good and proper ventilation provides light, fresh air, removes heat and increases air circulation. It is said at least 30 cubic feet of fresh air is necessary per person per minute and this increases with dust increases in fumes and the like. Fresh air should be introduced in a gradual and continuous manner and the economics and possibility of air conditioning may also be explored.

3. *Odours:* Bad and offensive odours increase labour turnover, absenteeism, poor morale, poor workmanship and lower productivity. They must be removed and masking agents, germicides, changes in ventilation, general cleanliness and maintenance should be adopted.

(f) Sanitary Facilities: They refer to washroom and toilet space and facilities, locker and shower rooms and drinking water facilities. The Factories Act 1948 requires these sanitary facilities, but unfortunately many sanitary facilities try to meet the bare minimum statutory requirements and leave much to be desired, particularly in washroom, toilet and drinking water facilities. Not much attention is paid to maintenance and general hygiene. But then there are many companies in U.S.A., who spend a good deal of money in providing these facilities and believe that they will pay and 'results justify the cost.'

(g) Plant Housekeeping: Daily and periodic clean-up and maintenance of available facilities and overhauling, repairing, painting, replacing of physical facilities must be carried on in a systematic scheduled way. Arthur D. Buschman reports[41] that The Perfection Stove Company of Cleveland follows the following steps in its clean-up programme: (1) Design of facilities for easy housekeeping; (2) Provision of adequate janitorial facilities; (3) Establishment of "off-hour" cleaning; (4) Unification of Janitor force; (5) Mechanisation of janitor jobs; (6) Provision of aid to good housekeeping; and (7) Organisation of the work.

In general, good working conditions improve employee morale, efficiency, productivity; they must promote healthy and desirable environment; and they promote good public relations. They attract and retain good persons and reduce labour turnover, absenteeism, tardiness and apathy. Professor John F. Mee, based on evidence gained through actual experience, maintains that a good industrial health programme:[42]

1. Assures healthy personnel.
2. Avoids entrance of potential human liability by preventing assignment of workers to jobs on which they should not work.
3. Improves efficiency of work.
4. Assures satisfactory products.
5. Reduces labour turnover.
6. Promotes safety.
7. Improves employee relations.
8. Reduces absenteeism on account of sickness.

9. Guards against fraudulent illness or accident claims.
10. Reduces the cost ratio of insurance.
11. Protects against public criticism.
12. Provides necessary date for decision as to employee physical fitness.
13. Affords proper job placement.
14. Makes for loyal and courteous employees.
15. Promotes community relations.
16. Improves the trade position of the company.

Safety — Total Loss Prevention

The new concept in management regarding safety and accident prevention is the total loss prevention where we are not only talking about the damage to human beings and injuries but also damage to the property of the Company and its prevention. The concept of total loss prevention transcends the narrow limits of individual safety and accidents and embraces the total concept of loss prevention on account of human injuries as well as property damages. The concept is a logical first step in the evolution from injury prevention to total accident control (damage to facilities, equipment, and material), fire prevention, industrial health and hygiene, pollution of air, water and soil.

Safety and accident prevention are of prime importance to management and the personnel administrators are deeply involved in organising and administering a safety and accident prevention programme. Public policy, unions, and management have attempted to combat the problem of accidents and safety. In India the Factories Act 1948 requires the employers to introduce safety measures relating to the fencing of machinery, casing of new machinery, testing and examination of appliances such as hoists, lifts, cranes, chains and pressure vessels, supply of protective equipment to workers, precautions against dust, fumes, gases and fire. The State governments are empowered to make special rules for certain dangerous operations specified by them. The Mines Act and The Indian Dock Labourers Act also stipulate various safety measures in mines and docks. The employer must be (1) sincerely interested in the promotion of safety; (2) must initiate sound safety policies and programmes, safety education and training; (3) must provide the necessary safety devices to protect the employee; (4) must have the complete co-operation and support of the union; (5) must furnish leadership and initiative in the introduction of safety programme; (6) must encourage the employees to offer suggestions to improve safety and to prevent accidents.

Safety Programme: Earl W. Wheeler has outlined the basic elements of a safety programme.[43] In any organisation the basic elements of a safety programme will be very much the same:

First, a safety policy statement by the management;

Second, competent staff direction;

Third, active participation by management;

Fourth, an all-inclusive personnel (safety) programme;

Fifth, inspection;

Sixth, accident records.

In some cases not all of these elements would be fully developed initially. Any successful safety programme, however, eventually contains all of these elements and the degree of success will be proportional to the completeness with which each is developed.

T.O. Armstrong comments more fully:[44]

"A few musts should be considered before (discussing) specific plans for safety organisation:

1. Safety must have top management approval, sanction and support.
2. Responsibility for safety must rest with the supervisory personnel.
3. Safety must be given equally important consideration with other factors of production.
4. Provision must be made for prompt action in the elimination of mechanical and personal hazards.

A definite programme should be developed to interest and educate all employees in safety and to secure their active co-operation in effect to eliminate accidents. Such a programme must be based on the full assumption of its responsibilities by the management. The programme must supply leadership and executive drive. Safety must be included in all phases of planning, purchasing, supervision and operation. Once these fundamentals are understood by management, and it fully assumes the responsibilities that are involved, the appropriate type of organisation can be evolved. But it is well to remember that whatever from the organisation takes, it will function effectively only if it is backed by executive interest and drive. Proof of this is furnished by the fact that each type of safety organisation is to be found among firms that have attained and continue to maintain a standard of first-rate performance in eliminating accidents."

Organisation of Safety: In larger companies there may be separate department of safety under the personnel division or under a medical division or it functions as an independent department reporting directly to the chief executive officer. But in general, safety is one of the functions of personnel management and there may be specialists in charge of safety under the personnel division. In some companies safety committees with representatives from labour and management are used to organise and administer safety programmes. The responsibility for safety lies with unions, employees and employer and these responsibilities are summarised by Harold C. Zulauf:[45]

In safety planning and programming the following principles are fundamental:

1. Safety primarily is the legal and moral obligation of the employer. The employer must have a sincere and continuing interest in providing for the safety of employees. This interest is demonstrated by:

(a) The initiation of a sound safety programme with the policies, procedures and staff necessary to make it effective.

(b) The provision of safe working conditions, machinery and equipment and personal safety protective devices and apparel where necessary.

(c) The development of effective training programme for supervisors and employees.

(d) The encouragement of employee interest and participation by making available channels through which employees may offer suggestions, advice and recommendations for the improvement of safety.

Management must have the authority necessary to carry out its responsibility. No steps should be taken which create confusion and uncertainty as to management's responsibility and authority.

2. Co-operation in the safety programme is the moral obligation of each individual employee. This is demonstrated by:

(a) Working safely at his job.

(b) Having regard at all times for the safety of fellow employees.

(c) Using his knowledge and influence to prevent accidents.

(d) Calling attention to unsafe conditions.

(e) Contributing his ideas, suggestions and recommendations for the improvement of safety.

3. In unionized plants the welfare of the employees places upon the labour union a moral obligation to co-operate in accident prevention, within the framework of its agreed-upon participation. This is demonstrated by:

(a) Taking its agreed part in the safety programme in the plant.

(b) Using its influence in encouraging the employees it represents to work safely.

(c) Promoting accident prevention through its publications, union meetings and educational course, with emphasis not only upon plant safety but also with due regard to safety in the home, on the highway and in other activities outside the plant.

TEN POINTS ON SAFETY FOR MANAGEMENT

1. Provide safe plant and tools.	6. Plan operational process with care.
2. Organise safety programme.	7. Place no new machines without full attention to safety.
3. Enforce safety recommendations.	8. Invite departmental reports.
4. Safeguard all machines.	9. Study statistical data on accidents.
5. Publish safety bulletins.	10. Conduct periodical plant inspections.

An outline of the activities of the safety department may be as follows:[46]

1. The maintenance of necessary accident records and data.
2. Collaboration in foreman and supervisory training.
3. Collaboration in job training programmes.
4. Stimulation of and assisting in the prevention of safe operating rules.
5. Preparation and supervision of the distribution of educational material as it pertains to specific hazards of the job.

6. Continually keeping top management advised of progress on the over-all programme.
7. Assisting in the design of machine guards, where such are necessary.
8. Describing and standardising the necessary personal protective equipment.
9. Collaborate with medical department on occupational disease, sanitation and related problems.
10. Either investigate or have investigated all injuries and accidents to determine causes and necessary preventive measures.
11. Collaborate with engineering and purchasing departments in reviewing plans and specifications with regard to safety.
12. Review job procedures regarding the details of how the job should be done, so that any hazards can be properly defined and corrective methods be incorporated in the job procedures themselves.
13. One of the specific duties of the person in charge of accident prevention activities would be to maintain and direct plant safety inspection.
14. The man in charge of the accident prevention programme fulfills a staff function. He should be given the authority to stop production only in those cases involving an immediate hazard where it is not possible nor practicable for him to handle the situation through the usual channels of the foreman or supervisor in the department involved.

The Southern India Millowners' Association (SIMA) has produced a brochure on Industrial Safety and Accident Prevention to help the member mills.

ACCIDENT PREVENTION

Perhaps it is well to remember that accidents do not just happen, but they are caused and they can be minimised, if not altogether eliminated. In order to do this an efficient programme of accident prevention provides the following factors:

(1) Establish reporting procedures of accidents, even minor ones.
(2) Study the accident rates.
(3) Study the people and departments involved in accidents.
(4) Study the accident environments.
(5) Analyse and tabulate all the facts concerning accidents.
(6) Determine course of action.
(7) Assign responsibility for action.

There are mechanical factors, environmental factors and personal factors which cause accidents and one summary lists all the causes of accidents:[47]

ACCIDENT CAUSES

I. Faulty Environment

1. *Hazardous Arrangement:*
   (a) Unsafe piling and storage.
   (b) Congested working space
   (c) Inadequate aisles, exists.
   (d) Unsafe processes.

(e) Overloading.
(f) No safe access to remote or high places.

2. *Unsafe material and equipment:*
(a) Rough and sharp-edged materials.
(b) Inherently slippery surfaces.
(c) Poorly designed and constructed equipment.
(d) Low material strength (floors, hoisting equipment, etc.)
(e) Weakening of parts by rust, corrosion and decay.

3. *Illumination:*
(a) Insufficient light.
(b) Unsuitable location of light sources.

4. *Ventilation:*
(a) Insufficient air change.
(b) Impure air source.
(c) Contamination by processes.
(d) Excessive heat.

5. *Moving machinery:*
(a) Unguarded.
(b) Inadequately guarded.

II. The Human Element

1. *Physical and mental characteristics:*
(a) Poor eyesight.
(b) Defective hearing.
(c) Muscular weakness.
(d) Slow mental reaction.
(e) Lack of co-ordination.
(f) Heart, circulatory or other organic weakness.
(g) Lack of nervous and emotional stability.

2. *Knowledge and skill:*
(a) Ignorance of correct methods.
(b) Faulty work habits.
(c) Insufficient experience.

3. *Attitudes:*
(a) Indifference.
(b) Inattention.
(c) Indolence.
(d) Arrogance.
(e) Recklessness.
(f) Hostility.

Accident Causes Are Found By

1. Investigation of accidents.
2. Study of plant accident experience.
3. Studying accident experience of other plants.
4. Plant inspections.
5. Suggestion systems.
6. Job analysis.

Measurement of Accidents: Accidents can be measured in a direct way or indirect way. Indirectly, accidents can be measured through production loss, absenteeism, increased costs, labour turnover, low quality products as a result of accidents. The more direct measures are the frequency rates and severity rates of accidents. Frequency rates can be measured through the formula:

Frequency rate of accidents (per 100,000)

$$\frac{\text{Number of lost-time accidents}}{\text{Total man-hours worked}} \times 100,000$$

Severity rate can be measured by adopting the formula:

Severity rate of accidents (per 100,000)

$$\frac{\text{Number of man-hours lost through accidents}}{\text{Total man-hours worked}} \times 100,000$$

Accident frequency and severity rates vary from industry to industry. In U.S.A. high frequency rates are common in coal mining, other mining, meat packing and woodworking. High severity rates are noted in coal mining, other mining, lumbering, construction and marine transportation.

Costs of Accidents: The National Safety Council (U.S.A.) calculations embrace the following cost items:[48]

1. The premium on compensation insurance or payments on compensation by self-insured companies.
2. Cost of wages paid for time lost by workers who were not injured.
3. Cost of damage to equipment.
4. Cost of wages paid for time lost by injured worker other than workmen's compensation payments.
5. Extra cost due to overtime work necessitated by the accident.
6. Cost of wages paid to supervisors while their time is required for activities resulting from the accident.
7. Wage cost due to decreased output of injured worker after return to work.
8. Cost of learning period of new worker.
9. Uninsured medical cost borne by the company.
10. Cost of time spent by higher supervision and clerical workers on accident investigation or processing compensation applications.
11. Miscellaneous unusual costs.

Cost calculation is an important element in accident analysis an in safety programme administration and evaluation.

Accident Proneness: There are some employees who are involved in accidents more than others and they are said to be 'accident prone.' It is important to detect such accident prone individuals and give them safety training and education and place them on safe jobs, where the chances of exposure to committing accidents are less. The proceedings of the President's Conference on Industrial Safety note:[49]

"To demonstrate the existence of accident proneness, it is, therefore, necessary to show that the accidents do not distribute themselves by chance among the total group. Two lines of evidence show that this is so. In the first place, there are more people with no accidents at all, and more people with multiple accidents, than would be predicted by chance. Secondly, there is a tendency for those individuals who have multiple accidents in one period of time to continue to have multiple accidents in later period of observation."

Some companies attempt to train and educate such accident-prone employees in safety matters; some go to the extent of providing psychiatric help also; and in extreme cases some companies discharge them. Many others believe in eliminating this problem at the selection process by careful job analysis, by testing general abilities, and by studying the worker's physical characteristics, particularly in relation to physical defects and limitations. This is an ideal approach of reduction of accidents by the elimination of accident-prone applicants in the selection process.

Safety Engineering: Safety engineering is an important aid in the minimisation of accident and promotion of safety and this may encompass the following aspects:

1. Provide for proper fences and safeguards for moving machines and machine parts.
2. Set up standards and provide necessary protective equipment for handling, transporting and using materials such as acids etc.
3. Provide proper illumination, ventilation, flooring, noise, colour and sanitation.
4. Avoid slippery, smooth, shining floors.
5. Provide safety clothing, glasses, shoes, respirators, gloves and other items.
6. Provide proper preventive maintenance and good plant housekeeping.
7. Develop safe operating methods and educate the worker to use them.

Safety Education: A safety education programme, designed to 'sell' safety and safety consciousness among all including executives, supervisors, line and staff employees, is necessary and it must have complete support and approval of top management. Enlisting the co-operation of all persons in the safety programme is part of safety promotion. Safety education may be imparted via posters, bulletin boards, house-organs, pay envelope messages, displays, cartoons, slogans and signs, and safety films. The employer must not only the persuaded to engage in safety education but also support in providing necessary safety equipment and in adequately maintaining them.

Safety Training: Safety training is part of safety education. Every new employee must be given safety training in the first week of his appointment and the older employees must also be provided with retraining. The supervisor plays a vital role in promoting safety consciousness through safety education and training. T.O. Armstrong has outlined the elements of a safety training programme:[50]

1. A safety method of performing each job operation or sequence of operations is developed and described in simple but adequate detail.
2. The various hazard points are brought to light clearly described, together with the relationship between these and the various steps in safety method.
3. The teaching is systematic and thorough. In the somewhat idiomatic English of one successful teacher it is:

(a) Tell him.
(b) Show him.
(c) Have him do it.
(d) Correct him until he has it.
(e) Supervise him to see that he keeps it.

4. The reason for requiring the wearing of personal protective equipment needed, if any, as goggles, safety shoes, hand protectors, and the like is explained and its proper use and care taught in full detail.
5. Specific safeguards needed for the protection of the worker or his fellows are similarly explained and their correct usage taught.

Through lectures, visual aids, demonstrations, meetings and conferences, safety training can be imparted. It is also desirable to publicise accident records and their costs to the employee, company and the community. Some companies dramatise this aspect to impress upon the workers the gravity of the problem.

Safety Contest: Inter-departmental and intra-departmental safety contests may also be held and the winning departments are given prizes and also given a good deal of publicity. Both monetary and non-monetary incentives may be offered to promote safety consciousness among employees.

Safety Rules and Enforcement: A set of safety rules must be prepared and communicated to the employees. These rules must be strictly enforced. Where there is an infringement of safety rules, disciplinary measures must be provided and the employees must know what is coming when they break safety rules. It is indeed surprising how so many people do not care for these rules and pay a penalty through a lost hand, stubbed toe, knocked out skull etc. Often safety goggles, or protective handgloves may be left unused by employees, but such carelessness must be effectively disciplined, before it hurts the employee badly — and the company too.

Finally safety measures and programmes must be constantly evaluated by checking the accident frequency and severity rates, production loss and by comparing with similar units. Safety performance appraisals must be used periodically. Fire extinguishing, plant protection and disaster combating techniques must also be emphasised in a safety programme. Safety always pays, provided you let it.

Safety Audit: It is pointed out that there has been a significant decline in the number of lost time accidents in the steel company after the Safety Engineering Department introduced a system of 'Safety Audit' in 1960. This Safety Audit consists of periodical inspections, noting safety hazards, reporting them on a standard form and follow-up action at specified intervals at different levels, namely, departmental heads, general superintendent, general manager and even the director, if need be. The company has also adopted a system of "Safety Communication Zone" according to which the steel works has been divided into different zones and the worker-steward and a member of the Safety Committee representing a particular zone are responsible for communicating all decisions and programmes concerning safety to the employees of their zone. These two systems have resulted in various improvements in matters like lighting, work practices, guarding of machines, and quality of safety appliances procured, etc.

In the steel company, there has been a marked decline in the number of fatal and non-fatal accidents from 5 and 1823 respectively in 1964 to 2 & 1559 in 1965; and to 9 & 771 respectively in 1996. The accident frequency rates have also steadily declined from 20.34 in 1964 to 14.1 in 1965 to 12.25 in 1966.

In conclusion, the following table is given to illustrate the practices prevalent in U.S.A. in the area of health and safety. This table is adapted from the NICB study:[51]

Table 12.3

HEALTH AND SAFETY PRACTICES

Practice	*Total Companies* No.	%
Total respondents	426	100
Companies that require employees to wear safety clothing	330	77
Companies that train employees in first aid	294	69
Companies that require exit physical examination for employees	27	6
Companies that require a pre-employment physical examination	364	85
Companies that require periodic physical examination	126	30
Companies that require a physical examination of employees returning to work after an illness	239	56
Companies that retain the following medical personnel:		
Doctor		
Full time	30	7
Part time	175	41
On call	170	40
Nurse		
Full time	211	50
Part time	4	0
On call	9	2
Psychiatrist		
Full time	2	0
Part time	1	0
On call	10	2
Dentist		
Full time	4	0
Part time	2	0
On call	8	2
Optometrist		
Full time	1	0
Part time	9	2
On call	26	6
Industrial hygienist		
Full time	12	3
Part time	1	0
On call	9	2
First aid attendant		
Full time	90	21
Part time	24	6
On call	21	6

Note: Other medical personnel retained include: X-ray technician (6 companies), psychologist (2 companies), skin specialist (1 company). Also 3 companies indicated that they operate a full-time hospital or clinic service. Out of some 276 companies (100%), without air conditioned facilities in the plant, 30 (11%) close early due to excessive heat or humidity. Out of some 68 companies (100%) without air conditioned facilities in the plant or office, 16 (4%) close early due to excessive heat or humidity.

5. EMPLOYEE MORALE AND WELFARE

There are a variety of services offered by the company to the employees, mainly with a view to improving worker morale and welfare as well as to maintain or increase the efficiency of the workforce, and these company services are usually referred to in our country as welfare activities. Employee services are typically non-financial and are sometimes called "non-financial services", unlike other employee financial benefits and services. Nevertheless, they cost money to the company and many employee services are called "non-wage payments" or "hidden payroll." These employee services are offered for a variety of reasons. Early paternalism of employers, statutory provisions, union demands, competition, management's desire to promote morale and welfare, and team spirit, union-management relations have all combined to produce a plethora of company services to the employees.

The Factories Act, 1948, requires the employees to provide various welfare amenities such as washing facilities, shelters, rest rooms, lunch rooms, canteens, creches, cycle sheds, spittoons, housing etc. In the mines, employers are required to provide creches, canteens, shelters for rest and taking food, separate lockers for men and women, sanitary latrines, showerbaths etc. In the plantation, they are required to provide canteens, creches, education facilities for the employees' children, recreational facilities, umbrellas, blankets, raincoats, etc. Usually there are welfare funds who finances come from the collection of fines and levies, which are utilised in defraying the cost of various welfare activities.

In the plantations every employer is required to provide housing to the employees and standards of housing are also fixed by the Plantations Labour Act, 1951. The government offers a subsidised Industrial Housing Scheme, from which employers are given a subsidy of 25 per cent of the cost of construction of houses for their workers and a loan assistance of 50 per cent of the approved cost. The loan is repayable in instalments.

Apart from these statutory provisions, many other employee services are offered.

Purpose of Employee Services

Yoder, Heneman Jr., Turnbull and Harold Stone enumerate the following general purposes:[52]

1. For the Company

1. Increase output.
2. Reduce turnover and absenteeism.
3. Increase employee morale.
4. Increase employee loyalty toward the company.
5. Increase employee participation in company affairs.
6. Reduce grievances.
7. Reduce influence of present or potential unions.
8. Increase welfare of employee in connection with his personal and social needs.
9. Improve public and community relations.
10. Facilitate recruitment and retention of employees.

2. For the Employee

1. Provide conveniences and facilities not otherwise available, or available, in less convenient form.
2. Provide assistance in solving personal problems.
3. Increase job satisfaction.
4. Contribute to personal advancement and well-being of individual employees.
5. Provide a means of becoming better acquainted with other employees.
6. Reduce feelings of insecurity.
7. Provide additional opportunities to attain status.
8. Provide extra compensation.

Some specific services are offered with specific purposes to meet certain specific needs. Often little attention is paid to this aspect of the needs, but any successful personnel activity must be dictated by the needs of the company and next by the needs of the employee.

Need Determination

The need for services may by determined through the following devices:

(1) Questionnaires, (2) exit interviews, (3) suggestions, (4) gripe sessions, (5) complaint letters, (6) interviewing and counselling, (7) training programmes, (8) activity committees, and (9) study and analysis of production records, scrap reports, labour turnover, absenteeism and grievances.

Companies are known to use one or more of these devices for the determination of a need for a particular employee service. In order to attract and maintain a capable workforce, it is essential to meet the needs of the employees. Only after determining the need for a certain employee service, it must be organised and provided to the employees.

Often a company starts a "package" programme because another company is operating them, but it is to be checked whether a certain item in the package is needed or not. Every service must be subjected to this "need test."

MANAGEMENT CHECKLIST

Management Check List for Determining Need For, And Planning For, Employee Service Activities.

1. What indication is there that a need for service activities exists?
2. What source or sources of information produced this evidence?
3. Has this evidence been checked by any other available means?
4. Is this a company as well as an employee need?
5. Does it appear to be a long-term need?
6. Is the need felt by a significant percentage of the employees?
7. Is the company the most logical agency to meet this need?
8. Is this the time to attempt a solution to need?
9. Is there a possibility of meeting this need through some service activity?
10. Would the needs of the company be met?
11. Would the real needs of the employees be met?
12. Are services seriously wanted by the employees?
13. Would the service be objectionable to any group of employees?
14. Is the service to be a maintenance, preventive, or curative measure?
15. Can this need be better satisfied through some other avenue?

Fig. 12.1

Source: John F. Mee (ed.), *Personnel Handbook* (New York: The Ronald Press Company 1955), p. 572.

Range of Employee Services

Earlier a complete range of employee morale building and welfare services is given and most common services are athletic and social events, service awards, credit unions, co-operative stores, recreational and cultural programmes, counselling and guidance, transportation, canteens or restaurants, savings and loan facilities, housing and townships. The other services and benefits like pensions, health, safety services etc. are already discussed. The following table, adapted from the NICB study,[53] gives the various services offered by American companies and the extent of their prevalence.

Table 12.4

EMPLOYEE SERVICES

Practice	*Total Companies*	
	No.	*%*
Total respondents	508	100
Companies having a company-sponsored recreation programme	300	59
Companies having an employee recreation association	124	24
Companies having a athletic or recreation field	72	14
Companies having a recreation club-house or separate recreation building	37	7
Companies having a recreation room (not a club-house or recreation building)	26	5
Companies having a library	186	37
Companies having clubs especially for retired employees	21	4
Companies sponsoring employee Christmas parties	210	41
Companies having employee picnics	222	44
Companies having open house programmes	40	8
Companies having religious activities	12	2
Companies having service award programmes	364	72
Companies having long-service clubs	161	32
Companies having parking facilities	487	96
Companies assisting with daily transportation	75	15
Companies assisting present employees to find housing	168	33
Companies having blood banks	192	37
Companies requiring employees to wear uniform	243	48
Companies that pay for cleaning or replacing of clothing soiled on the job	90	19
Companies with a cafeteria on the premises	237	47
Companies with a mobile lunch service	110	22
Companies with a special room (not cafeteria) for employees who bring their own lunch	204	40
Companies with vending machines for candy, soft drinks etc.	488	96
Companies having an employees' credit union	271	53
Companies making loans to employees under a company plan (not a credit union)	123	24
Companies paying temporary living expenses for newly hired employee and his family until they establish new residence	52	10
Companies paying all or some of the moving expenses for newly hired employees who must change residence to accept employment	262	50

Companies selling company products to employees at a discount on company premises or in a company store	53	10
Companies having an arrangement by which employees can buy company products at a discount from retailers in the local community	33	6
Companies having arrangement with local retailers (or wholesalers) for discounts on non-company products	94	19
Companies selling non-company products on company premises	50	10
Companies supplying the following special services (with or without charge):		
Notary Public	216	43
Loan of company equipment	109	21
Obtain theatre tickets	51	10
Post Office	44	8
Obtain Licences	41	8
Registration of voters	26	5
Hotel or travel reservations (non-business trips)	17	3
Obtain passports	12	2
Vacation planning	12	2
Barber shop	9	2
Laundry (other than uniforms)	7	1
Dry cleaning (other than uniforms)	3	—
Facilities for payment of utility bills	3	—
Beauty Parlour	1	—
Shoe Repair	1	—
Assistance in preparation of personal income-tax reports	74	15
Assistance in preparation of wills	18	4
Legal advice other than preparation of Wills and personal income tax	47	9

For purposes of discussion here these employee services are broadly categorised as follows: (1) Professional, (2) Recreational and social, (3) Employee conveniences, (4) Auxiliary.

1. Professional Services

In addition to professional help given in health and safety programmes, there are other professional services offered to the employees such as legal aid, vocational guidance, employee counselling.

Legal Aid: Employees may need legal assistance on various issues such as wills, income tax returns, traffic violations, financial matters, help in real estate matters, naturalisation procedures, instalment-purchase and other contracts, family problems etc. These services may be provided by at outside law firm or a company legal division. The employees may be directed and assisted in hiring legal experts in private practice.

Employee Counselling: Professional counsellors are provided to counsel and guide employees on a variety of personal problems, which may result in employee's absence, tardiness, grievances, turnover, accident etc. Such employees need professional help. Secondly, counselling is also used in induction interviews, exit interviews, communication programmes, transfer and promotions, appraisals, discipline and grievances. Thirdly, counsellors can train line people and supervisors in the art of counselling, because all of them will need to counsel sometime or the other. Fourthly, the counselling such as industrial minorities, women, veterans, old workers, physically handicapped, occupationally unadjusted people, economically unadjusted people and socially unadjusted people. Lastly, professional counselling for executive is also necessary.

Vocational Guidance: Vocational guidance experts are used for proper placement and selective placement, which will result in job satisfaction for the employee and efficiency on the job for the company. Such experts can help in transfers, promotions, selection and training. They provide occupational counselling to the employees. In order to promote efficiency in the allocation and utilisation of manpower, professional trained vocational guidance experts play a very useful role.

2. Recreational and Social Services

Recreation and social activities play a very useful role in an individual's life and they afford a sense of relaxation, teamspirit and togetherness. They include social get-togethers, informal associations, clubs, athletics and sports, picnics, welfare centres.

1. Clubs: Many companies organise a variety of clubs depending upon the interests of the employees. Some companies have *dramatic clubs*, where, the employees stage plays for the benefit of not only the company employees, but also the general community. Dramatic clubs are pretty popular and they may stage radio dramas. There may be a flying club. Some companies in U.S.A. have organised flying clubs for their employees, although this is flowers, vegetables and develop parks. They may conduct flower shows and competitions may also be conducted involving some prizes. In some companies employee orchestras are common and they may conduct concerts. They may play popular music or classical music. They perform on radio. There are dance bands, glee clubs and military bands.

Then there are a great many varieties of clubs catering to special interests of employees such as chess clubs, boxing clubs, bridge clubs, camera clubs, cards-playing clubs, tennis clubs, football clubs, cricket clubs, swimming clubs etc. For some of these clubs such as cricket, football, tennis etc. companies hire famous cricketeers, football players, tennis players, respectively and these players provide a great deal of advertising and publicity to the companies. Some companies also conduct state or national level tourneys or championships that bring enormous publicity to the company. The D.C.M. in Delhi conducts D.C.M. Football tourney at Delhi and the best teams are invited to play and lakhs of people come to watch the game and D.C.M. becomes very popular. The Lakshmi Mills of Coimbatore conduct at Kovilpatti a hockey tournament, which draws teams from all parts of India and which is a popular tourney.

2. Physical Facilities: Many companies provide physical facilities for these clubs in the form of club house, equipments, for the clubs such as footballs, cricket bats, balls, pads etc. There may be welfare centre, where all the facilities may be available.

3. Parties: Companies organise with the help of employees various social get-togethers and parties. Dance parties are common. Games and contests are popular and small prizes may be awarded. In U.S.A. Christmas parties, Halloween, Thanksgiving, New Year's parties are all very common. There may be parties on certain festival days like Puja parties, Deepavali parties etc. Employees and their families may participate.

4. Athletics and Sports: Organising athletic events, cricket matches, football matches, basket ball matches, table tennis matches, tennis matches, volley ball, bowling, soft-ball, golf matches for employees are very common during off-hours or during holidays and week-ends. These games and events are popular with employees who come in great numbers either to witness or enjoy the game.

5. Picnics: Picnics are a very popular practice with many companies. Picnics may be educational, for sightseeing, for pilgrimage, or just for entertainment and relaxation. Employees may bring their families among in some instances. There may be hunting trips, fishing trips, or gardening trips. Many employee participate in and enjoy picnics.

6. Welfare Centres: Some large units provide welfare centres where the employees can get together for their various club activities. Then there are film shows screened in these centres and they are very popular. Films of entertainment and educational value are shown widely patronised by the employees.

Organising a Recreational Programme

The Socony Mobil Oil Company offers the following suggestions for organising a recreational programme:[54]

A steering committee should be appointed to decide on the date and meeting place for launching and pushing the activity. Logically, its members should be drawn from the group that seems enthusiastic about the plan. The first meeting of this committee to lay the foundation for the activity should consider:

Organisation: Purpose of club; discussion and agreement on objectives and values; survey of existing and needed facilities and equipment.

Finances: Estimation of costs and probability of keeping within this budget.

Leadership: Selection of officers and committee; discussion of plans for constitution and by-laws, and conditions of membership — if club is to be formally drawn up and kept on business-like basis though its atmosphere may be informal.

Future Meetings: Time, place and frequency of future meetings.

Publicity: Personal contacts, house-organ write-ups, bulletin board, posters, notices, P.A. system announcements.

Follow-up: Letters of thanks to give credit and recognition to those who helped build spirit and unity in the group.

Other points to be discussed, settled and kept in mind: what one person is to be responsible for the care and storage of equipment?

What about practice time, company policies in regard to the activity, meetings on company time?

What assistance may be depended upon from management?

Could a citywide league or council be formed in this particular activity?

What safety factors must be taken into account?

How could this activity tie in with other activities — for example, in combination events?

Could movies, or talks by leading authorities in this or some related field, be effectively used as part of special planing events?

As far as possible, the executives of the company must show keen interest in these recreational and social programmes and actively participate in them. Executive participation is very healthy and stimulates a great deal of interest among employees. In organising these programmes, employee initiative and suggestions must be welcomed and they must be involved from the idea and planning stage in order to ensure the success of these programmes and to see that the expected beneficial results flow from these activities to the employees and the company.

3. Employee Conveniences

A great many variety of employee services are offered to promote employee comfort and convenience and here only the important convenience services are discussed. Most of these services are offered on management initiative, whereas some are required by law and some are demanded by unions.

Canteens or Restaurants: Canteens on a non-profit basis are required to be provided by Factories Act, 1948, in all the plants employing more than 250 worker and the Rules under the Act stipulate certain standards of construction, accommodation, furniture and other equipment, food-stuffs and charges and also require the setting up of a joint canteen managing committee with union and management representatives. A lunch break must be provided. In our country while there are some companies, who offer excellent canteen facilities, excellent food at subsidised rates, there are many whose canteen facilities are extremely poor, to put it mildly. IIPM notes:[55] "Both food and service in the canteen cause frequent problems for the personnel department, just because everyone is interested in food, and everyone has ideas about it, and is prepared to air it. Canteen committees are required by the Rules under the Factories Act, and obviously workers must be consulted if the service is to be satisfactory, but it is often difficult to get constructive suggestions from canteen committees, because what most people want involves additional expense. Canteen cost must be placed before the committee in order to overcome the suspicion that management is trying to save by cutting down canteen expenditure."

In U.S.A. in-plant feeding and food services are almost as old as industry itself and as early as 1928, 85 per cent of the factories with 5,000 or more employees had food services. Cafeteria and restaurant facilities are very common. The aims of the provision of in-plant food services were to improve employee health, morale, efficiency, lessen fatigue, decrease number of accidents and reduce apathy. Types of eating facilities are cafeterias or restaurants, lunch rooms, lunch stands, mobile lunch units, snack and coffee bars and recently vending machines. These facilities may be managed by management alone (usually personnel division) or by union-management or by unions alone or an outside caterer may run these facilities. Generally coffee, milk and other drinks, snacks, sandwiches, soups, desserts, vegetables, meat, beef, ham etc. are offered in these company restaurants. Please refer to the Table 12.4 for the practices in this aspect.

Most companies subsidise the operations of in-plant restaurants and provide relatively inexpensive but good food.[56] The subsidisation ranges from less than 10 per cent to 100 per cent and in dollars, from under $ 10 to $ 100 and over per worker per year. There are a few companies who offer meals free of charge. Out of 237 companies with cafeterias, 49 per cent try to operate them at a break-even point. But some 8 per cent of the 237 companies with cafeterias try to operate them at a profit. The meals provided in the cafeteria include breakfast, mid-morning snack, lunch, mid-afternoon snack, meals for overtime workers, meals for second shift, meals for third shift and meals for special meetings. Anywhere from less than 10 per cent to 100 per cent of the employees use the cafeteria.

The profits made from the vending operations by the companies are used for a variety of purposes by the 488 companies with vending machines. Some 26 per cent of 488 companies give all profits to an employee fund for social and recreational purposes; 15 per cent give some part of the profits to an employee fund for social and recreational purposes; 11 per cent give all profits to the concessionaire or vendor; 9 per cent retain all of the profits for employee activities, 7 per cent retain some part of the profits for employee activities. Some 9 out of 488 companies use the profits for such purposes as outside charity, employee welfare, local union, safety glasses, credit union, free coffee, scholarship fund, retired employees club, Christmas gifts, apprentices' living quarters and maintenance of room for vending machines.

Credit Unions: The credit unions are voluntary cooperative savings and loan organisations somewhat like a bank, where employees, after becoming members by buying shares worth $ 5 to $ 10, can deposit their savings, withdraw them when they need money, and obtain loans from the credit union. Professor Jucius[57] states that whereas there were only 5,000 credit unions in 1936, there were over 16,000 in 1957, when the loans outstanding amounted to nearly $ 3 billion. The majority of these unions are in the industrial states, with California, Illinois, Michigan, New York, Ohio, Pennsylvania and Texas each having over 800 credit unions and in California alone the memberships exceeds 1,000,000. In the Boeing Aircraft Company alone there are about 47,000 members in the credit union which has funds over $ 65 million.[58]

The employee credit union is managed by its members through an elected board of directors, who administer a credit committee, which screens the applications and sanctions loans; and supervisory committee, which audits all records and accounts. There is usually a full-time credit manager or treasurer. Some companies provide office space for the credit unions. The NICB study[59] found that 84 per cent (228 out of 271 companies) provided office space and some 28 per cent paid clerical assistance for the credit unions. The provision of check-off and advice and counsel are the other company services to the credit unions.

In an NICB survey, companies reported to following experience with credit unions:[60]

1. Advantages to employees — promotion of thrift, source of credit at lower rates than attainable elsewhere, relief from money worries, avoidance of illegal money lenders, and handling financial problems without embarrassment.
2. Advantages to employers — better employee morale, improved industrial relations, greater employee efficiency, elimination of requests for company loans and wage advances, and material reduction in wage assignments and garnishments.

3. Criticism of credit unions — in three-fourths of the companies, there were no adverse criticism. Some firms felt that loan policies were too lax — some felt they were too strict. A few companies reported that union officials spent too much time on clerical work for the credit union during working hours.

The companies are interested in the success of credit unions as they are one of the best ways of providing savings services to the employees, in addition to loans.

Company Stores or Co-operative Stores: Many companies operate a company store, where employees can purchase various provisions needed for them at a relatively low price when compared to market price. Some companies sell only company products in these stores at cost or at a wholesale discount or at retail discount anywhere from 5 per cent to 50 per cent. Some companies arrange for the sale of non-company products in these stores at cost, or at a discount on retail or wholesale price varying from 10 per cent to 40 per cent and they arrange for the retailers in town to sell company or non-company products at cost or discount rates. Several companies sell products in their stores at different prices ranging from a mere token payment to cost plus 10 per cent or wholesale plus 15 per cent. In some cases these stores facilities are provided for the retired employees also. Most sales are no credit basis which is recovered in instalments at wage source. These stores have been found to be very useful by the employees, who appreciate this service.

But in some cases the companies have exploited the situation where there were no other stores and where they would attempt to make money at the expense of the worker. Some view this as wage-cutting device. By offering credit they would keep the employee in debt for ever and make his mobility difficult. Many retailers are opposed to these stores, because they take away quite a bit of their business.

In our country a common service of this sort is the co-operative stores, where the employees, by virtue of membership through the purchase of share, enjoy the facilities provided by these stores. These stores are managed by a joint committee or a union committee or in some cases by the employer alone. Generally, these stores provide the essential commodities required by the employees, such as foodgrains, pulses, vegetables, edible oils, sugar etc., at a nominal profit, which may be ploughed back or distributed among the employee shareholders. Particularly when the prices in our country are rising constantly, the co-operative fair price shops are a help to the employees. Credit is given and recovered from wages in monthly instalment. Some collateral is required and the practice varies considerably.

Housing: In our country, as earlier pointed out, The Plantations Labour Act, 1951, requires the employer to provide housing and the Government offers the subsidised Industrial Housing Scheme to help the employers provide housing facilities for the employees. Housing is very serious and difficult problem, particularly in urban areas and the Housing Ministers' Conference in 1958 expressed disappointment at the poor response of the employers in utilising the Governmental assistance towards providing housing facilities. On the other hand, in some centres like Bangalore, Jamshedpur, Chittranjan etc. lovely industrial townships have come up providing very good housing facilities, along with educational, recreational, medical, cultural and sports facilities. In Bangalore the Indian Telephone Industries (ITI) and Hindustan Machine Tools (HMT) and TISCO and TELCO in Jamshedpur provide excellent townships with excellent facilities. Houses with basic and comfortable amenities are provided for low rent to the workers, usually on the basis of seniority. Apart from family quarters, bachelor quarters are also provided for the unmarried. Some companies operate plans for ownership of houses by employees and the most notable one, started as early as 1938, is the famous Harveypatti Housing Colony by the Madura Mills Company Ltd., at Madura. Operated by a co-operative society, whose funds come from the mills and the members and with a management representative as its president, the employee can own the house after paying rent for twelve and a half years.

Under the Five Year Plans, targets were established to increase industrial housing, plantation and mining housing, but Table 12.5 shows that most of the scheme have fallen short of targets.

In U.S.A. there has been a declining trend in the provision of company housing services; but this service is still prevalent in the textile, cement, auto, lumbering and mining industries. However, fewer and fewer companies are providing company-owned facilities, because the company wants to concentrate on production problems, not real estate problems; the employees don't want to live in a company township and want to choose their living places; employees do not like company supervision of their housing. The increasing trend is to encourage employee home ownership, which makes for desirable employees and these homes may be scattered over the entire community.

Housing Assistance: Most companies prefer to give various types of housing assistance in the form of loans and financial assistance and payroll deductions. The NICB study[61] reports that out of 168 companies that assist employees to find houses or apartments to rent or purchase, the methods used do assist employees are: (1) utilising notices on company bulletin boards (73%), (2) maintaining listing (49%), (3) publishing notices in company publications (19%), and (4) having real estate contacts and make referrals (17%). Some additional ways of aiding the employees are: Some 16 companies (out of 168) pay for advertisements in the local newspapers; 10 use the personnel department to assist employees; 6 give tours of living areas in the community; and 1 company holds the employee's home, pending sale.

Transportation: Transportation services play a vital role in a company's ability to obtain an adequate labour supply, particularly when the company is situated far away from the community. Some companies in our country operate company buses at nominal rates or at cost of transport employees back and forth. Some collaborate with public transit system and arrange for buses or trains to ply for the benefit of the employees. Some provide assistance to employees in the purchase of their own transport, usually cycles. Cycle sheds are required to be provided by law on company premises and some companies also provide a guard for the shed.

The aim in providing this service is to enable the employees to arrive on time in relative comfort at minimum cost without having to walk a great distance and to cut late coming, absenteeism, turnover and production loss and inefficiency.

Table 12.5

PARTICULARS OF HOUSING UNDER THE PLANS

	First Plan		*Second Plan*					*Third Plan*	
	Sanctioned	*Completed*	*Target*		*Sanctioned*		*Completed*	*Target*	
			Rs. crores	*Units '000*	*Rs. crores*	*Units '000*	*Units '000*	*Rs. Crores*	*Units '000*
1. Subsidised Housing	79.7	43.8		128	24.2	61	57	29.8	73
2. Low Income Group Housing	41,000	n.a.	40	68	37.8	45	53 (total since 1954)	35.2	75
3. Slum clearance Sweeper's Housing	—	—	20	110	9.9	50	n.a.	26.2	100
4. Plantation Workers' Housing	—	—	2	11	0.14	0.7	0.3	0.7	4
5. Miners' Housing	—	—	8	30	1.26	13	—	14	60

Source: Report of 10th Annual Convention of Hind Mazdoor Sabha, May 5-8, 1962, Coimbatore. p.142.

In U.S.A. most workers ride to work in their own cars or organise car pools and ride with co-workers. Principal company services in this respect are the provision of parking facilities, formation of car pools, collaboration with public transit system and other supplementary service. Some operate free bus service for the employees; some may subsidise employee bill of transportation, some provide taxi service, particularly for women late in the night.

Parking facilities are important and in the N.I.C.B. survey[62] 96per cent (487 out of 508) provide parking facilities and only 2 per cent (10 out of 508) charge the employees for the use of parking lot at $ 1 to $ 2 per week or $ 1 to $ 6 per month or $ 14 per tenure of employment. Parking lot guards are provided by some and some companies offer reserved areas for parking. Of the 487 companies with parking facilities 7 companies provide some services such as car wash or minor repairs on the parking lot. But only 15 per cent (75 out of 508 companies) give daily transportation assistance and only 3 companies operate company buses. This is mainly due to the fact that most of the employees own their cars and drive to work. For auto purchase the company may give financial assistance.

Music: In order to help overcome employee monotony, fatigue, boredom, emotional tensions and to provide relaxed, soothing and rhythmic atmosphere, in-plant music is provided by several companies. In U.S.A. one-eighth of the firms provide in-plant music and it is found to increase employee morale and productivity, to reduce accidents, to decrease rates of tardiness, absenteeism and turnover.[63] Generally music should be provided if a majority of workers desire it and the music must be that which is enjoyed by them. Music may be provided all the time, or at some regular intervals or during lunch or coffee breaks and employee tastes in music must be catered to. In our country though a majority of firms do not provide in-plant music, there are some who do.

4. Auxiliary and Miscellaneous Services

There are many other employee services that, for convenience sake and lack of better term, are categorised as auxiliary and miscellaneous and a brief description of the important ones is made.

Loan Services: Apart from the credit unions, some companies offer a loan service through their philanthropic foundations or through a Loan Fund Scheme. The purpose is to provide loans for employees, who need them for a variety of reasons such as illness, accident, death in the family, any financial emergency, education of employee or his children, marriage, child birth, home repairs or remodelling, home purchase or auto purchase. The loans are recovered through payroll deductions on monthly instalments and for bigger loans employees must produce security. Out of 508 companies in U.S.A. some 123 (24%) make loans to employees under a company plan.

Several companies operate an Employee Savings Plan to promote thrift and savings which will benefit the employees.

Educational Services: Under this category the most common are: (1) libraries, where there may be hundreds to thousands of books — general or technical or both; (2) reading rooms, where magazines, periodicals, journals, newspapers etc. are provided for employee use both for relaxation and education; (3) schools, where some companies may offer vocational schools, high schools, night schools and adult classes. Special lectures on family planning, health, personal hygiene, safety etc. may be given; (4) tuition aid, where companies may reimburse part or whole of the tuition fees either for the employee's or for his children's education; (5) film shows of educational and entertainment value are frequently shown; (6) information racks, where information about the company, safety, health, politics, government and nation, industry and economy are given. General Motors distributes over one million booklets a month to its employees.

Employee Publications: Many companies publish house journals for internal circulation giving a variety of personal, company, community and national matters. Employee handbooks, giving details about service conditions, holiday, working hours, overtime rules, company facilities, are common among American companies. Then some companies in India and many in U.S.A. give financial reports to the employees in a simple understandable way. Health, safety, training and other brochures, pamphlets, bulletins are supplied to the employees.

Community Service Activities: Companies co-operate with various community activities and the personnel administrators are asked to handle Red Cross and Community Chest drives, Prime Minister's Relief Fund and Famine Relief Fund and other charity drive and to provide assistance in community celebrations, festivals and carnivals. Blood Banks are organised and employees are encouraged to donate blood. Plant tours, furnishing speakers and other educational programmes for schools and colleges are organised by the personnel people. Then the open house programme, designed to impress the public and increase employee's pride in the company, is a popular one.

Long Service Clubs: Service award programmes, designed to recognise and reward the long service of senior workers, are common. The awards graduate with service and 72% (364 out of 508 companies) give awards varying $ 50 for 10 years service to $ 1,000 for 25 years or 35 years or 40 years or 50 years.[64] Many companies (55%) give watches and most of them (62%) at 25 years service. Other items used for service awards are pins and buttons, insignia jewellery (charms, tie pins etc.), silver trays, bowls etc. rings, clocks, radios, television sets, cameras, lighters, pen and pencil sets, china sets, book ends, wallets, plaques, Bibles, Birth certificates, company stock and bonds. Long service clubs are organised and they have some honorary, social, welfare and advisory activities.

Moving Aid: Several companies in U.S.A. provide moving expenses to the employees, who must change their residence. All or part of the expenses in relation to the transportation of the employee and his family or moving of household goods or incidental moving expenses, or loss on sale of house or real estate broker's commission are given by the company. Some companies pay temporary living expenses to the new employee and his family ranging from $ 5 to $ 12 per family of three persons (husband, wife and child). Some companies provide real estate help if the employee wants to sell his house or buy a new house.

Charm Course: Some companies provide charm or beauty courses to their employees, particularly girls, where they are taught about dress, postures, beauty care, personal hygiene, telephone etiquette, poise. Some operate beauty parlours where girls are given a shampoo and a hair dressing, and perhaps a new hair-do on Friday nights every week.

Gifts: On certain occasions like marriage of an employee, Christmas, birth of a child, retirement, illness, hospitalisation, Thanksgiving, Easter, Labour Day (in USA), Puja, Pongal, Deepavali, silver wedding anniversary, golden wedding anniversary, employee birth, death of employee or one of his family or a retired employee in India, gifts are given to the concerned employees. The companies send some small gift ranging from flowers at the time of illness or death to cash, bonds, radios at the time of retirement, to turkeys and ham at Thanksgiving. At the time of festivals, clothing is often presented to the employees. Work uniforms are provided by most and some provide laundry service also for washing the uniforms.

Company Religious Activities: Some companies sponsor and support religious activities for the benefit of the employees. A company temple, or Church or a Mosque is also provided. In the N I C B survey 65, out of 12 companies with religious activities, 4 have company chaplains, 7 religious activities, 3 religious counselling, 2 meditation and 2 Bible reading and films.

In most of the leading organisations in India prayer or bhajan mandirs are provided by the companies. For instance, in most of the units of the Mafatlal Group bhajan mandirs are provided for the employees to come together in order to pray and conduct pujas and bhajans on a regular basis.

In conclusion, it may be emphasised that:

1. Employee service must be built around employee needs.
2. Employees must be involved in the planning, organising and administering of these services.

3. These service programming must be kept in balance with other employee relations programmes.

The IIPM states the responsibilities of personnel people:[66]

"Welfare activities usually make heavy demands on the personnel or welfare officer, and involve much expenditure of his spare time. Positive results may sometimes seem rather disappointing, but it is through these activities outside his main job that the personnel or welfare officer can get into close touch with all the employees. The value also of personal visiting of worker's home cannot be overestimated. Through this personal contact the personnel officer will learn much about the background and normal reactions of the employees which he will never know otherwise. In welfare activities his task is to share in a joint endeavour that will deepen mutual comradeship. Leadership he must give, but it must be by way of influence rather than dominance, and most vital of all, he must have understanding. He must study the background, collect the necessary factual data, and then encourage workers and management in the formulation, planning and final execution of the welfare measures."[67]

REFERENCES

1. Robert H. Hoge, "Pinning Down The Problematic Fringe", *The Personnel Function: A Progress Report,* pp. 112-113.
2. *Ibid.*
3. See Austin M. Fisher and John F. Chapman, "The Big Cost of Little Fringes", *Harvard Business Review,* September-October, 1954.
4. Hoge, *op. cit.,* p. 114.
5. *Ibid.*
6. *Ibid.,* p. 115.
7. "Fringe Benefits — 1955", Washington, U.S. Chamber of Commerce, 1956, p. 10. See also: "Computing the Costs of Fringe Benefits", *Studies in Personnel Policy,* No.128, and "Fringe Benefit Packages", *Studies in Personnel Policy,* No. 143, New York, National Industrial Conference Board, 1952 and 1954 respectively.
8. See, for details, *The New Competition: International Comparisons* (New York: N I C B, 1961).
9. Pigors and Myers, *Personnel Administration,* p. 429.
10. Hoge, *op. cit.,* pp. 116-117.
11. Hoge, *op. cit.,* pp. 113-114.
12. See Yoder *et al., Handbook of Personnel,* pp. 17.3-17.6.
13. NICB, *Personnel Practices in Factory and Office, Studies in Personnel Policy,* No.194, pp. 25-28.
14. *Ibid.,* p. 24.

14A. See *Executive Digest,* January 1966.

15. NICB, *Personnel Practices in Factory and Office,* pp. 26-27.
16. *Ibid.,* p. 90.
17. Mary D. Owen, "The Contributions at Vacations to Employee Health", *Industrial Medicine and Surgery,* Vol. 19, No. 4, April 1950, p. 197.
18. See Dale Yoder, *Personnel Management*, p. 197.
19. L.J. Smith, *Collective Bargaining* (Englewood Cliffs, N.J. Prentice-Hall Inc. 1946), pp. 137-136.

20. NICB, *Personnel Practices... Studies in Personnel Policy No. 194,* pp. 88-96.

21. Everett D. Hawkins, *Dismissal Compensation* (Princeton, N.J. Princeton University Press 1940), pp. 5-6.

22. See *Studies in Personnel Policy, No. 194,* pp. 111-112.

23. See Richard A. Lester, "The Economic Significance of Unemployment Compensation", *Review of Economic and Statistics,* Vol. 42, No. 4, November, 1960, pp. 349-72.

24. *Studies in P.P. No. 194,* p. 110.

25. Detailed information regarding OASDI can be obtained from Social Security Administration, which maintains field offices in the main cities in the U.S.A.

26. See *Pension and Profitsharing Service* (Englewood Cliffs, N.J., Prentice-Hall, Inc.), Para 4000.

27. Yoder, *Personnel Management...*p. 518.

28. *Studies in Personnel Policy No. 194,* p. 111.

29. Jay V. Strong, *Employee Benefit Plan in Operation* (Washington, D.C., Bureau of National Affairs, 1951), pp. 116-119.

30. IIPM, *Personnel Management in India,* pp. 249-250.

31. W.E. Park, *Organisation of an Industrial Health Department in a Smaller Firm* (Minneapolis, Minnesota: 1951), pp. 1-2 (mimeographed notes).

32. *Ibid.*

33. Kenneth C. Copeland, "Costs and Profits of Industrial Medical Care", in "Practical Problems of Employee Relations", *Personnel Series No. 149* (New York: American Management Association 1952), p. 5.

34. Prentice-Hall, *Successful Employee Benefit Plans,* (Englewood Cliffs, N.J. Prentice-Hall Inc.), 1952 pp. 23-24. This volume and J.V. Strong's *Employee Benefit Plans in Operation* are two very useful volumes on the planning and administering of health and welfare programmes.

34A. See Harland Fox, "Company Group Insurance — who pays the bill", *Management Record,* Vol. 16, No. 11, November 1954, pp. 425-28.

35. Table adopted from NICB, *Studies in Personnel Policy No. 194,* pp. 98-110.

36. *A Nurse in Your Plant,* Minneapolis, Minnesota, Community Health Service (Visiting Nurse Service) p. 2.

37. See L.J. Murphy, "Build Plant Safety with Colours", *Mill and Factory,* Vol. 51, No. 5, November 1952, pp. 81-85; also Howard Ketcham, "Progress with Colour", *National Safety News,* Vol. 66, November 1952, pp. 28-29, 85-95.

38. See "How Colour Can Motivate Workers", *Management Methods,* May 1954, pp. 28-30.

39. See William C. Hunter, "New Acoustical Baffles Cut Our Noise, 35 Per Cent, Boost Productivity 7 Per Cent", *Factory Management and Maintenance,* Vol. 110, No. 3, March 1952, pp. 114-15.

40. G.L. Bonvallet and D.B. Callaway, "Noise Abatement" in "Industrial Noise", *Factory Management and Maintenance,* December, 1953, pp. 132-136.

41. See Arthur D. Buschman, "7 Keys to Cleanliness," *Factory Management and Maintenance,* Vol. 111, No. 5, May 1953, pp. 78-80.

42. John F. Mee, *Personnel Handbook,* p. 466.

43. Earl W. Wheeler, "Agriculture Speaks on Safety, 1: Basic Elements of a Safety Programme," *Personnel Administration,* Vol. 14, No. 5, September, 1951, p. 22.

44. T.O. Armstrong, in R.P. Blake (ed.), *Industrial Safety* (Englewood Cliffs, N.J. Prentice-Hall, Inc.), 1953, pp. 319-320.

45. Harold C. Zulauf, Chairman, Committee on Labour-Management Co-operation for Safety, U.S. Department of Labour, Bureau of Labour Standards, Proceedings of the President's Conference on Industrial Safety, Washington, Government Printing Office, 1949, pp. 146-47.

46. James E. Trainer, Chairman, Committee of Engineering, U.S. Department of Labour, Bureau of Labour Standards, *Proceedings of the President's Conference on Industrial Safety,* (Washington, Government Printing Office, 1949), pp. 77-78.

47. "Accident Causes", *National Safety News,* Vol. 60, No. 3, March 1950, p. 42.

48. "Determining Accident Costs: Part 1", National Safety News, Vol. 62, No. 2; August 1950, pp. 23-23,82.

49. William P. Yant, Chairman, Committee on Research, U.S. Department of Labour Statistics, *Proceedings of the President's Conference on Industrial Safety*, pp. 283-284.

50. T.O. Armstrong, "Safety Education and Training", in R.P. Blake (ed.), *Industrial Safety,* pp. 335-336.

51. NICB, *Personnel Practices... Studies in Personnel Policy No. 194,* pp. 115-119.

52. Yoder *et. al., Handbook of Personnel Management,* pp. 21-5.

53. NICB, *Studies in Personnel Policy No. 194,* pp. 64-86.

54. See William S. Wilcox, "Organising a New Recreational Activity" (New York: Socony Mobil Oil Company).

55. IIPM, *Personnel Management*, pp. 256-57.

56. All the material in this section is borrowed from the NICB, *Studies in Personnel Policy No. 194,* pp. 76-78.

57. Jucius, *Personnel Management,* p. 591.

58. Voice of America Breakfast Show Programme, Interview with Credit Manager, Boeing Aircraft Company.

59. *Studies in Personnel Policy No. 194,* p. 78.

60. Summarised from NICB *Studies in Personnel Policy No. 42,* pp. 14-17.

61. *Studies in Personnel Policy No. 194,* p. 73.

62. *Ibid.,* p. 72.

63. For details on the effects of music, See W.A. Kerr, "Experiments on the Effects of Music on Factory Production" (Stanford University Press, Applied Psychology Monograph, No. 5, American Psychological Association, 1945); and H.C. Smith, "Music in Relation to Employee Attitudes, Piecework Production and Industrial Accidents" (Stanford: Stanford University Press, Applied Psychology Monograph, No. 14, American Psychological Association, 1947).

64. NICB, *Studies in Personnel Policy No. 194,* pp. 70-71.

65. *Ibid.,* p. 69.

66. IIPM, *op. cit.,* pp. 275-76.

67. For greater details regarding the employee welfare services in the leading organisations in the co-operative, public and private sectors in India, please see M.N. Rudrabasavaraj, *Personnel Administration Practices in India.*

❑ ❑ ❑

CHAPTER 13

Human Relations and Motivation

In the words of the great Sophocles, "The wonder of wonders is man" and there is no doubt that man is the most dynamic animal. He has an infinite capacity to think, to create, to develop, to discover and invent, to produce, to feel, to love, to dream, to conquer, to master, to achieve, to give, to live, to respect, to play, to pray and to do as well as to destroy, to hate and to kill. He is the most complex being there is. His behaviour and conduct may also be most unpredictable. He can do infinite good and infinite bad as he chooses or as he is led to choose. But above all he is human although at times his conduct and actions may border almost on the inhuman side. He is not a machine. He is not merely a commodity that can be bought and sold.

This human element is the predominating factor that affects his relations with others in society, or in industry, or in business. This human element is perhaps the non-business character that greatly influences his business character and the two are inseparable. 'The whole man', who comes to the day shift, carries with him both the business character of a worker and also the non-business character of man, father, husband, brother etc. This whole man is a complicated human being with various emotions, aspirations, fears, desires and ambitions, likes and dislikes, prejudices and fads and he meets works with other men with similar or dissimilar feelings, emotions and aspirations in a factory. There is a constant interaction and interplay of these various dynamic human factors and it is the business of managers to harness these dynamic human factors and it is the business of managers to harness these dynamic forces and weld them together to work towards common goals of the company. The art and science of human relations movement after considerable research and study, have evolved various theories, tools and techniques for management to use in the industrial and business spheres. It is the major duty and responsibility of personnel administrators to assist and advise top and line management in this vital area of human relations. The discussion on human relations and personnel management proceeds under the following headings:

1. What is human relations in management?
2. Human relations and motivation.
3. How to handle human relations problems?
4. Personnel administration and human relations.

1. WHAT IS HUMAN RELATIONS IN MANAGEMENT?

The following are some of the authoritative definitions or descriptions of what is meant by human relations in management:

In the words of Yoder, Turnbull, Heneman Jr. and Harold Stone:[1]

"It is difficult to define the term 'human relations' because it appears to mean different things to many different people. In essence, the varying definitions appear to include the following 'essentials.' Human relations programmes represent an attempt to improve employee morale and motivations through improved three-way communications and through employee participation in decision-making processes. Human relations seek to emphasise 'employee' aspect of work rather than technical or economic aspects. In brief, human relations seek to make employment and working conditions less impersonal.

On the positive side, the *human relations approach* emphasises policies and techniques designed to improve employee morale and job satisfaction. It is believed that this will be accompanied by increased employee efficiency and reduction of employee unrest."

Professor John F. Mee defines human relations as follows:[2]

"Good human relations in business and industry is the medium for effecting the maximum satisfaction of the economic, social and psychological wants of all people having relations with an organisation which has the objective of increasing productivity. In a broader sense, human relations is the art of successful living. But it is the business and industrial definition of human relations with which the personnel programme and management are concerned...human relations is the medium through which both employees and the company mutually cooperate to achieve more production through higher morale, which, after all, is the economic purpose of all business and industry."

According to Mr. Robert Saltonstall:[3]

"Human relations is the study of people in action. Executives in upper or middle management, teachers, and students recognise that today's business organisation involves a complicated network of relationships among people. The manager's job is to co-ordinate the efforts of these people so that they will work together toward a common goal. To lead effectively he must understand these relationships and know how to build teamwork that leads to peak productivity. His decisions and actions always affect people. He must find ways to strike a proper balance between the needs of his people and the needs of the business. A proper understanding of human relationships will help him to do this."

Professor William G. Scott's definition is as follows:[4]

"Human relations is a process of effective motivation of individuals in a given situation in order to achieve a balance of objectives which will yield greater human satisfaction and help accomplish company goals."

"Human relations is the term commonly applied to the process of focusing the methodology and findings of a number of behavioural science disciplines on human problems. The human relations approach to problem solving is, therefore, labelled *interdisciplinary*. Management uses human relations to determine a course of action for unravelling problems of human conflict and human satisfactions in business. *Management action through human relations requires the application of behavioural science principles to promote human collaboration and social solidarity within the social system of the business organisation."*[5]

Simply stated, human relations is the art and science of accomplishing predetermined company goals, the process of which promotes individual efficiency and satisfaction and group solidarity and effectiveness as well as company productivity, profitability and growth and, in the ultimate analysis, the harmonisation of the interests and aspirations of the company on the one hand and individual and the group on the other.

Human Relations Research

Considerable research on human relations is being carried on by the universities, professional management associations, research institutions, companies in U.S.A. and some in India also.

The famous Hawthorne studies conducted by Professor Elton Mayo and his team of researchers and the findings of those studies represents the core of human relations theory and practice. Several books, that were the result of Mayo's experimentation for a period of more than a decade have remained as the important contributions to human relations literature.[6] It is well known that many of the concepts and hypotheses that are being tested through the above-mentioned researches originated in the field of psychology, sociology and anthropology. An interdisciplinary approach was evolved and the Table 13.1 suggests the interdisciplinary framework.

In 1947, the Survey Research Center, Institute for Social Research of the University of Michigan, initiated a ten-year human relations research based on direct observation of organisations with two major criteria to evaluate the effectiveness of organisations, departments or groups:

1. Productivity per man-hour, or some similar measure of the organisation's success in achieving its productivity goals.
2. Job satisfactions and other satisfactions derived by employees or members of work groups (as determined in most instances through opinion survey questionnaires).

Table 13.1

HOW SCIENCE BECOMES PRACTICE IN HUMAN RELATIONS

Science	*Techniques*	*A clinical point of view and method*	*Professional Practice*
1	*2*	*3*	*4*
Psychology	Applied psychology		Administration
Sociology	Applied sociology		
Anthropology	Applied anthropology	Human Relations	Personnel relations
Physiology	Applied physiology		
Engineering	Scientific management		Labour relations

Based on F.J. Roethimsberger, "Human Relations: Rare, Medium, or Well Done?" *Harvard Business Review*, January 1948, p. 103 adapted.

It is found that there is a consistent pattern of motivational principles and their application has found to be associated with higher productivity and job satisfaction, irrespective of the particular companies or industries that have been studied.

Professor Rensis Likert stated:[7] "The critical weakness of the scientific management approach, of course, are the resentments, hostilities and adverse motivational and attitudinal reactions which it tends to evoke. The underlying motivational assumption upon which scientific management is based is that it is only necessary to buy a man's time and he will then do willingly and effectively everything which he is ordered to do. Management textbooks emphasise authority and control as the foundations of administration."

The critical weaknesses of the scientific management approach occur at precisely the point where human relations research approach has its greatest strength — motivation. The great power of human relations research findings is in the understanding and insight which they provide as to:

1. The character and magnitude of the powerful motivational forces which control human behaviour in working situations.
2. The manner in which these forces can be used so that they reinforce rather than conflict with one another.

The fundamental problem, therefore, is to develop an organisational and management theory, and related supervisory and managerial practices for operating under this theory, which will make use of the tremendous resources of the scientific management concepts while fully utilising in a positive and reinforcing manner the great power of all the major motivational forces which influence human behaviour in working situations.

Human Relations Assumptions

The eight operating assumptions, which represent a consensus among writers on effective measures to improve and promote successful management human relations practice, are listed by Professor William G. Scott:[8]

1. Good human relations practice is the product of the manager using experience, intuition and interdisciplinary generalisations to guide him in the action he takes.
2. Employee participation is often essential to higher productivity and greater human satisfaction.
3. The role assumption stems from the variety of demands and individual "job-oriented role" and the "informal group-oriented role."
4. Communication has often been referred to as the nervous system of the organisation. Anything which impairs the functioning of the communication system will limit organisational effectiveness in terms of the accomplishment of business objectives.
5. Teamwork is an indispensable element of management practice for organisational survival. Teamwork is a matter of mutual anticipation and agreement on goals.
6. Man is *diversely motivated*; he has a hierarchy of needs which are quite changeable.

7. The plant or office is a social system. Viewing the work situation as a network of variable and inter-related elements is a major feature of modern human relations practice for the executive.
8. Executive skills in human relations practice can be developed. The executive can be trained to be aware, sensitive and competent to cope with the human problems of the organisation.

Professor William G. Scott maintains:[9] "Business is a framework in which the behavioural sciences have application. They combined anthropology, sociology, psychology, social psychology, political science and economics to offer a point of view of human behaviour. Business is a vehicle in which behaviour is subjected to the scrutiny of analysis to derive data and generalisation. From these data and principles, the executive may find information useful to him for understanding, predicting and motivating human action."

The essence of the human relations philosophy is to cultivate and develop an environment where the employees as individuals and in groups would wish to contribute their best to the organisational goals and this environment is cultivated and developed where there is an awareness of the needs, aspirations, feelings and emotions of the employees on the part of management.

With awareness comes a better understanding and explanation of the behaviour patterns of the individuals and groups and constant interaction between them and interpersonal relationships. Management must use this understanding to promote employee participation, to motivate employees and to remove human relations problems. Behind this whole philosophy of human relations lies the fundamental fact that employees are human beings entitled to certain amount of respect as individuals, who will contribute their best to organisation provided their needs are satisfied on the job. Managers must analyse the human relationships in a given environment related to a particular situation dealing with not merely individual but also interpersonal aspects at a given point of time in order to have a complete understanding of the total situation, which has its unique, unusual and special aspects that can be identified sometimes easily and sometimes not so easily. It is this interplay and interaction of so many forces that render understanding, analysis and evaluation difficult. But one may agree with Mr. Saltonstall when he observes:[10]

"It is obvious that human relationships present many pitfalls to the untrained observer who tries to draw quick and generalised conclusions about them. However, evidence is accumulating on all sides that executives can vastly improve their capacity to understand and deal with the bewilderments of human relationships and the problems that arise at home, at work and in the community.

"Instinct and guesses are giving way to reasoned understanding. Although certain rather clearcut skills of observation are called for and can be learned through practice and experience, perhaps the fundamental requirement is that the executive develop a sound, objective way of thinking about people including himself, in industry. This makes him naturally sensitive to behaviour of those about him. *He becomes interested enough in people as such to reflect on the causes of their behaviour and how they can be helped to work more effectively together.*"[11]

Mr. Saltonstall also suggests a framework for analysing a total human situation in the Fig.13.1.

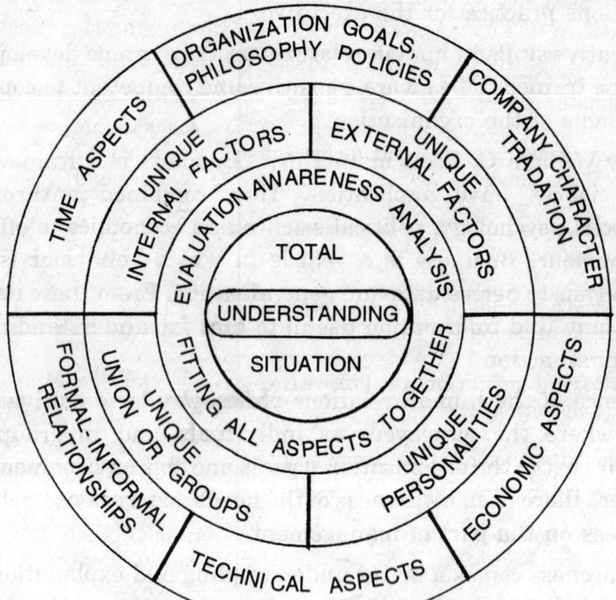

Fig. 13.1 Framework for Analyzing a Total Human Situation
Source: Robert Saltonstall, *Human Relations in Administration*, p. 278.

The result of human relations approach is the minimisation of conflict and misunderstanding, the encouragement of the will to collaborate and the promotion of solidarity in the social system.

2. HUMAN RELATIONS AND MOTIVATION

There is no doubt that motivation is the key to the promotion of proper good human relations. Rensis Likert calls motivation "the core of management which shows that every *human being earnestly seeks a secure, friendly and supportive relationship which gives him a sense of worth in face-to-face groups which are most important to him... a supervisor should strive to treat individuals with dignity and a recognition for their personal worth.*"[12]

It is needless to drive home the point that every individual, regardless of race, colour, rank, status, nationality, caste, deserves respect and recognition of his worth as a human being and craves for them. Deny him these, you have reduced his effectiveness on the job, because he is resentful and he has a deep but justifiable grouse. The ILO team, back in 1950s pointed out that human relations is the weakest point of management in India. The most serious lacuna in employer-employee relationship in our country is that management, save for a few cases, have largely not succeeded in communicating to the mass of illiterate migrant workers a sense of tremendous challenge, a sense of participation, a sense of national awareness and purpose and the worker has a significant role to play in the terrific transition that is taking place in India. When the worker does not get the necessary constructive guidance and leadership from the management, he turns to others, who may use him for their own ends. Addressing the Seventeenth Annual Conference of the Indian Institute of Personnel Management held at Coimbatore on March 11-13, 1967, Mr. R.S. Pande Resident Director of TISCO on the theme of "Maximising the effectiveness of Personnel Management", explained that the industrial worker is an "uncommon child" requiring guidance and leadership from management and through good human relations and proper motivational plans management must satisfy his needs so that he may become a productive industrial citizen.[13]

Motivation and Human Satisfactions

Life is a search for satisfactions. It is necessary to find out what satisfies the individual and to know something about what makes man to do what he does. If the motivations of the individuals can be identified, a good start is made. Various authorities have identified various drives, motives, or needs of the individuals which motivate them and management must strive to satisfy these motivations. It is said that attitudes pave the way for the development of motives and depending on a particular motive, a certain behaviour is chosen. Professor Roethlisberger developed "X" Chart, shown in Fig. 13.2, to portray the relationship of attitudes and behaviour.

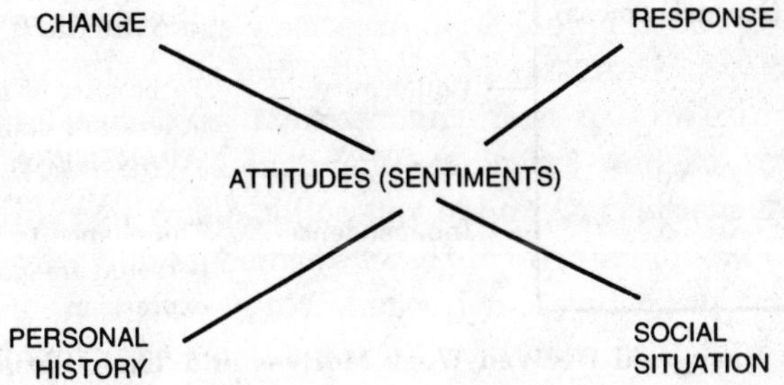

Fig. 13.2 The "X" Chart

Source: F.J. Roethlisberger, *Management and Morale*, p. 21.

The relationship of attitudes, motives and behaviour are shown in Fig. 13.3:[14]

Heredity / Experience / Environment → Make up an individual's Background → Attitudes → Motives → Course of Action Behaviour → goal

Fig. 13.3 The Relation of Attitudes, Motives & Behaviour

According to Professor Scott, motives imply that resulting behaviour will be consciously directed toward a goal. The goal may be viewed as a specific satisfaction for a specific motive. "Motives can be satisfied through numerous forms of activities including religion, education, social service, family life and many more. Of course, work is a channel of satisfaction of a number of learned human motives. Fig. 13.4 shows a system of classification of work motives illustrating their relationship to primary drives, basic and their ultimate requirement of satisfaction."[15]

Prof. Scott has interpreted Figure 13.4 as follows:[16]

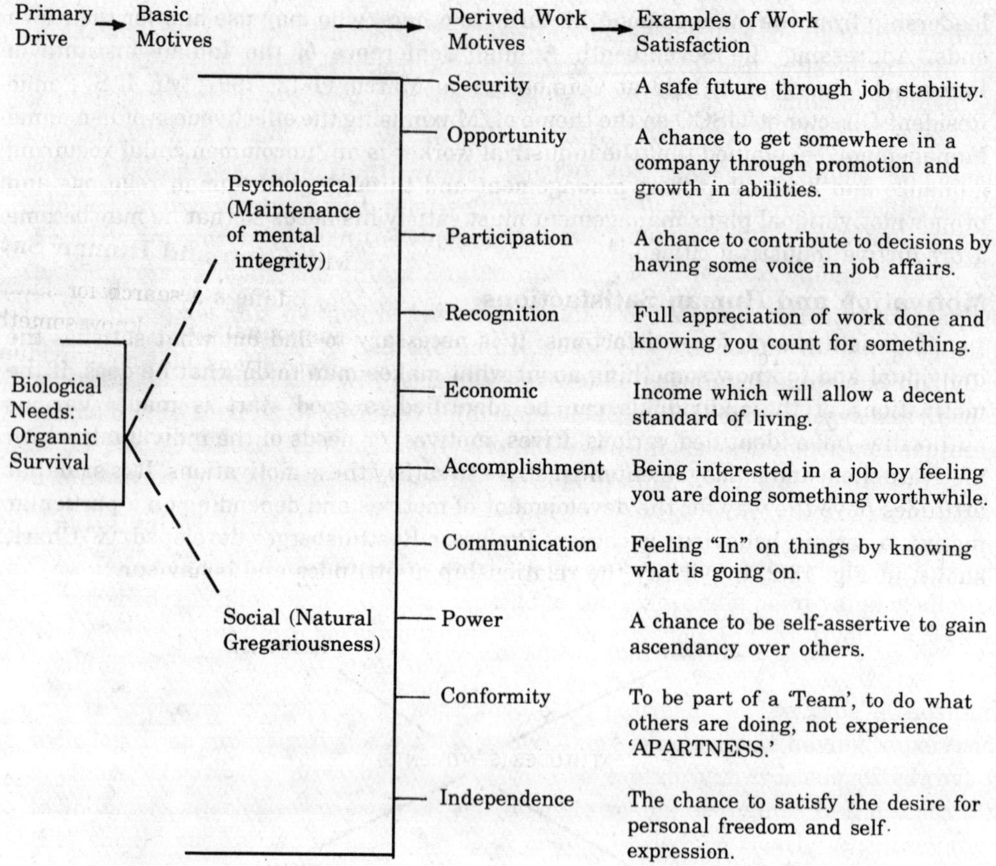

Fig. 13.4 Basic and Derived Work Motives and Their Satisfaction

Primary Drive: The biological drive, already mentioned, requires the satisfaction of these basic needs essential to maintain physiological integrity — organic survival. The nature of satisfaction for this drive is specifiable. The need for food, water, rest, air and elimination is necessary, for the survival of the human organism, even though the level of satisfaction of these biological requirements differs from person to person.

Basic Motives: There are two basic motives — psychological and social. The psychological motive results in a quest by an individual to maintain his mental integrity or balance. The social motive stems from the natural gregariousness of man and his need to associate with his fellow men.

Unlike the biological drive, it is impossible to generalise and predict the specific routes individuals will follow to satisfy these motives. Further, the satisfaction of basic motives is volitional. Although it was said that the social motive is basic for man in general, the example of a hermit or recluse comes to mind immediately to demonstrate the volitional character of this category of motives.

Derived (Work) Motives: This last category provides the richest source of motives underlying human behaviour. The ten derived work motives are only a few of many possible reasons why people work. These motives are derived from the basic social and psychological motives. But they are not connected in a specific way to one or the other basic motives. Who can say with any degree of certainty that the recognition motive is social or psychological in origin? The only possible way to find out is by studying an individual, not by generalizing to whole population.

Derived work motives have the interesting characteristic of being highly dynamic in nature. In this regard, (1) each person at a point in time has a certain hierarchy, a special ordering of importance of the derived motives; and (2) when the motive which is first on his "list" is satisfied, it slips in urgency and another motive takes its place.

Thus when research studies in worker motives turn up the "Discovery" that money is not on top of the list of motives for a group of employees, the obvious conclusion is not that money is no longer important, money is still vital but it is not the only reason for working. Once the basic income requirement is satisfied, for a time at least.

The Requirement of Satisfaction: Management is in part responsible for the satisfaction of derived work motives. The satisfactions are suggestive; and some satisfactions appear to be mutually exclusive of others. Each individual may interpret his requirement for the satisfaction of a particular motive differently. One job of manager who is attempting to improve his motivational ability is to determine what his subordinates expect in terms of satisfaction for their unique motives.

Generalizations will neither accomplish this job, nor will statistical studies of the hierarchy of employee motives. No substitute exists for managerial insight and sensitivity when it comes to perceiving the type of motive satisfaction required by each employee. Understanding individual motive is a day-to-day task.

Furthermore, motivation is a function which a manager performs in order to get his subordinates to achieve job objectives. It is not merely a management process and there is another side to it — the individual being motivated. Psychologists call individual motivation a state of tension. According to Viteles, motivation represents an unsatisfied need which creates a state of tension or disequilibrium causing the individual to move in a goal-directed pattern toward restoring a state of equilibrium by satisfying the need.[17]

Management should be aware that the strength of tensions, and therefore the strength of motivations vary. John W. Atkinson views motivation strength in the form of an equation:[18]

$$\text{Motivation} = f\,(\text{Motive} \times \text{Expectancy} \times \text{Incentive})$$

The strength of motivation to perform an act is a function of:

1. *The strength of the motive* which is the position of a motive in the individual's hierarchy of motives, representing a level of urgency for fulfilment.
2. *Expectancy* which is the probability that the act will obtain the goal.
3. *The Value of the incentive* which is the reward hoped for by obtaining the goal. The greater the rewards, the greater will be the motivational strength provided the other two factors remain equal.

Scott observes that[19] "motivation is not an automatic nor is it a one-sided management process. Individual motivational tensions are social, psychological as well as economic in origin. Knowing that unmet motives, expectancies and value systems of individuals provide management with the concrete information necessary to perform the *process* of motivation considered in the more traditional sense." An overall approach to motivation may be visualised in Fig. 13.5.[20]

Key questions, to ask about the employee and yourself

1. What are the employee's attitudes?
2. What are the employee's motives?
3. What is the strength of his motivation?
4. How do I, as manager, feel about his motives and attitudes?

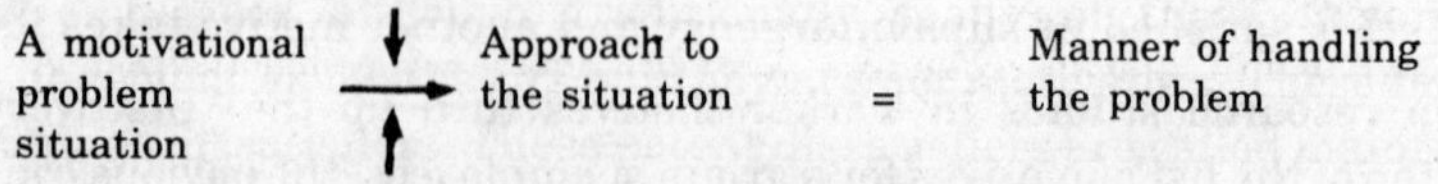

Fig. 13.5 An Approach to Motivation

Key Questions to Ask about the Work Situation

1. What factors in the physical and social job setting are relevant to the solution of this problem?
2. To what extent does the company policy circumscribe actions that might be taken to solve the problem?
3. Are there any outside organisations, like a union, which may affect the problem?

Professor Mee lists the following human drives which are to be satisfied by management:[21]

1. ***Hunger and Security Drive:*** Under this are included the human drives to secure food, shelter, security, to avert pain and to gain physical pleasure.
2. ***Sex and Family Drive:*** In this classification are included the love of the family, the gregarious drive, the drive of worship and sense of duty and the desire to be liked by one's fellow men.
3. ***Mastery and Self-Esteem Drive:*** The drives of mastery and self-esteem as a group classification include the drives for self-respect; rivalry drive; desire to be recognised, respected and liked by the group; the drive of pride; the desire of possession; and the desire of understanding.

Theories of Motivation

People go to work in order to satisfy their needs and aspirations. These needs are not constant but change according to circumstances, status, environment, society, groups. From *Prof. A.H. Maslow,* we have a theory of motivation where he identified a hierarchy of needs as shown in the Fig. 13.6 below.

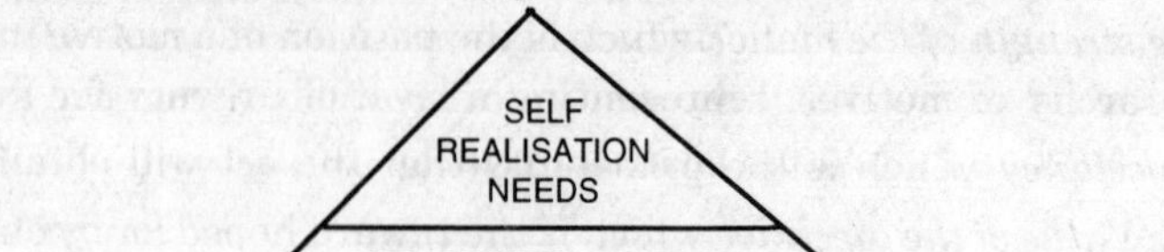

Fig. 13.6 A Hierarchy of Needs

First of all, the individual has the basic physiological needs such as food, shelter, clothing etc. and he works in order to earn to be able to satisfy these needs. Once these needs are satisfied he moves on to a higher plane of needs. Secondly, he has safety needs such as security, protection etc. Once these needs are met he moves on to work in order to satisfy the third type of needs called social needs, where he needs social acceptance. The fourth type is needs for self-respect and self-esteem. The last are the needs for realising the fullest stature of the individual or self-fulfilment and self-actualisation. When a person realises his fullest potentialities or has the opportunity to grow to his fullest stature he is completely satisfied.

Unsatisfied needs are motivators and satisfied need ceases to be a motivating force at a given point of time, under a given situation or set of circumstances.

Lower Order Needs: A person needs only so much food in order to satisfy his needs of hunger and thirst. Once this is met, he does not wish to have more food. Rather it becomes his wish to satisfy other needs and he moves on to seek to satisfy higher types of needs. The basic physiological needs and safety and security needs are considered to be the lower order needs which are primarily satisfied through economic behaviour. He earns money as a medium of exchange to purchase in order to satisfy physiological and security needs. As long as this lower order needs are not completely satisfied, the individual continues to strive to seek to satisfy these needs.

Higher Order Needs: His higher order needs, viz., social, self-esteem and self-actualisation needs, on the other hand, are primarily satisfied through symbolic behaviour of psychic and social content. While it is considerably easier to satisfy the lower order needs, it is difficult to achieve satisfaction in the area of the higher order needs, more particularly, the last need of self-actualisation. A very few people attain this goal in their lives. Secondly, to that extent, there is untapped and unexploited reserve of human capacity although this may vary from society to society depending on its sophistication of management and organisation. This, of course, is a serious problem in less developed countries like India where there is a tremendous under-utilisation of human capacity which results not only in a great loss to gross national product but also a great loss to personal psychic income of an individual. As Prof. Adam Curle, Harvard economist pointed out, the underdeveloped countries have remained underdeveloped, largely because the people are underdeveloped having had no opportunity to rise to their fullest stature and utilise their maximum capacities.

A study of managers in U.K. and U.S.A. reports that security, belonging, esteem and self-realisation needs are progressively less satisfied, according to the pattern of need-priority model. Another study of managers in the United States reports that their higher order needs are less satisfied than their lower order needs. In addition, first level supervisors feel less satisfied than middle managers. This relationship agrees with the need priority model because the supervisors have fewer privileges of office and therefore, are less likely to fulfil higher order needs. Another study supports the model by showing that managers and professionals in the United States highly value self-realisation, while service and manual workers value job security most highly.

The model also seems to apply to underdeveloped countries where the emphasis is mostly on basic physiological needs. A survey of 200 factory workers in India report that they give top priority to job security, earnings, and personal benefits — all lower order needs.

Motivation-Maintenance Theory: Based on original research in the Pittsburgh area by *Frederick Herzberg* and associates a significant development in motivation research is the distinction of motivational and maintenance factors in the work situation. Maintenance of hygiene factors are those which belong to company policies and administration, supervision — inter-personal relations — supervisors — working conditions, pay, job security, personal life, status. Herzberg propounds that these factors help in removing discomfort, dissatisfaction and discontentment on the part of the employees although traditionally many of these factors are perceived by management as motivators but they are not motivators. These factors are really more potent as dissatisfiers. These potent dissatisfiers are called maintenance factors on the job because they are necessary to maintain a reasonable level of satisfaction in employees. They are also known as hygiene factors because they support employees' mental health. But in themselves, they are not motivators according to Herzberg and his team.

The real motivators that primarily build strong motivation and high job satisfaction among employees are achievement, recognition, advancement, work itself, possibility of growth and responsibility. You may give a person fancy title, a large salary, thick carpets, fancy office, car and many other perquisites associated with the good life of an executive but remove challenge, achievement, growth, responsibility, recognition, the individual will not be motivated and he well feel a tremendous loss of personal challenge and worth.

In his book, *Work and the Nature of Man*, Herzberg presented his now famous Adam/Abraham summary of the two views of man's nature. As Adam, man is regarded as animal. He tries to satisfy basic needs — food, shelter, security, the hygiene factors. As Abraham, he is a human being with an intellect; he seeks to fulfil his talents by doing things that allow him to develop his potential — the motivational factors.

Herzberg also expounded his KITA principle. Traditional managers regard man as Adam, and they apply negative or positive KITA, prodding, or enticing him with hygiene factors to perform better. "Negative KITA is rape and positive KITA is seduction" he wrote. "Why is KITA not motivation? If I kick my dog, he will move. And when I want to move him again, what must I do? I must kick him again. Similarly, I can charge a man's battery and then recharge it, and recharge it again. But it is only when he has his own generator that we can talk about motivation. He then needs no outside stimulation. He wants to do it."

The Herzberg model adds something to the need priority model by showing the distinction between maintenance and motivational factors and showing that motivational factors are mostly derived from the work itself. Of the six motivational factors shown below, the first four are clearly intrinsic motivators and the remaining two are substantially intrinsic.

However, it must be mentioned that in less developed countries it is likely that workers will designate some of the maintenance factors or hygiene factors as motivators, since they are yet to meet some of their lower order needs.

Maslow's need-priority model	**Herzberg's motivation-maintenance model**
Self-realisation and fulfilment	Work itself Achievement Possibility of growth Responsibility
Esteem and status	Advancement Recognition
Belonging and social activity	Interpersonal relations — Supervision Peers Subordinates Supervision — technical
Safety and security	Company policy and administration Job security Working
Physiological needs	Conditions Salary Personal life

Goal Theory: Goal setting theory argues that the process of goal-setting and the possession of specific performance goals are in themselves motivating. Subsequent research in organisations[22] suggests that this only applies when the goal is perceived as realistic. This fits in with need achievement theory which suggests that for those high on need for achievement, challenging tasks, that is to say those of around 50 per cent probability, are more highly motivating than those which are very easy or very difficult.[23]

ERG Theory: The one major attempt to combine a new theory of needs with empirical research in the workplace has been made by *Clayton Alderfer* in the USA.[24] He took Maslow's theory as a starting point and suggested that Maslow's five levels of need could be amalgamated into three. These he has called 'existence, relatedness and growth' needs, resulting in his approach being termed 'ERG' theory. Existence needs include all forms of physiological and material desires. This subsumes Maslow's first two levels and also includes money. Relatedness needs include relationships with other people; and therefore cover Maslow's third level, esteem needs, which are derived from other people. Finally Alderfer proposes the existence of growth needs, which, rather like Maslow's notion of self-actualisation, are concerned with the desire to be creative and to achieve full potential is different in the existing environment.

Five into Three: Alderfer's theory is different from and more complex than Maslow's in a number of respects. First he rejects the concept of hierarchy and instead conceives of his three needs along a continuum, thus avoiding the implication that the higher up the hierarchy you are, the better. Secondly, he draws a distinction between chronic needs, which are situational and can alter according to the environment. This might help to explain behaviour such as the militant action of professional workers, which is sometimes a specific response out of line with their longer term needs and values. Thirdly Alderfer accepts that two needs can operate contemporaneously. To explain this he uses a frustration-regression model whereby, if a particular path towards the satisfaction of a need is blocked, the individual will both persist along that path and at the same time regress towards more easily satisfied needs.

Alderfer has tested his theory on a variety of American populations. Although the ERG theory has certain difficulties, at least it explains, the data better than Maslow's hierarchy and it does seem to provide a more realistic explanation of everyday work behaviour than the other theories of motivation which focus on needs.

Expectancy Theory: Expectancy theory, as applied to behaviour at work, has been formulated mainly by *Vroom*[25] and refined in particular by *Lawler*.[26] At its simpler level (see figure on next page) it argues that effort or motivated behaviour will only occur under certain conditions. These are:

1. That a relationship should be perceived to exist between effort and performance. In other words, if you display higher effort or motivation, this in itself is sufficient to exert a positive influence.
2. That a relationship should be perceived to exist between performance and reward. In other words, you can expect a higher reward, as a result of high performance.
3. That it is perceived that attractive rewards are available.

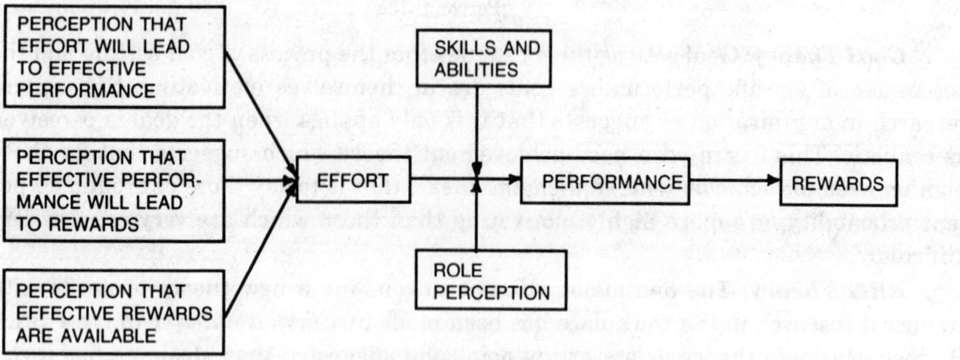

Fig. 13.7 Expectancy Model

Attribution Theory: A further development running parallel to, and to some extent arising out of, expectancy theory has been the growth of attribution theory. This hardly reaches the status of a theory, since it is more or less simply concerned with finding out to what people attribute their success or failure. If you had expected to be successful in obtaining a new job and failed, to what do you attribute this failure — it may be the system, bad luck, your own incompetence or that of the interviewer. Your attribution may then influence your future behaviour by altering your perception of the relation between effort, performance and reward.

Not surprising, what little work-related data there are suggested that people tend to take credit for success and to externalise the blame for failure. It is possible that there are some individuals who are more likely than other to believe that they, personally, influence their own performance and success. Such people will persist longer at whatever kind of task they are set.

Theory of High Expectations: High Expectations: It is interesting to note that the recent experiments conducted in the United States at the Metropolitan Life Insurance Company, A.T.T. by Harvard University and other organisations which revealed that the manager's expectations are the key to subordinate's performance and development. *Prof. J. Sterling Livingston,* who has done similar studies, states:[27]

"Some managers always treat their subordinates in a way that leads to superior performance. But most managers ... unintentionally treat their subordinates in a way that leads to lower performance than they are capable of achieving. The way managers treat their subordinates is certainly influenced by what they expect of them. If a manager's expectations are low, productivity is likely to be poor. It is as though there are laws that cause a subordinate's performance to rise or fall to meet his manager's expectations.

"The powerful influence of one person's expectations on another's behaviour has long been recognised by physicians and behavioural scientists and, more recently, by teachers. But heretofore, the importance of managerial expectations for individual and group performance has not been widely understood. I have documented this phenomenon in a number of case studies prepared during the past decade for major industrial concerns. These cases and other evidence available from scientific research now reveal:

1. What a manager expects of his subordinates and the way he treats largely determines their performance and career progress.
2. A unique characteristics of superior managers is their ability to create high performance expectations than subordinate's fulfilment.
3. Less effective managers fail to develop similar expectations, and, as a consequence, the productivity of their subordinates suffers.
4. The subordinates, more often than not, appear to do what they believe they are expected to do."

The important inference is that we have to have faith in our subordinates and colleagues and their capacities, as a result of which, if you have high expectations, they will always rise to our expectations. If you have low expectations because you do not have much faith in the capacities of your subordinates, their productivity and efficiency also will be low. It is more like the old saw: If you treat a person as a crook, sooner or later he will behave like one. And, of course, this is very well expressed in George Bernard Shaw's Pygmalion where Eliza Dolittle explains this to Freddie:

> "You see, really and truly, apart from the things, any one can pick up (the dressing and the proper way of pronunciation and so on), the difference between a lady and flower girl is not how she behaves, but how she is treated. I shall always be a flower girl to Professor Higgins, because he always treats me as a flower girl, and always will; but I know I can be a lady to you, because you always treat me as a lady, and always will."

Power Theory: A great many people, particularly executives, leaders, politicians and administrators are significantly motivated by power. Considerable work on power motivation is being done by Prof. David McClelland. According to him, these people have a high need for power and a high need for achievement. However, they have a low affiliation for people. Executives like to become a chairman of the company and strive all their lives to become a chairman largely because of their identification of power with that office. Thus, power motivation is a significant factor that drives them to achieve great heights and often in the process they may step over many people and also incur the wrath and displeasure of many of their colleagues for their tremendous power motivation and orientation. Because they have a low affiliation for people they could not care less about what other people thought of them and they continue to strive single mindedly to achieve their goals.

Praise Theory: The Harvard University Psychologist, Prof. Skinner has contributed a new concept of motivating people and the concept is variously called "behaviour technology", "behaviour modification" and "positive reinforcement." Prof. Skinner suggests that people perform better and gain better in psychological satisfaction on the job when they receive proper appreciation and praise for their good work. In effect Skinnerians says: "Don't play amateur psychologist. You do not care what a worker's basic needs are. What matters is what rewards he will work for. Just set out the job and its goals clearly and simply. Give the worker detailed feedback on his performance. Praise any positive achievements, even if you have to strain to find some thing to praise. This creates a pleasant environment in which the worker will strive for more recognition by doing better work."

"If criticism is needed, it should be sugar-coated. Rather than accusing a worker if he does poor work, you should note that objective feedback indicates something is wrong and 'we' should seek a way to improve things."[28]

While there has been a groundswell of interest in the idea, only a few firms report successful results as a result of the application of Skinner's theories. One such firm is Michigan Bell Telephone Company, a subsidiary of ATT. Skinner theories at Michigan Bell have been applied for the last ten years. The positive reinforcement through continuous and constant evaluation and feedback has helped Michigan Bell in improving productivity, in improving evaluation and feedback, in reducing absenteeism from 11 per cent to 2.6 per cent and in improving the rate of performance evaluation reporting from 20 per cent to 90 per cent, and in improving grievance settlements from 10 per cent to 80 per cent.

However, behaviour technology is not all carrot and no stick. At the outset, giving the employee full feedback on his performance against goals provides its own stick; he knows when he is performing poorly.

Mr. Grady of Michigan Bell observes: "Being positive does not mean we do not discipline. But first we discuss it as a mutual problem, then there is a verbal warning, then comes suspension and eventually dismissal. In fact, we probably fire more, because our standards are more explicit. We are less patient with an employee who has a poor record after a point of no return."

Professor Jucius has rightly observed that "there are many buttons beyond number. And many would give the same response. It is necessary to determine which buttons should be pushed — a compliment, a dollar raise, a smile, a promise of a raise, a new typewriter, a preferred location or a new desk? The theory does not tell an executive which button will provide the best spur under the circumstances."[29]

Jucius also states that differences such as the following must be considered when establishing motivating plans:

1. Personal background
2. Education
3. Age
4. Marital status
5. Financial status
6. Health
7. Political affiliation
8. Religious beliefs
9. Social relationships
10. Psychological make-up
11. Union affiliation
12. Company experiences

Steps of Motivation: Jucius has suggested the following steps of motivation:[30]

1. Size up the situations requiring motivation.
2. Prepare a set of motivating tools.
3. Select and apply the appropriate motivator.
4. Follow-up the results of the application.

It is necessary to find out whether the 'pay-off' of motivation has resulted either in higher output or lower costs or greater loyalty etc.

Rules of Motivation: Jucius lays down five rules of motivation:[31]

1. Self Interest and Motivation: People are selfish. When a person realises that his own interests are best served in the attainment of company interests, he is likely to give off his best.

2. Attainability: It is necessary to establish goals that are attainable and when such goals are achieved, it leads to employee satisfaction. Unattainable goals frustrate people.

3. The Human Element: Motivation appeals to emotions, importance of feelings. The executive, who is most successful as motivator, can trace his success invariably to his skill in dealing with people's feelings. He can bring out the best in people because he makes them feel good, feel significant, feel worthwhile and feel that they are growing.

4. Individual-Group Relationship: Motivation must be based upon group as well as individual-centered stimuli. Groups have terrific impact on individuals. Firstly, utilise motivational plans which do not run counter to group forces and secondly, seek change constructively the ideas of the group.

5. Managerial Theory: Management must base its motivational efforts on sound theory.

3. HOW TO HANDLE HUMAN RELATIONS PROBLEMS

The Twin City Chapter of the Society for the Advancement of Management recommend the following approach:[32]

1. Recognise basic individual needs. These include (1) recognition as an individual, (2) self-respect, (3) pride, (4) communication, (5) understanding, (6) confidence, (7) opportunity, (8) discipline.
2. Get background information about the individual, through (1) direct methods, such as, (a) man-to-man talks, (b) observation, (c) records analysis, (2) indirect methods, such as, (a) testing, (b) interviewing, (c) attitude surveys.

The Twin City SAM group[33] recommends the following in handling human relations problems:

1. Recognise that individuals are different.
2. Gather all information possible on a continuing basis.
3. For identical needs two individuals may have to be approached differently.
4. All information must be kept confidential.
5. Allow time for this in your daily activity.
6. Results will not necessarily be immediate or apparent.
7. Take immediate action wherever possible.
8. Eliminate or change the cause.
9. Know each individual so that rapport is established.
10. Keep informal notes on each case.
11. Separate facts from opinions.
12. Don't forget that you are involved and that you may have to change.
13. Do let suggestions for change appear to come from the individual.
14. Recognize that in some situations action by the supervisor is not appropriate, e.g., husband-wife relationships.
15. Do not express moral judgments — be objective.
16. Do not express surprise.
17. Find out what the individual wants.
18. Needs may be changed by changing conditions.
19. Ask for assistance from your own or other supervisors and from the staff.

Most human relations approaches emphasise increasing employee motivation through improved communication and through additional participation in solving problems found in the work situation. It is believed that improved morale will result from these practices.

Professor Scott in Fig. 13.7 illustrates that the data supplied by the analytical areas provide management with a basic understanding of human behaviour and organisational processes. With this information, management should have the technical insight necessary for the diagnosis, prevention, or cure of many human problems in business.[34]

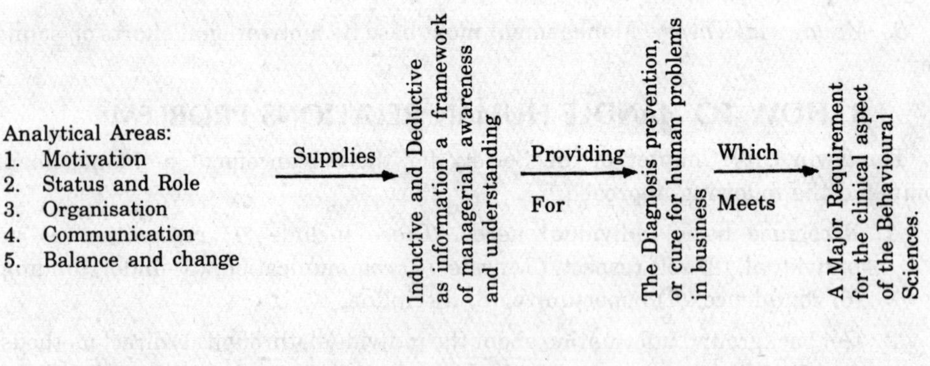

Fig. 13.7 Analytical Areas and Clinical Dimensions of Human Relations

Mr. Donald R. Shoen lists the following guides for a manager in human relations practice:[35]

1. He should understand and accept people as they are.
2. He should be aware and sensitive to another's point of view — along with an ability to maintain his own position.
3. He should be willing to understand and to respond to the feelings and attitudes of others which might not be purely logical from his own frame of reference.
4. He should be aware of himself and appreciate the scope of his influence on others.
5. He should appreciate the social structure or social system in which he is involved.
6. He should be realistic about his authority and status and aware of how they affect others.
7. He should attempt to predict (although the probability of occurrence of the outcomes he predicts may be low) how the organisation will respond to a change he introduces.
8. He should make use of experience and abstract generalisations about phenomena in taking action.

Management Attitude

Paradoxically enough, often it may be the apathy and non-involvement of management in human relations that may cause many problems. Only when matters come to a head, they realise that they had neglected this vital area. Then there are some who are domineering by nature and to them human relations approaches are an infringement on their own rights and prerogatives. There are some managers who regard labour as a 'cost, a commodity' or a machine and not as human beings, then there are "production-centred" or "efficiency-centred" managers, who are concerned only with increasing productivity or efficiency regardless of "the cost in human assets." There is another category of older executives to whom human relations is "a new gimmick" and they cannot cope with this new dimension, "after all I have been handling people all these years."

Most of these types of executives need exposure to human relations approaches, theory, practice, and best of all, "how it is working out in Sam's Company." Here is an area where the personnel administrator fits in perfectly. He must assist executives and supervisors in getting the necessary training, education and exposure to human relations concepts.

Professor Mee offers examples of common human relations problem and how to handle them in the following Fig. 13.8.

Problem	*Possible causes*	*Possible action*
1. Absenteeism.	Habit, lack of interest, trouble at home, dissatisfaction with job, transportation trouble.	Investigate, remove cause, personal talk, create interest in job, help obtain transportation.
2. Complaints about working conditions.	Jealousy, favouritism, actual poor conditions.	Better instructions, check supervision, transfer to other work.

3. Dirty work and work place.	Lack of interest, carelessness, toleration by management.	Personal talk, safety hazard explained, check supervisor's tolerance, allow clean up time.
4. Disloyalty.	Discontent, favouritism, lack of recognition.	Investigate Cause, give square deal, set up objective merit rating.
5. Complainer spreads discontent.	Work conditions, poor Wages, lack of recognition, poor leadership.	Transfer, investigate wages inequity, check to see if work has been recognized.
6. Excessive talking.	Lack of social outlet, idleness.	Investigate and recommend social outlets, redefine task, make employee realize that talking bothers others.
7. Insubordination.	Lack of interest, spite, jealousy, favouritism, personnel issue.	Investigate reason, transfer, if personal issue try to settle or transfer, buildup interest in job.
8. Misrepresenting the management or company data.	Ignorance of facts, dissatisfaction.	Better communication, give facts in understandable terms, buildup purpose of his job.
9. Not using safety aids.	Indifference, desire to turn out more work, device improperly designed.	Show safety movie, talk on personal danger, check time standards, check safety-aid design, penalty.
10. Plays on job.	Clownishness, desire to be important to group, lax discipline, not enough work.	Show safety hazard, get group action against, check task assignment, some social-play needed on job, allow break time.
11. Quality of work poor.	Lack of knowledge, laziness, desire to exceed piece rate.	Show importance of job to final product, proper motion instruction, emphasize need for quality, penalty for poor work, rework.
12. Rumour-Spreader.	Jealousy, curiosity, desire to seem important.	Investigate, recognition of work, and responsibility if merited, personal talk.
13. Quitting ahead of 5 p.m.	Habit, transportation, lack of washroom facilities, desire to get out rate too high.	Insist on quality of work, provide adequate washroom for all, check quitting time and bus schedule, allow employee to go to library so as to not interrupt work if task is done.
14. Soldiering.	Improper time standards, fear of rate cut, lax discipline, lack of interest.	Check time standards, maintain time rates once set, be firm, show importance of good job.
15. Theft.	Severity of discipline, natural dishonesty, low wage.	Cut opportunities for theft, lie-detector, tests are sure but serve discipline, send to psychiatrist, check home and money needs.
16. Wastefulness.	Laxness, lack of knowledge, lack of interest.	Place on waste committee, show importance of waste reduction to him, apply penalty.

Fig. 13.8 Examples of Techniques Useful in Solving Human Relations Problems.

Source: John F. Mee, *Personnel Handbook,* pp. 936-37.

Some Criticisms of Human Relations

1. Human relations assumptions are a useful way to view a certain class of problems. These are problems a manager faces when he turns inward to minimise conflict, to motivate, and to promote co-operation among his subordinates in the organisation.[36]

2. Human relations treatment of the plant or office workforce "community" or as a "social system" is not adequate for solving conflict problems which arise from larger institutional of industrial harmony, because of the "tight little social system" attitude expressed in the human relations assumptions is a serious one.

3. Mr. Harold L. Sheppard has four major criticism:[37]

(a) Human relations is a "systematic underestimation of economic and political determinants of industrial peace, either within or external to the factory." (b) Human relations restrict the area of observation to the factory "as if in a vacuum." It does not look beyond the social system of the organisation for causes of harmony or conflict. (c) Minimisation of conflict by the employer or manager does not come from redistribution of decision-making power or concessions to employee demands but from the application of social (manipulative) skills. The direction of manipulation is to get employees "to reinterpret their complaints in such a way as to eliminate the company as the object to hostility...." (d) Thus, industrial relations in the human relations perspective reduces itself to "person-to-person relations, primarily between worker and worker, worker and supervisor." The main source of conflict is found at this level.

4. Peter Drucker has observed that "it lacks adequate focus on work" and it places undue emphasis on interpersonal relations and the group. It is not the job that determines employee happiness, only the employee's relations to fellow workers according to human relations theory. However, he believes the functions people perform in an organisation are major determinants of happiness and that analysis of work and job is the sensible place to begin developing positive motivations for the people working in the organisation.[38]

5. Modern human relations tend to neglect the economic dimension of work satisfaction. While social and psychological needs and satisfactions are important, economic needs and satisfactions cannot be 'buried too deeply.'

6. The structure of human relations research suffers from short-sightedness in the sense that "most of what is known empirically about human behaviour, is a product of human relations research at the operative or at best, the first level of supervision in the company. The generalisations coming from such research are extended to higher levels of managements also without really knowing whether or not they are appropriate."

7. Then there is a tendency to go overboard on human relations in having too many "get together parties" or benefits, or services for employees without taking into consideration the cost aspects and the return accruing to the company from these activities. Too superfluous or manipulative behaviour in the name of human relations will not yield results either. Despite all these criticism, human relations has come to stay as a very useful tool for management to promote harmonious, productive, peaceful employee-employer relations. Now let us turn to examine the role of personnel administrations in the promotion of human relations.

4. PERSONNEL ADMINISTRATION AND HUMAN RELATIONS

Personnel administration has an enormous role to play in the promotion of good human relations in a company. At any given point of time there are always problems involving people that confront the operating management, who need expert help from personnel division to handle these human problems. The personnel staff must be sensitive to the needs and problems of operating managers and supervisors, *as they see them,* so that practical help maybe given as close to the source of needs and problems as possible but clear insights to long-term solutions come next. Personnel specialists achieve their major results through helping line managers become personnel administrators.

Mr. Saltonstall writes how personnel specialists can help operating managers:[39]

> "Perhaps the problem is one of training new workers, utilising engineers, absenteeism, safety, restriction of output, grievances, or labour cost controls. The personnel man should have the essential understanding and skills to work with line supervisors on those vital problems, which influence productivity and the supervisor's own success as a leader of men. By helping others to help themselves, the personnel specialist encourages realistic solutions for the never-ending stream of human pressures and misunderstandings that confront every organisation. Instead of dabbling in "the small stuff" the personnel executive should see his job in broader perspective as an integral part of the management effort. His sensitivity, his understanding of behaviour and his capacity to guide supervisors are important. His human skills make him a vital factor in policy making, organisation planning, supervisory development, and other activities that contribute to the productivity drive and sustained co-operation of the enterprise. Under these circumstances the focus of personnel department work is no longer "keeping people happy" or "efficiency" as such, but it becomes more the nurturing of better understanding, teamwork and more enlightened leadership by managers throughout the enterprise."

In India the personnel function is reduced merely to "keeping people happy" or "welfare" work and the "welfare officer" or "the labour welfare officer" is asked to take care of canteen, transportation, picnics, dramas, sports and clubs etc., all of which constitute just one type of innumerable functions that modern personnel executives perform.

The authors of a research study state the following:[40]

> "A third fundamental attitude is top management's acceptance of personnel administration — the management of the human organisation as "top drawer" responsibility of every member of line as well as staff management. Successful human relations cannot develop so long as top management is willing to say of some line subordinate: "He'll never learn how to handle people, but he gets out production." Nor can any healthy relations develop if management expects to dispose of the problems of personnel administration by delegating them to a staff department. The necessary attitude is one in which a high level of competence is demanded from all members of management in dealing with people, and in which those who cannot develop this competence are replaced. The problems of

personnel administration among the companies represented by our case studies are quite naturally given equal importance with the problems of finance and of technical operations."

Mr. S.A. Raube, the dynamic Vie-President, Personnel Division of National Industrial Conference Board, gives the following views of a company president:[41]

"The president...must make personnel administration the responsibility of every member of the management group. He pays the bill for a department of personnel administration to get specialised help and guidance for himself and all other members of management."

Personnel Functions and Human Relations

Jucius observes that "much of the mystery often associated with human relations can be removed by relating the human factor to the technical functions of personnel management. This means seeing how human relations ties in with procuring, developing, maintaining and utilising a labour force."[42]

He has suggested the following programme:

1. Procurement Function and Human Relations

(a) Lay emphasis upon human relations right from the start with a good selection process.

(b) Job specification, must not be restricted to technical qualifications, but also specify pertinent personnel adjustment and relationships by analysing jobs to ascertain such facts as the following:

1. Personal contacts that are involved.
2. Percentage of time spent with various classes of people.
3. Status and role implications.
4. Union, governmental and community associations.
5. Meetings with various groups and committees.

(c) Describe the kind of personality it takes to meet the specific human situations described for a particular job.

(d) Attract and screen good human relations prospects.

(e) Determine what sources of supply yield candidates with desired human qualities.

(f) Through good interviewing and testing, gather information about personality, emotional stability, social awareness, introvert and extrovert patterns, interests and the like.

(g) Emphasise in the induction and placement programme a relaxing friendly atmosphere first and then technical information, rules and regulations etc.

2. Development of Human Relations Potential

(a) Make arrangements to raise the understanding of employees regarding political, community and economic problems and affairs.

(b) Provide help (psychiatric, medical or expert) for those with marital or family difficulties.

(c) Provide help to such problem-individuals as the emotionally tense, kleptomaniacs, alcoholics etc.

(d) Provide guidance and counselling sessions.

(e) Provide religious facilities, if necessary.

(f) Establish contacts with community services and agencies.

(g) Provide books, magazines, newspapers and other literature to the employees.

3. Maintenance of Desirable Human Relations

(a) Establish appropriate policies and procedures to minimise sources of dissatisfaction.

(b) Establish morale-building programmes.

(c) Establish employee recreational, social and security programmes which provide an opportunity to exercise and indulge in a wide variety of human relations skills, desires and energies.

4. Utilisation of Human Relations

(a) Provide a well-designed workplace environment taking into consideration employee feelings, attitudes, status and social significance.

(b) Educate and train employees in work simplification and technical processes and designs.

(c) Explain to employees channels of promotion and opportunities for personal improvement.

(d) Train supervisors in human relations techniques and in using them.

(e) Encourage union participation and co-operation.

(f) Educate management in tolerating justifiable informal contacts among employees which are helpful in maintaining their status, roles and feelings.

The major emphasis of personnel department staff activity is to advise and assist all levels of the line organisation in fulfilling their responsibilities as leaders of people. The ultimate goal of the personnel department is to make good personnel administrators out of all supervisors and executives — line and staff — who direct the work of others. Thomas G. Spates, the well-known personnel expert, maintains that, "In order to be good personnel administrators, it is necessary that engineers, sales managers, controllers, plant managers, purchasing agents, foremen, presidents and chairmen of the board possess and apply talents, skills, understandings and comprehensions that exceed anything required by any art of which we have any knowledge...common sense won't do the job."

Mr. Saltonstall points out some of the major areas where the personnel department can help you — the line executive in handling your day-to-day relationships, opportunities, and problems with your superiors, subordinates and peers.[43]

1. As your Observer, Analyst, Diagnostician: Because of their training and background, our personnel specialists should spend upto half of their time out of their offices contacting supervisors and observing the multitude of changing conditions and relationships in the shops and offices. They must realise how these conditions are likely to affect productivity and morale in the immediate future and in the long run. As a skilled diagnostician, he can assist you in decision-making where people are immediately affected.

A decision to purchase labour-saving machinery that may mean layoffs and employee adjustments is a typical example. The responsible personnel specialist provides an extra pair of eyes, sensitive ears, an impervious nervous system and patient, wise advice to you and hard-pressed line executives.

2. *As your Adviser in Leadership:* The personnel specialist gets his results through you and the other line supervisors. He is in a position to pass along to you the know-how, the spirit, and the basic purpose of sound human relations, without interfering with your day-to-day leadership of people. With his specialised knowledge of the labour agreement, personnel policies, company rules and state and federal labour laws, he can give you sound advise or interpretations before you render a decision that may affect many people.

He knows that by helping you to develop your capacities as a leader of personnel he is spreading enlightened personnel administration throughout the company. In many ways he is management's conscience when leadership decisions involving people are made. He can help you gain deeper understanding and insights about your employees and co-workers and gradually guide you in the development of your own personal human relations capacities. His assistance will make you a better analyst, planner, decision-maker, and follow-up man — a more effective and understanding leader.

3. *As your Co-ordinator in Handling People:* Your personnel specialist is normally delegated the responsibility to initiate and to interpret personnel policies, and union agreement, which affect all departments and require uniform interpretation and administration.

As a co-ordinator, your personnel specialist may be responsible for sound wage and salary structures and their consistent administration through all departments. At other times he will co-ordinate hiring, lay-off and transfers in such ways as to stabilise employment. His knowledge of precedents established in grievance hearings in other departments will be invaluable to you. He co-ordinates information by acting like a sponge, absorbing employee points of view, union attitudes and strategies, supervisory viewpoints and top management thinking to the point where his objective conclusions can have real value for you, the line executive.

4. *As a Provider of Centralised Services:* Vital central communication services go both ways. The company house organ is normally under the guidance of your personnel specialist, and the employee suggestion filters through that office as well. His statistics on labour turnover, absenteeism, accidents and grievances help line officials to decide for themselves the action that needs to be taken to anticipate or correct unusual situations.

5. *As a Manager of Employee Services:* Your personnel specialist has direct responsibility for certain activities of interdepartmental interest to employees, such as food, beverage, canteen or cafeteria, recreation, social activities etc., which contribute to building employee morale. With the rise in employee benefits such as pensions, insurance plans, employee savings and stock ownership, the personnel people are often called upon to administer these increasing complex plans and deal with the technical problems involved.

6. As Skilled Liaison Man in Collective Bargaining: With the rapid growth of collective bargaining the personnel or labour relations specialist was literally swept into a position of major importance, requiring skills and knowledge and a new kind of understanding. He absorbs many of the shocks, listens to complaints, and maintains a constant liaison with the union in an effort to stabilise and interpret management goals and behaviour to union officials and vice versa.

His greatest contribution is to help you anticipate labour relations problems or when necessary, to guide you in finding the best long-range answers to frictions and misunderstandings.

7. As a Builder of Productivity and Morale: Your personnel specialist is focusing on the future, seeking better ways to achieve the company's productivity and profit goals through improved handling of people at the workplace. New plans, new policies, programmes and techniques, all require both internal company research and careful outside research information before management decision and action. Personnel specialists trained in the skills of painstaking staff work can make a major contribution to the line effectiveness by their imaginative, complete and accurate research into ways of improving teamwork and productivity. Mr. Saltonstall states the need for an over all coordinated approach to improve human relations:

> "In the past, management has placed too much emphasis on one-shot attempts to improve human relations and productivity. There have been many fads, many personnel techniques, and many limited theories on how to solve human relations problems in a hurry. One company will adopt job evaluation, another will promote an ambitious management development programme, a third will put in a profit-sharing plan, a fourth will focus attention on better communications, pensions may seem to be the answer for a fifth, whereas a labour-management committee, or some form of joint consultation will be adopted by a sixth. Each of these approaches in itself may be a worthwhile objectives, but unless it is tied in to a broader, over-all approach it is not likely to achieve worthwhile results." He gives Fig. 13.9 designed to provide a useful way for executives to think about their responsibilities for human relations. "Each of the ingredients in the diagram is important. They are interrelated. No one of them operating alone is likely to produce worthwhile long range results in an organisation of any size."[44]
>
> Interpreting the diagram, Mr. Saltonstall writes very eloquently:[45]
>
> "The centre of the circle identifies you, the operating line executive as a human being. Like other human beings you have a feeling of your own dignity as a person, like other people, created in the image of God. You want to be respected by other people. You want to be a good father. You want to lead a useful and productive life. You want to be the kind of leader who gets optimum results through coordinating the work of other people. This requires faith in yourself and in other people. You must understand the impact on your behaviour on other people whose outlook may differ from yours."

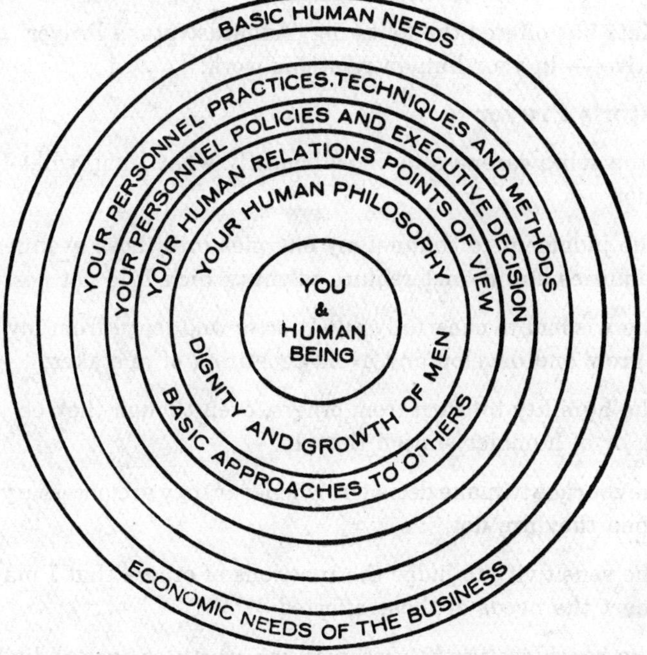

Fig. 13.9 Coordinated Approach to Human Problems

Source: R. Saltonstall, *Human Relations in Administration*, p. 450.

Personnel Philosophy and Human Relations

Management's attitude towards human relations is largely dependent upon the personnel philosophy of the employer and the line executive. If you respect human beings, realise their worth, require their willing cooperation and if you are one of those who believes that *"the basic purpose of the business is to serve society by building men"*, you are likely to take really seriously your responsibility to apply human relations coordinated approach in all phases of your family, business and community life. Your human relations philosophy will reflect itself in your personnel policies, followed by personnel programmes and procedures that activate your personnel philosophy and policies.

Considerable progress has been made through research, experiment and observation in our understanding of human relations in a fast changing business environment. Much has been learned through various researches about the kinds of organisation structure and leadership methods that release the untapped potential of people. We know more about the nature of human needs, as seen by people themselves, and we are learning what steps management can take to fulfil them in realistic ways.

Mr. Saltonstall concludes:[46] "Executives are learning that the firm but fair manager who 'runs a taut ship with an easy hand' cultivates respect and nurtures the best teamwork and sustained productivity. High morale and optimum productivity can go hand in hand when management established the kind of climate when men can grow through their work. Increasing number of executive have succeeded in integrating the engineering approaches of scientific management with the human relations approaches advocated in this book to the end that optimum results have been achieved, both for the company and for the people involved."

Robert L. Katz has offered the following "Administrator's Prayer" to help guide you — the executive — in your human relations work:[47]

An Administrator's Prayer

"Grant me the self-awareness to know honestly what I am, what I can do, and what I cannot;

Grant me the judgment to channel my energies into those avenues which best utilise my abilities and do not require talents which I do not possess;

Grant me the wisdom to cheerfully admit error and learn from my experiences, that I may grow and develop and avoid repetition of mistakes;

Grant me the humility to learn from others, even though they be younger, less experienced, or of humbler station than I;

Grant me the courage to make decisions whenever they are necessary and to avoid rashness when they are not;

Grant me the sensitivity to judge the reactions of others that I may modify my actions to meet the needs of those affected;

Grant me the consideration to recognise the worth of each individual, and to respect all those with whom I have contact, neither stifling their development nor exalting myself at their expense;

Grant me the perspicacity to acknowledge that I can be no more effective than my subordinates enable me to be, and to deal with them so that they can help me by helping themselves;

Grant me the tolerance to recognise mistakes as a cost of true learning, and to stand behind by subordinates, accepting my responsibility for their actions;

Grant me the insight to develop a personnel philosophy, that my life may have more meaning and satisfaction and that I may avoid capricious action under pressures of expediency;

Grant me the patience to live realistically with my circumstances, striving always for the better, but recognising the perils of too rapid or too drastic change;

Grant me all these things, dear Lord, that I may live a more useful life through serving my fellow men, and through them serve Thee."

Professor Mee has offered what he calls the "Ten Commandments of Human Relations" and they may be most useful to the executives:[48]

The Commandments of Human Relations

1. Give the employee the facts; keep him in the "know" in advance.
2. Do not dominate the employee; allow him his self-respect.
3. Promote competitive spirit among the employees, but avoid a fight.
4. Set an example for the employee; they like to respect their superiors. Train supervisors in human relations.

5. Consider the employee's sentiments and social situation; out of these his world is built.
6. Make the worker feel important; appeal to his mastery drive. Give him an opportunity not only for advancement but also for expression.
7. Provide reasonable security, and safe healthful working conditions.
8. Be firm; do not give concessions too easily; let the employee feel he has earned them fairly.
9. Treat each employee as an individual; determine what makes him valuable.
10. Make decisions as fairly as possible after considering the valuable facts. Be specially careful to be objective in making decisions.

REFERENCES

1. Yoder *et al., op. cit.,* p. 14.65.
2. John F. Mee, *op. cit.,* p. 893.
3. Robert Saltonstall, *Human Relations in Administration* (New York: McGraw Hill Book Company, Inc., 1959), p. 13.
4. William G. Scott, *Human Relations in Management* (Homewood, Illinois; Richard D. Irwin, Inc., 1962) p. 43.
5. *Ibid.,* p. 6.
6. Elton Mayo, *The Human Problems of an Industrial Civilisation* (New York: Macmillan Company, 1933); Elton Mayo, *The Social Problems of an Industrial Civilisation* (Cambridge, Mass: Harvard University, Graduate School of Business Administration. 1945); Fritz J. Roethlisberger and W.J. Dickson, *Management and the Worker* (Cambridge, Mass: Harvard University, 1939); Fritz J. Roethlisberger, *Management and Morale* (Cambridge, Mass: Harvard University Press, 1941).
7. See Rensis Likert, "Developing Patterns of Management", *Strengthening Management for the New Technology,* AMA General Management Series, No. 178, 1955, pp. 44-47.
8. William G. Scott, *op. cit.,* pp. 54-57 abstracted.
9. *Ibid.,* p. 73.
10. Robert Saltonstall, *op. cit.,* p. 278.
11. *Ibid.,* emphasis mine.
12. Rensis Likert, *Motivation: The Core of Management* (New York: American Management Association, Personnel Series, Number 155, 1953), p. 16. Emphasis mine.
13. R.S. Pande, "Maximising the Effectiveness of Personnel Management," 17th Annual Conference of Indian of Personnel Management, March,11, 1967.
14. William G. Scott, *op. cit.,* p. 77.
15. *Ibid.,* p. 80.
16. *Ibid.,* pp. 80-82.
17. Morris S. Viteles, *Motivation and Morale in Industry* (New York: W.W. Norton and Co., 1953), p. 73.
18. John W. Atkinson, "Motivational Determinants of Risk Taking Behaviour", *Psychological Review,* 1957, pp. 360-61.
19. William G. Scott, *op. cit.,* p. 84.
20. *Ibid.,* p. 85.
21. Mee, *op. cit.,* pp. 921-923. Professor Mee also points out how these human drives can be met by appropriate management programmes and action.

22. Latham, G.P., and Kinne, S.B., "Improving Job Performance through Training in Goal Setting", *Journal of Applied Psychology,* No. 59, 1974.
23. David Guest, "Motivation after Maslow", *Personnel Management,* March, 1976, pp. 29-32.
24. Alderfer, C.P., *Existence, Relatedness and Growth: Human Needs Organisational Settings*, The Free Press, 1972.
25. Vroom, V.H. *Work and Motivation.* Wiley, 1964.
26. Lawler, E.E., *Pay and Organisational Effectiveness,* Mc-Graw-Hill, 1971.
27. J. Sterling Livingstone, "Pygmalion in Management", *Harvard Business Review,* July-August 1969, pp. 81-82; also see, J. Sterling Livingstone, *High Expectations in Management*, Harvard University Press, 1972.
28. Jucius, *Personnel Management,* p. 45.
29. *Ibid.*
30. *Ibid.*
31. *Ibid.,* p. 53.
32. Summarised from R.C. Ingoldt *et al.*, "What the Supervisor can do in the Field of Human Relations to Encourage Teamwork and Efficient Operation" (Minneapolis: St. Paul Twin City Chapter, Society for Advancement of Management, 1950), pp. 2-4.
33. Scott, *op. cit.,* p. 72.
34. Donald R. Shoen, "Human Relation: Boon or Bogle?" *Harvard Business Review*, November-December, 1957, pp. 43-45.
35. Scott, *op. cit.,* p. 57.
36. Summarised from Harold L. Sheppard, "Approaches to Conflict in American Industrial Sociology", *British Journal of Sociology,* December, 1954, pp. 324-341.
37. Peter F. Drucker, "The Employee Society", *American Journal of Sociology,* January, 1953, pp. 278-280.
38. Robert Saltonstall, *op. cit.,* p. 132.
39. *Causes of Industrial Peace Under Collective Bargaining: A Final Report,* National Planning Association, Case Study No. 14, December, 1953, pp. 76-77.
40. S.A. Raube, "Personnel Administration: What, How, Why", NICB, *Management Record,* May, 1955, p. 185.
41. Jucius, *op. cit.,* pp. 39-45.
42. Robert Saltonstall, *op. cit.,* pp. 140-144.
43. *Ibid.,* p. 448.
44. *Ibid.,* pp. 449-450.
45. *Ibid.,* p. 450.
46. *Ibid.,* p. 456.
47. Robert L. Gatz, "Administrator's Prayer", *Harvard Business Review*, March-April, 1957, p. 40.
48. John F. Mee, *op. cit.,* p. 927.

❑ ❑ ❑

Union and Management Relations

CHAPTER 14

Union and Management Relations

Industrial peace and prosperity are largely dependent upon harmonious relations between unions and management. Unions, representing millions of employees, are here to stay and it is necessary for management to establish good and amicable relations with unions in order to get things done through the employees. Since personnel administrators are responsible to advise top management and line executives on all issues concerning personnel and handling manpower resources, they have to work closely with the associations of the workers — unions — in order to promote better union-management relations. It is interesting to note that there has been a coincidental development and growth of personnel administration and unionism in U.S.A., as pointed out by Pigors and Myers:[1]

> "The development of personnel administration has paralleled the growth of unions. During the First World War, labour shortages brought a recognition of the importance of sound hiring and employment practices, and through this personnel work got its start. Unionism also grew in strength, reaching a peak membership of 5,000,000 in 1920. Here the parallel breaks down, however, for union membership fell off drastically during the twenties, while personnel programmes continued to be more widely adopted. In fact, in many firms they were adopted as a device to weaken or avoid unionism. There were welfare schemes that smacked of paternalism, and many companies sponsored employee-representation plans. At the same time, government and courts were lukewarm, if not openly hostile toward unions. This attitude showed little change until about 1932. The depression of the thirties and the resurgence of unionism brought to personnel work renewed vitality and a new point of view. Widespread unemployment emphasised the social responsibilities of management, and collective bargaining through unions involved new management obligation. This was the period when personnel policies finally 'moved into the front office'."

They further add: "More especially, the growth of unionism has forced management to improve its own performance, to reconsider its personnel and labour relations policies, and to share the formulation of work rules (through collective bargaining) with an organisation representing the firm's employees. This development has also broadened the staff responsibilities of the personnel administrator."

Union-management relations are also known as industrial relations or labour relations and they are greatly influenced by public policy. The principal purpose of union-management relations is to establish an agreement regarding the conditions under which employees will render their services to the employer. The subject of union-management relations is discussed under the following sections:

1. Unions and their Role.
2. American and Indian Trade Unions.
3. Union and Management Relations.
4. Tripartite Machinery.

1. UNIONS AND THEIR ROLE

What is a Trade Union?

Sidney and Beatrice Webb[2] define a trade union as "a continuous association of wage earners for the purpose of maintaining or improving the conditions of their working lives." The Indian Trade Unions Act, 1926, provides this definition: "Trade Union means any combination, whether temporary or permanent, formed primarily for the purpose of regulating the relations between workmen and employers or between employers and employers or for imposing restrictive conditions on the conduct of any trade or business, and includes any federation of two or more Trade Unions."

Some Historical Aspects

Generally it is held that trade unions were the products of the Industrial Revolution and a factory system and its attendant evils and unions were protest organisations, attempting to combat the misery and suffering which resulted from the factory system where long hours of work for pitiful wages in extremely unsafe working conditions were all too common. Contrary to this popular notion, it is found that there were durable combinations of wage-earners in England nearly a whole century before the development of the factory system and the pioneers of the trade union movement were the extensive combinations of the West of England Woollen-Workers, and the Midland Framework Knitters around the 1650s. The historical processes, which explain the first institution of trade union movement are in the words of Sidney and Beatrice Webb:[3] "The essential cause of the growth of durable associations of wage-earners must lie in something peculiar to the later centuries. The fundamental condition of Trade Unionism we discover in the economic revolution through which certain industries were passing. In all cases in which trade unions arose, the great bulk of the workers had ceased to be independent producers, themselves controlling the processes, and owning the materials and the product of their labour, and had passed into the condition of lifelong wage-earners, possessing neither the instruments of production nor the commodity in its finished state. From the moment, that to establish a given business more capital is required than a journeyman can easily accumulate within a few years, a guild mastership — the mastership of the masterpiece — becomes little more than a name.... Skill alone is valueless, and is soon compelled to hire itself out to capital.... Now begins the opposition of interest between employers and employed, now the latter begin to group themselves together; now rise the trade society ... the rise of permanent trade combinations is to be ascribed, in a final analysis, to the definite separation between the functions of the capitalist entrepreneur and the manual worker.... It is often assumed that Trade Unionism arose as a protect against intolerable industrial oppression. This was not so. The first half of the eighteenth century was certainly not a period of exceptional distress.... Thus it is seen that seeds of growth of unionism lie in the historical evolution of the divorce of capital and labour, giving birth to a class of people permanently reduced to the status of wage-earners."

Although the employers fought tooth and nail to prevent the formulation of worker organisations or trade unions and the governments did not extend support in the initial stages by applying the doctrine of conspiracy, unionism slowly but steadily came into its own as a power to reckon with. There were always loose associations of workers, who, whenever they met, would discuss their wages and working conditions. Later a combination of evolving forces involving changes in the attitudes of the democratic governments, enlightened management, the initiative of craft unions, and the changing business and industrial scene contributed to the recognition and development of unionism.

Theories of Trade Unionism

*1. **Revolutionary Theory:*** Brilliantly expounded in the *Communist Manifesto,* the revolutionary explanation of Marx and Engles was that labour movements were the steps in reorganising society, overthrowing the capitalists, and substituting common ownership of all capital and property with economic equality for all. Trade unions were nothing but a preparation to bring about a revolution, which will result in the extinction of the capitalist class and the establishment of the paradise of the proletariat. Although this theory is accepted in the Eastern Totalitarian countries, it has no particular following in the U.S.A. and other Western countries.

*2. **Industrial Democracy:*** The theory of industrial democracy was put forth by Sidney and Beatrice Webb, who after a detailed study of early unions, concluded that unions represented a means by which workers can cope with the stronger political and economic power of employers and thus introduce democracy into working relations. Developing this theme, Professor Summer Slichter noted that members, through their unions, developed a whole network of work rules and traditions, a "system of industrial jurisprudence" and these rules become a means of protection to employees in their work, just as the system of public law protects citizens from arbitrary action by government.

*3. **Business Theory:*** Here the emphasis was on the economic, rather than the political power of worker associations. The early leaders of American Federation of Labour, particularly Samuel Gompers, its first president maintained that primary aim of unionism was to protect the economic interests of the worker through the unions. He was opposed to revolutionary unionism or political unionism.

*4. **Socio-Psychological Theories:*** Carlton Parker, Robert F. Hoxie, Clinton Golde and Harold J. Ruttenber have contributed these theories, where unions are regarded as instruments through which a broad range of human wants and needs, such as feeling of security, belonging, freedom, and strength, is realised.

*5. **Change Theory:*** It is Selig Perlman who concluded that the objectives of labour movements keep changing from time to time and no simple theory can explain the varieties of movements that have appeared.

Types of Unionism

Clark Kerr has identified 6 types of unionism in accordance with their broad economic purposes and their methods.[4]

1. Pure and Simple Unionism: Here the emphasis is on collective bargaining to raise money wage without the benefit of theories and formulas.

2. Wage-Policy (or Improvement) Unionism: Here the union bargains for a real wage (the escalator clause) and a share of increased productivity (improvement clause).

3. Managerial Unionism: Here the stress is on (1) Profit-sharing schemes; (2) "All or None" Contract; and (3) Union-Management Joint Control with union participating in price-setting, control of entry of firms etc.

4. New Deal Unionism: Here union policy is to develop political alliance with other forces for securing full employment economy through government action, while bargaining for higher money wages under improved economic conditions.

5. Labour-Party Unionism: Here the effort is to control distributive shares through governmental shares and not through collective bargaining, by means of progressive taxation and various forms of subsidy.

6. Direct-Controls Unionism: Direct governmental controls on a temporary or permanent basis are sought, particularly over prices. At a more sophisticated level, there may be a national bargain at the parliamentary level over "class shares" involving wages, prices, taxes, government benefits; and at the extreme a fully planned economy.

A BETTER LIFE FOR OUR WORKERS IN THE 21ST CENTURY

Our Progress

Singapore has done well as a nation. Since our independence in 1965, we have progressed from being a developing country to become a more advanced developing country all within a short span of 30 years. Our workers have contributed much to help make Singapore what it is today. This is an achievement our workers can be proud of.

Our Aim

We aim to do even better in the future. Our national vision for the 21st Century is to make Singapore our best home. We aim to become not just another developed nation, but a successful one with no unemployment or underemployment in our economy. We want our workers, and our future generations of workers to have better skills, better jobs, better working conditions, better wages and better quality. In short, we want our workers to live a better life and have a brighter future in the 21st century.

Rising to the Challenge of the Changing Environment

Sustaining healthy economic growth in future will not be easy. As we move up the economic ladder, we will face new challenges in including slower economic growth, keener and stronger competition, faster pace of technological changes and an ageing workforce. More companies will go through right-sizing exercises to remain competitive. We must prepare our workers and look after their interests as we go through this process of economic upgrading. We will work in partnership with the government and the employers in creating our future.

A Total Worker for the 21st Century

The vision of the labour movement is for every worker to possess better skills so that he can secure a better job, enjoy better pay and live a better life. We also want our worker to be one with a healthy body and a healthy mind, and one who cares for and shares with the society at large. Our blueprint to take the labour movement into the 21st century is based on these five key pillars:

* Enhance employability for life.
* Strengthen competitiveness.
* Build healthy body, healthy mind.
* Care more, share more.
* Develop stronger labour movement.

ENHANCE EMPLOYABILITY FOR LIFE

To grow, we have to go beyond what we have already mastered.

Our Aim

Our workers must be employable throughout their working life for them to live an enriching life. We must invest in the young and the not-so-young. Every worker will have the change to upgrade and update his skills through continuing education and training. We aim for 100 per cent skills certification in our workforce so that every worker will possess the skills needed to perform his job productively, now and in future.

Quality Workforce

Our government is pro-worker and pro-business. It is committed to attract more and better foreign and local investments to create good-paying jobs for our workers. Our workers must be multi-skilled, highly productive, adaptable and responsive so that they can take on these better-paying jobs of the future.

Better Skills, Better Wages

Even though many of our workers are not highly educated, we must recognise that undereducated workers are not necessarily under-skilled. Many of them have years of valuable experience. We will help them to keep with the pace of economic upgrading. They must have life-long employability in order to enjoy a more secure and enriching life.

Strategies

Skills Certification for All: Every worker will be trained and tested for specific skills, and given certificates that will be recognised at industry and national levels. We have started with 10 companies and 1,500 workers through the collaborative effort of the NTUC, EDB, PSB and IYE. We aim to expand this Skills Redevelopment Programme into a national programme for all workers, beginning with union members.

Productivity through Innovation: We must work hard and smart. Innovation in the workplace must go beyond the R&D laboratory to reach the production floor. We must bring out the creativity in our workers for them to become thinking workers.

A Learning Nation: We strive to make learning a way of life for all workers. We will help with training grants and by delivering training courses to their homes through the use of IT.

Employment Assistance through Information Link: Together with other government bodies, we will help workers affected by retrenchment by providing them with skills redevelopment and job matching.

Shared Responsibility: Realising the full potential of our workers is a shared responsibility of the government, employers, employees and labour movement. Our vision is for our workers to be multi-skilled, highly motivated and adaptable, and responsive to market needs. We call on Government and employers to help make this a reality.

STRENGTHEN COMPETITIVENESS THROUGH SHARED RESPONSIBILITY

Doing the common things uncommonly well in the first league.

Playing to Win

As we move up the economic ladder, we will compete with developing and developed economies for foreign direct investments. The tripartite partnership will come under greater stress due to greater uncertainty in the global economy. The labour movement, Government and employers must strengthen our tripartite partnership so that the economy can grow, companies can be profitable, and workers can be fully employed.

New Challenges

With more intense competition, employers will want greater flexibility in the deployment of workers to respond faster to changing market conditions. But employees will need employment stability so that they can commit themselves wholeheartedly to their employers. The tripartite partners will have to harmonise the interests of workers with the needs of companies. This can be achieved by building on our harmonious industrial relations climate.

Strategies

The tripartite partnership has worked well at the national level. We must build on this strong foundation and at the same time strengthen the partnership at the company level.

Mutual Dependency, Respect and Support: Employers and employees must share the same vision for their companies. We call on employers to have greater trust and confidence in the leadership of unions at all levels, and involve the labour movement in decision-making. We can achieve more together if we respect each other as equal partners.

Pro-active Industrial Relations: The labour movement believes in addressing key labour issues before they become major problems. We will continue to adopt a pro-active, enlighted and constructive approach in addressing industrial relations issues. We call on our tripartite partners to do likewise.

Adaptable and Responsive Workforce: To help strengthen our economic competitiveness, our workers must be prepared to adopt and respond to changes in work patterns. We will help our workers to save more during good times so that they will be more ready to make temporary sacrifices to help their companies recover from any temporary setbacks. We call on employers to do their part in sharing more gains with our workers during good times.

BUILD HEALTHY BODY, HEALTHY MIND

In our quest to be the best, we must also enjoy the race.

Work Hard, Play Hard

Our workers must be able to work hard, play hard, stay healthy and enjoy quality living to sustain a high level of performance. Workers with healthy bodies and minds will be better able to cope with stress, and stay employable throughout their working lives. We will develop and operate a variety of quality and affordable lifestyle facilities at convenient locations in Singapore and overseas for our workers to live a fuller life.

Strategies

We want our workers to have healthy, financially secure and fulfilling lifestyles.

Stretching the Dollar: Our NTUC Cooperatives, NTUC Club and SLF will continue to offer goods and services at prices that will help our workers stretch their hard-earned dollars. In this way, they can enhance the benefits gained through union negotiations. We will also find new ways to help their money grow. With more disposable income, our workers can enjoy the wide range of quality yet affordable social and recreational facilities.

Enhancing the Options: We will build more lifestyle centres. Our aim is to have one such centre in each of our major housing estates. We also propose to develop more holiday facilities abroad. Older NTUC Club branches and NTUC Fair Price outlets will be rejuvenated while newer and better ones will be added. We will continue to emphasise occupational health and safety and promote healthy lifestyle through wellness programmes, and health education.

THE NTUC FAMILY

NTUC's Main Objectives

(1) To improve the working conditions of workers and enhance their economic and social status;

(2) To promote good labour-management relations and industrial harmony so as to ensure the well-being of workers, and to achieve economic growth for companies and the nation;

(3) To secure opportunities for workers to upgrade their skills and productivity for their personal benefit as well as the benefit of their employers;

(4) To take part in the national decision-making process through tripartite bodies like the National Wages Council, representation on statutory boards, and the work of Labour Members of Parliament;

(5) To organise educational, cultural, recreational and other activities for the benefit of active and retired members and their families, as well as charitable activities to help the less privileged in society;

(6) To work with fraternal trade unions around the world in opposing various forms of social injustice and discrimination.

Overview

NTUC came into being at a time of industrial and political strife. In 1961, the year it was set up, there were 116 strikes, with the loss of over 4,00,000 mandays.

The first major step towards creating a more harmonious industrial relations climate came in 1965 when NTUC and employer bodies pledged to work for higher productivity and growth. Government was a signatory to this Charter for Industrial Progress. The three parties also signed a Productivity Code of Practice calling for the establishment of consultative councils at the workplace to promote productivity.

It took many more years before stable industrial relations became the norm, with tripartism as the guiding spirit. The establishment of the National Wages Council (NWC) in 1972 was a major step towards tripartite cooperation, and gave credence to the belief that tripartism can work.

With rapid economic growth, our unions were able to secure higher wages and improved employment conditions for our workers.

But when NTUC noted signs of a sharp economic downturn in 1985, its affiliates decided to forge wage increases that had been recommended by the NWC. The objectives was to help companies and our country ride out the storms of the impending recession.

During that recession many jobs were lost. NTUC decided to support the Government's move to reduce temporarily the employers' contribution to their workers' Central Provident Fund accounts from 25 to 10 per cent.

This cut, together with severe wage restraints, which NTUC, agreed to, led to a quick economic recovery. Since then, there has been a gradual restoration of the CPF cuts. Government and business leaders have openly acknowledged their appreciation of the role played by NTUC during the difficult period in the mid-1980s.

While protecting workers' rights remains the top priority of our trade unions, they have not limited their scope to just wage negotiations and settlement of disputes. Our unions are proud to be partners in the economic and social development of the nation. They actively promote skills upgrading, productivity growth, cultural development, a healthy lifestyle and nation-building.

The labour movement has also set up quality recreational facilities for our workers, such as the NTUC Pasir Ris Resort and NTUC Club outlets. By 1993, the Orchid Country Club, which will have golfing facilities, and the Sentosa Holiday Resort should be ready. Pasir Ris Resort will also be upgraded and expanded. These recreational facilities enable our workers to enjoy the fruits of the nation's success, to which they have contributed significantly.

NTUC has long enjoyed good rapport with workers. Our symbiotic relationship with the ruling People's Action Party and our tripartite partnership with government and employers have been key factors in our ability to represent and protect the long-term interests of our workers.

Remaining Competitive — A Joint Effort

"Remaining competitive is not only a matter of holding down wage costs, but also of raising productivity so that wages can go up without increasing business costs.

Management must find ways of raising productivity. One of these is improving the skills of workers. More and more, higher growth and incomes will depend on workers mastering new and more sophisticated equipment, and being able to diagnose and solve problems quickly and independently. This is the responsibility of both workers as well as employers. Workers must be willing to learn new skills, and take on expanded responsibilities. Employers must continually ask themselves how best to train and deploy workers, not just to raise profits, but also to create more challenging and satisfying jobs. I urge employers and workers to work together to strengthen our competitiveness, both by making realistic wage settlements and by investing in training and higher productivity. That is the way to secure a better future for ourselves and our children."

— Prime Minister Goh Chok Tong, May Day 1992.

Union Structure

Our trade unions are run along democratic lines. It is up to the workers themselves to choose whether they wish to join unions. In addition union leaders at all levels are elected by secret ballot. Major decisions on industrial action are also taken only with majority support expressed through a secret ballot.

There are three tiers of union leadership; the Branch Committee, the Union Executive Committee and, at the national level, the NTUC Central Committee.

Branch officials are elected by unionised employees of the branch. Key branch officials represent their branches at Union Headquarters as delegates. They have the right to vote or stand as candidates in elections to the Union Executive Committee.

Affiliated unions are represented at the NTUC Delegates' Conference, the supreme authority of the labour movement. The Delegates' conference is normally held twice in three years. During this conference, delegates review the work of NTUC and map out future directions for the labour movement.

Once in three years, the union delegates elect a 21-member NTUC Central Committee. The Central Committee members elect among themselves the Secretary-General, the President, the Vice-Presidents and the Secretary for Finance (treasurer). The Central Committee appoints other principal office bearers and the NTUC Secretariat.

Union leadership has been strengthened by the induction of professionals, including PAP MPs. These MPs are subject to elections, just as the other grassroot unionists are. Many other MPs, including Cabinet Ministers serve as union advisors.

Responsibilities

At Branch Level: The duty of branch officials is to serve members at the branch, or company, level. They try to resolve grievances through negotiations with management. Only when such problems cannot be resolved do headquarters officials come into the picture. Branch officials form part of the union delegation at collective bargaining sessions.

Another important role of branch officials is to serve as links between workers and leaders at union headquarters and the national centre. They help explain labour and national issues and get feedback on implementation of policies and matters of concern to workers. Branch officials also help mobilise workers for mass activities.

At Union Headquarters Level: The Union Executive Committee is responsible for the effective operation of the union. It coordinates the work of the various branches and maintains close contact with NTUC. The Executive Committee guides the Branch Committees in industrial relations and other matters and also takes an active role in collective bargaining. Where necessary, it can tap NTUC's expertise in carrying out complex negotiations.

Each Executive Committee appoints committees to deal with specific areas such as industrial relations, organising, financial matters, education, skills upgrading, occupational health and safety, social and welfare services, culture and recreation.

At National Level: The NTUC Central Committee is the highest policy-making body of the labour movement, subject only to the overriding powers of the NTUC Delegates' Conference. It oversees the work of the NTUC secretariat and other organisations set up by the labour movement.

The NTUC Secretariat, led by the Secretary General, is responsible for the day-to-day running of NTUC. It is made up of various departments dealing with:

- Administration
- Community Services
- Cooperatives
- Culture
- Finance
- Industrial Relations
- International Affairs
- Occupational Health & Safety
- Organising
- Productivity Promotion
- Skills Development
- Sports
- Women's Programme
- Youth

NTUC Central Committee

President
Vice-Presidents
Secretary-General
Deputy Secretaries-General
Assistant Secretaries-General
Treasurer
Committee Members
Committee meets monthly; it oversees the work of the NTUC Secretariat

NTUC Secretariat

Secretary-General
Deputy Secretaries-General
Assistant Secretaries-General
Secretaries (in charge of departments listed at right)

Departments:

- Administration
- Community Services
- Cooperatives
- Culture
- Finance
- Industrial Relations
- International Affairs
- Occupational Health & Safety
- Organising
- Productivity Promotion
- Skills Development
- Sports
- Women's Programme
- Youth
- Computer Services
- Legal
- Library
- NTUC News
- Planning & Research

Union representation at national level

The Central Committee is NTUC's highest policy-making body. Represented on this committee for 1991-1994 are 17 unions. To carry out this committee's decisions, executive functions are vested in the Secretary-general, heading the NTUC Secretariat, which is also responsible for the day-to-day running of NTUC.

NTUC also provides legal advice and management backing to affiliated unions. Other support services include a resource library, a computer department, and a publications department. Labour education and leadership training for union leaders is provided by the Singapore Institute of Labour Studies (SILS).

The Secretary-General, who is the Chief Executive of NTUC, and members of the Central Committee have regular dialogue sessions with leaders from affiliated unions to discuss important issues. Leaders from union headquarters hold similar sessions with branch officials, who in turn keep the ground posted on current developments.

TRADE UNIONS ARE DOWN BUT NOT OUT IN THE INDUSTRIALISED COMPANIES

Down but Not Out

Why union membership is dwindling in industrialised countries?

Changes in the Composition of the Labour Market: The falling share of manufacturing industries has led to fewer 'blue-collar' workers and more 'white-collar' employees who are less attracted to unions.

Competition from Developing Countries with Low Labour Costs: Has led to the gradual disappearance of low-skilled, labour-intensive jobs in the vulnerable industrial sectors of high-wage countries.

Impact of Globalisation: Rapid technological change and greater freedom of choice for enterprises in deciding where to set up their business are leading to changes in production and working methods and locations.

New Constraints on Macro-economic Policies: Have affected worker and union strategies.

New Strategies to Win New Members

- Provision of new services, such as supplementary social benefits, professional advisory services, and preferential rates such as discounts on loans, insurance premiums and credit cards for members.
- Recruiting new members to reach out to women, young people, workers in small and medium-sized enterprises, informal-sector employees and the jobless.
- Expansion of international cooperation.
- Forging new alliances.

THE NUMBERS IN 1995

Region	*Members*
Sub-Saharan Africa	10,027,000
North Africa and Middle East	7,338,000
North America	20,489,000
Central America	11,042,000
South America	22,431,000
Oceania	2,802,000
East and South-east Asia	23,930,000
South Asia	10,445,000
Northern Europe	7,527,000

Western Europe	23,749,000
Southern Europe	10,174,000
Central and Eastern Europe	13,993,000
Total	1,63,947,000

Source: International Labour Organisation, 1997-98, Annual Report.

UNIONS TAKE ON SOCIAL ROLES AS MEMBERSHIP DIPS

Some opening doors to those with no stable employment to stay afloat.

The trade-union movement has fallen on hard times.

Workers' organisations are facing serious difficulties almost everywhere and are losing members.

Some even had doubts about their future, said the International Labour Organisation (ILO) in its 1997-98 annual report.

New methods of production and communication, globalisation of the economy, new approaches to human-resource development, and stiffer competition all have a telling effect on states, companies and trade unions.

The ILO annual study showed that trade-union membership dropped sharply during the last decade, falling to less than 20 per cent of workers in 48 out of 92 countries surveyed.

It said that in 1995, some 164 million of the world's estimated workforce of 1.3 billion belonged to trade unions.

In only 14 of the 92 countries surveyed did the union membership rate exceed 50 per cent of the national workforce. In all but about 20 countries, membership levels declined during the last decade.

However, the 283-page report said that the downward trends had not meant a drop in influence. In most countries, trade unions had managed to consolidate their strength in core sectors, enlist members in emerging sectors and develop new collective-bargaining strategies, often on a global scale.

The report said that much of the decline was due to economic factors such as reduced public sector employment, increased economic competition and a falling share of manufacturing industries.

But the rise or fall was also linked to political changes or major legislative overhauls in many countries and regions.

For example, the drop was sharpest in central and eastern European countries, which saw an average dip of almost 36 per cent, much of which resulted from the ending of quasi-obligatory union membership following the break-up of the former Soviet bloc.

In contrast, the largest single increase in union membership — of 130.8 per cent — came in South Africa, especially during the post-apartheid era.

The ILO also noted that in countries such as the United Kingdom, Australia and New Zealand, declines in union membership stemmed partly from the weakening of laws protecting unions.

In the United States, 21.1 per cent fewer workers joined unions, mainly because of the introduction of new technologies.

Membership rise in East Asian and South-east Asian countries had also not been significant, except in the Philippines and Hongkong.

The report said that some governments "adopted a restrictive policy with regard to recognising unions in the hope of attracting foreign investment."

It added that while unions in most countries had moved "towards a less-adversarial and more-cooperative" approach, trade unions had shown themselves capable of wielding power in times of crisis.

For instance, in a number of recent industrial and political crises, unions proved decisive in reaching settlements in France, Germany and South Korea.

Turning to the future, the report said there was every sign that a whole new social dynamic was developing.

The most active trade unions were looking beyond the working population and opening their doors to those who had no stable employment, or no jobs at all.

Both in word and in deed, they were looking more and more like genuine social movements with a clear vision of how to defend and promote the interests of workers.

2. AMERICAN AND INDIAN TRADE UNION MOVEMENTS

A. American Labour Movement

A study of the American Labour Movement reveals four distinct stages of development: (1) Struggle for organisation of unions, (2) struggle for recognition of unions, (3) Success and accommodation, and (4) Consolidation and problems of consolidation.

1. Struggle for Organisation: In the beginning in the early part of 18th century, there was tremendous struggle for the organisation of unions. The employers were hostile to any association of wage-earners and they often resorted to violence to prevent the union organisation. The attitudes of the government and courts were also unhelpful. Labour agitation also became particularly violent, after the civil war when modern industrial growth began.

2. Struggle for Recognition: This phase of the struggle was to gain recognition of the unions and their rights to represent the employees and protect their interests. Through picketing, demonstrations, boycotts, and strikes, gradually unions forced the employers to recognise their existence. Instead of violence, often employers introduced paternalistic welfare schemes to keep the unions out.

3. Success and Accommodation: The growth of corporate power, the Great Crash in 1929 with its consequent evils, and the New Deal Administration, and the American ethos of providing a system of checks and balances and also responsible unions with mainly economic motives all combined to bring about public policy which required union recognition and there was a spurt in the following decade (1945-1955) in union growth and union membership growth from 3.5 million to 15.5 million.

4. Consolidation: Now the unions entered a period of consolidation where they were facing innumerable issues in the form of union democracy, union security, civil rights, union growth etc. They are attempting to establish and broaden the ethical bases and to combat corruption, fraud and ruse in the union movement. In this phase a study of unionism may perceive the gradual transition where, from merely the protection of economic interests of the membership, the unions are taking active interest in the political affairs, and international affairs.

Significant Milestones in American Labour Movement

In the incipient stage, there were unions and national unions belonging to one trade and the initiative in union organisation and development came from the craft workers. The significant dates and union formations are as follows:

1792 — National Union of Cordwainers (shoe makers) in Philadelphia.

1850 — National Union of Typographers.

1853 — National Union of Stonecutters.

1854 — National Union of Hatfinishers.

By the end of Civil War, there were at least thirty six union organisations. Then we notice the beginning of an era of the growth of inter-trade unions.

1866 — *National Labour Union* at Baltimore, which was an association of city central bodies, but they were weak and ineffective and short-lived, because of their dependence upon the city federations.

1869 — *Knights of Labour* at Philadelphia, which tried to amalgamate all unions and proposed to include skilled, and semi-skilled and unskilled members along with craft unions and their members. In 1886 they had a membership of about 703,000. The Knights of Labour had a broad range of goals representing diversified interests and also extensive political goals. These and a series of unsuccessful strikes led to its downfall eventually.

1886 — *American Federation of Labour (AFL):* In 1881 the skilled craftsmen came to feel so strongly that their interests were adversely affected by the huge masses of unskilled labourers, who belonged to the Knights, formed the Federation of Organised Trade and Labour Unions. Five years later, it came to be known as the American Federation of Labour (AFL) composing mainly of craft unions and its first president was Samuel Gompers, who was a dynamic leader and who kept the unions out of politics.

1935 — *Congress of Industrial Organisations (CIO):* The groups, who wanted to organise semi-skilled and unskilled workers, formed into the Congress of Industrial Organisations. For about 20 years from 1886 to 1935 the American Labour movement was sharply divided over the issue of craft and industrial unionism.

1955 — *AFL-CIO:* Finally the two organisations decided to merge into a new American Federation of Labour and Congress of Industrial Organisations, popularly known as "AFL-CIO".[5]

Union Objectives

Generally the objectives of trade unions are: (1) to defend and improve the wages and working conditions of labour; (2) to raise the status of the worker as a citizen of industry and of society; and (3) to extend the area of social control of the nation's economic life and participating in that control. The objectives of unions were explained by the first president of AFL, Samuel Gompers thus:[6] "The primary essential in our mission has been:

1. The protection of the wage-worker, now;
2. To increase his wages;
3. To cut hours off the long workday, which was killing him;
4. To improve the safety and sanitary conditions of the workshop;
5. To free him from the tyrannies, petty or otherwise, which served to make his existence a slavery. These in the nature of things, I repeat, were and are the primary objects of trade unionism."

Some Union Characteristics

1. A union normally represents members in many companies throughout the industry or occupation.
2. A union develops an industrial life of its own beyond the lives of the individual members. A basic objective of that development is strength, power and prestige of the union as such. Internal conflicts must be ironed out and members bound by a common philosophy and achievement.
3. A union is fundamentally an employer regulating device. It sharpens management efficiency and performance while protecting the interests of the membership.
4. A union is a part of the working class movement.
5. A union is a pressure organisation originating in the desire on the part of a group with relatively little power to influence the action of a group with relatively more power.
6. A union is a political institution in its internal structure and procedures.

Organising the Pros

A Conference Board research report states that two dramatic changes are altering the American labour force, an increase in the proportion of salaried professional and technical employees and a gradual "blueing" of the white collar professional as more occupations become unionised.

In recent years, professionals in education, government service, and non-profit organisations have reached for the union label. Teaching and nursing associations have evolved into collective bargaining units whose militancy has been clearly demonstrated, particularly in New York and other major metropolitan areas, by a willingness and ability to use the strike weapon. Over all, an estimated 40 per cent of all salaried non-managerial professionals are represented by collective bargaining agents, compared with 25 per cent of the labour force as a whole, according to the Board's new study on the unionisation of professional societies.

So far, however, scientists and engineers — private industry's largest professional employee group — have generally refrained from involvement in this trend towards increasing union activity. In contrast to the rapid increase in cohesiveness among other specialists, the report notes, the "proportion of unionised engineers and scientists has hovered between 5 and 10 per cent for about 20 years." But engineers and scientists constitute a unique group — "still relatively well paid, many with management aspirations, and still looking to their professional societies or their own individual efforts, rather than to any union effort, to improve and advance within the company."

But even these societies are changing, according to labour relations analyst Eileen B. Hoffman, who reports that "growing unemployment and income cuts among scientists and engineers have prompted the societies to lift their traditional taboos against dealing with employment security and compensation issues." Many of these societies have joined in issuing a set of employment "Guidelines for Engineers and Scientists." They also have developed placement programs, job-counselling workshops, and salary surveys and recommendations while pushing for employment contracts and legislation on behalf of job security and pension reform. As Hoffman sees the picture, a major segment of the upper-income work force is dissatisfied with some aspects of employer-employee relations, but is not yet ready to give up the status and perquisites of "professionalism" for union membership. "The attitudes as much as pressure from unions or corporate responses will determine the evolution of professional societies," the analysis notes.

Look at Britain

One need only look over to the United Kingdom to see how far the unionisation of professionals and managers can go. The British magazine *Management Today* describes the pace of white collar union growth as "amazing," and a research unit at Ashridge researchers Vivian Shackleton and Judith Davies, "White collar unions are not only finding new members among lower-paid non-manual workers, but are progressing well into the ranks of lower and middle management." After polling a panel of 500 managers from a cross-section of British industry, Shackleton and Davies wrote that the "results suggest that already at least half of those managers who are able to join a union decide to do so... (and)... given the snowball effect of an increasing proportion of managers joining unions, the field seems wide open for active unions. In the not too distant future, managers and other white collar workers may well be as heavily unionised as blue collar workers. Managers themselves seem to think so."[7]

The strength of the union movement in terms of membership is difficult to state with precision, though statistics are gathered by the Bureau of Labour Statistics in a biannual basis. The report for 1972 indicates that the total membership of national and international unions that had collective bargaining agreements with different employers in more than one state stood at approximately 20.9 million. After an absolute net decline during the 1960s, the union movement in recent years has slowly but steadily increased in numbers — 20.2 million in 1968, 20.7 million in 1970, and 20.9 million in the last reported period. However, the percentage of the United States labour force that this represents stands at 21.8 per cent, the lowest in the past three decades. The high percentage point for unionisation was reached in 1953, when 27.1 per cent of the labour force was organised.

Table 14.1
MEMBERSHIP IN AMERICAN LABOUR ORGANISATIONS, 1897-1960

Year	*Total Membership*	*Year*	*Total Membership*
1897	440,000	1929	3,625,000
1898	467,000	1930	3,632,000
1899	550,000	1931	3,526,000
1900	791,000	1932	3,226,000
1901	1,058,000	1933	2,857,000
1902	1,335,000	1934	3,249,000
1903	2,824,000	1935	3,728,000
1904	2,067,000	1936	4,164,000
1905	1,918,000	1937	7,218,000
1906	1,892,000	1938	8,265,000
1907	2,077,000	1939	8,980,000
1908	2,092,000	1940	8,944,000
1909	1,965,000	1941	10,489,000
1910	2,116,000	1942	10,762,000
1911	2,318,000	1943	13,642,000
1912	2,405,000	1944	14,621,000
1913	2,661,000	1945	14,796,000
1914	2,647,000	1946	14,974,000
1915	2,560,000	1947	15,414,000
1916	2,722,000	1948	15,600,000
1917	2,976,000	1949	15,800,000
1918	3,368,000	1950	15,800,000
1919	4,046,000	1951	16,750,000
1920	5,034,000	1952	16,750,000
1921	4,722,000	1953	16,948,000
1922	3,950,000	1954	17,022,000
1923	3,629,000	1955	16,802,000
1924	3,549,000	1956	17,490,000
1925	3,566,000	1957	17,369,000
1926	3,592,000	1958	17,029,000
1927	3,600,000	1959	17,117,000
1928	3,567,000	1960	17,049,009

Sources: John M. Brumm and Nelson M. Borz, "Brief History of the American Labour Movement", Release W-558. Washington, D.C. Bureau of Labour Statistics October 1947; Leo Wolman *Ebb and Flow in Trade Union,* New York: National Bureau of Economic Research, 1936. Subsequent directions of national and international unions and released by the United States, Department of Labour; Harry P. Cohany, "Membership of American Trade Union, 1960", *Monthly Labour Review,* Vol. 84, No. 12, December 1961, pp. 1299-1303.

Of the total union membership, 16.5 million are in unions affiliated with the AFL-CIO. Two of the three largest single unions are not affiliated with this national organisation — the Teamsters, with 1.86 million members, and the United Auto Workers, with 1.39 million, remains an affiliate of the AFL-CIO.

U.S. Union Membership Registers Steady Rise: The membership of 185 national unions headquartered in the United States increased by half million between 1968 and 1970 to a record of 20.7 million, the Bureau of Labour Statistics reported.

AFL-CIO affiliates reported a total membership of 15,916,000 in 1970, an increase of about 370,0000 over 1968. The total include 14,969,000 members in the U.S. and 1,220,000 outside the country, nearly all in Canada.

"Dire predictions regarding union stagnation appear unfounded," BLS said in a summary. "In the last six years, unions recruited an average of more than 460,000 (members) annually."

The increase in total membership was reflected in changes in most of the components of membership studied, BLS said. The number of women in unions rose by 342,000 over the two-year period to 4.3 million. White-collar union membership totalling 3.4 million reached a new peak in 1970, rising by 177,000 since 1968.

According to the BLS survey, national unions which had more than half a million members in 1970 were the Teamsters 1.829 million; Auto workers, 1.486 million; Steel-workers, 1.2 million; International Brotherhood of Electrical Workers, 922,000; Machinists, 865,000, and labourers, 580,000.

BLS reported that the most dramatic increases over the 1960-70 decade occurred in the government sector unions. In 1950, for example, three government unions — The Fire Fighters, Government Employees and Teachers — each reported fewer than 1,000,000 members. Ten years later, they ranked 37th, 17th and 27th, respectively, out of 48 unions in the 100,000 or over category.

Among the "big worth" unions and employee associations from 1958 to 1970 were AFGE with a 442 per cent growth rate during the period; State, Country and Municipal Employees, 122 per cent; Rental Clerks, 98 per cent; Service Employees 122 per cent and Communications workers, 65 per cent.[8]

Union Finances: Unions are financial healthy and sound and often unionism in U.S.A. is referred to as big business. Professor Yoder writes:[9] "Annual income from dues is in excess of 600 million dollars. About 280 millions of this total goes to the internationals. The Labour Management Reporting and Disclosure Act of 1959 has provided details on the financial aspects of American Unions. Monthly dues per member average about $ 3. Some 71 per cent of the reporting unions charge members less than $ 5 per month. Initiation fees range from no fee to more than $ 100, with one-fourth of all unions charging $ 5 or less. Approximately 10 per cent charge initiation fees of more than $ 100. A few unions charge transfer fees; more than half amount to less than $ 3; about 5 per cent charge more than $ 100. Work permit fees for non-members are issued by less than 10 per cent of reporting unions. Two-thirds of the monthly permit fees are less than $ 5.... International unions and the AFL-CIO are supported by per capita taxes paid by locals on behalf of their members. For AFL-CIO, locals pay a per capita tax of 4 cents per month. Internationals receive per capita taxes

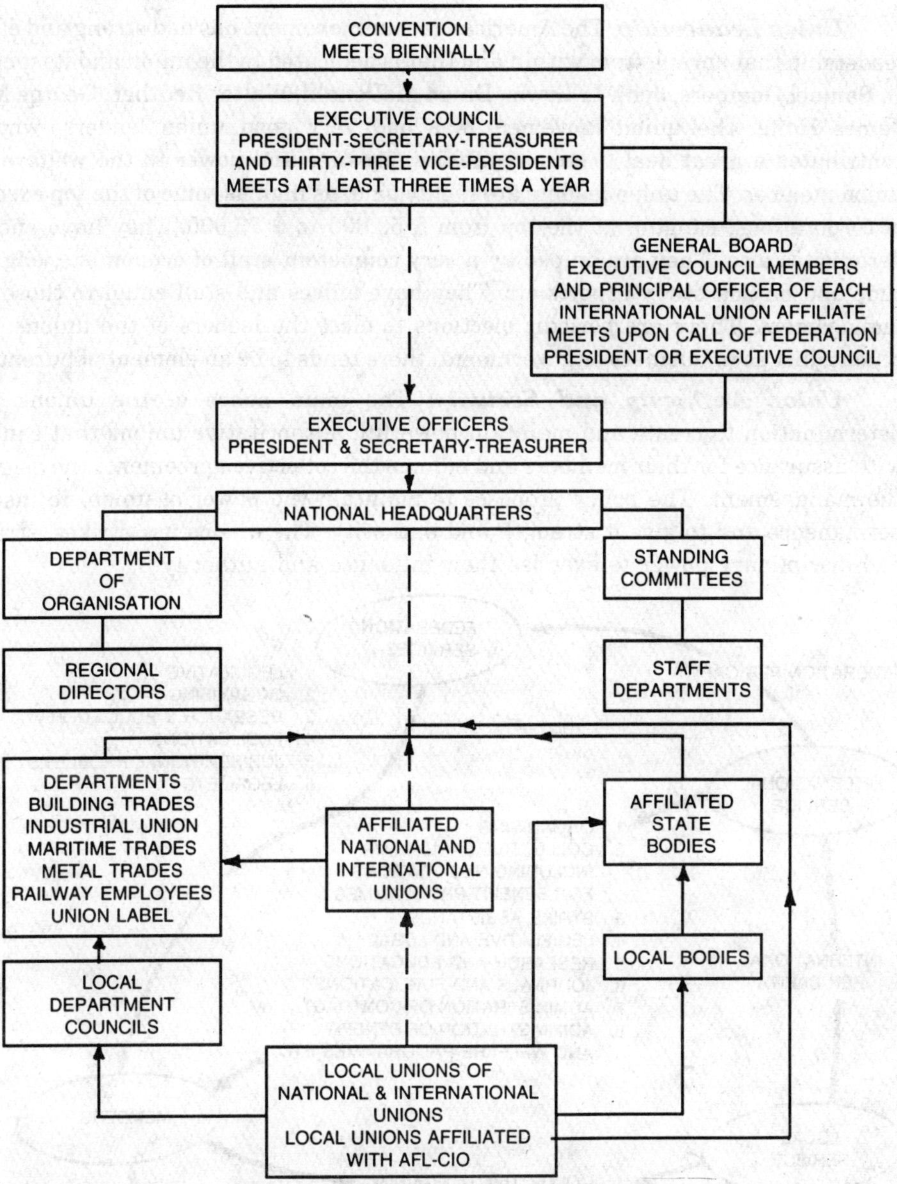

Fig. 14.1 Organisation of AFL-CIO

Source: U.S. Department of Labour, Director and National and International Labour Unions in the United States, 1971, Bulletin No. 1750 (1970) p. 64.

of 50 cents or more per month, depending largely on the range of benefits and services provided for their members." A summary of such services are outlined in Fig. 14.2.

As a matter of fact there is a trend where the unions are attempting to take over many of the company-operated services and benefits to the employees. Prominent among the services provided by the unions to their members are in the areas of health, education — economic and political training, research, safety, travel, rest homes, legal aid, etc.

Union Leadership: The American labour movement has had strong and effective leadership that sprang from within and that is dedicated to the union and its members. In Samuel Gompers, John L. Lewis, David McDonald, Walter Reuther, George Meany, James Hoffa, the union movement has had very good union leaders, who have contributed a great deal to union stability, prestige and power to the welfare of the union member. The union leaders are highly paid, as high as some of the top executives of corporations, ranging at the top from $ 50,000 to $ 75,000. They have enormous perquisites also. They are helped by a very competent staff of economists, engineers, time and motion study experts etc. They have offices and staff equal to those of the management. There are periodic elections to elect the leaders of the unions. In big unions, just as in business or government, there tends to be an element of bureaucracy.

Union Authority and Security: The main policy of the unions is the determination to create and maintain powerful, authoritative unions that can speak with assurance for their members and enforce the collective agreements they sign with the management. The policy proposes to maintain the power of union, to insure its permanence and to give it strength and authority. The unions use strikes, strike aid and disciplinary power to exercise their influence and authority.

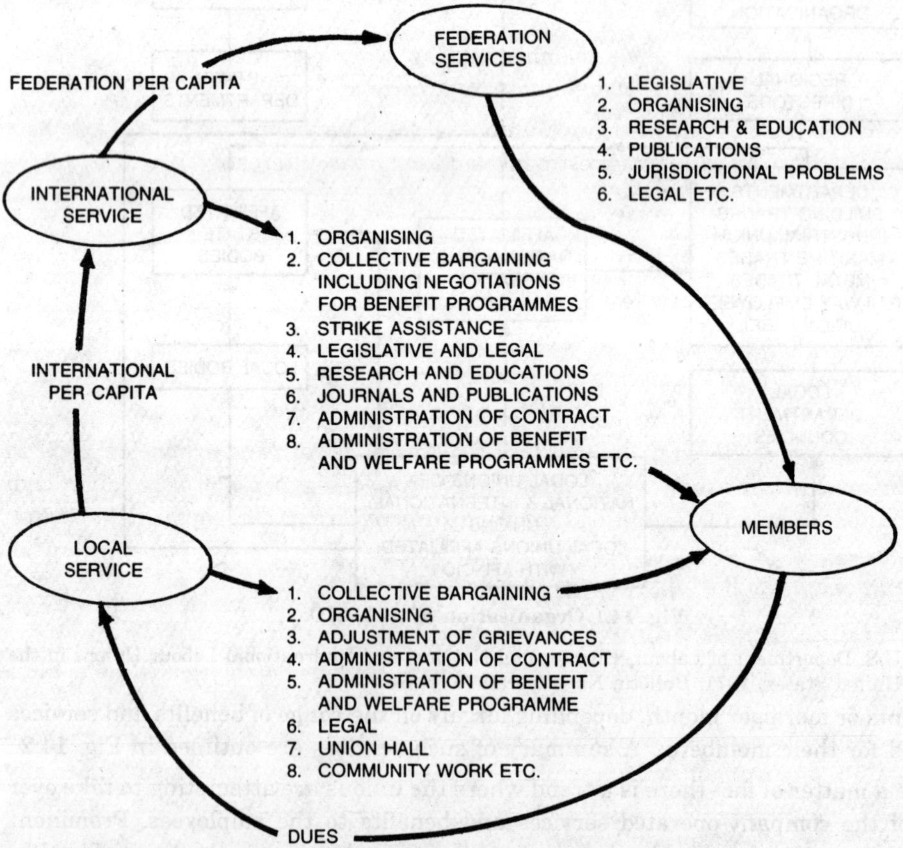

Fig. 14.2 Flow of Union Revenues and Services

Source: "Directory of Labour Unions in the United States", Bulletin. No. 1127, United States Department of Labour, 1953, 3.

Union Security: The union exercises its right to speak for its members in negotiating agreements and in enforcing the provisions of such contracts. The union is the agent of the employees.

Question of Recognition: Union demands employers to recognise the union as the bargaining agent. When several unions want to represent the employees, government, through National Labour Relations Act (NLRA) of 1935, has given the authority to the National Labour Relations Board (NLRB) to designate appropriate bargaining unit in interstate business. Many states provide State Labour Relations Board with similar authority in intra-state disputes. Federal and State labour Boards, in case of inter-union conflict, may call for membership authorisation cards or hold elections and designate one union as the *certified bargaining* agent of the unit.

Code of Ethical Practices: At the annual convention of AFL-CIO in 1957, the Code of Ethical Practices was adopted with a view to ensuring democratic controls and the protection of individual members as well as to fight racketeering and gangsterism in some unions. There are six codes:

Code (i) deals with the issuance of local union charters;

Code (ii) stipulates standards of behaviour in the handling of health and welfare funds.

Code (iii) is designed to force member unions to purge their organisations or racketeers, crooks, communists and fascists.

Code (iv) specifies principles to guide union officials in avoiding conflicts of interests arising out of their investments and business interests.

Code (v) requires appropriate accounting and auditing practices to insure that union funds and property are used as intended for the benefit of members.

Code (vi) deals specifically with democratic processes within unions, requires elections at specified periods, and requires that the conventions be open to public, and that safeguards be provided for the protection of individual members in expressing their views.

Union Problems: The American labour unions are facing various problems in the areas of union leadership, union democracy, union growth and expansion, right to work controversy, growth of white collar unionism at the expense of blue collar, civil rights, automation and retraining, inflation, union corruption and fraud, leisure, collective bargaining and negotiations, arbitration etc. There is still some amount of public and employer hostility toward unionism in U.S.A.

B. The Indian Trade Union Movement

The Evolution of Union Movement: Some form of trade union organisations came into existence after the establishment of factories in India after the 1860s. In 1875, a few social workers and philanthropists led by Sorabji Shapurji started a labour agitation in Bombay against the appalling condition of workers in factories, especially those of women and children and appealed to the authorities to provide legislative protection. There were sporadic agitations and strikes over the issue of wage rates and workers came together at the time of the strikes and again disintegrated. Between 1882 and 1890, twenty-five strikes were recorded in Madras and Bombay Provinces alone.

But these upheavals disappeared declined and was almost forgotten during the periods of famine, plague, and the consequent depression in the country at the end of nineteenth century.

In 1890 the first labour organisation was founded by N.M. Lokhande, who began his working life as a factory worker and started labour movement in India and the organisation was the Bombay Millhands Association, whose first president was Lokhande. The first working class newspaper *Dinabandhu* (Friend of Poor) was also started by Lokhande in order to place before the Government and employers the legitimate grievances of workers.

Between 1904 and 1911 there was a further advance in the organisation of unions, such as the Amalgamated Society of Railway Servants of India and Burma in 1897, the Printers' Union in Calcutta in 1905, the Bombay Postal Union in 1907 and the Kamgar Hitavardhak Sabha (Workers' Welfare Association) in 1910. The last named was formed by philanthropists, who also started a weekly called "Kamgar Samachar" (Labour News). This association did some good work in settling disputes and in sending petitions to the Government. That the labour movement in India was under the influence of "outside leadership", the freedom struggle and the swadeshi movement was underscored by the political strike for 6 days undertaken by four-fifths of Bombay's workers in protest against the sentence of six years' imprisonment imposed upon Lokamanya Tilak in 1908.

Factors Favourable to the Growth of the Union Movement: First, the economic distress caused during the First World War was responsible for a mass awakening and while the employers were amassing huge profits, the purchasing power of wages was going down as a result of rising prices. In the political field, the Indian National Congress had formulated a demand for immediate self-government and the political leaders were aware of the potentialities of the power of organised labour and wanted to use this power to their advantage. Another aspect of the First World War, that led to the rapid rousing of the consciousness of the working class, as that many soldiers, who had gone out to the West, came back with the news of good labour conditions, in other countries. Secondly, political leaders, social reformers and philanthropists assisted greatly in the formation and development of trade unions. The mass movements started by Lokamanya Tilak, Annie Besant and later by Mahatma Gandhi had tremendous influence on the incipient association of workers. In particular, the non-coopertion movement launched by Gandhiji in 1919-21 and his championing the cause of the peasants and industrial labour had profound impact on the mass of workers. Mahatma Gandhi was also largely responsible for giving a new orientation to the labour movement by establishing the Ahmedabad Textile Labour Association, which insisted on the settlement of trade disputes by negotiations and peaceful methods before resorting to direct action.

Thirdly, a more direct cause for the formation of trade unions in India was the establishment of the International Labour Office of which India was a founder-member and the annual International Labour Conferences.[10] The government had to consult the workers' and employers' organisations for the choice of nominees. This, among other things, led to the establishment of the All India Trade Union Congress, a central federation representing the various trade unions affiliated to it; this formation gave status to the labour movement and provided a platform where labour problems could be discussed and debated. Fourthly, the success of the Russian Revolution had its own favourable effects on the India trade union movement. The revolution brought good tidings of a new social order to the common man and a ray of hope to the worker.

All these had an effect on the working classes in the country and led to the formation of a number of trade unions. In the words of R.K. Dass,[11] "with the social mind surcharged with the war spirit, political agitation and the revolutionary ideal, the labour class could no longer remain patient and tolerant under the old social wrongs and new economic disabilities."

Unfavourable Factors: There were some unfavourable factors that inhibited the growth of unionism in India. First of all, most of the workers' associations served as *ad hoc* associations and strike committees and once they achieved their purposes, they went into oblivion. Secondly, the recognition of the right of association was also not forthcoming. The employers, just as in other countries, would not recognise the worker associations and often they blacklisted and victimised those who took the initiative in organising the workers. Above all, the nature of the labour force in India was a great handicap. The dearth of skilled labour and craftsmen as well as an educated work-force forced the workers to wait for "outside leadership" to take up their cause and lead them.

Union Movement From 1918: The first labour organisation on the lines of a modern trade union that was formed in India was the Madras Labour Union in 1918 by B.P. Wadia, an active member of the Indian Home Rule League and an associate of Mrs. Besant. Its was primarily an organisation of textile workers employed in the Buckingham and Carnatic Mills in Madras. But membership was not restricted to textile labour only and every type of worker could join the union. The union became powerful in a short period of time. In view of poor wages, unsatisfactory working conditions and lack of a system of redressal of grievances, B.P. Wadia argued:[12] "Why should not labour in India be made vocal so that it can agitate against the existing Factory Act and gain for itself a reduction in working hours and do other sundry things.... *Mass movements of a political nature* have to begin sometime in India and somebody has to tackle the problem. I think the time has come to make a start and why should I not be that somebody." The *political* nature and the political link was further emphasised by Wadia:[13]

"It is very necessary to recognise the labour movement as an integral part of the national movement. The latter will not succeed in the right direction if the working classes are not able to organise their forces and come into their own." And again the union, in a resolution, stated that "this meeting further urges the Congress, in its selection of delegates, to choose at least one who could speak with authority and knowledge of the grievances of Indian labourers and their representatives in the reformed India council."

This was a period when the first attempts at union organisation were being made all over India and there is a trace of the workers in Ahmedabad Cotton Mills forming a union in 1917 under the leadership for Miss Anusuyabehn Sarabhai, sister of the Chairman of the Millowners' Association who led a strike of the workers at Ahmedabad at this time. In 1920 at Ahmedabad, under the inspiration of Mahatma Gandhi, occupational unions, such as Spinners' Union and Weavers' Union, were established and they federated into the now famous Ahmedabad Textile Labour Association, that has been an example of probably the most successful union in the country, organised on a basis of class peace.

Scores of unions came into existence between 1919 and 1923. However, there was great infant mortality among these unions. In Madras there developed rivalries and dissensions within the Madras Labour Union, encouraged by the employers, which led to its dissolution. In 1920 Wadia was prosecuted by the Company for inciting the workers to go on strike and the resulting court proceedings and verdict forced Wadia out of the union. In Britain a deputation from the Trade Union Congress waited on the Secretary of State for India to protest against the injustice and regarded it as an attack on the fledgling trade union movement. In India, this court decision focused public attention on the handicaps of organised workers. N.M. Joshi, regarded as the father of the modern trade union movement in India, agitated for legislation giving protection to the trade unions in the same way British legislation protected the unions in that country. After persistent efforts, for five years, the Indian Trade Unions Act was passed in 1926 and this Act gave the trade union a legal status and immunity to its officers and members from civil and criminal liability for concerted action.

In 1919-20, as a result of a wave of strikes, and realising the ineffectiveness of isolated unions all over the country, the need for a central coordinating trade union organisation was felt, which was accentuated by the necessity of electing delegates to the annual International Labour Conferences. When the Bombay trade union leaders complained that Government did not consult them in selecting delegates, the government made the point that there was no central union organisation. In view of all these, the first all India body was established in 1920 known as the All India Trade Union Congress (AITUC) and this marked the first step towards the recognition of the general interests of the workers all over the country. At the first session of AITUC, B.P. Wadia, proposed for presidentship the name of Lala Lajpat Rai in view of "his unique experience as a president of the Indian National Congress, as a social worker and as a patriot." The political link with Congress was thus established and the AITUC was identified as a nationalist as well as industrial organisation and "Its first president was a social reformer, not a worker in the accepted sense of the term."[14] The other prominent Congress leaders were also associated with AITUC. The AITUC, from its very inception, followed the pattern of the Trade Union Congress in U.K. It represented the workers' interests — economic, social and political, and one of its chief objectives was to cooperate with and coordinate the activities of all labour organisations in the country and to give a lead for extension of all labour organisations in the country and to give a lead for extension of trade unionism in areas where it had not penetrated. In 1920, there were 64 affiliated unions with a total membership of 140,854 in AITUC and by 1925 the member of affiliated unions increased fourfold and the membership much more.

But the most notable absentee from AITUC was Ahmedabad Textile Labour Association, the reason being the fact that Gandhiji thought that the formation of the AITUC was premature. Commenting on this, Kanji Dwarkadas, a member of AITUC, stated:[15] "This was most unfortunate decision on Gandhiji's part because his keeping away from it and not getting the Ahmedabad Textile Labour Association to join it, prevented the more sober opinion in labour circles to be heard in the AITUC and left field open to more extremist, wild and irresponsible leadership to capture the AITUC. And this has impeded for all time to come the growth of a genuine and healthy trade union movement in India."

Between 1925-30, the trade union movement began to emphasise ideologies and to assume an international outlook resulting in the appearance of leftist or communist element in the AITUC. In 1926 at the Madras Congress delivering the presidential address, Dr. V.V. Giri discussed the role of the trade unions in the political field and concluded that the time was ripe for the formation of a labour party. Although a committee was appointed to frame draft proposals, nothing came of it as a result of the growing split in the AITUC one led by "rightists" and the other by "leftists", which was complete by 1927. This conflict had its evil effects on Indian Labour. Even in the major textile strikes in Kanpur, Bombay and the lockouts in Kharagpur, Golden Rock, Bombay and elsewhere, internal squabbles led to the failure of the strikes. Finally at the Nagpur session in 1929, the leftists won a victory by almost a snatch vote and the Trade Union Congress was captured by them. The minority then left the Trade Union Congress and formed the All India Trade Union Federation (AITUF) with a realistic policy, programme and objectives.

In 1931 the communists were forced out of the T.U.C., which was dominated by the Radicals and the Communists formed Red Trade Union Congress. Thus there were three central union organisations including All India Railwaymen's Federation (AIRF). After that, there was a reappearance of the leadership of the Indian National Congress and efforts for compromise were started in 1931 through the AIRF. A Trade Union Unity Committee was formed which put forward a "platform of unity." In 1934 at the annual session of AITUC a compromise was reached with the communists and the Red TUC was dissolved. In 1938 through the efforts of Dr. V.V. Giri, the AITUF also came back into AITUC which emerged in its full glory in 1940. Interestingly enough, the split took place in Nagpur and it was at Nagpur again they were united. N.M. Joshi, who was the general secretary of the AITUC when the rift took place, again became the general secretary of the reunited organisation.

The Second World War brought about many changes in the economic climate of the country. It created shortage of essential commodities and it provided an indirect protection to industries as the Indian market was denied the import of foreign goods. As a consequence, the activities of Indian industries began to increase and with them, the trade union activity also increased, as indicated in the progress in the number of both membership and unions.

This period also witnessed unity and disunity among trade union leadership. Differences arose on the question of the attitude of labour towards the War. A section of the leaders who did not approve the neutral and lukeworm policy of the AITUC and who wanted a more positive policy towards the war efforts, especially after the declaration of war by Germany on Russia, seceded from AITUC and formed the Indian Federation of Labour, which got financial support from the Government since it supported the cause of the British in the war. Thus there were two central organisations in India during the war. The nationalist elements in AITUC followed the line of the Indian National Congress and most of them were arrested and detained for a long time. The communists took full advantage of this situation by moving in to control AITUC. In 1944 the Government of India used the principle of rotation in respect of these two organisations and they were to represent India at the international conference alternately. A notable development of the war period was a definite change in the Government's attitude towards labour. Two facts were responsible for this change. The first was the government's anxiety to have increased production for supporting the war efforts, for which maintenance of industrial peace was essential. The second wars the sympathetic outlook with which the popular governments in the provinces viewed the problems of labour. For the first time, during this period government started joint consultations with the representatives of employees and employers on matters of a general nature affecting labour. The first tripartite labour conference was held in 1942. The important labour laws enacted during this period include those making provision for holidays with pay for factory workers and raising the wage limit in the Workmen's Compensation Act, the Industrial Standing Orders Act and the Weekly Holiday Act 1942.

The next important milestone in India was the attainment of independence in 1947 and as a result of the partition of the country, the socioeconomic problems became more acute and complicated by communal riots and large influx of population from Pakistan. Inflation caused the real wages of workers to go down and industrial unrest increased, manifesting itself in wave of strikes resulting in the highest ever recorded strikes and man-days lost during this period.

The Congress leaders, who assumed power after the war, wanted to restore normalcy in India on the labour front also and through Hindustan Mazdoor Sevak Sangh (H.M.S.S.) an attempt was made to gain control of A.I.T.U.C. and to influence it to conform to the political ideology of the Sangh and indirectly of Congress. When this proved abortive, Gulzarilal Nanda observed:[16]

> "Congressmen in general and particularly those working in the field of labour, have found it very difficult to co-operate any longer with T.U.C. which has repeatedly been adopting a course completely disregarding, or even in opposition to, the declared policy of the Indian National Congress."

The stage was set when the Congress leaders felt impelled to form a labour organisation, which followed Congress ideology and philosophy.

On May 3, 1947, a conference of leading Congress and trade union leaders met in New Delhi under the chairmanship of Sardar Vallabhbhai Patel and a resolution was passed pointing out the necessity of the formation of a central labour organisation, which would take concerted action to safeguard the workers' interests. Thus was born the Indian National Trade Union Congress (INTUC) and at the time of its inception the membership of INTUC was 5,75,000 workers from 200 unions. The kind of influence that Congress would have on INTUC was well expressed by Nehru:[17]

> "Technically the INTUC and the Indian National Congress are two separate organisations and neither is subordinate to the other. Still it goes without saying that the INTUC has been sponsored and nursed mostly by Congressmen and derives its strength from the moral and other support of the Congress. As such it is imperative that in all political matters all Congressmen working in the INTUC should treat the Congress as its supreme body and abide by its code of conduct."

The Ahmedabad Textile Labour Association, with about 55,000 members which had not joined any All India Organisation since its formation in 1918 now did so and formed the core of the original group. The TLA provided the INTUC with a strong membership nucleus, and a cadre with long experience. Both Nehru and Sardar Patel attended the inaugural session of INTUC. Around 1963 there were nearly 16,45,688 members in INTUC and at present INTUC is the largest federation in India.

When the INTUC was formed in May 1947, the socialist leaders felt that an organisation, toeing the line of Congress, would not be in the interests of the workers. Early in 1948, they left National Congress and in consultation with other leaders of IFL and an influential section of AITUC and some other trade unions, met in Calcutta on December 24, 1948 and decided to establish a new organisation call the Hind Mazdoor Sabha (HMS). At the time of its establishment, the HMS claimed 6,06,472 members from 427 unions and in 1963 its strength was 5,55,317.

Some trade union leaders with leftists views who attended the conference at Calcutta in December 1948, were not in agreement with the principles and objectives of HMS. They met again on December 27, 1948 at Calcutta and decided to call upon various trade union leaders to form a United Trade Union Committee. In a conference at Calcutta on April 30, 1949, a new organisation known as the United Trade Union Congress (UTUC) was formed. The membership of the UTUC in 1963 was 1,85,649.

Thus there are four central trade unions operating in India — INTUC, AITUC, HMS and UTUC — each with a different ideology and each with the backing and support of a political party and each toeing the line of its political godfather. Though all of them with characteristic forcefulness deny their subservience to any political party, it is as plain as daylight that the INTUC is the labour wing of the Congress, AITUC, that of the Communist Party (now split into two groups, Rightists and Marxist Communists), H.M.S., that of Praja Socialist Party and UTUC, that of heterogenous lefts socialists, mainly functioning in West Bengal and Kerala.

In recent years there has been a tremendous flux and constant splits among the various political parties including the Congress, the Communist Party etc., leaving its impact on the labour wings of these parties with the result that there have been emerging on the Indian trade union scene quite a few new trade union organisations owing allegiance to the splintered political parties.

Table 14.2

MEMBERSHIP CLAIMED BY CENTRAL ORGANISATIONS OF WORKERS AS AT THE END OF 1972

Organisation	*Membership Claimed*
1. Indian National Trade Union Congress	22,21,810
2. All India Trade Union Congress	claim not furnished
3. Hind Mazdoor Sabha	-do-
4. United Trade Union Congress	3,62,087
5. Bharatiya Mazdoor Sangh	6,27,968
6. Centre of Indian Trade Unions	9,12,327
7. United Trade Union Congress (Lenin Sarni)	2,48,594
8. National Labour Organisation	1,80,416

Source: From the reply of the Deputy Minister for Labour in the Lok Sabha on Nov. 22, 1973.

The IIPM notes:[18]

"Practically all through the history of trade unionism in India politics has played an important part in its development. According to some, the Indian Trade Union movement is the byproduct of the political movement. Before the appearance of N.M. Joshi, who tried to keep trade unions aloof from politics, the stalwarts of the Indian National Congress were prominently associated with the labour movement. Their association might originally have been from the humanitarian point of view, but the potentialities of organised labour could not possibly have been overlooked by the growing political organisation."

It was G.D.H. Cole[19] who stated that "...in each country, trade unionism is shaped not only by the form and stage of economic development, but also by the political conditions and by the general structure of the society in which it has to act." India falls into this general pattern. Considering the nature of economic and business sophistication and the largely unskilled and uneducated workforce there seems to be an absolute inevitability in the development of a labour movement sponsored and aided by social reformists, opportunistic politicians and humanitarian intellectuals. The aims and objects of these central organisations as stated in their constitutions are as follows:[20]

Aims and Objectives of INTUC

(I) 1. The INTUC sets before itself the comprehensive aim of establishing "an order of society which is free from hindrances in the way of an all-round development of its individual members, which encourages the growth of human personality in all its aspects, and goes to the utmost limit in progressively eliminating social, political, or economic exploitation and inequality, the profit motive in the economic activity and organisation of society and the anti-social concentration of power in any form."

2. To place industry under national ownership and control in a suitable form in order to realise the aforesaid objective in the quickest time.

3. To organise society in such a manner as to ensure full employment and best utilization of its manpower and other resources.

4. To secure increasing association of the workers in the administration of industry and their full participation in its control.

5. To promote generally the civic and political interests of the working class.

(II) 1. To secure an effective and complete organisation of all categories of workers including agricultural labour.

2. To guide and coordinate the activities of the affiliated organisations.

3. To assist in the formation of trade unions.

4. To promote the organisation of workers of each industry on a nationwide basis.

5. To assist in the formation of regional or provincial branches of the INTUC.

(III) 1. To secure speedy improvement of conditions of work and life and of the status of workers in industry and society.

2. To obtain for the workers various measures of social security including adequate provision in respect of accident, maternity, sickness, old age and unemployment.
3. To secure a living wage for every worker in normal employment and to bring about a progressive improvement in the workers' standard of life.
4. To regulate hours and other conditions of work in keeping with the requirements of the workers in the matter of health, recreation and cultural development.
5. To secure suitable legislative enactments for ameliorating the conditions of the workers and ensure the proper enforcement of legislation for the protection and uplift of labour.

(IV) 1. To establish just industrial relations.
2. To secure redress of grievances, without stoppages of work, by means of negotiations and conciliation and failing that by arbitration or adjudication.
3. Where adjudication is not applied and settlement of the disputes by arbitration is not available for the redress of grievances, to facilitate recourse, on the part of the workers, to other legitimate methods including strikes or any suitable form of satyagraha.
4. To make necessary arrangements for the efficient conduct and satisfactory and speedy conclusions of authorised strikes of satyagraha.

(V) 1. To foster the spirit of solidarity, service, brotherhood, cooperation and mutual help among the workers.
2. To develop in the workers a sense of responsibility towards industry and the community.
3. To raise the workers' standard of efficiency and discipline.

Means: The means to be adopted for the furtherance of the objects shall be peaceful and consistent with truth.

Aims and Objectives of AITUC:[21]

1. To establish a socialist State in India.
2. To socialise and nationalise the means of production, distribution and exchange, as far as possible.
3. To ameliorate economic and social conditions of the working class.
4. To watch, promote, safeguard and further the interests, rights and privileges of the workers in all matters relating to their employment.
5. To secure and maintain for the workers:
   (a) The freedom of speech;
   (b) The freedom of press;
   (c) The freedom of association;
   (d) The freedom of assembly;
   (e) The right to strike, and
   (f) The right to work or maintenance.

6. To coordinate the activities of the labour unions affiliated to the AITUC and
7. To establish political or economic advantage based on caste, creed, community, race or religion.

Means: The AITUC shall endeavour to further the aforesaid objectives by all legitimate, peaceful and democratic methods such as legislation, education, propaganda, mass meetings, negotiations, demonstration and in the last resort by strikes and similar other methods, as the AITUC may from time to time, decide.

Aims of UTUC

The formal aim of the UTUC is to establish a pure trade union movement, as free as possible, from any of the existing political parties.

Aims and Objectives of HMS:[22]

1. To promote the economic, political, social and cultural interests of the Indian working class;
2. To guide and coordinate the activities of affiliated and organisations and assist them in their work;
3. To watch, safeguard, and promote the interests, rights and privileges of workers in all matters relating to their employment;
4. To promote the formation of:
   (a) Federations of unions from the same industry or occupation; and
   (b) National unions of workers employed in the same industry or occupation;
5. To secure and maintain for the workers:
   (a) Freedom of association;
   (b) Freedom of assembly;
   (c) Freedom of speech;
   (e) Freedom of press;
   (e) Right to work or maintenance,
   (f) Right to social security; and
   (g) Right to strike.
6. To organise for and promote the establishment of a democratic, socialist society in India;
7. To promote the formation of cooperative societies and to foster workers' education;
8. To cooperate with other organisations in the country and outside having similar aims and objects.

Means: In the promotion and realisation of these aims and objects the Sabha shall employ all legitimate, peaceful and democratic methods.

After this brief historical review of the Indian Trade Union movement, it is only appropriate to discuss the contribution of the labour movement, the problems of our unions, and the issues facing them, before we proceed to an analysis of its relations with management and the role of personnel administrators in these relations.

Union Contribution

First of all, the Indian trade unions are here to stay as enduring labour institutions and they have overcome the nature of passing *ad hoc* associations. Thanks to political, economic, historical and international influences, they have attained legal status to represent the workers. They have succeeded in organising central union federations which help in the determination of principles, purposes, philosophy, ideology of the unions and give some sense of direction to an otherwise scattered and isolated numerous unions. This union organisation is a significant achievement.

Secondly, they have risen to a new status, where their voices are heard by the other two fundamental characters in any industrial relations system — the government and the employers. This they do, not only at the state level but also at the top level in the Standing Labour Committee and the Indian Labour Conference. They have gained a platform to air their views, policies and ideologies.

Thirdly, by this status, they have been able to influence public policy and labour and industrial legislation, which many a businessman would dub, more often than not, as anti-business and pro-labour. They are able to have their say on labour policy and on all matters concerning the interests of labour in the country.

Fourthly, they have made significant gains in the areas of wages, dearness allowance, bonus, health, safety, working conditions, hours of work and job security for the labourers in general and union members in particular.

Fifthly, the unions have played an important role in evolving some sort of a joint-consultation machinery to negotiate various issues between labour and management.

Sixthly, the trade unions are a power to reckon with and are not to be too easily dismissed as of no significant consequence.

Whether the trade unions have contributed to increasing industrial productivity, or to sharpening management performance and efficiency or in promoting efficiency or productivity consciousness among its membership and the labourers in general or not are all matters on which the evidence obtaining at present, in the light of no authoritative studies and research, does not warrant us to offer a definite set of observations and conclusions.

Union Weaknesses

Several students of trade union and industrial relations in India — both indigenous and foreign — have pointed out several weaknesses of our unions for purposes of brief discussion as follows:

1. Historical weaknesse.
2. Structural weaknesses.
3. Policy weaknesses.

1. Historical Weaknesses

This historical developmental and organisational process of unionism in India emerged with some built-in deficiencies. The initiative and leadership to organise workers came from reformist intellectuals, politicians and humanitarians and it has continued to stay with them. This "outside" leadership has had political affiliations, ideologies and interests, which have been superimposed on the Indian labour movement, sometimes at the expense of the labour's interests. The historical political character was perhaps something that was unavoidable in the initial stages of union development and growth. But it has been enduring. Unions and workers, whether they like it or not, are stuck with them and some unions claim that it is even essential to unionism in India. In one of its report, UTUC pointed out that without the politically influential leadership at the vanguard of the labour movement, unionism would be just a cry in the wilderness; but now its voice is heard in the policy-making circles. But this political orientation of unionism has lead to political unionism. N.F. Dufty makes this observation regarding the political forces in Indian union movement and their perpetuation:[23]

> "With very few exceptions, trade union leadership in India has come from the intellectuals; in the beginning, perhaps, from individuals with a strong social orientation, and later from those who had political ambitions as well. Operations at the industry and national level are more attractive to the average intellectual or politically-oriented individual than operations at the plant level. It is very likely that this type of leadership gave the Indian trade union movement its particular characteristics in its formative years. In any case, the general level of literacy of the workers was very low at that time, making it difficult for leadership to emerge from the work groups. This tendency was reinforced by caste prejudices which placed the working class trade union official, usually from a low rank caste, at pronounced disadvantage when dealing with members of management, who were usually from a higher caste. The all-pervading legalism which is characteristics of the Indian industrial relations system is another factor which increases the tendency for the union leadership to be drawn from the intellectuals. The present revolutionary-intellectual elite now in power has, naturally enough, not induced any change in the situation, rather has it been reinforced by the increasing degree of legalism and the growing importance of the trade unions as a political force, especially inside the Indian National Congress."

2. Structural Weaknesses

The main structural weaknesses of Indian trade unions are industrial unions, multiplicity of unions, poor finances, membership apathy, weak leadership.

Industrial Unions: The lack of craft unions, except in a few cases, on account of the dearth of skilled workers, has encouraged the formation of industrial unions. The craft unions could have provided a sense of purpose and direction from within and there could have been good initiative from the skilled workforce, as is exemplified all over the world. The unskilled workers and their low status have rendered the unions weak and ineffective at plant level and industry level.

Multiplicity of Unions: The political, social and religious affiliations of Indian workforce have resulted in the formation of numerous rival unions and this inter-union rivalry weakens the labour movement considerably. Sometimes the employers have encouraged such divisive tendencies to their own advantage and to break-up strong plant level unions. The political affiliations of union leaders encourage division, because every politically-backed union wants to have a foothold in unions at the plant level. Another characteristic weakness of the unions in India is infant mortality where many unions go out of existence very quickly. Often it may be because the union leader changes his mind and switches sides, taking along with him all the union members. Often the strength of unions is considerably weakened where there emerges a large number of small ineffective unions, instead of a small number of unions with large and effective membership. See Table 14.3 for this declining trend in the average size of the unions.

***Poor Finances*:** All the central union organisations complain that the affiliated unions are not paying their dues to them and the affiliated unions blame their members that they are not paying union dues of 25 Paise per member. The union facilities in the form of staff, libraries and reading rooms, buildings, offices etc. leave much to be desired. Anxious to increase membership, the union membership fees are fixed at a very low amount, but even this is not collected from members. Partly this is due to low real income of the union member, which leaves him with little surplus to pay for things other than his most urgent physiological needs.

Perhaps one of the most financially sound trade unions in India is the Ahmedabad Textile Labour Association, which spends 60 to 70 per cent of its income on social welfare work including compensation for accidents, medical aid, education, thrift and temperance work. Some of its welfare schemes include Day and Night schools, residential boarding houses for working girls, a hospital with a special maternity ward attached to it, libraries and reading rooms, and a physical culture centre.

Membership Apathy: A majority of the workers are apathetic and since most of them are illiterate and suffer from social and religious inhibitions, they take very little interest in their unions. Often they are members of more than one union in the plant — paying or non-paying — and naturally they do not have any strong feeling towards their membership of unions. The character of the migrant worker is another problem, because he is not committed to the industrial way of life in order to take active part in the union life.

The low real income of the worker also is responsible for his apathy, because his living conditions are miserable and they do not permit him to participate in the work of voluntary organisations. The social, religious, regional, community and cultural habits of workers are so different and diverse as to act almost as a disintegrating influence.

Weak Leadership: Leadership at the plant level has appeared to be weak and ineffective. The unions have lacked discipline, and it is alleged that the union executives seem to have neglected the shop-floor and plant level issues in favour of more glamorous political issues at the national level.

3. Policy Weaknesses

The Indian Trade Union Policies and programmes, it is felt, are influenced or even dominated by the political parties. Union policies are more preoccupied with the ideological and political issues and policies than with the economic issues affecting the workers. Political and ideological solutions are offered for economic problems. For example, to provide employment opportunities, INTUC advocates more and more small scale and cottage industries, sticking to the Gandhian ideology regardless of the

Table 14.3

Growth of Trade Unions and Membership, 1961-62 to 1971

Year	Workers' Unions			Employers' Unions			All Unions			Index No. of Trade Unions on Register (Base: 1961–62 = 100)
	On Register	Submitting returns	Membership (000's)	On Register	Submitting returns	Membership (000's)	On Register	Submitting returns	Membership (000's)	
(1)	(2)	(3)	(4)	(5)	(6)	(7)	(8)	(9)	(10)	(11)
1961-62	11,416	6,954	3,960	198	133	18	11,614	7,087	3,977	100.0
1962-63	11,620	7,114	3,667	207	137	15	11,827	7,251	3.682	101.8
1963-64	11,740	7,106	3,956	244	144	21	11,984	7,250	3,977	103.2
1964-65	12,744	7,380	4,441	279	163	25	13,023	7,543	4,466	112.1
1965 (Apr.Dec.)	12,948	6,771	3,763	300	161	24	13,248	6,932	3,788	114.1
1966	14,370	7,088	4,369	316	158	23	14,686	7,244	4,392	126.5
1967	15,024	7,381	4,503	290	142	22	15,314	7,523	4,525	131.9
1968	16,409	8,689	5,094	307	162	27	16,716	8,851	5,121	143.9
1969	18,460	8,254	4,866	377	169	34	18,837	8,423	4,900	162.2
1970*	19,915(E)	6,864	4,205	399(E)	138	37	20,314(E)	7,002	4,241	174.9
1971**	20,304(E)	3,662	2,232	372(E)	47	25	20,712(E)	3,709	2,257	178.3

Source: Annual Returns under the Trade Union Act. Indian Labour Statistics 1974 (Labour Bureau, Ministry of Labour, Government of India, Simla).

* Excludes Bihar, Kerala and Rajasthan.

** Incomplete — excludes, A.P., Assam, Bihar, H.P., Karnataka, Kerala, Rajasthan, U.P., W.B., and Delhi.

economic feasibility in contemporary industrial era. Similarly the panacea of our economic ills, according to AITUC, is the nationalisation of banks and state ownership, all stemming from Communist ideology.

A familiar charge is that the trade unions do no formulate their policies independently and this is to be expected in a situation where outside leaders have to toe the party line for their own survival. Rival unions often put forward conflicting proposals, which weaken the bargaining strength of the unions. The rivalry among unions forces them to adopt policies and programmes that weaken the labour movement as a whole. HMS observes that there is a lack of trade union consciousness:[24] "... in many cases trade unions still retain the tradition of being only strike committees, coming into fitful life at the time of a spontaneously generated labour dispute or when a bonus issue is raised. At such times of high tension, membership figures may swell only to subside in either eventuality, victory of defeat. This lack of trade union consciousness has party to be remedied by propaganda and education, teaching the value and importance of maintaining at all times, during periods of strife and stress and during periods of normalcy, an organisation, which would defend their interests."

The dearth of policies and programmes that sustain a healthy interest in union activities and work are perhaps conspicuous by their absence, save in a few cases.

While the INTUC adopts, naturally enough, a policy of cooperation in stimulating production and reducing work stoppages, the other unions adopt an agitational approach to various problems and they also resent the influence of Government on INTUC and tend to dismiss INTUC as the mouthpiece of the Government and ruling party. These policy and ideological differences among the central organisations have a tendency to confuse and frustrate the union membership all over the country and these differences tend to weaken the labour movement of India.

Mary Sur has observed that in many cases, unfortunately, rival unions object in principal to sitting together and will not recognise that they have a common economic purpose because their political allegiances are stronger than their economic outlook. In 1956, a unity call was extended by HMS to the other three unions on the following principles:

1. Freedom from external influence;
2. True and democratic elections of office bearers and committees; and
3. Resolution of existing rivalries through a free plebiscite of the workers concerned.

But INTUC would have no part in it and nothing came of it. The historical developments in the country that led to different political parties organising their trade unions, were responsible for the disunity in the union movement.

Union Issues: Briefly the major issues, with which unions are grappling, are the wage issues, rationalisation, joint consultant, social, security issues, rationalisation and job security, unemployment, trade union deficiencies, industrial relation issues, bonus issues, dearness allowance issues, inflation and low real income etc. With this brief review of the structure, aims, policies, strengths and weaknesses of trade union movements in U.S.A. and India, let us now proceed to an examination of union-management relations.

The National Commission on Labour has suggested that (a) The minimum number required for starting a new union should be raised to 10 per cent (subject to a minimum of 7) of regular employees, of a plant or 100, whichever is lower. (b) The minimum membership fee of a union should be raised from the present level of 25 paise per month to Re. 1 per month.

The instability of the trade union situation in India at the present time can be traced to three main causes: general immaturity and lack of experienced local leadership; political complications; and weak finances.[25]

Weak Trade Union Movement: In recent years the trade union membership has increased considerably. Today there are about 14,000 registered trade unions with an estimated membership of over 5 million workers. Looking to the size of the membership, the trade union movement is neither strong not stable. The reasons for the weak trade union movement are many which are summarised by a veteran trade union leader as follows:

(i) The membership is not stable. There is tendency amongst workers to become members of a union only when they have some grievances and demands. The income of unions is, therefore, not stable, and they cannot afford to engage efficient staff to run their offices.

(ii) There are rival unions in every industry and many a time in the same establishment. The rivalry and multiplicity of the unions have destroyed the solidarity of the working class.

(iii) The unions do not enjoy the right of recognition and, therefore, they cannot carry on negotiations with the management on equal footing.

(iv) On account of compulsory adjudication, many workers feel that the unions are redundant as wages and working conditions can be determined by the Courts, Tribunals and Wage Boards. Workers thus rely more on outside agencies rather than on the strength of their unions.

(v) Most of the unions are engrossed in questions of wages and other matters relating to employment and they do not engage themselves in any welfare, social, educational, or cultural activities for their members. The unions, therefore, have not penetrated into the life of the workers.[26]

3. UNION AND MANAGEMENT RELATIONS

The main aspects of union-management relations are: (a) Collective bargaining; (b) Settlement of Industrial disputes; and (c) Joint consultation. The settlement of grievances and the disciplinary action are studied in the following next two chapters. In India we have evolved a tripartite machinery under which the main characters of an industrial relations system — the Government, union and management representatives — are encouraged to meet together to discuss and exchange views on industrial relation matters and propose policies to meet the problems of industrial relations. We shall study this tripartite machinery in the next section. Now let us turn to collective bargaining.

(a) Collective Bargaining

What is Collective bargaining?

Selig Perlman explains that[27] "collective bargaining is not just a means of raising wages and improving conditions of employment. Nor is it merely democratic government in industry. It is above all a technique whereby an inferior social class or group carries on a never slackening pressure for a bigger share in the social sovereignty as well as for more welfare, security and liberty for its individual members."

The collective bargaining is a procedure in which compromise is reached through bargaining of opposed strengths. Only when this power is relatively equal and exercised with responsibility and discrimination can there by constructive negotiation between labour and management. The collective bargaining experiment is one which has been evolved in modern industrial societies after extensive discussion and consideration and current practice in U.S.A. is a result of the slow development of public policy to a point where collective bargaining has come to be regarded as desirable from the standpoint of society. In U.S.A. The National Labour Relations Act, 1935 (Wagner Act) and the Labour Management Relations Act, 1947 (Taft-Hartley Act) and Labour Management Reporting and Disclosure Act, 1959, clearly indicate public approval and insistence upon free collective bargaining, provide rules for determining bargaining units, and designating and certifying bargaining agent and outline several principles to be followed for free collective bargaining.

The aim of collective bargaining should be to arrive at wages and other terms of employment acceptable to both union and management for a given contract period. By taking a reasonable and supportable position at the outset of negotiations management can win union respect, while meeting its obligations to non-labour groups. Regarding profits, a positive approach must be taken so that the union regards profits as a goal of its own interests as well as managements.

Collective Agreement: The Collective Agreement, variously known as Labour Contract, or Union Contract, or Labour-Management Agreement or Contract is the end process of collective bargaining, and is the written statement of the terms and provisions of agreement. Many companies print them and make them available to all the covered employees and this booklet may act as guide for day-to-day relationships in the company.

In U.S.A. multi-unit and industry-wide bargaining is widespread and the contract period may extend from one to five years. The labour contracts are growing longer, more detailed and more complex every year.

Some general principles of collective bargaining: An experienced union negotiator regards the following as essential general principles of collective bargaining:[28]

Conditions Essential for Effective Collective Bargaining:

For both Union and Management

1. Collective bargaining should be made an educational as well as a bargaining process. It should afford union leaders an opportunity to present to management the wants, desires, grievances and attitudes of its employees

and enable management to explain to union leaders and through them, their employees, the economic forces that confront it.

2. Management and the union must conceive of collective bargaining as a means to find the best possible solution, not as a means of acquiring as much as one can while conceding the minimum. There must be a honest attempt to solve rather than to compromise.
3. Both parties must have enough bargaining power to command respect and to enforce the terms of the contract.
4. There must be mutual confidence, good faith and a desire to make collective bargaining work.
5. Honest, able and responsible leadership is necessary.
6. Parties must meticulously observe the national and state laws applicable to collective bargaining.
7. It is important that both parties realise that collective bargaining in a sense is a form of price-fixing and that successful collective bargaining in the last analysis depends on whether the union and management do a good job at keeping the price of labour properly adjusted to other prices.

For Management

1. Management must develop and consistently follow a realistic labour policy which should be accepted and carried out by all its representatives.
2. Because the union must feel that its existence is secure, management must grant recognition to union without reservations and accept it as a constructive force in the industry.
3. Management should not assume uninterrupted continuance of employee goodwill. It should periodically examine the rules and regulations — including those that supervisors use and enforce — by which the labour force is governed. These determine the attitudes, comfort and goodwill of employees.
4. Management should act upon the assumption that to make the union a responsible and conservative body it is necessary to treat it fairly and to establish such a satisfactory business relationship with its representatives that they and the union members will not lightly jeopardise that relationship.
5. Management should not wait for the union to raise grievances but should make every reasonable effort to prevent them from arising and to remove them promptly when they arise.
6. For any bargaining unit, management should deal with only one union, but where two unions seek recognition, no negotiations should be undertaken until one union establishes a majority.
7. In weighing the economic implications of collective bargaining, management should give more emphasis to social considerations.

For Union

1. In the light of the rights to organised labour in recent years, it is incumbent upon each union to eliminate racketeering and other undemocratic practices within its own organisation.
2. Union leaders must understand the economic implications of collective bargaining and realise that union demands must be met from the income and resources of the industry.
3. Union leaders should not conceive of their function as merely to obtain higher wages, shorter hours and better working conditions for their members. They and their members have an obligation to assist in eliminating waste and in improving the quantity and quality of production.
4. Union leaders have an obligation to remove restrictive rules and regulations on the part of union members since they increase cost and prices, reduce the amount that can be paid out as wages, tend to make for less employment, and in the long run, lower the standard of living of all groups in society.
5. Unions should resort to strikes only when all other methods have failed to bring about a satisfactory settlement of the issue or issues involved.

The Process of Negotiation: Collective bargaining has two fundamental phases and the first is the negotiation phase and the second is the phase of contract administration. Negotiation is a process of putting forth certain proposals, exploring the possibilities of their acceptance and arriving at mutually agreeable and acceptable proposals, after careful deliberation, consideration and criticism. The process of negotiation involves three stages:

1. Preparing for negotiations
2. Negotiation technique
3. Follow-up steps

1. Preparing for Negotiations

First the negotiation may be commenced at the initiative of either of the parties — labour or management. While some managements wait for the unions to put forth their proposals, some others resort to "positive bargaining" by putting forth their proposals. Many contracts provide that their party proposing changes in the existing agreement shall notify the other of the nature of such proposals usually 30 to 90 days before the termination date.

There is need for considerable amount of home work and preparation for negotiations and both union and management will have to spend quite some time preparing for negotiations or to initiate negotiations. They may need facts and figures on a variety of issues, such as wages, seniority, overtime, costs of living, economic conditions, union and management policies, productivity trends in the company, industry and the nation, agreements in other companies and patterns of agreement, legal controls and regulations etc.

Unions gather this information through their full time research staff of specialists from an analysis of contracts, employer pronouncements, public surveys and studies and reports of employer associations. Managements compile their data from their associations, government agencies and surveys undertaken by their research staff. In many large companies, the industrial relations department will study and analyse public statements of union leaders, proceedings of union conventions and conferences, and collective bargaining trends all over the country.

Both unions and managements prepare proposals and counter proposals on the basis of study and analysis of opinion of foremen and employees, current experience with the contract grievances, contract violations, arbitration awards, suggestion systems, morale surveys and contract amendments. These sources afford a great deal of ideas and notions to unions and managements.

2. Negotiation Technique

(a) The negotiation may be done by one representative or a committee and by a line or staff personnel. Negotiating committees may have 3 to 6 members or even more. Usually there is a bargaining team with a chief spokesman or principal negotiator. He must be one of the top executives and most commonly he is the person charged with top responsibility for labour or industrial relations. For some time negotiations were carried on by top line executives and Professor Jucius points out the error of that practice:[29]

> "For a number of years after the Wagner Act was passed, many top executives attempted to carry on the work of bargaining with unions. Although they recognised the need of experts in such fields as engineering, purchasing, sales, and production, they felt capable of handling personnel functions themselves. The results were as expected: The unions, with full time specialists on their staffs, gained many concessions unnoticed by the top executives, who seemed to think that wages alone were of importance in union negotiations. The advantages gained by unions in regard to such matters as grievances machinery, seniority rules and discharge rules are evidences of ineptness displayed by some top executives."

(b) While the committee plans negotiations, the chief negotiator should be principal spokesman and should direct strategy and tactics.

(c) Negotiations must be conducted in good faith, with courtesy and it must be educational to both parties.

The specific procedures to be followed in negotiation are suggested by Arnold F. Campo:[30]

For both Union and Management

1. Be friendly in negotiation. Introduce everybody. Relieve existing tension.
2. Be willing to listen. It is time enough to worry about how you will say "No" after you have heard the facts.
3. Give everyone an opportunity to state his position. This often discloses the real champion of the problem or grievance.
4. Know something about the personal history of the other party's representatives.
5. Always keep in mind the right and fair thing to do.

6. Both parties should strive to maintain an objective attitude. They should think rather than feel their way through the problem under consideration.
7. Don't attempt to guide the discussion along a straight line directed to solving the problem. Let it wander at times; don't hurry it.
8. Don't let negotiations reach a stalemate. Help to define the problem and to suggest the solution. Ultimatums are out of place in negotiations.
9. If facts disclose a need for doing more than solving the immediate problem, be willing to go as far as is justified.
10. Define each issue clearly and discuss it in the light of all available facts.
11. Avoid specific regulations and minute details in the contract to insure greater flexibility.
12. At all times search only for the correct and real solution.
13. Size of the conference should be kept as small as circumstances will permit. Small groups facilitate successful negotiations.
14. Avoid sharp practices.
15. Consideration should be given to fatigue and mental attitude in determining the length of the session.
16. Have a committee of employees present during the negotiations; it can be highly advantageous and is practical in case the bargaining unit is a single establishment.
17. Terms agreed upon should be in writing and parties should sign without mental reservations. Phrasing of contract should be realistic, not legalistic.
18. Arbitration in the making of agreements should be used only as a last resort.
19. Both parties should respect the right of the public at all times.

For Management

1. At the outset, management must make sure that the labour leaders are really the representatives of the workers in the bargaining unit.
2. Don't use lawyers as negotiators unless they have an intimate knowledge of industrial relations.
3. Don't limit contacts with the union to controversial subjects, but consider also matters of common interest.

3. Follow-up Steps

The agreement must be printed and communicated to all the employees. Supervisors must be made to understand the terms of the contract through meetings. This is vital. The records and notes made during the negotiation must be filed for future reference. Any language or semantic difficulties must be cleared.

Contract Administration: The other important phase of collective bargaining is contract administration, once the process of negotiation is completed and a contract signed.

Contract Coverage: The subject matter of the agreements cover the following aspects as indicated by the Industrial Relations Section of the California Institute of Technology:[31]

1. Industry
2. Geographic zone
3. Company size
4. Union affiliation
5. Bargaining unit
6. Shop granted; closed, union, preferential, maintenance of membership
7. Solicitation of members and/or dues
8. Picket lines, sympathetic strikes, boycott
9. Upgrading and transfer procedure
10. Grievance procedure
11. *Grievance adjustment:* arbitration, mediation, or conciliation
12. *Seniority:* types of clause, factor in layoff, in promotion
13. *Wages:* employee's pay basis, type of wage rates, wage-scales review, minimum call pay
14. Pay period
15. Annual wage
16. Dismissal compensation
17. *Premium wage rates:* shift differentials, overtime pay, holiday pay
18. *Hours of work:* hours worked per day, hours worked per week, offwork periods daily, shift schedules, guaranteed work week
19. *Vacations:* vacation pay, service requirement
20. Sick leave with pay
21. Medical care
22. *Returning servicemen:* seniority, accumulation of benefits, training programme.

The contracts also may include union security clauses, management prerogatives, renewal clauses, no-strike clauses, escalator clauses and automatic adjustment clauses, escalation rules, improvement factors, sweetheart clauses, arbitration. There is no "standard specification" of what should be included in the contract and what should not be, although some issues are sought to be fenced off collective bargaining as management prerogatives. A noted authority, Professor George W. Taylor writes:[32]

> "Any general specification of the scope of collective bargaining would ignore the fact that the exact subjects dealt with in joint dealing do vary widely between plants and between industries. In most situations for instance, hiring practices of employers are not even talked about in negotiations. In others, they comprise a major topic of joint dealing. Whether or not a subject of this nature is a matter of joint concern depends upon the problems of the industry and the reactions of the parties themselves. No decision about what constitutes a matter of mutual concern can possibly be made before hand by some general rule or by legislation." He further adds: "If joint dealing cannot be developed as a co-operative undertaking, concerned with changing subjects of mutual interest, then the fundamental idea underlying collective bargaining is erroneous."

Alexander R. Heron makes this observation on barring certain issues from collective bargaining: "It is probably poor tactics or a vain hope for any employer to contend that any phase of his relations and dealings with his employees will be found to be technically outside the meaning of the 'working conditions.' He is on weak foundation when he refuses to discuss any condition which his employees seriously demand, if he must rely on the doubtful technicality that the subject is not one on which he is legally required to bargain. He can make a better investment of his time and intelligence by studying the reason for the demand. He cannot afford to continue any practice which creates dissatisfaction and resentment, merely by reason of his supposed ability to bar the subject from the bargaining table...."

Living with the Contract: Once the agreement is signed, both management and union must endeavour to live by "not only the letter of the agreement but by the spirit of the contract also." Both Union officers and Company executives may have to explain the contract to the employees and supervisors and contract must guide day-to-day working relationships between union and management. Grievance and dispute settlement procedures will have to be laid down. Campo offers the following general principles to guide those who have the responsibility for contract administration:[33]

Policies and Procedures to be Used in Living Under the Agreement

For both Union and Management

1. Both sides should make a genuine effort to make the machinery for collective bargaining function. This requires a tolerant attitude, a spirit of accommodation, goodwill and a willingness to cooperate.
2. The channels for handling grievances must be observed. It is considered good practice to:
   (a) Instruct everyone as to its workings;
   (b) Handle all grievances promptly;
   (c) Put grievances in writing and indicate the factors on which both parties agree;
   (d) Hold meetings of grievances committees on company time;
   (e) See that supervisor and foremen are not short-circuited; to do so destroys morale;
   (f) Avoid cluttering the grievance procedure with matters that are not really grievances.
3. When conference over grievances reach an impasse the matter should be submitted to arbitration. Arbitrators should be selected with care.
4. Both parties should make sure that every commitment is scrupulously fulfilled. The use of a rigid follow-up guarantee observance is recommended.

For Management

1. Management should be available for conferences with workers' representatives so that it may be kept aware of changing attitudes and problems of employees.

2. Management must see that foremen and supervisors understand and carry out the terms of agreement.
3. Management should not short-circuit union representatives or undermine the union's authority. Any policies or proposed programmes involving the workers should be taken up with union representatives before they are made effective.
4. Management should give unions credit for the accomplishment whenever circumstances permit.
5. Management should avoid paternalism and strive to treat union representatives and employees as equals.
6. Many of the restrictive practices and what appear to be unreasonable demands of the union will disappear if management will strive to give its employees regular employment.
7. Management should maintain adequate employee records.

For Union

1. The union should see that its members understand the terms of the agreement.
2. The union should assume the responsibility to see that its members live up to the terms of the agreement.
3. Union representatives should make themselves available for conference when they are requested by management.

Historic Agreement in U.S.A.: Employer-employee relations practitioners and scholars have long sought ways to forestall strikes in U.S. industry. There is a growing feeling that traditional confrontation between labour and management should be softened in the direction of increased accommodation. An encouraging recent development is the agreement in the steel industry to use arbitration as a strike alternative.

In 1973 the nation's 10 major steel companies and the United Steelworkers of America (USW) ratified an agreement to eliminate strikes. It represented a milestone in an industry plagued by boom-bust cycles that were triggered by triennial negotiations of a nationwide collective-bargaining agreement. Success in preventing a strike in 1974, gave rise to an extension of the no-strike pact through 1977 negotiations. As such, the earliest a national strike will occur in steel is 1980.

The "Experimental Negotiating Agreement" (ENA) resulted from a weakening of the steel industry and USW caused by the negotiating cycle. Although the last steel strike was in 1959, for 116 days, steel users would begin several months before negotiations to stockpile steel. This entitled costly overtime payments by the steel mills to fill demand, and gave foreign producers opportunities to make inroads into domestic markets. U.S. production would subsequently drop, with or without a strike, as customers turned to their inventories and contracts with foreign suppliers. Discontinuous operation caused unemployment. The union president, I.W. Abel, estimated that the record 18.3 million tons of steel imported in 1971 represented the export of some 108,000 full-time job opportunities, and that stockpiling and related problems cost the companies $ 80 million annually.

Industry-union discussions to head off strikes began in the late 60s, but failed for lack of adequate support within the union. Continued worsening in position with foreign competition, layoffs and changes in union politics that provided a more solidly entrenched leadership, helped make the 1973 agreement possible. Also, a movie, "Where's Joe?", depicting job loss from imported steel, was shown on television in steel mill areas to gain employee support.

Under the initial ENA the parties agreed in advance of negotiation of the 1974 contract that some 350,000 represented employees would be guaranteed wage increases of at least three per cent each year from 1974-76. Employees also received a one-time bonus of $ 150 in recognition of the anticipated savings from avoiding the effects of stockpiling, as well as a cost-of-living escalator. The parties agreed that when negotiations took place in 1974, unresolved issues would be submitted to binding arbitration. While the agreement thus precluded a strike over national issues, local unions were given a right to strike over local plant issues. Such strikes, however, required approval of the national union president, and would not halt the nation's steel supplies.

ENA caused dissent among some union members, who filed a lawsuit in federal court claiming that the union violated its constitution and labour law by giving up strike rights without submitting the proposals to the full membership for ratification. The court rejected the claims, noting that the government of a union was a "representative democracy", not a "pure democracy." Since there was sanction by approved membership representatives the procedure was found "valid and legally irreproachable."

Labour/Management Councils: Although the arbitration panel was appointed in 1974, negotiations in that year did not require use of arbitration. The parties were philosophically committed not to use it, but praised its availability as a means of stimulating negotiations in the absence of a strike threat.[34]

Collective Bargaining and Agreements in India:[35] Although collective bargaining, as it is known and practised in U.S.A., is "virtually unknown in India", as a matter of a principle it was accepted for usage in union-management relations by the State:[36]

> "... the endeavour of the State has all along been to encourage mutual settlement, collective bargaining and voluntary arbitration to the utmost extent, and thereby reduce to the minimum occasions for its intervention.... The worker's right of association, organisation and collective bargaining is to be accepted without reservation as the fundamental basis of the mutual relationship."

However, because of the emergency — political and economic — the State was not prepared to encourage voluntary negotiations and the resulting show of strength by both parties; hence it armed itself with legal powers to refer disputes for settlement by arbitration and adjudication on failure of efforts to reach a mutually acceptable settlement. Apart from the Government, the trade unions, at the 1952 Indian Labour Conference expressed fears of unequal strength:[37] "... in view of the lack of bargaining strength of trade unions, it would be unwise to rely only on collective bargaining... if fair and proper justice between the parties is the aim, it is necessary to see that the advantage of any unequal position is not taken easily by any policy, and that this could be secured only if there is no provision for compulsory arbitration." Thus the unions thought that they required and asked for protection from the State. At the same conference V.V. Giri, champion of voluntary arbitration and collective bargaining and (then) Labour Minister argued:[38] "Compulsory arbitration has cut at the very roots of trade union organisation.... If the workers find their interests are best promoted only by combining, no greater urge is needed to forge a bond of strength and unity among them. But compulsory arbitration sees to it that such a bond is not forged.... Let the trade unions become strong and self-reliant and learn to get on without the assistance of the policeman. They will then know how to organise themselves and get what they want through their own strength and resources. That will also be the means of achieving greater self-respect. It may be that until the parties have learned the technique of collective bargaining, there are unnecessary trials of strength, but whoever heard of a man learning to swim without having to drink some gulps of water."

Despite all this controversy, collective bargaining is practised in some industries in our country and the essential prerequisites of effective collective bargaining are the following, according to IIPM:[39]

1. Existence of a truly representative, enlightened and strong union functioning strictly on constitutional trade union lines;
2. Existence of a progressive and strong management, conscious of its responsibilities and its obligations to the owners of the business, the employees, the consumer and the country;
3. Unanimity on the basic objectives and recognition of mutual rights and obligations;
4. Delegation of authority to local management, where there are several units of a company;
5. Acceptance of a fact-finding approach and willingness to use new method and tools, such as industrial engineering, for solution of industrial problems.

The IIPM suggests the following aspects to be included in the agreement:[40]

1. Purpose of the agreement, its scope, definition of important items;
2. Rights and responsibilities of the management and of the union;
3. Wages, bonus, production bonus, leave, retiring benefits, other benefits and terms and conditions;
4. Grievance procedure;
5. Methods and machinery for settlement of possible future disputes;
6. Termination clause.

Further, IIPM suggests some simple negotiation procedures:[41]

1. Appoint a negotiating team with top level executives and line and staff executives;
2. Make a good beginning and adopt a true spirit of "give-and-take";
3. Maintain continuity of talks with all the goodwill in the world;
4. Develop a problem-solving attitude;

5. Encourage leadership from the unions;
6. Bring in other Managers.

When there are serious differences of opinion and a conflict imminent, it is best not to aggravate the situation, to avoid loose talk, localise the conflict and not allow it to spread, and above all, to continue negotiations despite differences and disagreements. But N.F. Dufty believes that Government's policy is not conducive to collective bargaining:[42] "One of the paradoxes of the Indian Government's policy on industrial relations has been the large number of proclamations lauding collective bargaining. In practice, labour legislation does not favour collective bargaining and legislation designed to promote collective bargaining, although drafted and debated at length, has either not been enacted or allowed to remain in abeyance. These and other public proclamations may well have their roots in a natural desire to emulate Western Society's high material standard of living. This desire may in turn, have led to the assumption that industrial relations systems of the West also may be suitable for India, despite the many cultural and sociological differences between the two societies and in particular, the dissimilarities between their trade union movements."

Some Collective Agreements in India: Perhaps the earliest agreement was the one between Ahmedabad Textile Labour Association and the Millowners' Association for peaceful settlement of disputes through voluntary negotiations and arbitration, under the leadership of Mahatma Gandhi in 1920. In 1940, the Coir Factory Workers' Union and the Coir Mats and Matting Manufacturers' Association instituted a joint negotiating body called the Industrial Relations Committee for voluntary negotiation and settlement of all differences regarding terms and conditions of employment. In recent years the prominent ones are the Tata agreements, Hindustan Lever agreement, India Aluminium agreement, Bata agreement, National Carbon agreement, Reckett & Coleman agreement, Indian Tea Association agreement. A study of these agreements reveals these trends in collective bargaining and agreements: (1) Agreements are mostly unit-wise, but some are industry-wise agreements such as in textiles at Ahmedabad and Bombay; (2) The scope of the agreements is increasing and covering more aspects including bonus, productivity, modernisation, standing orders, voluntary arbitration, incentive schemes, job evaluation etc.; (3) Long-term contracts varying from two to five years are on the increase; (4) Each year the number of agreements is on the increase; (5) Joint-consultation in various forms is established in a number of a agreements and (6) Collective bargaining is feasible.[43]

The objectives and the basic philosophy of collective bargaining and agreement are well expressed in Article I of the Indian Aluminium agreement and it reads as follows:[44]

> "The purpose of this agreement is to provide orderly collective bargaining relations, to secure prompt and fair disposition of grievances, to establish fair wages and other working conditions, to maintain harmonious relationship between employees and the Company, to prevent strikes, lock-outs and slow-downs, to attain efficient and uninterrupted operation in the plant and to promote the stability and prosperity of the industry for the benefit of all who are dependent on this industry.

For achieving the above objectives the Company and the Union agree to encourage the highest possible degree of friendly, co-operative relationship between their respective representatives at all levels and with and between all employees. The Company and the Union believe that this goal depends primarily on attitudes between people in their respective organisations and at all levels of responsibility. Both parties believe that proper attitude must be based on full understanding of and regard for the respective rights and responsibilities of both the company and the Union."

Collective Bargaining Experience at Indian Aluminium:[45] More than a decade of collective bargaining in this company with plants in various states in India has revealed the following experience and results, as indicated by P.N. Krishna Pillai:[46]

1. A policy to promote collective bargaining and to avoid recourse to courts and tribunals was adopted, when a Central Personnel Division was set up.
2. It was decided that negotiations should be conducted with trade unions, regardless of their affiliations.
3. While the management was ready and willing to recognise trade unions and negotiate terms and conditions of employment with them, they were not willing to surrender their right to manage.
4. Though hesitant in the beginning, unions slowly gained confidence and signed long term contracts.
5. Unions became stronger both organisationally and financially.
6. The good functioning of joint consultative committees and the grievance procedure created a sense of good will and mutual confidence.
7. After adoption of voluntary negotiation policy, neither party took recourse to conciliation or adjudication to settle any industrial dispute concerning wages or terms and conditions of employment.
8. Though the Presidents of the various unions remain to be outsiders, an internal leadership of a non-political nature has developed in all the unions.
9. The best way to develop non-political internal leadership among workers is to encourage education through collective bargaining, joint consultation and proper grievance handling.
10. The unions and the management respected the no-strike and no-lockout clauses respectively.
11. Productivity, work standards, lay-off and retrenchments were also matters of mutual consideration.
12. Though the Presidents of the unions are outsiders with strong political allegiances, unions did not evince enthusiasm for central trade union affiliation, because the unions in various States were represented by workers having no political leanings and who are more interested in the economic issues and day-to-day problems of the plant than in political agitation.
13. This pattern has led to democratic election of office-bearers of the unions.
14. Both the union and management have learned that industrial peace does not rest on the signing of an agreement, but on fair joint dealing of problems of mutual concern.

Mr. P.N. Krishna Pillai adds:[47] "Collective bargaining pursued in the proper manner and spirit leads to the emergence of an identity of interests between parties. Though the interests of labour and management are not identical, there is an identity of interests. The same organisation is the source of sustenance, security and advancement for both labour and management. The fear in certain quarters that collective bargaining focuses class conflict is baseless. It is the absence of collective bargaining that will give a handle to those who want to propagate class conflict. This is evident from the experience of firms in this country which have maintained a long tradition of good relations through direct negotiations. It is in countries which effectively practise collective bargaining that class conflict is not the dominant feature of trade union thinking."

Policies and Procedures for Encouragement of Collective Bargaining in India: Proceeding with the assumption that collective bargaining is feasible in India, P.N. Krishna Pillai had advocated the following general principles to encourage collective bargaining:[48]

1. Legislation should lay down, wherever necessary, minimum conditions and the parties should be encouraged to negotiate themselves.
2. Conciliation machinery should set up a convention not to interfere in disputes generally before the parties try to settle the differences by mutual negotiation.
3. It should be made an unfair labour practice not to bonafide bargain with recognised unions.
4. Determine through proper and bold legislation the bargaining agent and the bargaining unit. The bargaining unit may be an industry or a plant.
5. Determine the bargaining agent on the basis of majority membership, which is decided by holding a plebiscite of all the workers in a unit or by verification of membership of the unions.
6. To conduct the plebiscite or to verify, judicial body, which will infuse confidence in the parties, should be set up for this purpose.
7. Only the majority union thus determined must have the right to negotiate with the management.
8. There should be provision for *de novo* election or verification of membership provided that any contending union other than the recognised bargaining agent could show a membership above a prescribed percentage of workers in a unit after the lapse of a prescribed time limit.
9. Provision can be made for registering contracts negotiated with recognised unions and making it illegal to resort to work stoppages during the term of such contracts.
10. Stress should be on collective bargaining and direct negotiations because it is the universal experience that settlement of disputes by third parties has never promoted internal harmony.

New Textile Wage Agreement: The New Textile Wage Agreement between the Bombay Millowners' Association and the Rashtriya Mill Mazdoor Sangh (representative union under the Bombay Industrial Relations Act, 1946) is based on the philosophy of give and take and mutual accommodation whereby a new wage pattern in Bombay Textile Mills is established. In the new wage pattern, an attempt has been made to evolve a production-oriented wage structure.

As the five-year period during which the majority recommendations of the Second Central Wage Board for the Cotton Textile Industry were to remain in force was coming to an end, the workers in the cotton textile mills at various centres launched agitations demanding wage increase. Another factor which influenced the agitation was the spiralling rise in prices of essential commodities resulting in erosion of real wages and purchasing power. The demand was also made by the workers in the Bombay Cotton Textile Industry. After negotiations between the Bombay Millowners' Association and the Rashtriya Mill Mazdoor Sangh, an industry-wise agreement was arrived at on 28th December 1973.

The agreement aimed at evolving a new basic wage structure and a new pattern of dearness allowance for employees in Bombay mills who are affiliated to the Association. The agreement fixed the revised minimum basic wage at Rs. 282.52 for a month of 26 working days for an unskilled operative which includes Rs. 221.60 being the full dearness allowance for 26 working days at Index No. 200 (base year 1960 = 100). It has also been agreed to relate the variable dearness allowance over Index No. 200 in percentage of the revised minimum basic wage of Rs. 282.50. The agreement further provides for giving an annual increase of Rs. 4/- on an average in each of the two years 1975 and 1976 to all permanent operatives and such of the badli operatives who work for not less than 240 days in the immediately preceding calendar year. The agreement came into force from 1st January 1974 and was to remain in operation for a period of three years ending 31st December 1976. The increase in the emoluments of the worker at the minimum level under the Agreement worked out to Rs.21/- per month and an average increase of Rs.25/- per worker.

As the leftist trade unions were not satisfied with the agreement, they exhorted the cotton mill workers in Greater Bombay to go on an indefinite strike which commenced on 30th December, 1973. The strike which lasted for 41 days was called off in response to an appeal made by Shri V.P. Naik, then Chief Minister of Maharashtra. The Chief Minister recommended that in addition to the increments mentioned in the above referred Agreement, an additional increment of average Rs.4/ — might be given from 1st April 1974, and that workers employed in Government-run mills should be given 50 per cent of benefits flowing from the above agreement and they should also get an additional increment as in the case of mills in the private sector. The appeal stated that in case management of any textile mill proposed to introduce 7 days a week working system it might be done after getting written consent of majority of workers and no one should oppose 7 days working started after such consent was given by majority workers of any mill.

The new agreement is expected to contribute to the production-oriented wage structure. A portion of variable dearness allowance linked to basic wage is also established, and an attempt has been made to place an indirect ceiling on the dearness allowance whereby even if the basic wage goes on increasing, there might not be proportionate increase in D.A. indefinitely. The problem of evolving the revised portion for piece rates is a delicate thing and is yet to be taken up. Another interesting feature of the new wage agreement was that considerable pressure was brought to bear upon on the bargaining parties, Bombay Mill Owners' Association and the RMMS by the direct intervention of the State and the Chief Minister with a view to promoting industrial peace.

Union Bargaining Pressures: The labour union, as the other bargaining member, has certain strategies and tacts that it utilises to extract greater concession from the employer. Union representatives use most of the particular tactics described for the employer above. They haggle, horse-trade, act, demand more in the expectation of getting less, and made tentative agreements subject to ratification by the membership. In addition to these manoeuvres there are certain stronger types of pressure which are sometimes used. These are strikes, picketing, and boycotts.

Strikes: A strike is a concerted and temporary withholding of employee services from the employer for the purpose of exacting greater concessions in the employment relationship than the employer for the purpose of exacting greater concessions in the employment relationship than the employer is willing to grant at the bargaining table. The strike, or the potential strike, is a basic part of the bargaining process. The possibility of a strike is the ultimate economic force that the union can bring to bear upon the employer. It is the power which offsets the employer's right to manage the firm and lock out the employee. Without the possibility of a strike in the background, there can be no true collective bargaining. When the strike is prohibited by law, some other mechanism, such as arbitration, must be established as a substitute for collective bargaining. There are various types of strikes. Among them are the following:

1. *Recognition Strike:* This is a strike to force the employer to recognise and deal with the union. This type of strike has been largely replaced by the consent elections administered by the National Labour Relations Board.
2. *Economic Strike:* This is the typical strike, based on a demand for better wages, hours, and working conditions than the employer is willing to grant.
3. *Jurisdictional Strikes:* When two unions argue about which has jurisdiction over a type of work and attempt to exert pressure upon the employer to allocate it to one or the other, a jurisdictional strike may ensue. For example, both carpenters and metal workers wish to hang metal doors. If either group strikes to force the employer to grant the work to its members, this is a jurisdictional strike. The employer is caught in the middle between two warring unions. Under the Taft-Hartley Act such strikes are illegal.
4. *Wildact Strike:* Wildcat strikes are the quick, sudden and unauthorised types of work stoppages. Such strikes are not approved by union leadership and are contrary to the labour agreement. They are sometimes viewed as a form of "fractional bargaining" by a subgroup of employees who have not achieved satisfaction through regular grievance processing or collective bargaining procedures. Rather than violations to be condemned out of hand, it has been suggested that they should be studied to determine whether existing procedures should be modified to make the bargaining relationship more realistic.

5. *Sit-down Strike:* When the employees strike but remain at their jobs in the plant, this is termed a "sit-down strike." Such strikes are illegal since they constitute an invasion of private property. Employees are free to strike for certain objectives, but they must physically withdraw from the company's premises.
6. *Sympathy Strike:* If other unions who are not party to the original strike consent to strike in sympathy with the original union, this is termed as "sympathy strike." It is an attempt to exert an indirect pressure upon the employer. This type of strike is also outlawed by the Taft-Hartley Act.

When any type of strike occurs, the employer should have a well thought out plan for functioning during the work stoppage. Among other items, he must make provision for the following: (1) Making sure that the plant is left in good physical condition; (2) Explaining the employer's side of the issue to the employees; (3) Giving a statement to the press; (4) Notifying suppliers and customers; (5) Notifying the appropriate mediation services; (6) Determining to what extent non-union personnel will be maintained on the working staff; and (7) Paying off striking workers for work completed in the past. There are few, if any, friendly strikes. Employers should do all in their power, short of violating law and public policy, to win the strike. Yet they must be aware of the fact that they have to live and work with these striking employees when the work stoppage is over. They should be wary of making permanent enemies of any large group of personnel. But if collective bargaining is to operate properly, there can be no automatic harmony after the strike. If harmony and cooperation are the sole objectives, the employer should have given up before the strike stage was ever reached.[49]

In India the unions have evolved their own pressure tactics which have compelled managements to give in often. Perhaps the biggest contribution in this area is the gherao which started in West Bengal which means for forcible detention of officers and managers by the union or employee groups. Often this is supplemented by a greater delay of violence which has taken such forms as stabbing, beating and denying officers water, food and bathroom facilities until the gherao is lifted. The gherao may last anywhere from a couple of hours to 2-3 days of forcible detention of officers.

The other forms of pressure tactics are: go-slow, work-to-rule, sit-in, sleep-in strikes, fasting-hunger strikes, satyagraha, slogan shouting, agitations, demonstrations, picketing, morchas, lightening strikes, intimidation, dharna, hartal, bandh, etc.

Indian unions have made their own contribution to the world of unions pressure tactics by giving to the world the gherao, the satyagraha, hunger strike, the bandh, hartal, work-to-rule and morchas.

(b) Settlement of Industrial Disputes

The Industrial Dispute Act, 1947, Section 2 (K) defines an industrial dispute thus: "Industrial Dispute means any dispute or difference between employers and employers; or between employers and workmen, or between workmen and workmen, which is connected with the employment or non-employment or the terms of employment or with the conditions of labour, of any person."

An industrial dispute carried to its logical end results either in a strike of employees or a lockout declared by the employers, both of which cause work stoppage and a production loss. Growing industrial unrest and increasing number of strikes in 1928 led to the conception of the Industrial Disputes Act 1929, whose main purpose was to bring the weight of public opinion to bear on industrial disputes in the belief that neither the employer nor the employees could afford to ignore its impact. Since then a series of amendments have been enacted with a view to strengthening the legal and governmental machinery to settle industrial disputes, it may be inappropriate to mention a brief explanation about the causes of industrial disputes in India.

Causes of Industrial Disputes: The major causes of industrial disputes in India are wages, bonus, personnel, leave and hours of work, and other. Tables 13.4, 13.5 and 13.6 present data, though not up-to-date, which illustrate the situation.

Settlement Machinery of Industrial Dispute: The basic philosophy supporting the settlement of industrial disputes in India is to discourage industrial disharmony, disputes, strikes and lockouts and to promote industrial peace and harmony through statutory machinery, if the union and management failed to settle their differences. This philosophy draws its inspiration partly from Gandhian doctrine of trusteeship and fundamental harmony and partly from the economic necessity of promotion of economic growth without interruptions to the productive machinery in industry and business.

Mahatma Gandhi declared:[50] "As all life, both individual and social, in its essence is one and undivided, the legitimate ends of its component parts should never be conflicting with each other. In an individual organisation, for instance, the legitimate interests of employers are never at variance with the legitimate interests of the employees."

And again:[51] "I have always said that my ideal is that capital and labour should supplement and help each other. They should be a great family living in unity and harmony, capital not only looking to the material welfare of the labourers but to their moral welfare also — capitalists being trustees for the welfare of the labouring classes under them."

Since Independence, the Government of India have initiated a massive industrialisation programme under the Five Year Plans with a view to promoting economic growth and raising the standards of living of the people and when this programme of economic reconstruction is in operation, the Government is determined to prevent industrial strife and unrest by providing an industrial dispute settlement machinery through conciliation and arbitration or adjudication. Stemming from Gandhism, the Government of the Congress Party was totally opposed to strikes and lockouts and Nehruji, Nandaji, Khandubhai Desai (the last two being prominent labour leaders for A.T.L.A.) declared time and again that strikes were outmoded in the present context. To quote Nandaji:[52] "It would be insensate cruelty to add to the agony and sufferings of the people of the country by stopping production... while it is possible to procure a reasonable settlement of the dispute by arbitration."

The Congress Working Committee, advocating a no-strike philosophy stated:[53] "The Committee feel further that it is necessary in the general interest to point out that avoidable strikes cannot have the backing of the public opinion, and in view of the dire need of the country for more goods and services, hasty or ill-conceived stoppages and the refusal to take advantage of the available means of settlement and negotiation, conciliation and arbitration, constitute a distinct disservice to the Community and the working class itself."

Table 14.4
Labour Situation in 1975 at a Glance

Sl. No.	State/Union Territory	No. of Industrial disputes referred to IRM	No. of failure reports received	Adjudication, Arbitration & Awards: No. of Disputes referred to for Adjudication	Arbitration	No. of disputes for which awards are available: In favour of workers	Against workers	Strikes & Lockouts: No. of Strikes & lock-outs	No. of workmen involved	No. of mandays lost	Works Committee: No. of works Committees required to be constituted	No. of workers covered in Col. 12	No. of works committees actually formed	No. of workers covered in Col. 14	Standing Orders: No. of establishments required to frame Standing Orders	No. of establishments having certified Standi Orders
(1)	(2)	(3)	(4)	(5)	(6)	(7)	(8)	(9)	(10)	(11)	(12)	(13)	(14)	(15)	(16)	(17)
1.	Centre	5,095	1,087	613	14	N.A.	N.A.	293	284,301	1,527,118	1,025	944,404	570	5,27,098	2,455(P)	2,403(P)
2.	Andhra Pradesh	N.S.	N.S.	N.S.	N.S.	N.S.	N.S.	35	18,070	295,415	N.S.	N.S.	N.S.	N.S.	N.S.	N.S.
3.	Assam	583	121	207	—	43	39	3	2,568	85,335	481	—	84	—	1,328	959
4.	Bihar	477	75	20	4	2	N.A.	54	13,288	255,588	152	1,37,261	76	1,22,739	107	95
5.	Gujarat	3,106	1,187	397	2	60	24	69	11,755	532,365	100	67,970	68	58,774	—	—
6.	Haryana	1,994	704	295	16	133	150	12	1,219	21,207	181	78,480	118	57,023	377	286
7.	Himachal Pradesh	N.S.	N.S.	N.S.	N.S.	N.S.	N.S.	N.A.	N.A.	N.A.	N.S.	N.S.	N.S.	N.S.	N.S.	N.S.
8.	Jammu & Kashmir	N.S.	N.S.	N.S.	N.S.	N.S.	N.S.	N.A.	N.A.	N.A.	N.S.	N.S.	N.S.	N.S.	N.S.	N.S.
9.	Kerala	N.S.	N.S.	N.S.	N.S.	N.S.	N.S.	71	11,304	429,696	N.S.	N.S.	N.S.	N.S.	N.S.	N.S.
10.	Madhya Pradesh	522	156	71	4	N.A.	N.A.	43	15,684	58,469	Nil	Nil	Nil	Nil	936	936
11.	Maharashtra	8,907	3,023	2,141	77	767	226	401	79,041	864,139	449	N.A.	239	1,95,293	—	—
12.	Manipur	N.S.	N.S.	N.S.	N.S.	N.S.	N.S.	N.A.	N.A.	N.A.	N.S.	N.S.	N.S.	N.S.	N.S.	N.S.
13.	Meghalaya	21	2	2	Nil	Nil	Nil	N.A.	N.A.	N.A.	2	3,587	1	700	38	2
14.	Karnataka	N.S.	N.S.	N.S.	N.S.	N.S.	N.S.	24	15,305	313,666	N.S.	N.S.	N.S.	N.S.	N.S.	N.S.
15.	Nagaland	Nil	Nil	Nil	Nil	Nil	Nil	N.A.	N.A	N.A.	Nil	Nil	Nil	Nil	Nil	Nil
16.	Orissa (P)	282	200	28	—	3	11	18	4,137	236.338	108	58,654	28	50,262	106	76
17.	Punjab (P)	4,932	2,392	1,973	7	836	655	2	87	1,748	166	55,000	94	42,790	1,550	280
18.	Rajasthan	1,065	612	644	9	N.A.	N.A.	27	4,890	26,562	101	N.A.	70	33,019	203	128
19.	Tamilnadu	7,550	911	444	21	—	—	176	70,117	1,102,057	485	2,86,815	357	2,14,971	6,114	1,880
20.	Tripura	N.S.	N.S.	N.S.	N.S.	N.S.	N.S.	1	23	667	N.S.	N.S.	N.S.	N.S.	N.S.	N.S.
21.	Uttar Pradesh (P)	4,853	3,474	2,686	15	913	649	100	27,989	919,665	17	7,315	17	7,315	1,630	1,407
22.	West Bengal	10,015	710B	436	N.A.	163	44	194	3,16,706	12,502,232	N.A.	N.A.	522(C)	96,725	N.A.	1,593
23.	Andaman & Nicobar Islands	N.S.	N.S.	N.S.	N.S.	N.S.	N.S.	6	1,992	1,992	N.S.	N.S.	N.S.	N.S.	N.S.	N.S.
24.	Arunachal Pradesh	Nil	Nil	Nil	Nil	Nil	Nil	N.A.	N.A.	N.A.	N.S.	N.S.	N.S.	N.S.	N.S.	N.S.
25.	Chandigarh	123	32	10	—	—	—	4	559	6,413	17	6,527	5	2,495	55	11
26.	Dadra & Nagar Havely	N.S.	N.S.	N.S.	N.S.	N.S.	N.S.	N.A.	N.A.	N.A.	N.A.	N.S.	N.S.	N.S.	N.S.	N.S.
27.	Delhi	3,045	1,154	926	5	448	185	15	5,525	33,060	N.A.	N.A.	22	23,861	155	125
28.	Goa, Daman & Diu	224	25	19	1	9	5	10	1,320	11,192	21	4,960	5	1,706	77	10
29.	Lakshadweep	N.S.	N.S.	N.S.	N.S.	N.S.	N.S.	N.A.	N.A.	N.A.	N.S.	N.S.	N.S.	N.S.	N.S.	N.S.
30.	Mizoram	N.S.	N.S.	N.S.	N.S.	N.S.	N.S.	N.A.	N.A.	N.A.	N.S.	N.S.	N.S.	N.S.	N.S.	N.S.
31.	Pondicherry	203	13	28	Nil	7	14	7	17,092	19,748	11	12,500	5	11,000	11	11
	TOTAL	52,997	15,878	10,980	175	3,384	1,995	1,565	902,972	19,244,472	3,316	16,63,473	12,311	14,45,771	15,142	10,202

P = Provisional. N.S. = Not supplied. N.A. = Not Available.

Source: Annual Report of the Union Ministry of Labour (1975-76)

Table 14.5

Percentage Distribution of Industrial Disputes by Causes

Causes	*1961*	*1962*	*1963*	*1964*	*1965*	*1966*	*1967*	*1968*	*1969*	*1970*	*1971*	*1972*
Wages and Allowances	30.4	30.2	27.8	34.9	33.5	35.8	39.9	38.4	36.0	37.1	34.3	31.8
Bonus	6.9	12.3	10.0	7.9	9.9	13.2	10.9	9.4	10.0	10.6	14.1	8.4
Personnel & Retrenchment	29.3	25.2	25.9	27.4	27.3	25.3	23.6	28.2	26.6	25.6	23.0	24.2
Leave & Hours of Work	3.0	0.7	4.6	2.0	2.5	2.4	1.0	1.9	2.2	2.1	1.4	1.4
Indiscipline & Violence	—	—	—	—	—	—	—	3.2	3.8	3.8	3.6	5.1
Others	30.4	31.6	31.7	27.8	26.8	23.3	24.6	18.9	21.4	20.8	23.6	29.1
Total No. of Causes	1,314	1,474	1,466	2,122	1,825	2,536	2,760	2,717	2,609	2,843	2,723	3,153

Source: *Indian Labour Statistics*, 1974, p. 157.

Table 14.6

Mandays Lost on Account of Industrial Disputes (Strike and Lockouts) Resulting in Work-stoppages by Sectors and by Cause during 1972, 1973 and 1974 (Provisional)

Causes	*1972*			*1973*			*1974 (Provisional)*		
	Public	*Private*	*Total*	*Public*	*Private*	*Total*	*Public*	*Private*	*Total*
Wages and Allowances	1,056,909	6,244,705	7,301,614	1,113,508	6,980,089	8,093,597	3,212,718	9,117,208	12,329,926
Bonus	1,392,953	789,598	2,182,551	251,521	1,249,393	1,500,919	941,978	494,753	1,436,731
Personnel	237,130	1,495,181	1,732,311	244,115	2362,239	2,606,354	240,444	1,631,297	1,871,741
Retrenchment	2,625	279,553	282,178	45,854	541,350	587,204	5,586	433,482	439,068
Leave & Hours of work	4,603	117,122	121,725	90,076	153,850	243,926	243,926	5,530	249,456
Indiscipline & Violence	144,646	1,810,181	2,954,827	73,552	2,201,910	2,275,462	100,458	2,297,411	2,397,869
Others	506,752	5,461,958	5,968,710	1,573,851	3,744,940	5,318,791	3,200,808	9,530,414	12,731,222
Total	3,345,618	17,198,298	20,543,916	3,392,477	17,233,776	20,626,253	7,707,522	23,562,965	31,270,487

Source: *Industrial Bulletin*, The Employers' Federation of India, March 1, 1975. p. 19.

In India the state-supported dispute settlement machinery consists of:

(1) Works Committees; (2) Conciliation Officers; (3) Board of Conciliation; (4) Courts of Inquiry; (5) Labour Courts; (6) State Industrial Tribunals; (7) National Tribunal. The first four are charged with the task of negotiation and conciliation; the last three with adjudication.

Procedures of the Settlement Machinery: Based on the principles and philosophy discussed in the above section, public policy provides a three tier machinery for the settlement of industrial disputes. The first tier constitutes voluntary negotiation and the works committees; second, conciliation officers; and third, industrial tribunals at the state and the central levels. In addition, under Article 227 of the Indian Constitution the High court has powers over all judicial and quasi-judicial bodies with respect to both judicial and administrative matters. Under Article 136, the Supreme Court is vested with extraordinary jurisdiction and Tribunals come within the scope of this. It has exceptional and overriding power where it concludes that the litigant has not been dealt with fairly. The Supreme Court has pointed out the limitations on the scope and authority of the Tribunal and the proper procedure to be followed.

Under the Industrial Disputes Act 1947, two new institutions, namely, the works committees and industrial tribunals, came into being for the prevention and settlement of industrial disputes. Every industrial undertaking employing 100 or more workmen is required to constitute works committees comprising of equal representative from management and the employees. Any dispute between the employer and employee is taken up for discussion and settlement in the work committee. Many trivial differences are settled at this level itself. When they fail to reach a settlement, then the conciliation machinery is brought in.

The dispute is referred to a Conciliation Officer, who tries to assist the parties to reach an agreeable settlement. If his efforts fail, he is expected to send a full report to the Government, who will then refer the matter to a Board of Conciliators. If the Board also is unable to bring about a settlement, the Government may refer the dispute to a Court of Inquiry to collect the necessary facts regarding the dispute. It is obligatory for the Government to refer the dispute to the Industrial Tribunal for adjudication, if the parties to the dispute jointly or separately apply for it. The adjudication award is binding on both the parties to the dispute and it becomes enforceable on the expiry of 30 days from the date of its publication in the Gazette and remains in operation for a period of one year in the first instance, but can be extended, unless termination is sought by either of the parties to the other.

The proceedings of the Tribunals are of a quasi-judicial nature and they may compel the production of documents, record evidence of parties and witnesses and afford the opportunity to cross-examine witnesses. They have wide powers than the ordinary courts as they administer a kind of law known as the law of industrial harmony. But a Tribunal is not a court of appeal which can substitute its own judgments for those of management. It can interfere only when there is a lack of good faith, where there is unfair labour practice, when a basic principle of natural justice has been violated or when the finding is completely perverse and baseless.

It was found that several Tribunals expressed conflicting views on various issues referred to them causing anomalies and discomfort to both the parties. To remove this defect, Government of India passed the Appellate Tribunal Act in May 1950, under which the Central Government was authorised to constitute one or more National Industrial Tribunals to deal with matters of national importance and issues concerning establishments located in more than one state. However, the Industrial Disputes (Amendment) Act of 1956 replaced the Appellate Tribunals Act 1950 and all the existing National Industrial Tribunals were abolished. Labour Courts were also appointed to speed up the settlement machinery, as the conciliation machinery was found to be slow and also because of the lack of finality at the end of the conciliation proceedings. The Labour Courts were to ensure impartial and relatively quick decisions in references regarding illegal changes, strikes and lock-outs and the complaints that either may bring about. The Labour Courts are also empowered to decide whether a strike or lock-out is legal or illegal. The 1956 Act prescribes the jurisdiction of the Labour Courts and Industrial Tribunals and the second schedule of the Act covers disputes in the general area of personnel management and the third schedule, matters relating to economic and technical factors.

Where the Tribunals exceed their jurisdiction, among other things, the remedies for the parties are available through *writs of certiorari, prohibition, and mandamus.* As pointed out earlier High Courts and Supreme Court have power to decide these issues.

The employer is not permitted to introduce any change in respect of certain matters relating to conditions of employment without giving the workmen concerned 21 days' notice. The Government can prohibit the continuance of any strike or lockout if the dispute is referred to a Board or a Tribunal or a Labour Court. Strikes and lockouts in public utility services are illegal if they are commenced or declared without giving a notice in the prescribed manner. All strikes and lockouts are illegal if commenced or declared during the tendency of conciliation proceedings before a Board, or a Labour Court or Tribunal. Financial aid in direct furtherance of an illegal strike or lockout is prohibited.

Recent Amendments: As a result of a recent amendment in the Industrial Disputes Act, it is now possible for individual disputes relating to dismissals or discharges of workmen to be directly processed under the Act without espousal of cause either by a union or a large number of workers in the company, as was required before. Another proposed amendment is to empower the courts to act as appellate authorities over management decisions concerning punishment of individual workers against misconduct. Both the amendments are backed by trade unions, not by the employers. A well-known labour journalist writes:[54] "From the institutional point of view of trade unions, it is really surprising that all the trade unions supported both the amendments which, in effect, are aimed at eroding the strength of the trade union movement. By making it possible for individual workman to get processed directly under the Industrial Disputes Act individual disputes without unions or fellow-workers espousing the individual worker's cause, the worker no longer needs the assistance of a union, as an organised institution. He could go to any individual with some knowledge of industrial law and procedures to process his dispute."

Instead of these amendments to enable the state to process individual disputes, he believes, a better alternative would have been to set up grievance redressal machinery with elected worker participation as in the case of the Works Committee. He adds: "This would have brought about a healthy revolution in the immediate emergency of democratic institutions within the industrial sector to deal with such problems and the experience gained in grappling with these problems at the factory level would have infused training to the ranks of workers in solving problems."

By an amendment to the Act in 1976 further curbs on law of retrenchment and closure have been placed on industrial establishments employing 300 or more workers.

Improvement in Industrial Relations: Industrial relations have considerably improved during the eighteen months of emergency. There has been a sharp fall in the number of mandays lost on account of work stoppages. As against 17.10 million mandays lost during the first six months preceding the declaring of emergency, the figure came down to 4.46 million during the following six months, namely, July to December, 1975. During the year, the number of mandays lost was only 6.03 million in the first half year as against 17.10 million during the corresponding period in 1974. The time loss during January-September 1976 has been only 8.37 million. This is no doubt a welcome trend.

The present trend is for increased emphasis on industrywise collective bargaining. In the industries like steel and coal and certain public sector establishments, the working of bipartism has resulted in industrial harmony and in settlement of differences by way of mutual discussions. Any measures that seek to promote collective bargaining and settlement of industrial disputes by the parties themselves needs to be encouraged so that reliance on statutory machinery such as adjudication is minimised.

It would be expeditious and simpler if more and more disputes and differences are sorted out by voluntary arbitration of persons who have reputation for bringing industrial harmony and who are in a position to give practical approach to the problems faced by the industry and the workers.[55]

Role of Law in Regulating Union-management Relations: Prof. John Dunlop the former U.S. Secretary of Labour looks at the role of law in regulating labour-management relations as under:

"In recent years, there has been a rapid expansion of Government controls, and at the same time a growing general dissatisfaction with the effects of regulation. At the outset, a distinction needs to be drawn between economic regulation of prices, rates or fees and related conditions of entry to a market, on the one hand, and social regulation affecting conditions of work such as discrimination, health and safety and the like, on the other. With economic regulation, it may be appropriate to raise the question of whether the interest of a sector and the public may not be better served by deregulation. But with social regulation, while some deregulation may be appropriate, the major concern is methods of regulation, the involvement of those affected, enforcement and compliance approaches, and communications with those affected; regulation to achieve a public purpose continues, but the central concern is the methods, approaches and mutual attitudes of the regulators and the regulatees.

Problems with Regulatory Approach: Whenever a problem has acquired national attention — as pollution, inflation and occupational disease have in recent years — the natural Congressional reaction has been to create a new regulatory agency to deal with it. There are problems with this approach.

First it encourages simplistic thinking about complicated issues.

Second, often times policies that appear straightforward will have unintended consequences which can create problems as severe as those with which the regulations were intended to deal.

Third, the rulemaking and adjudicatory procedures of regulatory agencies tend to be very slow, creating conflicts between the different groups involved, and leading to weak and ineffective remedies for the people the programmes aimed to help.

Fourth, the rulemaking and adjudicatory procedures do not include a mechanism for the development of mutual accommodation among the conflicting interests.

Fifth, a further problem is what is called "regulatory overlap", where a number of different regulatory agencies share some of the same responsibilities.

Sixth, regulatory efforts are rarely abandoned even after their purpose has been served.

Steps towards Improvement: It is not realistic to expect any reduction in the number of Federal regulatory programmes in the immediate future, but, as a practical matter, it is important that more attention be given towards improving the quality of regulation. As a first step in this direction, six considerations are put forth.

First, the parties who will be affected by a set of regulations should be involved to a greater extent in the development of those regulations.

Second, anachronistic and unnecessary regulations should be repealed and, in the future, rules should be promulgated with greater reluctance.

Third, greater emphasis should be placed on helping regulatees achieve compliance, especially through consultation.

Fourth, the activities of the various regulatory agencies need to be coordinated better.

Fifth, regulations must be made to reflect differences between industries, sectors, and geographic regions.

Sixth, the actions of the various regulatory agencies need to be brought into greater harmony with collective bargaining.[56]

Voluntary Arbitration: Before submitting an industrial dispute to a Board of Conciliation, or a Labour Court or a Tribunal, the parties may, by written agreement, refer it to arbitration, whose award they may voluntarily agreed to abide by. Except for a few instances, voluntary arbitration machinery has not become popular. This is due to the excessive reliance on compulsory adjudication. P.N. Krishna Pillai notes:[57] "What is fundamentally forgotten is that voluntary arbitration can thrive only in an industrial relations set up where a voluntary relationship between parties is established through free collective bargaining. Otherwise it is only an attempt to give another name to the present method of compulsory adjudication and to perpetuate the bitterness among parties caused by fighting before a third party."

Some Criticisms of the Dispute Settlement Machinery: The present machinery is very cumbersome and time consuming. Both the unions and managements are fed up with the inordinate delays and then the third party settlement never promotes complete harmony in the plant. Despite this, both parties resort to this adjudication machinery out of sheer helplessness and the hope that adjudication award may be favourable to one of them.

The reliance of trade unions on compulsory arbitration is a reflection of their weak bargaining power and their organisational and functional short-comings. According to many observers, this attitude has actually led to the weakening of labour movement. The employers prefer to abolish compulsory adjudication, because they believe that Tribunals favour unions most of the time. But there is a matching of unequal strength, as the employers are stronger than the unions in India. Another factor is that employers refuse to lay all their cards on the negotiation table and in the words of Dwarkadass:[58]

> "With the Damocles Sword of compulsory arbitration hanging over them the employers are afraid of offering compromise terms because once these terms are rejected and compulsory arbitration set in, the compromise terms offered by the employers become the minimum starting point.... The employers, therefore, take part in collective bargaining with mental reservation and do not lay their cards on the table."

An authority attempts to identify the causes of delay in labour adjudication in India and offers some suggestions for improvement as under:

1. There are three benches of the industrial court and three labour courts and a number of assistant commissioners of labour before whom the representatives of the parties are required to appear. The unions have a limited number of representatives and even the representatives of employers are also limited in number. Generally, the union representatives are social and political workers and have varied activities. This is also true to some of the employers — particularly when the employer is a local authority. Because of these circumstances many a time the cases are required to be adjourned to enable the parties to have their representatives before the courts.
2. Even when the cases come before the court, bearing in mind the scheme of the BIR Act and the I.D. Act, negotiations for amicable settlements are not discouraged. The negotiations between the parties take considerable time and for that purpose cases are required to be adjourned. They are adjourned as desired by the parties for this purpose.
3. The questions involved in some cases are sometimes linked with the questions arising in other cases and if negotiations for settlement are going on in either sets of such cases the other sets of cases are required to be adjourned. Even in such cases, the adjournments are given as desired by or at the instance of the parties concerned.
4. It is ordinarily not possible to give ex-parte awards in industrial matters, particularly in disputes regarding wages, bonus and a number of such other matters. It, therefore, becomes necessary to adjourn the matter from time to time to get the defaulting party before the court. This is equally true when the parties remain present but do not produce the relevant materials required for adjudication.

5. Cases regarding dismissal and discharge of the workers are given priority and disposed of early. But even in such types of cases when the parties desire that some amicable settlement should be arrived at, efforts are made for the purpose and such cases naturally require cooling period and are for that purpose delayed. In such cases the delay is generally in the interests of the workers and not the employer.
6. In many of the cases the representatives of the parties are not conversant with the court procedure and the requirements regarding the production of the necessary and relevant materials. In such types of cases the courts are required to discuss the relevant points with the parties and explain to them the materials required to be produced. Even when the evidence is brought before the court, the court has to see that the evidence is put in proper form and proper statements are prepared so as to help adjudication. Such methods are more helpful to labour than to the employers, especially when most of the available evidence is in the possession of the employers. All these naturally take considerable time.
7. In any case, if either of the parties to the proceedings desires early disposal, top priority is given to such cases and they are disposed of as speedily as possible.

Conclusions

"As it has already been indicated, delay in labour adjudication is caused by adjournments sought by both parties to a case. These are sought particularly at the evidence stage, since managements are usually unwilling to produce relevant material and the unions are unable to obtain appropriate information. Nevertheless, the adjournments are inherent in the procedures followed by the courts themselves. It has been pointed out by the Gujarat Labour Laws Review Committee.

"Largely in this State, Judges of the Labour Court and Industrial Court/Tribunal have been drawn from the civil judiciary, with the result that they carried with them their deep seated firm belief in advisory system followed in civil courts....The duty to bring evidence resting upon the parties which is an inseparable characteristics of civil justice administered through adversary systems, its malignable concomitant, namely, burden of proof and consequences of failure to adduce evidence by the party on whom burden of proving relevant facts rests, all came in its wake. Gradually over course of time, the methodology, the tardiness, the slow drift, the hypertechnical approach evident in Civil Courts raised their ugly head in these Tribunals too. Now, this may be a correct approach for the civil courts but it is certainly not a correct approach where parties are wholly unevenly balanced. The Committee suggested that the adversary system should be replaced by inquisitorial system, wherein the presiding judge should himself be made responsible for collecting necessary material to dispense justice to both parties.

"Another procedural problem relates to the appearance of legal practitioners before the courts. This system has in the past bred a legalistic approach in labour judiciary and has also been responsible for delays. Section 36 (4) of I.D. Act provides that a party to a dispute may be represented by a legal practitioner with the consent of the other parties to the proceedings and with the leave of the court concerned. The Committee suggested certain amendments to this provision. It argued that the appearance of legal practitioners should be severely restricted:

"The presiding officer (should) determine whether the case involves such complex issues of law which would necessitate assistance of legal practitioners, and if he is of that view, it would be necessary for the parties to apply and the Presiding Officer should make a speaking order permitting appearance of legal practitioners setting out reasons in support of his decision.

"In the final analysis, it is necessary to refer back to the total quantum of cases being handled by labour judiciary. With the possibility of the existing system of labour administration continuing for some time to come, one may confidently predict that the workload on courts may only increase in the future. Consequently there is also a case for increasing the number of courts in the State in step with the anticipated case load."[59]

The alleged cultural, status, class, sociological differences between the employers and employees do not promote the democratic mental processes that induce the employer to seek a rapproachment with the employees.

According to Van Dusen Kennedy,[60] one of the main reasons for the Government's adherence to a policy of protection for the trade unions and the imposition of an outside authority in the form of compulsory arbitration is its deep seated value of paternalism. This may be noted in the employer's attitude, but it has much stronger force in the Government as it has the moral sanction of a democratic society.

It has also been pointed out that the Indian worker has an ingrained tendency to let others rule his destiny and settle his disputes — the obverse of paternalism.[61] Furthermore, we may venture to add that among the people of India, there is an excessive love of litigation and those in industry are no exception. We would rather see the third party — courts — settle our disputes and we prefer to embrace the attitude: let the tribunals or the courts settle this.

In order to eliminate the inordinate delays, Mr. G. Ramanujam of INTUC,[62] delivering his presidential address, urged that the Government should fix a time limit of 90 days within which all write petitions and appeals against awards of Tribunals and Labour Courts should be disposed of. He also asked for the creation of a special cadre of judges with some training and industrial experience, if necessary, for manning the Tribunals.

The Supreme Court was also unhappy that its work was being held up by the industrial disputes and it felt that it would be better to create an industrial court with men of industrial experience to officiate as judges in order to do complete justice to the industrial disputes. Thus it is seen that everybody all round is unhappy about the statutory machinery, which, nonetheless, is resorted to more often than not.

Delivering his inaugural address at the seminar on the working of the Industrial Disputes Act, Employees' State Insurance Scheme and Joint Management Councils held in New Delhi in December 1966 organised by the Council of Indian Employers, Mr. Naval H. Tata said that collective bargaining and collective agreement were the only means of ensuring an amicable and lasting settlement. The statutory procedure should be a standby measure.... He added that more of bipartite agreements and less of adjudicated awards, more of voluntary codes and less of Labour Laws, more of self reliance on the part of the employer and the worker and less eagerness on the part of Government to interfere, might perhaps in course of time, put us on the path of an enduring industrial peace.

Recommendations of the National Commission on Labour: The National Commission on Labour (1969) considered the weakness in the working of the existing industrial relations machinery, viz., the delays involved, the expenditure, the largely *ad hoc* nature of the machinery, the discretion vested in the Government in the matter of reference of disputes and allegations of political pressures and interference. The Commission felt that reforming the industrial relations machinery was necessary towards making it independent in character, expeditions in its functioning and equipped to build up the necessary expertise, and accordingly recommended the setting up the Industrial Relations Commission at the national and state levels. Such Commission would combine in itself both the conciliation and adjudication functions as also certification of unions as representative Unions, thus ensuring interchange of knowledge, information and expertise.

The suggestion of the National Commission on Labour to set up IRCs found support from employers and the INTUC but have not found favour with the leftist trade unions nor with the State Governments, each for reasons of their own. However, the suggestion of the National Commission on Labour to set up Labour Court entrusted with the judicial functions of interpretation and enforcement of all labour laws, awards and agreements is likely to be implemented by the Government. At the Standing Labour Committee in July 1970 where AITUC and HMS did not participate, a decision, however, was taken to set up IRCs in States and the Centre with some modifications to the suggestions made by the National Commission on Labour.[63]

Tata Memorandum: Mr. J.R.D. Tata, in his memorandum submitted to the Central Government in May, has made a number of recommendations as to how best industrial growth could be stepped up within the framework of Government's socio-economic policies. The memorandum also refers to ways and means of curbing the current labour unrest in industry. The relevant extracts from the memorandum, which has attracted much attention in Parliament in 1972, are reproduced below:

"Government and Parliament have, over the past twenty-five years, devoted much time, energy, legislation and budgetary funds towards improving the lot of industrial and office workers. While this was a highly desirable objective, the attainment of which has made up for past neglect of workers' interests, it is an unquestionable fact that today in relation to the income of other categories of Indian citizens, including that, after tax, of managerial personnel at one end, and of unorganised workers agriculture and industry at the other, industrial and office employees in both the public and the private sectors are now getting more than a fair deal. They not only have fair wages, but good conditions of work and reasonable retiring benefits, none of which accrues to the vast majority of workers.

"We are glad to note, from recent public statements by government spokesmen, including the Prime Minister and the President, that the view is growing that efforts must now be concentrated on improving the lot of workers in agriculture and in the non-organised sector of industry.

"But there will still be the problem of minimising the excessive loss of production every year due to labour unrest. Partly for political reasons arising from the fact that the Indian trade unions are in effect arms of political parties, excessive advantage has been taken by unions in India of the known sympathy of Central and State governments towards labour. As a result, the country has suffered an appalling loss of mandays in recent years. These were 17.2 million in 1968, 19.0 million in 1969, 20.6 million in 1970, and about 15 million in 1971. It is true that there was recently been a marked improvement in Bengal, but indications are that the situation has begun once again to deteriorate in that part of the country.

"It is significant that loss of production through labour unrest has been much greater in the public sector than in the private sector, the obvious explanation for which is that employees of public sector enterprises and services are well aware that they can bring greater pressure on the management of public sector enterprises, including banks and public utility services, than in private sector concerns. This they achieve by being allowed to go over the heads of management and press their demands directly with government, and even Parliament. Labour's right to pursue their demands for further improvements in their emoluments or conditions of service within the framework of the Indian labour situation over recent years has been that the existing laws of the land have been consistently flouted without any action being taken by government. To our knowledge, there has been only a single instance of prosecution for illegal stoppage of work, and that was in Air-India in 1968, with immediate results.

"Of all countries in the world, India, at this critical stage of its development, can least afford the heavy loss of production and the gross public inconvenience repeatedly inflicted on it by labour unrest."

"While realising how difficult and at times intractable this problem is, we urge that in view of the commanding position government has acquired in the last Central and State elections, it should now take a firmer stand than it has been able to do in the past in the matter of labour disputes and discipline. Wherever appropriate, government should, we submit, not hesitate to invoke the rigours of the law, for there is no reason why violations of the labour laws should always be ignored or condoned, when violations of other laws are automatically subjected to punitive action."

"We also recommend that in labour disputes in public sector enterprises and services, government should refrain from intervening as has been too often done in the past, thereby undermining the authority of local management and destroying its morale. From long experience in both the private and public sectors, I plead for a greater realisation by government of the importance of morale in any organisation, whether private or public. Much of the poor performance of the public sector can be traced to poor morale at all levels, and this itself is usually due to a feeling of insecurity in the mind of management, caused by the lack of sufficient managerial autonomy and responsibility."[64]

Settlement of Industrial Disputes in U.S.A.: In U.S.A. the concept of free collective bargaining is widely accepted and also the unions and employers are permitted a great deal of freedom in the use of the strike or the lockout or other coercive techniques to put pressure on the other party to reach an agreement. The Government follows basically a policy of non-intervention, although in recent years it is using all its moral powers to force the parties to settle their disputes.

The Taft-Hartley Act 1947 established an independent agency, the Federal Mediation and Conciliation Service (FMCS), which provides a threefold service, mediation, conciliation, and voluntary arbitration.

Conciliation and Mediation: Only when the employers and employees fail to settle their disputes, the FMCS voluntarily or upon request may offer their services to mediate in order to bring about a settlement, but the suggested proposals are not binding on the parties. The FMCS also provides a list of qualified arbitrators whose names are given upon request to the parties. A majority of these arbitration cases involve disputes over the application or interpretation of terms of existing union contracts.

Voluntary Arbitration: Ninety-five per cent of all agreements in U.S.A. provide for voluntary arbitration which has come into extensive vogue since the Second World War. Mr. Francis A. O'Connell, Jr. writes[65] that "...the number of cases taken to arbitration through the American Arbitration Association increased by 151 per cent between 1945 and 1950 and by 125 per cent between 1950 and 1959. The latest figures from the Association show another 26 per cent increase thus far in 1960, and figures from the Federal Mediation and Conciliation Service indicate a somewhat greater increase for the year. The Bureau of National Affairs recently reported that about 95 per cent of all contracts now contain arbitration provisions."

Most disputes are settled by the parties through the grievance procedure; but a few unsettled disputes are referred to an arbitrator selected by union and management. Most arbitrators are selected on an *ad hoc* basis, but a few firms employee a permanent one. Arbitration is a desirable alternative to a strike or a lockout. In labour agreements, signed after the War, at least one consideration behind the inclusion of arbitration provisions was the inclusion of a no-strike clause and thus the character of arbitration as a substitute for a strike is preserved.

Pigors and Myers state:[66] "This voluntary nature of the arbitration is consistent with the essential philosophy of American industrial relations which emphasises the right of employers and unions to settle their differences by their own means, so long as the national health and safety are not seriously impaired by a strike or lockout."

As a matter of fact, voluntary arbitration has become too popular, as pointed out by Francis A. O'Connell, Jr:[67]

> "As arbitration became more familiar, it became more habitual. As contracts came to cover longer and longer terms, with consequently longer gaps between pyrotechnics of negotiation, arbitration was discovered by some unions to be a useful means of looking busy during the contract term. As shop stewards, and even rank-and-file employees, became more sophisticated in the uses of the labour contract and more aware of its potentiality for yielding windfalls the pressures to carry a given case through to arbitration became greater. Then somebody discovered the political uses of arbitration. Union leaders found they could avoid the unpleasant chore of telling a worker that his claim was groundless or his discharge justified by letting an arbitrator do it. (Management, too, I hasten to add, was not guiltless of this deplorable abuse of the arbitration process for political or tactical reasons.) Thus arbitration has gradually come almost to the

routine terminal point for a grievance, rather than an exceptional resort in a critical situation." In recent Supreme Court decisions the whole complexion of arbitration and arbitrator's responsibilities are changed and they have been given very wide latitude and powers.

Emergency Dispute Settlement: The national emergency provisions of Taft-Hartley Act 1947 invite the President of U.S.A. to intervene in a threatened nation-wide strike in a basic industry affecting the national health and safety. He is directed to appoint a Board of Inquiry which shall report the "facts with respect to the dispute, including each party's statement of its position, but shall not contain any recommendations." Upon receipt of the report, the President may direct the Attorney General to seek an injunction, which may last a maximum of 80 days, popularly known as the "cooling off period." During the first 60 days, the FCMS tries to settle the dispute, and the Board of Inquiry is reconvened to report the President on the status of the dispute, including a statement of the employer's last offer of settlement. The NLRB then conducts a secret ballot of employees on the employer's last offer, and the result are reported to the Attorney General within 20 days. Following this, the injunction is dissolved, and a strike or lockout again is legal. If the dispute is not settled, the President is required to report to Congress with recommendations "for appropriate action."

Government intervention in labour-management relations in U.S.A. is steadily increasing, more in the nature of establishing "the rules of the game."

(c) Joint Consultation in India

Joint consultation in India discussed in this section refers to the Works Committees and the Joint Management Councils designed to promote a bipartite machinery (union-management) to handle problems of mutual interest in direct furtherance of the doctrine of fundamental harmony and the philosophy of no-strike followed by the Government of India.

Works Committees: As mentioned earlier, the Works Committees came on the industrial scene as a result of the Industrial Disputes Act 1947. They were to promote measures for securing and preserving amity and good relations between the employers and the workmen and, to that end to comment upon matters of their common interest or concern and endeavour to compose any material differences of opinion in respect of such matters. The scope of the Works Committees was so wide that they were unable to fulfil the ends for which legislation created them. In view of mutual distrust and suspicion on the part of both employers and employees, these committees were reduced to a form where grievances were aired by the parties freely. To quote IIPM:[68] "The idea was sound, but in practice it rarely worked out as intended. Some blamed the legislators for not defining more closely the objects and functions of the Works Committee; but the fact remains that one cannot compel people by law to co-operate. They can be forced to sit together, but that does not produce joint if the spirit is not there behind the legal machinery. Management, with a few exceptions, were sceptical of the value of joint consultation; the trade unions were frankly suspicious." Both the parties are always on the defensive; but organisations where labour-management relations were amicable, the working of the Committees was smooth and useful.

There was also an attempt to introduce a scheme of Joint Production Committees, which was not successful either. Poorly defined functions of Works Committees, poor preparation for meeting, worker illiteracy and educational problems, lack of collective bargaining and agreements, and lack of voluntary negotiation philosophy, mutual distrust and suspicion have rendered the Works Committees weak and ineffective.

In 1959, a tripartite committee of the Indian Labour Conference attempted to define the functions and it suggested the areas with which the Works Committees should deal and with which they should not.

I. List of items Works Committees could deal with:

1. Conditions of work such as ventilation, lighting, temperature and sanitation including latrines and urinals.
2. Amenities such as drinking water, canteens, dining rooms, creches, rest rooms, medical and health services.
3. Safety and accident prevention, occupational diseases and protective equipment.
4. Adjustment of festival and national holidays.
5. Administration of welfare and fine funds.
6. Educational and recreational activities such as libraries, reading rooms, cinema shows, sports, games, picnic parties, community welfare and celebrations.
7. Promotion of thrift and savings.
8. Implementation and review of decisions arrived at meetings of Works Committees.

II. List of items Works Committees will not deal with:

1. Wages and allowances.
2. Bonus and profit sharing schemes.
3. Rationalisation and matters connected with the fixation of workload.
4. Matters connected with the fixation of standard labour force.
5. Programmes of planning and development.
6. Matters connected with retrenchment and lay-off.
7. Victimisation for trade union activities.
8. Provident Fund, gratuity schemes and festival holidays.
10. Incentive schemes.
11. Housing and transport services.

Mr. P.N. Krishna Pillai pointed out:[69] "The Works Committees or similar joint consultative bodies have not taken deep roots in the industrial relations set up in our country since there was a lot of misconception about them from the very beginning. Some people thought that this machinery provided in the Industrial Relations law in the country could be used to bypass trade unions and the unions in many instances were non-cooperative. Works Committees and other joint consultative bodies were functioning in our country where they are established in consultation with trade unions and with their co-operation." But it is observed that the functioning of the Works Committees has been successful where they have confined themselves to the areas of welfare amenities and social activities and working conditions and have avoided discussion of any subject which is normally a matter of negotiation between the employer and unions.

Joint Management Councils: During the Second Five Year Plan at the fifteenth sessions of the Indian Labour Conference the programme of "workers, participation in management" was launched with a view to creating an industrial democracy in the long run and harmonious relations between labour and management as well as an active commitment on the part of the worker to the company for which he is working. Joint Management Councils were constituted in some 27 undertakings both in private and public sector in 1958. At present the scheme is reported to be in operation in some 90 firms.

This programme also has not been very successful, because of management apathy, the unions charge. INTUC reported:[70] "In some cases the management went to the extent of creating a situation where it was impossible for the workers to extend their co-operation. The scheme aims at achieving relationship of equal partnership based on mutual goodwill, and, as it is, it cannot be enforced by an Act of legislation." HMS also noted that there was no interest on the part of management for the scheme of workers' participation in management. "In many cases," remarked Mr. B. Tulpule,[71] "the meetings of the Joint Management Councils are held at long intervals. Often, the meetings are not convened at all or dispersed without transacting any business. The explanation given is that there are no subjects for the agenda for the council meetings."

In a similar view the managements complain that unions do not trust them and that they are apathetic and uncooperative. Mr. Nanda, when he was the Labour Minister, admitted that the progress of the scheme was far from satisfactory. Interestingly enough many of the big undertakings in private and public sector refused to come forward to adopt this programme.[72] In October 1965, the then Union Labour Minister, at the Indian Labour Conference, admitted that there was no enthusiasm for the scheme from the management side or the union side. But he prodded the employers to give the scheme another try. "The Joint Management Councils have been given a say only in regard to items like administration of welfare facilities, supervision of safety and so on. For the rest it is largely a matter of sharing of information and joint consultation on all important matters of the undertaking which are of mutual interest to labour and management."

The study group on worker participation in management appointed by the Government of India in 1957 reported that "a firm impression left with us was that worker participation in management could be successful only as a supplement to a well established system of collective bargaining." Furthermore they pointed out that "the first interests of workers are wages, conditions of work, security, and a fair grievance procedure and if there is bitterness over these, no real participation is possible. Satisfactory arrangements for collective bargaining and for the settlement of unresolved disputes are, therefore, essential for the success of worker's participation."[73]

Then, of course, there are those who claim that it is only association of labour with management and that unions do not really want to manage along with the employer, particularly in the function of control, but their interest in management is limited to their area of operation such as working conditions that affect their working lives. But it appears that unions want more than that, as INTUC proclaimed, "workers' participation in management is a tremendous and thrilling experiment in the field of democratic industrial progress. It deals with the whole aspect of industrial economics and specially its psychological impact on the workers."[74] It must not be forgotten that union leadership, though not the workers, has grandiose visions of industrial democracy, social ownership, co-partnership and similar notions. While the worker's interests in India are geared to his immediate physiological needs, the union leadership's sights are trained on grand designs, far removed from the mundane aspirations of their membership.

It is interesting to note that the strongest trade unions in U.S.A. do not aspire for any participation in management and they want the management to do a good job of managing and getting the best results, so they may demand a share in those results. To many trade unions in U.S.A., U.K. etc., where the labour movement is strongest, worker participation in management is irrational.

When asked, "what would you do if you were made the President of the company, and you were asked to make (better)", a worker in U.S.A. replied: "If I were the President, I'd go nuts." [75] He would rather have the President manage the company. Perhaps it is understood there that managing an enterprise calls for professional know-how, competence, and expertise. This idea, not a revolutionary one, holds good even in our country.

Finally, Mr. P.N. Krishna Pillai points out that the "same fundamental mistakes associated with our concept of Works Committees are discernible in this scheme also. The illusion still nurtured in certain quarters that a scheme of worker participation in management or a joint management council scheme can function successful without strong and effective collective bargaining is at the root of failure of the whole scheme." Raising the question why neither the unions nor managements are enthusiastic about the scheme, he answers: "Because as the report of the study team has cogently pointed out, the first interests of the workers are wages, conditions of work, security and fair grievance procedure" and in the absence of a system for collective bargaining in this area, "no real participation is possible." When the workers are not interested in the scheme of joint management councils why should the employers be enthusiastic about it? As in the case of works committees, in this regard also the universal experience of industries that joint consultation can only succeed as a supplement to joint negotiation on wages and terms and conditions of employment, has been affirmed in this country.[76]

The New Scheme of Participation: What are the main causes of the failure of the Joint Management Councils? First, the failure was in their non-acceptance by big industrial concerns even in the public sector. Most of the concerns selected for this experiment were small-sized and as such they could not make any impact. Government could have used its large undertakings as laboratories for this experiment. Secondly, the JMCs had functions of minor importance and even there the decisions taken unanimously had no mandatory force. Minor functions often make the institution unimportant. Thirdly, participation was not properly defined. It was mostly at lower levels of health, safety, welfare and production. Fourthly, the spirit of participation was absent. Institutions were created without creating the necessary congenial and constructive climate, where each party would trust the *bona fides* of the other and would respect its rights. As a result, the JMCs were used as a platform where management and trade unions showed distrust of each other; there were charges and counter-charges about deliberate delays in setting up JMCs, utilising them for their own ends, apathy and indifference, shirking responsibility and unnecessary intervention in labour matters by the State.

The New Scheme: Against the background of this earlier experience, "the scheme for workers' participation in industry at shop floor and plant level" may be examined. The factors which held to the failure of the Works Committees and Joint Management Councils have to be avoided to ensure the success of the new scheme.

The present scheme has been kept "flexible so as to allow variations to suit local conditions and hence will be implemented through executive action." However, Government's Resolution, relating to the new scheme, states that legislation would be considered after adequate experience has been gained. Normally, legislation implies some coercion from a third party, and hence is inimical to industrial democracy.

The scheme initially applies to "manufacturing and mining industries" and thus excludes many sectors, particularly services. It also applies to units having 500 or more workers. The Work Committees were for industrial establishments with 100 or more workers, whereas the Joint Management Councils were voluntarily set up in units, most of which had less than 500 workers.

In the Twenty-Point Programme, emphasis was "particularly at the shop floor level" and hence the shop council was a step in the right direction. Both the Works Committee and the Joint Management Council dealt with the problems of the whole unit and thus indirectly neglected the shop floor problems. The new scheme envisages workers participation right from the shop floor.

The role of recognised trade unions (or the various registered trade unions) in the election of employees' representatives is not clear and may lead to inter-union conflict. Similarly, the practice of taking all decisions on the basis of consensus (and not by a process of voting) may generate difficulties, particularly when some of the employees' representatives decide to take a rigid stand.

A happy feature is that the decisions of the Council would be implemented within a month. The failure of Works Committees and Joint Management Councils was partly due to the fact that even their unanimous decisions were not mandatory.

The functions of the Shop Councils relate to production and productivity absenteeism, general discipline, health, safety, welfare and working conditions. Collective bargaining issues are excluded from the scope of the functions of shop councils. The Joint Councils, which are to deal with matters relating to the entire unit, have broadly the same procedures and functions as those of the Shop Councils.

Composition: In view of the considerable diversity in the situation prevailing from unit to unit in different industries and also in departmental undertakings and public enterprises under the same Ministry of the Central Government, no uniform pattern for the constitution of shop councils, particularly relating to the representation of workers, could be laid down. Hence, the Government Resolution recommends that the management, in consultation with the workers, should evolve the most suitable pattern of representation so as to ensure that the representation of the workers results in their effective, meaningful and broad-based participation.

Communication: The Government of India attaches great importance to communication, for its Resolution states: "For any scheme of workers' participation to succeed, there must be an effective two-way communication and exchange of information between the management and the workmen. It is only then that the workers would have a better appreciation of the problems and difficulties of the undertaking and of its overall functioning. With this end in view, each unit should devise a suitable system of communication within the undertaking.

Implementation: The National Press Agency, Samachar, conducted a national survey regarding the implementation of the worker participation scheme and found that nearly two and a half million industrial workers were covered by it. The scheme was applicable to 1,795 unions of which 1,249 implemented it by the end of October 1976.[77]

4. TRIPARTITE MACHINERY

In 1942, the Government of India started the Indian Labour Conferences which brought together the representatives of labour, employers, and the Government and which set up a tripartite machinery, whose constitution drew its inspiration from I.L.O. with 22 Government, 11 Workers' and 11 Employers' representatives. The objectives of this tripartite machinery were as follows:[78] (1) the promotion of uniformity in labour legislation; (2) the determination of a procedure for the settlement of industrial disputes; and (3) consultations on all matters of industrial interest affecting the country as a whole. The organisation consists of a Standing Labour Committee and a Plenary Conference, which meets at least once a year, both being presided over by the Union Minister of Labour. The tripartite Indian Labour conferences have become a regular annual feature of Indian Industrial Relations system and they play an important role in the formulation of labour policy and in the promotion of consultation and exchange of ideas and views. They have considerably influenced labour legislation as well as other matters of industrial interest in India. Between 1947 and 1957 there was a spate of labour legislation on various matters.

Since 1957 a series of tripartite codes or conventions were evolved at the labour conferences and the inspiration for these codes came from Mr. Gulzarilal Nanda, Labour Minister in 1957. Nandaji, who was a trade union leader of Ahmedabad Textile Labour Association and who was greatly influenced by the Gandhian ideology of trusteeship and fundamental harmony, was opposed to excessive resort to compulsory adjudication and litigation of industrial relations matters. He was keen that labour and management should evolve their own codes of conduct or "rules of the game" which were acceptable to them and according to which they would "play the game." The following are the codes or conventions reached at Indian Labour Conferences beginning with 1957:[79]

1. Code of Discipline in Industry.
2. Agreed Criteria for Recognition of trade unions.

3. Code of Inter-union Harmony.
4. Grievance Procedure.
5. Model Agreement for Joint Management Councils.
6. Code of Efficiency and Welfare.

All these codes are established with a view to reducing industrial strife and unrest and to promoting harmonious employer-employee relations. The Government also claimed that the codes, particularly the code of discipline, were responsible for improving the industrial relations situation in the country, when there was a gradual decline in the number of mandays lost due to strikes and work-stoppages from the peak of 77.98 lakhs in 1958 to 32.68 lakhs in 1963. Then there was a steep rise in 1964 to 77 lakhs man-days lost, which really bothered the whole tripartite machinery. Patriotism prompted the workers in 1962 during the Chinese aggression to stick to their jobs and again during Indo-Pakistan War. But it appears that the Codes have been unable to achieve the ends for which they were evolved, mainly because of the built-in internal deficiencies of the labour movement, and in the union-management relations. Inter-union rivalries, distrust and lack of confidence between employers and employees, differences between local and central union leadership and lack of the spirit of voluntary bilateralism established by collective bargaining and negotiations proved to be too strong for the various codes to overcome.

Besides, the Codes received a mixed reception from the unions (though they agreed to the codes in the conference). Regarding the Code of Discipline, only INTUC was enthusiastic. "Code of Discipline has been a great step towards the preservation of healthy and peaceful industrial relations." INTUC favoured collective bargaining and voluntary arbitration. The Gandhian approach of no-strike and no-lockout followed by INTUC came in sharp conflict with the approach by AITUC. In so far as Code of Discipline attempted to deprive the worker the legitimate right to strike, demonstrate and agitate, AITUC was not agreeable to the Code. "We cannot agree", said AITUC,[80] "to this as it will lead to a ban on all strikes and demonstrations and deprive the workers of their only weapon of defence." UTUC did not think much of the Code of Discipline.[81]

1. the code of discipline has been a dismal failure.
2. the code of discipline has been utilised to suppress the trade union movement.
3. the evaluation and implementation machinery does not function in some States; and
4. in those States, where they function they move so tardily and ineffectively that only the employers stand to gain by it.

HMS did not think that the Code of Discipline had reduced industrial disputes and they opposed the Code of Efficiency and Welfare altogether. HMS thought that the India Labour Conferences were not very useful either:[82] "It has been our experience during recent sessions of the Indian Labour Conference and Standing Labour Committee that there is a tendency on the part of the Government to avoid frank and full discussion on controversial subjects. The inevitable polite talk and no decision of any practical importance is reached."

Mr. P.N. Krishna Pillai makes this observation regarding the Code of Discipline:[83] "The code is a magnificent document affirming well accepted principles in industrial relations. It endeavours to eschew coercion, threat, illegal stoppage of work, slowdown, victimisation and to promote joint negotiation, conciliation and voluntary arbitration. It is also recognised in the code that litigation in industrial relations is to be avoided. It is however regrettable to note that the code has not brought any material change in the strife-ridden situation in industry in general." A sort of an explanation was offered by Mr. C. Subramaniam, when he was the Minister of Steel and when there was a strike in the Bhilai Steel Plant as a consequence of inter-union rivalry:[84] "No doubt, we have got codes of conduct at the highest level. I am sure when the labour leaders enter into them, they do so sincerely and genuinely and they also try to implement them. But what about the lower level? They are not interested in the rational leadership entering into these codes of conduct. They want to be the dominating tussle going on." Perhaps the Honourable Minister was hinting at the futility of the codes in view of the basic problems with the labour movement. Unless these codes were made acceptable at the plant level, the national agreements do not ever amount to anything of consequence.

In the 24th session of the Indian Labour Conference held in New Delhi on the 29th and 30th July 1966, both the labour and management representatives agreed that the Code of Discipline was ineffective:[85] INTUC argued that (though it believed in the spirit of the code) the Code might be scrapped because the parties were interested in their rights only and not in meeting their obligations under the Code. AITUC complained that both management and Government, as a major employer through public sector, failed to honour the Code and charged that the Government had no moral right to ask others to follow the Code. Besides, unions were not getting recognition under the Code and the Implementation Committees were not even meeting. AITUC said that unless special measures were taken, "it was better to bury the Code and abolish compulsory arbitration."

The management representatives were also not happy with the Code for different reasons. Their complaint was that the unions dishonoured the Code and some unions openly preached strife and violence. Another argument advanced was that unions blamed the employers whenever the Code hurt them. The Government representatives, in a characteristic manner, came up with their favourite recipe of some more "appropriate statutes" with the principles of the Code incorporated in them. In view of no better alternatives, Government claimed that neither the Code nor compulsory adjudication can be abolished. Thus the uneasy life of the Code is prolonged.

Industrial relations both in the Central and State spheres, have registered a significant improvement during the last one year. This has been possible mainly due to various measures taken by the Centre as well as by the State Governments to promote industrial harmony and peace with a view to increasing production and productivity.[86]

The mandays lost due to lockouts and strikes, which stood at 17.10 million in the first half of 1975 came down to 4.46 million in the second half of the year. Yet another significant feature of the post-emergency period was that there had been no strike in railways, ports and docks, defence and other Central Government undertakings.

The industrial relations machinery, both at the Centre and the state level, continued to make efforts to minimise work stoppages through informal mediation, conciliation, adjudication and arbitration. This was possible under the existing statutory provision and voluntary arrangements.

To ensure that the private sector also played the assigned role and to develop a system of bipartite consultation between the organisations of employers and workers, the National Apex Body was set up with 23 members representing employers and workers. Based on the deliberations of this body, bipartite industrial committees at the national level for some industries were set up. The apex body sorts out problems of industrial relations and motivates workers towards increasing production, productivity and ensures efficiency.[87]

Personnel Administrator in Union-Management Relations

Though not responsible for naming policy on union-management relations, the personnel administrator has a key role in advising the top and line management in the areas of negotiation process, contract administration, settlement of disputes, conduct of proper grievance procedure and redressal. In many large companies these matters are the concern of Labour Relations or Industrial Relations or Employee Relations Director in the personnel administration division.

The personnel executives concerned with union-management relations study and analyse union's policies, the statements of union leaders, policy statements of central union organisations, labour policy and legislation of the Government. Furthermore, they study and analyse the grievances and complaints and opinions of employees and supervisors, and executives regarding the labour agreement, and employee suggestions. On the basis of this study and analysis they make recommendations and they may help in the formulation of management strategy and help to negotiate the union contract. The personnel administrator may represent top management at some stage in the grievance procedure. But he must play his staff role and let the line managers make the decision and assume responsibility.

The personnel division may train supervisors in handling personnel problems within the framework of the union contract or the company policies. The personnel people at The Timken Roller Bearing Company, Canton, Ohio, U.S.A., offered HOLMAW, a company training course on "How Our Labour Management Agreement Works".[88] In this course all the articles in the agreement, particularly the most important ones from the viewpoint of the foremen, were carefully explained and the foremen were examined to see whether they had followed the instruction. Then they explained the changes in the agreement that had taken place during negotiations. They used flannel boards, flip charts, colour slides etc. as training aids. All supervisors of operating department and plants covered by the agreements as well as all the middle-management personnel of these same plants were given the full course. They prepared a booklet on HOLMAW, which the foremen use as a handy reference in their day-to-day activities.

Mr. John Newmann claims the following results for his training programme — HOLMAW:[89]

1. A definite improvement in the handling of complaints and grievances.

2. An over-all improvement in our day-to-day employee and union relations on the plant floor.
3. A feeling on the part of our first and second line operating managers that they are definitely a part of management.
4. A much better understanding among these same managers of the critical importance, in relation to various articles of the agreement, of many of the things that happen in the plant each day.
5. A noticeable decline in the tendency of some of our foremen and general foremen to become needlessly involved in plant grievances.

In conclusion, we may quote Professor Pigors and Myers with regard to the role of personnel administrator in union-management relations:[90] "The personnel administrator has a number of tasks and opportunities. He can help to influence and formulate the company's policies in dealing with the union. He can assist top management in communicating these policies to lower levels of management, particularly to first-line supervision. He can advise and assist the different levels of management in handling labour relations problems that are bound to arise in unionised firms. Beyond this, he may also be called upon to be the company spokesman in contract negotiations, although in this role he is almost certain to appear as a 'line' representative. In the long run, he will be more effective if he assists line management in contract negotiations and grievance settlements, leaving the responsibility for decision-making where it belongs."

REFERENCES

1. Pigors and Myers, *Personnel Administration*, pp. 81-82.
2. See Sidney & Beatrice Webb, *The History of Trade Unionism* (New York: Longmans, Green, 1935 rev. ed.)
3. See Sidney and Beatrice Webb, *op. cit.,* pp. 6, 10-11, 22-26, 41-56.
4. Clark Kerr, "Labour's Share and the Labour Movement," in E. Wight Bakke, Clark Kerr & Charles W. Anrod, *Unions, Management and the Public* (New York: Harcourt, Brace and Company, 2nd ed., 1960), pp. 498-506.
5. See James O. Morris, *Conflict AFL: A Study of Craft versus Industrial Unionism* (Ithaca, N.Y.: Cornell University Press 1958) and also, Walter Galesnson, *The CIO Challenge to the AFL* (Cambridge, Mass: Harvard University Press, 1960).
6. See Samuel Gompers, *Labour and Common Welfare* (New York: Dutton, 1919), pp. 7-8, 20.
7. *Personnel* (American Management Association), September-October 1976, pp. 5-7.
8. *Industrial Bulletin,* Employers' Federation of India, July 15, 1973, p. 55.
9. Dale Yoder, *Personnel Management,* p. 193 and also pp. 194-195.
10. See V.K.R. Menon, "The Influence of International Labour Conventions on Indian Labour Legislation", *International Labour Review,* 73, June 6, 1956, p. 571.
11. See R.K. Das, *The Labour Movement in India* (Berlin: de Gruyter, 1923).
12. A.S. Mathur and J.S. Mathur, *The Trade Union Movement in India*, (Allahabad: Chaitanya Publishing House, 1957), p. 231, Emphasis mine.
13. C.B. Kumar, *The Development of Industrial Relations in India* (Bombay: Orient Longmans Ltd., 1961), p. 92.
14. See N.F. Dufty, *Industrial Relations in India* (Bombay: Allied Publishers Private Ltd., 1964) p. 34.

15. K. Dwarakadas, *45 Years With Labour* (Bombay: Asia Publishing House, 1962), p. 21.

16. R. J. Soman, *Peaceful Industrial Relations,* Their Science and Technique (Ahmedabad: Navjivan Press,1957), p. 310.

17. *Times of India,* December 20, 1953.

18. IIPM, *op. cit.,* p. 150.

19. G.D.H. Cole, *An Introduction to Trade Unionism* (London: Allen and Unwin 1953).

20. Constitution of Indian National Trade Union Congress (Delhi: 1947 Annual Report, Proceedings of the Inaugural Conference of INTUC, May 3, 4, 1947), pp. 3, 31-32.

21. Constitution of AITUC (Delhi: All India Trade Union Congress, 1958).

22. Constitution of HMS, Proceedings of 1953 Session of Hind Mazdoor Sabha.

23. N.F. Dufty, *op. cit.,* p. 157.

24. *Report of the 7th Annual Session,* Hind Mazdoor Sabha, 1958, p. 27.

25. *Personnel Management in India*, pp. 171-172.

26. Y.B. Bhonsle, *Personnel Management — The Indian Scene,* New Delhi, S. Chand & Co., 1977, p. 117.

27. See Selig Perlman, "The Principle of Collective Bargaining", *The Annals of the American Academy of Political and Social Science,* March 1936, pp. 154-59.

28. See Arnold F. Campo, "A Collective Bargaining Check-list", *Advanced Management,* Vol. 14, No. 2, June 1949, pp. 73-75.

29. Jucius, *Personnel Management,* p. 482.

30. Arnold F. Campo, "Outline for Collective Bargaining: A Union Man's Checklist", *Industrial Relations Paper,* No. 2, Division of Industrial Relations, Stanford University, January, 1949, pp. 2-3.

31. See Yoder *et al., Personnel Handbook,* pp. 4.39-4.41.

32. See George W. Taylor, *Government Regulation of Industrial Relations,* pp. 347-348.

33. Arnold F. Campo, *op cit.,* p. 75.

34. Paul D. Staudohar, "The Steel Industry's Agreement to Eliminate Strike", *Training and Development Journal*, December 1976, pp. 44-41.

35. For a detailed discussion, See chapters 14 and 15 in IIPM, *Personnel Management in India*, pp. 175-290.

36. Planning Commission, *First Five Year Plan Report,* Government of India (New Delhi: Government of India, 1953), p. 573.

37. Cited by Kumar, *op. cit.,* p. 142.

38. *Proceedings of Indian Labour Conference* (12th session) (New Delhi: Government of India, 1952), pp. 6-7.

39. IIPM. *op. cit.,* p. 175.

40. *Ibid.,* p. 178.

41. *Ibid.,* pp. 178-181. See the details in these pages.

42. N.F. Dufty, *op. cit.,* pp. 119-20.

43. For an excellent study on Collective Bargaining, See Mary Sur, *Collective Bargaining — A Comparative Study of Development in India and Other Countries* (Bombay: Asia Publishing House, 1965).

44. Quoted by IIPM, *Ibid.,* p. 190.

45. Most of the material for this section is borrowed and adopted from the Acceptance Address of P.N. Krishna-Pillai at the time of receiving Sir Jehangir Ghandy Gold Medal for Industrial Peace and published — P.N. Krishna Pillai, "Industrial Relations in Retrospect", *Industrial Relations,* Vol. XVIII, No. 4, July-August, 1966, pp. 149-162.

46. *Ibid.,* pp. 158-162.
47. *Ibid.,* pp. 160-161.
48. *Ibid.,* pp. 161-162
49. *Principles,* pp. 494-496.
50. Quoted by R.J. Soman, *Peaceful Industrial Relations, Their Science and Technique,* (Ahmedabad: Navjivan Press, 1957), p. 25.
51. *Ibid.,* p. 60.
52. See P.P. Lakshmanan, *Congress and Labour Movement in India* (Allahabad: All India Congress Committee, 1947), p. 88.
53. *Ibid.,* pp. 65-66.
54. S.R. Mohan Das, "Industrial Disputes and Industrial Disputes Act Amendment," *Machine Tool Engineer,* Vol. VII, No.3, July-September 1966, p. 42.
55. Indian Institute of Personnel Management Bombay Branch, *News Letter,* February 1977, p. 6.
56. *Industrial Bulletin,* June 1, 1976, p. 1.
57. P.N. Krishna Pillai, *op. cit.,* p. 154.
58. Dwarakadas, *op. cit.,* pp. 84-85.
59. *Industrial Bulletin,* March 15, 1977, p. 21.
60. See Van Dusen Kennedy, "The Conceptual and Legislative Framework of Labour Relations in India", *Industrial and Labour Relations Review,* 11, 4 July 1958, pp. 487-505.
61. B. Shiva Rao, *The Industrial Worker in India* (London: Allen and Unwin, 1929), p. 162.
62. G. Ramanujam, Presidential *Report* of the Tenth Annual Session, INTUC, February 1959.
63. *Personnel Management in India,* pp. 103-104.
64. *Industrial Bulletin,* September 15, 1972, pp. 69-70.
65. Francis A. O'Connell Jr., "Has Labour Arbitration Lost Its Value to Management?" *Industrial Relations Forum,* AMA Management Report Number 54, Personnel Division, AMA 1961, p. 15.
66. Pigors and Myers, *op. cit.,* pp. 104-105.
67. Francis A. O'Connell, Jr., *op. cit.,* p. 14 Study this article for the trends in arbitration in U.S.A.
68. IIPM, *op. cit.,* pp. 161-162.
69. P.N. Krishna Pillai, *op. cit.,* p. 152.
70. *Report* of the Tenth Annual INTUC Session, p. 7.
71. B. Tulpule, General Secretary's *Report,* HMS 1962 session, p. 82.
72. See Gyan Chand, "Joint Councils of Management", Fifth All India Labour Economics Conference, Dharwar, December 1961, p. 20.
73. Report of the Study Group on Worker Participation in Management (Delhi: Government of India Publications), pp. 47 and 76.
74. *Report* of the Twelth Annual Session, INTUC, p. 10.
75. See Frederick C. Crawford, "Good Communications for Good Human Relations", *Tata Review,* Vol. 1, No. 1, October 1965, p. 22.
76. P.N. Krishna Pillai, *op. cit.,* pp. 152-153.
77. S.D. Punekar, "Worker's Participation in India", in S.D. Punekar *et al.*, *Economic Revolution in India,* Bombay, Himalaya Publishing House, 1977, pp. 404-407.
78. IIPM, *op. cit.,* p. 47.
79. See the Appendix in IIPM's *Personnel Management in India,* for the text of some of these Codes.

80. *Report* of the Twenty-sixth Session of AITUC, Jan 6-12, 1961, p. 58.
81. Sreekantan Nair, Presidential Address, *Report* of 1960 Session of UTUC, p. 21.
82. General Secretary's Report, *Report of 1962 Session of HMS*, p. 76.
83. P.N. Krishna Pillai, *op. cit.*, p. 153.
84. See *Capital*, Bombay, 16 April, 1964.
85. See A.D. Singh, "Indian Labour Conference", *Industrial Relations,* Vol. XVIII, No. 5, September-October, pp. 215-216.
86. *The Indian Express*, December 26, 1966.
87. *Industrial Bulletin,* July 1, 1976, p. 49.
88. John Newmann, "HOLMAW": A Company Training Course On Labour Management Agreement, *Industrial Relations Forum*, AMA Management Report No. 54, pp. 89-92.
89. *Ibid.*, p. 92.
90. Pigors and Myers, *Personnel Administration,* p. 94.

❑ ❑ ❑

CHAPTER 15

Labour Legislation

In this chapter we shall proceed to deal with the important legislative measures that a personnel administrator has to be familiar with in order to see that the company does not run foul of the laws of the State. The mills of labour and industrial legislation have been pretty busy since Independence and many laws have been enacted to improve working conditions, worker welfare, safety and health in industrial establishments.

According to Indian Institute of Personnel Management:[1] "During the last two decades there has been a tremendous spate of labour legislation, and it is probably true to say that more labour matters are now covered by legislation in India than in any other country. The great speeding up in labour legislation since Independence is accounted for by the urgency of industrial development and the determination of government to achieve in a few years what it had taken other countries decades to build up by normal growth. Just as the pace of industrialisation had to be speeded up by expansion of the public sector industry, so the pace had to be forced in order to change the outlook of management on labour matters in accordance with the Government's policy of achieving a 'socialistic pattern of society'."

It is noticeable that Indian labour legislation since Independence has been strongly influenced by the work of the I.L.O. and in fact India has been able to ratify a large number of the I.L.O. Conventions, although she entered comparatively late into the industrial field.

Matters pertaining to labour other than regulation of labour and safety in mines and oil fields are included in the "Concurrent List" of the Constitution of India and, therefore, both the Central Government and the Governments of States have power to frame laws concerning them. However, in order to ensure uniformity in essential matters almost all important Labour Acts have been enacted by the Central Government. The State Acts are either supplementary in their nature, or cover the field left out by the Central laws.[2]

The administration of these labour laws, however, is generally the responsibility of the State Government, who have been given wide rulemaking powers to enable them to supplement laws and determine the details.

Let us now turn to the important Labour Acts and the salient provisions of these legal measures. Labour legislations could be studied under four main categories as suggested by IIPM.[3]

1. Laws dealing with working conditions in factories, mines and plantations, shops and establishments.
2. Laws dealing with wages.
3. Laws dealing with industrial relations.
4. Laws dealing with social security.

The important provisions of the important Acts under each of the above categories are discussed briefly.

1. FACTORIES ACT

Legislation for regulating working of Factories is among the earliest measures taken by the Government to prevent exploitation of Labour. The first Factories Act was passed in 1881. The Act was amended or replaced periodically in 1891, 1911, 1922, 1934 and 1946. The Factories Act of 1948 has been amended in 1976 and the provision of the amended Act came into force on 26th October, 1976. Considering that even the present Act is stated to provide only the minimum requirements, one can easily imagine, how the conditions in factories in 1881 would have been.

The Factories Act is intended to assure the health, safety and welfare of the workers. These provisions are to be adhered to by factories irrespective of their financial position.

A place where manufacturing process is carried on with the aid of power and providing employment for ten or more persons is a factory. Where no power is used, the minimum employment should be of 20 persons. The Factories Act covers workers employed directly or through an intermediary like a contractor. The responsibility for implementing the provisions is placed on the "manager" and in certain cases on the "occupier."

According to the Factories (Amendment) Act, 1976, Worker means a person employed directly or by or through any agency including a contractor with or without the knowledge of the principal employer whether for wages or not in any manufacturing process or in cleaning any part of the machinery or premises used for a manufacturing process or in any other kind of work incidental to or connected with the manufacturing process, but does not include any member of the armed forces of the Union.

In computing the number of workers all persons working in different relays in a day will be taken into account.

Provision Relating to Health

Cleanliness: Factory premises should be kept clean and free from effluvia arising from drain, privy or other nuisance. The floor and benches in work-rooms must be swept daily and dirt and refuse must be removed. The floor is to be washed with disinfectant. Effective drainage to avoid floors becoming wet should be provided. Painted surfaces should be repainted once in five years and white washing or colour washing should be done once in fourteen months.

The Act enjoins upon an occupier to make effective arrangements for the treatment of waste and effluents due to the manufacturing process carried on in the factory so as to render them innocuous and for their disposal.

Ventilation: Adequate ventilation by circulation of fresh air should be ensured. This is to safeguard the health of the worker from deterioration. Walls and roofs should be of such material as will keep the temperature as low as possible. Special precautions are prescribed where the nature of work generates excessive heat or dust or fume.

Artificial Humidification: Where Artificial humidification is resorted to for purposes of manufacture, the obligation on the occupier relates to the using of water from a public supply, any other source of drinking water or purified water.

Overcrowding: Overcrowding to an extent likely to injure the health of the workers is prohibited. Factories built before 1948 should provide working space of 350 cubic feet per worker. Post-1948 factories should provide 500 cubic feet of per capita workspace.

Lighting: Sufficient and suitable lighting, to the satisfaction of the authorities should be provided and maintained, gazed windows and sky-lights must be kept clean. Glare is to be avoided. Shadow formation is to be avoided.

Drinking Water: Adequate supply of wholesome drinking water must be ensured at convenient points.

Latrines and Urinals: Sufficient latrine and urinal accommodation of prescribed types are to be provided with separate enclosed accommodation for men and women. Adequate lighting and proper maintenance of such accommodation and sweepers for cleaning are to be provided. Where strength exceeds 250 better standards are prescribed.

Spittoons: Sufficient number and proper maintenance of spittoons are to be provided. Workers are not free to spit elsewhere.

Provisions Relating to Safety

The provision regarding safety are meant to prevent injury to workmen while at work and are considered to be a minimum requirement to be complied with by employers. Though the adequacy of many of the provisions is left to the satisfaction of the executive, a fairly strict compliance is expected to be adhered to.

It is obligatory on the occupier of a factory wherein 1000 or more workers are ordinarily employed, to employ a Safety Officer. It is further provided that in case of a factory wherein, in the opinion of the State Government, any existing manufacturing process or operation involves any risk of bodily injury, poisoning, of disease or any hazard to health of workers, the State Government can direct the occupier to appoint a Safety Officer. The State Governments have been empowered to prescribe the duties, qualifications and conditions of service of Safety Officers.

Fencing of Machinery: All moving parts or other dangerous parts of machinery are to be securely fenced by safeguards of substantial construction which shall be kept in position while the parts of the machinery they are fencing are in motion or in use.

Work on or Near Machinery in Motion: Where it is necessary to work in or near machinery in motion, it must be done by specially trained adult male worker wearing tight fitting clothing. Particulars of such working are to be kept in prescribed registers. Moving parts of the other prime movers and fly wheels directly connected to them must be securely fenced irrespective of their position.

Transmission Machinery: Devices or appliances for promptly cutting off the power from the transmission machinery must be provided in every place where work is going on.

New Machinery: New machineries cannot be installed in any factory now unless certain more stringent requirements of safety provisions are conformed at by the manufacturers.

Hoists or Lifts: The safety provision in respect of these relate to good condition, maintenance and other safety measures where human beings are carried therein.

Additional safety requirements are prescribed in respect of hoists and lifts installed after the commencement of the Act. Similar safety provisions are prescribed in respect of lifting machineries and tackles, revolving machinery and pressure plants. These are detailed in Sections 29 to 31.

The precautions in respect of floors, stairs and means of access relate to sound construction, proper maintenance and provision of substantial hand rails where necessary.

Fixed vessels, drums, tanks and pits are to be securely covered or fenced.

The maximum weight to be lifted or moved by adults — men and women, adolescents and children — may be specified by the State Governments. Where the nature of work carried on in a factory is likely to cause risk of injury to eyes either due to particles or fragments thrown off or due to excessive lights, the State Government is empowered to frame appropriate rules for protection.

Precautions against dangerous fumes include prohibition against workers entering congested or closed space likely to contain dangerous fumes unless it is provided with a manhole of adequate size or other means of egress.

If fumes or gas arising from manufacturing process are likely to explode on ignition all practicable measures shall be taken to restrict the spread and effects of explosion.

The Act prohibits the use of portable electric light or any other electrical appliance of voltage exceeding 24 volts for use inside any chamber, tank, vat, pit, pipeflue or other confined space.

The Act prohibits the use of lamp or light other than that of flameproof construction, if any inflammable gas, fume or dust is likely to be present in such chamber, tank, vat, pit, pipeflue or other confined space.

Precautions in case of fire consist of means of escape, provision for warning and free passage way to means of escape.

The safety of building or machinery is a matter to be decided by authorities and their instructions in this behalf are to be observed.

Provisions Relating to Welfare

While health and safety provisions are strictly enforced on all factories, one finds that the welfare provisions, except the essential ones, are made obligatory on bigger factories.

Common to All Factories Irrespective of Size: Washing Facilities should be adequate and separately screened for male and female workers.

Facilities for storing of clothes not worn during work and for drying of wet clothing should be provided.

Facilities for Sitting for workers obliged to do their work in standing position to take advantage of any opportunity for rest has to be given. If the Chief Inspector of Factories is of opinion that any particular work can be done equally efficiently in a sitting position, he may direct the occupier to provide sitting facilities.

First-Aid: First-aid box and cupboards at least one for every one hundred and fifty workers are to be provided and to be kept in charge of a responsible person trained in first-aid.

Where there are 500 workers and more, an ambulance van with prescribed equipment must be made available.

Provision for Bigger Factories — Canteens: Where 250 workers or more are employed, Rules may require establishment of a canteen, the foodstuffs to be served therein and the charges to be made therefore and the management of the canteen.

Shelters, Rest Rooms, Lunch Rooms: If more than 150 workers are employed rest rooms and lunch rooms with provision for drinking water and sufficiently lighted and ventilated are required.

Creches: If more than 30 women workers are ordinarily employed, a creche is to be maintaining for use of the children below the age of six years, and the same has to be incharge of a woman trained in the care of children and infants.

Welfare Officers: Where 500 workers or more are employed, the occupier will have to employ such number of welfare officers as may be prescribed. This aspect has been discussed earlier.

Working Hours of Adults and Young Children

Adults: Normal weekly hours of work are 48. A weekly holiday is a must. If a worker works on his normal weekly holiday, he is to be given a substitute weekly holiday within 3 days prior to or after the weekly holiday and information to authorities to that effect must be given. No worker should be made to work for 10 days continuously without giving him a weekly holiday.

Daily hours should not exceed nine.

Maximum working at a stretch should not exceed five hours and a minimum rest of half an hour thereafter must be provided.

Spread-over of work including rest interval should not exceed 10½ hours and with the permission of Chief Inspector of Factories it may be increased to twelve hours.

Overlapping of shifts are prohibited. This provision is to prevent abuse of clauses relating to maximum daily hours of work.

Overtime: Twice the rate for work done for beyond 9 hours a day or 48 hours a week is to be paid.

The total number of hours of overtime shall not exceed 54 in any one quarter.

Double Employment: Working in more than one factory on any day is prohibited.

Display of Notice Regarding Hours of Work: Display of hours of work is provided for as means of letting the workers know the correct position and for easy check up during inspection by authorities. A Register of adult workers is also to be maintained.

Young Persons: No child who has not completed his fourteenth year shall be required or allowed to work in any Factory.

Between 14 to 18, employment is conditional on certificate of fitness granted by certifying surgeon and on his carrying a token giving reference to such certificate.

Employment of a child is restricted to 4½ hours a day or during night.

Notice of working hours of child workers should be displayed and register of child workers to be kept.

Annual Leave with Wages

A worker, who has worked for 240 days or more in a factory is to be allowed leave with wages at the rate of one day for 20 days of work (adults).

One day for 15 days of work (child). To be eligible for leave with pay a worker must have put in 240 days of work in the firm.

(1) Days of lay-off, (2) Maternity leave not exceeding 12 weeks, (3) Leave earned in the previous year, shall be deemed to be days worked for computation of eligibility but not for grant of leave.

Workers entering service after 1st of January shall be given leave at the same rate if he has worked for two-thirds of the number of days in the remainder of the year.

If a worker is discharged or dismissed from service or quits his employment or is superannuated or dies while in service during the course of a calendar year, he or his heir or nominee, as the case may be, shall be entitled immediately before his discharge, dismissal, quitting of employment, superannuation or death at the prescribed rate even though the worker had not worked for 250 days in the calendar year or for two-thirds of the total number of days in the remainder of the calendar year, as the case may be.

Carry over of leave may be done for one year subject to a maximum of 30 days. If the leave applied for is refused, it could be carried forward without any limit.

If a worker applies for earned leave on 15 days notice (30 days in the case of Public Utility services), he shall be granted the leave.

It is open to employers to frame a scheme, with the approval of authorities, for granting of leave without affecting continuity of work.

It is open to a worker to adjust earned leave against a period of sickness without giving prior notice to employer.

The rate of payment for earned leave is on the basis of his earnings in the month prior to the taking of leave. The payment should be in advance if the leave granted exceeds 4 days.

The mines and plantations have their own Acts, which largely follow the pattern of the Factories Act. The Shops and Establishment Acts of various States also regulate hours of work, conditions, holiday, etc. The Dock Workers Regulation of Employment

Act, 1948, Motor Vehicles Act 1939, Indian Railways Act 1890 as amended in 1956, The Indian Merchant Shipping Act, 1923 as amended in 1956, Air Corporations Act, 1953 regulate the working conditions of the respective workers.

2. LAWS DEALING WITH WAGES

There are three central laws relating to wages, viz.:

(a) The Payment of Wages (Amendment) Act, 1975;

(b) The Minimum Wages Act, 1948; and

(c) The Equal Remuneration Act, 1976.

The last Act has been passed in conformity with the Directive Principles of State Policy embodied in the Constitution of India, which stipulates that there should be equal pay for equal work regardless of sex which is also an I.L.O. convention which is ratified under the Act.

(a) The Payment of Wages Act, 1975

This Act is intended to regulate the payment of wages to certain classes of persons employed in industry. It applies to all factories and to certain establishments.

Employed persons drawing over Rs. 1000/- per month are outside the scope of the Act.

The object of the Act is to secure to 'workmen' wages due to them. New rights cannot be agitated or obtained by workmen by recourse to this Act. Existing rights can be processed. If the employer contends that the wages are not due, it is open to the authority to go into the facts and find out the terms of employment.

With the availability of Section 33-C(2) of the Industrial Disputes Act which is an omnibus provision, the remedy provided under this Act has become redundant.

Scheme of the Act: Wage Periods is to be fixed by employer and cannot exceed a month, e.g., payment of wages could be done weekly, fortnightly or monthly but not quarterly.

Payment of wages are to be made within 7 or 10 days of the close of the wage-period according to the number employed, being less than or over 1000.

Wages can be paid by cheque or by crediting wages in bank account after obtaining written authorisation from the employees concerned.

Any deduction from wages is to conform to those sanctioned under the Act and mentioned hereunder:

Deduction	*Conditions for Enforcing the Same*
1. Fines	(i) List of acts and omissions for which fine could be levied to be certified by authority and exhibited. (ii) Any opportunity to show cause to be given. (iii) Total fine in wage period not to exceed three paise payable. (iv) No fine for workers under 15 years of age. (v) Register to be maintained; and accumulation to be spent for purposes beneficial to workmen and approved by authority.

2. Absence from duty	(i) Deduction is only for absence from workspot and shall be of wages payable for the actual period of absence. (ii) Where there is absence of 10 or more workers employed in concert (strike) without due notice and without reasonable cause, deduction may be 8 days' wages, if due in lieu of notice as per terms of employment.
3. Damage or Loss	(i) There must have been express entrustment of goods and loss of the same due to neglect or default of worker. (ii) If it is money, the person employed should have been accountable therefor. (iii) Amount of deduction not to exceed amount of loss. (iv) Register of deduction to be maintained.
4. House accommodation or Services rendered to workers	The house accommodation or other amenity provided should have been accepted by the person employed as a condition of employment.
5. Recovery of advances	(i) Advance not to exceed two months wages. (ii) Recovery limit — one-fourth of wages payable if total wage is less than Rs. 100/- and one-third if wages exceed Rs. 100/-. (iii) Deduction to be spread over not more than 12 months.

Other deductions not listed above include:

(i) Deduction of income tax at source.

(ii) Deduction as per order of court or other competent authority.

(iii) Deduction of subscription to Provident Fund (P.F.) or for repayment of loans taken from P.F.

(iv) Deduction for payment to co-operative societies or for Insurance premia.

(v) Deduction from wages can be made with written authorisation from a worker towards contribution to Prime Minister's Relief Fund or to such other fund as may be notified.

Remedies: (within a period of twelve months) Section 15 provides for moving prescribed authority on two grounds:

(i) Non-payment.

(ii) Deduction not falling under the provisions of the Act.

The authority exercises a judicial function and hence should hear the parties before pronouncing orders. If he finds that the non-payment of wages is made out, he may direct payment of same and also compensation not exceeding ten rupees. If delay in payment is due to *bona fide* reasons, no compensation can be ordered. If deduction made is against the provisions of the Act, compensation may go up to 10 times the deduction made.

If the worker's recourse to the authority is found to be malicious or vexatious, penalty not exceeding Rs. 50/- may be levied.

Appeal: Appeal lies to District Courts (Small Causes Court in Madras City):

(i) By employer, if total sum directed to be paid is more than Rs. 300/- or such direction has the effect of imposing on the employer or the other person a financial liability exceeding one thousand rupees.

(ii) By worker, if the amount exceeds Rs. 50/-.

(iii) By worker, if directed to pay a penalty.

Amounts determined by authority may be recovered by distraint.

Where delay may defeat justice a conditional attachment of properties of employers enough to satisfy the claim of workers may be ordered by authority in suitable cases.

No Civil Court can take cognizance of a case which has been or could have been agitated under this Act.

Contracting out of the Act is prohibited and such contracts, if entered into, shall be void.

(b) The Minimum Wages Act, 1948

The Indian Constitution by its Article 43 provides that the State shall endeavour by legislation or otherwise to secure to all workers a living wage and conditions of work ensuring a decent standard of life. It is one of the directive principles of State Policy. The Minimum Wages Act is an attempt, albeit a feeble one, in that direction.

The Act provides for fixation of minimum rates of wages for employment in certain occupations listed in the Schedule. The list includes both industrial and operations.

Workers employed through contractors are brought within the purview of the Act and the principal employer made liable for payment of minimum wages.

Any contract by which an employee gives up his rights to minimum wages prescribed under the Act is null and void.

The Government is not obliged to fix any minimum rates of wages for the schedule employment if in the whole State the total number employed is less than one thousand.

The minimum rates of wages fixed by Government are subject to periodical review, once in five years.

It is open to the Government to fix a "minimum time rate", a "minimum piece rate", a "minimum fall-back rate" and "overtime rate."

The minimum rates of wages may be a consolidated rate or divided into basic wages and cost of living allowance. Before fixing or revising minimum wages under the Act, the Government shall either form committees to advise it in respect to fixation or revision of minimum wages or shall give two months' notice of its proposals by publication in the official Gazette so as to give the parties likely to be affected a right to make representations.

An Advisory Board shall be constituted by the Government for the purpose of coordinating the work of the Committees appointed for particular employments and to advise the Government generally in respect of minimum wages.

The Committees appointed under the Act shall bear a tripartite character (employees, employers and government).

Minimum Wages have to be paid in cash unless the Government by notification permits payments in kind on the basis of custom or usage.

The Government may also fix the hours constituting a normal working day and also provide for weekly day off.

Overtime wages at prescribed rates are payable for work done beyond a normal working day. If a worker works for less than a normal working day, he is nevertheless entitled to payment of minimum wages fixed for a normal working day unless the failure to work was occasioned by his unwillingness to work.

The Act provides for appointment of inspectors with powers of entry and inspection to secure the proper enforcement of the provisions of the Act.

A remedy by way of application to a prescribed authority has been given to a worker complaining of non-payment of minimum rates of wages. If the complaint is made out the authority may direct payment of compensation also. If the claim is malicious, the worker may be directed to pay a penalty. The applicant has to approach the authority within six months of the claim becoming due.

As earlier pointed out, in our country the tribunals, labour courts, adjudicators, wage boards etc., have played an important role in the fixation of wage rates and other conditions of employment. As far as people in Government service are concerned, central pay commissions are appointed from time to time and they lay down the principles according to which pay for Central Government employees are fixed.

(c) The Equal Remuneration Act, 1976

The Equal Remuneration Ordinance, 1975 was promulgated from 26th September, 1975. It was passed into an Act without any changes and published in the Gazette of India, "Extra-Ordinary", Part II, Sec. 1 dated 12th February, 1976. The Act is deemed to have come into force with effect from 26th September, 1975.

The establishments or employments to which the Act will apply are notified in the official Gazette by the Central Government from time to time. The process of enforcement of the Act is proposed to be completed in 3 years' time.

The Act has already been made applicable to plantations, local authorities, employments under Central and State Governments, employments in banks, insurance companies and other financial institutions, employment in education, teaching, training and research institutions, etc.

The Act provides that while making recruitment for the same work or work of a similar nature, no discrimination can be made against women except where the employment of women in such work is prohibited or restricted by any law in force. However, this provision will not affect any priority of reference for schedule castes or scheduled tribes, ex-servicemen, or any other class of employees in the matter of recruitment to the post.

Men and women have to be paid by the employer equal pay for performing the same kind of work or work of a similar nature. If the rates are different only on ground of sex, the higher or the highest rate of wages is payable to men and women workers.

Difference in remuneration to men and women workers in any establishment or employment is not based on sex, and if the appropriate Government is satisfied to that effect, it may declare that such difference in remuneration will not be a contravention of the Act.

Payment of Bonus Act

'Bonus' was initially regarded as an ex-gratia payment made at the discretion of the employer. The evolution of industrial law, especially the 'Social Justice' concept, has lifted 'bonus' to a higher status and has defined it as a share of the working class in the prosperity of the concern.

The contribution which a worker makes to the earning of profits has been made the basis of his claim for Bonus.

In the year 1950, the Labour Appellate Tribunal evolved a formula for computing Bonus. This formula came to be known as the LAT formula or the Full Bench formula. It recognised certain claims of industry and shareholders as being superior to the claim for Bonus. They were: (i) Return on Paid-up capital; (ii) Return on the Reserves; (iii) Depreciation and rehabilitation; (iv) Income tax. If there were profit left after meeting the above prior charges, a bonus was payable out of the surplus. If there was no surplus, there was no bonus.

Labour agitated for a revision of the formula and a tripartite Bonus Commission was appointed. The Commission retained the core of the LAT formula. It provided for higher returns on capital and reserves but negatived the claim for rehabilitation. It also provided a minimum and maximum bonus with a right to set on or set off.

The Government of India made some alternations in the recommendations by enhancing the rate of return on capital and reserves. On this basis the Payment of bonus act was enacted in the year 1965. The Act also provided under Section 34(2) for the safeguarding of higher bonuses paid in the past and compelled the employers to pay bonus, wherever more advantageous to workers, in the same proportion to gross profits on a comparison with a base year.

The employers questioned the validity of the provision for minimum bonus but the Supreme Court struck down as unconstitutional Section 34(2) relating to the retention of higher bonuses paid in the past.

The right of workers to payment of a bonus over and above 4% will depend on the level of profits. Out of the profits the following appropriations are just made:

1. Dividends payable on its preference share capital.
2. Return on paid up capital at 8.5%.
3. Return on Reserves 6%.
4. Depreciation as per I.T. Act.
5. Development Rebate as per I.T. Act.
6. Income tax.

If after meeting there claims, these is still a surplus, it is called 'available surplus.' 60% of the available surplus is called 'allocable surplus' and is distributed as bonus.

The Payment of Bonus Act 1965 was superseded by the Payment of Bonus (Amendment) Ordinance 1975, which was later replaced by an Amendment Act. The Amendment Act came in to force on 25th Sept., 1975, the day on which the Bonus Ordinance came into force. The salient feature of the Amendment Act is that minimum bonus of 4% is payable only if there is an allocable surplus. However, an exception was made for the financial year 1975 for paying minimum bonus of 4% irrespective of allocable surplus. In case of availability of higher allocable surplus proportionately higher bonus will be payable but subject to the maximum of 20%. If minimum bonus of 4% is less than Rs. 100/-, then the minimum bonus payable is Rs. 100/- for an adult employee and Rs. 60/- for employee below the age of 15 years.

For calculating allocable surplus, amount of set on and set off in the three immediately preceding accounting years and in the accounting year in respect of which bonus is payable shall be taken into account in the manner illustrated in the third schedule appended to the Act.

There is a provision for payment of bonus to employees upto 20% under an agreement reached before or after the Amendment Act if such bonus is linked with production or productivity, in lieu of bonus based on profits payable under the Act.

New establishments are not required to pay bonus for the first five accounting years following the accounting year in which the employer sells goods or renders services unless such establishments have allocable surplus in any particular year of the first five years.

For the sixth accounting year allocable surplus will have to be taken into account after considering the set on or set off of the 5th and 6th accounting years. For the 7th accounting year set on and set off of the 5th, 6th and 7th accounting years will have to be taken into account. From 8th year for calculating allocable surplus amount of set on and set off in the three immediately preceding accounting years and the accounting year in respect of which bonus is payable shall be taken into account in the manner illustrated in the third schedule.

The Act is not applicable to certain classes of employees such as employees employed in Central and State Government services, in L.I.C., Reserve Bank, Banks and other Financial Institutions set up by the Government, Departmental Undertaking of the Government, Indian Red Cross Society or any other Institution of like nature, Universities and other Educational Institutions, Institutions, including Hospitals, Chambers of Commerce and Social Welfare Institutions, Establishments set-up not for purposes of profit etc. Similarly, public sector undertakings which sell goods produced or manufactured by them or render any services in competition with establishments in private sector and income from such sale or service is less than 20% of the gross income of such public sector undertakings, then such public sector undertakings are not required to pay bonus. By amendment of Section 36 of the Income Tax Act 1961, a provision has been made under which any bonus paid in excess of the amount payable under the provisions of the Bonus Act will not be admissible for purposes of Income Tax relief. The employers will have, therefore, to pay tax on any bonus amount which is paid in excess of statutory bonus.

All employees drawing a salary not exceeding Rs. 1600/- per month are eligible for payment of bonus but for those drawing above Rs. 750/- per month (and less than Rs. 1600/-) bonus will be paid as if their monthly salary was only Rs. 750/-.

All employees who have worked for at least 30 days in the year will be entitled to bonus. Workers who have not worked on all working days during the year will be entitled to bonus proportionately.

The bonus is to be disbursed to the employees within 8 months of the close of the financial year of the concern. The Government may extend this time in suitable cases.

If there is any dispute about the bonus payable, the Government may refer the dispute for adjudication by an Industrial Tribunal.

3. LAWS DEALING WITH INDUSTRIAL RELATIONS

These laws relate to (1) Trade unions, (2) Standing orders, and (3) Settlement of Industrial Disputes.

1. The Indian Trade Unions Act, 1926

This is a statute enacted by Central Government and is intended to provide for registration of Trade Unions and allied matters.

The real purpose of the Act was to provide immunity from civil and criminal action in courts to trade union official legitimately exercising their function of organising labour. Both in England and India, civil courts had given decree for damages against trade union leaders organising strikes in factories. Once the right of labour to organise themselves for collective bargaining is conceded, the immunity would appear a natural sequence. The immunity is contained in Sections 17 and 18 of the Act.

The Act provides for registration of trade unions with the Registrar appointed for the purpose (Sec. 3). Any trade union with several members may apply for registration (Sec. 4).

A trade union seeking registration should comply with certain formalities. Important among the formalities is to have rules providing for the objects of the unions, purposes for which funds may be utilised, conditions of admission, selection of office bearers, safe custody of funds and annual audit (Sections 5 and 6).

A trade union which is registered is entitled to a certificate of Registration from the Registrar.

A certificate of Registration may be cancelled, if it has been obtained by fraud or mistake, if the union has ceased to exist, or has contravened the rules. Before cancellation, the trade union should be heard by the Registrar (Sec. 10).

A right of appeal to a civil court is given by Sec. 11 to a person aggrieved by non-registration or cancellation.

A trade union is a body corporate; it can sue or be sued (Sec. 13).

Section 15 stipulates the objects on which trade union funds may be expended. Important among these are (i) administrative expenses, (ii) conduct of trade disputes, (iii) publishing of union magazine, and (iv) compensation or allowance to members.

A separate fund may by constituted for political purposes, viz., sponsoring a candidate for elections etc. No member of a trade union shall be compelled to pay for this special fund and no benefit should be denied to any member by reason of his not contributing to the fund (Sec. 16).

At least one-half of the total number of officers of a registered trade union should be from employees of the industry (Sec. 22).

The Act also provides for amalgamation of Trade Unions and matters incidental thereto.

A trade union may be dissolved in accordance with the rules of the Trade Union. Notice of dissolution shall be sent to the Registrar within 14 days and shall be registered by him. Dissolution shall have effect from the date of Registration. Funds of the trade union in the absence of any specific provision in the rules shall be divided among members (Sec. 27).

Annual Returns in the prescribed form (audited statement of income and expenditure; assets and liabilities) shall be sent to the Registrar by a prescribed date (Sec. 28).

The Government is empowered to make regulations for the purpose of carrying into effect the provision of the Act.

Non-compliance with the provisions of the Act is made penal.

2. Standing Orders[4]

The Industrial Employment (Standing Orders) Act 1946 requires all the employers with 100 or more workers working for them to draw up a set of standing orders regulating the day-to-day relations between the employers and the workmen. The States are empowered to extend the scope of the Act to undertakings employing less than 100 workmen. In Assam the Act has been extended to industrial establishments employing 10 or more workers, in Bombay and West Bengal to establishments employing 50 or more workers and in U.P. to those employing less than 100 workers.

Procedure: Employers are required to submit draft standing orders which they propose to adopt for their industrial establishments within six months from the date of application of the Act to the certifying officer appointed for the purpose. Standing Orders can be drawn up either by an employer or a group of employers. The draft standing orders should provide for all matters mentioned in the schedule to the Act and should conform to the Model Standing Orders, wherever, prescribed.

The schedule covers the following matters:

1. Classification of workmen, e.g., whether permanent, temporary, apprentices, probationers, or budlis;
2. Manner of intimating to workmen periods and hours of work, holidays, pay days and wage rates;
3. Shift working;
4. Attendance and late coming;
5. Conditions of procedure in applying for, and the authority which may grant leave and holidays;
6. Requirement to enter premises by certain gates, and liability to search;
7. Closing and reopening of sections of the industrial establishment, and temporary stoppages of work and the rights and liabilities of the employer and workmen arising therefrom;

8. Termination of employment, and the notice thereof to be given by employer and workmen;
9. Suspension or dismissal for misconduct, and acts or omissions which constitute misconduct;
10. Means of redress for workmen against unfair treatment or wrongful exactions by the employer or his agent or his servants; and
11. Any other matter which may be prescribed.

The standing orders become operative on the expiry of 30 days from the date on which the Certifying Officer sends the authenticated copies to the parties. The text of the certified Standing Orders is to be posted by the employers in English and in the language of the majority of the workers near the factory entrance and also in all the departments where workers are employed.

3. The Industrial Disputes Act

The Industrial Disputes Act was enacted in the year 1947 and is one of the major Acts intended to benefit labour by redressal of their grievances.

The Act was further amended in 1976 which contains special provisions relating to layoff, retrenchment and closure in certain establishments.

Where any employer discharges, dismisses, retrenches or otherwise terminates the services of any individual workman such disputes or differences between that workman and his employer shall be deemed to be an industrial dispute notwithstanding that no other workman nor any union of workmen is a party to the dispute.

By an amendment to the Act in 1971, Labour Courts, or Tribunals have been empowered to review the cases of discharge or dismissal of workmen when such cases are referred to them and if Labour Court or Tribunal as the case may be, is satisfied that the order of discharge or dismissal was not justified it may by its award set aside order of discharge or dismissal and direct reinstatement of workman on such terms and conditions, if any, as it thinks fit or give such other relief to the workman including the award of any lesser punishment in lieu of discharge or dismissal as the circumstances of the case may require. However, the Labour Court or Tribunal will have to rely on the materials on record and cannot take any fresh evidence in relation to such matter.

By an amendment to the Act in 1976 further curbs regarding lay-off, retrenchment and closure have been placed on industrial establishments employing 300 or more workmen. These restrictions are applicable only to factories as defined in the Factories Act, mines as defined in the Mins Act or Plantations, as defined in the Plantations Labour Act. In other words commercial establishments etc., are excluded from the new restrictions.

Before an industrial establishment wants to lay-off any workman (other than a Badli workman or a casual workman), it has to seek the permission of the authority as specified by the government unless such lay-off is due to shortage of power or natural calamity. It is for the authority specified, after making such enquiry, as he thinks fit, to grant, or refuse, giving necessary reasons, the permission applied for in writing. If the permission or refusal is not communicated to the employer within two months from the date of application, permission would deem to have been granted. Lay-off without seeking permission or where it is refused would be deemed to be illegal.

It is important to note that if an industrial establishment wants to lay-off the workmen because of break-down of machinery, shortage of raw materials, accumulation of stock etc., it cannot do so immediately because previous permission is necessary in such cases. In view of this maintenance of plant and machinery, proper planning of inventory control, sales planning etc., would be essential.

Another departure from the original provisions is that even if lay-off is due to strike or slowing down of production on the part of workmen in other part of the establishment the previous permission for the lay off from the authority is necessary.

Broadly speaking the Act provides for investigation of the grievances of organised labour by governmental machinery in the first instance through the medium of Conciliation Officers and failing which by reference of appropriate cases for adjudication to the authorities set up under the Act. The Act envisages a three tier system under which disputes of certain types are referred for adjudication by Labour Courts while certain types of other disputes are referred for adjudication to the Industrial Tribunal. Both these authorities function at State level. There is also the National Tribunal intended for adjudication of disputes of a character involving repercussions all over the country, e.g., Oil Company disputes; other industries situate in more than one state; Banking companies.

The Conciliation Officer tries to bring the parties together by making them meet at his table and discuss the differences between them. If the dispute is amicably settled at his level, a settlement is entered into between the parties and this is called a conciliation settlement. A settlement thus effected determines the dispute. If there is no settlement a report is sent by the Conciliation Officer to the appropriate Government and the Government after a perusal of all the relevant circumstances including the report of the Conciliation Officer may refer a dispute or not and in the absence of *mala fides* the decision of the Government is final and cannot be questioned in a court of law. If the matter is referred to adjudication, the authority goes into the matter and pronounces an award which is forwarded to the Government and is published in the gazette. Thirty days after the publication the award becomes enforceable. The Act also provides for the recovery of monies due to the employees from the employer under an award or otherwise. The relevant provisions are Sec. 33(c)(1) and (2).

The Act prohibits strikes and lockouts in certain circumstances and in certain industries. There is further provision for the payment of compensation for lay off, retrenchment or closure. For contravention of any of the provisions of the Act by either party, penalties have been provided which may be a fine or imprisonment.

What is an Industrial Dispute: The Act as mentioned already provides for the investigation and settlement of 'industrial disputes.' In other words, the Act as originally conceived did not provide for the espousal of the individual disputes. The entire object of the Act being to preserve industrial peace, it was in consonance with this basic objective that only collective disputes were considered suitable for the application of the provisions of the Act. Individual disputes were more or less ignored other than discharge, dismissal, retrenchment or termination of service of individual on workman. An industrial dispute has been defined in the Act. Judicial decisions on the subject have been held that an 'individual dispute' may become an 'individual dispute' if a body of workmen of the establishment or a substantial number of them make a common cause with an employee who is unfairly dealt with. It is when they take up the matter that an individual dispute takes the characteristic of a collective dispute. What is 'substantial number' has been left to be decided according to the circumstances. In other words, the question is a question of fact to be dealt with in respect of each individual case. No hard and fast principles have been laid down but it has been stated that 'substantial' does not necessarily mean majority. Even as low as 15% or 20% have been held to be a substantial number. Where particular workmen belong to a special category like the clerical staff, the question whether the dispute is an individual dispute or an industrial dispute should be dealt with by applying the test of 'substantial support' to the members of the clerical staff only and not to the totality of the workers including operatives (B. & C. Mills case).

What is an Industry: The term 'industry' has been defined very widely in the Act. If the definition in the Act is alone taken hardly no form of activity would escape this definition. Judicial decisions have allowed certain cases for finding out where a particular activity constitutes an industry or not. The tests are the following:

1. There should be co-operation between the employer and the employee;
2. Such co-operation should be in carrying on an operation or activity;
3. The operation or activity should be directed with a view to the satisfaction of material human needs or rendering material services to community at large or section thereof; and
4. The operation or activity should not be casual but systematically or habitually carried on in an organised fashion.

Applying the above tests, the following have been held to be industries:

- Textile Research Association;
- Hospital;
- Sugarcane farm attached to Sugar factory;
- Dispensary run by Municipality.
- Conservancy service run my Municipality.

The following forms of activities have been held not to constitute an industry.

- University;
- Chartered Accountant's establishment;
- Solicitor's establishment;
- Charitable Institutions.

Dismissal of Workmen: One of the most common items in respect of which industrial disputes are raised, relate to dismissal of workmen. Tribunals have laid down that the employer should normally be allowed to take necessary disciplinary action against erring employees. But that such action should be preceded by a full and fair enquiry. An order of dismissal could be interfered with by the Labour Court only if any of the following ingredients are present:

1. Where there is want of good faith;
2. When there is victimisation or unfair labour practice;
3. When the management has been guilty of a basic error or violation of a principle of natural justice; and
4. When on the materials the finding is completely baseless or perverse.

Defective Enquiry or no Enquiry: Where the enquiry has been defective or there has been no enquiry into the charges by the management, it is nevertheless open to the management to adduce evidence before the Tribunal to justify its action and in such a case it is for the Tribunal to judge whether the action taken by the management is justified or not.

Wage Fixation: The concept of wages has been defined under three different heads: viz., (1) The Minimum Wage, (2) The Fair Wage and (3) The Living Wage.

The minimum wage is a wage which is necessary to keep the body and soul of a workman together and it has been held that any industry which cannot pay a minimum wage has no right to exist. The fair wage is the lower limit of the living wage and is intended to provide the workman with a measure of frugal comfort including the education of his children while a living wage is the ideal wage and is intended to provide the workman with a comfortable means for livelihood. Both the fair wage and the living wage depend on the capacity of the employer to pay unlike the minimum wage to its workmen. The wages fixed by the employer on contract with workmen are liable for interference by the Tribunal on properly raised industrial disputes and it is open to the Tribunal to refix the wages on the basis of the capacity of the industry to pay and the wage rates prevailing in similar industries in the same region.

Lay-off Compensation: The provision relating to lay-off compensation was put on the statute book in the year 1954. It provides for payment of half the basic wages and dearness allowance if workmen are denied employment on account of shortages of power, or raw materials, or the accumulation of stocks or the breakdown of machinery or other reasons similar to the above. The provisions for payment of compensation do not apply:

(a) To industrial establishments in which less than 50 workmen on an average per working day have been employed in the preceding calendar month; or

(b) To industrial establishments which are of seasonal character or in which work is performed only intermittently.

It is for the Government to decide whether a particular establishment is of seasonal character or not.

Any worker who has put in continuous service of one year which has been defined to mean service for a period of 240 days in any of the working year is entitled to the payment of compensation.

A workman is not entitled to lay-off compensation:

1. If he refuses to accept alternative employment either in the same establishment where he has been working or in any other establishment belonging to the same employer situated in the same town or village within a radius of 5 miles;

2. If he does not present himself for work at the establishment at the appointed time during normal working hours at least once a day;
3. If such laying off is due to strike or slowing down of production on the part of workmen in another part of the establishment.

Retrenchment: Industrial establishments which are factories, mines or plantations as defined in the Factories Act, Mines Act or Plantations Labour Act as the case may be, employing 300 or more workmen will have to give three months' notice or three months' pay in lieu of three months' notice to the workmen affected by the retrenchment. Here also the permission of authority as specified by the government is necessary before retrenching any workmen. It is for the authorities to grant or refuse permission after giving reasons in writing. However, no period has been mentioned for serving notice on the appropriate government for the purpose of seeking permission for retrenchment. But if the specified authority does not communicate within three months from the date of receiving the application, the permission for the retrenchment will be treated as illegal and the workmen will be treated as if they are in continuation of service. The rate of retrenchment compensation is the same as in the case of other establishments, i.e., 15 days average pay for every completed year of service.

In the case of closure the employer is required to give 60 days' notice of his intention to close down the undertaking in the prescribed manner on the appropriate government mentioning clearly reasons for the intended closure of the undertaking. This provision is not applicable to industrial establishments employing less than 20 workmen or the undertakings set up for construction of buildings, bridges, roads; canals, dams or for other construction work or projects.

The industrial establishments which are factories, mines or plantations as defined in the Factories Act, Mines Act, or Plantations Act, as the case may be, will have to give 90 days' notice of closure in the prescribed form to the government stating reasons for the intended closure. The government has reserved the power now to direct the employer not to close down the undertaking. Where the permission has been refused for closure, the closure will be treated as illegal and the workmen as if in continuation of service. If permission for closure is granted the workmen will have to be paid retrenchment compensation as in the case of retrenchment.

Penalities by way of imprisonment and fines for lay-off, retrenchment or closure without permission have been laid down.

Retrenchment Compensations: Retrenchment though defined widely in the Act, really means the discharge of the surplus. An employer can decide to run his establishment in any manner he wants and may restrict the size of his labour force. The decision to retrench must, however, be *bona fide.* If a case for retrenchment is made out, normally the junior most workmen of each category should be discharged. In other words, it is not open to the employer to pick and choose the employees to be retrenched. The rule of 'last come first go' should normally be applied but may be departed from for reasons to be recorded in writing. The reasons are open to scrutiny by a Tribunal in a dispute. The payment of compensation calculated at 15 days' wage for each year of service should be made before the actual retrenchment takes place. Since this is a condition precedent, failure to pay beforehand would render the retrenchment null and void. It is open to the employer to set off any amount paid by way of lay-off compensation during the period of one year prior to retrenchment against the retrenchment compensation due to the workmen. (Retrenched workers should be given preference if the employer finds the necessity to recruit additional hands at a later date.)

Transfer of Ownership and Closure: Service is always considered personal and therefore, a transfer of an undertaking severs the employer-employee relationship *ipso facto*. It has, therefore, been provided that on the transfer of an undertaking workers will be entitled to retrenchment compensation unless the transferee agrees to keep the workmen in service on the same terms and conditions applicable to the workmen before the closure and also agrees to pay retrenchment compensation for the previous service also in the events of any future necessity for retrenchment.

It was held by the Supreme Court that discharge of workmen on closure did not amount to retrenchment. The Act was, therefore, amended to provide for compensation to workers discharged on closure in the same manner as in the case of retrenchment.

Sections 33 and 33 A: These two sections come into play during the pendency of an industrial dispute which is referred for adjudication. The underlying object appears to be that workmen should not be victimised for raising industrial disputes. In other words, these sections are intended to ensure that the legitimate right of workers to raise industrial disputes is not frowned upon by the employer. It is, therefore, that Sec. 33 requires an employer, who wishes to dismiss an employee during the pendency of an industrial dispute, to pay the worker concerned a month's wages and also to file a petition for approval of the action so taken. The Tribunal or Labour court to whom such application is made will give its approval only after satisfying that a *prima facie* case has been made out and there has been no victimisation of the worker. The limits of jurisdiction of the court in ascertaining a *prima facie* case are more or less the same as the limitations placed upon the Tribunal in dealing with an industrial dispute. Where a full and fair enquiry has been held and there is no evidence of victimisation a *prima facie* case is said to be made out and the employer will be entitled to the approval of his action.

Where an employer does not comply with the provision of Sec. 33 where it is applicable, a right has been given to the worker concerned individually to file a petition under Sec. 33-A of the Act. In such a case the application made by the worker is deemed to be an industrial dispute and dealt with accordingly. (This provision is against the general tenor of the Act that only collective disputes as distinct from individual disputes will be referred for adjudication). Obviously, this right has been given to an individual worker because the exercise of it is conditional upon the employer having contravened the law in the first instance. In dealing with Section 33-A application the Supreme Court has held that it is not enough for the Tribunal to go into the *factum* of contravention alone. It has got to go into disputes on the merits and pass order accordingly. An employer who has dismissed his worker for valid reasons will be entitled to have his action upheld in a petition under Sec. 33-A notwithstanding his contravention of Sec. 33. The only damage he suffers is a possible prosecution for violation of the Section.

Section 33C(1) and (2): These provisions are intended for working out the rights of employees in terms of money. Under Sec. 33C(2) a worker is entitled to make a petition to the Labour Court for computing the money value of any benefit due to him from his employer and the amounts so computed may be recovered by applying to the Government under Sec. 33C(1) of the Act. This section empowers the Government to recover the money due as if it is arrears of land revenue by distraint.

The Supreme Court has held that the section is very wide and covers any benefit which a worker may be entitled to, whether it is under an award or otherwise. It has also held that the law of limitation does not apply for cases coming into under Sec. 33C(2).

[By an amendment in the year 1964 a limitation of one year has been provided for seeking recovery of money due under Sec. 33C(1).]

These two sections were not initially put in the 1947 Act but experience of the working of the Act proved that while workers were declared entitled to benefits by awards, there was no easy method of making a recalcitrant employer to honour the obligations in time. These sections, therefore, fulfil a great need. It is, however, to be noted that these sections may be used only for processing existing rights of workers and cannot be interpreted as displacing the need for Sec. 10 of the I.D. Act, which relates to the reference of disputes. In other words, an industrial dispute cannot be processed under Section 33C(2), but where the right of the worker has already been declared or otherwise not in doubt, the scope of this section comes into play.

Strikes and Lockouts: A strike has been defined as a cessation of work by a body of workmen in pursuance of a common understanding. It denotes only concerted refusal and not individual actions. If 100 workers abstained from work on the ground that the day was the Tamil New Year's Day, it cannot be called a strike even though the abstaining number was large and employer might have been put to hardship thereby; but if 10 workers join together and refuse to work demanding that, that day should be declared a holiday it will amount to a strike. To constitute a strike there must be a 'concerted refusal.' Similarly a lockout is the shutting down of the place of employment or the suspension of work by an employer. A lockout may be used as an offensive weapon or in retaliation for a strike.

The Act does not favour the rights of the parties either to strike or to lockout. While recognising the rights of the respective parties, it has put sufficient embargo on the use of these accepted but costly methods of solving industrial disputes. In respect of public services (by which is meant industries in the running of which the public is closely interested, e.g., textile industry, motor transport industry etc.) strikes and lock-outs have to be preceded by a fortnight's notice. Otherwise they would be illegal. The idea of this notice is only to set in motion the conciliation machinery. Once conciliation starts there is a prohibition against indulging in strike or lockout. Incidentally, the prohibition on strikes and lockouts during pendency of conciliation proceedings and during pendency of disputes referred before Tribunals or Labour Courts applies to public utility services as well as other industries. The requirement of a notice is, however, confined to public utility services only. The Act provides deterrent penalities for illegal strikes and lockouts. A lockout declared in pursuance of an illegal strike or a strike declared in pursuance of an illegal lockout is not illegal. It is open to Government to ban a strike or lockout in existence on the reference for adjudication of a dispute in respect of which the strike or lockout was resorted to.

Works Committees: The Act also provides for the constitution of works committees. In any industrial establishment in which 100 or more workmen are employed, the appropriate government may by general or special order, require the employer to constitute a works committee consisting of equal representatives of employers and workmen. The workers' representatives are elected while the employers' representatives are nominated. The election has to take place in consultation with the trade union of workmen if any. The duty of the works committee is to promote measures for securing and preserving amity and good relations between the employer and the workmen and to that end, to comment on matters of common interest and endeavour to compose any material differences of opinion in respect of such matters.

4. LAWS DEALING WITH SOCIAL SECURITY

Under various social security laws, the employers are required to accept certain obligations with a view to promoting the interests of their workers. These social security laws are:

(a) Workmen's Compensation Act, 1923;

(b) Maternity Benefit Act, 1961;

(c) Employees' State Insurance Act, 1948; and

(d) The Employees' Provident Funds Act, 1952.

(e) The Payment of Gratuity Act, 1972.

The first two Acts are measures of social assistance whereas the latter two are measures of social insurance.

(a) Workmen's Compensation Act, 1923

This Act was the first social security statutory measures which required the employer to pay compensation to workers for disablement — temporary or partial — for a period exceeding three days and death. Compensation is also payable for certain occupational diseases. The Act applies to workers whose monthly wages are less than Rs. 1000 and who are employed as regular workers in factories, mines, plantations, transport and construction work, railways, and certain specified hazardous occupations. Schedule II mentions the list of persons who are covered under the Act. The State Governments are empowered to extend the scope of the Act to any class of persons whose occupations are considered hazardous and some states have extended the Act to other sectors of employment. A series of amendments to the act has increased the scope, title to and amount of compensation, classes of dependents entitled to benefit, and also the number of scheduled occupational diseases.

The enforcement of the Act is entrusted to the Workmen's Compensation Commissioners who are given wide powers regarding the settlement of claims to compensation and the allocation of compensation to dependents. The awards of compensation of the Commissioners are generally accepted, although the aggrieved parties are given the right of appeal in the High Court, which is, however, restricted to questions of law.

The amount of compensation depends on the nature of the injury and the average monthly wage of the worker concerned. In the case of death, total permanent, partial permanent and temporary disablement, the employee is compensated according to the

Schedule of the Act. Where Employees' State Insurance scheme is applicable, the liability of the employer under this Act is transferred to the E.S.I. Corporation.

(b) The Maternity Benefit Act, 1961

This Act is a central statute enacted in the year 1961 and applicable to all states. The Act is intended to regulate the employment of women in certain establishments for certain periods before and after child birth and to provide for maternity benefits and certain other benefits.

The employment of women during the six weeks immediately following delivery or miscarriage is prohibited. A women worker may also absent herself from work for a period of six weeks prior to the expected delivery.

Wages are to be paid by the employer for the period of actual absence of the worker immediately before and following the delivery. The liability of the employer to pay wages is limited to twelve weeks in all. A worker who has worked for at least 160 days in the twelve months prior to the date of delivery is entitled to the payment of wages.

If the worker concerned is in receipt of maternity benefit under the Employee's State Insurance Scheme, the employer need not pay under this Act.

A woman worker receiving maternity benefit under this Act is also entitled to the payment of Rs. 25/- as medical bonus from the employer if no pre-natal confinement and post-natal care is provided by the employer free of charge.

In case of miscarriage, a woman worker will be entitled to payment of wages at the rate of maternity benefit for a period of six weeks immediately following the day of her miscarriage.

A woman suffering from illness arising out of pregnancy or miscarriage will be entitled in addition to other benefits eligible under the Act to leave with wages for a maximum period of one month.

Women returning to duty after child birth shall be allowed two breaks for nursing the child till the child is fifteen months old.

Dismissal on the ground of absence caused by maternity is prohibited.

Any contract between the employer and workman giving up the right to maternity benefit is not valid.

The Act also provides for an inspectorate whose duty is to see to the proper enforcement of the provisions of the Act. The inspectors appointed under the Act have powers of entry, inspection and also to issue directions for payment where due.

Penal provisions have been enacted making non-compliance or violations of the provisions of the Act punishable.

This is a social welfare legislation and is one of several measures taken by the Government for achievement of the Welfare State contemplated under the Constitution of India.

(c) Employees' State Insurance Act, 1948

The welfare of the common man is one of the objectives of the Constitution of India. Workmen working in factories and establishments suffer from hazards of employment injuries, sickness and fortunes which press on them at sometime of their lives. Social insurance is a remedial step in this direction. Workmen's Compensation Act and State Maternity Benefit Act were pieces of legislation intended to give social security. The most important development in the field of social security was, however, the passing of the E.S.I. Act in 1948. The Act was amended in 1968 and in 1975. The Act applies to factories having 20 or more employees, where manufacturing is carried on with power. The Government has power to extend the provisions of the Act to any other establishment by issuing a notification or after giving six months' notice.

All the employees drawing salaries upto Rs. 1000/- are covered under this scheme.

Finances: The E.S.I. Scheme is financed by the contributions from both employers and employees and from the State and Central Governments. The State Government share most of the medical treatment and attendance on the insured persons. The Central Government met two-thirds of the administrative expenses of the Scheme for the first 5 years.

Contribution: Both the employers and the employees are required to contribute to the scheme. The rate of contribution has been specified in the Schedule I. The employer's minimum contribution is 75 paise and the maximum contribution is Rs. 7.50 per week. The employees' contribution is nil for those who are getting below Rs. 2/- as average daily wages and the maximum contribution is Rs. 3.75 per week, for those who are getting Rs. 2/- and above as average daily wages.

Administration: The administration of the Insurance Scheme is entrusted to an autonomous body called the E.S.I. Corporation. This consists of representatives of Central and State Governments, employers, employees, medical profession and Parliament. A smaller body known as standing committee works as the executive of the Corporation. A Medical Benefit Council advises the Corporation on the medical side of the Scheme. Local Committees function at Regional level to advise on the local problems.

Benefits: The following benefits are provided under the Act:

1. Sickness benefit;
2. Maternity benefit;
3. Disablement benefit;
4. Dependent's benefit;
5. Funeral benefit; and
6. Medical benefit.

(1) to (5) are cash benefits while (6) is benefit in kind. The cash benefits approximate to half the daily average wage and the can be availed of for a maximum period of 56 days in a year in cases of sickness. In case of tuberculosis, the benefit is extended to 18 weeks at a reduced rate.

Maternity Benefit: Payment to full wages for a period of 12 weeks — six weeks on either side of the confinement, to eligible and insured employees.

Disablement Benefit: This is payable to an insured person suffering from temporary or permanent disablement as a result of an employment injury.

Dependent's Benefit: This is payable in the event of the death of a worker to his dependents, i.e., wife and children. In the absence of widow or children, parents or other dependents may claim the benefit.

Medical Benefit: This is a free medical treatment. Treatment Dispensaries, visits by doctors to the home of the insured person, inpatient treatment in hospital form part of the medical benefit.

Medical benefit may also be extended to families of workers.

General: The E.S.I. Scheme is a well thought-out scheme which affords a good deal of social security to the working class. The working of the scheme is, however, not satisfactory as the medical side of the scheme is controlled by the State Government while the other aspects of the scheme are administered by the Corporation. Due to dearth of doctors, the service is not satisfactory and at present the scheme only helps the workers to malinger. Nevertheless the utility of the scheme cannot be underestimated.

(d) The Employees' Provident Fund Act, 1952

The introduction of the statutory provident fund for industrial workers serves the twin purpose of providing for their retirement and also for cultivating among the workers a spirit of saving something regularly. Further it was thought that the institution of contributory provident fund would encourage the stabilisation of a steady labour force in industrial centres.

The Employees' Provident Fund Act 1952 provided for the institution in the first instance of contributory provident fund in six major organised industries. Subsequently this list has been considerably added to. The original requirement that the Act would apply to establishments in specified industries employing over 50 persons has also been watered down to 20. It has also been clarified that once the number required is employed and the Act becomes applicable to an establishment, it will continue to apply notwithstanding the number subsequently going below the specified number. There is also a provision for empowering the Central Government by notification to apply the Act to industrial undertakings employing less than the stipulated number. Section 6 of the Act provides for contribution at the rate of 8% of the basic wages and dearness allowance (and retaining allowance, if any in erosional industries), while the provision empowers the Central Government after making due enquiry to increase the contribution to $8^1/_3$%. The employer has to contribute at the same percentage as the worker.

To avoid any hardship to new establishments provision has been made for exempting them for a period of three years from the date of setting up, for the establishments employing more than 50 workmen and five years for the establishments employing more than 20 but less than 50 workmen. Judicial decision have consistently taken the view that this concession is applicable only for an infant establishment and not for one which is a mere rebirth of a defunct establishment.

Where an establishment manufactures several items one of which comes within the Schedule I listing the industries to which the Act is made applicable, then the applicability of the Act is considered not with reference to the number employed in manufacturing the item coming under the schedule but the overall number employed in the establishment itself. In other words, all the employees will get the benefits of this scheme, even though quite a number of them are not manufacturing any article which will come under the schedule.

Where an establishment consists of different departments or has branches which constitute in the same place or in different places, all such departments or places are to be treated as parts of the same establishment.

The employer is to pay the contribution of the employee also in the first instance but recovery thereof is permitted from current wages. There is no option given to the employee to fall out of the Act and Scheme.

The vast funds collected under the Provident Funds Act are administered by a Central Board consisting of a Chairman, Central Government officials, State Government officials and representatives of labour and employers. They function as board of trustees. Provision has also been made for the constitution of board of trustees at State level to deal with certain matters to be specified by Central Government.

The amounts standing to the credit of any member cannot be assigned or charged and are not liable for attachment under any decree or order of Court. The protection against attachment extends even in the case of insolvency of the member.

When the employer is adjudicated insolvent or being a company is wound up the amount due from the employer towards contributions payable to the fund are to be paid in priority to all other debts in the distribution of the assets of the insolvent or the company being wound up as the case may be. The employer shall not reduce the wages payable to the employee by reason only of the scheme coming in to force and his liability to contribute therefor. If a provident fund scheme is already in existence in any establishment to which the Act becomes applicable, the appropriate government may give exemptions after considering whether the existing scheme is, taken on the whole, not less favourable to the employers than the statutory scheme. This exemption could be given either for the entire factory or for a class of employees.

The Central Government has been given the power to give the necessary clarifications where doubts arise in respect of the applicability of the Act either to factories or to any person employed therein. Its decision is final.

The provident fund scheme contemplates the enrolling of all employees drawing salary upto Rs. 1600/- per month as members once they put in a service of 120 days within a period of six months or less, in factories and establishments to which this scheme applies. Even when an employee quits service in one establishment he continues to be the member of the fund so that if he joins another factory he can straight away start contributing to the fund. If, however, he withdraws the money his membership stands terminated and he will have to qualify once again for the new employment by putting 120 days of service within a period of six months or less.

Family Pension Scheme

The Act was amended in 1971 with a view to providing Family Pension and the life assurance benefits to employees of any establishments or class of establishments to which the Provident Fund Act is applicable. Accordingly the family pension scheme was framed and a family pension fund was set up from and out of contributions paid by the employers and employees each month under the Provident Fund Scheme. A part of the contribution representing $1^1/_6$ per cent of the employee's pay along with an equivalent amount of $1^1/_6$ per cent from and out of the employer's contribution has to be credited to the family pension fund. Central Government is also required to contribute at $1^1/_6$ per cent of the salary of the members to the family pension fund. A member of the family pension fund will continue to be the member of the family pension fund till he attains the age of 60 years or till he retires or quits the services and withdraws and becomes entitled to withdraw the benefits to which he is entitled under the scheme or dies during the period of his service in respect of which contributions are payable, whichever is the earliest.

Under the scheme following benefits are payable:

1. Monthly Pension: Monthly pension to the family of a member who dies during the period of his service in respect of which contributions are payable before fund for at least two years. The rates of pension vary depending upon the age of entry into service, length of his membership and the salary of the member.

2. Life Assurance Benefits: A lump sum amount is also payable to the family of the member as life assurance benefit when a member dies during the service period in respect of which contributions are payable. The amount is Rs. 1000/- to those who become the members of the scheme at the age of 25 years or below and this amount gradually goes down to those members who become the members of the scheme after the age of 25 years.

3. Retirement Benefit: On completion of the age of 60 years, a member of the scheme, who has contributed to family pension fund for at least two years will be paid a lump sum of Rs. 4000/- and thereafter will cease to be a member of the family pension fund.

4. Withdrawal Benefit: When a member ceases to be a member of the family pension fund having contributed to the fund for not less than two years, before attaining the age of 60 years for reasons other than death, he is entitled for withdrawal benefit at the prescribed rates. If a member has contributed to the family pension fund for less than two years and ceases to be a member of the family pension fund then he will be entitled to get back his own contribution to the family pension fund together with interest thereon at 5½ per cent per annum.

Details of the Scheme: The Provident Fund scheme contemplates the enrolling of all employees drawing salary upto Rs. 1600/- per mensem as members once they put in a service of 120 days in six months or less in factories and establishments to which this scheme applies. Even when an employee quits service in one establishment he continues to be the member of the fund, so that if he joins another factory, he can straight away start contributing for the fund. If however, he withdraws the money, his membership stands terminated and he will have to qualify once again in the new employment by putting in 120 days in six months or less of service.

The administrative side of the fund is looked after by Regional Commissioners with a central Provident Fund Commissioner as the co-ordinating authority. There is a large inspectorate which inspect establishments covered by the Act frequently and ensure the strict compliance by employers of the various provisions of the Act.

This Scheme provides for nomination by members conferring the right to receive the amount to any family member. Withdrawal from the fund is permissible once in every six months to make payments for life insurance premia. In such cases, the policy is assigned to the board as security for the payment of the amount withdrawn.

Withdrawal is also permissible at the discretion of the Commissioner of an amount not exceeding 12 months basic wages or his own total contributions with interest thereon whichever is less for the purchase of a dwelling house or dwelling site. Advance may also be made from the fund towards allotment of tenement constructed or to be constructed under subsidised housing schemes for industrial workers. Employees who have completed 7 years membership of the fund and having a minimum contribution of 500 rupees uptodate may be sanctioned an advance for the acquisition of a site or construction of a house under the low income group housing scheme. In cases of severe hardship resulting from the closing down of the factory for more than 30 days, non-recoverable advance can be given from the provident fund and interest thereon. Non-refundable advance is also permissible for purchasing shares in consumer co-operative societies.

Full amount standing to his credit may be withdrawn by an employee:

(a) On retirement from service after attaining the age of 55 years.

(b) On retirement on account of permanent and total incapacity for work due to physical or mental infirmity, duly certified by the Medical Officer of the company.

(c) Immediately before migration from India for permanent settlement abroad.

(d) On termination of services in the case of mass or individual retrenchment.

In all other cases, the following provisions apply in respect of withdrawals:

(i) 75% of the employers' contribution and interest is forfeited if the period of membership in the fund is less than 3 years.

(ii) 50% is forfeited for membership between 3 and 5 years.

(iii) 25% is forfeited for membership between 5 and 10 years.

(iv) 15% is forfeited for membership between 5 and 15 years.

In case of death of member the accumulations are payable to the nominee or in case where there is no nomination, to members of the family who are dependents of the deceased. Where a member is dismissed for serious and wilful misconduct, a portion of the employer's contribution upto a maximum of two years' contribution may be forfeited to the fund.

Employees Deposit Linked Insurance Scheme 1976

The Employees Deposit Linked Insurance Scheme 1976 has been framed under Section 6(C) of the Employees Provident Fund and Miscellaneous Provisions Act 1952. The scheme came into force from 1st August 1976. The scheme has been framed for the purposes of providing life assurance benefit to employees engaged in factories and other establishments (including contract labourers who are covered by the Provident Fund Scheme 1952).

The scheme provides for the payment of life assurance benefit together with the provident fund accumulation to the deceased employee's nominees or heirs, as the case may be. The life assurance benefit will be equal to the average balance in the provident fund amount of the deceased member during the preceding three years provided that such an average balance is not below Rs. 1000/- at any time during the preceding three years. However, the amount of life assurance benefit is restricted to Rs. 10,000/-

Contributions of both employees and employers and interest thereon will be included in calculating the average balance.

In relation to other covered employees under the scheme the employees will have to pay contribution to the fund at 50 paise per Rs. 100/- of the salary to the member. In addition, the employer is also required to pay administrative charges to the fund at 10 paise per Rs. 100/- of the salary of the member.

The employee is not required to pay any contribution.

(e) Payment of Gratuity Act, 1972

Until the passing of the Payment of the Gratuity Act 1972, there was no law governing the payment of gratuity to the employees except in Kerala and West Bengal where a legislation for the payment of gratuity was enacted in 1970 and 1971 respectively. It was paid either by agreements or by awards and in some organisations no gratuity was paid at all. Even though the payment of gratuity was voluntary in character it had led to several industrial disputes.

The Payment of Gratuity Act was passed in 1972 which came into force from 16th September 1972.

Salient Features of the Act: The Act is applicable to the factory, mine, oil field, plantation, port and railway company as defined in the Factories Act, Mines Act, Plantations Act, Oil Fields Act, Indian Ports Act, or Indian Railways Act, as the case may be and every establishment and establishment to which Shops and Establishments Acts are applicable in which 10 or more persons are employed. The Central Government can extend the provisions of the Act to any other establishments or class or establishments in which 10 or more persons are employed by issuing a notification. The Act is applicable to the employees drawing wages upto Rs. 1000/- per month, but excludes employees employed in managerial or administrative capacity. The employee should have put in minimum of five years continuous service before he becomes entitled to the payment of gratuity. However, the completion of five years of continuous service is not necessary where the termination of the employment of any employee is due to death or disablement. Gratuity is payable to the employee (a) on his superannuation, or (b) on his retirement or resignation, and (c) on his death or disablement due to accident or disease. The rate of gratuity payable is at 15 days wages (basic and DA) based on the wages last drawn by the employee concerned. In seasonal establishments the employers are required to pay gratuity at 7 days wages (basic and DA) for each season. The Act lays down that the amount of gratuity payable to employee should not exceed 20 months wages. The Act also protects the interest of the employees who are entitled to receive better terms of gratuity under any award or agreement or contract with the employer. If any employee's services have been terminated for any act of wilful omission or negligence causing any damage or loss to or destruction of property belonging to the employer, then the employer has the right to forfeit gratuity to the extent of the damage or loss so caused to him. However, the whole amount of gratuity can be forfeited if the services of an employee have been terminated for his riotous or disorderly conduct or any other act of violence on his part or any act which constitutes offence involving moral turpitude provided that such offence is committed by the employee in the course of his employment.

The appropriate government is required to appoint any officer to be a controlling authority who will be responsible for the administration of the Act and different controlling authorities may be appointed for different areas. If the amount of gratuity payable under this Act is not paid by the employer within the prescribed time to the person entitled there to, the controlling authority shall, on an application made to it in this behalf by the aggrieved person, issue a certificate for that amount to the Collector, who shall recover the same together with compound interest rate thereof at 9% per annum, from the date of expiry of the prescribed time as arrears of land revenue and pay the same to the person entitled thereto.

REFERENCES

1. IIPM, *op. cit.,* p. 88.
2. See Administrative Staff College, *Employers' Obligations Under Labour Laws,* 1941, p. 1.
3. IIPM, *op. cit.,* 88-89.
4. For this section, most of the material is borrowed from *Employers' Obligation Under Labour Laws,* published by Administrative Staff College, pp. 31-33.

❑ ❑ ❑

CHAPTER 16

Employee Grievance Redressal

There is hardly a company where the employees do not have grievances. Real or imaginary, valid or invalid, truthful or not, employees have grievances with regard to some aspects of the company. It may be a grievance against a foreman, or a machine, or the plant atmosphere, the food in the canteen, workloads, the job, the work environment etc. The grievance produces unhappiness, frustration, discontentment, indifference, poor morale and ultimately it hurts employee concentration, efficiency and productivity. A discontented workforce is a sure sign of potential turmoil affecting adversely the interests of the organisation. Some companies attempt to ignore employee grievances hoping that, if they do not pay attention to them, they will solve themselves. Nothing can be farther from the truth. On the other hand there are companies who after careful consideration, have organised a grievance redressal procedure. We shall proceed to discuss:

1. What is a grievance?
2. Causes of grievances?
3. Grievance redressal procedures.
4. Evaluating grievance procedures.

1. WHAT IS A GRIEVANCE?

Giving the broadest scope to the term, Professor Jucius defines grievances as "any discontent or dissatisfaction, whether expressed or not and whether valid or not, arising out of anything connected with the company that an employee thinks, believes, or even 'feels' is unfair, unjust or inequitable."[1]

Professors Pigors and Myers[2] use, instead of using only the term "grievance" three words "dissatisfaction", "complaint" and "grievance" indicating the stages of employee dissatisfaction.

They define an employee dissatisfaction as "anything that disturbs an employee, whether or not he expresses his unrest in words. A complaint is a spoken or written dissatisfaction, brought to the attention of his foreman or his shop steward.

"The complainant may or may not specifically assign a cause for dissatisfaction; and a grievance is simply a complaint which has been formally presented, in writing, to a management representative or to a union official in the language of labour relations from management's angle." Management also has grievances against employees or unions. Unrest of either party accuse poor morale.

Personnel administrators must assist the line executives, particularly foremen and supervisors in handling employee grievances. They must study and analyse the grievances and the pattern of grievances. Then they may help the top management plan policies, procedures and programmes to handle grievances and they may train supervisors and other line executives in handling grievances and dealing with unions.

2. CAUSES OF GRIEVANCES?

The U.S. Department of Labour has provided the following check list of typical grievances and common causes.[3]

The following sample list indicates the kind of grievances which workers bring up frequently and some of the causes which give rise to them:

TYPICAL EXAMPLES OF WORKERS' GRIEVANCES

Type of Grievance	*Common Causes*
(Listed with reference to frequency)	The worker feels that
A. WAGES	
1. Demand for individual wage adjustment.	He is not getting what he is worth. He gets less than other people doing work requiring the same degree of skill.
2. Complaints about job classification.	His job is worth more than it pays and should be reclassified. He deserves to be upgraded.
3. Complaints about incentive system.	The method of figuring his pay is so complicated that he does not know what his rate really is. His piece rates are too low. His piece rates are cut when his production increases.
4. Miscellaneous.	Mistakes are made in calculating pay. Methods of paying are inconsiderate.
B. SUPERVISION	
1. Complaints against discipline.	Foremen does not like him and picks on him. Company has it in for him because he is active in union. His mistakes were due to inadequate instruction.
2. Objection to a particular foreman.	Foreman is playing favourites. Foreman is trying to undermine union. Foreman ignores complaints.
3. Objection to general method of supervision.	There are too many rules and regulations. Rules and regulations are not clearly posted. Supervisors and/or time study men do too much snooping.
C. SENIORITY DISCHARGE ETC.	
1. Loss of Seniority.	He has been unfairly deprived of seniority.
2. Calculation of Seniority.	He has not received all the seniority due him.

3. Interpretation of seniority.	Clause in contract has been unfairly interpreted by company (Clauses often vague).
4. Disciplinary discharge or lay-off.	He has been penalised unfairly or at least too severely. Company wanted to get rid of him anyway for union activity or other reasons.
5. Promotions.	Seniority clause has been violated. Company would not promote him because of union activity. He goes not have a chance to advance himself.
6. Transfers to other departments or shifts.	He has more than his share of dirty work or graveyard shifts.
D. GENERAL WORKING CONDITIONS	
1. Safety and health.	Toilet facilities are inadequate. Dampness, noise, fumes, and other unpleasant or unsafe conditions could be corrected. He does not have enough time for personal needs.
2. Miscellaneous.	He has to lose too much time waiting for materials. Overtime is unnecessary. He is being unfairly denied an employment release (certificate of availability). Lunch room facilities are inadequate.
E. COLLECTIVE BARGAINING	
1. Violations of Contract.	Company is stalling or putting obstacles in the way of grievances settlements.
2. Interpretation of Contract.	Company won't give supervisors authority to grant any concessions. Company has disregarded precedents and agreed upon interpretations.
3. Settlement of grievances.	Company fails to discipline supervisors where disciplinary action is necessary and has been promised.

TYPICAL EXAMPLES OF MANAGEMENT COMPLAINTS

Type of Grievance	*Common Causes*
A. DISSATISFACTION WITH INDIVIDUAL WORKER	
1. Complaints concerning discipline.	Disregard of plant rules. Disregard of supervisor's orders. Disregard of safety regulations. Repeated tardiness or absenteeism. General irresponsibility.
2. Complaints concerning work.	Soldiering on job. Slowing down for time studies. Poor work.
B. COLLECTIVE BARGAINING	Company thinks that the Union.
1. Violations of contract	Lacks good faith. "Cooks up" complaints.
2. Disputes over interpretation of contract.	Fails to obtain facts before presenting grievances.

3. Complaints about grievance settlements.	Spends too much time on grievance work. Would not give stewards authority to make concessions to the company.
4. Alleged failure of unions to live upto promises.	Disregards precedents and agreed upon interpretations. Fails to take disciplinary action against union member or representative where necessary.
C. MISCELLANEOUS	
1. Questionable methods of soliciting union members.	Misrepresents management's attitude toward new employees.
2. Union rules conflicting with terms of agreement.	Interferes with management's freedom by passing restrictive rules in conflict with the agreement.
3. Irresponsible charges against management by union leaders in press, leaflets, or public speeches.	

In India, an analysis of 200 complaints, brought to the labour officer of a firm of 3,000 employees between May and July 1953, illustrates the types of problems which the individual workers had in the company.[4]

Complaint Concerning	*Per cent*
Medical advice and treatment	13
Housing accommodation in the company colony	12
Admission to state insurance hospital	9
Retirement	8
Granting or non granting of leave	8
Financial aid	7
Shortage of water in company housing	6
Lack of work (for part-time workers)	6
Employment of relatives	4
Repairs of quarters in company housing	3
Cattle nuisance in company housing	2
Transfers from one department to another	1
Miscellaneous	21

Grievances may be caused by a variety of factors and the causes of grievances are important because without studying and analysing the exact nature and causes of grievances, employee dissatisfactions cannot be overcome. Superficially one may think that he has settled a grievance, but soon the problem will crop up again and again, because the causes underlying the grievances are not eliminated. Grievance is a symbol of some malfunctioning or maladjustment and the able and skilful management representative must seek out the real and submerged causes or difficulties. Some grievances are unexpressed, but they are there and they are real, in so far as they affect the work of the individual. The worker behaviour, attitudes, expressions, habits and mannerisms betray employee dissatisfaction and grievance, without the individual worker ever having to express them orally or in written fashion.

Similarly there are complaints, which appear, on first glance to have no overt basis; but "the real difficulty may be a health condition, or a family situation, or a long standing personality problem.... In a day when more than 60 per cent of the visits to the doctor's offices in the country are found to have a psychic rather than a purely physical basis, it should not be surprising that a large proportion of grievances of individual employees should also have their roots in psychic difficulties."[5]

Grievances may also be anticipated. Instead of waiting till somebody presents a grievance, it may be a good idea to carefully observe changes in employee conduct or behaviour to detect possible or potential dissatisfactions.

The foremen, supervisors, managers — line and staff — must watch their actions, behaviour, instructions, and mannerisms in order to see that they do not give rise to any grievances. A potential area of dissatisfaction is alleged discourtesy of superiors toward employees. "I wish him 'Good Morning', but he just ignores me. What does he think he is?" Thinks the employee and the seeds of a potential grievance are sown. "They never speak the truth around here", complains another employee. "You can never trust them", concludes another. Such simple minor matters build up and have a cumulative effect and finally blow up. So the potential consequences of a gesture, action, speech of the supervisor or manager may have to be weighted in order to prevent the occurrence of employee grievances.

When grievances come into the open, they must be settled. Usually well-organised companies institute a grievance procedure whereby employee grievances are redressed. Let us take a look at these procedures.

3. GRIEVANCE REDRESSAL PROCEDURE

Grievances must be settled (1) promptly, (2) as near as possible to the point of origin, (3) on merit only, (4) with as many facts as possible and (5) with an attitude of mutual confidence and respect. Hasty actions, without proper facts do not settle grievances and if anything, they will aggravate the situation. Hence it is better to have a systematic methodical grievance procedure.

A systematic grievance redressal procedure must:

1. Be simple, fair and easy to understand.
2. Encourage employees to put forth their grievances.
3. Function promptly.
4. Gain employee confidence.
5. Promote healthy relations between employee and the company.

William Simkin provides the following suggestions for setting up a systematic grievance procedure:[6]

1. At low levels, let all gripes into the procedure.
2. Restrict scope, if at all, at arbitration level.
3. Do not have unnecessary steps — you can test this by seeing if few grievances are actually settled at certain steps.
4. Give as much authority as possible to settle at each step.
5. Set time limits for each step.
6. Have regular meetings of the grievance committee.

Although grievance procedures are made available to all employees — both union members and non-union members — the practice may generally be different in unionised plants from that of non-unionised plants. In U.S.A. and NLRB (National Labour Relations Board) ruling provides that unions certified as exclusive bargaining agents must handle grievances for employees, who are not members of the union and must do so without charging any fee. Most collective agreements provide for regular grievance procedures, which are sometimes not dealt in the union contract.

The number of steps in a grievance procedure may vary depending on the size of the company and the number of employers. The larger the company with large number of employees the more may be the steps in the grievance procedure. Smaller companies may have less number of steps in the redressal procedure. The terminal point is usually arbitration. The number of steps may vary from one-step to five-step grievance procedure. The U.S. Bureau of Labour Statistics has given in Figures 15.1 and 15.2 a typical three-step and a five-step grievance procedure for use in smaller and larger plants respectively.

STEP NUMBER	UNION REPRESENTATIVE		EMPLOYER REPRESENTATIVE
One	Shop Chairman (Steward)	Takes up grievance with	Representative of the Employer (Foreman)
Two	Union Representative (Business Agent)	Takes up Grievance with	Firm (Owner or Manager)
Three	Arbitration by Impartial Chairman		

Fig. 16.1 The Typical Grievance Procedure for Small Factories

Fig. 16.1. Typical grievance procedure for small factories. Provided in the standard agreement between the Amalgamated Clothing Workers of America and the Laundry Workers' Joint Board of Greater New York, A.C.W.A. and the New York Laundry Industry. (From "Settling Plant Grievances", Washington, Government Printing Office, U.S. Department of Labour, Bulletin 60, 1943,). p.12.

STEP NUMBER	UNION REPRESENTATIVE		EMPLOYER REPRESENTATIVE
One	Aggrieved Employee and District Committee man (Steward)	Attempts to settle with	Foreman

If this fails, then grievance is written out and

Two	Committee man	Attempts to settle with	Higher Supervision

If this fails, then Steward's Council decides whether to appeal. If so

Three	Shop committee committee where it exists	Attempts to settle with	Plant management

If this fails, Regional Director of Union decides whether to appeal.

If so grievances is considered by the Appeal Committee consisting of

Four	Regional Director and Chairman of shop Committee of plant involved	and	Two representatives of General Motors Corp.

If this fails and the question is one which the Umpire is authorized to rule, then

Five	Arbitration by permanent Impartial Umpire

Fig. 16.2 GM & UAW Grievance Procedure

Fig. 16.2 Five-Step grievance procedure. Provided in contract between General Motors Corporation and United Automobile, Aircraft, and Agricultural Implement Workers of America-CIO, 1942 (from "Settling Plant Grievances", Washington, Government Printing Office, U.S. Department of Labour, Bulletin 60, 1943), p. 14.

To serve as an illustration of another general pattern of grievance redressal machinery in a unionised plant, the following Figure 16.3 is given below:

NUMBER	UNION REPRESENTATIVE		EMPLOYER REPRESENTATIVE
One	Steward & Aggrieved employee or Steward alone or Aggrieved employee alone	To	Foreman
	Additional appeals may be made by the steward to higher line supervision or the foreman may consult his superiors before giving the steward his answer.		
Two	Union Business Representative (Business agent) Chief Plant Steward or Chairman or Grievance Committee	To	Industrial Relations Office Or High line supervision
Three	Plant Grievance Committee (May be assisted by an International Representative)	To	Top Local Management Or Industrial Relations Office
Four	International Office of Union (Regional or District Representative)	To	General Office of Corporation
Five		Arbitration (Conciliation where arbitration is not provided)	

Fig. 16.3 Grievance Machinery in Unionised Plant — General Pattern of Grievance Machinery

Source: Lawrence L. Bethel, Franklin S. Atwater, George H. E. Smith, and Harvey A. Stackman, Jr., *Industrial Organisation and Management* (New York: McGraw-Hill Book Company, Inc., Ist ed. 1945), p. 5.

The following joint action grievance redressal procedure serve as a good example of the care with which the machinery is specifying each step, people and time involved at each step.[7]

1. Any difference between the employer and employee involving the meaning of the provisions of this agreement shall constitute a grievance and may be taken up in the manner hereinafter set forth.
2. The company may utilise the following procedure upon any grievance against the union or any or its members:

   First — Presentation of complaints in writing to the officials of the Union.

   Second — If no satisfactory adjustment is obtained within seven working days, then the company shall have the right to have the matter handled in accordance with the procedure outlined above for appealing grievances to the impartial referee.
3. The union and the company shall establish and maintain joint committees to review by mutual agreement hourly wage rates of employees, in each department upon completion of each individual six month period of continuous employment with the company. Each wage review committee shall consist of six members, three from the union and three from the company, who are company officials. One of the union members shall be rotated so that the union committee man of each department can serve as a member of the committee during the time the rates of his department are being reviewed. If a wage review committee fails to reach an agreement in regard to any case brought before it, then and in that event, the matter in question shall be referred in writing within twenty-four hours to a general wage committee, consisting to three men from each party to his agreement. Within five days after the general wage committee has received a deadlocked case, a decision shall be handed down. In the event the general wage committee is unable to reach an agreement, the matter shall be submitted to arbitration as provided for in this agreement. In accordance with past practice, the company will approve interim individual increases when justified by proof of the individual involved that he has been performing work, which work calls for a higher rate, job, or wage classification to the satisfaction of his foreman. In all such cases, the foreman and the union committee man shall be consulted prior to the granting of such increases.
4. The umpire, to whom any grievance shall be submitted in accordance with the provisions of this section, shall have jurisdiction and authority to interpret and apply the provisions of this agreement in so far as shall be necessary to the determination of such grievance. But he shall not have jurisdiction or authority to alter in any way the provisions of this agreement.
5. The company may discipline or discharge any employee for just and proper cause, except that before any employee is disciplined or discharged, there shall be a hearing and mutual agreement between the shop committee (of the union) and a representative or representatives of the management appointed for such hearings, the decision, if mutually agreed upon, shall be final and binding upon both parties.

Non-unionised Plants and Grievance Procedure

A NICB survey of grievance procedures in 57 non-unionised companies showed the following typical practices for non-union employees:[8]

1. The majority put no limit on what can be considered a grievance.
2. Four-step procedures were most common; smaller companies have fewer steps; bigger companies have more.
3. First step is usually appeal to foreman.
4. In most cases employee may have fellow worker accompany him or represent him.
5. Most companies require grievance in writing at some step.
6. Final step in most companies is president or chairman of the Board.

In these companies, managements, in order to keep the unions away from the plant, attempt to provide a fair grievance procedure and impress upon the worker the fairplay of the employer and that he can depend upon the employer for protection of his legitimate interests.

Some companies follow an 'open door' policy where they encourage the worker to go to the top man and tell him about his particular problem or grievance. This policy seems to work well in some companies. But this policy may also create other organisational morale problems, because this policy bypasses various levels of line authority, who may not be quite happy with the employee going over their heads to reach the president directly.

Grievance Redressal Machinery in India

The IIPM lays down the following principles regarding grievance procedure:[9]

1. A grievance should be dealt with in the first instance at the lowest level, i.e., an employee should raise his grievance with his immediate superior.
2. It must be made clear to the employee what the line of appeal is, so that if he cannot get satisfaction from his immediate superior, he should know the next higher authority to whom he can go.
3. It is essential that grievances should be dealt with speedily.
4. It must be clearly understood in establishing a grievance procedure that, if the grievance is against an instruction given by a superior, in the interests of order and discipline, instruction must be carried out. Only then can the employee register his protest and set in motion the procedure.
5. It should be agreed that there will be no recourse to the official machinery of conciliation unless the procedure has been carried out and there is still dissatisfaction, and moreover, there must be no direct action on either side which might prejudice the case or raise tempers while the grievance is being investigated.

In many small companies and quite a few big ones also, there is no systematic grievance procedure at all. In most cases authority is centralised at the top and even the workers know that there is no use talking to the supervisors or welfare officers or production managers about their dissatisfactions or grievances. They are too timid to go to the top boss, who, of course, may completely ignore employee problems till such time as he cannot any more. But most of the time the aggrieved employees go about their chores dispirited and devoid of enthusiasm and in some extreme cases resort to sabotage and worse to take revenge upon the employers.

But there are other companies, though small in number, who have excellent grievance settlement machinery, which works very well. The following grievance procedure adopted by a large firm in our country serves as an example:[10]

1. The worker brings his complaint to the plant personnel officer who discusses it with the foreman and superintendent, although the personnel officer may transmit it to the worker and his union steward.
2. If dissatisfied, the worker and the union representatives go to the General Superintendent or the Deputy Director of Personnel. They take up the problem with the full time General Secretary of the Union.
3. Unsettled grievances then go to plant works committees which have four management and four union representatives elected by the union executive committee. These plant committees have the power to investigate the facts in the case and try to reach a decision. If the decision is unanimous it is usually accepted by both the union and management. The committees meet weekly.
4. A central works committee, composed of four representatives of top management and four top officers of the union, meets weekly to handle grievances on which the plant works committees have split. Unanimous decisions are binding.
5. Final authority to decide a grievance rests with the managing agent, who, however, gets few cases, since a great majority are decided at the joint committee level.

Indian Labour Conference and Grievance Procedure

Realising the importance of grievance procedure in the promotion of good employee and employer relations, the Indian Labour Conference held at Nainital in 1958 evolved certain guiding principles of grievance procedure and appointed a sub-committee, to draw up a scheme which came up with a procedure to settle grievances in our companies in India. The text of these principles and the grievance procedure is given below:[11]

Guiding Principles for A Grievance Procedure

Existing labour legislation does not provide for a well defined and adequate procedure for redressal of day-to-day grievances in industrial units. Clause 15 of the Model Standing Orders in Schedule 1 of the Industrial Employment (Standing Orders) Central Rules 1946 specifies that "All complaints arising out of employment including those relating to unfair treatment or wrongful exaction on the part of the employer or his agent, shall be submitted to the manager or the other person specified in this behalf with the right to appeal to the employers."

In some industrial units, however, detailed grievance procedures have been worked out by mutual agreement. In the absence of a satisfactory grievance procedure, day-to-day grievances are allowed to pile up with the result that the accumulated discontent culminates sometime or the other in cases of indiscipline, strikes etc. In what follows, therefore, an attempt has been made to draw up guiding principles of a grievance procedure. It is realised that it may not be possible to apply all these principles in respect of each and every industrial unit. However, all units should endeavour to conform, as much as possible, to these principles.

Complaints affecting one or more individual workers in respect of their wage payments, overtime, leave, transfer, promotion, seniority, work assignment, working conditions, and interpretation of service agreement, dismissals and discharges would constitute grievances. Where the points at dispute are of general applicability or of considerable magnitude, they will fall outside the scope of this procedure.

A Grievance Procedure should take note of the following principles:

1. *Conformity with existing legislation:*

   A Grievance Procedure forms part of the integrated scheme intended to promote satisfactory relations between employer and workers. This procedure should be designed to supplement the existing statutory provisions and it may, where practicable, make use of such machinery as is already provided by legislation.

   The grievance machinery can be availed of on the receipt by the worker of the order causing a grievance. The operation of the order, however, need not be held up till the grievance machinery is completely exhausted. Wherever possible, attempts should be made to complete the grievance procedure between the time the order is passed and when it is acted upon.

2. *Need to make the machinery simple and expeditious:*

   (a) As far as possible grievances should be settled at the lowest level.

   (b) No matter should ordinarily be taken up at more than two levels, i.e., normally there should be only one appeal.

   (c) Different types of grievances may be referred to appropriate authorities.

   (d) A grievance must be redressed as expeditiously as possible and towards this end, the employer, in consultation with the workers, should decide upon the time limit required for settling a grievance.

3. *Designation of authorities:*

   The workmen must know the authorities to be approached and it should, therefore, be incumbent on the management to designate the authorities to be contacted at various levels.

   It may be useful to classify grievances as those arising from personal relationship and others arising out of conditions of employment. In the former case, a grievance should be taken up, in the first instance, with the authority in the line management immediately above the officer against whom the complaint is made. Thereafter, the matter may go to the grievance committee comprising representatives of management and workers. The size and composition of the committee shall be decided at the unit level. (See Annexure).

   Other grievances should be taken up, in the first instance, with the authority designated by the management. Thereafter, reference may be made to the Grievance Committee.

   Where the matter goes to the Grievance Committee, in the first instance, an appeal shall lie with the top management.

ANNEXURE

Constitution of Grievance Committee.

1. In the case where the Union is not recognised.

Two representatives of management plus a Union representative and the Union Departmental representative of the Department in which the workmen concerned work.

2. In the case where the Union is not recognised or there is no Union but there is a works committee.

Two representatives of management plus the representative of the Department of the workman concerned on the Works Committee plus either the Secretary or Vice-President of the Works Committee (this is in case the Secretary of the Works Committee is also the workman's departmental representative).

It is suggested that in the case of the management, their representative should be the Department Head plus the Official who dealt with the matter at the first stage, or the personnel officer should act as an adviser.

The size of the "Grievance Committee" should be limited to a maximum of four to six; otherwise it becomes unwieldy.

Mr. Krishna Pillai believes that this "recipe for harmonious relations at the plants" will work "only in an atmosphere of good industrial relations" and that "a uniform procedure copied from some collective agreements in the country for grievance handling and processing and superimposed from above does not necessarily work, since the climate of trust engendered by collective bargaining is just not there."[12]

As earlier mentioned, there are some companies where the grievance procedure is spelt out with great care and consideration. The following procedure in a leading textile mill in India serves as good example.

Grievance Settlement Procedure of Mani Mills

Whereas it has been represented by the representatives of the workers of the Mills that a definite procedure should be laid down in order to establish a more speedy and effective method of settling all industrial disputes concerning individual workers or sections of workers and whereas the Management feels that such a procedure could well be of benefit to the workers as well as to the Management in maintaining good industrial relations, the Management have, therefore, agreed that the following procedure will be adopted in the case of all industrial disputes relating to individual workers or sections of workers:

1. The Union shall annually nominate a departmental representative of workers from amongst the workers from each shift in each of the main departments of the Mills. In the case of small departments, they will be conveniently grouped and departmental representatives nominated for such groups of departments.

The representatives so nominated shall hold office till the next general election of the executive committee of the Union or till after the expiry of 15 months after their nomination as departmental representatives, whichever is earlier. A departmental representative shall cease to hold office if the Executive Committee of the Union passes a resolution that he has ceased to represent it. In such an event, there shall be a fresh nomination. Fresh nominations shall also be made if a representative ceases to be an employee of the Company or resigns his office.

2. If any individual worker has a grievance relating to his wages, leave, promotion, hours of work, overtime, seniority, work assignment, or working conditions, he may make a representation to the departmental head through his departmental representative. Such preliminary negotiation should be started within 7 days of the date of the cause of action of the grievance. Departmental representatives may, if they so desire, personally record their complaints in the register maintained in the Department. For this purpose, Departmental representatives may seek the assistance of the Assistant Welfare Officer or the Administrative Assistant.

3. The departmental representative shall be shown by the departmental officer, records, such as attendance, production and seniority registers as may be necessary to understand the merit or otherwise of the grievance he is representing. The departmental officer shall have the right, however, to refuse to show any document or give any information which he considers to be of a confidential nature.

4. The departmental representatives may meet the departmental officers on any working day at a specified time to be mutually agreed upon between the departmental officer and the departmental representative except when compelling circumstances require immediate representation of a grievance.

5. A brief record shall be kept by the department officer of all preliminary negotiations between himself and the departmental representative and the result of the negotiations. This register shall be signed by the departmental officer and the departmental representative. The Departmental Officer's decision on any complaint brought by the Departmental representative is recorded in the Register of preliminary negotiations as soon as possible. However, if the Departmental Officer requires more than two days' time to communicate his decision, he shall record the same and the reasons therefore in the Register of preliminary negotiations. If the Departmental representative requests, the Departmental Officer shall record his decision and furnish a copy of the same to the Departmental representative.

6. Where the departmental representative is not satisfied with the decision of the departmental officer he may note his dissent in the register of preliminary negotiations maintained by the departmental officer and then report the matter to the workers' representative in the Mill Labour Advisory Committee who shall examine the complaint and upon being satisfied that the decision of the departmental officer is not acceptable, he may notify the Secretary of the Mill Labour Advisory Committee of his desire to have the matter placed before the next meeting of the Mill Labour Advisory Committee.

7. (i) There shall be one Mill Labour Advisory Committee, the constitution of which shall be as follows:

(a) Labour Officer — Chairman

(b) Four representatives of the workers to be elected by the departmental representatives from amongst themselves.

(c) Four management's representatives to be nominated by the Manager.

(d) Assistant Labour Officer — Secretary.

(ii) The Committee may call any departmental representative for participation in discussion relating to that particular department.

8. The Mill Labour Advisory Committee will meet once a week at the Labour Office during office hours. The workers' representatives on the Mill Labour Advisory will normally meet on Thursdays. The workers' representatives on the Mill Labour Advisory Committee may, however, request the Secretary to call a special meeting of the Mill Labour Advisory Committee by giving the Secretary at least 24 hours' notice and for any such special meeting there shall not be more than one item on the agenda. If any such special meeting is held in any week, the next normal meeting during that week will be postponed to the following week.

9. The Mill Labour Advisory Committee shall examine all complaints referred to it by either side and will send its recommendation to the Manager whose decision will be conveyed to the workers' representatives on the Committee through the Labour Officer normally within 7 days of the meeting and in the case of a special meeting normally within 3 days of the meeting. If, however, the Manager is unable to give his decision within the time specified above, he shall convey to the workers' representatives on the Committee through the Labour Officer the reasons for the delay and the date by which he will communicate his decision.

10. The Manager may before arriving at a decision on any matter referred to him by the Mill Labour Advisory Committee consult the concerned workers' representative in the Mill Labour Advisory Committee and the Labour Officer.

11. If the decision of the Manager is not acceptable to the workers' representative in the Committee he may notify the Secretary of the Central Labour Advisory Committee of his desire to have the matter placed before the Central Labour Advisory Committee. The grievance, however, will only be accepted for consideration by the Central Labour Advisory Committee provided the subject matter is fully covered by the provision of paragraph.

12. The Central Labour Advisory Committee shall consist of the following: (a) A Director of Mills-Chairman; (b) Manager and two other representatives nominated by the Management; (c) Four representatives of the workers to be elected by the departmental representatives; (d) Labour Officer who will act as the Secretary to this Committee and as a Liaison Officer.

13. The Central Labour Advisory Committee shall meet twice a month. At the end of each meeting the Chairman shall in consultation with the members of the Committee, fix the date for the next meeting.

14. (a) Workers' representatives on the Central Labour Advisory Committee may include not more than two official of the recognised union who are not workers of the Mills.

The four elected representatives of workers on the Central Labour Advisory Committee may elect one official of the recognised union who is not a worker of the Mills as an alternate member in the absence of another official of the recognised union who is not a worker in the Mills Departmental Representatives as a member of the Central Labour Advisory Committee.

(b) Workers' representatives on the Central Labour Advisory Committee have the power, if necessary, for any particular meeting to co-opt an additional departmental representative.

(c) Whenever an agenda for a Central Labour Advisory Committee meeting is sent to the Secretary, the member sending the agenda may ask for any relevant information that he may require on the items in the agenda. The Secretary, in consultation with the Chairman, shall furnish the information to the extent approved by the chairman as soon as possible but in any case not later than 24 hours before the meeting.

15. The recommendation of this committee will be sent to the Management whose decision shall be communicated in writing to the workers' representative on the Committee within 7 days of the meeting.

16. If the decision of the Management is not acceptable to the workers they may pursue the matter in accordance with law.

17. Matters that may be referred to the Central Labour Advisory Committee will be confined to individual grievances of an important nature or involving a principle or the interpretation of the Standing Orders or legislation or those affecting the rights and privileges of workers generally. If the workers' representatives on the Central Labour Advisory Committee and the Chairman of the Committee agree that any matter is very important and urgent, it may be brought up for discussion before the Central Labour Advisory Committee without first being discussed by the Mill Labour Advisory Committee.

18. Negotiations regarding complaints which affect the workers of the Mills as a whole or which affect the whole industry, such as, general revision of wages, bonus, dearness allowance, etc., will not be initiated by departmental representatives, and will not be covered by this procedure. Such questions may be taken up by any recognised union directly with the Managing Agents without going through the above procedure.

19. No recognised union will take up any matter covered by this procedure nor will there be a stoppage of work by workers unless the above procedure has been fully gone through. Violation of this clause will render this procedure null and void and the rights of the workers under this procedure will immediately lapse.

Rules for the Conduct of the Meetings of the Mill Labour Advisory Committee and the Central Labour Advisory Committee

1. Subjects to be included in the agenda for the meetings of the Mill Labour Advisory Committee shall be sent to the Secretary before 9 a.m. on Monday.

2. Subjects to be included in the agenda for the meetings of the Central Labour Advisory Committee shall be sent to the Secretary at least 7 days in advance.

3. The agenda for the meetings shall be prepared by the Secretary in consultation with the Chairman and circulated to the members at least 2 days in advance.

4. Subjects not included in the agenda shall not be discussed at the meeting.

5. Discussion at meetings shall be on an informal basis but the decision of the Chairman on the conduct of the meetings shall be obeyed by all members and all members will co-operate in the orderly conduct of meetings.

6. Minutes of the meetings shall be made by the Secretary and circulated to members. One copy of the Minutes translated into vernacular will be given to one of the workers' representatives in the Labour Advisory Committee, provided that in the event of any discrepancy between the English and the vernacular copies of the Minutes, the Minutes as recorded in English shall always prevail. After the minutes have been passed by the Committee and signed by the Chairman they shall become final and kept on record.
7. There will be no voting on any subject discussed at the meetings but the result of the discussion will be recorded in the minutes with such details as are necessary to follow the trend of discussions.
8. Two members elected by the workers and two members nominated by the Management shall form a quorum for all meetings.

The Southern India Millowners' Association has suggested the following grievance machinery for use in the member Mills:[13]

Grievance Procedure of Sima

Bearing in mind the set up in member mills, it is considered that a simple three stage procedure would fit into the working of the mills. Accordingly a three system is considered in this draft, but where larger organisational factors enable a more detailed and comprehensive procedure such cases may be considered specially.

The procedure is intended only for redressal of grievances of disputes of individual workers, but does not cover issues where section or a body of labour is involved giving rise to general matters such as policy matters and other issues affecting the rights and duties of workers generally in departments of categories. Such issues would stand to be handled at management-union level.

The first and foremost purpose of this procedure is to provide an opportunity for discussing grievance at the earliest stage and subsequent handling thereof failing redressal at the earliest stage, of individual cases only.

Stage I: Therefore a worker who believes that he has a justifiable request or complaint shall first discuss his point of view with his immediate superior, who supervises his duty. If it is not resolved within the authority of the said supervisor, be he a jobber, mistry or spinning master then a grievance may be deemed to exist and it shall be handled as prescribed in this procedure.

If the grievance which is not settled within 2 days of earliest intimation by the worker to his immediate supervisor, it shall then be submitted in writing in the form prescribed to that immediate superior duly signed by the employee.

Stage II: On receipt of such a written complaint, the same should be transmitted to the higher authority, namely, the manager or the officer at the managerial level. In transmitting this grievance to the higher authority, the Supervisor, Jobber or Mistry shall report the circumstances applicable to the case in his view together with the representation of the worker. Within two days of receipt of this representation, the manager shall summon a meeting of the worker and/or his representative, the immediate supervisor concerned and the departmental head, i.e., the Spinning Master or Supervisor, if any. At this meeting the workers' case shall be heard and the subject fully discussed.

The management's view is also to be explained to worker. The proceedings of this meeting shall be recorded and the decision of the manager communicated to the worker in writing.

Stage III: If the worker is not satisfied with the reply as rendered by the Manager, he is given an opportunity to the Managing Agent, or Managing Director, as the case may be. Upon such an appeal, the entire records will be considered by the Managing Agent or Director and unless the worker has raised any new issue or altered his stand in his appeal to the Managing Agent or Director, then it may not be found necessary to hold a formal meeting and discuss the subject in the presence of the worker. But the Managing Agent or Director is to exercise his own judgment and pass orders thereon. Such orders shall be communicated to the worker within 24 hours of passing the order. The Managing Agent or Director shall deal with the grievance and communicate his orders within 7 days from receipt of the appeal from the worker. This worker who is not satisfied with this decision may then take action according to law.

The procedure shall cover only the following types of workers' grievances. This list could be modified to suit special cases.

1. Complaints regarding wages that they are not paid in accordance with the contract, award or settlement.
2. Complaints in regard to classification or designation.
3. Complaints in regard to any differences in wages due and actual payment.
4. Complaints in regard to seniority, promotion and transfer.
5. Complaints resulting from non-observance of the Factories Act, Employees' Provident Funds Act, Employees' State Insurance Scheme, affecting the worker prejudicially.
6. Complaints against superiors in their enforcement of standing orders, duty assignments and discipline.

Every mill shall publicise translations of the procedure in the local language.

Every mill shall notify the workers to nominate the 'Grievance Man' for each department or groups of departments (depending upon the size of the Unit) of their establishment. These 'Grievance Men' may represent grievances on behalf of the workers and participate in meetings summoned and discuss the subject of grievance filed as prescribed in this procedure.

Scope of the Procedure

Complaints affecting one or more individuals in respect of their wage payments, overtime, leave, transfer, promotion, seniority, work-assignment, working conditions, adherence to acts and regulations, interpretation of service agreements would normally fall within the scope of the above procedure.

In the case of any grievance arising out of discharge or dismissal of a workman the above procedure shall not apply. Instead, a discharged or dismissed workman shall have the right to appeal either to the dismissing authority or to a senior authority who shall be specified by the management within a week from the date of dismissal or discharge. At the time the appeal is heard, workman may, if he so desires, be accompanied by either an official of the recognised union or a fellow worker as the case may be.

Mode of Grievance Procedure

*A. **Grievance Machinery:*** A Grievance Machinery will be required to be set up in each undertaking to administer the Grievance Procedure. The minimum requirements of such a machinery would be as follows, except where an established procedure is already working to the mutual satisfaction of either party. Even in the latter case, every effort shall be made to bring the procedure in conformity with the Guiding Principles.

For the purpose of constituting a fresh Grievance Machinery, workers in each department (and where a department is too small, in a group of departments) and each shift, shall elect, from amongst themselves and for a period of not less than one year at a time, departmental representatives and forward the list of persons so elected to the management. Where the Union(s) in the undertaking are in a position to submit an agreed list of names, recourse to election may not be necessary. Similar is the case where Works Committees are functioning satisfactorily since the Works Committee Member of a particular constituency shall act as the departmental representative. Corresponding, the management shall designate the persons for each department who shall be approaching at the first stage and the department heads for handling grievances at the second stage. Two or three of the departmental representatives of workers and two or three departmental heads nominated by the management shall constitute the Grievance Committee. In the case of appeals against discharges or dismissals the management shall designate the authority to whom appeals could be made.

*B. **Grievance Procedure:*** While adaptations have to be made to meet special circumstances with such as those obtaining in the Defence Undertakings, Railways, Plantations and also small undertakings employing a few workmen, the procedure normally envisaged in the handling of grievances should be as follows:

1. An aggrieved employee shall first present his grievances verbally in person to the officer designated by management for this purpose. An answer shall be given within 48 hours of the presentation of complaint.

2. If the worker is not satisfied with the decision of this officer or fails to receive an answer within the stipulated period, he shall, either in person or accompanied by his departmental representative, present his grievances to the Head of the Department designated by the management for the purpose of handling grievances. For this purpose, a fixed time shall be specified during which on any working day, an aggrieved worker could meet the departmental head for presentation of grievances. The Departmental Head shall give his answer within 3 days of the presentation of grievance. If action cannot be taken within that period, the reason for delay should be recorded.

3. If the decision of the Departmental Head is unsatisfactory, the aggrieved worker may request the forwarding of his grievance to the "Grievance Committee" which shall make its recommendations to the Manager within 7 days of the worker's request. If the recommendations cannot be made within this time limit, the reason for such delay should be recorded. Unanimous recommendations of the Grievance Committee shall be implemented by the Management. In the event of a difference of opinion among the members of the Grievance Committee, the views of the members along with the relevant papers shall be placed before the Manager for final decision. In either case, the final decision of the management shall be communicated to the workman concerned by the personnel officer within three days from the receipt of the Grievance Committee's recommendations.

4. Should the decision from the management be not forthcoming within the stipulated period or should it be unsatisfactory, the worker shall have the right to appeal to management for a revision. In making this appeal, the worker, if he so desires, shall have the right to take a union official along with him to facilitate discussions with management. Management shall communicate their decision within a week of the workman's revision petition.

5. If no agreement is still possible, the union and the management may refer the grievance to voluntary arbitration within a week of the receipt by the worker of management's decision.

6. Where a worker has taken up a grievance for redressal under this procedure, the formal Conciliation Machinery shall not intervene till all steps in the procedure are exhausted. A grievance shall be presumed to assume the form of a dispute only when the final decision of the top management in respect of the grievance is not acceptable to the worker.

7. If a grievance arises out of an order given by management, the said order shall be complied with before the workman concerned invokes the procedure laid down for redressal of grievance. If, however, there is a time lag between the issue of order and its compliance, the grievance procedure may immediately be invoked but the order nevertheless must be complied within the due date, even if all the steps in the grievance procedure have not been exhausted. It may however be advisable for the management to await the findings of grievance procedure machinery.

8. Workers' representatives on the Grievance Committee shall have the right of access to any document connected with inquiry maintained in the department and which may be necessary to understand the merit or otherwise of the workers' grievances. The management's representatives shall have the right, however, to refuse to show any document or give any information which they consider to be of a confidential nature. Such confidential document(s) shall not be used against the workmen in the course of the grievance proceedings.

9. There shall be a time limit within an appeal shall be taken from one step to the other. For this purpose, the aggrieved worker shall, within 72 hours of the receipt of the decision at one stage (or if no decision is received, on the expiry of the stipulated period), file his appeal with the authority at the next higher stage, should he feel inclined to appeal.

10. In calculating the various time intervals under the above clauses, holidays shall not be reckoned.

11. Management shall provide the necessary clerical and other assistance for the smooth functioning of the grievance machinery.

12. If it is necessary for any worker to leave the department during working hours on call from the Labour/Personnel Officer, or any other officer of the established grievance machinery, previous permission of his superior shall necessarily be obtained.

Subject to this condition, the worker shall not suffer any loss in wages of the work-time lost in this manner.

13. If, however, there be any complaint against any individual member of the staff, who is nominated by the management to handle grievances at the lowest level, the workman may take up his grievance at the next higher stage, i.e., at the level of Departmental Head.

14. In the case of any grievance arising out of discharge or dismissal of a workman, the above-mentioned procedure shall not apply. Instead, a discharged or dismissal workman shall have the right to appeal either to the dismissing authority or to a senior authority who shall be specified by the management, within a week from the date of dismissal or discharge. At the time the appeal is heard, the workman may, if he so desires, be accompanied by either an official of the recognized union or a fellow-worker, as the case may be.

Attitude of Unions

In the smooth functioning of the grievance redressal machinery, the unions play a key role in unionised plants. Their co-operation is essential for the success of the procedure. When they co-operate, they can "squelch" many a grievance in the very budding stage. Complaints without merit or imaginary grievances may be settled by a union representative who could advise the worker and put him on the right track. Of course, this calls for strong union leadership. Sometimes unions are afraid that, if they do not support the worker *'under all circumstances'* they may lose the support of the membership. So all sorts of grievances — merit or not merit — are brought forth before management and often this may clog up the work of the grievance machinery and cause delay, frustration and cynicism.

Some union leaders may entertain grievance solely with the purpose of "looking busy" and impressing the members that they are at it. This is alleged to have happened in U.S.A. as well as in India. In U.S.A. another tactic adopted by some unions is to open up new issues not dealt with in the labour agreement through the grievance machinery. Then it is possible that unions may adopt the attitude that it is their "duty to oppose" management and thus attempt to sustain unmeritorious grievances against management. These are some of the union attitudes that are not very helpful to the smooth functioning of a grievance procedure and that come in the way of settlements and harmonious relations between the parties.

Should the grievance procedure be held during working hours? To accelerate the pace of redressal, unions argue that union representatives should be permitted to investigate, present, discuss and settle grievances on company time, i.e., during working hours. They argue that this is in the interests of the employer as well as the employees and that to compel the handling of grievances outside of working hours makes an unreasonable demand upon the non-working time of both employees and executives. While many employers share this viewpoint, some others point out the problem of misuse and the consequent repercussions on production.

Advantages of a Systematic Grievance Procedure

A well planned and well-operated grievance redressal procedure has many advantages. It serves as a:

1. Channel through which any aggrieved employee may put forth his grievance.
2. Procedure assuring a systematic handling of every grievance.
3. Device whereby the aggrieved employee can relieve his feelings.
4. Means of assuring promptness in the handling of grievances.
5. Means by which employee satisfaction is obtained.
6. Device to locate problem situations in the relations between a union and management and to discern difficulties within both organisations.
7. Channel of communication where information is channelled both ways between the top and the bottom of the hierarchy.
8. Device to interpret the provisions of the labour agreement, to apply the agreement to the new and changing aspects of everyday relations between a union and a management.
9. Machinery to promote harmonious and peaceful employee-employer relations.

In the words of Mr. G.Y. Mangrulkar,[14] formerly Chief, Management Planning and Development, Tata Iron & Steel Co., a Grievance Procedure is essential because it brings uniformity in handling grievances. It gives confidence to the worker that if he feels he has not got a fair deal, he knows what to do and whom to approach. It also gives him confidence that his complaint will be investigated and a decision given in reasonable time.

4. EVALUATION OF GRIEVANCE REDRESSAL MACHINERY

Pigors and Myers suggest the following test questions that a personnel administrator should ask if he is keen on evaluating the success of the redressal machinery on any given grievance.[15]

1. Was the case handled in such a way that the parties directly involved were able to identify, and agree upon, what was at stake?
2. Was the incident closed with a sense of satisfactory adjustment by everyone immediately concerned with the original complaint?
3. Was the case handled in a way that strengthened line authority, especially at the level immediately above that at which dissatisfaction was first expressed?
4. Did the solution result in a better mutual understanding and a better mutual adjustment between a superior and his subordinates?
5. Was there any spread of understanding, as a result of this case, to other people (in management and in the union — if there is one — as well as among other employees) who were not directly involved in the original complaint?
6. Did the solution contribute to operating efficiency?

Thc Role of Personnel Administrator

It is necessary for the personnel administrator to carefully study the grievances in order to discover any patterns in them and the sources of dissatisfactions must be brought under scrutiny. If a series of grievances emerge from the interpretation of a clause the individual or the department respectively may deserve special attention.

Grievances may disclose weaknesses in planning, in handling materials, in assigning work, or in supervision and these weaknesses may have to be remedied. It would be also a good idea to analyse the difference between grievers and non-grievers in terms of personal characteristics, types of grievance, and results.

One of the most important requirements of a systematic grievance machinery is carefully kept adequate records which help analysis and research to improve the redressal machinery.

In conclusion we may emphasise that the personnel administrator must help the top and line managers, particularly supervisors in the formulation and implementation policies, programmes and procedures in handling grievances. But they must never make decisions for the line authority and they must help strengthen line management by proper and timely advice and guidance. Personnel division may provide training for executives and supervisors in handling grievances and they may also enlighten the supervisors on contract provisions.

The personnel administrator may help remove employee dissatisfactions — present and potential — by assisting management in the establishment and implementation of a machinery that will bring about a redressal of employee grievances quickly, cheaply, and satisfactorily.

REFERENCES

1. Jucius, *op. cit.*, p. 490.
2. Pigors and Myers, *op. cit.*, p. 242.
3. U.S. Department of Labour, "Settling Plant Grievances", *Bulletin* No. 60, 1943, pp. 1-8.
4. See Charles Myers, *Industrial Relations in India* (Bombay, Asia Publishing House, reprinted 1960) p. 230.
5. See John T. Dunlop and James J. Healy, "The Grievance Procedure", in *Unions, Management and the Public,* p. 302.
6. Abstracted from "Handling Grievances", *Institute of Labour and Industrial Relations* (Urbana: University of Illinois, 1952) pp. 10-11.
7. Jucius, *op. cit.*, pp. 507-508.
8. See James J. Bambrick, Jr., and J.J. Speed, "Grievance Procedures in Non-unionised Companies", NICB *Studies in Personnel Policy,* No. 109, September, 1950.
9. Abstracted from IIPM, *op. cit.*, pp. 172-174.
10. Charles Myers, *Industrial Relations India,* p. 227.
11. See *Indian Labour Gazette,* January 1959, p. 552.
12. Krishna Pillai, *op. cit.*, p. 154.
13. The author is much indebted to the Southern India Mill Owners' Association for giving permission to reproduce this here.
14. G.Y. Mangrulkar, "Effective System of Communication for Employee Discipline", *Industrial Times,* Vol. IX, No. 1, January 1, 1967, p. 31.
15. Pigors and Myers, *op. cit.*, p. 254.

❑❑❑

CHAPTER 17

Employee Discipline

The promotion and maintenance of employee discipline in an organisation is essential to its progress and growth. It is said that the government, which is best, is that which governs least. Similarly it may be said that employee discipline is at its best when there is a great amount of self-discipline on the part of the employees. In order to realise that state of affairs it is necessary to promote and retain high morale which makes for high self-discipline in the organisation among the employees. In an ideal situation there may not be any need to enforce rules and regulations, penalties and disciplinary actions, because every employee is highly disciplined in the sense that he follows the rules and regulations of the organisation willingly. But whenever the employee does not follow the rules or instructions or causes acts of indiscipline to occur, he requires to be disciplined. Enforcement of discipline is a management function — an important function at that. An employee, when he is dissatisfied or has a grievance, he is given an opportunity to air his grievance and get it when the management is dissatisfied with the conduct, behaviour and attitude of an employee, it is the management's duty to use the disciplinary measure to correct the situation and the employee. Just as the grievance procedure, so also as in the disciplinary matters, management must enlist the co-operation of the Union, where there is one. The personnel division plays a key role in this area also as it is closely associated with the disciplinary programme at the policy-making, programme developing and implementing, and discipline-administering levels within the organisation.

The important aspects of employee discipline are discussed under the following sections:

1. The problem of alienation.
2. Principles of maintaining discipline.
3. Areas of indiscipline and types of penalties.
4. Disciplinary procedure.
5. Role of personnel administrator.

1. THE PROBLEM OF ALIENATION[1]

The central problem of modern business and industry is how to create a work environment and an organisational climate that will contribute to the employee fulfilment, motivation and self-actualisation. In recent times the progressive sophistication and automation, an excessive specialisation and division of work in industry have increasingly created a great amount of apathy, non-involvement and indifference among the employees. In short, employee alienation has become a serious and mounting problem. Employee alienation results in low productivity, efficiency and output. It also increases social costs of human input.

There are several manifestations of such employee alienation. On the one hand, it may be expressed by passive withdrawal — turnover — absenteeism, tardiness, and inattention on the job. On the other hand, it is expressed also by active attacks — sabotage, deliberate waste, pilferage, assaults, gheraos, violence and other disruptions of work routines. People feel alienated when their jobs cease to provide any sort of creative job satisfaction and when their jobs are being chopped into several meaningless pieces and there is no more meaningful and purposeful work content in their jobs. In addition the employees' dissatisfaction is fuelled by the changing employees attitudes and aspirations, rising educational levels and also the rising expectations. More than sharing the gains of productivity and profits, the employee as a unique human being seems to be crying out for a more meaningful and creative type of work that would provide opportunities for self-actualisation and self-fulfilment. People want to be involved and they want to have a say in things that affect them, their work and their lives.

Causes of Alienation

Prof. Walton identifies some of the major causes of employee non-involvement and alienation:[2]

1. Employees want challenge and personal growth, but work tends to be simplified and specialities tend to be used reportedly in work assignments. This pattern exploits the narrow skills of a worker, while limiting his or her opportunities to broaden or develop.
2. Employees want to be included in patterns of mutual influence; they want egalitarian treatment. But organisations are characterised by tall hierarchies, status differentials, and chains of command.
3. Employee commitment to an organisation is increasingly influenced by the intrinsic interests of the work itself, the human dignity afforded by management, and the social responsibility reflected in the organisation's products. Yet, organisation practices still emphasise material rewards and employment security and neglect other employee concerns.
4. What employees want from careers, they are apt to want right now. But when organisations design job hierarchies and career paths, they continue to assume that today's workers are as willing to postpone gratifications as were yesterday's workers.
5. Employees want more attention to the emotional aspects of organisation life, such as individual self-esteem, openness between people, and expressions of

warmth. Yet organisations emphasise rationality and seldom legitimate the emotional part of the organisational experience.

6. Employees are becoming less driven by competitive urges, less likely to identify competition as the "American way." Nevertheless, managers continue to plan career patterns, organise work, and design reward systems as if employees valued competition as highly as they used to.
7. Furthermore, concepts of industrial democracy, workers' participation in management and social justice have contributed to a situation where the current organisational structures and designs, work routines and excessive division of work and bureaucratic hierarchies are increasingly becoming inadequate to counter the problem of employee alienation and to the promotion of optimum human resources utilisation.

2. PRINCIPLES FOR MAINTAINING DISCIPLINE

Disciplinary measures have serious repercussions on the employees and they must be based on certain principles in order to be fair, just and acceptable to the employees and the union. The most important principles to be observed in the maintenance of discipline are outlined by Yoder, Heneman, Turnbull and Harold Stone:[3]

1. So far as possible, all rules should be developed in cooperation and collaboration with representatives of employees. If they have a hand in formulating the rules, they will be much more likely to observe them.
2. All rules should be appraised at frequent and regular intervals to be sure that they are and remain appropriate, sensible and useful.
3. Rules should vary with working conditions. The rules for office workers, for instance, may well vary from those affecting employees in the shop.
4. Rules must be uniformly enforced if they are to be effective. They must be applied without favouritism or exceptions.
5. Penalties for violations should be stated in advance, as should procedures for enforcement. Employees have a right to know what to expect. To that end, both rules and procedures may well be published in employee's handbooks.
6. Disciplinary policy should have, as its objective, the prevention of infractions rather than the simple administration of penalties, however just. It should be preventive rather than punitive.
7. Extreme care must be taken to assure that infringements of rules are not encouraged, if not actually required, by supervisors or company policy.
8. If violations of any particular rule are numerous, the circumstances surrounding these infractions should be carefully studied to discover the source of difficulty.
9. Recidivism must be expected. Certain offenders will almost certainly occasion far more than their proportionate numbers of violations. These or problem cases may require extensive consideration and attention.
10. Definite and precise provision for appeal and review of all disciplinary action should be expressly provided in the employee handbook, collective agreement, or otherwise.

Almost a similar set of principles of industrial discipline is provided by Mr. V.K.R. Menon, former Director of I.L.O. in India:[4]

1. Whenever there is a case of individual indiscipline or group indiscipline, a searching examination of its cause should be made.
2. Rules should be framed after proper consultation with the workers or their representatives.
3. If any rule is infringed frequently, the cause of such infringement should be looked into.
4. There should be no rigidity or finality about the rules, and they should be considered as means and not as ends.
5. There should be a periodical check-up of the rules, to see whether any changes are necessary in the light of experience gained.
6. In the enforcement of rules, there should be no favouritism or bias.
7. Managements should see that those who are responsible for ensuring the observance of rules are themselves setting an example by following them strictly, where the rules concern them.

In developing a set of rules of discipline it must be borne in mind that as far as possible, a legalistic and a punitive approach should be avoided. Rules must be simple, easily understood and to a minimum. When rules are framed with elaborate legalistic caution giving scope for too many different interpretations and they are long-winded, the very purpose of rules is lost, because they are not easily understood and observed.

A Policy Statement of Employee Discipline

Professors Pigors and Myers have suggested the following policy statement: "because (1) It expresses the main ideas that belong in an organisational policy for discipline; and (2) It uses the kind of language that distinguishes a policy from a procedure or a rule":[5]

A Suggested Policy for Discipline

It is the intention of management to promote, at all times, and throughout the whole employment relationship, the high morale that makes for self-discipline in every work team. When it is necessary for management representatives to resort to discipline, such action should demonstrably implement two related purposes: (1) To inform, remind and encourage employees in regard to accepted standards of work and of conduct; and (2) To prevent an unruly minority from exercising an undue influence on standards of behaviour. In other words, our disciplinary procedure should be used, whenever possible, in such a way and at such a time as to reinforce in employees the desire and ability to meet accepted standards of work and of conduct. Punitive action, such as discharge, should be taken as a last resort. In case of doubt as to the facts, suspension should be used, pending further investigation.

The responsibilities which all employees are expected to meet are summarised on a minimum of rules for efficiency, safety and good conduct. These rules are to be carefully explained to every new employee, re-emphasised — if necessary — in follow-up interviews by supervisors, and promptly and impartially enforced.

No management representative should, at any time or for any reasons, overlook disobedience, either of these rules, or of a supervisor's order. Even if an employee should feel that either a rule or an order is unsuitable, this does not alter his duty to obey it. He has recourse to the grievance procedure by entering a complaint with his representative on the Grievance Committee.

Any act of clear-cut disobedience (where the facts have been established) shall be considered a ground for disciplinary action. The scope of such action shall depend upon the supervisor's judgment as to the seriousness of the offence, in relation to the various rules, or to the gravity of the situation. It should be set in motion by the supervisor in charge and should depend on what disciplinary steps, if any, have previously been taken, with the employee.

This policy shall be implemented by a written procedure for discipline and an established disciplinary process; both of which should be made known to all employees at the time when they first joint the organisation.

Disciplinary policy must provide the employee with an opportunity to explain his idea of the case and also a recourse to an appeal, if he feels that an unjust punishment is being meted out to him.

Accurate records of disciplinary cases and the measures taken have to be maintained for use in the future. While the disciplinary action is generally taken by the line executives, in some companies personnel administrators are asked to take the ultimate disciplinary measures such as discharge or dismissal.

Next major phase of employee discipline is to consider the areas and types of indiscipline and the type of penalties administered.

3. AREAS OF INDISCIPLINE AND TYPES OF PENALTIES

The disciplinary cases are in the areas of attendance, punctuality, regularity, insubordination, loafing, fighting, drunkenness, stealing, breaking or defacing company property, smoking, etc. "An analysis of major types of disciplinary cases made by Allis-Chalmers Company showed that 323 cases went beyond the initial warning stage. This is for a 1 year period, in an operation with 18,000 employees working 35 million manhours. Of these cases, 44 per cent involved absenteeism, 26 per cent involved horseplay and fighting, 26 per cent involved insubordination and loafing and 4 per cent were for theft, drunkenness, and other abuses."[6]

Pigors and Myers list all the possible areas of misconduct and indiscipline:[7]

A List of Offences

Using liquor on the premises. Drunkenness. Fighting or attempting to injure others (aggressor only). Stealing from company or from any employee. Falsifying time cards and production records. Immoral behaviour. Unauthorised possession of weapons. Engaging in a strike or group stoppage of work of any kind, slowdown, sabotage, picketing, or failure to abide by the terms of the union agreement or by the award of the impartial arbitrator. Wilful destruction of company property. Insubordination or wilful disobedience in carrying out reasonable request of the supervisors. Gambling and bookmaking on the premises. Refusing to accept job assignments. Unexcused absence for period of 3 consecutive working days without notification to the supervisor or the employment department. Inefficiency, i.e., failing to do the amount and quality of work that was expected of the employee when he was hired. Defacing company property. Violation of safety rules. Occasional unexcused tardiness and absenteeism. Horseplay and practical joking. Smoking in prohibited areas.

Most of the disciplinary problems do not occur overnight, but they gradually develop and many of the tendencies toward misconduct or indiscipline could be remedied if proper and timely action is taken by the supervisors. As pointed out by G.Y. Mangrulkar, formerly Chief, Management Planning and Development of TISCO,[8] "Most problems leading to slack behaviour or workmanship can be sensed or sized in advance. Wasting time in the canteen, not starting work on time, carelessness about materials and tools or gossiping away during hours are lax attitudes which have developed over long periods because they were tolerated. If the supervisor is watchful and looks for signs of faulty leadership or funny behaviour amongst workers, he can take action in time and there is no need to be unpleasant about it. In other words it is like putting out fires while they are small and yet to spread."

Another important aspect is not to get carried away by the outward symptoms and superfluous causes of indiscipline or misconduct. But it is essential to probe in order to find out the basic underlying causes that give place to disciplinary problems. the deeper underlying causes beneath the outward manifestations or disciplinary problems have to be explored and pinpointed and they must be alleviated.

A Set of Penalties

Deterrent and preventive disciplinary measures are very important in the prevention of internal indiscipline and offences. In order to do that, it is necessary to formulate a list of penalties that will be meted out for certain types of offences and every employee must be made aware of these penalties through an employee handbook, or house organ or bulleting boards etc. The employee, who knows that he will be discharged if he is found drunk on the job, is less likely to commit this offence than an employee who is not told what is coming to him if he comes to work drunk. If the employee knows, when he joins duty in a company, that if he steals company property or the property of a fellow employee, he will be immediately discharged, he is not likely to steal.

The major types of disciplinary action include the following: (1) Correction. (2) Show-cause. (3) Warning (Oral). (4) Written warning or reprimand. (5) Fines. (6) Suspension. (7) Lay-off. (8) Transfer to a hardship post or to less attractive work. (9) Discharge, dismissal, or termination.

The NICB survey of 473 companies revealed the following disciplinary practices for a variety of disciplinary problems:[9]

In case of insubordination, disciplinary action is immediate discharge in 167 companies (35%); one warning, then discharge in 160 firms (33%); two warnings, then discharge in 90 firms (18%); immediate suspension, subject to discharge in 18 (4%); and some 105 companies (21%) mentioned that the disciplinary action varies case by case.

The disciplinary action for *employee dishonesty* is immediate discharge in 361 companies (77%); one warning, then discharge in 59 (12%); two warnings, then discharge in 14 (3%); and varies, no set practice in 39 (8%).

Disciplinary action for *malicious damage* is immediate discharge in 356 firms (75%); one warning, then discharge in 46 (9%); two warnings, then discharge in 17 (4%); immediate suspension, subject to discharge in 8 (2%); and varies case by case in 84 (17%).

Disciplinary action for *intoxication* is immediate discharge in 266 companies (56%); one warning, then discharge in 116 (25%); two warnings, then discharge in 43 (9%); immediate suspension, then discharge in 10 (2%); and varies case by case in 92 (20%).

Disciplinary action for *carelessness* is immediate discharge in 5 companies (1%); one warning, then discharge in 106 (22%); two warnings, then discharge in 239 (51%); immediate suspension, subject to discharge in 23 (5%); warning, suspension, then discharge in 13 (3%); and varies case by case in 130 (27%).

Disciplinary action for *fighting* is immediate discharge in 266 companies (56%); one warning, then discharge in 114 (24%); two warnings, then discharge in 32 (7%); immediate suspension, subject to discharge in 14 (3%); and varies case by case in 87 (18%).

Disciplinary action for *safety violation* or breaking safety rule is immediate discharge in 5 companies (1%); one warning, then discharge in 47 (11%); two warnings, then discharge in 161 (40%); warning only in 24 (6%); warning, lay-off or suspension, then discharge if chronic offender in 36 (8%); and varies case by case in 296 companies (69%). Some 95 companies (20%) reported that *employee theft* of tools, equipment, materials, or company products was a real problem. Nearly 15 companies (3%) charge the employees for the breakage of tools and equipment. For loss of tools and equipment some 122 companies (26%) charge the employees anywhere from replacement cost to actual cost of the original article.

Apart from such written disciplinary rules, regulations and penalties, traditional conventions and controls lay down certain unwritten, nevertheless important, regulations, as observed by Yoder, Heneman, Turnbull and Harold Stone:[10]

> A large part of all modern industrial discipline, like modern social discipline, takes no such formal shape as written regulations. Much of it is a matter of unwritten, traditional rules. The very fact, for instance, that the worker does not assume any direct right to the product upon which he has worked is an expression of the recognition of basic traditional rules respecting the nature of private property in the productive process. It is only where traditional rules do not extend, where situations beyond the scope of established convention require control or where traditional controls must be changed that formal regulations are necessary.

Then there are employees who may repeat acts of indiscipline or misconduct and they must be met with increasing penalties. When a person is found sleeping on his job, he may be warned. If he is found sleeping again, he may be asked to go home for the rest of the day, in which case the penalty is the loss of pay for time not worked. If he repeats the offence, he may be suspended for 3 days. And on another repetition, he may be laid off for a week, with a warning that he will meet with the ultimate penalty of dismissal next time if he repeats the misconduct. The Figure 17.1 serves as an example of increasing penalties with growing number of repetitions.

DISCIPLINARY PENALTIES

19	Posting or removal of any matter on bulletin boards or company property at any time unless specifically authorised by Industrial Relations Department.	1 day off	3 days off	Discharge		
20	Theft or removal from the premises without proper authorisation of any company property or property of the Government or of any employee.	Discharge				
21	Gambling or engaging in lottery on company premises.	Discharge				
22	Misusing, destroying, or damaging any company property or property of an employee.	Discharge				
23	Deliberately restricting output.	Discharge				
24	Making false, vicious, or malicious statements concerning any employee of the company, or its product.	Warning	3 days off	1 week off	Discharge	
25	Provoking or instigating a fight or fighting during working hours or on company premises.	1 week off (or) discharge	Discharge			
26	Drinking any alcoholic beverage on premises or on company time.	1 week off	Discharge			
27	Reporting to work obviously under the influence of alcohol or drugs.	1 day off	3 days off	1 week off	Discharge	
28	Engaging in sabotage or espionage.	Discharge				
29	Violating a safety rule or safety practice.	Warning	1 day off	3 days off	1 week off	Discharge

30	Immoral conduct or indecency.	Discharge				
31	Interfering or refusing to cooperate with plant protection officers in the performance of their duties.	Discharge				
32	Sleeping on the job during working hours.	Discharge				
33	Entering restricted areas without permission.	Warning	1 day off	2 Week off	Discharge	
34	Refusal to show badge at the request of any member of supervision or plant protection.	Discharge				
35	Leaving plant during work shift without permission.	1 day off	1 week off	Discharge		
36	Insubordination.	1 week off or Discharge	Discharge			
37	Failure to observe parking and traffic regulations on premises.	Warning	1 day off	3 days off	1 week off	Discharge
38	Mistakes due to lack of knowledge.	Warning	1 day off	Demotion		
39	Leaving work area without permission before final whistle blows indicating end of shift.	Warning	3 days off	1 week off	Discharge	
40	Failure to report for overtime work without good reason after being schedule to work according to overtime policy.	Warning	1 day off	3 days off	1 week off	Discharge

Fig. 17.1 Disciplinary Penalties

Source: "Simplified Discipline Procedure", *Factory Management and Maintenance,* Vol. C, VIII, No. 10, p. 458.

4. DISCIPLINARY PROCEDURE

A systematic disciplinary procedure is essential to maintain established standards of work, conduct and discipline. Professor Jucius has suggested the following steps in a disciplinary procedure:[11]

1. Accurate statement of the disciplinary problem.
2. Collection of full information on the case.
3. Selection of tentative penalties to be applied.
4. Choosing among the alternative penalties.
5. Application of the penalty.
6. Follow-up of the case.

Professors Pigors and Myers have suggested the following steps:

1. Preliminary investigation.
2. An informal, friendly talk.
3. An oral warning or reprimand.
4. A written or official warning.
5. A series of penalties, such as disciplinary lay-off, demotional downgrading, or transfer, and — as a last resort — discharge.

In our country the following steps in a disciplinary procedure may be said to be in vogue:

1. Calling for explanation.
2. Consideration of explanation.
3. Show-cause notice.
4. Notice of holding the enquiry.
5. The holding of enquiry.
6. Punishment.
7. Follow-up.

Calling for Explanation: When an employee's conduct falls short of established standards of work and behaviour and when there is an act of indiscipline or misconduct entailing disciplinary action, management must, with particular care, frame the charges against the employee. The charges of indiscipline or misconduct should be stated clearly and precisely, giving details of offence, time and date of its commitment. The charge-sheet may be served personally or by post. It is not always necessary to draw up a formal charge.

The employee must be asked to give an explanation as to his conduct or behaviour and sufficient time, anywhere from 24 hours to 48 hours, must be given to the employee to come up with an explanation. If the employee requests for some more time, it may be granted.

Consideration of Explanation: If the employees 'submits an unqualified admission of the charges levelled against him' there is no need for any further enquiry and suitable disciplinary measure may be taken against the employee. Or if the employer is satisfied with the explanation of the employee, there is no need for any disciplinary action. If the management is not satisfied with the explanation tendered by the employee, there arises a need to take the third step of serving a show-cause notice.

Show-Cause Notice: With the show-cause notice, which may be in English or in the regional language, the employer provides another opportunity to the employee to explain his conduct and rebut the allegations made against him. The show-cause notice is issued by the manager, who intends to punish the employee. The following figure serves as an example of a show-cause notice.

After careful consideration of your explanation to the letter of charge issued to you on............ it is found that your explanation is unsatisfactory. You are given another chance to rebut the allegations. You are hereby required to show-cause against allegations given below. Your reply should reach the office by.................... at the latest.

Dated .... 19 .... Manager/Employer

Fig. 17.2 Show-cause Notice

If the employee is unable to give proper explanation to rebut the allegations charged against him or his act of indiscipline is grave, a regular enquiry must be held.

Notice of Holding the Enquiry: A notice, giving the name of the Enquiry Officer, time, date and place of enquiry into his conduct is served on the employee who is expected to give relevant information or produce evidence in support of his innocence or contention.

Holding of Enquiry

The institution of enquiry is to be in conformity with the principle of "natural justice" that "no man shall be condemned to consequences resulting from alleged misconduct, unheard and without having opportunity of making his defence." The industrial courts have evolved a procedure of departmental enquiry based on rules governing discipline for those employed by Government under Article 311 of the Constitution of India, according to which no person employed by the Union or a State Government shall be dismissed or removed "until he has been given a reasonable opportunity of showing cause against the action proposed to be taken in regard to him." It is necessary for the employer to hear the employee before he proceeds to take action against him.

The alleged violations of the employee must be stated and a reasonable opportunity to rebut the charge must be given to the employee. He should be allowed to cross-examine witnesses and rebut charges. If the worker wants to produce his own evidence or witnesses he should be given an opportunity to do so by the Enquiring Officer. The enquiry must be just and fair and all reasonable opportunities must be given to the employee to present his case. All the procedural rules of properly recorded by the Enquiring Officer. The procedural rules of enquiry must be strictly followed. The Enquiring Officer must make his report stating his findings as to whether or not the charges levelled against the employee are substantially supported by evidence. Then he may also recommend the nature of action to be taken.

Punishment: When the charges are proved, the necessary disciplinary measure may be taken by management keeping in view the employee's previous record. The manager may conform to the recommendations of the Enquiry Officer or may reject them. It is the management's duty and responsibility to discipline the employee. There is no inherent right to appeal unless the law provides for it.

Follow-up: After the disciplinary action is taken it is necessary to be vigilant and to see whether the disciplinary measure has had a desirable effect on the employee. This is with a view to preventing the employee from repeating this offence. If the employee feels that he is unjustly punished and feels that the enquiry was not in proper order or that he was not given a reasonable opportunity to present his case, there must be recourse for him to appeal.

Dismissal and Discharge: In our country the terms "dismissal" and "discharge" connote different meaning and concepts, though the result of either dismissal or discharge is the same, namely, termination of employment. Discharge is a punishment less severest punishment. In the words of D.N. Vohra[12], "Discharge represents release from contractual obligation. The implication of discharge in industrial employment is nothing more than termination of service where the employee gets full benefit of provident fund, gratuity, etc. whereas dismissal is punishment depriving the workman of all or many benefits. In discharge, a notice is to be given but no notice need be given in the case of dismissal. Dismissal is a punishment inflicted on the employee for misconduct but discharge may not be by way of punishment in all cases. It may be discharge *simpliciter*."

IIPM also observes:[13] "Many standing orders, however, make a distinction between discharge and dismissal and provide for discharge with one month's pay in lieu of notice. The Supreme Court has held that discharge in accordance with such a clause may be valid without an enquiry, if it is bona fide termination of employment only and not a punishment or victimisation. But it must be remembered that termination of employment in this manner would normally bring it within the scope of retrenchment section of the Industrial Disputes Act."

The Model Standing Orders lay down the procedure for dismissal, "No order of dismissal shall be made unless the workman concerned is informed in writing of the alleged misconduct and is given an opportunity to explain the circumstances alleged against him. The approval of the manager of the establishment or where there is no manager, of the employer is required in every case of dismissal and when circumstances appear to warrant it, the manager or the employer may institute independent enquiries before dealing with the charges against a workman."

The Model Standing Orders prescribed the following grounds of misconduct for which a workman may be suspended for a period not exceeding 4 days at a time or dismissal without notice:[14]

(a) Wilful insubordination or disobedience, whether alone or in combination with others, to any lawful or reasonable order of the superior.

(b) Theft, fraud, or dishonesty in connection with the employer's business or property.

(c) Wilful damage to or loss of employer's goods or property.

(d) Taking or giving bribes or any illegal gratification.

(e) Habitual absence without leave or absence without leave for mere than 10 days.

(f) Habitual late attendance.

(g) Habitual breach of any law applicable to establishment.

(h) Riotous or disorderly behaviour during working at the establishment or any act subversive of discipline.

(i) Habitual negligence or neglect of work.

(j) Frequent repetition of any act or omission for which a fine may be imposed to the maximum of 2% of the wages in a month.

(k) Striking work or inciting others to strike work in contravention of any law or rule having the force of law.

A New Approach to Employee Discipline

Mr. G.Y. Mangrulkar of TISCO cites an interesting example of a new approach to employee discipline adopted by an American company:[15]

The company evolved a new philosophy about discipline and punishment. They believed that certain personality traits exercised a decisive influence on a person's record for high standards of workmanship and disciplined behaviour. Demotion, suspension, and similar form of punishment was not an effective method for dealing with lapses of discipline or unsatisfactory work.

They believed that each individual must be given a reasonable chance to play a positive role in the company's operations. They felt, however, that it was possible to play a role if the individual had adequate self-respect. In a person with adequate self-respect, lapses in work or discipline will happen rarely and will stop promptly if brought to his attention in a friendly manner.

The company decided that if such friendly methods did not produce the desired result and an individual repeated his lapses within a short interval, it could be taken as an indication of lack of adequate self-respect. When such a regrettable conclusion had been reached about an individual, the company would not wish to keep him in its employment.

This company believed in influencing employee performance and conduct through such motivational factors as self-respect, financial gain, job interest and respect for superior and they did not wish to "drive" the employee by the instrument of "fear." Then they developed the following simple procedure for maintaining employee discipline.

A Simple Procedure: In the first place — the foreman gives the worker a causal and friendly reminder on the job.

If another incident arises within 4 or 6 weeks, the foreman will again correct it casually on the job, but later call the man to his office for a serious but friendly chat. If the foreman feels that the lapse was unintentional, he will inform the employee that the matter is closed. In case of further incidence within about 6 weeks, this step is repeated with some variation.

The employee who perpetrates another incident within 6 to 8 weeks of the above step is called off the floor into the foreman's office and is directed to go home for the rest of the shift and consider seriously whether he does or does not with to abide by the company's standards. He is informed that he will get full for the time and also that another occurrence of this nature within reasonable time will lead — regretfully — to termination.

If another incident should occur within reasonable time, the employee's service is terminated.

It is reported that the system has worked well. During nearly eight months of its introduction three individuals were processed to the last but one step, i.e., sent home for the rest of the day with pay. Two of them returned to work but left the company within a few weeks. The third genuinely regretted his lapses and assured his foreman that there would be no more trouble.

The Union's role in this context must be appreciated. The management explained to them the background for its decision to eliminate all forms of punishment and expressed the hope that it would get the support of the Union in its efforts to deal with grown-up people as men and not as a collection of schoolboys. The Union did not seem too pleased with this unexpected turn of events but found it difficult to argue the point.

One can well agree with Mr. Mangrulkar when he notes that "... the respect the management has for its workers, the respect the workers have for their management and above all, the respect an individual worker has for himself, provides a strong motivating factor and this fact can be utilised for ensuring high performance and good discipline instead of resorting the measures which bring bitterness and antagonism of the workforce."

5. THE ROLE OF PERSONNEL ADMINISTRATOR

The personnel administrator has an important role to play in fostering proper and effective employee discipline and the following responsibilities of a personnel administrator may be enumerated:

1. He must advise and assist top and line management in the adoption and development of a proper constructive management philosophy regarding the employees and their conduct.
2. He must assist in the formulation of an effective and positive disciplinary policy and procedure.
3. He must help in the communication of the same to all the employees in the organisation.
4. He must see that disciplinary policy and procedure conform to the legal provisions of the state.
5. He must see that the procedure is strictly followed by the management, in every case.
6. He must see that the disciplinary action is fair and consistent with sound principles of personnel administration.
7. He must train executives and supervisors in handling disciplinary problems and cases.
8. He must involve the Union and the employees in the formulation and implementation of disciplinary process and measures.

9. He must help develop standards of self-discipline among the employees.
10. He must help win the confidence of employee in company policies and discipline.

Explaining the role of personnel administrator in the area of employee discipline, IIPM states:[16] "In advising management whether to proceed with a disciplinary case, the personnel officer must give a careful thought to the likely repercussions on discipline and general relationship in the organisation. Even when there is a *prima facie* case against an employee, it is to be considered whether an enquiry, with all publicity and excitement that it causes, is advisable, or whether some other line of action might not prove more effective in improving discipline for the future, such as consultation with the trade union or the works committee in the hope that social pressure may be brought on the delinquement to apologise and not to repeat the offence." It further adds: "Because he has to be familiar with the correct procedure and with tribunal rulings in disciplinary cases, the personnel officer is often felt by top management to be the most suitable person to conduct an enquiry. He has the advantage of being removed from the direct line of production, and he is also well-known to both employees and union. It is generally he who makes the preliminary investigation, and he may be asked to give his views on the enquiry report, even if he does not himself conduct the enquiry."

Happiness Boys

There is another problem, where the personnel manager wants to be popular with the employees and one of the ways he may choose to remain popular is to dissuade the supervisor and line executives from taking any disciplinary action even in the face of gross violation of rules or established standards of work and conduct. This attitude of the personnel executive is, in the long run, harmful to the organisational interests and indirectly, to the interests of the employees. However unpleasant it may be at the moment, disciplinary action must be made to be taken by management, for misconduct condoned is misconduct encouraged, which will have grave repercussions on the organisational morale and discipline. You do not promote harmonious employer and employee relations or union-management relations by encouraging (indirectly) insubordination or some such misconduct on the part of the employee. Neither do you promote any respect for management or company policies on the part of the employees. Employee discipline must come first and personnel administrator must encourage and foster self-discipline among the employees.

Stressing self-discipline, the American Management Association observed:[17] "Until human nature attains greater perfection, the fullest measure of individual freedom of action can be realised only within the framework of an *expressed* discipline. In the social situation, this takes the form of laws; in industry, it is manifest in standards. Firmness in securing conformity in both instances is wholly consistent with our democratic approach. But the requirements must be fair, the reasons behind them must be clear, and in so far as possible, they must be arrived at cooperatively. This is the road to self-discipline; this is the aim of a wise leadership."

REFERENCES

1. M.N. Rudrabasavaraj, "EAM — An Experiment in Indian Businesses", *Indian Management*, May, 1974.
2. Richard E. Walton, "How to Counter Alienation in the Plant", *Harvard Business Review*, November-December, 1972, p. 70.
3. Yoder *et. al., Handbook of Personnel Management,* pp. 14.60-14.61.
4. V.K.R. Menon, "Industrial Discipline", quoted in IIPM, Coimbatore Branch, *Newsflash.*
5. Pigors and Myers, *Personnel Administration,* pp. 323-324.
6. Yoder *et. al., Handbook of Personnel Management,* pp. 14.59-14.60.
7. Pigors and Myers, *op. cit.,* p. 327.
8. G.Y. Mangrulkar, *op. cit.,* p. 31.
9. NICB, *Personnel Practices in Office and Factory,* Personnel Policy Study No. 194, pp. 133-139.
10. Yoder *et. al., op cit.,* p. 14.59.
11. Jucius, *op. cit.,* p. 515.
12. D.N. Vohra, *Law Relating to Dismissal, Discharge & Punishment in the Private Sector* (New Delhi: Labour Law Publishers, 1961), p. 79.
13. IIPM, *op. cit.,* pp. 134-135.
14. D.N. Vohra, *op. cit.,* p., 88.
15. G.Y. Mangrulkar, *op. cit.,* p. 32.
16. IIPM *op. cit.,* pp. 128-129.
17. *Constructive Discipline in Industry,* American Management Association, Special Research Report, 3, 1943, p. 36.

❑ ❑ ❑

PART FOUR

Management of Human Resources — Recent Trends

CHAPTER 18

New Trends in Human Resources Management

In the Part IV we shall deal with the areas, perhaps, for the first time in any text or reference volume on the subject of human resources management in this country or anywhere else. The areas at once relevant, complex and futuristic. These areas constitute six new chapters of Part IV and they are:

1. New Trends in Management of Human Resources.
2. Human Resources Management Education.
3. Computer Applications in Human Resources Management.
4. Children by Choice and Personnel Administration.
5. Evaluation of Human Resources Administration.
6. Challenge of Tomorrow.

Let us begin with the new trends in the field of human resources management. We shall discuss the chapter under:

1. The new role.
2. The new concern.
3. The new professionalism.

1. THE NEW ROLE

There are three important shifts in the role and responsibilities of human resources management areas. First of all, it is realised that people are not merely a cost centre but a great potential profit centre. Managing and converting human resources into human assets is an important responsibility of management, not just personnel executives and in this process the key role of personnel administrators is to proselytise all managers into effective resources in order to maximise productivity, efficiency and profits. Secondly, thanks to the State and public policy, unions, labour legislation, and also his own professional competence, the personnel executive is moving into the inner sanctum sanctorium of power and decision-making and assuming the role of a director on the Board and demonstrating that he knows company's business and can contribute to its strategic decisions as do the directors of fiance, marketing, and manufacturing. Increasingly he is getting involved in long range corporate planning. Thirdly, more important, he is assuming the role of conscience-of-the-corporation and moving into the general management area by assuming the role and responsibilities of general manager, chief executive, managing director and chairman of organisations and this is increasingly happening in Indian industry and elsewhere in other countries, although the usual promotion route to the top used to be through finance, production and marketing. The Fortune in a recent article referred to the personnel executives as the new super corporate heroes in American business. The Harvard Business Review dwelt at length in two articles, the new importance of the role of personnel function.[1]

These changes in the role of personnel function are, according to an authority, due to changing mix of the workforce, changing values of workers, changing demands of employers, and changing demands of government. Last but not the least, is the changing character of professionalism among the HRD practitioners.

Why the New Role and the New Concern?

Observing the American Business scene, Ted Mills writes about the new movement — its timing and deep-seatedness:[2]

"In 1973, At & T produced a film entitled, 'The Quiet Revolution', which was about business's new concern for the quality of human performance at work. Senator Charles H. Percy has labeled this same concern, 'the quality of work phenomenon.' Leonard Woodcock, President of the United Automobile Workers (UAW), refers to it as 'the quality of work life.' John Taylor, Undersecretary of commerce, calls it, 'human productivity.' An early 1973 conference about it in New York was entitled 'The Changing Work Ethics', and a late 1973 American Assembly called it 'The Changing World of Work.' David Jenkin's book refers to it as *Job Power,* while Judson Gooding's book calls it *The Job Revolution.*

"Whatever you call it, something of apparently considerable and growing dimensions, and certainly something unusual in the conduct of business, seems to be happening throughout US industry. In the past three years, there has been a steady increase in US managerial concentration on the human factor in the production of goods and services. With a gathering momentum that is in itself intriguing, a concern at the corporate level for better management of human resources at work seems to be mushrooming. Two reasons make the sudden emergence of this concern of special interest." One is its timing. It is happening at a time, when the then chairman of the Federal Reserve, Arthur Burns could warn in May 1974 that "the very future of our nation is in jeopardy." The second factor is the apparent deep-seatedness of the emerging concern. Human potential and productivity is receiving the great attention in the light of scarce capital. The Swiss playwright, Max Frisch, may have synthesised the new concern eloquently when he wrote, "We sought workers, and human beings came instead."

Ted Mills offers generally accepted four hypotheses and then his own hypothesis to explain the emergence of what he calls the human resources development phenomenon.[3]

Four Hypotheses — The Emergence

1. Alienation, Boredom and Job Dissatisfaction: "One of the prevalent explanations of the need for and emergence of HRD cluster of concerns was that workers were becoming alienated from their jobs and wanted greater satisfaction at work." Perhaps the dramatic example of this was voiced by an auto worker: "All that I do shift after shift, day after day, year after year is fix seven bolts. What do you think will happen to me. I will go nuts."

2. Decreasing Motivation and Increasing Counter-productive Behaviour: "This school dwells on the so-called wane of the Protest work ethic, with its injunctions about diligence, sweat and hard, uncomprising work. Counter-productive behaviour manifests itself overtly (in absenteeism, tardiness, phony sickdays, errors, or quitting) or covertly (in sabotage, slow-down, or secretly diminished output, drug abuse or alcoholism at work)."

3. "Rising Expectations and Declining Institutions: The premise here is that the richer our society becomes in money and education, and further we move from traditional allegiance and moral values, the greater our expectations from demands on the work experience will be. This contemporary shift in values and the uncertainty this has brought to young and old outside the work place cannot help having a profound impact inside that seriously affects the performance of work."

"One major institution after another, including the military and the Catholic Church, is facing a steady decline of authority and respect. They point to rising divorce, homosexuality, crime and drug abuse rates as aberrant manifestations of growing social contempt for tradition and authority."

4. Dying Mechanism and Changing Ideas: The fourth explanation is that we are moving into a brand new post-industrial anti-mechanistic era "which our children are trying to identify for us, and which they say should be manifested by environmental protection, zero growth and a fuller use of knowledge and leisure."

The concept of gross national product as a measure of a nation's well-being and prosperity is being replaced by the concept of net economic welfare.

5. ROI Hypothesis: "This school contends that HRD provides a high potential rate of return on a relatively low-cost, low-risk investment of resources. The ROI school differs significantly from the other four in that it suggests the source of the HRD phenomenon is in business, which itself has discovered — perhaps to its astonishment — that HRD efforts work. It is simply sound management.

"They suggest that senior officers of U.S. business are turning more and more to HRD, not so much for remedial action against various troubling socio-economic disorders, but rather for action towards better management of a conspicuously underdeveloped business resource: its people. They see HRD's emergence in the past few years as a creation of U.S. managers, who have themselves begun to perceive positive bottomline results from HRD activities — results such as significantly diminished accident, absenteeism and error rates and significantly increased morale, quality of product or service, and their important by-product, productivity.

"This school has strong pragmatic reasons such as 'growing awareness of the competitive advantages accruing from HRD innovation', 'rising cost of labour' and 'to seek and develop ways to cut labour cost by fuller development of workforce' and 'to derive new benefits from intelligence, education, and even feelings (i.e., motivation) of employees as well as from their hands. Improved quality of work life can mean improved performance'."

"Perhaps this school's most impressive argument, however, is that investment in HRD provides a high potential rate of return. In researching this article, I talked to a director of a large paper company who strongly believes in this argument. He told the story of a board meeting, convened late, in 1974, at which the 'bewilderment at best and fear at worst' mentality was overwhelming, and at which reports of rising inventories and falling sales in many product lines added to the gloom."

"During the meeting, the management presented a proposal for a new plant to the board. The board decided to put off its construction and, instead, at approximately one fiftieth of the cost, approved replacing some old capital in the existing plant and quadrupling the already begun HRD activity in that same plant. The board became convinced its decision would deliver from the old plant at least the same productivity anticipated from the new. 'If it works', the director said, 'we will get our ROI from investment in people, and we are convinced we will."

Ted Mills identifies six distinguishing characteristics of the companies moving into the HRD field in the mid-1970s.[4]

Six Characteristics

There seem to be six distinguishing characteristics of the companies moving into the HRD field in the mid-1970s.

1. The first is size; emergent companies, like those at the New York conference, seem to be well up in Fortune's "500" list. (This appears to be a trend; before 1970, the noteworthy companies in the field — Lincoln Electric, Donnelly Mirrors, and R.G. Barry — were small.) Although these small companies would dispute it fiercely, one rueful small-business president asserts that big companies can afford large HRD staffs and small ones cannot.

2. The second characteristic of companies in or entering the HRD field is that they tend to be conspicuously well-managed and have consistently high past performance and earnings. Most of these companies have been innovative in other fields as well, so their interest in HRD may be part of a long commitment to advanced business practices.

3. Another common characteristics among HRD companies, one hardly surprising in efforts relating to human concerns, is a high proportion of social psychologists, usually trained in organisational development, on HRD staff and consultant teams. In three years, General motors has reportedly increased the number of such professional in its field operations alone by 2,000% from 6 to 110, excluding its large Detroit headquarters staff.

4. Another interesting and unexpected characteristics of much current HRD effort is that decisions to become active in it frequently seem to be made at senior management levels, and are expressed as policy that works downward into organisations through structural change. Rarely is HRD activity "sold" upward from an individual plant or office as a way to solve some local problem in morale or operations.

5. Perhaps the most distinguishing characteristics of true HRD efforts is its preoccupation with the nature of work itself (a favourite term of HRD people at AT & T). In marked contrast to the concerns of traditional personnel and employee relations departments — concerns such as recruiting and training, housekeeping, compensation and benefits, and labour relations — HRD's professionals are concerned with the organising (or reorganising), designing (or redesigning), and structuring (or restructuring) of line functions and the people and machines performing them.

Peter Drucker has observed that "it is not human nature but the structure of job and work that, in effect, determines how people will act and what management they will require." While this observation, with which Frederick Herzberg would probably agree, is basic to the HRD approach, to many HRD professionals, it does not go far enough. It omits a critically important ingredient in the performance of work: the striking differences between the aptitudes and attitudes of individuals. No two people are exactly alike; the response of one to an improved job structure may differ greatly from that of another.

To most HRD professionals, therefore, the social systems involved in line functions (the allocation of individual and group involvement in decision-making and self-management the degree and nature of supervision, the degree of autonomy in job performance, and so on) are as important to workplace performance as is the structure of the tasks required of people. To HRD experts, an optimised workplace is one that views work as made up of both social and mechanical systems whose elements are in dynamic and effective balance.

6. Until recently, a sixth common characteristics has been the surprising absence of organised labour in HRD advocacy, planning, and implementation.

Although curiously developed up to now, in the years ahead trade union presence may be crucial to facilitating and accelerating HRD efforts.

Union Attitudes in Transition

Union leaders have expressed publicly a variety of reasons why most unions have thus far viewed the movement with attitudes ranging from suspicion and hostility to apathy. There seem to be five common concerns:

1. More efficient, "advanced" work organisations such as Procter & Gamble's (non-union) Lima, Ohio plant or General Foods' famous (non-union) Topeka, Kansas dogfood plant considerably reduce the size of work forces required.
2. In organised companies, most managements refuse to invite union participation in HRD planning.
3. The intellectual sounds made by "bleeding heart" HRD ideologies about the "poor worker" alienate union leader and members alike.
4. A 'happy' work force might diminish labour militance, grievances, and other forces contributing to allegiance to unions.
5. There is an unexpected, but central absence of signal is upward from rank and file workers indicating that improved quality of work life is an important worker concern — one worth going to the mat for.

In just the past year, despite rising union preoccupation with growing unemployment, such negative (win-lose) attitudes toward HRD activities have shown signs of change in many levels of the labour movement.

Two historic turning points in the labour toward HRD have occurred in the last three years. One is the remarkable agreement between the Steel-workers, under I.W. Abel, and the steel industry to form new labour-management bodies now called "employment security and productivity committees." These committees are now in operation in every workplace in the basic industry's "big ten" companies. Using the threat of dangerous foreign competition as powerful glue, the committees substitute a new win-win collaborative effort for the classic win-lose adversary one between management and workers. Today, both the USWA and the industry point with pride to the achievements of these committees improving work and work life, and to a soaring productivity rate in the steel industry."

The other turning point in labour history occurred in the 1973 negotiations between the Automobile Workers under Leonard Woodcock and the "big three" automakers for a new contract. Long an advocate of union leadership and participation in HRD activity in the industry, the UAW demanded that new contract provide for establishment of a joint labour-management "quality of work life committee" in each company. Some of the managements fought the notion as an incursion into management's right to manage. The UAW's victory and the establishment of functioning joint committees in General Motors, Ford and Chrysler was big labour's first bargained-for commitment to active participation in HRD determinations. Today, as in the steel industry, both the managements and the unions express satisfaction with the beginning achievements of these committees.

In addition to these two unions, at least a dozen major international service and manufacturing unions have agreed to participate actively and jointly with management in industry and government in the demonstration project organised by the National Quality of Work Centre. In each pilot project labour-management committees like the USWA's and the UAW's are formed to improve performance and the quality of work life in various kinds of workplaces through collaborative union-management HRD participation.

2. THE NEW CONCERNS OF HUMAN RESOURCES MANAGEMENT

In addition to dealing with the basic concerns of personnel function, such as selection, manpower planning, training and development, industrial relations, there are new concerns in the field of human resources management, which are receiving a great deal of attention and experimentation.[5]

Personnel's New Approaches

If the personnel function is properly integrated within the organisation, the director ought to consider developing or refining expertise in the following human resource activities: attitude surveys or other upward communication programmes, the changing work life; Job design; career planning and development; pay and benefits; and supplemental uses of the workplace.

Attitude Surveys of Other Approaches

Rather than waiting for union organisation drives or other indications of morale problems to occur, companies should be regularly assessing and evaluating their employee's attitudes.

As a senior official of the company points out Marriott's management considers the money well spent:

"Over the long period of years we have been in business, the top management of our company has guaranteed fair treatment to employees and has spent a lot of money making attitude surveys and having personnel representatives follow up on personnel problems. I think our attitude has been like IBM's Tom Watson's. We have thought that employees were our most important asset."

Another effective approach is what one organisation calls "sensing." Certain managers (usually from personnel but not always) hold regular group meetings of 30 to 50 employees at each of this company's plants to identify problems and concerns. This provides both an outlet for employees and information for management.

One leading non-union U.S. employer has started a resident ombudsman programme. Senior personnel are assigned to all of the company's divisions and are available to discuss whatever problems or concerns the employees wish to raise.

Often companies and unions only meet during times of conflict, whereas the parties ought to meet regularly, not just during contract negotiation and administration periods. In one company, for example, the personnel director meets each Friday with the union officers to discuss mutual concerns. Personnel managers must never forget, however, that the union is, and has to be, first and foremost a political organisation.

Changing Work Week and Work Life

The initial rush of enthusiasm for the four-day week in the United States has passed. After some experience with the three-and-four-day schedules, several companies that tried these have returned to a standard five-day week. Nonetheless, the shorter work week does make sense in some carefully selected situations.

Some companies that want to guarantee full utilisation of computer time find the three-day week (three twelve-hour days) works well. Also, some companies have found that the shorter work week can be an attractive recruiting item. Some employees clearly like working longer on some days and having an extra day off, even when it is not the same day each week.

Flexible working hours is a concept imported from Germany, where it was adopted not to satisfy employee needs, but rather in response to urban traffic congestion. Under this kind of system employees arrange their own hours around certain core times when they must be at work each day and around a maximum amount of time that can be carried out from week to week or month to month. The flexible hours system fits well with different lifestyles and with parents' needs to be at home before and after their children's school day. Because it conveys trust and allows an employee a little more freedom in scheduling his own time, flexible working hours can be special form of job enrichment.

Another form of job enrichment also results from a more flexible working system when some employees who do certain kinds of work are allowed to work at home. For example, one company has given its programmers computer consoles for their use at home. And some managers say that on certain types of projects, like report writing, they can work more effectively at home where they are not interrupted by the telephone and other office distractions. In addition to the savings employees can make in commuting time and costs, the company can use its costly office space more efficiently.

Flexible working hours can also provide another job modification, part-time work, that is particularly attractive to women with young children. As well as enhancing a company's affirmative action programme, part-time work can be a solution to boring jobs that, though they are tolerable for four hours may not be tolerable for eight. Also, part-time work frequently meets the needs of students as well as older people who might want to work past retirement and still receive their social security benefits, and it allows couples to share a job.

Not only are the hours most U.S. workers spend at their jobs shifting according to individual schedules, but also the number of years people work is no longer standard. Some unions have won "30 years and out" agreements and some companies have lowered their mandatory retirement ages.

Meanwhile, personnel departments will also have to do a better job of getting the young into business (possibly through the distributive and business education programs in the high schools, and through part-time work), and it will have to do a better job of helping employees find other work or second careers through outplacement programmes. In addition, it will have to help employees adjust to retirement through counselling.

Job Design

As people have become more interested in quality of life issues, it is natural that the quality of working life should also be a concern. Because people spend so much of their waking hours at work, what happens there significantly affects their lives. There is growing evidence that family and community life are both positively affected by improved conditions at work.

The experience so far indicates that job redesign can increase employee satisfaction and productivity. The DowChemical Co. has issued a booklet called "Happiness Is a Whole Job," which stresses the importance of fitting jobs to people rather than the reverse. At AT & T modules of work for some employees provide them with territory or a set of internal or external clients for whom they are responsible. The employees are provided with direct feedback on their performance and with additional opportunities for growth and development.

Other approaches to job design involve creating work teams, involving employees in problem-solving and goal-setting sessions, and in new planning and control activities that give them additional responsibilities. Indicative of the dilemma faced by companies is a comment of Henry Kissinger's: "People think responsibility is hard to bear. It is not — I think that sometimes it is the absence of responsibility that is harder to bear."

Career Planning and Development

To the person who has been in the same job for a long period of time, career development might mean the opportunity to go to a conference. To someone else it might mean a sabbatical to be used for a executive development programme or for independent study. To the young woman or minority person it might mean a realistic career ladder.

One organisation investing career development approaches for affirmative action discovered that there were certain pivotal jobs that most top line managers had been in during their careers. This company is now taking action to see that women and minorities have the opportunity get into those key developmental jobs.

Some organisations are asking their managers to state their career goals in writing. One company is asking its people to define their next two jobs in the company (a very hard but worthwhile assignment for most managers, particularly women) and then assisting the individual in achieving his or her career goal. Other companies are offering "life planning" courses to employees in their forties so that they can plan more thoughtfully for the future.

From the company's viewpoint, career development should be of interest because it provides an orderly succession of talented people who are ready for openings as they occur. Not to be confused with manpower planning, career development grows out of performance improvement and evaluation programmes. These developmental programmes should be supported with information systems, in career advisory services, and — where practical — with a formalised job-posting procedure.

For a number of years, Polaroid and other companies have engaged in career counselling and have recently begun career development workshops. At these voluntary workshops, individuals are given tools to help them better evaluate their own abilities and interests as well as information about various job and career possibilities within the company.

Pay and Benefits

Yet as we live in times of rapid technological and social change, companies are beginning to build personal growth and learning criteria into their pay systems. In some new plants, people are paid for the number of jobs they know how to perform and what they might do rather than precisely for what they do. This pay plan adjustment encourages people to learn more jobs and additional skills, providing them with added mobility and a more satisfying work experience. And it also gives the company added flexibility.

Group bonus plans are being introduced in some companies, which is a visible sign of the importance of team work for some interdependent tasks. Profit sharing and Scanlon-type plans also need to be considered, since they are quite consistent with a number of the work life changes being tried. In addition to rethinking compensation plans along these dimensions, companies should consider revising their system to reflect rapid inflation, depressed stock prices, and changing employee preferences.

The new pension reform legislation, expected action in the health area (such as the Kennedy-Mills bill), additional holidays, longer vacations, and a rising social security base, are causing benefit costs to approach 40% of payroll. Within the next ten years, this figure may exceed 50%. While benefits are, from a tax viewpoint, attractive to the individual, they are still pretty much taken for granted, and few employees recognise the amount the company contributes.

A flexible benefits system can help both the company and the individual.

To be consistent with attempts to recognise individual employee needs, companies could investigate another way of providing private benefits to individuals; supplemental use of the workplace and working time.

Supplemental Uses of the Workplace

Companies have had long and favourable experience with services that provide collective benefits to members of the work groups (such as baseball teams, bowling leagues, organised car pools, credit unions, discounts on company-made consumer products, and travel clubs) as well as with services that provide benefits to the larger community (such as United Fund, blood drives, and so on). What we may see more of in the future are services that provide private benefits to individual workers.

Examples of appropriate private benefits might be company-subsidised day-care centres, time off for non-emergency professional appointments, shopping, going to the bank, barber shop, or beauty parlour, and personal use of company telephones, copying machines, or other equipment, could be done by a company telephone operator. These services would be appreciated by the factory worker, the nature of whose work often requires that he be away from it during his shift.

To benefit employees, some companies permit outside firms to sell gasoline in their parking lots. The employee signals his or her desire for a full tank by leaving the windshield wipers up; each is billed by the gasoline company through the license plate number. A final example of individual benefits is the practice of a small midwest company that allows its office and professional employees to use its WATS line for personal long distance telephone calls after normal working hours. This practice, which costs the company little, is appreciated by the company's employees who have family and friends in distant places.

None of these services are major items, nor do they entail high cost, but some times in the greater scheme of things little touches can be very important. They not only demonstrate employer interest in the employee as an individual but also show recognition of his problems. In these days of inflation, social unrest, urban transportation problems and just the complexities of modern-day living, these extra considerations can become more and more important.

Pressures on top management from within the organisation as well as from without are forcing it to reconsider not only the nature of the services human resources departments ought to be providing, but also the role of human resources in the organisation. Whether the CEO is willing to delegate his own responsibility for the quality of life in the company, he can make sure that his personnel director and staff are able people to whom he gives the freedom necessary for the expanded role. Good work from able people will produce over time the necessary respect and confidence of line management.

With a good staff the personnel director ought, with top management's support, to take the lead in researching and defining the company's human problems and in forming an alliance with top management to solve them. If personnel assumes this proactive role, it can contribute substantially to the company's ability to implement its strategy. Furthermore, line managers will recognise and appreciate the expertise of this source help provides.

As the famous philosopher Charlie Brown has said, "There is no heavier burden than a great potential." This potential is surely the case with respect to personnel today. Personnel has the opportunity to help make the corporation more of a community by assisting in managing human resources in ways that will both increase productivity and enhance the quality of working life.

Flexible Hours

Another interesting experiment that is catching the imagination of managements all over the world is the flexible hours, what with the tremendous problems of commuting, transport systems and stresses and strains.[6]

Study of Flexible Working Hours Scheme: A study of experiments with flexible working hours has been conducted by the Unit of Manpower Studies of the Department of Employment of the United Kingdom.

A report on the result of study was published in January 1975. A system of flexible working hours is defined in the report as one that allows employees to choose, within certain limits: the starting and ending times for work, as long as they work during certain core-time periods and accumulate a specified total number of hours worked per week or month.

Organisation in the United Kingdom first introduced systems of flexible working hours in 1971. It is estimated in the report that by the start of 1974 approximately 500 British organisations with about 100,000 employees had adopted some form of flexible work time.

Most of these firms were in the pharmaceutical, engineering, and food, drink and tobacco industries, in the insurance industry or in public services, local authorities and public utilities; most workers involved were in white-collar occupations.

Five categories of flexible work schemes are identified in the study:

1. A certain number of hours must be worked per day;
2. A certain number of hours must be worked per week;
3. A certain number of hours must be worked per month;
4. Flexibility between months exists and credit hours must be taken off outside core-time; or
5. Credit hours can be taken as half or whole days off. Most schemes restrict flexibility somewhat when the workload requires it.

The study notes three major problems to be anticipated when establishing a flexible working hours scheme: practice regarding existing privileges, such as medical visits during working hours; definition of overtime; and method of time-recording.

Attendance practices and reactions of employees to the schemes were gauged in several surveys. It was noted that between one-third and one-half of all employees questioned worked hours very similar to their previous fixed hours. Many workers amassed credit hours (where there they could be carried over), while there were very few instances of carryover of debit hours. In general, the employees surveyed expressed great satisfaction with the operation of the schemes; the most popular advantages were better balance between work and private life, avoidance of rush-hour traffic, and ability to finish a task before leaving work. Most workers questioned found no great disadvantages to the schemes; the most widely disliked feature of the schemes was the time-recording requirement.

Employers were found to be generally satisfied with the schemes though that report advises that employers' judgments are impressionistic since most data collected concern attendance and not performance comparisons. Several benefits of the schemes were cited by employers; elimination of time-keeping losses, quicker starts upon arrival at work; removal of the need for petty discipline; increased responsibility among staff; and a better working climate. While a substantial minority of managers questioned felt that productivity had improved, most felt there had been little change, and a very few felt that productivity had declined. None of the firms surveyed were considering a return to fixed hours.

The report mentions briefly the increased difficulties of devising an efficient flexible working hours scheme for production workers, though it indicates that several firms have introduced successful schemes in some production departments.

The study concludes by noting that flexible working hours might well develop as a normal feature of employment in a significant part of the economy. It is stressed that an interested organisation should embark on a flexible work time scheme only after consultation with employee representatives and that results of the scheme should be monitored carefully.

Flexible Organisations

All over the world there is a great demand to change the traditional authoritarian organisational structure of pyramid, because there is a general erosion of authority and a general revolt against behind subservience to hierarchy and authority.[7]

What do a beehive, doughnut, a bell, a super griddle and a ladder have in common? The answer is they are all organisation structures that are being used to overcome the inadequacies of the pyramid, that most faithful of all hierarchical designs.

"In a time of rapid market and technological change, growing complexity and a shift of emphasis to individual aspirations, top management can no longer rely exclusively on the pyramid," says Neville Osmond, development manager for Management Selection Ltd. (MSL), a personnel consulting firm in the UK.

"The company pyramid only shows the static picture. What really matters are the dynamic aspects of how an organisation works and the personal inter-relationships", says John McDonald, head of the Dusseldorf office of McKinsey & Co., US management consultants.

"In today's technologically dominated world, pyramidal concepts no longer have any credence," says Ronald Hainsworth, a salaries expert at Esso Petroleum Co. in the UK.

These are just a few of the experts who cite the limitations of the pyramid and who believe it embodies outmoded concepts. They are not suggesting that the pyramid has completely outlived its usefulness and should be abandoned entirely.

The Bell

The result is a variety of variations on the pyramid theme, which have been dubbed with such names as 'beehive' and 'doughnut.' These fanciful terms help to visualise in a simple and evocative way something which is much more complex.

The structural variations aim primarily at toning down the strict autocratic nature of the pyramid accentuated by its sharply defined apex. The 'bell' for example is a company structure depicting the idea of collegial management. The apex of the pyramid is broadened by a top management team of leaders.

Collegial management is highly popular among European concerns such as Demag AG of Duisburg, West Germany's heavy machine building company, and Switzerland's AG Brown, Boveri & Cie., one of the world's leading manufacturers of heavy electrical equipment.

The Beehive

The 'beehive' company structure also attempts to soften the pinnacle of the pyramid by blunting it.

But the beehive is designed to do more than accommodate the trend away from autocracy. It also tackles the problems of trying to indicate the human relationships that do not show up in the pyramid.

The three-dimensional beehive, consisting of a series of concentric circles, overcomes this pyramidal inadequacy. The innermost circle represents the apex of the management hierarchy. The surrounding bands constitute the supervisory echelons and correspond to the various levels of management. Pie-shaped segments represent the company's principal operating divisions or functions.

The chief executive's symbol is placed in the middle circle, but not necessarily in the exact centre. If he trends, for example, to favour one particular division — perhaps because he was promoted out of it — his symbol is placed closer to it.

A similar system is used at lower management levels. If a manager is close to his boss, his symbol is placed near the inner rim of the band. Where the reverse is true it is placed at the outer rim. If two managers within a department are congenial, their symbols are placed side by side. When they are on bad terms a space is left between the symbols, reflecting the degree of hostility.

The Ladder

Some companies see the 'ladder' as the answer to the problem of where to locate the swelling numbers of specialists being added to their staffs. John Argenti, a British management consultant suggests lifting all the management services out of the pyramid and placing them in a neutral ladder apart from the hierarchy.

This leaves executives free to call for the advice of any specialist without having to go through the hierarchical channels. It also releases the executive communication network from the obstruction of specialist departments. The specialists, on the other hand, are left to their speciality instead of being forced to climb to positions in the company they are incompetent to fulfil.

Most of the attempts to modify the pyramid reflect a growing trend towards more democratic forms of management. Employee participation and job enrichment are highly fashionable, and the growing complexity of company operations is forcing the delegation of authority to lower reaches of the hierarchy.

Meanwhile authority is gravitating towards where the information is.

This has led to what one company expert calls 'bottom-up-management.' There has been a shift from the downwards relationship characterised by participative and supportive management.

A good example of this approach is the inverted pyramid structure that has been adopted by Jewel Companies Inc., the US supermarket chain. It reverses the normal boss-subordinate relationship.

"Each of our executives is the first assistant to the person in line below him," explains Franklin J. Lunding, Jewel's chief financial officer. "He is charged not so much with directing and supervising, as with offering assistance to those reporting to him. The effect is to turn the organisation chart upside down."

Now companies are beginning to think in open systems terms. Open systems theory takes into account that the company with all its inter-linked sub-systems is itself part of the larger social system in which it exists. This has led to the realisation that the company is open to the surrounding influence of the outside world."

The new awareness of the influence of the social environment has prompted some of the larger companies, such as the oil and chemical firms, to think about the kind of organisation structures they are likely to need by the year 2000. They are particularly interested in assessing what demands and constraints are going to placed on their companies in the future by the aspirations of their employees.

Peter Drucker, the US management theorist, suggests that the well balanced company organisation should encompass a three-way relationship. In addition to the top-down and bottom-up relationship, there should be a sideways relationship between one department or colleague and another.

As the limitations of the pyramid become increasingly apparent to a growing number of companies the rush to institute more flexible alternatives is likely to intensify. But McKinsey's McDonald warns that companies considering a structural change should not think that there is any pre-packaged solution to their problems. While at first sight a doughnut or a beehive might seem to fit bill, there are almost always factors which make every company unique in its requirements.

Flexible Pay and Benefits

Increasingly the cafeteria approach to compensation plans and benefits emphasising flexibility is being talked about in order to attract, retain and motivate people. D.A. Leader Jr. observes:[8]

"We shall also have to show flexibility in designing compensation plans; payments in both cash and benefits will increasingly be tailored to individual needs. The young married man recently out of school and possibly in debt will need more cash and more life insurance to get his career and family started than the older person, who will need more medical insurance and perhaps deferred compensation for tax advantages. These individually adjusted compensation programmes will probably be more expensive than what we are accustomed to, and strong opposition from controllers can be taken for granted. However, if personnel managers are to lead and guide, rather than follow and float into the future, they must initiate these new plans and demonstrate their effectiveness and long-run payoff; ultimately, that should silence the opposition.

It looks as if comptrollers are also going to have to adjust to new benefit costs. Like their employees, large organisations are ceasing to view fringe benefits as competitive leverage in employment and view them instead as a standard corporate obligation. "Standard," in the 1970s, will probably include dental insurance, prepaid drug plans, more complete psychiatric coverage, and more comprehensive employer-paid insurance for employees and dependents. Other new areas covered may be education and day care for children and even hitherto private concerns such as insurance against unexpected or large legal bills. (The American Bar Association has a pilot programme under way to identify individual legal needs and what people would have to pay in premiums to take care of them.)

HRD Scene in India — New Trends

1. The traditional role of a "Canteenwala" or "Show-cause-noticewala" of personnel specialists is fast disappearing in Indian Industry and business and is being replaced by young competent professionals, who have made significant contribution not only to their discipline and field of operations but also general management processes and enterprise problems so much so, in several cases, they have risen to become chief executives, managing directors and chairmen of their corporations.
2. By virtue of their expertise and competence they have become valued members of the board of directors.
3. A new crop of young competent professionals are moving the function away from the traditional areas of welfare and industrial relations into such new areas as OD, manpower planning, management development, compensation systems, organisation structures, communications, long range planning, managerial styles, joint consultation machinery, ergonomics, quality of work life and job designs etc.
4. There is a trend towards appointing specialists in such areas as manpower planning, selection and recruitment, training and development organisation, communications, compensation systems, career planning, industrial relations etc., who will be better qualified to provide the necessary expertise and competent advice and service to the organisation and management.
5. The larger business houses have been setting the pace in this field and providing opportunities for greater varieties of experimentation and evolving sound progressive personnel policies, systems and procedures.
6. The multinationals operating in the country have brought along with their technical know-how a great deal of managerial know-how, particularly in the area of human resources management.
7. Closely related to size is the sophistication of management. As our organisations grow large, higher will be the sophistication of management as witnessed in public sector, multi-nationals and large private business houses. Greater the sophistication of management, greater is the sophistication and experimentation in the area of human resources management.
8. Some of the corporations, especially personnel experts, visualise great opportunities in the computer applications in the personnel area and some

routine applications such as payroll, selection, manpower inventory etc. have already been started in the country. More interesting and technical applications are likely to follow in the near future.

9. The Indian Institute of Personnel Management, National Institute of Labour Management, Xavier's Institute of Labour Relations, Tata Institute of Social Sciences, Institutes of Management have started a whole of process of completely revamping the entire educational pattern of post-graduate courses in personnel management with a view to preparing the aspiring students for the new role, responsibilities and challenges of a personnel career.
10. Human resources managers will be increasingly called upon to play the role of facilitation in the process of joint consultation and workers participation in management and the shop floor.
11. Flexible organisations with a view to maximising managers' participation in management, breaking down the hierarchical pyramidical structures, facilitating decentralisation and delegation will be a major preoccupation in the profession. As a corollary to this is the need, for systems of motivation for the managers, supervisors and employees and designing a motivation mix for these categories in order to attract, retain and challenge them to reach their maximum potentialities.
12. There is a great demand for managers in view of the increasing industrialisation as well as increasing sophistication of business and the generation of executive leadership will be a major challenge for the personnel people.
13. The optimum utilisation of human capacity and conversion of the abundant human resources into human assets will be an increasing concern in the future.
14. Career planning succession planning, and manpower planning will be a major pre-occupation.
15. Designing innovative compensation system, particularly in areas like linking bonus with productivity and production will tax the ingenuity of personnel specialists.
16. Collective bargaining and industrial relations will continue to be the bread and butter issues.
17. Employee alienation and discipline will pose to be a serious problem area.
18. With increasing cost of manpower, fringe benefits and employee services, there is an increasing demand from organisations particularly the top management for an evaluation of the impact and effectiveness of human resources management in terms of some kind of cost-benefit analysis. The human resources expert would have to develop tools and indices to measure the effectiveness of his function and highlight his and his division's contribution to the organisation's productivity, profits, effectiveness and growth.

One of the personnel managers presenting his paper, The Personnel Man in Prospect, at an annual Conference of NILM, observed:[9]

One of his primary responsibilities will be to participate in the process of change and make the acceptance of this change smooth and orderly. This can be illustrated by a look at some of the fundamentals of an enlightened personnel policy in any economic endeavour of size today. They are:

(a) Provision of an effective organisation structure capable of achieving the economic and social objectives.

(b) Managing the organisation with the right personnel and ensuring reasonably decent working conditions.

(c) Creating and maintaining a level of morale in the enterprise which promotes the fullest participation of every employee in the common endeavour.

(d) Encouraging everyone in the enterprise to develop and grow remembering every employee has a potential-worth aspect.

(e) Securing maximum operational efficiency and providing easily seen rewards to employees.

(f) Ensuring a behaviour of cooperation between individuals and groups within the organisation and preparing them for changes.

My image of the Human Resource-Man of tomorrow is this:

* He will be found in the mainstream of Management responsibility in industry and will have adopted the basic economic goals of the enterprise as his own.
* He will have acquainted himself with the economics of the enterprise and with its product lines and markets.
* He will read the Company's balance sheets in the belief that business is meant for economic results, which alone can sustain social gains.
* He will know about the technical processes involved in his enterprise, foresee the human consequences of technological innovations and will become an instrument of the acceptance of the changed process.
* He, from his base in Management, will make the people employed also as the business of the Management and help his colleagues secure employee and group participation in the fulfilment of objectives.

Lastly,

* He will keep his organisation chart up-to-date by mentioning the latest strength of men employed in the organisation and keep reminding the Management Group to get so concerned about costs that losses and gains in human values figure as prominently in their calculations as the material ones.

3. THE NEW PROFESSIONALISM

To fulfil the new role and responsibilities and new concerns and challenges of the contemporary human resource management function, the essential pre-requisite is professionalism. In the not too distant past, this function has suffered considerably from the lack of it. Richard Anton, Vice-President of General Telephone, aptly states:[10]

"For too many practitioners in the employees relations field tend to neglect basics in favour of the latest fad; and to the degree that this is true, they do a disservice both to the profession and the business they serve. As a result, I think you will find many companies very weak in the development and articulation of a philosophy concerning their approach to their employee relations (or human resources) work. From my own observations, many employee relations people fail or never try to identify and reconcile employee and company objectives. One of the results is that too often employee relations programmes do not effectively support company business objectives or, sometimes, do not even reveal an awareness of their existence. "This observation also holds good in our situation also. The general criticism of the human resources function is that there is no participation in the mainstream of business operations and the personnel people are pretty lightweights in terms of pulling their weight in the policy-making and decision-making process of business and do not even bother to read the balance sheet."

However, of late, there is an interesting trend in India of isolated enclaves of great competence and besides their own field, these personnel executives have pulled their weight in the highest councils of business so much so that they have pushed themselves in to the driver's seat, occupying the positions of Chairmen, managing directors, chief executives and general managers. Even if such dynamism cannot be expected universally, a certain sense of professionalism in the field is a *sine qua non*. Improvement of professionalism in the field of human resources management would entail the observation of the following five aspects:

1. ***Education and knowledge of the modern concepts, tools and techniques of human resources management:*** This is so crucial that we have discussed at some length and detail in the next chapter.
2. ***A period of practical training and apprenticeship:*** While this is not formalised and institutionalised as in some of the older professions like law, medicine, in most progressive organisations, there is a period of training and apprenticeship as some kind of trainee varying from 16 months to 24 months.
3. ***A code of ethics:*** The Indian Institute of Personnel Management has drawn up a code and it is necessary for the practitioners to observe the code fairly and squarely.
4. ***Contribution to the organisation:*** It is necessary to make a contribution to (1) optimum utilisation of human capacity; (2) converting human resources into human assets; (3) increasing productivity and efficiency; (4) improving the quality of work life; meeting the physiological, safety, social, self-esteem and self-actualisation needs of people, particularly the basic human needs (which are still to be met in most cases in our country); (5) encouraging and supporting creativity, innovation and dynamism; (6) improving the quality of life.
5. ***Contribution to society:*** A profession must serve the society at large and service to society is altruistic. A profession has to internalise the dominant values and goals of the society and thus make a contribution to the national and social purposes. Removal of unemployment and poverty, optimum utilisation of human capacity, converting masses into human assets,

population control are some of the immediate and urgent challenges to which the personnel professional must address himself to and make a contribution.

Mr. Naval Tata the founder president of National Institute of Labour Management addressing the members deplored the fact that while National Institute of Labour Management has made great strides from its inception more than 25 years ago, the Institute has failed to make any significant impact on the national scene in terms of influencing the state policy, in this vital area of human resources management and he requested the members and the Institute to come out and express themselves on vital issues of State government policy, labour legislation and current problems of human resources management and thus influence policy-making and decision-making at the highest level in the nation.

The professional associations, Indian Institute of Personnel Management and National Institute of Labour Management must assume a great responsibility in not only enhancing the effectiveness and image of the profession but also influence the public policies. The Institutes of Management and Personnel Management need to make a contribution to the generation of first rate professionals in the human resources management field through better education, research, experimentation and testing. The Central and State Governments, who indeed gave so much fillip to the profession in its formative years, can provide greater opportunities to the professionals to influencing policy, encourage professionalism and experimentation and also provide all facilities for education, training and development. There is of course tremendous scope for experimentation, research and practice in the Government, because, as Robert McNamara put it, the state is the largest single management complex.

However, in the ultimate analysis, it is the professionals who have to carry the ball and make a contribution to human endeavour by their competence, expertise and practice. David Leader Jr. highlights six courses of action that can be taken now by the professionals to prepare the future.[11]

1. Do some organised long-range planning. For example, at Rand Corporation each of the supervisors is responsible for his own research and recommendations for the future. At least once a year the personnel staff has a series of meetings to talk about what is new and the direction our work should take.
2. Sharpen your reporting skills to help management make a better personnel decisions. At Rand, this is done through an annual report to top management covering not only employment, salary and benefit statistics, but also analysis of significant activities and trends.
3. Get young people into positions of responsibility sooner. One way is through a well-planned summer employment programme for college student, which gives them not only an opportunity to earn money, but also a preview of what regular employment with your company is like.
4. Give a generous amount of time and thought to the development of your own staff. Do not neglect your own department in your efforts to work out programmes for others. Staff development activities should include educational assistance and encouragement to attend professional meetings, conduct research and present papers, associate with contemporaries in their working environments elsewhere in the company.

5. Reorganise your personnel staff members on a project basis, so they would not be isolated in purely functional areas. For example, the benefits administrator should have an extensive background in insurance, legal areas, and data processing, with some knowledge of medical terminology, and so forth. He should be a specialist, not a broad generalist, but his full potential will not be realised if you restrict him to benefits work. At Rand recently, to prepare a study of our fringe benefits programme for management, a team was formed with the associate personnel manager as project leader. The benefits administrator was an indispensable member of the team, of course, but so were the salary administrator and several other specialists in the personnel department.
6. Take steps now to adjust to the changing nature and composition of the workforce from social, racial, and economic standpoints. Attitudes and ways of handling what used to be routine matters will have to respond to increased number of minority employees, and, in particular, hard-core hires.

To help our supervisors handle these new responsibilities, at Rand we arranged a series of administrative meetings with them to discuss work standards in the context of habits and attitudes of new employees from varying cultural, educational, and work backgrounds.

To summarise, these six action areas for the future are long-range planning, analytical reporting to top management, giving more responsibility to young people, development of the personnel staff itself, organisation around problems rather than around specialised, isolated functions, and building a personnel staff sensitive to the changing social world and representative of the company's employee mix. In implementing these ideas, a planned, but flexible, response to change is essential.

By closely observing the entire group personnel department, Peter Honey was able to pinpoint the changes in behaviour which would bring the personnel in U.K. to his model of professionalism.[12]

"The extent to which the personnel function can be 'professional' depends, in the main, on:

The enlightenment of line managers (including managing director and group directors), because as consumers of personnel services they are so influential in shaping what those services should provide.

The Phase of development of the Company, because there are differing pressures, depending on whether it is in the "establishing itself/entrepreneurial phase", or the 'consolidating/bedding down phase or the slimming for survival phase' etc.

The funding of the personnel function, because this largely determines the sort of expertise personnel can hire and/or retain, the sheer number of hands and brains in the function and so on.

The Trade unions, because they make a vast difference to what personnel spends its time on.

The professionalism of the personnel director, because "The buck stops there."

The personal credibility of corporate personnel with the managing director, the group personnel managers and various demanding line managers, who tend to exert pressure on corporate personnel as a way of leapfrogging the local system.

The personnel function is faced with 'crunch' dilemmas, the chief ones currently being:

Whether to be 'warm' or 'cold', or in other words, to what extent personnel is in business to influence the business plan or provide various caring services for the company's human resources.

What to centralise and what to decentralise, it poses the 'classic' organisation problem.

What balance to strike between long-term and short-term activities, the temptation to do the short-term activities is too strong often.

What satisfactions to go for and / or admit to, personnel is a thankless job, because personnel successes are claimed by the line as theirs where personnel failures are attributed to personnel.

What to do and what not to do, it has a critical priority, problems, because it cannot do all that it would wish to do and, therefore, forced to make choices.

"However, I think there should be an attempt to articulate standards, if only as mechanism for 'straightening-out' relationship between people who have to work together."

"Setting Priorities: A personnel manager should be able to determine and state his current priorities unhesitatingly, showing how they relate to the short and long term needs of the business, to the resourcing, situation and to the credibility of the personnel function."

"Shaping Activities in the Light of Priorities: A personnel manager should be able to demonstrate that the activities he is engaged in are consistent with the priorities. As a guide, I would expect a minimum of 60% of his time to be spent on activities directly related to priority areas, a further 25% to maintain the day-to-day administration aspects, leaving a 15% 'cushion' for development activities."

"Comprehension of the Business: A personnel manager should be able to rattle off the vital statistics of the industry correctly, he should be able to describe the business objectives the latest performance indices and the current concerns of the 'the line' correctly."

"Involvement: A personnel manager should be sufficiently acceptable to line management that they voluntarily invite his involvement in problem-solving and decision-making more often he has to 'gatecrash.' As a guide I would expect him to be present during all discussions involving change in the management of human resources.

Public Relations: A personnel manager should demonstrate that he understands the importance of being seen to do things well — Additionally I would expect him continually to create feasible ways of publishing the achievements of the day-to-day maintenance or administrative part of his function (to maintain his credibility in the eyes of line management)."

"Use of Explicitness: A personnel manager should be able to distinguish correctly between models and charts, and between goals, objectives, and plans, not shrug it off as mere semantics."

"Being Clear about Line/Staff Responsibilities: A personnel manager should be to articulate the criteria he uses to decide who is responsible for what. I would expect him to demonstrate that he is clear about the implications of the personnel department taking on too many line responsibilities."

"Reinforcing Line Cooperation/Help: A personnel manager should possess at least 75 per cent of the following 'winning ways' when interacting with line managers:

Being a 'good listener.'

Using probes that get to the heart of the matter but not in a threatening way out to prove you wrong/inadequate way.

Showing problems are understood by summarising them in such a way that the line manager agrees without having to correct them.

Being positive far more than negative by suggesting solutions to problems rather than explaining why things cannot be done.

Remaining inadequacy and errors in such a way that line managers conclude they are safe to trust and respect the personnel manager.

Merging in with the style of the line managers in a non-dominating way.

Professional Credibility: A personnel manager should be able to demonstrate that he can talk sensibly and authoritatively about at least 75 per cent of the following:

Administrative systems	Manpower planning
Appraisal systems	Organisation planning and development
Behavioural sciences	Pensions
Business planning/corporate planning	Personnel administration, policies and procedures
Career development	Profit centre management
Communication techniques and systems	Personnel records and research
Compensation packages	Recruitment and selection practices
Ergonomics and environmental planning	Redundancy procedures
Induction	Retirement packages
Industrial relations	Safety and health
Job enlargement and enrichment	Salary structuring and reviewing
Job evaluation	Trade unions
Legislation	Training and management development
Management by objectives	Training needs analysis
Management succession planning	Welfare and counselling.

REFERENCES

1. Fred K. Foulkes, "The Expanding Role of the Personnel Function", *Harvard Business Review*, March-April 1975, p. 71, and Ted Mills, "Human Resources — Why the New Concern?", HBR, March-April, 1965, p. 120.
2. Ted Mills, *Ibid.*, pp. 110-121.
3. *Ibid.*, pp. 128-34.
4. *Ibid.*, pp. 124-127.
5. Fred Foulkes, *op. cit.*, pp. 78-84.
6. Employers Federation of India, *Industrial Bulletin*, Jan. 1, 1976, p. 1.

7. See David Oates, "Is the Pyramid Crumbling?" *International Management,* July, 1971.

8. D.A. Leader Jr., "Personnel Policies for the 1970s", *Personnel*, Sept-October, 1968, p. 13.

9. S.C. Bakshi, "The Personnel Man in Prospect" in Y.B. Bhonsle (ed.), *Personnel Management — The Indian Scene,* Delhi, S. Chand & Co., 1977, pp. 70-71.

10. Fred Foulkes, *Op. cit.,* p. 77.

11. *Ibid.,* pp. 14-17.

12. Peter Honey, "On the Trail of the Personnel Professional", *Personnel Management,* Institute of Personnel Management, U.K., pp. 33-35.

❑ ❑ ❑

CHAPTER 19

Human Resources Management Education

Considering the challenges facing human resources management now and in the near future, it may not be sufficient to possess any university degree or a diploma in Social Science of recognised institution with a law degree, as many companies require to become personnel executives. The current social science and labour welfare bias supplemented by labour legislation expertise is woefully inadequate to discharge the new and complex responsibilities of the personnel function. With the management movement gaining momentum, with the growth of management institutes and with the growth of professional management in India, the future human resources management executives would have to be specialised in human resources management along with some allied courses in management. A new programme of education is clearly called for.

A NEW PROGRAMME OF EDUCATION

The following courses may be suggested to those aspiring for human resources management career:

Considering the challenges facing personnel administrators in the near future it may not be sufficient to possess any University degree or a diploma in Social Science of a recognised institution, with a law degree, as many companies require, to become personnel executives. With the management movement gaining momentum in India and with the growth of management institutions it may not be impracticable to expect the future personnel executive to have specialised in personnel management and industrial relations with some allied courses in management. The following courses may be suggested to an aspiring personnel administrator.

English	Cost-Benefit Analysis
Two or three Indian Languages	Manpower Planning
Economics	Research Methodology
Statistics	Personnel Management
Psychology	Industrial Relations
Political Science	Labour Legislation
Legal Controls of Business Enterprise	Time Study

General Management
Human Relations
Labour Problems
Business Policy
Production Management
Finance Management
Materials Management
Computer Applications
Collective Bargaining
Wage and Salary Administration
Testing
Job Analysis
Job Evaluation
Supervision
Industrial Sociology
Ethics

The Indian Institute of Personnel Management devoted their entire national conference in 1971 to Education and Training in Personnel Management and after three days of detailed deliberations suggested the following curriculum to Universities and Institutes of Management.

CURRICULUM DETAILS EVOLVED AT THE CONFERENCE

PART I — PRE-REQUISITES

1. **Mathematics:**

Algebra
Indices
Quadratic Equations
Logarithm
Arithmetic and Geometric Progressions
Summation of Series (Finite and Infinite)
Permutation and Combination
Binomial Theorem
Determinants and Matrices Application to Solution of Simultaneous Equations
Integral and Differential Calculus including of Simple Differential Equations
Elementary Trigonometry — Trigonometric Ratios, Reading Trigonometric Tables.

2. **Quantitative Analysis:**

Concept of Statistics — Its Meaning, Scope and Place in Quantitative Analysis
Methods of Presenting Statistical Information
Methods of Presentation of Statistical Information by Graphs, Charts and Tables
Frequency Distribution, Measures of Central Tendency
Mean, Median, Mode, Measures of Dispersion, Standard Deviation
Variance, Quartile, Mean Deviation Range
Probability Theory, Definition of Probability
Independent and Dependent Events — Mutually Exclusive Events
Theoretical Distributions —
Binomial, Poisson and Normal Continuous and Discrete
Chi Square Test
F Test
Simple, Random Sampling
Stratified Sampling

S.Q.C. Techniques

Forecasting Techniques:

Curve Fitting and Methods of Least Squares

Correlation and Regressive Theory — Multiple and Partial Cemelation

Factor Analysis, Time Series, Secular Trend, Cyclical

Seasonal and Irregular Fluctuations

Index Numbers — Analysis of Variance, Linear Programming

Elementary Accounting and Financial Concepts

Book Keeping, Profit and Loss Account — Balance Sheet

Basic Techniques of Financial Accounting:

1. Earning Power Analysis
2. Break-even Analysis
3. Analysis and Costs for Managerial Decisions
4. Presentation of Costs for Performance Appraisal and Control

Budgeting:

Types of Budgets

Budget Procedures

Methods, Preparation, Operation and Control of Budgets

Alternative Choice Problems — Future Costs and Differential Costs

Make or Buy Decisions

Capital Expenditure

Return on Investment and the Concept of Present Value

3. Principles of Economics:

Nature, Scope and Significance of Its Study

Economics and Related Sciences

Limitations of Economic Laws

Methods of Economics Analysis

Production Process

Factors of Production

Land, Labour, Capital and Organisation

Industrial Location

Demand — Meaning of Demand — Law of Demand

Demand Schedules and Curves — Elasticities of Demand

Supply — Meaning of Supply, Law of Supply

Supply Schedules and Curves — Elasticities of Supply

Assumptions of Perfect Competition

Short and Long Period Supply

Supply under Monopolies

Fixation of Price

Money: Theory of Money

Concept of National Income and Gross National Product (GNP)

Concept of per Capita Income

Theory of Wage

Theory of Interest

Study of Organisations Affecting Money System

O.I.N.F., World Bank (IBRD), I.C.I.C.I., R.B.I. and similar organisations

Problems of Underdeveloped and Undeveloped Countries

Economic Planning in India

(a) National level

(b) Industrial level

4. **Effective Communication:**

Written Communication:

Exercise in problem analysis and report writing to improve the skills of written exposition through a clear, concise, convincing and correct writing style.

Oral Communication:

Purposive Group Conversation

Conference Leadership

Business Speech.

PART II — BASIC CORE

1. **Social Work Methodology:** (Social Case Work, Individual, Group and Community):

Basic Concept of Social Case Work

Development of Case Work Process

Application of Case Work Method to Personnel Problems

Methods of Case Study

Social Group Work — Role of Social Group Work in Personality Development

Principles and Methods

Group Work in Industrial and Business Setting

Principles of Community Organisation

Community Organization as a Method of Social Work

Adjusting Social Welfare Resources to Social Welfare Needs within the Functional Field.

Problems Raised by Individual and Group Differences in: Language, Caste, Culture, Age, Sex, etc.

2. **Organisational Behaviour:**

Basic Concepts of Social Sciences in Relation to Business and Industry.

Understanding of human behaviour — Needs, goals, habits — Learning, aptitudes and abilities and personality.

Individuals in relation to others — Social and task-roles — Role conflict and resolution — Maladjusted relationship — Improving social relationships.

Groups at work — Formal and informal groups — Origin of group dynamics, Group cohesiveness — Group pressures and standards — Individual motives and group goals — Effect of cooperation and competition — Group factors and workers' productivity.

Formal and informal organisation — Task oriented group — Structural balance — Organisational goals and interaction process — Management of change — Role interdependence — Leadership — Power relations — Authority and group-emotion — Influence without authority — Communication — Participation — Competence — Creativity and organisational effectiveness — Human behaviour at work.

3. Business Law:

Purpose of Law and Conception and Justice

Indian Judicial Structure and Process

Legal Forms of Association

Joint Enterprise, Partnership, Indian Company Law

Rights of Property

Building Regulations Including Dangerous and Obnoxious Industries and Trades

Elements of Commercial Laws and their Influence on the Running of a Business

Law of Contracts and Conditions of Contracts

Sale of Goods — Claims and Disputes

Transportation of Goods

Laws Affecting International Trade

Import and Export trade.

PART III — RELATED CORE

1. Business and Social Environment:

Political: Political Philosophy — Socialistic Pattern of Society

Parliamentary Democracy and Roles of Political Parties

Leadership Succession

Economic: Monetary, Fiscal, Industrial and Labour Policies of the State and their Impact on Business

Social: Cultural Background

Castes and Communities

Joint Family System

Linguistics and Religious Groups and National Integration

Profession and Communities

Migration of Population

Literacy Standards

Co-operation in Community Life

Population Growth

Standards of Living

Income Groups

Impact of Foreign Cultures

Social Reforms

Changing Social Values.

2. Principles of Industrial Engineering:

Productivity Techniques used in place of Industrial Engineering

Method Analysis

Motion Study Techniques — Process Charts

Flow Process, Operator Process

Simultaneous Motion and Man and Machine Charts

Work Measurement

Work Measurement in Office-Benefits of Work

Measurement — Technique of Work Measurements

Time Study, Work, Sampling, Time Records, Predetermined Time Standards, Work Estimation, MTM-Application of Work Measurement Techniques.

Job Evaluation:

Job Analysis and Specification — Job Evaluation Methods;

Ranking Methods, Job Specification Method, Job Classification Method, Factor

Comparison Method, Point Method — Job Evaluation and Merit Rating

Cost Benefit (Value) Analysis of Activities, Techniques of Quality Control

Value Analysis:

Techniques — Principles, Procedures, Measurement and Implementation

Input-output Analysis

Measurement of Labour, Capital and Management Productivity

Learning Curves.

3. Principles and Practices of Management:

Nature of Management — Definition — Science or Art

Field of Management — Managerial Structure of a Joint-stock Company — The functional areas

Evolution of Management Thought — Contributions of Taylor, Gilbreth, Cant, Elton Mayo

Planning Process — Statement of problem, Determination of alternatives, Collection of facts, Analysis, Decision on action and execution. Hierarchy of planning — Group or Sectional, Departmental or Divisional, Functional and Company-wise Planning.

Organising:

Grouping of activities.

Creating a network of relationships through determining the authority and responsibility of the positions created.

Line relationship — Delegation of authority, chain of command, Span of control;

Staff relationship — Advisory services and relationship with 'line';

Staffing the positions — Determining the kind of personnel required, Selection process, Compensation, Executive succession.

Directing:

Motivating — Factors affecting performance — Leadership techniques — Delegation of authority as a motivating factor.

Decision-making:

Controlling (Measuring):

Concept of managerial control — Control of personnel versus performance;

Areas of performance control — Product, finance, morale;

Process of control — Standards, Appraisal and collective action;

Control aids — Good organisation structure, Clarity of objectives and policies, Methods, Procedures, Budgets, etc.

Management in India — Historical analysis — Position of executives in India, Recent trends in management thought — Management a profession.

PART IV — INDUSTRIAL RELATIONS

Labour Laws:

Growth of Labour and Industrial Laws in India.

Salient features of the following legislation:

The Factories Act

The Bombay Shops and Establishment Act

The Payment of Wages Act

The Minimum Wages Act

The Workmen's Compensation Act

The Employees' State Insurance Act and the Scheme

The Employees' Provident Fund Act and the Scheme

The Payment of Bonus Act

The Industrial Disputes Act

The Bombay Industrial Relations Act

The Industrial Employment (Standing Orders) Act, and

The Trade Unions Act

Study of Case Laws

Trade Union:

Labour Movement — Concept of Labour Movement and Union Organisation — Trade Union Movement and Various Phases of the Movements — Trade Unions and Policies — Unions in Relation to Welfare and Management — Purpose and Functions of Trade Unions — Problems of Membership and Finance — Union Leadership — Unions and Personnel Officers — Union Recognition and Its Methods — Problems of Unionisation in Small Units in Agricultural, Co-operative Sector, Public Sector, Government Employees — White Collar Workers — Trade Unions and Economic Development.

Development of Trade Unionism in India — A Historical Retrospect — Central Organisation of Workers in India.

International Labour Movement; I.C.F.T.U., W.F.T.U., I.L.O., History, Objectives and Functions; Conventions and Recommendations; Brief History and Important Characteristics of Trade Unions in U.K., Canada, U.S.A., U.S.S.R., Germany, Sweden, Japan and Asian Countries including Burma, Malaysia, Philippines, Ceylon and Pakistan.

Industrial Relations and its Machinery:

Concept of Industrial Relations; Social Obligations of Industry; Role of Government, Employers and the Unions in Industrial Relations. Industrial Relations Machinery — Works Committee, Conciliation, Adjudication, Voluntary Arbitration.

Collective Bargaining:

Object of Collective Bargaining; Attitudes of parties to Collective Bargaining; Process of Collective Bargaining; Advantages and Disadvantages of Collective Bargaining.

National Policy on Labour:

Concept of Social Justice; Directive Principles of State Policy; Industrial Truce Resolutions; Conclusions of Tripartite Conferences; Legislation for Investigation and Settlement of Industrial Disputes and Governmental Machinery for the same; Wage Boards — Reports of various Wage Boards; Report of National Commission on Labour; ILO and Other International Bodies; Employers' Organisations.

PART V — PERSONNEL ADMINISTRATION

Introduction to Human Resources Management:

Patterns and Philosophies of Management and Their Implications on Personnel Function.

Evolution of Theory and Practice of Human Resources Management with Reference to India.

Concept, Definition and Scope of Human Resources Management Management and Administration — Inter-disciplinary Approach, Its Relationship with other Social Sciences.

Personnel Department — Its Role, Function and Its Organisation, Human Resources Management Policy — Manuals.

Human Resources Planning:

Concept of Manpower Planning, Assessment of Manpower Needs of an Organisation; Manpower Inventory (succession planning).

Factors Influencing Manpower Planning — Rate of Growth of Organisation/industry.

Techniques of Manpower Planning.

Personnel Section:

Importance of Systematic Selection, Traditional Selection Methods.

Scientific approach to selection — Designing application blank. Steps in systematic selection:

— Assessment of job requirements through job analysis and job descriptions.

— Recruiting

— Screening of Applications

— Preliminary Interviews (Types of interviews)

— Testing (Abilities, Aptitudes, Personality and Achievement)

— Group Discussion

— Panel Interview

— Medical Test

Human Resources Development:

Need for training and development, Objectives of training, Ascertaining training needs, Induction, Training at three levels — (i) Workers, (ii) Supervisors, (iii) Executives.

Personality development — Trait approach, Overall approach.

Methods — (i) On-the-job (ii) Class Room Method — Lecture, Conference, Case study, Role play, Programmed instruction, Demonstration, Simulation, Business game, Incident, etc.

Training within the organisation — Establishment of a training department.

Training by outside agencies, Institutes like NITIE, CLI, Productivity Councils, Staff Colleges, Consultants.

Employee Appraisal:

Need of Employee Appraisal

Purpose of Employee Appraisal — Development, Promotion, Salary administration

Employee Appraisal Forms (For different levels of employees)

Raters — Their Training

Periodicity of Appraisal

Follow-up — Counselling.

Wage and Salary Administration:

Nature and scope of salary administration — Its problems

Determinants of wages fixation — Job evaluation (quantitative and non-quantitative methods) Industry-cum-region basis

Methods of payment — Piece rate and time rate and their relative merits

Differentials and incremental time scales

Allowances

Production and efficiency bonus

Incentive payment

Different types of wage incentive plans — Halsey, Rowan, Cutt, Emerson, Scanlon, etc.

Wage patterns (scales of pay), wage boards, perquisites for managerial cadre.

Employee Benefits and Services:

Historical development of concept of welfare

Scope of welfare activities

Statutory regulations — Canteen, creche, safety etc. Their organisations and administration

Non-statutory welfare activities — Medical facilities, housing, transport, supply schemes, education, recreation, family planning etc.

Benefits — Scholarships, travel allowances, uniforms, discounts on products, encashment of leave, long service awards, advance (Loans)

Social Security — In India and Foreign countries

Retirement benefits

Role of I.L.O.

Role of Welfare Officer

Relevant Legislation

Field Work and Project Work

Human Relations:

Concept of Human Relations, Distinction between Human Relations and Industrial Relations, Evolution of the Concept of Human Relations, Effect of Different Philosophies and Discipline on the Concept. Reasons for growing importance and its place in day-to-day working.

Factor Affecting Human Relations — Working conditions, Organisational atmosphere and Role of an executive.

Understanding Human Behaviour — Individual and group; Individual differences; Effects of sociological aspect of human behaviour; Considerations in dealing with people — Subordinates, colleagues and boss.

Communication — Its role in better understanding the people and the problems in view of the organisational goals.

Motivation — Job satisfaction and morale — Their role in organisational atmosphere conducive for human relations.

Delegation — Concept and its emergence in industrial setting — Organisational expansion and technological changes vs. human capacities. Factors to be considered in the process of delegation — Whom to delegate and what?

Counselling — Meaning as different from types and suggestions. Counselling as a process of understanding problems of maladjusted cases. Factors responsible for maladjustment in the organisation. Types of counselling for mild cases of maladjustment. Major counselling for serious maladjusted cases.

Role of an Executive — Concept of Leadership, Formal and Informal Leadership, Leader's attitude towards employees' empathy, Self-awareness, Objective attitude towards behaviour objectivity, Man to man relation, Development of leadership — Different approaches, Types of leadership, Leader as a key to Human Relations.

Employment Administration:

Service rules — Conditions, Salary scales, Leave provisions, Disciplinary rules, Time office — Organisation of time office, Its role and effectiveness on company's policies and objectives.

Personnel Records and statistics

Accident Statistics

Records as may be required under the Statutes.

Application of Industrial Legislation and Laws in View of the above Factors.

Safety and Security Measures.

Health and Hygiene.

Co-ordination.

FIELD WORK

FIRST TERM

1. **General Information:**
   (a) History and Development of the Organisation
   (b) Manufacturing Processes and Products
   (c) Organisational Set up and Functional Chart
   (d) Time Office
2. **Social Work Practice**

SECOND TERM

1. **Industrial Relations:**
   (a) Standing Orders
   (b) Grievance Procedure
   (c) Shopfloor Supervision
   (d) Joint Committees.
2. **Labour Legislation:**

   Students will also study the working of the following Acts:

   Factories Act, Standing Orders Act, B.I.R. Act, Employment Exchanges Act, Apprentices Act.
3. **Social Work Practice**

THIRD TERM

1. **Industrial Relations:**
   (a) Standing Orders Administration
   (b) Grievance Settlement Problems
   (c) Domestic Enquiry Procedure

(d) Discipline and Supervision

(e) Joint Consultation

2. Labour Legislation:

Students will study the working of the following Acts:

E.S.I. Act, Payment of Wages Act, Employees' Provident Funds and Family Pension Fund Act, Trade Unions Act (Central and State) Industrial Disputes Act, Payment of Bonus Act, Contract Labour Act.

3. Human Resources Management:

(a) Recruitment Procedures

(b) Job Descriptions

(c) Transfer and Promotion

(d) Personnel Records and Statistics

(e) Retirement Provisions

4. Labour Welfare and Employee Services:

(a) Plant Layout

(b) Working Conditions

(c) House-keeping

(d) Canteen

(e) Creche

(f) Safety Administration and Education

(g) Accident Statistics

(h) Industrial Health and Hygiene

5. Project:

Selection of the topic and preliminary preparation including review of literature.

1. Human Resources Management:

(a) Selection Techniques and Psychological Tests

(b) Induction and Placement

(c) Wage and Salary Administration

(d) Executive Compensation Plans

(e) Communication System

(f) Employee Evaluation and Merit Rating

(g) Training and Management Development

(h) Job Evaluation, Incentives, Work Study, Industrial Engineering

2. Industrial Relations:

(a) Works Committee

(b) Trade Unions and Their Organisations

(c) Disputes and Their Settlement:

(i) Conciliation

(ii) Arbitration

(iii) Adjudication

(d) Collective Bargaining and Agreements

(e) Labour Management Co-operation.

3. Project

Collection of Data, Analysis and Report Writing.

Tools for the Field Work Process:

1. Observation and attendance in work situations
2. Discussion with officials
3. Interviews with employees
4. Study of files, reports, manuals, personnel records, etc.
5. Actual participation in work situations
6. Recording of experience in field work journals
7. Reporting of experiences in field work seminars
8. Participation in class seminars with constructive criticism

Methodology for Social Work Practice:

During the field work placement in an industrial organisation students will be required to devote one day per week for the study of individual problems in the areas of Labour Welfare and Personnel Management from the standpoint of social work practice and to handle such cases with social work skill and techniques as indicated below:

1. Individual problems arising out of:
   (a) Adjustment to job, working conditions, health, canteen, creche, accidents and rehabilitation
   (b) Standing orders
   (c) Transfer, promotion and any other problems related to work and work relationships
2. Personal problems such as:

   Indebtedness, alcoholism, absenteeism; emotional disturbance or disorder
3. Family problems such as:

   Illness, family planning, interpersonal relationship, etc.

   Social group work practice is possible where housing is provided as well as in the plant.

In view of the knowledge explosion as well as the growing and changing complexities in the field of management and human resources management, a retread in education is a *sine qua non* to any specialist in this area. Fortunately in India there are a great many institutions such as the Universities, Institutes of Management, Tata Institute of Social Sciences, National Productivity Council, All India Management Association, Administrative Staff College of India, Indian Institute of Personnel Management, National Institute of Labour Management etc., which can provide a retread in education through seminars, conferences, programmes, workshops to the personnel specialists. I hope organisations also provide a forum to share experiences, ideas and views, update knowledge and education and thus enhance the effectiveness of the specialists.

Increasingly the personnel executives will have to operate by theory, principles and codified knowledge, using inter-disciplinary management concepts, tools and techniques. The new human resources management education will make a great contribution in the generation of the much-needed talent and expertise in this vital area of converting human resources into human assets for the organisation in particular and the nation in general.

❑❑❑

CHAPTER 20

Computer Applications in Human Resources Management

Electronic data processing (EDP), computer applications and automated data systems open up great vistas in human resources management. Although computer applications in personnel are fairly common for more than a decade in advanced countries like USA, they are still uncommon in most organisations in India, except for payroll accounting, which is quite widespread in the leading organisations in the country. However, in the coming decade, we shall witness a steady rise in the computer applications in such areas as selection, manpower planning, manpower inventory, compensation and benefits systems, management development, career and succession planning, morale and attitude surveys, absenteeism and turnover analysis, long range planning and the list could go on and on. In addition to the micro personnel applications, there are great possibilities in the area of macro manpower planning systems, national manpower data banks, matching jobs and men on national data network systems, spotting talent and file searching, optimum utilisation of human resources, industrial unrest, strikes, lockouts, disputes, productivity, inter-firm and inter-industry comparisons of labour productivity, various types of ratio analyses and many other stupendous new frontiers. In India, we have not even began to scratch the surface and the sky is the limit. Which increasing applications of computer and EDP, there are three things likely to occur, which will transform, in a manner of speaking, the entire human resources management function. First, the personnel function will be integrated in a more positive way in the general and top management policy-making and decision making role. Secondly, the function itself will be rendered more objective, effective and systems-oriented. Thirdly, the personnel experts will sharpen their own concepts, tools and techniques and make a more direct contribution to the general processes of industry and business. Observing the trend in USA, Richard T. Bueschel states:[1]

Real-time data processing has been used in the personnel function only since 1965. However, its development will change many of the concepts and practices now prevalent in the personnel area, and several predictions can be made as to the future direction of this function. Forward planning by the personnel departments will be accelerated, and personnel managers will have an opportunity to participate more in top management decisions that affect the future planning of the corporation.

The concept of a global data base, now made possible by time-shared computers, will tie the personnel department into the mainstream of the company's activities to a far greater extent that might seem possible to the personnel manager today. Interaction with other departments will expand. Personnel services, particularly to line management, will be significantly broadened. Response will often be in real time.

Employment may take a different form if nationwide systems are successfully implemented. Competition for skilled personnel will be extremely keen, and more emphasis will be placed on training and development activities to compensate for the difficulties in employing new talent. Motivating and retraining those employees within the organisation will be stressed as the labour market becomes more mobile.

A broader business background will be a prerequisite of the personnel manager of tomorrow. The successful personnel manager will be judged more objectively for his contribution to the firm than he has been in the past. This trend, already in evidence, will become more apparent through the use of real time in the personnel department.

Application in Personnel

Elizabeth Lanham conducted a survey of 333 firms on EDP in the personnel department covering nine major areas:[2] (1) extent in EDP utilisation, (2) reasons, (3) administrative arrangements, (4) selection, (5) training, (6) personnel records and reports, (7) EDP cost aspects, (8) problems and (9) advantages.

1. Extent of Utilisation

The 333 firms covered, 254 utilised EDP in one or more phases of their operations. Moreover, only 35 respondent companies had no plans to use EDP; the others not using it either reported definite plans for EDP or had it under serious consideration.

2. Reasons for Utilisation

Various reasons were cited for installing personnel EDP systems. The major ones were: (1) to expedite records and report preparation, (2) to provide facts quickly, (3) to improve quality and timeliness, (4) to provide for rapid and accurate classification and reclassification of data, (5) to establish systematic and efficient procedures, (6) to provide more comprehensive data, (7) to improve overall control, (8) to permit cross-comparisons of inter-departmental data, (9) to reduce costs, and (10) to improve long-range planning.

3. Administrative Arrangements

Responsibility for overall control of personnel EDP systems was most frequently assigned to someone in the personnel department, usually the director, assistant director, or a personnel systems analyst. Of these, the director of personnel carried the responsibility in the majority of companies. A number, however, placed control under the computer centre EDP specialists rather than anyone in the personnel department, and some also used the services of a representative from the EDP equipment manufacturer in planning and designing their record and report system.

4. Employees for Personnel EDP

Number and Skill Level Required: Only a few personnel departments found it necessary to add more employees as a result of switching to the computer. The number of employees remained the same after the changeover in the majority of cases; and the workforce was actually reduced in all the rest. Most personnel departments did not experience a rise in the ratio of skilled to unskilled employees, although a few reported some increase.

Source: Employees for personnel EDP work were found primarily within the department's own ranks in the majority of cases. When additional staff was needed, about equal numbers of companies said they made selections from other departments within the company and from external sources.

Prior Experience Requirements: The firms were also about equally divided between the practice of requiring prior experience in EDP and in not requiring it for the personnel EDP jobs. Approximately one-half of those with experience requirements specified one year or more as the minimum. The rest were about equally divided on the requirement of one to three months, three to six months, and six months to a year.

Prior Training Requirements: No prior training in EDP was specified for employees in about half of the companies. The majority of the others required only "partly" trained employees; a few hired fully trained workers only.

Testing for EDP Employment: Special tests were not given to evaluate applicants for EDP jobs in most of the organisations. A few did, but general practice was to use no such selection procedure.

5. Training for Personnel EDP

Responsibility for Training: Company EDP training specialists were the most popular choice for training employees for personnel EDP jobs. Personnel department training specialists and manufacturer's representatives ranked second and third, with the former holding only a slight lead over the latter. A few firms had a "personnel system analyst" in the personnel department, and assigned the training to him.

Location of Training Area: Four locations for training employees for personnel EDP work were reported with about equal frequency, manufacturer's training center, company computer center, personnel department, and company training department. A fairly large number of the respondents used a combination of locations, with the particular locations selected depending on the content to be taught.

Training Methods: On-the-job training for EDP was by far the most common procedure reported. Two other fairly popular methods mentioned with about equal frequency were tours of the computer center and group lectures. A few companies had vestibule schools for trainees, but their number was relatively insignificant.

Content and Length of EDP Training: Most of the respondents covered a variety of areas of information in their training of employees for personnel EDP work. The primary ones were: personnel records and reports; personnel policies, operations, and procedures; EDP equipment use and application; company policies, operations, and procedures; computer center policies, operations, and procedures, refresher training in EDP; and programming.

One to three months was usually the formal training period. However, few companies extended it to three to six months, six months to one year, or one year and over.

6. Computerised Records, Reports

The major classifications of employee records and reports processed electronically were: selection and placement, classification and analysis, changes of status, lateness and absences, merit ratings, suggestions and grievances, health and safety, education and experience, and payroll.

Most of the companies processed a variety of records and reports under each of these major classifications. Typical of the selection and placement category were additions to company personnel; employee history cards; selection data for promotion, transfer, layoff, recall and demotion; roster of applicants and their qualifications; job specifications; and test score analyses.

For general classification and analysis purposes, such information as employee census reports, male and female differentiation, skills inventory profiles, communication media effectiveness, and attitude survey analyses were among the data covered.

Included in the employee change-of-status classification were personal history cards, new-status registers, transfers in and out of various jobs and locations, and termination analyses.

Individual employee, department, division, and company records of lateness and absenteeism were commonly detailed under a separate heading.

Merit rating reports usually included scores made by individuals on the respective traits evaluated, and these records were usually kept for departments, divisions, and the company as a whole.

A tally of suggestions and grievances was usually classified by individuals responsible, then by departments, divisions, and the overall company.

Individual employee, departmental, divisional, and companywide reports on sickness and accidents were the major EDP records in the health and safety groupings.

Records of education and experience often processed electronically included individual employee, departmental, divisional, and companywide reports, as well as overall manpower development analyses.

By far the greatest use of EDP was for payroll data. Tax reports such as OASI and income and deductions from employees' earnings were processed most frequently. Other records often incorporated in the EDP system were payroll registers, cumulative payroll, costs, individual employee payroll records, labour cost distribution, salary payroll, overtime earnings, day or hourly payroll, pension recipient records, fringe benefit records, average wages or salaries, wage survey data analyses, profit sharing and bonus reports, commission earnings, sick leave costs, incentive earnings, and illness and accident costs.

Most of these payroll records and reports were kept on the basis of individual employees, jobs, departments, divisions, and over-all company classifications in order to provide the detail required for effective payroll administration.

Of the 142 companies using data processing in the personnel function, 104 allotted regularly scheduled machine time to personnel. Thirty-three made no such provision, and the remaining five allowed some time but not as much as was requested. Nevertheless personnel records and reports were usually processed in a responsible length of time. Only a few personnel administrators complained that their work on the computer was unduly delayed.

7. EDP Cost Aspects

Most of the companies kept records of several types in order to determine how much their EDP systems cost. The four primary ones were: Machine hours, programming, man hours on machines, and selection and designing costs.

Over half of the organisations had found that processing personnel records and reports electronically cost less than manual processing. A few found the EDP cost higher, and the rest reported the same cost for both methods.

8. What are the Problems?

Inevitably, a variety of problems had been encountered in operating personnel EDP programmes. Over half of the 142 respondents had some trouble in controlling the accuracy of input information; a little less than half had run into difficulties in foreseeing their requirements with respect to records and reports and in planning in advance for them. Changing over to EDP, coordinating and designing records and reports and the tailoring EDP to fit personnel needs were other trouble spots often cited.

9. Advantages of EDP

Despite the problems, over three-fourths of the companies said that personnel EDP installations improved payroll accounting, speeded up handling of personnel information, and made possible less expensive and more accurate personnel records and reports. Uniform data, improved cross-comparisons and analyses of data, more accurate forecasting and planning, tighter control of personnel operations, and better managerial decision on personnel matters were also benefits many companies pointed out.

Judging by the experience of these organisations, personnel administration is a fertile field for EDP, a system as yet only partly utilised. The records and reports required in sound planning, operating and controlling personnel areas continue to grow in number and complexity. Effective and prompt decision cannot be made without facts or with partial facts only, and EDP provides an orderly, systematic, and fast approach to gathering, coordinating, and reproducing vast areas of personnel information far superior to manual operation. And it does so at less cost in more cases than not.

Steven Mayer maintained that "the computer is being successfully utilised as a tool within the personnel function and as such its applications are becoming increasingly complex and diverse," based on a mid-1970 survey of 375 major U.S. corporations.[3]

To what extent and in what ways are computers presently employed to facilitate the personnel administrative process? Which personnel functions are the most adaptable to computerisation? Which yield the most valuable benefits? What variables affect the implementation of computer-assisted personnel programmes? How do personnel executives perceive the relative status of the personnel function within the corporate computer activity? What will be the probable future role of computers in personnel work?

A mid-1970 survey based on a random sample of 375 major U.S. corporations and analysis of the findings provide some answers to these questions.

Extent of EDP Use

As might be expected, computer utilisations are not as extensive in personnel as in most other functional areas of large U.S. corporations. Survey participants' numerically force ranking (1 through 7) of functional areas by the degree of current and future computer usage showed comparatively low status of personnel. (See Figure 20.1).

What is significant here is not only the fifth-place ranking of personnel, but its unchanged future status. Evidently, even personnel executives were convinced that the utilisation of personnel-oriented computerised programmes would increase only negligibly, when cast into the perspective of corporate growth.

Surprisingly, the ranked position of each functional area remained constant when correlated with industry-type and population size variables. Although computerised personnel systems applications tended to grow as population size increased, it was determined that the overall computer capacity of companies increased as well, a parallel that offset any possible shift in the rank position of personnel.

Types of EDP Use

The variety of computer utilisations in personnel is limited for the most part by the imagination of the personnel administrator and the data storage/retrieval capacity available to him. Computerised personnel systems range from simple payroll and record-keeping programmes to complex and fully integrated information systems, generating sophisticated displays such as historical personnel profiles, graphic salary diagrams and monitors, and manpower-planning forecasts based on economic data put into mathematical models using a library of statistical techniques. To simplify analysis, a specific data fields were identified with five functional personnel areas. The survey revealed the order of areas by degree of full implementation of computerised personnel programmes, shown in Figure 20.2.

Of course, the information fields in records administration may overlap those in other functional areas, but applications in the remaining areas generally utilise information independent of each other; for example, job evaluation data used in compensation are seldom used in employment, and vocational objectives data used in manpower development are seldom used in compensation. Hence, each of these functional areas will be considered separately, after the following explanatory notes:

The degree to which specific personnel data fields were incorporated in the data bases was correlated with three variables: employee grouping (job family), industry type, and population size. First, the employee groups of managerial, administrative, technical, and clerical personnel were found to be clustered together in establishing data bases. (The last was deleted as more specific data were required by skill inventory programmes.) Another grouping, however — unskilled and semi-skilled personnel — was included to a significantly lesser degree in the overall information system.

Second, industry type had a slight bearing on the degree of implementation of personnel systems. Life insurance was the leader, followed by industrials, banks, utilities, retailing and transportation. Third, population size apparently was not an immediately significant variable, because no direct relationship was detected until population increased to the 75,000 level, after which the degree of system implementation became greater as population increased.

Records Administration: Current personnel information (personal data, present wage, and present job) was put into a data base by 89 per cent of the survey participants, but only 68 per cent were utilising historical personnel data (salary/wage history, work history of positions held, and educational data such as data and type of degree). This difference is explained by the fact that current data are the fundamental element in a computerised payroll system, whereas historical data, involving record storage and retrieval, are more difficult to establish and more expensive to maintain.

Information such as present employee performance rating and performance history was maintained by only 33 per cent of the respondent companies. The confidential nature of this rating, even to the employees themselves in some companies, tends to limit incorporation within a computerised personnel system.

Compensation: The areas of computer utilisation within the compensation function were varied. A number of system of applications included within it utilised data described under records administration, such as payroll, salary forecasting, audits, and internal comparison systems. The rest focused on specifically compensation-oriented data, such as that having to do with job evaluation (Figure 20.3).

Figure 20.4 shows, in rank order of incorporation with a computer data base, the types of data utilised within the compensation function.

A trend toward integrated compensation systems was evidenced by the fact that an additional 45 per cent of the companies surveyed were planning to incorporate salary survey data within their current systems. However, 43 per cent of the firms had no intention of including job evaluation data.

Manpower Development: One kind of manpower development-oriented data-current employee population data — had been implemented within and generated from a computerised personnel information base to a very high degree (84 per cent) to facilitate the corporate manpower planning effort. The remaining system applications surveyed were utilised in varying degrees (Figure 20.5).

The high figures for educational resources and skills inventory programmes were predictable, since these system applications lay the foundation for a sound manpower development programme. The last three applications were not similarly utilised primarily because of the many variables that must be considered in designing those applications. Without the constant input of updated information, they are often impractical.

Figure 20.1

Functional Areas	*Aggregate Numerical Rankings*	
	Today	*5-Year Projection*
Controller-accounting	1.6	2.3
Production-Manufacturing	3.4	3.0
Production/material control	3.6	3.1
Sales and Marketing	3.7	3.3
Personnel	4.5	4.5
Engineering	4.9	5.3
Research & Development	5.5	4.6

Figure 20.2

Functional Area	*Degree of Implementation*
Records administration	High
Compensation	
Manpower development	
Employment	
Labour relations	Low

Figure 20.3

Type of System	*Degree of Implementation*
Payroll services	89%
Internal salary comparisons	58%
Salary action audits	41%
Salary forecasting	35%

Figure 20.4

Type of Data	*Degree of Implementation*
Classification mix	59%
Pension planning	51%
Labour costing	38%
Insurance claim	35%
Salary survey	29%
Job evaluation	23%

Figure 20.5

Type of Application	*Degree of Implementation*
Educational resources	49%
Skills inventory	48%
Manpower forecasting	29%
Backup/replacement charting	10%
Organisation charting	5%

Figure 20.6

Type of Application	*Degree of Implementation*	*No Intention of Implementation*
Turnover analysis	49%	16%
College relations results	19%	38%
Applicant data retention	16%	36%
Position openings data	14%	40%

Figure 20.7

Type of Application	*No Intention of Implementing*
Employee disciplinary record	92%
Grievance record data	84%
Suggestion programme	80%
Attitude/morale survey data	63%

Figure 20.8

Variable	*Rank Position*
Cost vs. benefit	2.3
Top management viewpoint	2.5
Employee population size	3.5
Present computer capability	3.6
Personnel staff size	4.4
Type of industry/business	5.0
Union/employee resistance	6.8

Employment: Although a number of employment-oriented system applications have been defined, only a minority of the surveyed firms were currently utilising the major types of applications in this area. (Figure 20.6).

It can be seen that turnover analysis had been implemented by almost half of the companies, while the last three applications had been implemented by fewer than one out of five companies. Moreover, almost two out of five firms had no intention of considering implementation of these last three applications, perhaps because the costs of such applications are hard to justify; College relations results data have only a limited use, generally in determining the college visit schedule. Applicant data retention is an application that produces voluminous output but firms that utilise this system usually restrict it to exempt job candidates. Position openings data are also of limited usefulness in developing recruiting plans, so incorporation in a system makes sense only if the employment function is centralised and responsible for filling a large number of position openings.

Labour Relations: With the exception of absenteeism control (which was implemented by 26 per cent of survey respondents), system applications to assist the labour relations function seemed to elicit scant interest. In fact, most companies had no intention of considering implementation in the areas shown in Figure 20.7.

The first two of these system applications utilise data that are critical in maintaining sound labour-management relations, but one could easily envision union resistance to the "impersonality" of computerisation. This was not the case, however; the personnel administrators queried did not cite "union/employee resistance" as an objection to putting these data on the computer. It is much more likely that such utilisations cannot be justified on a cost-versus-benefit basis and that they are low on the priorities lists of personnel managers anyway.

Variables in EDP Use: In attempting to identify the factors influencing the degree to which computer applications in personnel are adopted and implemented, several key influences were identified and personnel executives were asked to rank these variables 1 through 7. (Figure 20.8).

A number of respondents indicated that, in spite of employee population growth and cumbersome manual systems, the cost savings of computer utilisations in personnel administration had to be made clear at a higher managerial level than did computer applications for other functional areas of the company. Further, the quantitative clarifications of costs versus savings played a persuasive role in altering the viewpoint of top management. EDP personnel systems were often said to be perceived as "expensive, big adding machine" utilisations of the computer. To avoid formulating proposals that would only invite such negative reactions at higher levels, personnel administrators must realistically deal with the cost-versus-benefit argument. However, it appears that the overriding restriction will continue to center on the optimal employment of variable computer time.

Apart from internal cost and attitudinal variables, company employees population size and present computer capability were reported to be the most influential factors in implementing personnel EDP programmes. Logically, personnel systems become more adaptable to computerisation as increasing numbers of employees make manual record keeping and reporting more burdensome. Therefore, to get their share of present computer capacity, in addition to demonstrating cost advantages of immediate proposals, personnel administrators should conceptualise the design and associated costs of more comprehensive systems with an eye to computer storage and time privileges after their firms increase their computer capability.

The type of industry/business did not emerge as an important variable, since the personnel department is generally charged with the same responsibilities across industry lines. It follows that concepts of computerised personnel systems are transferable across the same industry lines; for example, the skills inventory concept developed initially among life insurance companies was quickly translated into applications among industrials.

As was noted earlier, union/employee resistance to the implementation of personnel computer systems was considered inconsequential. Early negative relations to "putting people in computers" are now minimal, according to the personnel executives queried. Experience with such systems, especially the payroll and record-keeping ones, has demonstrated to employees that the computer can play an effective role in personnel administration without dehumanising the company's view of its people.

SOME SPECIFIC APPLICATIONS

(1) G.M. Application on Selection of Trainees

NOTE ON TECHNICAL TRAINEE SELECTION

Introduction

The technical trainee application forms will be processed through our computer for preliminary short-listing the candidates. Selection will be by group discussion and panel interview, the weightage being 80% on the initial application, 20% on panel interview so that the human error and subjectivity is minimised. On the basis of the total marks secured from three variables, a ranked list will be prepared to select the trainees.

How we go about?

An application form is designed in such a manner as to send the filled up form directly for computer operations and to prepare a register differentiating the department, degree or diploma and area preferred and ranking the candidates on our agreed variables.

The weighted variables are broadly as follows:

	Total Marks
1. Age	5
2. Language	5
3. Physical	5
4. Leadership Skills	5
5. Social and Cultural Skills	5
6. Practical Experience	5
7. Technical Education	50
8. Formal Education	20

1. Age:

Total marks	—	5
	Degree	*Diploma*
21 years and below	5	5
22 years	5	4
23 years	4	3
24 years	3	2
25 years	2	1
26 years	1	0
27 years and above	0	0

2. Language Skills:

Total Marks	—	5
	Degree	*Diploma*
1. Hindi	1½	1½
2. Marathi	1½	1½
3. Gujarati	1½	1½
4. Other Languages	½	½

3. Physical Stamina:

Total Marks	—	5
1. Play physical stamina games (Football, Cricket, Basketball etc.)	1	1
2. Represented College	3	3
3. Represented District	5	5

4. Leadership Skills (N.C.C.):

Total Marks	—	5
1. Rank 3		
2. 3 star Under-Officer & above	3	3
3. 2 star Group Captain	2	2

4. 1 star Corporal	1	1
5. Certificate C	2	2
B	1	1

5. Social and Cultural Skills:

Total Marks		*5*
1. President	5	5
2. Secretary	4	4
3. Vice-president	3	3
4. Asst. Secretary	2	2
5. Class Representative	1	1

6. Practical Experience:

Total Marks		*5*
	Degree	*Diploma*
1. 3 years and above	5	5
2. 2 years	3	3
3. 1 year	2	2

7. Formal Education:

Total Marks	—	*20*
The marks allotted to:	*Processing*	*Text Tech / Engineers*
1. S.S.C.	8	15
2. 1st year	—	—
3. Int. Sc. pre-Final	4	5
4. B.Sc.	8	—

We shall give weightage for each University differentially but for S.S.C. No distinction will be made for any school.

8. Technical Education:

Total Marks	—.	*50*
The marks allotted to each year as follows:		
	15	15
3 years	15	15
	20	20

Those applicants whose results are not published, the average index will be simulated for final year and marks thus allotted. There will be a rating factor for different Universities and institutes of the country which will be taken into consideration.

RATING FOR THE INSTITUTES/UNIVERSITIES

Spinning/Weaving:	*Percentage*
I.I.T., Delhi	100
V.J.T.I., Mumbai	100
M.S. University, Vadodara,	95
Chennai	90
Bangalore	90
T.I.T. (Bhivani)	85
Calcutta University	85
Others	80

Engineering:	
All I.I.T.'s	100
V.J.T.I., *Mumbai*	95
Mumbai University	95
Jadavpur University	95
M.S. University	85
All Regional Colleges	85
Others	80
Processing:	
U.D.C.T., Mumbai	100
V.J.T.I., Mumbai	90
R.C.T.I., Gujarat	85
Vadodara (M.S. University)	85
Others	80

(2) ESSO on Wage Systems

See the form printed (Fig. 20.9).

(3) IBM Personnel Data Systems

At IBM, the complexities inherent in these activities led some time ago to the development of computer systems designed specifically to assist in personnel work. Those earlier systems have evolved into a comprehensive personnel data system (PDS) that is proving to be an effective tool in supporting corporate objectives, even as it helps fulfil the more traditional personnel functions.

Personnel Data Base: PDS begins with the same basic material required for an efficient information system — a data base with complete, accurate information on each of the 150,000 individuals employed at IBM locations within the United States. (It does not include IBM employees in other countries.) With a growing company population of this size, dispersed throughout a number of operating divisions with their own plants, warehousing, sales, and other facilities, record-keeping alone takes on a new dimension. The chances for error are multiplied, and employees transferred from one location to another can more easily be 'lost'. Uniformity becomes a problem, since different personnel managers will have their own ideas about the information that should be gathered and the format in which it should be maintained.

In a complex organisation, uniformity cannot be imposed from above. IBM marketing divisions have very specific personnel information needs relating to sales performance, sales clubs achieved, and special awards. The manufacturing divisions are heavily involved with suggestion award winners and training programmes. The research division, as another example, requires data on professional society memberships, patents pending and issued, and professional papers published. A company wide personnel system cannot be effective unless it accommodates all these varying needs.

Two Kinds of Files: After extensive studies, interviews with functional staffs at the division and corporate levels, and a thorough analysis of existing records at each location, it was decided that each laboratory, plant, marketing region, division headquarters, and so forth should maintain its own personnel file. Within this file is what is called a "mirror image" of the information required at corporate headquarters. Basically, this includes data such as the individual's name, social security number, location, salary, position code and level, latest performance appraisal, home address, military status, data employed, and relocation information.

EM(9-72)

PAYROLL ADVICE

SERIAL NO. ________

PAY OFFICE | TYPE ADVICE [1] NEW EMPLOYEE | [2] CHANGE | [3] SEPARATOR

NEW EMPLOYMENT OR CHANGES

EMPLOYEE RELATIONS DEPARTMENT

ORGANISATION

EMPLOYEE NAME (22) | EFFECTIVE DATE | EMPLOYEE NO.

1 POSITION//TITLE PRESENT | OFF./DEPT./LOCATION/SECTION PRESENT

POSITION/TITLE/REVISED (22) | OFF./DEPT./LOCATION/SECTION REVISED (20)

2 ADDRESS LINE1 (22) | ADDRESS LINE2 (15)

ADDRESS LINE 3 (15) | ADDRESS LINE4 (15)

3 EDUCATIONAL QUALIFICATIONS 10 × (4)

4 PROFESSIONAL COURSES 14 × (3)

5 TRAINING COURSES 14 × (3)

6 LANGUAGES AND PROFICIENCY 8 × (5)

DATE OF BIRTH	DATE JOINED CO.	SEX	MAR. STATUS	CHILDREN	POL.STATE	NATIONALITY	RELIGION	ACC. INS.	MED. INS.
14	20	26	27	28	30	32	33	34	35

7

SALARY GROUP	DATE OF S.G.	HS.TYPE	HOUSE RENT
36	36	42	43

PAYROLL

8

RATE OF PAY	P/R CLASS	X - D - CC - LOC - SEC	DA	RATE CH	STATUS	M.O.P.	EMP. BANK A/C REF.
14	21	23	31	33	34	35	39

PF	EPF NO.	E.S.I.C. NO.	JOB CL	WK. SCH	DIV./CR
49	50	54	64	66 (0 8)	67

EMPLOYMENT STATUS

[1] REGULAR [2] TEMPORARY FROM ____ TO ____ [3] TRAINING ASSIGNMENT [4] LOANED

[5] RETIREMENT [6] RESIGNATION [7] TERMINATION [9] DEATH [0] TRANSFERRED TO EEI/ESRC

RATE CHANGE

TYPE RATE CHANGE	FROM	INCREASE	TO	NEW SALARY GROUP
LAST CHANGE	DATE	AMOUNT		TYPE

REMARKS

if space provided is inadequate, please use the reverse of this form.

RECOMMENDATIONS AND APPROVALS

SIGNATURE	SIGNATURE	SIGNATURE
DATE	DATE	DATE
SIGNATURE	SIGNATURE	SIGNATURE
DATE	DATE	DATE

PAYROLL SECTION

PREPARED BY ________ CHECKED BY ________ PUNCHED BY ________ VERIFIED BY ________

Fig. 20.9 Esso on Wage Systems

These basic data, covering the 150,000 IBM employees in the United States, constitute the corporate PDS file. It is maintained on magnetic disk storage units that are part of a dual System/360 model 50 installation at corporate headquarters. Here, 108 "pieces" of data are kept on each individual; in contrast, a division's personnel file may include up to 400 data elements on each individual. There is no conflict, because each otherwise separate file includes an "image" of the PDS data base, in its required format.

The PDS file is updated according to payroll frequency at each location, and transaction data are transmitted by way of cards, magnetic tapes, or telecommunications. Those divisions that generate a large number of changes send them in by way of a high-speed tape-to-tape link. All changes are accumulated on tape, and passed against the PDS file to bring it up to date.

Accuracy Checks: A number of techniques are used to ensure the accuracy of the data base, including audits and programmes computer checks. Sixteen data elements have been identified as critical, and these are checked every month. They include the individual's last name, age, social, security number, current salary, and amount of the last salary change. The other pieces of information are checked periodically. We have found that the combination of these techniques has yielded a file that is better than 99 per cent accurate.

With the data base established, the next steps were to provide for ready access and for use of the data to extract the information needed for current and future management planning. Retrieval is handled in two ways: through remote terminals that have access to the data base directly and either display the data on TV-like screens or print it out, and through a Select/360 inquiry programme that provides over-night services. Depending on the specifics of each individual request for information, Select/360 can run as many as nine simultaneous searches in one hour. A huge range of information can be provided according to factors such as division, department, salary, and position codes.

For requests that require a fast response, on-line terminals linked directly to the computer are used. Tight security is maintained through codes issued only to those people authorised to tap the file; data cannot be obtained without these codes, which are changed monthly.

On-Line Data Manipulation: Another on-line arrangement for retrieval of PDS data uses a hookup between corporate headquarters and a large-scale System/360 Model 91 at the IBM Research Division in Yorktown Heights, N.Y., where a "copy" of the PDS file is maintained on magnetic disk, also under tight security. A small System/360 Model 20 at corporate headquarters serves as a terminal to the large System/360 Model 91.

Maintained on the Model 91 is a PDS matrix programme, which permits retrieval, formatting, and manipulation of information in one dimension, or up to a six-dimensional matrix. Matrix requests are handled in a minimum of four minutes time, with an average response time of a half-hour. Requests are entered through the Model 20 and transmitted automatically over high speed wire communications to the Model 91 for processing, and results are returned to the Model 20 to be printed out.

Here are just a few examples of the capability of this programme: A one-dimensional matrix might list number of employees by age; a second dimension would add service; a third would add salary; and a four-dimensional matrix would list number of employees by age and service, within salary, within education level. Up to 50 ranges or breakdowns can be handled for each variable. If the variable were length of service, the possible ranges would include less than a year, 1 year, 2 years, 3 years, 4 to 10 years, 11 to 15 years, 16 to 20 years, and over. And within these variables and ranges, entire divisions or specific locations can be excluded, as well as employees hired after a specified date.

At this point, the capabilities for meaningful data manipulation become self-evident. The accurate current-data base provides the essential core of information, and the variety of user-oriented programming systems avoids the need for formal programming while facilitating access to the information. With these facilities, the stage was set for regular application of sophisticated management science programmes that use techniques such as linear programming and model building to analyse current and project future requirements.

Pension Plan Evaluation: An excellent illustration of this kind of work is IBM's retirement benefits evaluation system. Originating with a study of alternative benefits and evolving over a period of time, this series of programmes now permits analysis of many proposed improvements for a given plan. Each alternative — representing the entire U.S. IBM work force — is run on the computer in ten minutes.

The system has three phases. In the first, or plan design, phase, the yield to the employee from the pension plan plus social security is calculated in terms of a percentage of the employee's final pay, and in absolute dollars. Since the effect on employee yield of any number of alternatives can be studied through fast computer runs, through model-building techniques the enormous number of computations needed to redesign a pension plan is reduced to manageable proportions.

The results, or output, of this design phase become input for the second phase, which examines projected costs for the plan over the next 30 years. This is done by simulating the employee population, the pension fund, actuarial, computations, and other factors affecting the pension plan, including new hires, employee turnover, mortality, accumulation of pension fund interest, increase in salaries over future periods, and retirements at age 65. Various options in the area of retirement are easily incorporated.

Output from this second phase then becomes input for the pension trust fund phase, which simulates trust fund activity to determine the net contribution required for the new plan. It takes into consideration current investment performance, appreciation of fund assets, investment of pension trust funds in various media with different rates of return, and financial implications of the new or changed plan. In so doing, it can take into account the impact of a recession, the implications of different investment mixes, and similar factors.

With this capability, corporate pension plan objectives are readily studied in great depth — and at reasonable cost in terms of staff and computer time required — to project their impact on IBM employees and on the company. Top management can be presented with a variety of alternatives, along with the different implications inherent in each one.

Studies are also made of vacation plans and their cost, group life insurance, death benefits, and the cost of paid holidays. Soon to be included are studies of survivor benefits.

Other Applications: The same techniques are applied in other areas, such as manpower and long-range salary planning. Company growth will mean that at different times in the future more people with certain skills will be needed. It can be expected that some skills will be available in the future labour marketplace, but others will be developed, perhaps through in-house training programmes. Intelligence that identifies those areas of future needs is instrumental in helping to assure that the necessary labour force will be on hand when it is needed. Similarly, long-range salary planning is important in helping to assure that people will be properly compensated.

The importance of this ability to manipulate data and develop meaningful analyses and projections cannot be overstated. If PDS did no more than make this possible, it would have been well worth the effort, but its impact is felt in every area of personnel management.

PDS has proved invaluable in meeting these different responsibilities. It has assisted in assuring that company policy in such matters are relocation of individuals and maintenance of position code salary ranges is adhered to. It even provides the mailing list through which internal publications are mailed to employees.[4]

(4) GE-GEDAN System

How GE Does It: The development of such a computer programme has been the direction taken by General Electric's corporate employee relations staff. By building on prior operating component experience, a piece of software called GEDAN (an acronym for generalised data analysis) was created, capable of giving access to any automated data base (that is, punched cards, magnetic tape, drum, or disc) to identify data elements relevant to the problem at hand, to isolate special categories of records, to sort, list, count, or calculate. Simple, easy-to-master, English-language commands, "program" GEDAN. This piece of highly generalised but simple, self-tutoring software enables anyone to employ the computer as a clerical processor of data with a few hours' practice and little or no technical assistance.

Behind the development of this software was the realisation that the process of analysing data really involves very little more than exploring an existing data base to see what it reveals or what light it can shed on hypotheses raised by existing operating problems. Analysis is, in its simplest form, the process of reorganising existing data in order to get different perspectives — to see something that could not be seen before. For instance, the assumption that turnover and absenteeism rates for women employees are higher than for men may go unchallenged until someone realises that women tend to fill different kinds of positions and therefore reorganises turnover and absenteeism data by job classification. The perspective one is able to get on the data in this case may change one's understanding of the problem completely.

The ability to manipulate data very rapidly and very inexpensively is the key to expanded, lower-cost analysis and use of any kind of existing data base. If, in the turnover and absenteeism example above, it took 35 clerical man hours or 20 high-cost computer programmer hours to get the new perspective, that expense alone would probably be sufficient deterrent to a re-examination of the problem, but if the same thing could be done by posing the question directly to a computer, at a cost of $5, $ 10, or even $ 25 in computer time, personnel men to whom the question occurred would almost certainly ask it.

The GEDAN system is so flexible and inexpensive to use that it can be applied to virtually any kind of personnel or other data base and thus has become a highly generalised data management tool for use by people who have no background whatsoever in computer technology. It is, in effect, a do-it-yourself data management kit.

(5) Matching of Jobs and Men

The Mark II system is also used by National Manpower Register, in New York City, the first of several computer-powered registers that were established by private companies to build up "banks" of jobs and/or job applicants from all around the country and provide them to employers, agencies, or applicants. NMR, which specialises in engineers, scientists, and other technical personnel, has more than 20,000 active job applicants in its data base, and plans to open a file of 5,000 technical openings on its computer this spring.

"Lost" Applicants, Openings: Established in 1966, NMR was not at first computerised. "But as the number of applicants grew, so did the need for computerised retrieval," says Tom Jackson, NMR's president. "Without the computer, too much information and too many applicants were being overlooked. Also, the sheer amount of paperwork necessary to file applicants was overwhelming. Many applicants should be filed under five or six headings, because they can function in that many areas."

Using the computerised system, NMR has made more than a thousand job placements in the last twelve months. It differs from other registers in two respects: First, it does no charge applicants, and second, it does not give information directly to employers or job seekers, a practice called "naked retrieval," but provides it only to placement agencies, about 80 of which around the country subscribe to its services.

"The cost of employers of the 15 million placements and replacements this year will be $ 3.5 billion," Mr. Jackson predicts. "That's an average of only about $ 230 per person, but a professional placement generally costs over $ 1,000 through an agency and when an employer in a technically-oriented industry hires directly without an agency, the cost can run up to $ 3,000 if one or two ads fail to produce. We all accept the fact of job mobility today, but may be the pattern would be less mobile, and less costly, if more of the right jobs and right people would be brought together in the first place."

To illustrate the point, Mr. Jackson cites a recent placement made by an agency near Seattle, which had a job opening for a chemical engineer with the Schlumberger oil companies in Paris. The agency searched the NMR register and retrieved five possible candidates, all of whom said they were eager to relocate in Paris. Screening by the placement counsellor, man hired, less than a week later, was from Idaho Falls, and it is unlikely that he would have heard of the job were it not for the computer, but it was agency screening that saved the company the time and cost of interviewing five candidates and possibly hiring someone who would not stay for any length of time.

What it Costs: Other computerised registers have come into this field since NMR pioneered in it. The National Registry, in New York City, charges applicants $ 15 a year plus a $ 1 service charge to update a resume. It provides applicants with monthly printouts of suitable openings obtained from employer subscribers.[5]

Now electronic data processing and computer equipment are slowly becoming popular in personnel work. Richard T. Bueschel tells us the main advantages of these equipment and how they are improving the personnel functions.[6]

"Despite the varied nature of the reports provided, all are produced from the same file of information so that the data are recorded only once. This is one of the advantages of EDP — multiple causes can be made of a single file. Among its other significant advantages are the reduction of clerical workloads; the provision of more timely data for decision-making; the supply of broader information for salary comparison, forecast and simulation purposes; and increased accuracy of personnel reports.

"One of the most interesting automated systems in this area is SPARTAN (System for Personnel Automated Reports, Transactions and Notices), which has been developed by the Bureau of Census. Here, information on employee changes is taken from a request for Personnel Action form and inserted into the computer. Though some of the information is keypunched on to cards before entry into the system, most data is "read" into the computer by a machine known as FOSDIC (Film Optical Sensing Device for Input to Computers).

"The system provides a number of reports on employees. Additionally and more unusual, the computer prepares and addresses memos to managers alerting them to the imminence of certain events, or activities that have been accomplished by the computer. Scheduled step increases, time and salary limits on appointments, eligibility for retirement, sick leave limits, eligibility for service awards, performance rating periods, placement and training followups, probation periods and so forth are among events that are thus examined by the computer and reported upon as required."

At Honeywell, employment records have been automated by means of a programme that prints out, twice a week, the status of all applicants and visitors. The system is also designed to identify, once a week, all files that have exceeded certain time limits. Some of the tasks this programme performs are:[7]

1. Provision of a complete report on the status of all resumes and applications, so that delays can be spotted and decisions made quickly.
2. Elimination of over 22 separate posting and routing activities previously performed by clerical help, thereby freeing their time for more productive work.
3. Printing and updating of a complete set of indexing cards that provide cross-reference to all files placed in storage, thus eliminating a posting job that formerly required over 20 clerk hours a week.
4. Provision of a highly selective system of retrieval on all applicants who visit the plant.
5. Speed-up the preparation of reports on employment activities.
6. Measurement of the effectiveness of different recruiting sources, such as advertising and employment agencies, based on source-of-hire data.

7. Provision of up-to-the-minute budget information, cost-of-hire figures and other pertinent cost data.

Increasingly, personnel administration to be more effective and to gain more top management attention must talk "turkey" to them. They must spend more time henceforth in finding ways to measure the contribution of personnel division to profits, productivity and growth of the concern. They must interpret their contributions in more tangible terms, say in terms of rupees and paise. They must find ways to answer these questions raised by Albert F. Watters:[8]

1. How can statistical and other personnel data be presented to top management to best reflect their impact on business in dollar-and-cent terms?
2. Does personnel administration, like research, require investments which some times have only long-range potential? If so, how can we sell this concept to top management and how can we make it clear that not every expenditure is a cost — that some are investments?
3. What corporate characteristics and factors indicate the point upon which a personnel programme must focus for maximum effectiveness?
4. What are "human value judgements", and how does the work being done at MIT, Harvard, and other educational institutions in the fields of theology, philosophy, psychology, axiology, and so forth, contribute to our understanding of human value judgement and of their force and effect in business?

(6) Computer Checklist

The value of a personnel data system can be determined only by itemising and appraising what the system actually does for the personnel function. In general, of course, such a system should:

— Replace present clerical operations.

— Make possible a level of control and information retrieval and analysis that could not be achieved with conventional clerical method.

— Provide tangible and intangible dollar savings.

Assuming a good data base and retrieval system, here is a checklist of the basic functions that characterise and measure a "real" personnel data system.

1. Data must be continually edited for you by your system. Most elements of data are checked as they are entered to see that they are in correct form. For example:

   — A cost center code must match an actual cost center number.

   — Dates are checked within realistic ranges.

   — Numeric fields such as salary are rejected if they contain alpha characters.

   — A five-digit code is rejected if only digits are entered.

   In short, the system should alert you to data that do not conform to edit standards for each field.
2. The system should generate or complete data for you. If you change an employee's job code, for example, the system should automatically change his job title, salary range, salary minimum, salary maximum, midpoint, job

grade, salary review date, and other data dependent on job code. If you change a man's department number, his department name, manager's name, location telephone number, and cost center may be automatically updated by the system.

3. Salary increases and pay changes require special attention. Your system should reject them or at least warn you if they are too soon, below the minimum, above the maximum, an excessive per cent, or inconsistent with other company policy or job code. You should be automatically notified when an increase is overdue or inconsistent with an appraisal rating, or if it is violation of a probationary period. A salary increase may also automatically trigger an updating of other information or plans.
4. Maintenance of the work history section. Work history statements on each employee should be updated by the system as status changes are entered. For example, a salary increase, bonus, transfer, promotion, and educational or other leave of absence should not only change the base of information related to an employee but should also produce a new work history statement on his profile form.
5. Management by exception. The testing of data and transactions against criteria established by the personnel department or company policy provides a long list of audits and edits that the system should automatically conduct. A signal should be produced for any variance, non-conformity, or exception to these criteria.
6. Specific programmes monitored by the personnel department should be accommodated. For example, if personnel is responsible for scheduling appraisal interviews, or salary reviews, the system should handle all the mechanical aspects of the schedule. Each month a new schedule by department is produced and addressed to the responsible manager by the system.

   Excessive overtime, lost time, tardiness, vacation time, and sickness and accident time can be detected and signalled automatically.
7. Monthly reconciliations of manpower. Manpower on board and requisitions should be balanced against each department's or division's authorised budget of head count. This reconciliation should agree with the controller's figure produced from the payroll and budgeting system.

   Special conditions of labour union contracts, such as seniority privileges, bumping schedules, special rights for certain job codes, changes and benefits based on payroll increases, or other changes geared to a calendar date should be incorporated in the system.
8. Tailored records or secondary history files of information should be automatically created. It is extremely helpful to accumulate a separate file on certain transactions of importance, such as employees who are terminated, leave the company, or retire. These files can then be processed separately.
9. Education data. Especially important for employees who are in school and raising their educational level is the function of updating educational data.

This may be automatically accomplished from tuition refund or other related procedures.[8]

Some 'Do's and 'Dont's

We should first look at the personnel man's usual approach to human relations problem-solving and decision-making. In a way, he is a self-contained data processing unit. In his daily contacts with employees and managers he keeps his senses tuned to every nuance of information supplied to him: He hears the words being spoken, but he also observes facial expressions and postures and looks for signs of tension or abnormality. He instinctively weighs all these impressions against his experience in the business setting to reach decisions about what actions are needed to solve the problems that have come up or keep the operation on an even keel. He seldom reflects on problems at length; rather, he reacts to them. If asked to explain his decision-making process, he probably won't make much sense to anybody who has not had the same kind of experience, because so many subtle assumptions and specific experiences hard to articulate underlie his decision-making.

To the scientific purist, this way of arriving at decisions is too loaded with subjectivity to be anything but irrational and perhaps corrupt, but the fact is that such science as exists in the field of human relations decision-making covers only the most rudimentary kinds of decisions. Indeed, most business decisions are most efficiently made in an insightful fashion by a person with the judgment that comes from experience.

Personnel data systems are only subsystems of other, larger systems. In fact, the entire personnel operation can be thought of as a system in its own right, with the personnel data system merely a new type of sub-system designed to permit the personnel man to handle certain kinds of logical data management problems more efficiently than he could in the past. In practice, though, one of the biggest problems in installing a workable personnel data system is the failure of the system implements to see the need to fit disparate systems together. The personnel department is a system designed by and for insightful problem solvers, and machine-based systems are designed by and for logical problem solvers, yet the problems of reconciling the two have often not been recognised, much less solved.

Speaking Two Languages

Experience has shown that the abstract terminology that systems architects use to describe their work is so far divorced from the day-to-day realities the personnel man deals with that it is almost impossible for them to communicate at first. And, in an effort to try to bridge the different perspectives, they too easily both oversell and overbuy computerised personnel data systems. Because systems men lack experience with the complexities of the personnel man's job they are inclined to oversimplify the job of building the systems that are supposed to serve the personnel man's needs. At the same time, the personnel man is so often buried under the complexities of his administrative chores that he is too ready to believe that the computer can lift or at least substantially ease that burden. It therefore, behooves him to keep a firm grasp on reality, to keep working back to clear-cut examples of the real problems that need to be solved at every step in the development of his data systems.

Data vs. Information

Another trap the entrant into the field of computerised personnel data systems must be wary of is the assumption that if you gather data you automatically obtain information. Actually, data are facts, knowledge per se, but information is knowledge for the sake of taking purposeful action. You do not automatically end up with information merely by gathering data; there is an intermediary process of making sense out of the data by relating it to goals. Computerised personnel data systems that merely collect data but do not allows for extensive, low-cost examination and exploration of the data collected to find out what they mean in terms of business goals and objectives are bound to be of minimal value.

Managing Data

The data management process has eight clearly defined elements:

1. Identification of relevant data elements
2. Gathering of data elements
3. Storage of data
4. Isolation of relevant categories of records
5. Sorting (or ranking) of records
6. Listing of records (Preparing rosters)
7. Performing counts
8. Performing simple calculations (basic per cent and ratios).

The largest part of "systems activity" is concentrated on elements 2 and 3 — data gathering and storage, and form a technical point of view, these processes are easy for the computer and the computer technicians. However, all the other elements of the process are of at least equal importance and deserve approximately equivalent effort and attention. The first item, for instance — identifying relevant data elements — will largely set the limits on subsequent utility of the data. What is relevant and what is not, however, only a skilled personnel man can really say. In fact, it would be foolish to take it for granted that even he can identify all the elements of data that are relevant to the personnel function.

One of the first steps in building a personnel data system, then, is to begin shaking loose old concepts of what is relevant and to expand awareness of characteristics and events within the work environments that are potentially relevant to the problems of personnel work and human relations.

The remaining five elements of the data management process (4 through 8) are largely ignored by present-day personnel data systems, or at best, addressed in a very mechanical way, on the premise that these kinds of activities can be carried out only with the aid of an experienced systems man or programmer. Yet these are very simple, straightforward operations. They are, in fact, the kind of jobs that we expect any experienced clerks to perform: furthermore, a computer can do them at very low cost and very high speed. Because they are standard processes of a very general nature, they are activities that can readily be programmed in a generalised form on any medium-to-large-size computer, so the user himself can instruct the computer to carry out these clerical functions in much the same way that we would instruct a clerk to do them.[10]

FUTURE AHEAD

Personnel and Systems Men

True a systems man who can acquire intensive experience inside the personnel operation in a matter of a few months can, under favourable circumstances, turn out a first-rate-job. If the personnel manager is willing to bring a man with systems experience into his organisation and teach him the personnel ropes, such an approach may turn in fine results. Otherwise, the usual result of the systems organisation's efforts on behalf of the personnel department will be a clerical ornament, and the personnel man will have to depend on someone else to make sure that this elaborate tool runs right.

Systems and computer offer an opportunity for the personnel man attuned to reliance on insight to learn a new set of problem-solving and decision-making skills. If he refuses to "get his hands dirty" with the do-it-yourself part of the systems and computerised data operation, he is probably merely replacing low-cost clerical labour with high-cost programming labour to do the same job.

Ultimately, whether a computerised personnel data system becomes a boon or a burden to the personnel man is a matter of his own choice and involvement in the total process. If he does get involved, however, he must not put aside this.

Personnel men should insist that their systems counterparts actively engage themselves in an understanding of the personnel man's problems and problem-solving techniques, and systems men should insist that personnel men gain a sound working understanding of systems' problem-solving skills and techniques. Tough "acceptance tests" for application of a system when it is delivered should be worked out in advance by the personnel people; if possible the option to pay for the system only when it is delivered should be worked out in advance by the personnel people; if possible, the option to pay for the system only when it is delivered and is found to meet the personnel department's requirements should be negotiated in advance. Tough-minded, pragmatic attitudes — insistence that system architects deliver meaningful results and take a chance on a certain amount of penalty for failure to deliver those results — are essential in developing a workable computerised personnel system of any kind.

The risks are high but the potential rewards are great. But then, that is the way business is and will always be. The personnel manager who demonstrates the initiative and ability to chart his course into the unfamiliar waters of systems and computer technology is simply proving himself to be an effective businessman.[11]

REFERENCES

1. Richard T. Bueschel, *EDP and Personnel,* AMA Management Bulletin, No. 86.
2. Elizabeth Lanham, "EDP in the Personnel Department," *Personnel*, March-April,1967, pp. 17-22.
3. Steven J. Mayer, "EDP Personnel Systems: What Areas are being Automated?", *Personnel*, July-August,1971, pp. 29-36.
4. Wesley R. Liebtag, "How an EDP Personnel Data System Works for Corporate Growth", *Personnel*, July-August, 1970, pp. 15-20.
5. Edward P. Dear, "Computer Job Matching Now & Tomorrow," *Personnel*, May-June, 1970, pp. 60-61.

6. Richard T. Bueschel, "How EDP is Improving Personnel Function," *Personnel*, Sept-Oc 1964, pp. 60-61.

7. *Ibid.,* p. 63.

8. Alert F. Watters, *op. cit.,* p. 10.

9. William E. Berry, "What a Personnel EDP System should Do," *Personnel*, January-Februar 1969, pp. 18-21.

10. Glenn A. Bassett, "EDP Personnel Systems: Do's, Dont's, and How-To's," *Personnel*, July August, 1971, pp. 20-26.

11. *Personnel*, July-August,1971, pp. 27-28.

❑ ❑ ❑

CHAPTER 21

Human Resources Management and Family Planning

Talking about preparing for the new century, Professor Paul Kennedy, who is the Yale Professor of history with a focus on modern strategic and international affairs and who is also the Co-director of UN committee to chart out the role of UN, by the Secretary-general Mr. Boutros Ghali, has published a thought-provoking new book, *Preparing for the Twenty First Century,* where he shares ideas on how.[1]

"In his last best selling book, *The Rise and Fall of the Great Powers* (1988), Paul Kennedy looked mainly back in time to consider the forces within nations that led to their decline.

A. PREPARING FOR THE 21ST CENTURY

In his latest book, *Preparing for the Twenty-First Century,* the Yale University history professor projects forward, upto 30 years ahead to AD 2025. He analyses the major forces for change now affecting the world and discusses their implications. He examines the different regions of the globe and their respective capacities to deal with new challenges and cope with the next century.

Human history has always been shaped by the growth and migration of populations, by the opportunities and constraints provided by the environment. Today, these forces are enmeshed in a state of unprecedented turbulence. World population has more than doubled in the past 40 years to reach 5.5 billion, and it will exceed 8 billion and perhaps even 10 million early next century.

How will these vast numbers reshape the world's borders, strain an already fragile ecosystem and remake politics?

Doomsday Scenario Again?

In 1798, English curate Thomas Malthus argued pessimistically that the world's population would increase at a higher rate than man's ability to feed and sustain himself from the Earth's resources.

The Big Baby Boom

Mr. Kennedy plucks out some alarming demographic statistics:

- World population has risen from about 1 billion in 1825, to 2 billion in 1925, to 4 billion in 1976, to 5.3 billion in 1990. Estimates for 2025 range between 7.6 billion and 9.4 billion.
- 95 per cent of the world's population growth will take place in the developing nations, between now and 2025.
- In 1950, the population of Africa was half of Europe's. By 1985, it had drawn level and in 2025 it will be three times Europe's.
- China's population may rise from today's 1.13 billion to about 1.5 billion in 2025.
- India's population may rise from 853 million to 1.5 billion too. India, may even have the largest population in the world by 2025, eventually reaching 2 billion.
- Developed nations will reach these projected figures without any corresponding increase in resources — indeed, with resources shrinking.
- Developed nations will place far greater stress, per capita, on Earth's resources. "The average American baby represents twice the environmental damage of a Swedish child, three times that of a Brazilian, 35 times that of an Indian and 280 times that of a Chadian or Haitian because its level of consumption throughout its life will be so much greater," says Mr. Kennedy.

Rampant population growth combined with limited resources will lead to migration within developing countries, from the country-wide to the city, and from developing to developed countries.

The last should help both sides, but it has been resisted within the developed countries because of unemployment, racism and so on.

The Rise of the MNC

The world economy is becoming more integrated and richer overall, although creation and enjoyment of wealth is very uneven. The main creators and controllers of technology have increasingly become large, multinational corporations "with more global reach than global responsibility."

Rather than narrow the gap between rich and poor, the way international business and finance develops may result in the "have-nots" becoming ever more envious of the "haves."

The Biotech Farming Revolution

Can a new agricultural revolution avert the threatening population explosion in developing countries, as it did (in part) in Britain in Malthus' time? Mr. Kennedy is inconclusive. There may be major advances in agricultural productivity, but this may hurt traditional farmers and the benefits may not reach those who need them most.

Farming as it is now is on its way out because it cannot meet demand. The answer must lie in biotechnology — which both eases and complicates the global dilemma. It seems unlikely that global society can handle the economic and social consequences of a large-scale shift to biotech farming and food processing.

The Robotics Revolution

Can human labour be replaced with robots, just as machinery and mechanical power replaced it in the first Industrial Revolution? On use of robotics, Japan is way ahead (176,000 robots in 1988) of Western Europe (48,000), the United States (33,000) and the rest of the world (23,000).

Like the biotech revolution, the robotics revolution will benefit developed countries and MNCs more than developing countries.

Environmental Dangers

The environmental problems of the past were localised and escapable, at least by the rich. Future problems will have a much greater scale and are harder to focus because of national interests. Past efforts by developing countries to harness technology in agriculture have harmed the environment, and in some cases are being reversed.

Future of the Nation-state

What do the projected demographic, technological and environmental changes — all transnational in nature — mean for the future of the nation-state, the organising unit that people normally turn to when challenged by something new?

If the nation-state is unable to handle these problems, is it redundant and should it be replaced by another type of unit? Mr. Kennedy concludes that it will remain the key unit in responding to global damage, "even if the autonomy and functions of the state have been recorded by transnational trends."

Japan's 'Plan' for a Post-2000 World

Complete isolation from the "fallout" from global trends is impossible, but the Japanese will try harder than other countries. Japan will continue to be successful because of its social and racial coherence, and the subordination of individual wants to the collective good.

Japan can handle a technological revolution, but is less well-placed to cope with its own demographic future, still less with global population trends. Its higher life expectancy and lower fertility rates will result in a smaller work force having to support a graying population.

Winners and Losers in the Developing World

There are growing differences between rich and poor developing nations. For example, in the '60s, South Korea and Ghana had the same GDP; today, South Korea is 10 to 12 times as prosperous.

The most successful are those of East Asia, which can be divided into:

- Japan;
- The newly industrialised economies of Singapore, Hong Kong, Taiwan and South Korea (sec story above);
- The larger South-east Asian nations of Thailand, Malaysia and Indonesia, which, stimulated by foreign investment, are becoming involved in manufacturing, assembly and export; and
- The stunted and impoverished communist societies of Vietnam, Cambodia and North Korea.

Will the progress of the NIEs last into the 21st century? Politically, Hong Kong's future is completely uncertain; Taiwan remains a diplomatic pariah because of Beijing's claims; and South Korea still feels threatened by the unpredictable military regime in the north. On Singapore, Mr. Kennedy is silent.

He is scathing on developing countries in the Muslim world: "Far from preparing for the 21st century, much of the Arab and Muslim world appears to have difficulty in coming to terms with the 19th century, with its composite legacy of secularisation, democracy, laissez-faire economics, transnational industrial and commercial linkages, social change and intellectual questioning."

The Erstwhile USSR and its Crumbled Empire

It is very difficult to estimate the ability of the former USSR and Eastern Europe to prepare for the 21st century because, as Mr. Kennedy puts it, "so severe and complex is the crisis (the splintering of the Soviet Union) that the only certain fact is the existence of innumerable uncertainties."

A triple crisis lies at the heart of the Soviet problem, consisting of economic distress caused by years of dictatorship and inefficiency; the lack of a legitimate political system and consequent mass alienation; and the re-emergence of the nationalities problem.

Mr. Kennedy concludes the former Soviet Union is headed for more trouble, no matter how the new splintered states fare, as they clearly are unprepared for the new forces of global change.

Europe's Future

Although the European Community appears relatively comfortable now, it is uncertain that Europeans can continue to enjoy their present way of life. Its problems are greater because it is not a united country like the US or Japan.

Hence two questions:

- What organisational form will Europe assume as it approaches the 21st century?
- Whatever its shape, how will the region fare as it grapples with the transnational changes described in Part One?

Mr. Kennedy believes that instead of merely building a large trading consortium, integration is the only way to go for Europe.

The American Dilemma

The US economy is a mix of strengths and weaknesses but the single most important fact is that rates of growth have slowed considerably in the final third of this century. This means the US may be unable to continue to fund the same level of military security and attend to its social needs and repay its debts.

The US population is forecast to grow steadily, and there will be more old people and more non-Caucasians (through legal and illegal immigration). Some favour more immigration, to fuel the economy and avert the "greying" of America.

Mr. Kennedy says that the US may not be a loser in the face of global changes, as many desperate societies in the developing world will be. But, because of its social and economic structure — altering demographic pattern, environmental problems, educational and social deficits, political — constitutional gridlock, fiscal problems — it could be less than a clear winner.

Mr. Kennedy closes by noting that the desire of politicians and the public to consider short-term general benefits will hinder responsiveness to change. He lists three key elements in any effort to prepare global society for the 21st century.

- Enhancing the role of education (especially in developing countries);
- Improving the status of women and reducing population growth; and
- The need for political will on controversial decisions to effect change.

It is interesting that Mr. Kennedy has gathered his information from a wide range of sources — not only academic works but also computer databases, press clippings and ephemera.

Preparing for the twenty first century begins with a bleak, even dire prediction, but this is not maintained throughout. The author ends on an uncertain, even suggestively optimistic note:

"Because we do not know the future, it is impossible to say with certainty whether global trends will lead to terrible disasters or be diverted by astonishing advances in human adaptation."

As an incurable and ambitious optimist, I have great faith in human action and adaptation. Here is an interesting US study that identifies the circumstances which are most conducive to change and the key element of leadership with a vision.[2]

When Do Economic Reforms Work?

"The Institute for International Economics, a think-tank based in Washington DC, recently commissioned research into 13 cases of radical economic change. In terms of the political setting, these ranged from Chile's reforms, carried out after 1983 by a brutal authoritarian regime, to Spain's, which was carried out after 1982 by democratically elected socialists.

The main question the researchers addressed was this: How, if at all, did governments maintain the political support that made reform possible? These studies, edited by Mr. John Williamson, have now been published by the institute as "The Political Economy of Policy Reform."

It is fascinating volume — not least for the angry exchange between Mr. Jeffrey Sachs and an IMF official over the Fund's role in reforming ex-communist economies. Unlike that, some of the book's findings may come as a surprise.

In 11 of the 13 countries, governments succeeded in making a radical, and with luck, partly irreversible, move towards more liberal economic policies. These were Australia, Chile, Colombia, Indonesia, Mexico, New Zealand, Poland, Portugal, South Korea, Spain and Turkey.

The two failures were Brazil and Peru. The successful countries achieved lower inflation, thanks to better control of monetary and fiscal policies; they privatised state-owned enterprises and otherwise liberalised their economies and they opened their markets to trade.

Such reforms have been tried in many other places at many other times, and failed either at once or soon. What can be learned from the countries that made the changes stick? Of all the factors examined, only one applied in every successful case; the government drew on the advice of a "coherent and united economic team."

In India, one of the most important factors impeding economic growth and preventing the standards of living of our people from rising is the problem of "multiplying millions." Here is an area where intelligent and imaginative personnel administration can yield rich dividends in the factory and office alike through a personnel measure to promote family planning and the Ideal Family concept. This author's contention is that there is an imperative need for management in general and personnel administration in particular to assume a more "creative role" in promoting the economic health of the organisation and the economic growth of our nation. The subject matter of this chapter is divided and discussed under the following headings:

1. Family planning scheme of the government.
2. A personnel programme.
3. Children by choice, not by chance.
4. Have you a family planning service?

1. FAMILY PLANNING SCHEME OF THE GOVERNMENT

The problem of the multiplying millions in our country received its much delayed but much needed share of attention only since Independence under the inspiration of our late Prime Minister, Mr. Nehru and somewhat systematic efforts were initiated with family planning programme as the cornerstone.

National Population Policy

Dr. Karan Singh, who announced the National Population Policy in April 1976, outlined the following measures to make family planning a success:

1. A law will be enacted to raise the minimum age of marriage to 18 for women and 21 for men.
2. Upto the year 2001, representation in the lower House of Parliament and in State Legislatures will remain frozen as determined on the basis of the 1971 census.
3. Upto the year 2001, wherever population is a factor in determining the share of the State in Central resources (for example, in the allocation of assistance for States plans, devolution of taxes, and grants-in-aid), the 1971 population size will be used as the basis.
4. Eight per cent of the Central Government's assistance to State Plans will be allocated on the basis of performance in the area of family planning.
5. Special measures will be undertaken to raise the level of education among females and to improve the nutritional status of children.
6. The Union Cabinet will review in depth the performance of States in the area of family planning at least once a year.
7. Monetary compensation by the Centre to the States for sterilisation procedures (both vasectomy and tubectomy) will be raised to Rs. 150 for

procedures on persons with two or fewer living children, Rs. 100 for persons with three living children, and Rs. 70 for persons with four or more living children. These amounts are intended to cover the cost of drugs, dressings, and other related expenses. The net amount received by individual acceptors of the programme will be somewhat smaller.

8. Group incentives will be introduced for the medical profession, teachers, co-operative societies, labour in the organised sector and panchayats at the districts and lower levels.
9. Individual States are free to introduce special measures designed to encourage the adoption of family limitation by State Government employees and others (for example, preference to acceptors in the allottment of houses and loans). Employees of the Central Government will be expected 'to adopt the small family norm" and their service and conduct rules will be changed "to ensure this."

In this connection, it may be mentioned that the Finance Act of 1976 has already provided that donations for family planning to Government, local bodies, institutions and associations shall be entitled for 100 per cent rebate while computing the income of the donor for the purposes of income-tax. This has been done with a view to generating enough funds to finance family planning programmes, the success of which has now become essential for national survival.[3]

"The revised family planning programme includes opening of 5,200 family welfare and planning centres and 30,000 sub-centres. It is envisaged to open at least one family planning bureau in each district to coordinate the work in towns and villages. One of the main features of the enlarged programme is to provide a greater supply of free contraceptives. To implement this programme, the indigenous production of contraceptives will be stepped up. About 6,000 beds will be provided in hospitals for sterilisation cases.

"The goal is to reduce the birth rate from the present 41 per 1,000 of population to 25 by 1975. This is further sought to be reduced to 18 during the next ten years. The new programme lays stress on making family planning methods known more widely and readily acceptable by the people.

"With only 2.2 per cent of the world's land area, India has 12.8 per cent of the world's population. While the death rate has been steadily declining, the birth rate continues to be 2.5 per cent. This means 12 million more months are added to the population every year. The Government has now decided to go ahead with a crash programme of family planning."

Despite the verbosity, lavish allocations, and elaborate trappings, the national family planning programme in the last 15 years is yet to gain the necessary momentum, to say the least, and its performance is pathetic, to say the worst.

Apart from the phenomenal increase of 78 millions over the 1951 population (an increase of 21%), Indians will multiply themselves to the tune of another 133 millions between 1966 and 1976 according to the estimates of Central Statistical Organisation.

The problem of feeding, clothing, sheltering, educating, and employing all these millions would be a Herculean task.

Mr. R.A. Gopala Swamy, former Director of Manpower Research Institute, in Delhi in a seminar, maintained that our salvation lay mainly in cutting down the birth rate by 53% just as Japan halved its rate of population growth in a decade from 3.5% to 1.7%. In order to do something like that it is not enough to primarily depend on governmental programmes and there is a need for community self-help programmes. The industry and business houses in India have a moral responsibility and a social obligation to meet this vital problem through some of their own efforts.

2. A PERSONNEL PROGRAMME

Now a legitimate question may be asked: Where does personnel management fit in with the population problem? What can personnel administration do about it? We believe that personnel management can and should make a distinct contribution in combating this birth bulge by propagating family planning and the Ideal Family concept in the factory and office. Such a personnel measure has a five-fold purpose:

1. To promote individual and family welfare;
2. To sharpen individual efficiency;
3. To contribute to the national efforts on birth control;
4. To accelerate the process of economic growth; and
5. To raise the standards of living of our people.

Top Management Support: First of all, the personnel department must win the unequivocal support of the top management for a personnel programme that is designed to promote planned families among its labour, clerical and managerial forces. Because this measure aims at moulding the individual life, particularly in its vital areas, the personnel department would be on safe ground if it has the complete backing of the top brass, before indulging in selling the concept of planned parenthood on the premises.

Without this support, the personnel administrator is hardly likely to succeed for obvious reasons.

Once having "sold" the family planning concept to the top brass, the personnel manager must start a whole-hearted family planning campaign and it is not a campaign of coercion but one of persuasion. It is to persuade the worker, the typist, the clerk and the manager to restrict the size of the family through the use of various contraceptives or vasectomy, or intrauterine device, which is both effective and economical. The firm must provide expert medical help to perform sterilisation operations and to suggest the use of contraceptives, either on the premises or in a nearby clinic.

A campaign of education, as to the benefits of having an Ideal Family, which should consist of a father, mother, two or three children, must also be started and it must not neglect to emphasise the impact of the problems of having too many children like educating, feeding, clothing, and employing them on the individual as well as the State. The education plan must be skilfully planned and geared to persuade the individual to overcome his traditional values, religious beliefs, and social mores. This is easier said that done. But then, this only should enhance the significance and value of the personnel 'mission.' Here it is necessary to underscore the economic and social 'disincentives' of unchecked birth bulge.

Incentives: Probably the best way to fight population explosion in the country is not by issuing edicts in the factory and office, or by preaching ponderous platitudes on the evils of uncontrolled procreation, but by providing for certain monetary and non-monetary incentives for the individual who pays heed to the appeal.

As far back as a decade ago, a motor-dealer concern in Madras introduced a welfare measure whereby they induced their employees to undergo vasectomy operation conducted by company doctors for a monetary remuneration of Rs. 30 plus a day's paid holiday. The firm also provided free contraceptives to its employees.

On similar lines, each company, depending on its finances, may evolve its own monetary incentives programme to spread the concept of family planning and may also offer free contraceptives.

Various non-monetary incentives may also be resorted to fruitfully. Recognising ideal families and according wide and conspicuous publicity to them as model families to be emulated by the rest, introducing them at company's and workers' meetings, awarding them nominal prizes, celebrating an Ideal Family Week (when one or more ideal families are prominently introduced and given an opportunity to speak about their good fortunes in having ideal families) and decorating them with distinctions are some of the ways through which individuals can be induced to adopt family planning techniques without cash remuneration.

Education Campaign: The campaign of education and persuasion with regard to the policy, process, programme and procedure of family planning may be channelled through the following media of communication:

1. Personal contacts.
2. Bulletin boards.
3. Employee hand books.
4. Notice boards.
5. Posters.
6. House Magazines.
7. Wall Newspapers.
8. Brochures and pamphlets.
9. Broadcast messages.
10. Medical and health bulletins.
11. Meetings and conferences.
12. Exhibitions and films.

The communication campaign must highlight the following:

1. Why family planning should be adopted?
2. How it can be adopted?
3. Where it can be adopted?

4. What are the benefits of adopting it?
5. What is the contribution of the individual to the country by adopting it?

Here a ticklish but vital point to bear in mind is the language used in these media and it is most advisable and preferable to use such language as is commonly used in the region in order not to defeat the very purpose of communication.

Undoubtedly all this is going to cost money and the personnel department with the help of the expert medical assistance, must prepare a careful estimate of costs and a budget keeping in mind the financial facilities of the firm. The Government may also be approached for some help in this area of operations and the State can also ask its family planning centres and clinics to collaborate with the company concerned in various ways. For example, they can provide literature, films, free drugs, the use of their centres and expert help and clinic facilities and financial aid, if necessary.

The main thing is to cast the first stone and here the personnel administrators must give the initial lead.

3. CHILDREN BY CHOICE, NOT BY CHANCE

Under the auspices of the "New Life Movement" started in 1953, the Japanese employers, considering family planning as crucial factor for improving workers' living conditions started family planning as the core of whole campaign. By 1960, one hundred and fifteen companies provided family planning services to work employees. Stewardesses were appointed to work with family planning instructors and help wife groups. All advice relevant to family planning was provided to every wife when necessary. By 1954 wherever such guidance was given birth control acceptance increased by 15% and wherever individual advice was given by 43.6%. In the third year of the campaign the project was extended to all factories, in Tokyo. Employers could bear the expenditure of this programme as it was offset by non-payment of family allowances, maternity and other benefits usually met by the company when children were born.

In India, the Government offered tax concessions on amounts spent by industries on family planning facilities but the owners of industry feel that the relief is meagre and marginal and not worth the trouble of keeping the necessary records and accounts. Let the Government of India increase this tax relief considerably so that population control may really become successful in India.

The industrial employers in India offered family planning services in order to get the benefit of reduction in maternity benefits, family allowances and absenteeism. Godrej and Tata groups have introduced family planning facilities in India. The Railway Board of India has 60 family planning medical officers at both Central and Zonal levels. Its field workers are carrying on publicity and information campaign. Their employees and public get information on family planning from railway time-tables, coaches, exhibitions by advertisements and posters at the railway stations.

The railway family planning staff carry out door-to-door motivation campaign. During April-December 1973 itself 8,380 sterilisations and 2,016 insertions were carried out by F.P. staff of the Railway Board.

Certain individual private employers and firms are giving cash incentives and paid leave for undergoing vasectomy and tubectomy though according to Family Planning Association of India the two or three days' leave on pay is too short.

The South Indian Plantations have opened a joint account in the joint name of the company and the women employees. The company deposits a certain sum in the account every month the woman is not pregnant. After the child bearing age has passed the sum is given to the woman, if she becomes pregnant meanwhile, the sum is used by the company to cover their costs to be incurred according to employees maternity law. Then after the child birth, the woman can rejoin the scheme.

In all the above cases family planing is made the business of social and health services provided by the business companies and thus was made simple and inexpensive as a part of existing health and clinical structure. Accustomed to their employer-companies the workers are readily willing to accept family planing information at their place of work from their own employer. When the family planning programme is propagated without being made a part of health and clinical structure and also without any other benefits, it is resented by the workers even in Japan where the New Life Movement also faced opposition for the same reason. Smaller firms can come together to give Family Planning facilities, with the help of Family Planning Associations and Training Institutes. In Tunisia some firms have paid overtime allowance to employees when they help family planning association in organising their educational lectures. In many countries the industrialists are allowing their business premises to be used for conducting sessions to motivate workers for adopting birth control measures and also allowing their workers to attend their sessions during working hours. Iran's Family Planning Association is enlisting workers and trade unionists as volunteers to facilitate family planning work. Several Family Planning Associations like that of Grenada, Malaysia and Bangladesh are taking representatives of industrialists into their executive. National concern, increased productivity and attendance resulting from the introduction and adoption of family planning is influencing many employers to cooperate.

International Labour Organisation

I.L.O.'s education programme has considerably stimulated family planning in the industrial sector. The United Nations Fund for Population Activities (UNFPA) is financing this scheme of ILO from 1967 when the educational programme for family planning was begun. This expenditure has risen from $ 25,000 in 1970-71 to $ 2 million in 1973. The ILO population control education programme is three fold: (1) Steps to stimulate the participation of social security and medical services in family planning for workers. (2) Research on demographic aspects of population growth. This is done as a part of world employment programme to consolidate and expand knowledge on the interaction between population and employment growth. Income distribution, labour market pressures, wage rates and other relevant problems are studied. In 1972 a project was started to study the contribution of social security (like family benefits) to population policy. (3) Promotion of information and educational activities in the field of family planning and population. More emphasis is laid on this third aspect. I.L.O. is helping to organise seminars on population control, family welfare and welfare tasks by workers' organisations, in different parts of the world.[2]

Some organisations in our country have already introduced family planning programmes and they have provided monetary and non-monetary incentives.

Family Planning at TELCO

TELCO has introduced this scheme and many employees have embraced this scheme. TELCO gives great publicity to families, which have adopted family planning in its house journal, TELCO News. The proud and happy father and mother along with their children beam at you from the well-got-up TELCO News — a house journal that can be compared with any of the best in the world. In one issue TECLO News exhorts its employees:[5] "Almost 2,000 fellow TELCO workers have now had the entirely painless family planning vasectomy operation. Now what about you? Ask any of these 2000 TELCO Workers and they will all tell you about the safe, harmless and entirely painless operation that brings nothing but happiness and peace for the family. This operation does not in any way affect subsequent sexual relations or manhood. If for some reason at a later date an additional child is required, this can be easily had by another operation. 2000 TELCO families are now happier because they no longer have the worry and anxiety of another mouth to feed in these hard and difficult days. Just ask any of them. The late Pandit Jawaharlal Nehru and our Chairman Mr. J.R.D. Tata have been emphasising the point again and again that family planning is India's single biggest problem. Each one of us in TELCO has it in his power to do something about this. There is no excuse for being complacent."

In another issue TELCO requests its employees to take to family planning thus:[6] "Just you ask... any of the 2000 people that have had the family planning operation in TELCO. They will tell you that it is entirely safe and has no harmful after-effects whatsoever and that it does not affect your sexual powers or manhood in any way. Just you ask them. If you have two or more children have this operation straight away."

At Indian Telephone Industries (ITI)

ITI tells its workers that family planning "is essentially meant to benefit a family and in a cumulative way the country. It is a necessary measure to safeguard the health of the mother, for the healthy development of the child as also for the proper gearing up of the family economy." The motto "children by choice and not by chance" fully sums up the virtues of family planning in that it helps a family to have a child when wanted and not when it does not want it for various reasons.[7]

ITI also gives information with regard to its scheme, the incentives involved and methods to be used:[8]

> "Since family planning affects the private life of a couple, whatever measures the Government may adopt at huge expense cannot succeed unless each and every couple realises the importance of family planning as a necessity. Family planning advice and facilities are today available throughout the country. The ITI General Hospital is running a family planning centre since 1960, where trained lady doctors advise mothers on family planning and on the latest technique of the loop. Willing mothers are fitted with loops after examination. Further follow-up is regularly done to check up the safety and effectiveness of the various contraceptive measures.
>
> "For those families having more than three children, sterilistaion (vasectomy for the male and salpingectomy for the female) operations are advised and these operations are carried out if the couples are willing. These operations do not

produce any untoward effects and are one hundred per cent effective. While salpingectomy for women is a major operation requiring hospitalisation for about 15 days, vasectomy for men is a minor operation needing no hospitalisation at all. The ITI provides a week's extra leave to those who undergo the operation and the ITI hospital has facilities for both these operations.

"The State Government pays Rs. 25 for the person who undergoes the operation and family planning advice in family planning clinics and government hospitals is free. Contraceptive material is either made available free or at a nominal cost depending upon one's income. There are a number of methods of birth control available today and those commonly advocated because of their safety and effectiveness are the condoms, loops and oral tablets. Condoms are rubber sheaths which are one hundred per cent safe and effective. Loop is a plastic coil which after sterilisation is inserted into the uterus of a woman. This technique is simple, safe, cheap and effective to about 98 per cent. One advantage of the loop is that it is a reversible operation. That is if a mother desires children, the loop can be easily removed. The oral tablets are hormone tablets which are taken by the woman. Starting from the fifth day of menstruation, one tablet should be taken daily for 20 days. Five days after the stopping of the tablets, the woman will have her usual periods. The tablets should be taken regularly to avoid pregnancy and this method is safe and one hundred per cent effective."

A Case Study:[9]

Mahindra & Mahindra Ltd. (M & M) which won the first prize for outstanding family planning endeavour in industry during the two year period from 1970-72 is selected for an objective appraisal.

Evolution and Evaluation: It was realised very early that organised establishments could make a singular contribution to the National Family Planning Programme. Central and State Governments were trying to coax employers through circulars. Policies were proclaimed in employers' conferences and seminars. But only a few inspired employers of textile mills like Hindustan, Kohinoor, Century, Bombay Dyeing and business houses like Tata, Godrej and Hindustan Lever made a purposive effort. For most others, it was a routine circular which evoked no obligation. Moreover, Government which was the biggest employer had no model family planning programme for its employees which could be considered as an example for emulation. The lonely exception was Bombay Division of Western Railway which towered in contrast. Under the circumstances most of the employers were apathetic.

Family Planing Programme as an unprecedented marketing endeavour called for the application of relevant principles of management. If the target population is considered as the total potential market, then the workers in organised sector constituted a well-defined major market segment — relatively better organised, more homogeneous in nature and, easily accessible to communication. But the employers were reluctant to invest money and time for the remote gains offered by family planning through mental health, morale and productivity. Bombay District Family Planning Bureau tried to trigger action by co-operative employers by offering a free package of health and family planning drive consisting of inaugural speeches and pledges, exhibition, films, medical check-up and care, immunisations, etc., finally culminating into family planning camps. Help was sought from Rotary Clubs, Lions Clubs, Chambers of Commerce and other Employers' organisations to motivate their member-employers and friends. As a short-term commitment with no financial implications, the programme found favour with a number of large-scale establishments some of whom were generous to give time off to workers for this purpose. It is in this context that the first contract with Mahindra & Mahindra Ltd. (M & M) was established, in 1969.

The management of M & M decided to play an active role to enable the employees to lead a better and happier life by restricting the size of their families and also conform to the national objective. On September 3, 1969, they declared a cash incentive of hundred rupees (Rs. 100) plus 6 days special casual leave to any worker undergoing vasectomy. They also decided to establish an ideal family planning centre within the factory premises. This centre was declared open by Mr. Keshub Mahindra on August 19, 1971. Dedication, dynamism and drive of a farsighted management had materialised in the form of a pleasant, well-equipped family welfare and planning centre staffed with experienced medical and paramedical personnel working as a team under the guidance of its medical advisor Dr. S. L. Balse. It covered in the beginning 5500 employees of M & M. Recently the services have been extended to 3000 additional workers employed in three sister concerns in the area, bringing up the total coverage to 8500 workers. In the near future it is hoped that the centre will also offer family planning services to people living in the neighbourhood. A most logical development when an employer identifies himself with the problems of his workers, community and country, is prone to use his facilities and know-how for furthering a solution. Unfortunately such instances are rare. Very few large employers had good family planning services very often coupled with general welfare services. The smaller employers did not display the interest required, and their workers were left to rely on the family planning services at the community level. It is recognised that there are several constraints, organisational and financial, in the way of effective action by employers in family planning. These difficulties are much more enhanced in the case of smaller and medium-sized industrial establishments. Employers are not aware of any confirmed formula of financial assistance to organise family planning programmes in their establishments and the little interest they may evince dies a natural death in the absence of guidelines. Hence it is very essential that such a formula be evolved and communicated by concerned top officials to employers to accelerate meaningful effort. Willingness should be re-inforced with a built-in component of requirement. A survey schedule for industries may reveal the needs of each industrial establishment and the lacunae in individual situations can be bridged by personalised attention.

Money and time are the twin problems that hinder progress. The finances for the programme in M & M are borne by the management, augmented with the resources of district family planning bureau wherever available. Of course, the revenue expenditure is allowed to be deducted as business expenditure and 20 per cent of the capital expenditure each year for a period of 5 years is also allowed to be deducted as business expenditure for tax purposes. This concession is availed of by the management of M & M to provide an ideal family welfare and planning centre for its workers. It may be mentioned that statutory welfare funds can also be utilised by employers for this purpose. The most urgent need therefore is a possessive conviction which can translate ideas and opportunities into action. Programme policy and planning, staffing pattern and recruitment was done in consultation with the Director, Family Planning, Mumbai. An experienced surgeon, a gynaecologist, a pediatrician, a male social worker, a female social worker, a nurse, a ward boy, a female attendant and a sweeper were appointed to ensure the smooth and efficient functioning of the centre. M & M had 5500 employees of whom 150 eligible men had already been sterilised as a result of enhanced incentive of hundred rupees. The inauguration of the new family planning centre was accelerating the process of decision because of the convenient location of total facilities. The problematical disparity between desire and practice was fast diminishing. All the 5500 workers were surveyed, their needs were identified and through repeated contacts of the 1350 eligible couples 638 had been motivated to undergo sterilisation by March 1973. The scope of the programme was not however limited to sterilisation. Individual counselling, group talk and mass media were geared to promote and provide total family planning services in a comprehensive health care setting. Health of mothers and children and improvement of family life received special emphasis as family planning and family survival were two sides of the same coin.

Organisation and Administration: A committee consisting of the chief executive, administrative manager, personnel and industrial relations officer, medical adviser and family planning social workers organises and administers the programme. Involvement of top officials has the salutory effect of communicating the serious intent about the project. Frequent review meeting take it still further. The committees sets the policy, the personnel of the family planning centre undertake the motivational campaign, medical officers and the nurse conduct the clinical services and the social workers cover the target audience of workers and their families. Lower level committees have not been formed so far. Nor the trade unions and workers are represented in the decision-making process.

Trade unions are institutions through which the organised sector of the working population can be reached and motivated. Trade union leaders of varying political and ideological affiliations have expressed support for national population programmes. Nevertheless, the fact remains that trade unions have brought limited direct contribution to these activities so far. Perhaps this may be due to lack of means or lack of interest or both. Unions occupy a crucial position in favourably influencing the workers' attitudes and acceptance of these programmes. Yet management is always shy to invite unions in committees as they are afraid of conflicting opinions which may lead to idle controversies. It will be helpful if the trade union movement could be made to reach a common understanding that activities relating to population matters — which benefit both the society and the worker — would not be used as an issue in inter-union rivalries and disputes. Though the potential role by trade unions is immense, cautious approach of the management in not rushing representatives of trade unions and workers on these committees till the programme attains maturity, reflects the dilemma which needs to be resolved as early as possible. A beginning should be made by appointment of trade union leaders in central, state and district level family planning programme implementation committees. Simultaneously, a dialogue of involvement can be started through orientation training programmes for trade union leaders and workers. Interested individuals can then be invited to play their rightful role in family planning councils at plant levels. Willing trade unions can also be given material help for more structured programmes.

Strategy: The campaign strategy in M&M is simple and direct. Opportunities for education and motivation of workers and their families are systematically exploited. The workers are approached directly through their respective departmental heads by the social workers on company time. Other informal occasions such as Dassera celebrations, Republic day and Annual Social Gathering when employees and their families get together are gainfully utilised to nourish the common goal of welfare through children's parties, baby shows, healthy mother contest and other themes of improved family living. Selected workers and their families are invited by rotation to the Activity Centre maintained by the company for picnics which bring them together in pleasant surrounding to discuss problems of mutual interest. In addition to Employees State Insurance Service (ESIS), a dispensary with a full-time works doctor is available to all workers in need of medical attention. Company also offers comprehensive medical service to all others not covered by ESIS. Medical personnel utilise every contact with the worker and his family to spread the message of family planning. Gynaecologist promotes family planning when workers' wives are brought to the centre for antenatal and postnatal advice. Women and their husbands are highly motivable during this period. Pediatrician instils confidence by improving child health and survival. Social workers visit workers' homes for follow-up and maintain family folders on health including which are utilised to promote labour health and welfare services of which family planning forms an important integral element.

Even though medical facilities to industrial workers are now the responsibility of Employees State Insurance Service (ESIS), the organisation does not give enough attention to family planning. ESIS with its vast field network extending to several major industrial areas to motivate and provide service to workers in industry is in a particularly powerful position to promote family planning. In view of the close links with employees and workers, the ESIS personnel are the right people to play a leading successful role. For example, if all 1850 insurance medical practitioners in Greater Bombay were to contribute inspired effort, family planning in the industrial complex of Greater Bombay will be a greater reality. Unfortunately this does not happen as no firm emphasis has yet been placed on the prevailing concept that family planning is an integral part of health and medical care. ESIS machinery should be geared to implement family planning motivation and action through its numerous medical contacts in the clinics of insurance medical practitioners, its diagnostic centers and hospitals. Of course, medical practitioners should be oriented for the job, facilities should be provided and their performance should be regularly evaluated.

Motivational Methodology: Workers constitute the ultimate target population. Influencing the attitude of workers and impelling them through mass and group communication techniques and individual persuasion to adopt one or the other family planning methods is a stupendous task affecting as it does their intimate and personal lives and age old prejudices. But, it has been achieved at M&M with concerted efforts. Tradition and illiteracy are recognised impediments in engineering any social change. But the greatest hurdle in family planing is Fear. The most deep-rooted fear of insecurity. Tradition of many children have roots in hoary past when the family unit was the only insurance against improvidence. Death was around and life was a struggle for survival. High infant mortality rates and death rates induced a desire for more children as a reaction to insecurity. Talk of decreasing death rates cannot easily overcome these hang-overs from the past in as much as infant mortality rates continue to be higher than 100 per 1000 live-births in developing countries. Moreover, poorly developed social security measures do not engender the necessary confidence to accept a small family norm. Under the circumstances family planning as a programme of family welfare can be meaningful only through improved survival. Improved health care of mothers and children at M & M, it is hoped, will lead to greater acceptance of family planning.

Other common fears which militate against acceptance of family planning methods are fear of body injury, fear of sex injury, fear of family injury, fear of moral injury and fear of group injury. No method is one hundred per cent safe, and the occasional complication provides a factual basis for dissemination of rumours. The necessary vigilance is exercised at M & M to reduce the complications to a minimum as the total resources of the company are mobilised to treat the complications that may occur through proper follow-up. Safety to a method lies in its effective demonstration. Satisfied acceptor is a very good example and every effort is made to make them communicate with other potential acceptors. Fear of body injury is also overcome by permitting individuals to see the procedure and appreciate its simplicity. Another frequent fear which explains the existing disparity between desire and practice is fear of sex injury. Sex is deep-rooted, the driving force. Males are more sex-conscious than females and fear of sex injury dissuades many from contraception. Complication of hirsutism in females associated with oral contraception with pills of high oestrogenic content led to non-acceptance during the earlier period. Sex dissatisfaction is the major drawback of condom. Fear of possible impotency is decelerating the progress of vasectomy programme. Adequate emotional support to the individuals will help overcome these problems. One of the barriers to the acceptance of sterilization is the fear of death of children or spouse as sterilistaion is considered as a drastic irreversible method. This fear of family injury has been overcome by making reversal of vasectomy and tubectomy, i.e., Recanalisation operation, a reality. Of the 638 sterilised individuals from M & M, not a single individual has requested a reversal proving that instance of childlessness after one year of age are very rare today if the children are given proper care and attention. Fear of moral injury has roots in religion and ethics and is a formidable handicap against family planning. In its extreme form, it manifests in the shape of religious objection. Efforts are made to convince individuals that it is the greatest moral sin to bring an unwanted child into a home of chronic want and misery. Approach is to the parents; group approach through religious leaders is not attempted at present as it is frought with uncertainty. But the greatest iceberg in family planning is differential acceptance by various religious, regional and socio-economic groups — fear of group injury. Unfortunately, generalised family planning programme tends to be a programme of convenience rather than a programme of conviction. Willing families are planned and the resistent continue to breed. Personalised attention in a closed working community permits deployment of greater inputs into areas of higher resistance to make the programme representative in character. Indebtedness of the workers is also utilised to bring home the small family norm.

Management including the labour welfare personnel, medical and paramedical personnel, acceptors of family planning methods and interested worker-leaders are the principal motivational inputs in M & M programme. Considering that the programme is young, the achievement is commendable, but falls short of the requirements. Qualitative and quantitative increase in the inputs by strengthening the rank of motivators and organising formal training programmes for them may lead to sustained success. Motivation, incentives, disincentives and compulsion are the four methods of moulding human behaviour. In a democratic society, compulsion has no place. But along with motivation and incentives, disincentives can also be tried to focus attention of irresponsible parents. Though no penalty is imposed on workers, M & M restricts maternity benefits and schooling facilities in the company's school to the first three children. Disincentives are justifiable to save democracy from the clutches of population explosion. Trade unions and workers must realise that their growing demands can be met when society is not encumbered with unwanted children.

Conclusion

Acceptance without controversy has been the prominent feature of family planning programmes in Mahindra & Mahindra Ltd., and few other pioneering industrial endeavours. Success has been proportionate to the degree of involvement of management, workers and trade unions and the support extended by government. This raises hopes for a massive attack against improvidence. A tripartite declaration that family planning is an integral part of Labour Health and Welfare will go a long way in improving the quality of life of workers and their families in particular and community in general. Orientation training programmes for the various components of the industrial team should be instituted to channelise effort in this war for survival.

4. HAVE YOU A FAMILY PLANNING SERVICE?

The Federation of Indian Chambers of Commerce and Industry has taken active interest in 'selling' the family planning scheme to the industrialists and businessmen of India. They have published a brochure:[10] "Have You a Family Planning Service?" which should be very useful to the businessmen in introducing family planning programmes.

Some Hurdles

The first hurdle, more often than not, is inertia and personnel executives and top managers would rather leave this area well alone than take the initiativc in introducing a measure that is going to taper with the pattern of individual life. But it is a social responsibility of management in an over-populated country like ours to propagate the evils of unmitigated growth of population and the advantages of having planned families.

The second hurdle is more serious and that is the set of religious beliefs and traditional values, which view birth control as "contra-divine" arrangement that is to be frowned upon. It is only through education that individuals can be persuaded to overcome traditional taboos.

Human Resources administrators must take up this challenge and make a very useful contribution by stemming the increasing numbers of our people, by giving a fillip to national efforts and by accelerating the economic growth and progress of India.

REFERENCES

1. Steve Thompson, reviews the book, Preparing for the Twenty-first Century, The Life, *The Straits Times,* Singapore, 8-4-1993, p.2.
2. The Economist, when do Economic Reforms Work? Reproduced in *The Straits Times,* 22-1-1994, p.4.
3. *Economic Revolution in India* (ed. S.D. Punekar), 1977, Himalaya Publishing House, Bombay, pp. 526-527.
4. *The Indian Worker,* January 1977, pp. 15-17.
5. *Telco News*, Vol. XIV, No. 3, 1965.
6. *Telco News,* Vol. XIV, No. 4, 1965.
7. Dr. N.K. Maheswarappa, "The Economics of Family Planning", ITI Magazine, Vol. 18, No. 2, June 1966, p. 20.
8. *Ibid.*, p. 11.
9. D.N. Pai, *Family Planning — Role of Industry and Labour,* 24th All India Conference of Personnel & Welfare Officers, The National Institute of Labour Management, Pune, pp. 5-15.
10. "Have You a Family Planning Service?," a Brochure published by FICCI, July 22, 1966.

❑❑❑

CHAPTER 22

Evaluation of Human Resources Management

One of the most neglected areas in the field of human resources management is the evaluation of the impact of the function and there is very little analytical literature on the concept or the methodology or the choice of techniques with regard to this critical aspect. While this lacuna was tolerated when not much responsibility, status and challenge was conferred on the function of personnel administration in the past, it cannot be now in view of the increasing importance and criticality of the function in total management process. First of all, it is an important activity and function and an integral part of the total management. Secondly, a great deal of time, money and effort is invested by all managers in this function as a part of their managerial responsibility and position. Thirdly, all manages have to depend on the advice, and service provided by the personnel specialist in discharging their responsibilities and functions. Fourthly, thanks to the changing attitudes of people, public policies, labour legislations, concepts of work, quality of working life and quality of life, the function has come to occupy a pivotal place in the management of organisations.

In the light of this advancement, it is only natural to raise the issues:

— What is the contribution of personnel function to productivity, efficiency and profits of the organisation?

— How do we evaluate the function and its impact and effectiveness?

— What are the indices through which we can measure, evaluate and review the function?

— What are the methodologies and the choice of techniques that can be used?

— Is it possible to develop relevant ratios and use ratio analysis?

— What kind of questions should we raise when we think in tems of evaluation of the function?

— What sort of problems are we likely to encounter in the process of evaluation?

Perhaps for the first time, we shall take some tentative steps in defining the problem, clarifying the choice of techniques and pose some indicators to measure, evaluate and review the function.

We should like to submit that this is not the last word and people more competent than the present one, I am sure, would certainly come forward with more lucid, accurate and quantitative techniques to arrive at a solution to the problem of evaluation of the function.

We shall discuss the chapter under the following sections:

1. The problem of evaluation.
2. The process of evaluation.
3. Cost-benefit analysis (questions; indices; ratios).
4. Everybody a personnel administrator.

1. THE PROBLEM OF EVALUATION

Until now, the general rationalisation has been that it is not possible to evaluate the function of personnel because it is a staff function, an advisory function and a service function. It can only advise, but it lacks the line authority to enforce its counsel in the organisation, except for the legal requirements in the area of human resources management. While he is designated the Personnel Manager, he is not directly in-charge of the personnel, except his own departmental people and he is in fact assisting, advising and guiding the line managers to manage their people. While the personnel manager assists in the procurement of personnel, he is not responsible for some of those personnel leáving the organisation or coming late or not performing upto the norms, as they are directly under the charge of some line manager, who is actually responsible for their utilisation and evaluation of their performance. However, the line manager, busy and expert as he is in respect of his function, lacks the necessary know-how and competence as to how to motivate his subordinates, utilise their full capabilities by integrating their needs with those of organisation, appraise their performance, train them, compensate them etc. This is where the responsibility of the personnel manager lies; to provide the expertise, guide, counsel and coach in all aspects of human resources management. On the other hand, the line manager cannot absolve himself of all responsibility for turnover, absenteeism, tardiness, poor productivity, efficiency and performance of his departmental personnel and throw the entire blame on personnel department, just as the personnel department cannot be silent spectator to what is happening in the area of human resources. Both the postures would tantamount to basic irresponsibility on the part of line and staff specialists. This is amply illustrated by the case where the General Manager of a foreign subsidiary walked into the office of the Personnel Manager and told him: "Look, the absenteeism is extremely high in the factory this month. What are you doing about it? This is your problem, because it deals with personnel." The Personnel Manager shot back: "Don't shove this absenteeism thing into my lap as my problem, because it concerns personnel. In fact it is your problem. It is the problem of the entire factory and management. Let us be first aware of this situation. Now if you want to tackle this problem, let us both sit together and we can come up with ways to lick this problem. I am here to assist you." Then they sat together along with the other heads of departments and the union and worked out a solution.

It is the responsibility of the personnel department to monitor the entire human resources programmes, policies and practices, in the ultimate analysis guide, train, coach and help line managers to manage their people according to company personnel philosophy, policies and procedures. If this principle is conceded, then it is possible to find a way around the problem of effectiveness of the personnel function and we shall turn to the methodologies that can be adopted with a view to assessing the contribution of personnel and evaluating its effectiveness.

Now we shall suggest a process of evaluation with a certain choice of techniques.

2. THE PROCESS OF EVALUATION

We suggest a three point evaluative process of human resources management in organisation:

(1) Asking the right kind of questions, to monitor the activities and the inputs.

(2) Suggesting critical indices, to monitor the effectiveness of the function and its impact through output.

(3) Using ratio analysis, to monitor norms and standards of performance.

(1) Questions

There must be considerable soul-searching and self-analysis and evaluation. All personnel functions, programmes and policies must be constantly subjected to close scrutiny, evaluation and review. After identifying all the major functions and sub-functions, the next step is to assess each activity in the light of the following questions suggested by Prof. Robert D. Gray:[1]

(1) What is the philosophy underlying the function?

(2) What principles of management are being followed in carrying it out?

(3) What policies have been established for this function?

(4) What procedures have been established? Are they in line with philosophy, principles and policies?

(5) Are the procedures, policies, management principles and philosophy of each function consistent with those of other, related functions?

Who will be asking these questions in the formal evaluation, and how? There are at least five agents and methods to choose from, and, in fact, all or any combination may be used:[2]

(1) Observation by higher management.

(2) Formal appraisal by higher management.

(3) Group discussion among "customers" of the personnel department.

(4) Opinion polls.

(5) Use of a consultant.

In every function or activity of the personnel division at every major step such questions as the following must be raised and answers sought:

(1) What is being done?

(2) How it is being done?

(3) Who is doing it?

(4) Where is it being done?

(5) How much is it going to cost?

(6) What is the return?

(7) Is it a worthwhile investment?

(8) How does it affect people?

(9) Do we know of a better way of doing it?

(10) Who will be responsible for it?

(11) Are we achieving the results we planned to achieve?

(12) How do the results compare with the objectives?

(13) What modifications are necessary in the light of experience or more knowledge?

Constant vigilance is necessary in personnel administration, because people are dynamic and unpredictable. Before you know, programmes may be rendered obsolete and you are left behind.

After these omnibus questions, we shall suggest some specific questions in various activities and sub-functions of human resources management.

(A) Personnel Philosophy

(1) Is there a well-defined and written statement of personnel philosophy of the organisation?

(2) Is it unique and relevant to meet the peculiar needs of the people of the organisation, industry, region and nation?

(3) Does everybody understand and operate by the philosophy?

(4) Are there checks and balances in the statement to take care of the contingencies, deviations and emergencies?

(5) Is it the 'Bible' for the organisation?

(B) Personnel Policies and Procedures

(1) Is there a written statement of policies and procedures for the organisation?

(2) Do they meet the needs of the organisation and the people?

(3) Does everybody understand and operate by the policies and procedures?

(4) Is there a systematic periodic review and monitoring system?

(5) Is the statement based on the state of the art consideration?

(C) Human Resources Planning (HRP)

(1) Is there a good system of HRP involving the key executives to a sufficiently long perod, say 5 years or 7 years or 10 years?

(2) Is it dovetailed to the corporate business plan?

(3) Does it achieve the objectives of forecast demand and supply, career and succession planning, and promotion?

(4) Does it highlight trouble spots early enough to take necessary action?

(5) Does it generate enough resources internally to meet the needs of the organisation?

(D) Selection

(1) Is there a scientific selection process and procedure?

(2) Does it place the right man on the right job?

(3) Are all relevant line and staff executives trained and involved in the process?

(4) Does it utilise properly the appropriate instruments of selection and objectively?

(5) Is it reasonable and cost effective?

(6) Is it legal and non-discrimination oriented?

(7) Does it induct and follow-up properly?

(E) Human Resources Development

(1) Is there a good system of HRD involving all people at all levels in the process of developing their subordinates?

(2) Are the strategies appropriate?

(3) Does the system generate and provide for people at all levels — skilled, supervisory, managerial — wherever necessary and assure a steady source of supply of a well trained and developed people at all levels?

(4) Does it use the right techniques and pedagogical approaches to develop people?

(5) Is it reasonable and cost effective?

(6) Is everybody committed to the developmental approach?

(7) Does it meet the needs of expansion and diversification?

(8) Does it meet with the individual and organisational needs of growth?

(F) Promotions, Transfers and Performance Appraisals

(1) Is there written statement of policies of promotion, transfers and appraisals?

(2) Does everybody understand and operate by the objectives, criteria and policies in these areas?

(3) Does the system yield the right kind of people at the right places?

(4) Are individual and organisational interests achieved?

(5) Does the system result in the promotion and retainment of people in the organisation?

(6) Are the executives well trained in these activities?

(G) Morale

(1) Is there a system of attitude and morale surveys in order to measure morale among personnel?

(2) Is there a morale improvement programme?

(3) How effective is it?

(4) Are people trained in the scientific and technical aspects of morale measurement and improvement?

(5) Does morale result into increased productivity and efficiency?

(H) Communications and Suggestion Systems

(1) Do people understand Company policies and operation clearly enough to make a contribution to the organisation?

(2) Is there a three way flow of communication — top down, bottom up and horizontal?

(3) Is there a proper understanding, cooperation and coordination among people, departments and union and management?

(4) Does the system generate suggestions, ideas and solutions to take care of productivity, efficiency, profits, costs, and quality of working life?

(5) Do people believe official communications or only rumours and grapevine?

(I) Wage and Salary Administration

(1) Is there a good system of wage and salary administration?

(2) Does the system provide adequate incentives for people to give off their best as well as stay with the organisation?

(3) How does it compare with those in the same industry, region and community?

(4) Does it reward the outstanding and punish the poor performer?

(5) Does it have enough flexibility to take care of the peculiar needs and situations in the organisation?

(6) Is it based on job evaluation system?

(7) Is there a systematic periodic review of the system, based on surveys and research?

(8) Does it meet with the legal requirements?

(J) Employee Benefits and Services

(1) Is there a good system of benefits and services based on the needs of the people and the organisation?

(2) Does it meet with all the statutory requirements?

(3) Does it promote the health, safety and welfare of the employees?

(4) How does it compare with those of the industry, the region and the community?

(5) Does it improve employee morale, productivity, efficiency and motivate them to do their best?

(6) Is there a cost benefit analysis done?

(7) Does it retain the personnel?

(K) Human Relations and Motivation?

(1) Is there a good system of human relations and motivation?

(2) Do employees take pride in their organisation because of its human relations policy?

(3) Is there job satisfaction, job security and job enrichment?

(4) Is there a system to understand and take care of the attitudes, motives, feelings and needs of employees and evolve motivational systems?

(5) Are people treated with individual dignity, respect, and decorum?

(6) Does the system lead to self actualisation and individual fulfilment?

(7) What is the correlationship between human relations, motivation and high performance, efficiency and productivity?

(L) Union-Management Relations

(1) Are Union-Management relations smooth, peaceful and harmonious based on the philosophy of bipartism?

(2) Are there long-term agreements which regulate their relations?

(3) Are they able to solve their disputes across the table?

(4) Is there an effective joint consultation machinery?

(5) Is there a continuous dialogue between union and employees and management on all matters of mutual interest?

(6) Does the system promote industrial peace and prosperity?

(M) Labour Legislation

(1) Is there a system to monitor the compliance of the company with all the legal and statutory requirements?

(2) Do the people understand and operate by the statutory provisions?

(3) Are the people trained to observe and follow the statutory provisions?

(N) Employee Grievance Redressal

(1) Is there a formal system of grievance redressal?

(2) Are the employee grievances redressed speedily and satisfactorily?

(O) Employee Discipline

(1) Is there a system for the promotion of employee discipline based on individual dignity and self-respect?

(2) Are the rules and regulations and disciplinary procedure clearly stated and understood by the employees?

(3) Does the system promote order, discipline and decorum in the organisation and prevent acts of indiscipline?

(4) Are domestic inquiries technically and legally correct?

The list of questions can go on, but the point is that the questions are to assist in the assessment and evaluation of the activities and inputs within the personnel function.

(2) Critical Indices

The critical indices help to monitor the effectiveness of the personnel function and its impact through outputs, which are the outcome of human behaviour in the organisation. They are indicators or act as barometers of the impact and effectiveness of the function. For instance, if there are frequent strikes in an organisation, it is index of the poor state of union-management relations, even though it is conceded that some of the causes are beyond the function of personnel and even management. Nevertheless it affects the economic health of the organisation and presents a serious problem to management and personnel executives. Similarly an attempt is made to suggest some critical indices which highlight the effectiveness (or the lack of it) of the function in the organisation in the following table:

Table 22.1

EFFECTIVENESS OF PERSONNEL FUNCTION

Activity	*Indices*	*Effectiveness*	
		High	*Low*
(1) Manpower Planning Selection	The rate of turnover	Low	High
	The rate of internal promotions	high	low
	Cost of selection	low	high
	The rate of response to ads	high	low
	The rate of retention	high	low
(2) Human Resources Development	The rate of internal promotions	high	low
	The employees promoted to management cadre	high	low
	The rate of direct recruitment	low	high
	The number of potentials	high	low
(3) Promotions	The rate of internal promotions	high	low
	The rate of direct recruitment	low	high
	The rate of turnover	low	high
(4) Transfers	The rate of transfers	low	high
	The rate of retention	high	low
	The rate of turnover	low	high
(5) Performance Appraisal	The rate of promotions	high	low
	The rate of retention	high	low
	The number of potentials	high	low
	The rate of turnover	low	high
(6) Morale and Motivation	The rate of turnover	low	high
	The rate of retention	high	low
	The rate of absenteeism	low	high
	The rate of productivity and efficiency	high	low
	The rate of rejections, rework	low	high
	The rate of tardiness	low	high
	The cost per unit	low	high
	The rate of accidents	low	high
	The number of strikes	low	high
	The rate of disciplinary problems	low	high
	The rate of grievances	low	high
	Frequency of unrest	low	high
(7) Communication	The rate of rumours	low	high
	Frequency of unrest	low	high
	Rate of suggestions	high	low
(8) Wage and Salary Administration	Rate of turnover	low	high
	Rate of retention	high	low
	Rate of grievances	low	high
	Rate of satisfaction	high	low
	Morale	high	low

Activity	*Indices*	*Effectiveness*	
		High	*Low*
(9) Industrial Relations	Rate of strikes	low	high
	Rate of mandays lost due to strikes	low	high
	Frequency of unrest	low	high
	Rate of closures & lockouts	low	high
	The term of contract	long	short
	Frequency of disputes	low	high
	No. of cases pending for adjudication	low	high
	Morale	high	low
	Rate of production and efficiency	high	low
(10) Employee Benefits and Services	The rate of turnover	low	high
	The rate of absenteeism	low	high
	The rate of tardiness	low	high
	The rate of sickness	low	high
	The rate of accidents	low	high
	The rate of satisfaction	high	low
	Cost of services per unit	low	high
	The rate of investment on service	high	low
(11) Labour Legislation	The rate of disputes	low	high
	The rate of adjudication matters	low	high
	The rate of strikes, closures and lockouts	low	high
	No. of cases in court	low	high
	Rate of show cause notices	low	high
	Rate of domestic enquiries	low	high
(12) Employee Grievance Redressal	Rate of grievances	low	high
	Rate of companies	low	high
	Rate of turnover	low	high
	Rate of satisfaction	high	low
	Rate of grievance redressal	high	low
(13) Employee Discipline	Rate of turnover	low	high
	Rate of dismissals	low	high
	Rate of domestic enquiries	low	high
	Rate of show cause notices	low	high
	Rate of grievances	low	high
	Rate of satisfaction	high	low
	Rate of punishments	low	high

In addition, there may be some other indices, developed on the state of the art, for example, the level of sophistication of the personnel function, the level of complexity of services provided, the number of times the top and line management seeks the counsel of specialists, the level of compliance with the statutory and corporate stipulations.

(3) The Ratio Analysis

The third methodology of evaluating the effectiveness of personnel function is by suggesting certain ratios:

(1) Assets per employee.

(2) Sales per employee.

(3) Employee productivity to total productivity.

(4) Cost of employee to total costs.

(5) Employee efficiency to total efficiency.

(6) Employee generated loss, damage, scrap, waste to total loss, damage, scrap, waste.

(7) Cost of employee benefits to total costs.

(8) Cost of employee welfare to total costs.

(9) Cost of employee development to total costs.

The above kind of ratio analysis would enable top and personnel executives to evaluate the effectiveness of human resources management. If this ratio analysis is done on a inter-firm comparison, it is a real eye opener for organisations and necessary decisions can be made to improve the effectiveness of the personnel function.

3. COST BENEFIT ANALYSIS

The cost benefit analysis is another important management tool to assess the effectiveness of the personnel function. Generally the charge is that personnel administrators are rarely aware of the cost implications of some of their proposals and projects and not even budgets and cost estimates, let alone benefits analysis, are formulated before undertaking a personnel project. The major business consideration in any project, including that of personnel, is what is the cost of the project and what are the benefits likely to accrue to the organisation and only after such a cost-benefit analysis projects are to be undertaken. Here we present an interesting case of cost effectiveness programme of a large multinational, which should serve as a model to organisations interested in maximising their personnel effectiveness.

"The purpose of this is to describe a framework which top operating and personnel executives can use to channel the resources of the personnel function to the most worthwhile undertakings. This framework first implemented at Xerox in 1971 as part of a long range manpower planning strategy, is currently being used to develop operating budget proposals for selected personnel units throughout the company. Here are the key procedural steps that I shall discuss:

(1) Define and describe each personnel programme — whether proposed or ongoing — in a discrete package.

(2) Separate for special treatment those programmes that are legally required.

(3) Evaluate all programmes on the basis of these factors:

(a) "state of the art," (b) ease of implementation, (c) net economic benefits, (d) economic risks of not acting.

Developing a Framework

The President of our business products group asked us to review our manpower requirements and to indicate what programmes were underway or were needed to ensure achievement of the plan. To accomplish this objective, we had to:

- Review our group's present and projected revenue and profit economics.
- Identify and understand the ways that major groups of employees (managers, scientists, salesmen, servicemen, clericals, and hourlies) affected our economic situation.

- Specify action programmes that could increase productivity or help avoid major manpower risks and unnecessary costs.

There is nothing fundamentally new about the four-part approach we developed. For years, bankers have used systematic screening standards to evaluate creditworthiness. More recently, managers in virtually every business function other than personnel have used decision frameworks or models to assist them in selecting alternate investment or project opportunities. Usually, these techniques are quantitative, sometimes, they are subjective. But in either case, they share a systems approach. The idea, then was to apply the systems approach and programme management concepts to our personnel operations. Let us not turn to an examination of the key steps in Xerox's programme management framework.

1. Define and Describe

The first step is for each staff specialist responsible for a particular programme to describe his efforts — whether ongoing or proposed — in discrete packages. He specifies the programme's objectives, target population, implementation schedule, and any other considerations that might have impact on the programme's success. (Exhibit I shows a condensed form of the basic document used in our evaluation process for all programmes.)

The personnel programme manager, who is responsible for coordinating the entire department effort, assists the staff specialist. The two work as a team, so that each individual's capabilities complement the other's. For example:

— On the one hand, the staff specialist (in the case of Exhibit 22.1, a job enrichment specialist), (please see Exhibit 22.1, Program Evaluation Form, HBR, May-June 1973, p. 99), is the most knowledgeable about the programme's objectives and technical aspects, the behavioural subtleties of the target population, and the scheduling problems that might inhibit timely implementation.

— On the other hand, the personnel programme manager can provide details on manpower levels, salaries, productivity, absenteeism and turnover rates, and spans of control, as well as the costs and profit economics implied by each.

2. Identify Legal Requirements

Many of the resources of a personnel staff must be allocated to programmes required by law. Most manpower legislation and regulations have been enacted in the past decade in such areas as pension plans, minority hiring, labour relations, and wage controls. Moreover, such legal requirements will probably increase in future years, particularly among larger organisations, as the traditional economic role of business is enlarged to include a social one.

Obviously, the job enrichment programme detailed in Exhibit is not a statutory necessity. But other programmes — in areas such as labour relations, and reporting, and payroll — clearly are legal requirements. Legally required efforts are handled separately from all other proposals and assigned the highest priority. Here are just a few illustrations from the spectrum of manpower regulations:

Exhibit 22.1
PROGRAM EVALUATION FORM

1. Define and describe the program

PROGRAM NAME: Service Force Job Enrichment Program — Program No. 16

DESCRIPTION (objectives, target population, implementation schedule):

To extend the job enrichment program for the service force — as piloted in Spring Falls, Avon Hills, and Maplewood branches — to all branches between 1972 and 1976.

2. Identify and segregate legally required efforts

Is program legally required — Yes [ ] No [X]

3. Evaluation feasibility:

(a) State-of-the-art implications — STATE OF THE ART: [X] High [ ] Medium [ ] Low

(b) Ease of implementation. — EASE OF IMPLEMENTATION: [ ] High [ ] Medium [X] Low

(c) Net economic benefits ... — ECONOMIC BENEFITS: [X] High [ ] Medium [ ] Low

Identifiable benefit:	Potential revenue impact	Probability of occurrence	Probable gross benefit (cost)
Reduction in service force turnover of 1 point	$ 450,000	.2	$ 90,000
Extension of 1.2 point reduction in absenteeism, as demonstrated in pilot project.	$ 2,132,500	.8	$ 1,706,000
Extension of 5% increase in service force productivity, as demonstrated in initial efforts.	$ 85,500,000	.1	$ 8,550,000
Total benefits	$ 88,082,500	.12	$ 10,346,000
Tangible costs to Xerox of acting:			
Group personnel staff time to develop program, and line management time to implement program in all branches.	($ 472,950)	.9	$ 425,655
Total costs	($ 472,950)	.9	$ 425,655
Probable net benefits (cost)			$ 9,920,345

... and intangibles — Intangible benefits

Increased morale in service force, with improved customer service and satisfaction.

"Contagious effect" of job enrichment to other groups, e.g., sales and clericals.

Improved service manager development with concurrent sharpening of their motivational skills. As an extreme example, one manager at Avon Hills increased his team's productivity 70%.

(d) Economic risks — ECONOMIC RISKS: [X] High [ ] Medium [ ] Low

Possible consequences of not acting:

Continued escalation of service costs as a per cent of revenue

ASSUMPTIONS AND OTHER CONSIDERATIONS:

Cost estimates assume 4.4 man years of group staff time, 26 man years of branch manager time, and 15.8 man years of service manager time to implement program in a population of 1,053 service managers.

Benefit estimates assume elimination of 3 days absenteeism per month for each of 1,053 service teams, favourable productivity, and that turnover experience in pilot branches can be cascaded to all branches

— Reporting programmes to maintain records of hours, earnings, overtime, union dues collected, and the financial health of existing or proposed pension plans.

— Affirmative action plans to hire and upgrade the skills of minority groups and women.

— Any validation efforts needed to insure that pre-employment selection tests or standards comply with the guidelines set by the federal government.

— Programmes to insure a safe work environment and to eliminate recognised hazards likely to cause death or injury.[3]

3. Evaluate Feasibility

The feasibility evaluation of any programme focuses on several distinct issues. These are:

— Determining the state-of-the-art requirements. Are the necessary skills available?

— Determining the ease of implementation. Will line management accept and execute the programme?

— Determining the net economic benefits. Will the programme be cost effective?

— Determining the economic risks. Can the company afford not to act?

State of the Art: The resolution of this issue requires an in-depth assessment of a programme's technical problems as well as the skills available within the personnel department or outside the company (e.g., consultants) needed to overcome these problems. If data processing support is necessary, programming complexity and the availability of equipment must also be determined.

In the case of the job enrichment programme shown in Exhibit, qualified technical talent was already available on our staff; thus we could evaluate the state of the art as "high."

For comparative purposes, the technical feasibility of all programmes must be consistently evaluated against the same standards. Part A of Exhibit II (Please see Exhibit II, Standards for feasibility evaluation, HBR, May-June 1973, p. 101) shows these standards, which I feel are generally applicable to most companies.

Ease of Implementation: This is the most critical stage of the feasibility evaluation. It involves such elements as line management attitudes, corporate policies, organisation structure, opening environment, and management styles. These elements are difficult to change, particularly when programmes are in new areas such as job enrichment, organisation development, assessment centers, and selection research.

The key to successfully implementing such advanced concepts hinges on the willingness of line management to corporate. Reorienting personality traits and management styles (which many of the new techniques require) is more challenging than gaining acceptance of a new production process, a new marketing programme, or a new billing system. Most of the latter are more tangible and can be "sold" exclusively on their economic merits. But convincing managers of the need to change their behaviour is not only difficult but also crucial to programme implementation.

Because of the potential resistance, however, our evaluation of the ease-of-implementation factor was a qualified "low" — a market that injected a sobering element should the programme pass its other tests and be given the green light.

Exhibit 22.2

STANDARDS FOR FEASIBILITY EVALUATION

	A. State of the art	*B. Ease of implementation*
Evaluation	*Standards*	*Standards*
High	Program appears simple. Skilled manpower available in company. EDP programming is simple. Hardware available in company.	Implementing program requires little or no effort to effect a change in line management attitudes and styles, and in organisation policies, structure, and operating environment. Implementing program does not imply a radical departure from historic company practices.
Medium	Program appears complex. Skilled manpower not available in company but is available outside. EDP programming is difficult. Hardware not available in company but is on the market.	Implementing program requires moderate efforts to effect a change in line management attitudes and styles, and in organisation policies, structure, and operating environment. Implementing program implies some departure from historic company practices.
Low	Program involves new or unfamiliar effort. Personnel not available on staff or outside company. EDP programming is very complex. Hardware not available.	Implementing program requires substantial efforts to effect a change in line management attitudes and styles, and in organisation policies, structure, and operating environment. Implementing program implies a radical departure from historic company practices.

Note: Standards for evaluation of the net economic benefits and the economic risks have not been included in this exhibit since they are not generally to other companies.

Finally, as with the state-of-the-art evaluation, consistent standards must be applied when evaluating programmes for ease of implementation. These standards are shown in Part B of Exhibit 22.2 (HBR, May-June 1973, p. 101), again, I feel they are generally applicable to most business enterprises.

Net Economic Benefits: At this stage of the evaluation, we use cost/benefit analysis, with modifications that are appropriate to the unique needs of manpower management, to determine whether a programme will be cost-effective.

For the programme shown in Exhibit 22.1, our job enrichment specialist, assisted by the personnel programme manager, identified potential benefits and costs, estimated the probable occurrence of each benefit and cost, and calculated the probable dollar impact. In this case we were fortunate. The pilot project mentioned earlier gave us quantitative data regarding job enrichment's effect on turnover, absenteeism, and productivity.

For many other programmes, however, it is particularly difficult to estimate potential benefits and to establish a direct linkage between them and the programmes. To overcome this problem, we estimate benefits by one of these two approaches:

(a) Identifiable Benefits: These are used whenever possible. They must be tangible and clearly attributable to implementing the programme. An example of an identifiable benefit is the direct savings achieved by eliminating redundant functions in a proposed reorganisation.

In other cases, we contrast the cost (for value) of the existing approach with that of the proposed approach. For example, one of our employment managers felt he could achieve significant savings by relying less on outside employment agencies. His identifiable benefit was developed using the present cost of fees paid to these agencies. The projected costs of additional staff and advertising were substracted from this present cost to develop a net economic benefit for his proposal.

Finally, if a pilot test has been conducted on a small group of employees with favourable results, a plausible benefits estimate can be developed by projecting the savings identified in the pilot tests to the entire organisation.

(b) Target Benefits: These are used in the absence of identifiable benefits. In essence, they are derived from a preliminary estimate of results to which the personnel manager is willing to commit himself, if he is given the resources to do a pilot test of his proposal. An example of a target benefit is a 1% increase in revenue or a one point decline in turnover projected for a given programme.

In some cases, the personnel manager develops such estimates for each of his programmes with assistance from the programme manager, the controller's staff, or the long-range planning staff. In other cases, our staff managers are able to make sound cases for target benefits by consulting their colleagues in other companies or by reviewing the professional literature. The benefits detailed for the job enrichment programme in Exhibit 22.2 are identifiable benefits. They are based on the pilot project, and assume that the results of that effort can be extended to other locations. Intangible benefits and risks are also described at this stage of the feasibility evaluation.

Economic Risks: In the final stage of the feasibility evaluation, we consider the economic impact of not implementing the proposal. For example, a failure to continually re-evaluate the company's pre-employment selection standards could result in the hiring of more marginal employees. (The cost of subsequent declines in productivity could be estimated.) Or a failure to increase productivity could result in unacceptable costs. (This approach was used to assess the job enrichment programme.)

Our standards for classifying economic risks, ranging from over $ 1,000,000 for "high" to under $ 1,00,000 for "low" are unique to our company. Other companies may have higher or lower standards, depending on their size or industry. Banks and insurance companies, for example, would probably have substantially higher risk standards than oil or chemical companies have. (The revenues of the former are highly sensitive to payroll costs). Similarly, service organisations, such as airlines, are more vulnerable to strike losses than hard good enterprises. (The latter can hedge such risks with inventory).

4. Allocate and Deploy Resources

After each programme has been evaluated on its own merits, its over all feasibility must be determined. The decision table shown in Exhibit 22.3 (please see, Exhibit 22.3 — Decision table for determining programme feasibility, HBR, May-June 1973, p. 103),

Exhibit 22.3

DECISION FOR DETERMINING PROGRAM FEASIBILITY

Step 1. Evaluate feasibility and economic benefits/risks

Using predefined standards, separately evaluate each program's state-of-the-art implications, ease of implementation, net economic benefits, and economic risks of not acting. The Service Force Job Enrichment Program was evaluated (see Exhibit I) as follows:

State of the art	- High
Ease of implementation	- Low
Net Economic benefits	- High
Economic risks	- High

Step 2. Compare technical (state-of-the-art) with operational (ease-of-implementation) feasibility.

1. The "high" state-of-the-art evaluation ... is matched against "low" ease of implementation.

State of the art	Ease of implementation		
	HIGH	MEDIUM	LOW
HIGH	Very desirable	Very desirable	Marginally desirable
MEDIUM	Very desirable	Moderately desirable	Marginally desirable
LOW	Marginally desirable	Marginally desirable	Not worthwhile

Step 3. Compare Step 2 evaluation with net economic benefits.

2. Results of this evaluation are compared to "high" net economic benefits

Step 2 evaluation	Net economic benefits		
	HIGH	MEDIUM	LOW
Very desirable	Very desirable	Moderately desirable	Low desirable
Moderately desirable	Very desirable	Moderately desirable	Marginally desirable
Marginally desirable	Marginally desirable	Marginally desirable	Not desirable

Step 4. Compare step 3 evaluation with economic risks to determine overall feasibility

3. Results of this evaluation "high" risks ...
4. ... to determine overall feasibility category of "moderately desirable."

Step 3 evaluation	Economic risks		
	HIGH	MEDIUM	LOW
Very desirable	Very desirable	Moderately desirable	Moderately desirable
Moderately desirable	Moderately desirable	Moderately desirable	Marginally desirable
Marginally desirable	Moderately desirable	Marginally desirable	Not worthwhile

serves as a convenient tool to accomplish this. It allows each programme to be categorised into one of the following overall feasibility categories: (a) very desirable, (b) moderately desirable, (c) marginally desirable, or (d) not worthwhile.

Note that the table is structured so that a high rating on any factor will not conclusively decide in favour of the programme, but a low rating on any factor could eliminate the programme from consideration. For example, Exhibit 22.3 shows that while the job enrichment proposal was rated "high" on three of the four individual feasibility characteristics, the single "low" rating (for ease of implementation) resulted in an overall feasibility assessment of only moderately desirable.

When all programmes have been classified in the foregoing manner, they are ranked on the Programmes Priorities Schedule shown in Exhibit 22.4. (Please see Exhibit 22.4, Programme Priorities Schedule HBR, May-June 1973, p. 104). The legally required programmes appear at the top of the schedule. All other programmes are ranked, within the appropriate overall feasibility category, according to their economic benefits. (Note that the job enrichment programme is ranked third after the legally required programmes.) Those programmes evaluated as "not worthwhile" appear at the bottom of the schedule for elimination. And, if management limits the budget or mandates as austerity programme, other programmes can be cut, starting with those of lowest priority. The Programme Priorities Schedule has become our basic tool for allocating and deploying staff resources.

Trim Marginal Programmes: This is often difficult for management to do since it may involve cutting some sacred cows (e.g., the executive jet or weekend retreats). But the fact remains that eliminating marginal programmes is one key way of achieving the primary objective of business-profitable operations.

Allocate and deploy staff resources toward the most worthwhile project.

Timely programmes implementation requires that staff resources be deployed only toward the higher-ranked projects. For some programmes, staff members might be transferred from areas that have been trimmed, for other programmes, particularly in highly technical areas, new people might have to be hired. Furthermore, additional resources might be allocated to worthwhile projects in order to speed up their implementation date.

Evaluate all new programme proposals and reorder priorities as necessary.

To be successful the evaluation procedure must be viewed as dynamic and ongoing. As new proposals are developed, they must be evaluated and ranked, then accepted or rejected by the same standards applied to all other efforts. Thus priorities may be changed, and staff resources may be redeployed, as circumstances warrant.

Reevaluate existing programmes.

Programme priorities must be changed not only to accommodate new programmes but also to reflect alterations of existing programmes. For example, the appointment of a new key executive in an operating department may alter the ease-of-implementation evaluation of a particular programme. Similarly, the personnel staff may achieve a key break-through that raises the state-of-the-art evaluation. In short, any of a number of events could trigger a chain reaction of reordered priorities by altering the feasibility evaluation on one aspect of a given programme.

Exhibit 22.4
PROGRAM PRIORITIES SCHEDULE

ACTION PROGRAM	Priority	Timing (1972 1973 1974 1975 1976 1977)	Net annual dollar benefit	Cost/ benefit ratio (1 : n)
LEGALLY REQUIRED PROGRAMS				
Labour Relations Strategy	x		($ 619)	n/a
Protected Right to Select Employees	x		($ 86)	n/a
Continue validation of Selection Tests	x		$ 35,000	78.17
Redesign Personnel Data System	x		$ 273	1.78
Develop Part-Time Female Employment Approaches	x		$ 227	4.16
VERY DESIRABLE PROGRAM				
Restructuring Service Force	1		$ 14,608	9.6
Service College Coop. Program	2		$ 4,490	2.74
MODERATELY DESIRABLE PROGRAMS				
Service Job Enrichment	3		$ 9,920	24.3
Assessment Center	4		$ 4,946	15.40
Education & Training Center	5		$ 4,780	3.57
Clerical Selection Program	6		$ 1,799	19.94
Develop College Campus as Primary Employment Source	7		% 834	2.06
Interfunctional Moves & Fast Track Program	8		$ 679	7.54
Selection Standards for New Sales/ Tech. Rep. Types	9		$ 520	11.6
Improve Economics of Field Employment Operations	10		$ 472	1.42
Build Better Technical Recruiting/Selection Capability	11		$ 222	2.48
Monitor Sales & Tech/Rep. Selection Tests	12		$ 211	9.05
MARGINAL BUT DESIRABLE PROGRAMS				
Implement Executive Search Functions	13		$ 177	1.67
Refine Career Path Guides	14		$ 110	1.75
Continue National Trend Attitude Surveys	15		$ 107	1.33
Re-evaluate Overall Organisation Approach	16		$ 93	2.37
NOT WORTHWHILE				
Executive retreat	x		($ 450)	n/a
Corporate Jet	x		($ 769)	n/a
Savings Plan	x		($ 75)	n/a

1. Legally required efforts come ...

2. ... then other programs are ranked by overall feasibility category

3. ... and within feasibility category by net benefit

4. Priorities are indicated here.

5. Starting from the lowest priority program, marginal efforts may be trimmed as required by the budget

6 In any case these programs are eliminated

||||||||||| Program and design development

▬ Program Implementation

Monitor Progress.

The execution of each programme must be carefully monitored to identify bottlenecks as they develop, chart alternatives where necessary and ensure timely implementation and achievement of planned benefits. This task should be the permanent and ongoing responsibility of a personnel programme manager or a manpower planning manager.

AQA ASSESSMENT RESULTS

A growing evaluation method in Australia is the assessment against the Australian Quality Awards (AQA) criteria:[4]

In completing this assessment it is important to remember this is an assessment of the Human Resources Business Unit and the effects of their strategies/operations in the organisation. So we are looking at HR in a two fold manner. Example for the "Leadership" criteria.

How effective is HR at leadership as a business unit and how effective is HR in developing this criteria across the organisation (relevant to their accountabilities). *Note:* Only extracts from the assessment are provided due to time constraints.

1. Leadership

Strengths	*Opportunities*
1.1 Senior Executive • The HR director and direct reports are participating in leadership training • There is a leadership program for the Executive team	• HR director to operate at a more strategic level and make greater use of KPIs • To strengthen the people orientation across all levels of management by adopting a more participative style of management
1.2 Leadership throughout the organisation • Managers are currently undertaking leadership training • HR team have developed a respected program. • Staff are reviewing position descriptions to incorporate more responsibilities and quality initiatives.	• For managers at all levels to improve their understanding of empowerment and quality principles and learn how to put them into practice • HR to further deploy the understanding of empowerment • Management to dedicate 20% to developmental/quality activities • HR to seize opportunities for education
1.3 Leadership in the Community • Strong emphasis on ethical behaviour • HR is actively involved in industry forums	• To communicate key HR initiatives in a planned way, to staff and the wider community about performance in this area

2. Strategy, Policy and Planning	
Strengths	***Opportunities***
2.1 Organisational Values • HR has a vision and mission to provide direction • HR has its own value that drive their decisions and are in alignment to the corporate values • HR policies are up-to-date and well communicated	• More input from the organisation for the next policy up-dates • Conduct value audits to ascertain the importance of values and how they are being demonstrated
2.2 The Planning Process • HR has a strategic, annual and operational business plan • HR is a member of the Strategic Planning council	• To incorporate KPIs and other performance measures in the plan to drive improvement • To involve people in the planning, seeking input prior to execution of the Annual Plan
3. Information and Analysis	
Strengths	***Opportunities***
3.1 Scope and Collection of Data and Information • There is a computer system for HR data • Priority has been given to enhance the operation of the computer system • Visits from the international business units comparing information and operations	• The HR system could include basic staff information requirements • Develop the HR system to be user friendly • HR need to enhance their environmental scanning process to capture a broader range of information, and easier to access • Commence benchmarking program-link into institutes with data, and participate in benchmarking teams
3.2 Analysis and Use of Data and Information • There is a considerable amount of data collected based on the needs of some of the customers • Simplified some of the processes of data collection.	• Data needs to be presented in a more comprehensive manner for the line managers, in line with their information needs • Train the key managers in interpreting HR data • Seize opportunities to present HR data in trend analysis and comparison to industry norm.
4. People	
Strengths	***Opportunities***
4.1 Human Resource Management Planning • A number of strategies are implemented to enhance the management of people objectives in the organisation, e.g., Competencies analysis, Training Plan, Employee Handbook	• Communicate HR plans and policies to all staff • Develop a HR Procedure Manual and make it available to staff • Ensure Managers are aware of their HR roles and responsibilities

4.2 Employee Involvement ● Training program that support use of teams and continuous improvement culture ● Use of staff in forum for development of key process ● Workplace Safety and Communication committees ● All HR staff develop the Business Plan and work in teams to improve their processes	● Use regular staff meetings to communicate information and as a means of seeking staff input — enhance two way communication in a more effective timeframe ● Encourage more face to face communication by managers at all levels ● Develop other avenues for employee involvement
4.3 Performance Management ● Performance management exists for senior staff and key specialist positions ● Competencies based performance system is under development, facilitated by HR and completed by the staff ● User friendly documentation in place to deploy the performance appraisal process to managers and leaders ● Enhancement of the Career Development program	● Develop a process to more effective evaluation of the performance appraisal system — from the evaluates' perceptive ● Train managers in linking business plans to performance appraisals ● Review succession planning process due its current ad-hoc approach
4.4 Education and Training ● Staff are encouraged and supported in external training ● Training program is becoming more focussed and flexible — much closer link to business plans ● Most courses offered are accredited ● x% of dollars are dedicated to training	● Develop training program closely to the time of preparation of business plans per business unit ● Upgrade training facilities and resources ● Monitor the effectiveness of training and create a performance measure for this area
4.5 Wellbeing and Morale ● There is a social club, picnic days, gym and celebration events all sponsored by HR ● OH & S policy and committee ● Counselling and health check services	● Collect trend data on indicators of absenteeism, turnover, sickness by business unit ● Involve staff and seek input early in the process when altering policies
4.6 Communication ● Staff survey has been conducted yearly to help understand the attitudes of staff ● There are newsletters and bulletins that openly discuss all major changes in the organisation ● Open door policy of HR	● To provide more timely feedback and actions from the staff survey concerning HR issues — publish actions and outcomes throughout the year ● To evaluate if all managers are utilising the Staff Survey for improvement and communication opportunities
5. Customer Focus	
Strengths	***Opportunities***
5.1 Knowledge of Customers' Needs and Expectations ● Visits per quarter to each Business Unit by dedicated HR staff member ● File on each of the business units capturing key information	● To develop a more planned methodology for ascertaining the customer's requirements ● Develop a set of service standards for each business unit ● Collect more extensive data on each business unit

5.2 Customer Relationship Management • Forums are held to ascertain how HR can be of greater assistance • HR offers many courses that focus on Customer Relationship Building	• Need to develop a more effective process for relationship management • Need to dedicate time to relationship management with Senior team as the balance is currently mostly with line staff
5.3 Customer Satisfaction • An annual survey is undertaken to ascertain levels of customer satisfaction with HR • All values focus on satisfying the customer	• Survey needs to be report by business unit for clarity of needs instead of just one overall result • Need to formally survey the HR customers more often — program to be developed
5.4 Competitive Comparisons • Attend forums of other HR areas to learn about their performance and initiatives • Memberships to numerous HR programs	• Determine cost of services and compare to outsouring • Commence benchmarking program • Visit leading organisations to compare work practices, levels of productivity and strategic direction • Develop a report to report on HR effectiveness
5.5 Design and Innovation • Introduction of new technology to handle many HR manual processes and support cross referencing of information • Development of "working from home"	• Development of the Learning Center • Further time dedicated into exploration into work practices of the future — attend more conferences dedicated to information in this field.
6. Quality of Process, Product and Service	
Strengths	***Opportunities***
6.1 Supplier Quality Improvement • There is a criteria for selection of suppliers for HR needs • HR have valuable information on the organisation and its aims for suppliers	• Suppliers performance should be reviewed within and at the end of the contract period by a variety of personnel
6.2 Improving Process Performance • HR staff work in teams both within HR and in the organisations • All HR staff are trained as Facilitators and regularly support terms & Yearly goals are established for each product/service of HR	• Identify the priorities of HR processes for review • Process map the core business activities of HR, identifying non-value adding activities and key performance indicators
6.3 Quality of Products, Process and Services • Staff survey and forums are used to initiate improvements in HR • HR review its business unit through process management principles	• Seek data on international best practices • Each HR process to have KPIs • Conduct specific customer forums on each process to develop the service standards

7. **Organisational Performance (Business Unit)**

Strengths	*Opportunities*
• Business plans drive the operations of HR • The focus on HR financial reporting has significantly improved • HR utilises the data for development of business plans	• To utilise activity based costing for key processes • To provide reports on the value of HR services compared to external providers • HR to report via KPIs at organisational level, specifically HR performance, not organisational issues that are HR related (e.g., turnover)

Lessons Learned for the Evaluation Process

- Be trained in all the aspects of the AQA criteria, both in what each criterion means and the methodology of assessment (i.e., ADRI-Approach, Deployment, Results and Improvement). Too often issues were seen quite differently depending upon whether ADRI was considered.
- Use of an external facilitator was a valuable factor. Numerous issues were raised that had been taken as resolved or of little consequence.
- Customers were more open and direct in feedback through the use of the external facilitator.
- Customer research should have been featured early in the process. Many targets and plans were not considered relevant by customers, especially senior management.
- The Business Planning workshop was considered extremely worthwhile as all team members agreed the information needed to be formalised in such a plan to ensure action was taken and measurable.
- Conducting the AQA work first and then determining what needs to be involved in benchmark was the best approach as it highten your "quality thinking" and provides a criterion for priorities.
- Build in a business planning process and ensure planning is completed prior to the budgetary process otherwise new key plans miss the process of budget review and support.
- Utilise data currently available through key organisations — don't reinvent the wheel. HR team was surprised how much benchmarking data are easily available.
- Weakest link was the availability of financial data on HR activities — few, if any, systems in place that could be specific to defined activities — only budgetary data. New paradigm for the HR team to be seen as a cost or consider charging for services.
- Customers were delighted to see HR completing an assessment — in increase of their profile in the organisation. For the first time they were viewed as having to report like all other divisions in a more serious/appropriate manner.
- HR link to environmental issues was weak and reactive. A system for scanning information in a proactive manner is currently being developed. They were surprised how far the development of some HR units had progressed.

- Major planning and review should not be left to once a year annual workshop. HR has developed a schedule to review each of the criterion every four months to ensure actions remain timely and strategic.
- Data collected were not specific enough to track down the source of problems — it was organisational wide, but now needs to be customer driven to be of any real assistance.

The best lessons learnt was the responding support of the HR team to this form of assessment. Initial talks of evaluation were met with little interest. It was like another Staff survey — lots of data and little action. At the presentation of their results the HR team concluded the assessment taught them about business management and quality, easy to apply to the unit, and added value to their planning process. Most satisfying was the acceptance of their work by the Executive team, as they view the process as strategic in process and outcomes.

Conclusion

The framework for evaluating and ranking personnel programmes has enabled us to allocate resources to those programmes that should significantly improve productivity and profit performance. (A brief review of the benefits column in Exhibit IV underscores the magnitude of this improvement potential.) One of the key advantages of this framework is the discipline it instills in the personnel staff. It encourages staff members to rigorously assess their programmes' benefits and to evaluate the likelihood of achieving them. The procedure is by no means perfect, but I doubt that an optimal approach will ever be developed — particularly for staff projects. However, it does provide personnel management with a simple and systematic way to allocate resources in an area where good intentions, hunches, and poor information have cost many companies heavily in lost opportunities."

4. EVERYBODY A PERSONNEL ADMINISTRATOR

In the ultimate analysis, the impact and effectiveness of the personnel function depends on how well the top and line managers operate in the field of human resources management. The real challenge is not only in the personnel managers operating at a very high level of the state of the art in introducing human resources concepts, systems, policies and procedures but also in enabling all executives and supervisors to operate at a very high level of efficiency in managing people by utilising all the personnel systems in the most productive way. In other words, the personnel manager must convert every executive into an effective personnel manager and therein lies the maximum effectiveness of his function and contribution.

REFERENCES

1. Robert D. Gray, "Evaluating the Personnel Department," *Personnel*, March-April 1965, p. 47.
2. *Ibid.*, p. 49.
3. For a more complete discussion of this subject, see Willard A. Lewis, "The Personnel Manager as Compliance Officer," *Personnel Journal,* December 1971, p. 907.
4. Natalic Clare Verdan, *Developing and Evaluating the Strategic Role of the Human Resources Division,* Singapore, HRD Asia 1996, pp. 54-58.

❑❑❑

CHAPTER 23

The Challenge of Tomorrow

"As in the past, our future depends upon people, what they do and what they accomplish. In 1960s and beyond, wherever we look or think, the answer is human beings. Those of us who are interested in perfecting the processes of business must always think first in terms of the men and women who work for us. However obvious all of this may be, no part of it can be taken for granted", wrote Mr. Carter L. Burgess, President of American Machine and Foundry Company, New York City.[1] He went on to list "just a few of the many factors" that make personnel administration and 1960s "an important combination."[2]

The fact that more than 90 per cent of all the scientists and engineers whoever existed are alive today. This highlights the constantly shifting "manpower mix" of technical, skilled and administrative personnel requirements which will increase greatly in this important decade.

Albert F. Watters, Vice-President of Personnel and Public Relations, General Foods Corporation lists the following "fundamental problems" caused by changes in organisation structures and in basic management philosophies:[3]

(a) Changes in population centres as the trend toward urbanisation continues and causes a shift in distribution patterns in a number of consumer goods industries. (b) The increasingly large role of the corporation in politics at local, state and national levels. (c) An increase in the number of mergers and the human problems associated with them. (d) The vital problems of new and expanded industry in fields related to nuclear energy and the space age — in war or peace. (e) The increasingly large role of American business in world markets. (f) Greatly increased emphasis on science and research, with greater interest in the needs and importance of the people engaged in this work.

Dean Courtney C. Brown of Columbia's Graduate School of Business cited three factors which placed "unprecedented demands on the personnel resources of the successful businessman".[4]

1. Greater size of administrative units, made possible by accelerated change in production and control technology. (2) The progressive emergence of human factors in the operation of a business. (3) The ideological as well as the production role played by business in the cold war.

In India, while some of our problems are similar to those quoted above obtaining in U.S.A. relating to expansion, sophistication, diversification, complexity of business, etc., we face some more fundamental problems in the area of personnel administration.

(1) "Selling" personnel administration to the doubting upper echelons of management. (2) Increasing the effectiveness of personnel functions. (3) Raising to the full stature of a personnel administrator from that of a mere welfare officer. (4) Evolving appropriate training and education programmes to produce personnel administrators. (5) Getting out of legal quagmires into which personnel administration has descended. (6) Generally winning friends and influencing top and line executives, union leaders and employees.

These are some of the vital issues that the people interested in the profession of managing human resources in our country will have to face in the coming decade. Personnel administration, in order to play its proper role along with the other areas of management, will have to surmount these fundamental problems. While the day for lip service or disregard for personnel effort is past in U.S.A. it is not yet so in our country. Only in some progressive firms in India personnel administration policies, programmes and procedures have received considerable attention from top management and the personnel administrators are heard in the upper chambers of management. But there is a great need to "sell" personnel administration to the top and line management in our country.

In this chapter we shall deal with:

1. Tomorrow's manager and management.
2. The job ahead.
3. The challenge.

1. TOMORROW'S MANAGER AND MANAGEMENT

"In the past 30 years technological changes have helped to double the gross national product, and in the next 30 they will more than double it again. In the field of human knowledge, we are told that four times as much is known today as was known 30 years ago and that scientists will learn as much more in the next 15 years as in all of previous history. As for population in USA we can expect to grow from a country of 200 million people to 226 million by 1975 and 245 million by 1980."

"To those engaged in business management generally and in the personnel function particularly these prognostications have a special significance, because all these goods, all this knowledge, all these people will be the concern of a shrinking proportion of the population. The group from which our executives and decision-makers and drawn, the age group from 35 to 55, will have dropped from 57 per cent of the total productive age group to 38 per cent by 1980. Roughly, this means that three managers will be doing the work that four are doing today."

Tomorrow's Manager

To understand what this means for the personnel function, we have to consider first what tomorrow's manager will be like and what kind of work he will be doing. We can be reasonably sure that he will have to know more and learn more than his counterpart today, and that he will be supervising more sophisticated people than he does today. Professor Harold Leavitt of Carnegie Tech predicts that tomorrow's manager will be more of an intellectual, that he will make more of his decisions on the basis of systematic analysis and less by off the cuff methods. There is evidence that this is already happening. Not long ago, the American Telephone & Telegraph Co. studied the records of 17,000 college graduates in the Bell companies and learned that the single most reliable indicator of their success was class standing on graduating from college, and more recently the Prudential Insurance Co. of America came to the same conclusion.

Tomorrow's manager will also be supervising a different kind of work force. Between 1950 and 1960, the number of professional and technical people employed in business increased 47 per cent, and for the first time white-collar workers in industry exceeded the number of blue-collar workers. This trend is expected to continue. The supervision of primarily professional, technical, and other white-collar employees will require a kind of manager different from the one who is now typical in factory management.

At the same time, despite the best possible preparation for his present job, tomorrow's executive may find himself threatened with obsolescence in mid-career. With "knowledge" compounding at such a rapid rate, no manager can be sure that his skills will continue to be needed or even that his job will exist tomorrow. As MIT's Professor Charles Myers has observed, "It is becoming impossible to learn a skill that will continue for a lifetime." In some companies there is even talk about preparing executives for a second career.

Shifts in Personnel Emphasis

Can Personnel specialists meet the needs of tomorrow's manager?

Speaking about the new tasks of the professional manager at the 15th CIOS International Management Congress at Tokyo on the theme of *The New Role of Management: Innovation, Integration and Internationalisation,* Professor Peter Drucker went straight to the heart of the problem of the developing economies:[5]

> "It can be said without too much oversimplification that there are no 'underdeveloped countries.' There are only 'undermanaged' ones. Japan a hundred years ago was an 'underdeveloped' country by every material measurements. But it very fast threw up management of great competence, indeed of excellence. Within twenty-five years Meiji Japan had become a 'developed' country, and indeed in respects, such as literacy, the most highly developed of all countries. We realise today that it is Meiji Japan, rather than 18th century England — or even 19th century Germany — which has to be the model of development for the underdeveloped world. This means that management is the prime mover and that development is the consequence.
>
> "All our experience in economic development proves this. Wherever we have only contributed the economic 'factors of production' especially capital we have not achieved development. In the few cases where we have been able to generate management energies (e.g., in the Cauca Valley in Colombia) we have generated rapid development. Development, in other words, is a matter of human energies rather than of economic wealth. And the generation and direction of human energies is the task of management."

Our experience with national economic planning and development over a period of a quarter century goes to prove Professor Drucker's contention and also has underlined the tremendous importance of the crucial input of competent professional management for the promotion of growth both at the microlevel and the macrolevel. The third Five Year Plan progress report stated clearly that the success of the business enterprises in India was largely prejudiced by the dearth of competent professional managers and that this had been the greatest singular stumbling block to the growth of enterprises.[6]

The central challenge and opportunity facing the developing economies is the promotion of optimum utilisation of human capacity, potential and assets, since the condition of underdevelopment in an eccnomy is a function of undermanagement of its resources, more particularly the human resources; for underdeveloped countries, maintains Professor Adam Curle, the Harvard Economist, have remained underdeveloped largely because the people are underdeveloped having had no opportunity to realise their maximum potentialities and capabilities. While optimum utilisation of human capacity and the promotion of human resources development may be a global problem, it is particularly acute in a country like India where the asset of the teeming millions is yet to be capitalised because of the problem of undermanagement or what is popularly called the management gap.

Organisational Renewal Experiment

As a consequence of the several forces mentioned earlier, the major problem facing organisations is employee alienation and organisational effectiveness. In the era of knowledge industry, knowledge worker and professional manager, the traditional pyramid is considered to be ineffective in motivating employees and, hence, the problem of employee alienation. In a time of rapid market and technological change, growing complexity and shift of emphasis to individual aspirations, top management can no longer rely exclusively on the pyramid.

Hence, this traditional structure is giving place to a beehive, a doughnut, a bell, a super girdle, a ladder, cell, matrix forms of organisations. There is a new concept of man and a new concept of power based on collaboration and reason, replacing power and coercion. There is also a new concept of organisational values — humanistic, democratic ideals, replacing mechanistic value system of bureaucracy. John Argenti, a British Management Consultant, suggests the cell and matrix organisational pattern and also lifting all the management service out of the pyramid and placing in a neutral ladder apart from the hierarchy in order that executives are left free to call for the advice of any specialist without having to go through the hierarchical channels.

Most of the attempts to modify the pyramid reflect a growing trend towards a more democratic form of management. Employee participation and job enrichment are highly fashionable and the growing complexity of company operations is forcing to lower reaches of the hierarchy. These organisational renewal experiments have tremendous implications for the trainer and his strategies of training and development.

Despite the criticism frequently levelled at it, the traditional pyramid will probably be around for a long time to come. But not long ago, a survey of the Fellows of the Academy of Management, a group of distinguished senior management professors in USA, attempted to forecast the shape of the organisation in the future.

The result was a 75 per cent probability prediction that the dominant organisational structure in 1985 will still be the classical pyramid. However, there are persistent various modifications to the classical pyramid.

1. The Behavioural Model of Organisation

Here an attempt is made to overcome some of the mechanistic-structural objections to the classical organisation. The model assumes the objective of economic productivity output as given, but it adds to a new dimension — employee satisfaction. The pyramid is likely to be modified into more "horizontal systems" in which control is loose, power diffused, and centres of decision-making widespread.

2. The Organic Model of Organisation

The behavioural organic approach to organisational design goes one step further in that it addresses itself to the fundamentals of structure and specialisation of tasks. Warren Bennis, its foremost proponent, summarises his proposal thus:

> "First of all, the key word will be temporary. Organisations will become adaptive, rapidly changing temporary systems. Second, they will be organised around problem-to-be-solved. Third, these problems will be solved by groups of relative strangers who represent a diverse set of professional skills. Fourth, given the requirements of coordinating the various projects, articulating points or "linking-pin" personnel will be necessary who can speak the diverse language of research and who can relay and mediate between the various project groups. Fifth, the groups will be conducted on organic rather than on mechanical lines; they will emerge and adapt to the problems, and leadership and influence will fall to those who seem most able to solve the problems, rather than according to the programmed role expectations. People will be differentiated, not according to rank or roles, but according to skills and training.... Though no catchy phrase comes to mind, it might be called an organic-adoptive structure."

3. The Team Approach

How can the essential characteristics of the organic model — described as temporary, flexible and accommodating to change — be achieved within the traditional pyramidal structure? The answer is the team approach which has several versions. The one called project management is widely used; matrix management and venture teams management are evolving.

Project Management: To tackle problems of development and design of a new product, deeper market penetration of existing product, cost reduction, acquisition of or a merger with an outside company, management development, construction of a new plant, etc. where coordination of two or more functional departments such as accounting, finance, marketing, engineering are required. The organisation device is to have a project manager with complete and diluted authority for all aspects of the project with responsibility for planning, work scheduling, budgeting and controlling and to get the project completed within an established standard of time, cost and technical specifications.

Matrix Management: Matrix organisation gets its name from the fact that a number of project managers exercise planning, scheduling, and cost control over people who have been assigned to their projects, while the functional managers exert line control, in terms of technical direction, training, compensation, and the like, over the same workers. Thus, there is shared responsibility for the worker, and he must please two bosses.

Two excellent examples of this kind of management in operation can be found at Honeywell and Texas Instruments. When General Electric decided to quit the computer business, Honeywell acquired the pieces. It set up 20 managerial task forces, made up of about 200 people from both its own staff and GE's to integrate manufacturing, marketing, field services, personnel, software, and the inventory of actual product lines. Honeywell's chairman called it a textbook exercise in how to merge painlessly.

In the case of Texas Instruments, matrix management is a way of life, and has been carried to a high degree of sophistication. Broad company objectives are broken down into a series of strategies and methods for achieving them, and those strategies, in turn, are translated into several hundred tactical action programmes (TAPs). Each TAP has a project system.

Venture Teams: The venture team is somewhat like the project matrix management team in that its personnel resources are obtained from the functional departments. Other similarities include organisational separation, the team of multi-disciplinary personnel, and the goal-directed effort toward the achievement of a single result, here, product development and introduction. The venture team also may have a flexible life span, with a completion time loosely defined by broad time and financial goals. To be successful, members of venture teams have to be generally well accepted by others in the organisation, because the interaction of the venture manager with those in other segment is considerable.

4. The Contingency Model

The contingency model seeks to answer the question of what factors, forces or variables — contingencies — should be considered in deciding how to design an organisation structure. The most important are: (1) the manager, (2) the work, (3) environment, (4) the individual contributors. Thus, all these innovative and adaptive organisation experiments are designed to provide (a) a more democratic attitude on the part of managers, (b) more participation in major decisions at lower levels, (c) decentralisation of decision-making as far as possible, (d) less emphasis on hierarchy and authority delegation, (e) less narrow specialisation of work tasks.

The challenge facing the trainers is to train and develop people into working together effectively, in interdisciplinary and multi-functional teams in temporary, flexible and adaptive organisations under more open and democratic systems of management. It will be necessary for the managers to recognise, evaluate and largely satisfy the often conflicting demands, of consumers, shareholders, employees and most importantly, governments and citizens. How well we meet the changing needs of the organisation and the changing roles of the managers will determine the place and importance of the training function in an organisation.

In the milieu of an innovative organisation, knowledge industry and knowledge worker, I suspect that the top management will be increasingly taking interest in the training and development of people in order to promote both managerial and organisational effectiveness. Increasingly, they will call upon the training function to identify the changing needs and aspirations of people as well as develop, administer and evaluate training and development programmes. The interaction between the trainer and the top management is likely to increase considerably. Increasingly, the promotion of optimum utilisation of human resources will be the concern of top management and this concern has to find its expression in the efforts of trainers and educators. There will be more emphasis on training, education and development effort and the department of training and development will increasingly play a key role in promoting both managerial and organisational effectiveness, because of the pace of change, it will be necessary for us to react, devise and more effectively attend to the identification of needs of training and developing people.

Although, there are two schools of thought whether training function should be an independent function, or should be a part of the personnel function, I suspect that training and development will continue to be part of the total human resources management function, although it will play a major role. Because of the challenge, complexity and sophistication of the function of management development and human resources development, the status, responsibilities, compensation and importance of the people involved will be on an increase. They will interact closely with the top management and coordinate their activities more closely with the line management. In order for the trainer to become more effective, the organisation staffing and budgets of executive development and human resources development will have to be strengthened.

Instead of the routine training packages, the top management will increasingly call upon the personnel and development experts to assist them in development of:

1. New styles of management — Open, consultative, democratic and participative.
2. New systems of management — Cellular, matrix, venture teams.
3. New knowledge of management — New concepts, tools and techniques emerging from research, experimentation and testing.
4. New roles of management — Entrepreneurial, developmental, innovative.
5. New goals of management — Service, social responsibilities, national objective.
6. New philosophy of management — Humanism, man and the quality of life.

It is also necessary for us to increase our own professional competence particularly understanding the new concept of a man, the new concept of power in addition to training strategies, technologies and methodologies. Most people want a challenge and want to be recognised by themselves and others as achievers. Many people want to do their own thing, i.e., to be their own boss. It is necessary for us to discover such innovative and entrepreneurial resource and nourish and nurture them and to encourage entrepreneurship not only for the organisation but also for the nation.

Professor Yoder observes:[7]

"What may be most disconcerting is the fact that business leaders, after 200 years of experience with the free enterprise system, have been unable to come to a consensus on a plausible explanation of what makes for effective employment teamwork in a democratic society. Only a few respondents see enthusiastic, participative work teams of free men as implicitly requiring voluntary compacts and acceptance of leadership. Only a few are aware of the clear emphasis upon demonstrated managerial competence as the essential key to acceptance of managerial leadership. Similarly, only a few respondents acknowledge the importance of employee status and personnel security, based on competence, as a source of enthusiastic participation for rank-and-file employees, supervisors, middle managers, and executives. In the absence of such an accepted theory or philosophy, many managements fail to recognise their opportunities in employee development and agency management where employers and managers are identified as agents of employees)."

Other evidence, he adds, however, suggests the wide acceptance of agency management philosophy where managers propose to coach and develop team members and to help them maximise their value, contribution and earnings. Such policies implicitly recognise that enthusiastic participation can be expected only from employees who want to play their best game, on the team of their choice. "Similarly the mass migration of managers into management development programmes, conferences and seminars, evidences implicit acceptance of what may be called the 'special competence' theory of leadership and management. It implies that managers, supervisors and executives can expect to be accepted as leaders only if they have shown evidence of special competence."

The personnel administrators either in India or U.S.A. will have to come up with valid answers to three questions raised by the President of American Machine & Foundry Company, Mr. Carter L. Burgess:[8]

1. How do we keep the *right people* that we have?
2. How do we get the other *right people* that we need?
3. How do we energise all the *right people* to accomplish bigger and better objectives?

The personnel policies, programmes, planning, tools and techniques, that we have already discussed, will need constant review, refinement, evaluation and improvement. Companies are keenly aware of the cost of turnover at all job levels. The cost of hiring, training and providing proper tools and facilities makes nearly every employee-loss a matter of real concern. While the deadwood must be eliminated from a progressive organisation, the great preponderance of *good and right employees* must be provided with every inducement to remain; opportunity for development, good personnel administration, as much employment stability as business will permit, and awareness that their future and that of the organisation are inseparably entwined. In brief, the retention and growth of employee depends on an enlightened management whose concern for its people is as great as, or greater than, its concern for its buildings and facilities. It was Alfred P. Sloan Jr., who maintained that if an organisation lost its machines and buildings, those could be replaced; but if it lost its loyal, well-trained employees, the organisation would be doomed.

In the opinion of Albert F. Watters:[9] "One of personnel's most important responsibilities is to help management identify the individuals and groups to contribute most to profitability and who must be qualified, not only to keep pace with the foreseeable changes, but to set the pace and provide a forward push. A searching study in this area will...lead surprisingly often away from the assumption that an employee groups is of primary importance merely because it is numerically large. Individual contributors such as the researcher, the engineer, the marketing specialist, the manager, and the salesman make contributions to corporate growth and profitability which far outweigh the percentage of the payroll they receive.

"From a total human relations viewpoint, the needs of such people must be considered in a new light and from a different point of view than that traditionally taken with respect to mass groups of factory and office employees. The fundamental job of personnel is to help top management select, develop, utilise and motivate the kind of people who will have the ingenuity and good judgment necessary to develop new processes and products; the acumen necessary to administer sound business programmes; the alertness necessary to perceive shifts in distribution patterns; and the ability necessary to exact the maximum voluntary growth and productivity from each individual.

"To do this job, personnel administration requires a vastly higher degree of professional competence than has thus far been generated in most organisations. Only real professionals can achieve the broader focus so vital to such an effort. Also needed is a much more clearly defied set of objectives for function itself. Here, too, only professionals — line and staff — with deep convictions and high principles can rid personnel people of the reputation of being good starters and good talkers, but poor finishers."

The personnel administration must sharpen its techniques in understanding and analysing the needs and aspirations of more and more white collar employees such as programmers, analysts, workstudy men, engineers, scientists, technologies etc., help and advise top management in evolving programmes and communications systems that motivate these individuals and groups to do their best and in the process, derive great personal satisfaction and pride. The most serious problem will be in understanding the motivations of many of these new breeds of employees and in harmonising their aspirations with the company goals. Individuality must be reconciled with conformity and creativity with the organisation chain of command.

Mr. Dorr C. Snoyenbos, Director of Personnel, AC Spark Plug Division of General Motors, points out some of the radical changes taking place in the personnel field:[10] "Each area of the personnel field is undergoing radical change today. The safety department can no longer be content to see that machines are properly guarded, that ladders are safe and that scaffolding is properly erected. It must now concern itself with the effects of radiation, the problems of heat transmission, the proper checkout equipment for electrical machine controls, and the lack of concern on the part of skilled and semi-skilled personnel for safe practices. The medical department finds itself more than a first-aid station. It now has to contend with beryllium reactions, radiation exposure, hypertension, and many other matters which were of little concern or no concern to the medical director of ten years ago.

"Sound wage and salary administration, as it applies to well developed job content, is a matter of major concern. The large variety of new skills, for which there is no known job description, being introduced to modern industry makes this field a rapidly expanding activity.

"The days of the old plant guard or watchman are gone. In place of these familiar figures is a new group of well-trained and disciplined security patrolmen whose functions carry them into every part of the plant and who must, therefore, have some understanding of the new types of fire hazards deriving from the new metals, the espionage problems to nation security, and the possibilities of sabotage to equipment which they had never seen before. And they have in addition such small problems as keeping the prestige of the technical man in mind when assigning parking lot space."

There will be a greater urgency and necessity to apply the scientific method and tools in personnel work. Mr. D.J. Moffie, Vice-President, Industrial Relations of Hanes Hosiery Mills Company makes these observations regarding the application of scientific method:[11]

"Decisions in the personnel area should be based on carefully thoughtout principles and on facts gathered and evaluated by the most modern techniques. Personnel methods have relied too long on hunches, guesses and past experience. It is time for the scientific method to be applied. Scientific management implies decision-making based on facts. The new science of mathematical programming is an attempt to fulfil these objectives, and it can be applied in the various areas of personnel work.

"A sound personnel programme is not merely sweet-talk, smiling, and back-slapping. It is realistic, firm, and in line with the objectives of good business, and it can and should be an integral part of company growth and development. To accomplish these goals we must first establish an awareness of objective data. Statistical tools of evaluation can be used on quantitative data only; feelings, emotions and hunches are not subjects for such analysis. Second, personnel people must be willing to learn what the scientific method is, and what is implied in a coefficient of correlation, in an analysis of variance, or even in a "T" test. They must know how to systematise procedures so that data may be collected over a given period of time for such analysis."

They must find ways to answer these questions raised by Albert F. Watters:[12]

1. How can statistical and other personnel data be presented to top management to best reflect their impact on business in dollar-and-cent terms?
2. Does personnel administration, like research, require investments which sometimes have only long-range potential? If so, how can we sell this concept to top management and how can we make it clear that not every expenditure is a cost — that some are investments?

3. What corporate characteristics and factors indicate the point upon which a personnel programme must focus for maximum effectiveness?
4. What are "human value judgments", and how does the work being done at MIT, Harvard, and other educational institutions in the fields of theology, philosophy, psychology, axiology, and so forth, contribute to our understanding of human value judgments and of their force and effect in business?

Only by providing answers to such questions can personnel administration make an adequate impression on top management who must be made to feel that personnel is their most important problem and programme, like this statement from President Carter L. Burgess:[13]

"In my company, I want everyone in management in the job of making personnel the No. 1 programme. I would like to see our Personnel Department act as the control center and the great persuader, in making certain that we gather the right facts and project requirements — in short, that we draw up the necessary maps and plans to coordinate the action and score the results. Beyond that, each of us in management must assume our rightful share of the responsibility under such a programme for assuring that people, in the decade ahead, are truly our greatest assets. There is no room in the picture for lip-service boys, for slogan makers, or for the line manager who leave all his people problems on the personnel department's doorstep. People are 24 hour-a-day job, and we had all better make it so we face the stern and relentless competition, the changes, and opportunities and even the dangers that mark the course of the 1980s."

Delivering his address on "Maximising the effectiveness of Personnel Management in Industry" Mr. R.S. Pande, former Managing Director of TISCO maintained that personnel administration is the most difficult area of management and winning the willing and enthusiastic co-operation of employee is a constant ever present challenge to management.

What's Ahead?

In addition to these development there are signs of other changes, some of which may have a profound effect on the purpose, staffing, status and organisation of the personnel department in the future. Four related changes of particular significance are: (1) the growing profit orientation of the personnel function; (2) the shift in personnel work from a mechanistic concept to a creative, innovative one; (3) the interest in furthering an organisation, rather than just maintaining or servicing it; and (4) the more direct involvement of top management in the development of the human resources of the business. Just what are the implications of these trends?

1. The personnel function will assume a more important role in the management of the business. It will do more planning and policy-making in the areas of the manpower, organisation, structure, and compensation, among others. It will have more functional authority, especially in large, complex and growing organisations. In becoming increasingly oriented toward growth and profits, instead of merely administering personnel activities, it will search out profit-improvement opportunities.

This new awareness will mean that personnel people will view their role in a different light. For example: In selecting people, more weight will be placed on what a candidate has accomplished than on the jobs he has held. In management development, more stress will be placed on identifying company and departmental needs and objectives and training people to attain them. In compensation, it will be important to relate pay to performance and to its motivational impact, as well as to make sure that rates are competitive. In the area of employee benefits, there will be more consideration of the fact that a large part of expenditures are going to people who are not working in the form of retirement benefits, life insurance payments, medical plans and the like.

In appraising performance, there will be more emphasis on accomplishment against expectations, and appraisal results will be more closely tied to a man's compensation. In organisation planning, there will have to be major emphasis on aligning responsibilities and relationships in the individual company to obtain maximum results with the least manpower, instead of seeking symmetrical or conventional organisation patterns or uncritically following principles of organisation laid down by others.

In summary, the personnel function will no longer be able to justify itself to top management by citing numbers or listing activities, the number of people interviewed or trained or counselled, the number of reports prepared or of records maintained, the number of job descriptions written, or the rate of employee turnover. Rather, personnel will demonstrate its effectiveness by raising the qualification levels of the employees hired; reducing the turnover among key managerial and professional people; recommending or drafting plans, policies, and programmes that are adopted by operating management; and initiating organisational and staffing changes.

2. The personnel function will become more creative, less mechanistic. In the future, disparity between the paper programmes and actuality will have to be eliminated. The deficiencies of rigid, packaged "personnel programmes" will become increasingly apparent.

Most of us are familiar with companies where "management development programmes" have been conducted for years, yet half of their top managers are over 55 years old and there are few successors in sight, and the companies go outside to find people for many higher-level jobs; where management positions are invariably staffed without consulting the head of the personnel department; and where although the companies have performance appraisal programmes, half the executives do not even bother to complete the required forms.

In such corporations, most of the top management group have had experience in only one function of the business; there are no inventories of management resources, no plans for management succession, and only a dim notion of future management requirements or how to meet them; participation by top executives in outside management development programmes is almost non-existent; a high proportion of the more promising men recruited on college campuses leave the company within two years; and numerous corporate departments are involved with compensation and employee benefit plans, but no department is responsible for overall policy or co-ordination in these areas and, for that matter, the compensation plan does not apply to a sizable group of executives in the top levels.

There will be less me-tooism, less concern with imitating industry practice or matching industry averages, and more attention to what's actually required to help the company meet its goals. There will be more concern with ends rather than means, with substance rather than forms, with accomplishments rather than activities. There will be increasing emphasis on what the operating people find workable instead of what is theoretically best or easiest for the personnel department to administer. We already see this trend in the adoption of less complicated job-evaluation plans and in the movement away from automatic merit increases and appraisal based on an employee's activities or traits and towards appraisals based on performance measured against company goals or standards.

3. The personnel function will be responsible for furthering the organisation, not just maintaining it. Personnel people will devote more time to proposing and promoting changes than to protecting the *status quo*. Instead of a miscellany of diverse specialities or activities, the personnel department will be regarded as an integrated general management function, responsible for the effective development of the firm's human resources, and, as it becomes more oriented to the requirements of the organisation, it will view the needs of individuals in the light of their compatibility with those of the organisation.

The personnel managers will recognise and encourage sound management practices, fostering concepts like management-by-objectives and team problem-solving approaches. They will seek new ways to awaken the talents that lie dormant in every organisation by searching out opportunities and providing training experiences that are challenging and meaningful, rejecting a commitment to human relations as an end in itself.

In planning and developing his company's human resources, the personnel man will have to raise his sights to plan the form of the future organisation and of the firm's manpower requirements; to structure and integrate the work; to identify and select management talent; to appraise and reward performance; to provide learning experiences to ensure growth of both the individual and the organisation; and to rotate, transfer, and promote people into appropriate positions.

To handle this responsibility, the personnel man will have to be an individual of singular breadth and influence, sensitive equally to the needs and capabilities of people and to the requirements of the business. How many personnel departments or personnel people today perform this role or qualify for it? Apparently, not many. Some companies establish a separate unit within the personnel department to carry out this creative policy-making and programme-planning function. In others, a small, high-level staff, responsible for organisation planning and development is created to work directly with the chief executive officer and his key subordinates, while personnel services for supervisory and employee groups are provided by the regular personnel department.

4. Top management will become more directly involved in the deployment and development of human resources. The chief executives of a growing number of companies are spending a good deal of time thinking about the people in the organisations, reviewing management manpower needs and resources, assessing the performance and potential of their executives, and planning their future experiences.

After identifying all the major functions and sub-functions, the next step is to assess each activity in the light of the following questions suggested by Professor Robert D. Gray:[14]

1. What is the philosophy underlying the function?
2. What principles of management are being followed in carrying it out?
3. What policies have been established for this function?
4. What procedures have been established? Are they in line with philosophy, principles and policies?
5. Are the procedures, policies, management principles and philosophy of each function consistent with those of other, related functions?

Finally, I must make a mention of the deliberations of 17th All India Conference of Indian Institute of Personnel Management held at Coimbatore in march 1967 and one of the themes of the conference was — very appropriately and timely "Maximising the effectiveness of Personnel Management in Industry." In all the three syndicates (for one of which the present author was the chairman) some 162 personnel executives coming from all parts of India and various industries participated in the syndicate's deliberations and gave suggestions as to how to maximise the effectiveness of personnel management in industry. The down-to-earth comments, suggestions, and recommendations of these practising personnel executives concerned with many of the issues, that were resolved long ago in a country like U.S.A., but they were yet to be resolved in our country. The recommendations adopted at the plenary session of the conference were as follows:[15]

I. Formulation of Personnel Policies

(a) There should be a well-defined personnel policy.

(b) The Chief of Personnel Division should be associated with top policy-making body of the company.

(c) There should be an effective communication of the personnel policies to all the employees, executives — line and staff, supervisors etc.

(d) The Personnel Executive must assist in the implementation of personnel policies.

(e) The personnel policies must be subjected to periodic reviews and evaluation to ensure that the organisational objectives are achieved.

(f) The personnel policies recommended by the employers' organisations or associations should be capable of being adopted by member units depending on regional needs and problems peculiar to them.

II. Functional Areas

The Personnel Management in Industry has three broad functions, viz.:

(a) Advisory Function.

(b) Service Function.

(c) Control Function.

1. In large companies, personnel officers can be posted in units/departments to assist and advise the unit manager/head of department.
2. Personnel managers must play a positive role by developing a "creative" industrial relations policy. This can be achieved by various measures such as creating a sense of confidence and goodwill among the employees.
3. Settlement of personnel problems should be expedited particularly where centralised decisions are taken.
4. Each personnel manager should review whether he is accomplishing the tasks already assigned to him. In progressive organisations, top management will be willing to give more and more responsibilities to personnel managers depending on their success on the present assignment.
5. Apart from formal communications, informal communications must be considered equally important.
6. The duties and responsibilities of line management and personnel managers must be clearly demarcated to avoid any conflicts that usually arise between line and personnel.
7. The Personnel Department in its functioning must contribute to the objectives of the company.

III. Professional Nature of Personnel Management

Ways and means of improving the professional nature of Personnel Management:

1. A proper course of professional education and training including apprenticeship is suggested for the people who wish to enter the profession of Personnel Management. This education and training must in addition to the specialisation on the functions of Personnel Management, also give to the personnel executive a working knowledge of other functional areas of management such as, production, sales, marketing, finance, accounting etc. The institute may endeavour to prepare and recommend a suitable syllabus for Personnel Management Education.
2. *Code of Ethics:* Steps may be taken to evolve a Code of Ethics for the profession of Personnel Management (in India).
3. *Professional Training:* Professional training for a period of two/three years is recommended before a personnel man takes up a permanent position in a personnel department. Non-personnel executives should also be given orientation courses on the need and significance of personnel functions.

IV. Productivity

1. To a large extent, the effectiveness of Personnel management is reflected in higher productivity and in that process giving satisfaction to employees concerned.
2. Where it is feasible, the services of specialists such as psychologists, job analysis, interviewers etc. must be utilised in the personnel department.
3. Employee productivity could be augmented by joint consultation and by co-operation between employees and management.

4. The personnel managers may help create a proper atmosphere and environment where a worker would 'want' to contribute his best to the organisation.

V. Research

1. The personnel department for its effective functioning should have proper liaison and constant contact with research institutions in India and abroad dealing with Personnel Management research.
2. Exchange of views, information and experiences must be encouraged.

5. The Challenge

The job ahead in this vital area of management of human assets is clearly a difficult and challenging one and the men in this field must rise to the occasion and acquit themselves credibility. They will need more technical competence and better professional training. They will need to identify and develop potential leaders and this process of identification and development may require constant sharpening of their tools of selection. They must develop the ability to see through clearly the kind of problems, needs, aspirations and motivations of people and have the sagacity to aid management to deal with people successfully. They must be aware of the latest literature, experiments, tools and techniques, theories and principles in their chosen avocation and endeavour to use the constantly growing body of knowledge and learning to improve personnel functions. They must be men of compassion in their dealings with people — workers, union leaders, supervisors, executives. They must have the patience to look at their problems as they see them and gain insights into the working of their minds. They must be men of principles and courage. But above all they must be very competent and capable of giving sound advise to their "customers." There is no room for complacency at all in this field and they must keep in touch with increasing labour legislation, changing labour conditions and union demands.

What is expected of the personnel administrators of tomorrow? What should be the qualities, qualifications and competence of these men? What should be their major concerns? How can they raise the status and prestige of their calling? What and how can these men contribute to company productivity and profitability? To these very relevant questions here are some answers provided by top executives, top personnel people and academic authorities on the subject:

Mr. Albert F. Watters, Vice-President of Personnel and Public Relations of General Foods Corporations, U.S.A. writes:[16]

"Someone once said that the first requisite for successful personnel work is the willingness to lose one's job. I doubt, however, that personnel administration has any monopoly on that requirement. All leaders — and that is what personnel people purport to be when they endeavour to influence and lead management thought and philosophy in connection with the "people processes" — must be individuals of high integrity. If the personnel function is to achieve a posture of confidence and courage, and if not only personnel people but all management people are to recognise personnel administration as a legitimate management function, we must send out the kind of personnel technicians who really know their business and who command respect for that knowledge. Only that kind of emissary can help personnel emerge from the isolation ward to which some managements have banished it; only that kind of individual can truly integrate personnel managers with the other company leaders.

"When I say 'send out', I mean just that one of my own requisites for good personnel people is that they have strong legs and rabbit ears; the first to carry them out from behind their desks and into the plants, offices and the field where their job really are located; and the second to listen for what the people who actually run the business have to say about their problems and the kind of people and policies they need to solve them. Only by circulating and by listening can we hope to come up with the needed plans, programmes and philosophies. Only in this way can we equip ourselves to evaluate accurately the degree to which human relations problems are valid and justify attention. There are, in short, no substitutes for knowledge, intelligence and sensitivity. In personnel, as in other phases of any undertaking, mediocrity produces only more of the same. We need personnel people who are good businessmen, sensitive to profitability and knowledge of return on investment. To assure the introduction of this kind of person into the personnel field, our selection standing must be raised and our approach to the development of personnel people more thoughtfully organised."

Mr. R.S. Livingstone, Vice-President, Thompson Ramo Wooldridge Inc., Cleveland, Ohio, U.S.A. points out the responsibility of the personnel man in "creating a new state of mind" among the workgroups:[17]

> "The constructive forming of employee opinion should be made the primary duty of the personnel man, working with his chief executive.
>
> "As I have indicated, conditions in industry are generally good. The techniques for determining wages and for monitoring working conditions are established and known. These activities can now be delegated to specialists within the personnel department.
>
> "The top personnel executive should make his principal task the problem of developing and applying appeals to the mind, mental concepts that will include the people who comprise the nation's business to give more fully and freely of their human energy.
>
> "In this effort, the personnel man — to repeat — must work side by side with his chief executive. He must become familiar with the chief's thinking, with his plans for the growth of this business and then interpret to the organisation, not only those plans, but also the hopes and fears and fortunes of the company as events transpire. The personnel executive must be backed up by a good staff writer — possibly even two or three. The shaping of men's minds for constructive purposes is one of the most advanced and difficult of the arts. (Witness the bungling and ineffective efforts of management to date). It cannot be handled by journalistic beginners, people to whom you pay $ 400 or $ 500 a month. Nor can it be by cynical, slapdash, artists who cannot make the grade in the journalistic profession.
>
> "Editorial objectives in written company bulletins, newspapers, handbooks, supervisory publications and letters to the homes have to be carefully determined in advance. What are you trying to accomplish by each one? Every items should

be written in such a way that some worthwhile fact about business economics is demonstrated by the company's own circumstances.

Mr. Clarence Francis, Chairman of Studebaker-Packard Corporation, speaks of the vital role that is before the personnel administrators:[18]

"You whose avocation is selecting, training, understanding and rewarding men realise, I am sure, your great responsibility. I wonder, though, if your bosses fully appreciate the great importance of your office. I am here to evaluate the office, not the man. The Office, in my judgement, is so vital as to demand close proximity to the chief executive....

"There are, in fact, certain qualities which seem to me to be more highly developed in the more successful administrative leader. High on my list, I place:

Initiative: the will to start; the dominant will to do.

Decision: the courage to conclude and act.

Judgment: the ability to think wisely (without judgment, initiative; and decision could be very costly).

Human Understanding: the ability to elicit the best efforts of others by humane methods (under this heading could come tolerance, generosity, recognition and the like).

Imagination or Vision: the ability to create, to dream; the key to horizons yet unseen.

Faith: in one's self, in one's associates, in one's civic and religious beliefs; the key to the future.

"Men with these qualities will lead, not drive. They will inspire confidence, not fear. They will believe in the dignity of the individual, and their belief will become infectious. Men will work in support of such men and taken pride in so doing.

"The responsibilities of management to understand men, to know the stimuli to which they will respond, and to create a proper climate in which they will put forth their best efforts is great indeed. Without it, this industrial machine will not approach its full potential. With it, not only the corporate welfare but the well-being of the individual will be insured.

"Some years ago I made a statement which seems to have stood the test of time. Here it is again:

"You can buy a man's time. You can buy a man's physical presence in a given place. You can even buy a measured number of skilled muscular motions per hour or per day. But you cannot buy enthusiasm.... You cannot buy initiative.... You cannot buy loyalty.. You cannot buy the devotion of hearts, minds, and souls. You have to *earn* those things!

"Such conditions are yours as personnel administrators to create. Your contribution to industrial peace in this nation can be as great as you are great.... The responsibility for the future welfare of our country rests in large measure with today's leaders in public service, industry, in private life — leaders with faith and the will to do. The responsibility for selecting, training, and inspiring, such men is clearly your field of activity. To fulfil this role is a great challenge and a great opportunity."

Professor Dale Yoder paints the difficult picture of challenges and opportunities available to the men who deal in human resources:[19]

"In short, the future for those who specialise in managing human resources look both bright and threatening, for it is likely to be both rewarding greater and demanding. Several current trends appear certain to lead toward greater opportunities, more acceptance and increasing influence for the employee relations staff. At the same time, however, the road has rough spots. Some of the challenges of the future will be met only by hard thinking, planning and rigorous self-development, on the part of industrial relations staff members. To achieve growing acceptance and meet greater responsibilities, current practice in several activities must be sharply improved; pressure for such changes may be expected to increase as manager are brought into these programmes. Research will be given top priority in the improvement of current practice.

"Of even more importance, these trends indicate that industrial relations staff members must continue to lead the whole management group up the long, difficult road to professional competence. Industrial relations managers must spark the progress of professionalisation through both precept and example. This means that they must continue their individual professional development so as to achieve acceptance and status on the basis of specialised competence. At the same time, they must help all managers to understand the elementary, basic requirements for the enthusiastic participation of free men in work-teams and they must take the lead in continuing studies of employee attitudes, morale, enthusiasm and loyalty."

Under the auspices of the U.S. Agency for International Development (US-AID), the National Productivity Council and the various Local Productivity Councils in India organised a Personnel Management Team consisting of senior personnel drawn from well-known private and public sector industries, a trade union, and a teaching body, who visited Japan, U.S.A. and U.K. to study the personnel management philosophies and practices. Before proceeding abroad the Team visited some twelve organisations in India — ten industrial undertakings and two training institutions. In the Team's recommendations "for bringing the personnel management practices obtaining in this country in line with the advanced techniques and thinking in this field" the following comments and suggestions were made:[20]

"In India, the personnel department does not enjoy as high a status as in U.S.A. or England. In U.S.A. especially, the personnel officer is equivalent to a Vice-President or a Director. In England, too, he enjoys a high position. His functions are advisory. The personnel officer plays a very useful role in initiating and co-ordinating the functions relating to recruitment, induction, training, welfare services, promotions etc.

"In India, a personnel officer, or whatever designation we may give him, is differently situated. Employers tend to combine in as many personnel and industrial relations functions as possible, in addition to purely welfare work. Moreover, the *Factories Act* which prescribes the appointment of the welfare officers provides for a very comprehensive set of functions embracing a wide range of personnel management.

"The position is further worsened by the fact that employers and labour in India tend to be litigous, and the poor labour and welfare or the personnel officer is sometimes used as a buffer by the management. Quite often he is utilised by some unenlightened managements to pursue and realise anti-labour policies — as far as possible in a constitutional manner wherever statutory enactments provide loopholes. Thus his time, in many cases, is wasted in the law courts and special tribunals. Labour legislation in India is becoming quite a considerable body of literature with ever increasing case law and complicated procedures. It is suggested here that earnest consideration be given to the idea of codifying welfare and social security measures now found scattered in various enactments.

"There are some enlightened managements who entrust the work of the personnel department to separate sections: industrial relations, legal affairs and welfare. In such patterns of managements, the purely legal matters tend to be separated from the welfare functions, and from purely personnel functions, so that the personnel officer is able to devote his time to recruitment, training and development of personnel, while retaining overall co-ordinating and administrative control over the said departments. But such management patterns are few and far between. Hence, it is proposed here that the labour and welfare officer should be relieved, as far as possible, of court work and legal matters. The personnel officer should be invested with status and dignity consonant with the functions and responsibilities and purposes pertaining to his department. To achieve this it will be necessary to associate him with the policy-making decisions of top management...."

"India has been pre-eminently a land of human values. That man should realise his being and destiny through proper work has been stated eloquently in the Bhagawad Gita. Yet it is said to note that this philosophy is now more practised in the United States and in England than in India. We should now accept that work influences the character and the career of the whole man. The personnel officer has great opportunities to discover aptitudes and abilities of men and place them in suitable jobs. A worker is a growing person: so too is a job a growing situation. Opportunity should be provided to the man to develop into a person worthy of high responsibilities. A man should be trained to operate in a job efficiently and build up and develop the job too."

"A job should be visualized as a challenge to the employee to utilise and invest his creative talents. The personnel department should provide and sustain a climate in which the colleagues of the worker, the supervisors and all the other officers uphold and realise the supremacy of human values. Managements should be friendly and sympathetic to the employees. Through appreciation and respect rather than through punishment and humiliation, it is possible to get more co-operation from the worker. Huge machines and large groups of workers have made personal approach to employer-employee relations difficult. Hence, human relations should be re-discovered and practised between employees and employees, and employers and employees. The success of this human relations approach lies in the belief in man, his capacity to grow and respond to goodwill. In the United States, this belief is seen in the working conditions, workload assignments, overtime payment."

Mr. R.S. Pande, Former Managing Director of TISCO observes:

1. The personnel executive must assist in the implementation of company personnel policies.
2. He must educate and train line executives in personnel policies.
3. He must understand the role of line executives.
4. He must promote bipartite negotiations between labour and management, and respect for unions.
5. He must adopt a human approach and use human relations approaches.
6. He must respect the individual and get to know so well as to inspire confidence and trust, for "trust begets trust."
7. He must attempt to know the family of every employee intimately.
8. He must constantly strive to promote willing and enthusiastic co-operation of employees.
9. He must report to the top executive.
10. He must be on par with the managers of other functional areas, as per ILO's recommendations.

Mr. A.K. Sen, Former Managing Director of Indian Oxygen, refers to the new dimensions in personnel management and new requirements for personnel experts:[21]

"I have referred to the new dimensions in Personnel Management and I have no doubt that with the progressive development of social values and traditions, these dimensions will grow further. To keep pace with them, future personnel managers must be men of better ability, not only conversant with the techniques of Personnel Management but also capable of understanding and appreciating the wider issues and problems. At present, Personnel Management definitely does not attract the best brains. In fact, a career in Personnel Management does not rank very high in the list of choices of bright young men. However, I feel that there are signs which encourage us to take a more optimistic view of the future. Daily pinpricks involved in dealing with problems of industrial relations are no doubt tiresome and frustrating and may deter young talent from taking up Personnel Management as a career; but the growing new dimensions should prove intellectually challenging and socially purposeful. Further, the financial rewards in a career in personnel are gaining in attractiveness and the status of Personnel Managers is also improving. I would, therefore, urge the Personnel Managers to be alert in taking full advantage of the opportunities that lie ahead by fulfilling satisfactory the top management's expectations of them. What then are these expectations? I have drawn up a list and though it is rather long, I do not propose to prune it.

1. Personnel Managers should be adept in the art of communication, both in speech and in writing.
2. He needs to be an extrovert, a skilful negotiator, good at selling his ideas and persuading others to his way of thinking.
3. He should have imagination to anticipate events; he should take prophylactic action instead of trying to solve problems as and when they arise.
4. He should be resilient as his work is crisis-oriented.
5. He should be calm in emergencies and able to think on his feet in an urgent situation.
6. He should have sincerity of purpose and should command respect for his fair-mindedness.
7. He should have courage of conviction and should not be afraid of putting forward his views even at the risk of disagreeing with the top management.
8. He must have an appreciation of the financial implications of the decisions relating to his function. He should at least have a working knowledge of the techniques like organisational methods, work study, incentive schemes and so on. Personnel function cannot be satisfactorily discharge in an isolated manner as it is very closely linked with other functions, particularly finance and production.

"Almost every problem in a business has a 'personnel angle', 'personnel consciousness' should, therefore pervade the whole organisation. Personnel matters are not the sole preserve of the personnel department only, but they are also the concern of all managers who have men working under them, although it is primarily the responsibility of Personnel Managers to train, guide and advise other managers. As for cost control, there should be cost consciousness throughout the organisation; so, for the proper discharge of the personnel function, the recognition of the personnel angle to problems must spread throughout the enterprise."

Lastly, Mr. C.A. Efferson, Manager — Organisation Planning, Kaiser Aluminium & Chemical Corporation, U.S.A., believes that the future will usher in a new breed of personnel administrators, who operate as "working philosophers" bearing in mind a higher purpose and eternal values that kindle the path of human beings:[22]

"How can we best characterise, then, this age which we are entering and to which we eventually must adjust? Unless we concede defeat and become relatively unimportant personnel technicians doing small chores for a people-conscious management, we must become more and more 'working philosophers'.

"Will good profit-conscious managers pay for philosophy? Practical philosophy, I feel sure, they will see as being more and more necessary, and they will become more and more glad to pay for it. In fact, I think they will see, as they become more mature in all the facets of management, that assistance is necessary to set a basic, broad long-range course with their people — a course that comprehends all the many sciences and their complexities. Only philosophy has the breadth to cover all these things, and they will see it as being more worthy than the relatively insignificant contributions in technique and superficial theory that some of us have been guilty of espousing in the past. Many personnel people in the past two decades have been little more professional and mature in what they have been doing that a child at a beach trying to dip all the ocean out on the sand with a spoon....

"The personnel man of the future will also assume that physical security has some worth, and he will certainly agitate for more of it for people as he sees it practical to do so. But he will also embody in this thinking a simple principle known to philosophers for centuries: The true wellspring of security is in a man's spirit, not in his bank, and there may be no connection between the two.

"These personnel men of the future will also continue to realise that to be healthy and at their best, men must receive recognition. Here, too, however, they will see what philosophers have known for centuries: True recognition comes from the individual's evaluation of the extent to which he has met his own standards as a man. Providing this man with a suggestion system through which he may pass superficial ideas about machine or work processes may have no bearing whatever upon his true feeling of work. These practical, working philosophers will concentrate less, it seems to me upon class categories in their thinking, such as "what do workers want?" or "what do managers want?". They will concentrate more upon the nature of the individual man wherever he is. These working philosophers will recognize that corporation such as we have today, and labour organisation as we know it, have been here only a short time — hardly more than a historical blink of an eye. They will recognize that, in scarcely more than another blink, corporations and all our other institutions will evolve to something so different that the kinds of issues we struggle with today will appear as unimportant as those of two hundred years ago now look to us. They will work on today's problems with this perspective.

"These personnel men of the future and their managers will calculate with much greater care which of the total of man's need the corporation should strive to fill; what functions should more properly be left to other institutions; and what problems should be left to the individual alone. For, I think, these philosophers in business will recall another truth of long standing: The truly great issues have never been group debates or battles, for group issues, like leaves, die and are replaced by others. Groups and their issues are often only a convenient maze in which individuals can show their purpose more meaningfully. The only issue of any permanent account is the age-old inevitable battle within the individual mind and spirit as each person struggles within himself, searching consciously or subconsciously for the true reason of his being and for his true work. I think that, in later years, we in personnel will better comprehend this phenomenon in each man, and have more awe and respect for it. We will be less inclined to tamper with it in others and we will desire the wisdom that it can bring to ourselves."

The personnel administrators — present and future — must realise this important aspect that the leaders of industry and business have great expectations, which have to be fulfilled if the personnel executives wish to win the esteem, respect and confidence of leaders not only for themselves but for their avocation also. In order to fulfil these rising expectations, personnel administrators must clothe themselves with competence, character and courage and act with humility, tact and sagacity.

3. THE CHALLENGE

In India at the present juncture we are passing through one of the most exciting and challenging (often maddening) periods in the life of any nation with the ultimate of raising the standards of living of all our people through a democratic and peaceful socio-economic revolution. In one of his most memorable speeches, our beloved leader and the architect of Modern India, Jawaharlal Nehru gave expression to the challenge of our times:

> "A moment comes, which comes but rarely in history, when we step out from the old to the new, when an age ends and when the soul of a nation, long suppressed, find utterance. It is fitting that at this solemn moment we take a pledge of dedication to the service of India and her people to the still larger cause of humanity."

What we are attempting now transcends even the unique and unparalleled struggle for freedom that we staged and won and never before in our history has anything like this ever been attempted. Everyone in India, be he an industrialist, a businessman, a scientist, an engineer, a manager, a worker, an administrator, a civil servant, a typist, a union leader, a party leader, a farmer, a secretary — whatever maybe his avocation — everyone of us has a great stake and a great role in this stupendous task of national reconstruction and in this pilgrimage towards progress and prosperity. This is the challenge of our times. The fundamental challenge facing the personnel administrator in India is: how to communicate this challenge to his associated, superiors, subordinates and workers; and how to touch that sense of sacrifice for an ideal, for truth, for faith, for country and honour which is there in every one of us.

The Macro and Micro Issues

The macro economic and management issues facing the Indian economy and business is the removal of the twin evils of unemployment and poverty. How to remove these twin evils and promote optimum utilisation of human capacity would be a major concern of not only the Government of India but also Indian business and management. In addition to this following are the major macro and micro issues that would pose serious problems to Indian business and it is time that the personnel administrators face the challenge of these issues and make a contribution to solving these issues.

1. Capacity utilisation — machine as well as human.
2. Combating inflation and holding price line.
3. Motivation involvement and consultation.
4. Population control.
5. Meeting basic physiological needs.
6. Reducing absenteeism, accidents, loss and damages.

7. Generating executive leadership.
8. Human assets accounting and profits and growth.
9. Eliminating strikes and lockouts through voluntary arbitration.
10. Job re-designing, enlargement, enrichment.
11. Promoting health, self renewal and creativity.
12. Promoting exports and economic growth.
13. Conservation of resources — renewable and non-renewable.
14. Increasing the productivity of finance.
15. Waste and cost reduction.
16. Promoting arts, culture, religion, sports and leisure activities.
17. Adoption of villages and community.
18. Promoting entrepreneurship, barefoot entrepreneurs and managers.
19. Eliminating discrimination of all types.
20. Promoting a sense of national identity, awareness and contribution.
21. Promoting industrial and national security.
22. Quality of working life.
23. Quality of life — wellrounded personal and professional life.

The major challenge facing personnel experts is how to convert the enormous human resources in the country into human assets that can promote not only corporate growth but also national economic growth.

Then there are other challenges with which the personnel administrator will be concerned in the coming years and some of them are the following:

1. How to win the confidence and respect of top management and line management.
2. How to influence management and employer philosophies regarding human beings.
3. How to convince employers and managers that people are also their business.
4. How to evolve policies and programme that have tangible and material results, whose statistical and quantitative values can be represented in money terms to management.
5. How to promote harmonious relations between labour and management through bipartite negotiations.
6. How to deal with multiplicity of Unions and inter-union rivalry.
7. How to reduce the dependence of the company, management, unions and employees on law.
8. How to bring the existing differences between union and management out into the open with a view to arriving at solutions.
9. How to win the confidence and respect of employees and unions.
10. How to improve the tools and techniques of selection, training, and development.

11. How to spot good employees among thousands of applicants; how to enthuse them; how to train and develop them.
12. How to compensate people for their services — people like managers, engineers, scientists, programmers, systems analysts etc.
13. How to raise the status and prestige of their profession.
14. How to increase and improve their technical competence and professional education and training.
15. How to develop a code of ethics — and some canons of conduct for the profession.
16. How to apply science and scientific method.
17. How to understand, analyse and interpret the psychology, needs, aspirations of people.
18. How to introduce technological change — automation, rationalisation — and how to communicate it.
19. How to infuse zeal into people for bigger and better goals.
20. How to realise their (personnel administrator's) own potentialities and to grow in the service of people.
21. How to satisfy people — managers, employers, workers, union leaders.
22. How to adjust not only to the fast changing environment but also play a role in bringing about progressive changes.
23. How to maximise the effectiveness and efficiency of the profession of personnel administration.
24. How to contribute to the productivity and profitability of the organisation and thus ultimately to national growth and development.
25. How to appeal to the basic essential goodness in man.

Perhaps we could extend the list endlessly, but it is enough to note that people — countless people with countless beliefs, problems, ambitions, needs, motivations and several other factors that go to make people — are the business of personal administration and it is its business to educate employers, managers — line and staff — and supervisors to place a high value on the dignity and work of the individual-human being. It was that authority on personnel matters, Mr. Thomas G. Spates, who declared in "Leadership and Human Relations at the Places where People Work":

> "For the attainment of those goals for which people everywhere have been striving since the early dawn, there is no substitute for sound personnel administration. The stand it takes is universal and creative and fulfils the needs of human beings. Sound personnel administration stands for principles that mankind has evoked out of hope and love for centuries...."

In short, the challenge of human resources management is people — their development, their well-being, and their fulfilment. Personnel administrators are dealing with people — the most dynamic beings and their avocation must be dynamic enough to cope with people. They must realise and then communicate and convince other top and line managers that people are not mere "machines", "commodities" or "cost" or "things" and that people — workers, machinists, sweepers etc. — are just as human beings are and in every human being there is a divine spark. People should not be lightly dismissed.

Some employers and management have recognised this important aspect and are assigning greater and greater importance to the personnel divisions. More functions and responsibilities are added to the existing ones in personnel and some of the recent functions assigned to personnel departments are the following:

Long range planning,	Work and Job Redesign,
Organisation planning,	Evaluation of employee morale,
Management development,	Attitude surveys etc.,
Public relations,	Special problems of engineers
Personnel research,	and scientists and problem employees,
Net Economic Welfare (NEW).	Quality of working life,
	Quality of life.

One expert who has predicted future developments in personnel administration wisely concludes:

"The field of personnel administration in the future will be a constantly expanding universe which will always keep one step ahead of us no matter how fast we run."

Let me quote Dr. Charles Malik, a statesman from Lebanon, who said in the mid-fifties "we do not see our involvement enough. We do not know them, we do not recognise their souls. We do not meet them as person to person. As a result, we know them only as moving animals producing and wanting an economic good. The society that thus reduces man to the level of 'economic animal' and does not show sufficient active concern for his soul can never know peace. For peace is to be in the truth that man expects primarily by his reason and conscience so that if these are neglected there is no end to the social havoc that his distorted being will produce."[23]

There are times when a personnel executive may feel frustrated in his work with people — either the boss, or a line executive, or a union leader, or a supervisor, or some worker, or some colleague; then it is time for him to pause and think about his wonderful statement of Mr. Nehru — an affirmation of faith in man:

"How amazing is the spirit of man. In spite of innumerable failings, man throughout the ages has sacrificed his life and all he held dear for an ideal, for truth, for faith, for country and honour. That ideal may change, but the capacity for self-sacrifice continues, and because of that much may be forgiven in man, and it is impossible to lose hope for him. In the midst of disaster he has not lost his dignity or his faith in the values of cherishes. At the mercy of Nature's mighty forces, less than a speck of dust in this vast universe, he has hurled defiance at the elemental fires and with his mind, cradle of revolution, has sought to master them."

The mission of human resources management is to be concerned with the amazing spirit of man and inspire others to have immovable faith in the powers of man Its mission is to create a humane and worthy environment in industry and business where every individual human being — employer, employee, manager, supervisor — is able to, wants to and is willing to make his maximum contribution and in the process, grows to his fullest realising his potentialities and deriving immense satisfaction.

Its mission is to place before the people of India and the world the exciting challenge of national reconstruction and to touch that amazing spirit of man which can move mountains, and harness it in the cause of our country. Its mission is to uphold the honour, dignity and worth of the human being.

REFERENCES

1. Carter L. Burgess, "Personnel: Our Principal Asset in the 1960s", *The Personnel Job in the 1960s,* AMA Management Report No. 63, AMA, 1961.
2. *Ibid.,* pp. 5-6.
3. Alert F. Watters, "Some Personal Thoughts on the Personnel Function — Past, Present and Future", *The Personnel Function: A Progress Report,* p. 8.
4. *Ibid.*
5. Peter Drucker, "Management's Role in the New World", in *The New Role of Management: Innovation and Integration,* Proceedings of 15th CIOS International Management Congress (Tokyo, Kogakusha Co. Ltd., 1969), p. 24.
6. Planning Commission, *The Third Five Year Plan Progress Report,* Government of India, p. 238.
7. Dale Yoder, "Looking Ahead in Employment Relationship", *The Personnel Function: A Progress Report.*
8. Burgess, *op. cit.,* p. 7.
9. Albert F. Watters, *op. cit.,* pp. 8-9.
10. Dorr C. Snoyenbos, "Personnel Procedures in a Space Age Enterprise", *The Personnel Job in the 1960s,* pp. 28-29.
11. D.J. Moffie, "Applying the Scientific Method in Personnel Work", *The Personnel Function: A Progress Report,* p. 11.
12. Albert F. Watters, *op. cit.,* p. 10.
13. Carter Burgess, *op. cit.,* p. 12.
14. Robert D. Gray, "Evaluating the Personnel Department", *Personnel,* March-April, 1965, p. 47.
15. Recommendations adopted at The Plenary Session on "Maximising Effectiveness of Personnel Management in Industry", IIPM 17th All India Conference, Coimbatore 12-3-1967. The author played a humble role in drafting these recommendations with the able guidance and assistance from the other two chairmen, Mr. J.A. Panakal of TISCO and Mr. G.V. Subbra Rao of Western India Match Company.
16. Watters, *op. cit.,* p. 9.
17. Livingstone, "Employee Attitudes and Productivity", p. 20.
18. Clarence Francis, "Management and Men — The Challenge of Changing Times", *The Personnel Job in 1960s,* pp. 118-119.
19. Dale Yoder, "Looking Ahead in Employment Relationships," pp. 38-39.
20. *Personnel Management in Japan, U.S.A. and Britain,* Report of Indian Productivity Team, (New Delhi, India: National Productivity Council, March 1963), p. 55.
21. A.K. Sen, "The Role of Top Management is Personnel Management", Text of talk delivered at the Second Annual Conference of IIPM Calcutta Branch, pp. 4-5.
22. C.A. Efferson, "Charting the Course of Personnel Administration", *The Personnel Function: Progress Report,* pp. 29-30.
23. Please see John Marsh, "To making, working and living more acceptable", keynote address at the silver anniversary conference of the American Society for Personnel Administration, San Juan, Puerto Rico, June 1973.

❑❑❑

